spotlights

✔checklists

W9-BHJ-486

Welcome to

Contemporary Business Communication

SIXTH EDITION

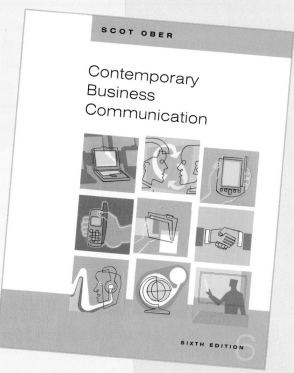

Dear Colleague:

In teaching business communication for more than twenty years, I've learned that students appreciate a textbook that fully prepares them for the real world of business. That is why I have designed a text that provides students with a solid, practical guide to business communication and an accessible, engaging look into the real business world.

I've often said, "Students learn to communicate by communicating—not by just reading about communicating." The Sixth Edition of *Contemporary Business Communication* continues to uphold this principle in a variety of ways. While the text is conceptually rich and grounded in real-world examples, it also provides ample opportunities for students to apply what they have learned and reinforce basic skills. The companion CD and Eduspace tutorials take this a step further, providing additional practice as well as virtual experience of the world of work.

On the following pages, you will find an introduction to the key features of the student text and Instructor's Annotated Edition, as well as a description of the support items available with the text for both you and your students.

Cordially,

Scot Ober
Ball State University
scotober@comcast.net

Helping students communicate …

Opening profiles are based on actual interviews and provide insight and advice about business communication on the job.

Spotlights on technology, diversity, and ethics enhance student awareness of the key issues in business communication today.

First draft/second draft examples show how a document evolves through rewriting and refining. Final draft **annotated models** help students develop basic writing skills.

---

7 Routine Messages

Communication
OBJECTIVES

...you have finished this ... you should be able to

... Compose a routine request.

... Compose a routine reply.

... Compose a routine claim ...

... Compose a routine adjustment letter.

5. Compose a goodwill message.

Writing letters on behalf of her bunny mascot takes up a good portion of entrepreneur Ann Withey's time. Withey is cofounder of Annie's Homegrown, a $10 million business that makes packaged all-natural macaroni and cheese products. The company is Withey's second business venture, started after she and a partner sold their first business, Smartfood Popcorn, to Frito-Lay for $15 million in 1989. These days, she lives with her family on an organic farm in Connecticut and, in between weekly visits to the company's Massachusetts office, stays in contact with employees via phone, fax, and e-mail.

Competing against corporate giants, Withey has built her business through social responsibility and folksy communication, seeking to connect with customers on a more personal level. That's why every package carries information about social causes along with a chatty letter signed "Annie" and a drawing of Bernie, the "Rabbit of Approval." "One of the things that attracts people to our products is that Annie is real and not a made-up Madison Avenue icon," Withey explains. (Bernie is real, too; his niece, Scout, recently succeeded him as company mascot.)

While another staff member handles e-mail messages, Withey responds to roughly 1,500 letters every month. Most are requests for free information about one of the causes promoted on product packages, such as a listing of scholarships or a "Be Green" bumper sticker. Although these items are routine requests, "90 percent of the

ANN WITHEY
Cofounder, Annie's Homegrown

an insider's perspective

226

... **ROUTINE MESSAGES** **227**

... pasta," she says. In re... ich opens with an expres... lly. The letter refers to the ... h Bernie's picture next to ..., this routine reply also ... d products and commu...

products. Before I write, I try to envision that person sitting at the kitchen table writing to me," she says. "This helps me plan a genuine, unique letter that addresses each person's concerns." She first thanks the reader for his or her support, then picks out a specific detail from the original letter that she can discuss in her response. Finally, she closes on a friendly note by thanking the reader for "bringing a smile to my face." Withey's highly personal approach to communication reflects her overall business philosophy: "I'm a customer, too, and I treat people the way I would want to be treated."

> *"Before I write, I try to envision that person. . . . This helps me plan a genuine, unique letter that addresses each person's concerns."*

---

spotlight2
ON TECHNOLOGY

Overcoming Information Anxiety

Executives, like nearly everyone else in this information-laden society, are being bombarded by more data than they can absorb. According to Richard Wurman, author of *Information Anxiety*, to function in business, we are being forced to assimilate a body of knowledge that is expanding by the minute.

For example, consider these statistics:

- The total amount of unique information generated worldwide each single year is about 1.5 exabytes (one exabyte is 1 followed by 18 zeroes). Stored on floppy disks, this amount of information would stack 2 million miles high.

tween data and knowledge. Here are some symptoms of information anxiety as Wurman describes them:

- Nodding your head knowingly when someone mentions a book, artist, or news story that you have actually never heard of.
- Feeling guilty about that ever-higher stack of periodicals waiting to be read.
- Feeling depressed because you don't know what all the buttons on your VCR do.

Wurman believes that "the System" is at fault—too many people are putting out too much data.

---

sion holds a weekly staff meeting at which the three managers (Jean, Larry, and Eric) exchange information about the status of their operations.

Horizontal communication is important to help coordinate work assignments, share information on plans and activities, negotiate differences, and develop interpersonal support, thereby creating a more cohesive work unit. The more that individuals or departments within an organization must interact with each other to accomplish their objectives, the more frequent and intense will be the horizontal communication.

---

model 8

PERSUASIVE REQUEST—ASKING

National Multiple Sclerosis Society

January 21, 20—

Ms. Tanya Porrat, Editor
Autoimmune Diseases Monthly
1800 Ten Hills Road, Suite B
Boston, MA 02145

Dear Ms. Porrat:

Subject: Program Planning for the Multiple Sclerosis Congress.

"The average person has about 1 chance in 1,000 of developing MS," comment of yours in a recent interview in the *Boston Globe* made me ... and think.

Your knack for exploring little-known facts like that would certainly ... interest to those attending our annual congress in Washington, DC. ... As the keynote speaker at the banquet at the Mayflower Hotel on A... would be able to present your ideas on current initiatives to the 200 ... You would, of course, be our guest for the banquet, which begins a ... 45-minute presentation would begin at about 8:30 p.m.

We will reimburse you for any travel and hotel accommodations. ... nonprofit association is unable to offer an honorarium, we do offe... opportunity to introduce your journal and to present your ideas to ... of major autoimmune groups in the country.

We'd like to announce your presentation in our next newsletter, w... press on March 1. Won't you please call to let me know you can ... have a large, enthusiastic audience of medical researchers waitin...

Cordially,

May Lyon

May Lyon, Banquet Chair

... **Grammar and Mechanics Notes**

... increase readability, do not italicize publication titles ... *Boston Globe*: Italicize the titles of separately published w... ... azines, and books.

... *you can come:* Use a period after a courteous request.

4 Do not include reference initials if the letter writer also ...

---

figure 8.1
An Ineffective Persuasive Request

278

Uses a subject line that is too specific

Begins by directly asking for the favor, using me-attitude language.

Omits important information (such as: Who will be attending the conference? How many attendees? How long will the presentation be?).

Identifies the obstacle in a selfish manner—without including any reasons to minimize the obstacle.

Gives a deadline for answering—without providing any rationale.

Closes with a cliché.

January 15, 20—

Ms. Tanya Porrat, Editor
Autoimmune Diseases Monthly
1800 Ten Hills Road, Suite B
Boston, MA 02145

Dear Ms. Porrat:

Subject: Request for You to Speak at the Multiple Sclerosis Congress

I have a favor to ask—a rather large one, I'm afraid. Having served as editor of a professional journal myself, I know how busy editors are, but I was wondering if you would be willing to fly to Washington, DC, on April 25 and speak at the closing banquet of our annual Multiple Sclerosis Congress.

The problem, of course, is that as a nonprofit association, we cannot afford to pay you an honorarium. I trust that this won't be a problem for you. We would, however, be willing to reimburse you for air travel and hotel accommodations.

Our conference attendees would benefit tremendously from your vast knowledge of multiple sclerosis, so we're really hoping you'll say yes. Just let me know your decision by March 3 in case we have to make other arrangements.

Please call me if you have any questions.

Cordially,

May Lyon

May Lyon, Banquet Chair

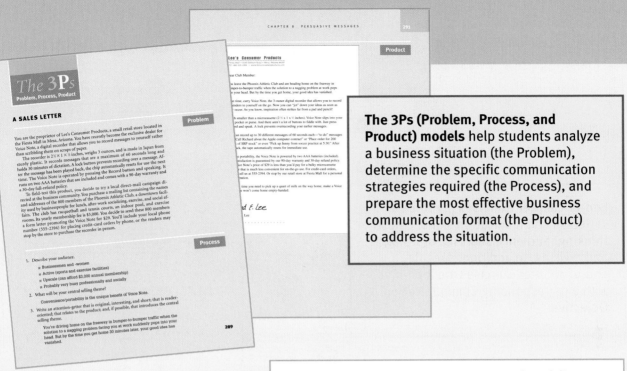

The 3Ps (Problem, Process, and Product) models help students analyze a business situation (the Problem), determine the specific communication strategies required (the Process), and prepare the most effective business communication format (the Product) to address the situation.

Checklists recap essential points for student review.

✓checklist 3

Evaluating the Quality of Internet Resources [5]

Criterion 1: Authority

✓ Is it clear who sponsors the page and what the sponsor's purpose in maintaining the page is?

✓ Is it clear who wrote the material and what the author's qualifications for writing on this topic are?

✓ Is there a way of verifying the legitimacy of the page's sponsor; that is, is there a phone number or postal address to contact for more information?

✓ If the material is protected by copyright, is the name of the copyright holder given?

Criterion 2: Accuracy

✓ Are statistical data in graphs and charts clearly labeled and easy to read?

✓ Does anyone monitor the accuracy of the information being published?

Criterion 3: Objectivity

✓ For any given piece of information, is the sponsor's motivation for providing it clear?

✓ Is the information content clearly separated from any advertising or opinion content?

✓ Is the point of view of the sponsor presented in a clear manner, with well-supported arguments?

New! The **"Ask Ober"** feature encourages direct dialog between you or your students and the textbook author. This feature is based on actual e-mails to and from the author.

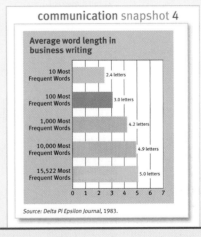

A S K Ober

Dear Dr. Ober:

I am currently a student at Baker College and am very interested in a business mentioned often in your text. I would like some further information on Urban Systems and an address and phone number where I would be able to reach them. Do they have a website?

—Michelle

Dear Michelle:

Urban Systems is a completely fictional company that I "created" to illustrate important business communication concepts. It is, however, a composite of the many small companies I've consulted with over the past 25 years, and the situations depicted in the case problems are all typical of those encountered in small companies operating in the contemporary business environment. The people in the photographs that accompany these end-of-chapter case studies are just actors.

—Scot

E-mail your questions and comments to askober@ober.net.

communication snapshot 4

Average word length in business writing

10 Most Frequent Words	2.4 letters
100 Most Frequent Words	3.0 letters
1,000 Most Frequent Words	4.2 letters
10,000 Most Frequent Words	4.9 letters
15,522 Most Frequent Words	5.0 letters

Source: Delta Pi Epsilon Journal, 1983.

New! Communication Snapshots present up-to-date factoids about contemporary business communications.

End-of-chapter exercises reinforce a variety of communication skills: critical thinking, audience analysis, drafting, and revising. In addition, specific end-of-chapter exercises are identified with a corresponding Communication Objective.

The continuing case on Urban Systems allows students to experience the unique and complex communication challenges posed by workplace policies and organizational dynamics. It also correlates directly to the Urban Systems CD-ROM that is packaged with each text.

Visit the **BusCom Online Learning Center** (at http://college.h for additional resources to help you with this course and with y career.

Summary

co1. Specify the purpose of your message and analyze your audience.

co2. Compose a first

Before writing, identify the purpose of your intended message. Carefully audience (or audiences) and determine what information to includ whether a direct or indirect organizational plan will help you achieve you Select an appropriate environment for drafting, and schedule enoug centrate on getting the information down, without worrying about format. Leave a time gap between writing and revising the dr ... st for content—to determine whether all the needed inform ... d information) have been included. Then revise for style, ... in which you present your ideas is effective. Finally, revise for ... to avoid any errors in grammar, mechanics, punctuation, and ... nerally accepted format for your letters, memos, e-mail, and ... ciency for the writer, readability for the receiver, and a co ... through your document to ensure that the document makes ... st for typos. Finally, visually inspect the document for appro

Key Terms

...should now be able to define the following terms in your ow ... riginal example of each.

... ence analysis (198)   organization (203)
... storming (203)   primary audience (198)
... fting (203)   revising (207)
... (208)   secondary audience (198)
... writing (206)   writer's block (205)
... nd mapping (203)

Exercises

■ Suggestions and sample solutions for exercises appear in the Instructor's Resource Manual.

1 The 3Ps (Problem, Process, and Product) Model: Communi ... at PriceWaterhouseCoopers' *Executive Perspectives* ... all five steps in the writing process when he prepares an ... company's *Executive Perspectives* online magazine. He tak ... proofreading because he is writing for a global audience of ... uments on the screen. Only after two colleagues and a professional proofreader have proofed an article does it appear on the magazine website.

Product

Format your revised draft, using plain paper and a standard memo format. Then proofread and submit to your instructor both your memo and your responses to the preceding questions. If requested to do so, submit both documents as an e-mail message to your instructor.

co1. Specify the purpose of your message and analyze your audience.

3 Communication Purpose   Compose a specific goal for each of the following.

a. A memo to a professor asking him to change a grade.
b. A letter to MasterCard about an incorrect charge.
c. A letter to the president of a local bank thanking her for speaking at your student organization meeting.
d. A memo of reprimand to a subordinate for leaving the warehouse unlocked overnight.

4 Communication Purpose and Reader Response   For each of the following communication tasks, indicate the specific purpose and the desired response.

a. A letter to a state senator about a proposed state surcharge on college tuition.
b. A memo to your payroll department head about an incorrect paycheck.
c. A letter to the college newspaper discussing the quality of the cafeteria food in recent months.
d. A memo to your assistant asking about the status of an overdue report.

5 Audience Analysis   Assume you must write an e-mail message to your current business communication professor, asking him or her to let you take your final examination one week early so that you can attend your cousin's wedding.

a. Perform an audience analysis of your professor. List everything you know about this professor that might help you compose a more effective message.
b. Write two good opening sentences for this message, the first one assuming that you are an A student who has missed class only once this term and the second assuming you are a C student who has missed class six times this term.

6 Audience Analysis Revisited   Now assume the role of the professor (see Exercise 5) who must reply to the request of the student with the C grade who has missed class six times. You'll tell the student that you are not willing to schedule an early exam.

a. Perform an audience analysis of yourself (as the student). What do you know about yourself that would help the professor write an effective message?
b. Should the professor use a direct or an indirect organization? Why?
c. Write the first sentence of the professor's message.

7 Audience Reaction   Read the following situations and decide what the audience reaction would be and whether a direct or indirect organizational plan would be better. Explain your answers.

a. As the manager of a small retail clothing store, you are preparing a memo to let the employees know they are getting a 50-cent-per-hour raise.
b. As the assistant manager of a hotel, you are writing to a customer letting her know that the jewelry she left in her room when she departed has not been found.
c. As a newly hired advertising director, you are e-mailing the president of the company requesting a 10 percent increase in your advertising budget.

APPENDIX TO CHAPTER 1
Urban Systems, Inc.

The Company

Urban Systems, Inc. (US) is a small "start-up" company whose primary product is Ultra Light, a new, paper-thin light source that promises to revolutionize the illumination industry. The company employs 178 people at its corporate headquarters in Ann Arbor, Michigan, and in a completely automated manufacturing plant in Charlotte, North Carolina. It is incorporated under the laws of the state of Michigan, with all stock privately held by the founders and their families.

Urban Systems has annual sales in the $30 million range, with a net profit last year of $1.4 million. It is considered a progressive company by the investment community, with good management and good earnings potential. The local community considers US to be a good corporate citizen; it is a nonpolluting firm, and its officers are active in the local chamber of commerce and in community affairs.

Urban Systems headquarters in Ann Arbor, Michigan.

The Product

Ultra Light is a flat, electroluminescent sheet of material that serves as a light source. It is capable of replacing most fluorescent, neon, and incandescent light fixtures. Physically, Ultra Light is a paper-thin sheet of chemically treated material laminated between thin layers of clear

36

plastic. In effect, it is a credit-card-t ... bendable and that can be produ ... shapes and sizes. Operated by eith ... rent, it generates a bright white or c

Ultra Light is cost-competitive with ... ventional lighting, and its life expec ... years. All of this, combined with i ... thin profile, battery operation ("us ... evenly distributed light it produce ... conform to a variety of physical ... Light a new product with a lot of po

Company History

US was founded in 2001 by two brot ... Kaplan. Dave was a chemical en ... Chemical, Inc., when he developed ... Ultra Light while working on anothe ... was not interested in pursuing the ... marketing of this product, Dave bo ... Light from IC and patented it in ... younger brother Marc, formerly a m ... an advertising agency in Chicago, s ... in an empty warehouse in Midland,

The company received start-up fu ... investments of $50,000 by Dave Ka ... Marc and a $68,500 five-year loan from the United States Small Business Administration. Because of Marc's advertising background, the company's five-year business plan focused on marketing Ultra Light initially for advertising purposes—to illuminate signs, point-of-purchase displays, and the like. Later, as the company became better established in the marketplace, plans were to expand into industrial, office, and consumer applications. Hence, a company name—Urban Systems—was selected that was broad enough to encompass a variety of products.

After a somewhat uneven start, US had become profitable by the end of its fourth year of operations and had outgrown its original building. The company recently built an 11,000-square-foot facility in an attractive office park in Ann Arbor, Michigan, to house its administrative, marketing, and R&D functions. The company also moved its

The Instructor's Annotated Edition helps you to see *at a glance* the supporting materials available for use in the classroom.

Author-created PowerPoint slides are reproduced in the margins of the IAE for easy review and selection.

Cross-references to other teaching materials, such as handouts in the *Instructor's Resource Manual*, provide additional support.

Cartoons in every chapter provide humorous examples of business communication problems and opportunities to enhance the classroom experience.

Teaching tips and interesting business examples offer additional resources for enriching your lectures.

Instructor Supplements

 **Instructor's Resource Manual** The *Instructor's Resource Manual* provides additional teaching materials including special student handouts for each chapter, chapter overviews, lecture and discussion notes, supplemental lecture notes, suggested answers to and/or teaching tips for all writing exercises and case problems, additional 3P (Problem, Process, and Product) exercises with solutions, answer keys, solutions to all letter writing assignments, and sample long report and memo report. Additional teaching tools include Suggested Scoring Rubrics, Portfolio Assignment, and SCANS correlation table. The IRM is available on the instructor website and on HMClassPrep.

 PowerPoint Slides More than 150 PowerPoint slides include summaries of key concepts, paired good/bad examples, and supplementary information, including answers to selected exercises.

 Eduspace® Powered by Blackboard™ Houghton Mifflin's online learning tool is a customizable, powerful, and interactive platform that provides text-specific online courses and content. Instructors have the ability to create all or part of their course online using the widely recognized tools of Blackboard and quality text-specific content. Content includes Lab Manual diagnostic tests, auto-graded quizzes based on BusCom Writer Tutorials, and supplemental study materials. Instructors can modify that content or even add their own. BusCom Writer Tutorials are a special component of the Eduspace program accompanying *Contemporary Business Communication*. Each of these self-paced tutorials, based on the textbook's 3Ps (Problem, Process, and Product) model, presents students with a business situation and guides them through preparing a finished product.

 Instructor Website The BusCom Online Teaching Center can be accessed via a free password provided to instructors using this text. The site provides a monthly newsletter with additional teaching tips and current event items, detailed lecture and supplemental discussion notes for each chapter, additional application exercises and cases, PowerPoint slides to preview and download, and a forum in which to exchange ideas with the author.

 Test Bank and Computerized Test Bank The Test Bank and HMTesting contain approximately 1,200 test items including multiple-choice, short answer, true/false, revisions, and writing items. HMTesting is software that lets instructors prepare examinations.

 HMClassPrep with HMTesting All instructor resources, including the complete IRM, PowerPoint slides, and HMTesting, are provided on this CD-ROM.

Instructor Supplements, continued

  Video Program   Video case studies of real-world companies reinforce text concepts by directly relating them to the footage being shown. In addition, discussion questions and suggested writing assignments are provided.

 Overhead Transparencies   Nearly 100 electronic overhead transparencies are available on the instructor website, including summaries of key concepts, writing examples, text figures, and answers to selected exercises.

 Blackboard and WebCT   Houghton Mifflin provides this option for instructors who want to create and customize online course materials for use in distance learning, distributed learning, or as a supplement to traditional classes. This service helps you create and manage your own website to bring learning materials, class discussions, and tests online. Houghton Mifflin provides all of the basic content for an introductory course in business communication using Ober's *Contemporary Business Communication*.

Tools for Student Success

Urban Systems CD-ROM   A CD-ROM packaged with each text brings the world of Urban Systems to life. Each case scenario is simulated so that students can virtually experience the situation and actively solve the problem. Immediate feedback is provided by the program. Additional scenarios allow students to work independently, while still receiving guidance when needed.

 BusCom Writer Tutorials   Eduspace provides a set of interactive computer modules that guide students through the development of 15 basic business documents. Based on the textbook's 3Ps (Problem, Process, and Product) model, each module (1) presents students with a unique business situation; (2) guides them through the process of analyzing the situation, developing communication goals, and preparing the document; and (3) prompts students to proofread and revise the finished product to meet proper writing guidelines. A multiple-choice quiz helps students assess their understanding of the tutorial.

 Student Website   The BusCom Online Learning Center provides students with a one-stop guide to the world of online business communication. Here they can learn more about the Internet, locate business information, get help with writing problems, complete ACE quizzes designed to assess students' understanding of chapter and Lab Manual content, test vocabulary knowledge with flash cards, and get information about employment communication, available jobs, and employers. They can also "Ask Ober" questions about business communication through a direct e-mail line to the author.

Table of Contents

For more information on Houghton Mifflin products, services, or examination copy requests:

- Consult the College Division online: **www.hmco.com/college.**
- Call or fax the Faculty Services Center: **Tel: 800/733-1717 Fax: 800/733-1810.**
- Contact your Houghton Mifflin sales representative.

Contemporary Business Communication

SIXTH EDITION

Contemporary Business Communication

INSTRUCTOR'S ANNOTATED EDITION

Scot Ober
Ball State University

Houghton Mifflin Company
Boston   New York

To my wife and five sons, with deep affection: Diana, Jeff, Andy, Ken, Tony, and Casey

Publisher: Charles Hartford
Editor in Chief: George T. Hoffman
Associate Sponsoring Editor: Joanne Dauksewicz
Development Manager: Susan M. Kahn
Senior Development Editor: Chere Bemelmans
Project Editor: Andrea Cava
Senior Composition Buyer: Sarah Ambrose
Senior Art and Design Coordinator: Jill Haber
Senior Photo Editor: Jennifer Meyer Dare
Manufacturing Coordinator: Chuck Dutton
Executive Marketing Manager: Steven W. Mikels
Marketing Associate: Lisa E. Boden

Cover image: © CSA Images Illustration / Veer Incorporated

The model letters provided on authentic company stationery have been included by permission to provide realistic examples of company documents for educational purposes. They do not represent actual business documents created by these companies.

Credits appear on pages 634–635, which are considered extensions of the copyright page.

Printed in the U.S.A.

Library of Congress Control Number: 2004113917

Student Text ISBN: 0-618-47252-5
Instructor's Annotated Edition ISBN: 0-618-47253-3

1 2 3 4 5 6 7 8 9-DOW-09 08 07 06 05

brief contents

contents

3 Communication Technology 96

Part Three ■ Basic Correspondence

9   Bad-News Messages   304

Part Four   Report Writing

10   Planning the Report   343

Part Five ▢ Oral and Employment Communication

15 Employment Communication 528

Reference Manual

preface

Scot Ober

Students don't have to be convinced of the need for competent communication skills. By the time they enter the business communication class, they already know enough about the business environment to appreciate the critical role communication plays in the contemporary organization. They're also aware of the role that communication will play in helping them secure an internship or get a job and be successful at work.

To sustain this inherent interest, students need a textbook that is current, fast-paced, and interesting—just like business itself. Thus, a major objective of the sixth edition of *Contemporary Business Communication* is to present comprehensive coverage of real-world concepts in an interesting and lively manner.

This edition of *Contemporary Business Communication* has been considerably revised to provide students with the skills they need to communicate effectively in the complex and ever-changing contemporary work environment. The revision was based on helpful feedback received from current users around the country (and, indeed, around the English-speaking world), changes in the discipline, and changes in the workplace itself. As illustrated later, specific numerous refinements have been made to various features of this edition. Two important and global changes, however, are the move to an objective-based organization and the complete revision and updating of the end-of-chapter exercises.

Objective-Based Organization   To a greater extent than is true for most other business courses, the content and organization of the basic business communication course differs markedly, depending on the institution at which it is taught, the department that teaches the course, the level of the student, and the like. For example, some institutions place major emphasis on business report writing, while others give the topic scant coverage. The same is true, of course, for other topics such as oral communication, basic English skills, and employment communications. Even more important, there are topics within chapters that, because of time constraints or coverage in other courses, some instructors choose not to cover. Thus, every chapter communication objective (CO) may not be relevant for every business communication class.

The sixth edition of *Contemporary Business Communication* lets instructors easily customize their course to meet their particular needs. Each communication objective that is presented at the beginning of each chapter has been defined to cover an important element of that chapter's content. Each chapter is then organized around these objectives, and the particular objective being covered is identified in the margins. All content relating to one objective is presented before moving on to the next consecutive objective. Further, the chapter summary is organized around each objective, as are the end-of-chapter exercises.

This means that instructors can easily assign an entire chapter or only components of the chapter, based on the communication objectives, and then easily identify the related end-of-chapter exercises and test-bank items.

New Student Exercises   No matter how effective a student exercise is, it begins to lose its effectiveness over time. Long-time users of *Contemporary Business Communication* will be pleased to learn that all application and assessment exercises have been revised for this edition, including the following:

- More than 100 totally new end-of-chapter exercises and minicases have been added to this text. The ones that have been retained have been revised and updated.

- All of the exercises for the LAB (Language Arts Basics) modules at the end of the book are new. The old exercises have been placed on the BusCom Online Teaching Center (http://college.hmco.com/business) for instructors to download and use for additional practice materials for students.

- Test items in the printed test bank and computerized test bank have been completely updated—with hundreds of completely new items; others have been extensively revised. The test items are now organized according to the communication objectives they cover.

The following discussion highlights the features of this complete teaching and learning system:

- Business communication—in context
- Work-team communication
- Focus on contemporary issues
- The 3Ps (Problem, Process, and Product) Model
- Annotated models and checklists
- Basic skills first

Business Communication—In Context

Business communication problems in the real world do not occur in a vacuum. Events have happened before the problem and will happen after the problem, affecting its resolution. Thus, in addition to typical end-of-chapter exercises, three learning tools in this text provide more complete long-term situations that provide a "slice-of-life" reality students will actually face on the job.

An Insider's Perspective   Each chapter begins with an on-the-job interview with a manager from a multinational company (such as 3M), a small entrepreneurial company (such as Hilliard-Jones Marketing Group), or a nonprofit organization (such as the Wilderness Society). All opening vignettes continue at the end of each chapter with a 3Ps (Problem, Process, and Product) activity.

New to this edition are chapter-opening interviews (and new end-of-chapter exercises) with the following business managers:

- Gilbert C. Morrell Jr., President and CEO, The Nucon Group
- Scott Roller, Internet Marketing Director, Texas Instruments
- Gary Davis, Vice President, Corporate Communications, World Wrestling Entertainment, Inc.
- Bobbie Kroman, General Manager, Barnes & Noble, College Division

- Noel McCarthy, Editor-in-chief, *Executive Perspectives*, PriceWaterhouseCoopers
- Patrick Vijiarungam, Sales Representative, Wurzburg, Inc.
- Anne K. Cobuzzi, Senior Brand Planning Manager, CV, AstraZeneca
- Todd Mesek, Director of Marketing and Communications, Rock and Roll Hall of Fame and Museum
- Sara González, President and CEO, Georgia Hispanic Chamber of Commerce
- Jeff Taylor, Founder and Chief Monster, Monster.com

Continuing Text Examples and End-of-Chapter Exercises   Continuing examples are often used throughout the chapter (and sometimes carried forward to the next chapter) in both the text and end-of-chapter exercises. For example, in Chapter 7, students first assume the role of buyer and write a claim letter. Later, they assume the role of seller and answer the same claim letter by writing an adjustment letter. In Chapter 8, students write a persuasive request from a subordinate; and in Chapter 9 (about bad-news messages), they assume the role of superior and turn down the well-written persuasive request.

Such situations are realistic because they provide a sense of following a problem through to completion. They are interesting because they provide a continuing thread to the chapters. They also reinforce the concept of audience analysis because students must first assume the role of sender and later the role of receiver for the same communication task.

Urban Systems: An Ongoing Case Study   Every chapter ends with a case study involving Urban Systems (US), a small entrepreneurial start-up company whose primary product is Ultra Light, a new paper-thin light source that promises to revolutionize the illumination industry. A company profile is contained in the Appendix to Chapter 1, and each chapter presents a typical communication problem faced by one of the employees. As students systematically solve these 15 case studies, they face communication problems similar to those typically found in the workplace. The continuing nature of the case studies provides these positive learning experiences:

- Students are able to use richer contextual clues to solve communication problems than is possible in the shorter end-of-chapter exercises.
- Students become intimately familiar with the managers and the company and must select what is relevant from a mass of data, thereby learning to handle information overload. For added realism, each case includes an action photograph illustrating that particular communication situation.
- Because the same situations frequently carry over into subsequent chapters, students must face the consequences of their earlier decisions.
- Many cases require students to solve the same communication problem from two different perspectives—thereby enhancing the concept of audience analysis.
- The cases provide realistic opportunities for practicing work-team communication and critical-thinking skills.

Work-Team Communication

Fed by global competition and global opportunities, contemporary organizations are making extensive use of project management, continuous process improvement, and work teams to encourage their employees to work and communicate collaboratively to solve complex workplace problems. Thus, competent communicators need to develop high-level interpersonal skills for working in small groups as well as for writing and presenting collaboratively.

Because many instructors assign group projects right from the beginning of the term, work-team communication competence is one of those "up-front" skills students must have to benefit completely from the discussion of other business communication topics. Unfortunately, however, instructors often erroneously assume students already know how to work together effectively.

Chapter 2, "Work-Team Communication," introduces these topics:

- The role of conflict, conformity, and consensus in work teams.
- Proven methods for giving constructive feedback, including commenting on peer writing.
- Work-team intercultural diversity that stresses diversity within the United States—for example, ethnicity, gender, age, and physical abilities.

Numerous end-of-chapter exercises provide students the opportunity to work together in teams to solve typical business communication problems.

Focus on Contemporary Issues

Throughout the text, boxed features called Spotlights illustrate how business communication is affected by three contemporary issues: the increasing international and intercultural nature of today's business world (with an emphasis on demographic diversity within the U.S. work environment), technology in the workplace, and the growing importance of the ethical dimensions of communicating.

Spotlights are specifically designed to reinforce criteria from AACSB (Association to Advance Collegiate Schools of Business) for teaching the international, technological, ethical, and demographically diverse dimensions of business. Because these are contemporary issues, all Spotlights have been updated.

New to this edition are "Communication Snapshots"—colorful graphics that present up-to-date factoids about issues directly relating to contemporary business communication.

Today, if there is one business buzzword, it has to be "technology"—and with good reason. Every aspect of contemporary business communication—from determining what information to communicate to processing the information and sharing it—depends on technology. In *Contemporary Business Communication* students learn to:

- Compose, format, and manage e-mail.
- Evaluate the quality of the information accessed from the Internet.
- Format electronic and HTML résumés and search online for jobs.
- Give electronic presentations, including preparing effective audience handouts.
- Cite electronic sources such as Web pages, online journals and directories, e-mail, and other Internet sources in business, APA, and MLA formats.

Throughout, the text places major emphasis on newer technologies (such as teleconferencing, videoconferencing, and video and electronic presentations). In addition, numerous end-of-chapter exercises provide experience in obtaining, evaluating, and using Internet data sources.

The 3Ps (Problem, Process, and Product) Model

The 3Ps (Problem, Process, and Product) models and activities, with their step-by-step analyses of typical communication tasks, have been one of the most popular features of previous editions. These models comprise the *problem* (the situation that requires a communication task), the *process* (step-by-step guidance for accomplishing that task), and the *product* (a fully formatted finished document).

The 3Ps activities require students to focus their efforts on developing a strategy for any message (including e-mail messages) before beginning to compose it, and they serve as a step-by-step model for students when they compose their own messages.

The 3Ps activities within each chapter all contain the solutions to the process questions. The 3Ps exercises at the end of the chapter (plus additional ones in the *Instructor's Resource Manual*, on the instructor's website, and in Eduspace in the BusCom Writer tutorials) pose process questions and then require the students themselves to provide the solutions, thereby more actively engaging the student in the problem-solving process.

Annotated Models and Checklists

Full-page models of each major writing task appear in this edition, shown in complete ready-to-send format, so that students become familiar with the appropriate format for every major type of writing assignment. Each model provides marginal step-by-step composing notes as well as grammar and mechanics notes that point out specific illustrations of the grammar and mechanics rules presented in the Reference Manual.

The 19 Checklists recap the essential points for composing each major type of communication and serve as a blueprint when students compose their own documents.

Basic Skills First

Language Arts Basics (LABs)   No one can communicate effectively if he or she cannot communicate correctly. It is an unfortunate fact of life that many contemporary students today have not had the advantage of the nuts-and-bolts grammar and mechanics instruction that their instructors took for granted in their own education. Students must learn these basic skills at some point, and the collegiate business communication course is probably their last opportunity.

The six LAB exercises in the appendix of *Contemporary Business Communication* systematically teach and test the most frequently occurring and most frequently misused rules of English grammar and mechanics:

1. Parts of Speech
2. Punctuation—Commas
3. Punctuation—Other Marks
4. Grammar
5. Mechanics
6. Word Usage

Each chapter in the text ends with a LAB test that systematically reinforces the language arts rules presented in the appendix. Instructors can use the LAB exercises and LAB tests as needed to ensure that their students have an opportunity to demonstrate their strategic business communication skills without allowing grammar and mechanics deficiencies to interfere with their communication goals.

SCANS Competencies   In its report *Learning a Living*, the U.S. Department of Labor Secretary's Commission of Achieving Necessary Skills (SCANS) defined the skills U.S. workers need for workplace success. Clearly identified in this report were needed workplace competencies in using resources, acquiring and processing information, developing interpersonal skills, understanding and working with systems, and using technology. Since then, numerous state higher education commissions have required that postsecondary textbooks indicate the extent to which they teach and apply these competencies. The *Instructor's Resource Manual* identifies every SCANS competency taught and applied in *Contemporary Business Communication*.

Revising—The Real Communication Skill   Students learn at least as much from revising as from drafting their documents. The *Instructor's Resource Manual* provides handout masters for "Help Wanted" exercises for Chapters 7 through 15. These exercises present a sample student-written draft, marked up with typical instructor or supervisor comments, which students then revise and resubmit as homework.

The purpose of these exercises is to provide students with guided editing practice. The content is a complete business document (instead of isolated sentences), and guidance is provided regarding the writing weaknesses to look for (instead of just providing a complete "bad" document and asking students to revise it). Both rhetorical and stylistic weaknesses are identified for students to correct.

In addition, annotated first-draft/second-draft models in the correspondence chapters show how a document evolves through rewriting and refining.

Unprecedented Instructor Support

The sixth edition of *Contemporary Business Communication* provides unprecedented instructor support.

Ask Ober   *Contemporary Business Communication* takes the concept of communication to a new level. The "Ask Ober" feature (e-mail: askober@ober.net) permits and encourages direct dialog between you or your students and the textbook author. Whenever you or your students have a question or comment about this text or about the business communication curriculum, ask Ober. Add this e-mail address to your own contacts list and include it in your course syllabus. (Please ask students to copy you on any e-mail so that both you and your students receive a personal response from the author.) You and your students have never been so connected.

New to this edition is an "Ask Ober" column in each chapter. This column contains actual questions received from the hundreds of instructors and students who have made use of this unique form of communication—along with the author's responses.

Instructor's Annotated Edition   In the typical collegiate business communication department, a large number of faculty are adjunct instructors—often with extensive work experience but with less experience actually teaching business communication. The *Instructor's Annotated Edition* provides specific, accessible teaching aids, such as these:

- Miniature copies of the PowerPoint slides and handout masters shown in the text margins of the IAE so that instructors can see immediately what enrichment materials are available for each section of the text.
- Marginal notes that reference related sections in the teaching support package for suggested solutions to text exercises and additional exercises.
- Teaching tips and interesting business examples that offer resources to enrich lectures.

Instructor Website   The BusCom Online Teaching Center (http://college.hmco .com/business) can be accessed via a free password provided to instructors using this text. The site contains detailed lecture and supplemental discussion notes for each chapter, additional application exercises and cases, PowerPoint slides and handout masters to preview and download, and a forum in which to exchange ideas with the author, publisher, and other instructors around the country teaching this course.

PowerPoint Slides   The PowerPoint program consists of more than 300 author-prepared slides, including summaries of key concepts, paired good/bad examples, and supplementary information such as answers to selected exercises. For added interest, the examples used in the slides are all different from those used in the text.

Instructor Newsletter   An online monthly newsletter features additional teaching tips and hot-off-the-press current event items that illustrate business communication concepts. Through a new listserv provided by Houghton Mifflin Company, instructors may now also request that the newsletter be sent to them regularly via e-mail.

Eduspace® Powered by Blackboard™   Houghton Mifflin's online learning tool is a customizable, powerful, and interactive platform that provides instructors with text-specific online courses and content in multiple disciplines. Eduspace gives an instructor the ability to create all or part of their course online using the widely recognized tools of Blackboard and quality text-specific content. Content includes Lab Manual diagnostic tests, auto-graded quizzes based on BusCom Writer Tutorials, and supplemental study materials. Instructors can modify that content or even add their own.

BusCom Writer Tutorials are a special component of the Eduspace program accompanying *Contemporary Business Communication*. Each of these self-paced tutorials, based on the textbook's 3Ps (Problem, Process, and Product) model, presents students with a unique business situation and guides them through preparing a finished product.

Blackboard and WebCT Support   Houghton Mifflin provides specific assistance for instructors who want to create and customize online course materials for use in distance learning or as a supplement to traditional classes. This service helps instructors create and manage their own websites to bring learning materials, class discussions, and tests online. Houghton Mifflin provides all the necessary content for an introductory course in business communication using *Contemporary Business Communication*.

Instructor's Resource Manual　　The *Instructor's Resource Manual* includes sample syllabi, correlation of SCANS competencies to text material, grading rubrics (objective forms to help instructors evaluate student work), and suggestions for guiding students in developing a writing portfolio. In addition, the manual provides chapter overviews, lecture and discussion notes, supplemental lecture notes, suggested answers to and/or teaching tips for all writing exercises and case problems, additional 3Ps (Problem, Process, and Product) exercises with formulated solutions, an answer key to grammar and mechanics exercises, fully formatted solutions to all correspondence assignments, and a sample long report and memo report.

Also included are 70 handout masters, which include in-class worksheets, checklists that can be used as evaluation forms (grading rubrics) for student writing, model assignments, and "Help Wanted" editing exercises.

Test Bank and HMClassPrep with HMTesting　　HMClassPrep with HMTesting contains all instructor resources including the complete IRM, the PowerPoint slides, the Test Bank, and HMTesting. The Test Bank and HMTesting contain approximately 1,200 test items, including multiple-choice, true/false, and short-answer items, most of which are new or extensively revised. HMTesting is software that allows instructors to prepare examinations of any quantity and combination of questions from the Test Bank. The instructor can produce a test master with alternative versions for easy duplication.

Overhead Transparencies　　Nearly one hundred color transparencies are available on the instructor website, including summaries of key concepts, writing examples, text figures, and answers to selected exercises.

Video Program　　Video case studies of well-known companies reinforce text concepts by directly relating them to the footage being shown. In addition, discussion questions and suggested writing assignments are provided for each video.

Innovative Student Support Materials

A wealth of additional learning materials completes the sixth-edition package.

- **Student Website.**　The BusCom Online Learning Center provides students with a one-stop guide to the world of online business communication. Here they can learn more about the Internet, locate business information, get additional help with writing problems, complete ACE quizzes designed to assess students' understanding of chapter and Lab Manual content, test vocabulary knowledge with flash cards, take practice chapter tests, and get information about employment communication, available jobs, and employers.

- **Urban Systems Case Study CD-ROM.**　This innovative case study simulation provides a total immersion experience for students. Based on the Urban Systems end-of-chapter continuing case, the CD-ROM brings business communication challenges to life by allowing students to virtually experience the situation and actively solve the problem. Within each of the 15 modules, students take on the role of an employee at Urban Systems who needs to solve a basic communication problem. In keeping with the text's overall emphasis on technology and real-world experience, each scenario involves a series of daily communication tasks encountered in any modern office—reading e-mail, listening to voice mail messages, and sorting through a variety of in-box materials. The CD program provides immediate feedback for all exercises, as well as additional guidance when students work independently to address the communication challenge at hand.

Acknowledgments

During the revision of this text, it has been my great pleasure to work with a dedicated and skillful team of professionals at Houghton Mifflin, including Audrey Bryant, Andrea Cava, and Joanne Dauksewicz. I gratefully salute them for the major contributions they have made to the success of this text. I also wish to express my sincere appreciation to Ron and Carolee Jones, Duane Miller, Keith Mulbery, and Marian Wood for the many elements they contributed to this and previous editions. What a genuine pleasure it has been to work with this talented and dynamic team. In addition, I wish to thank the following reviewers for their thoughtful contributions:

Carl Bridges, *Arthur Andersen Consulting*
Annette Briscoe, *Indiana University Southeast*
Mitchel T. Burchfield, *Southwest Texas Junior College*
Janice Burke, *South Suburban College*
Leila Chambers, *Cuesta College*
G. Jay Christensen, *California State University, Northridge*
Connie Clark, *Lane Community College*
Miriam Coleman, *Western Michigan University*
Anne Hutta Colvin, *Montgomery County Community College*
Doris L. Cost, *Metropolitan State College of Denver*
L. Ben Crane, *Temple University*
Ava Cross, *Ryerson Polytechnic University*
Nancy J. Daugherty, *Indiana University-Purdue University, Indianapolis*
Rosemarie Dittmer, *Northeastern University*
Gary Donnelly, *Casper College*
Graham N. Drake, *State University of New York, Geneseo*
Kay Durden, *The University of Tennessee at Martin*
Phillip A. Holcomb, *Angelo State University*
Larry R. Honl, *University of Wisconsin, Eau Claire*
Kristi Kelly, *Florida Gulf Coast University*
Michelle Kirtley Johnston, *Loyola University*
Alice Kinder, *Virginia Polytechnic Institute and State University*
Emogene King, *Tyler Junior College*
Richard N. Kleeberg, *Solano Community College*
Patricia Laidler, *Massasoit Community College*
Lowell Lamberton, *Central Oregon Community College*
E. Jay Larson, *Lewis and Clark State College*
Michael Liberman, *East Stroudsburg University*
Julie MacDonald, *Northwestern State University*
Marsha C. Markman, *California Lutheran University*

Diana McKowen, *Indiana University, Bloomington*
Maureen McLaughlin, *Highline Community College*
Sylvia A. Miller, *Cameron University*
Billie Miller-Cooper, *Cosumnes River College*
Wayne Moore, *Indiana University of Pennsylvania*
Gerald W. Morton, *Auburn University of Montgomery*
Jaunett Neighbors, *Central Virginia Community College*
Judy Nixon, *University of Tennessee at Chattanoga*
Rosemary Olds, *Des Moines Area Community College*
Richard O. Pompian, *Boise State University*
Karen Sterkel Powell, *Colorado State University*
Seamus Reilly, *University of Illinois*
Jeanette Ritzenthaler, *New Hampshire College*
Betty Robbins, *University of Oklahoma*
Joan C. Roderick, *Southwest Texas State University*
Mary Jane Ryals, *Florida State University*
Lacye Prewitt Schmidt, *State Technical Institute of Memphis*
Sue Seymour, *Cameron University*
Sherry Sherrill, *Forsyth Technical Community College*
John R. Sinton, *Finger Lakes Community College*
Curtis J. Smith, *Finger Lakes Community College*
Craig E. Stanley, *California State University, Sacramento*
Ted O. Stoddard, *Brigham Young University*
Vincent C. Trofi, *Providence College*
Deborah A. Valentine, *Emory University*
Randall L. Waller, *Baylor University*
Maria W. Warren, *University of West Florida*
Michael R. Wunsch, *Northern Arizona University*
Annette Wyandotte, *Indiana University, Southeast*
Betty Rogers Youngkin, *University of Dayton*

Scot Ober
askober@ober.net

Contemporary Business Communication

1

Understanding Business Communication

After you have finished this chapter, you should be able to

1. **Describe the components of communication.**

2. **Identify the common forms of written and oral communication.**

3. **Explain the directions that make up the formal communication network.**

4. **Describe the characteristics of the grapevine.**

5. **Identify the major verbal and nonverbal barriers to communication.**

6. **Explain the legal and ethical dimensions of communicating.**

Look to the Communication Objectives (COs) as a guide to help you master the material. You will see references to the COs throughout the chapter.

2

an insider's
perspective

DEBRA SANCHEZ FAIR
Vice President,
Corporate Communications,
Nissan North America, Inc.

These on-the-job interviews give you a snapshot of the reality you will face in the workplace.

Steering communication upward, downward, horizontally, and across business and borders—at full throttle—is part of a race that never ends for Debra Sanchez Fair. As vice president of corporate communications for Nissan North America, she and her 43-person staff drive all communications for the automaker's operations in the United States, Mexico, and Canada. Communication is considered so critical to building internal and external relationships that Fair reports to North American senior management, the global head of communications, and directly to Nissan's CEO in Tokyo; she is also part of a six-person team handling the corporation's overall communication strategy. Fair always maintains a global perspective because Nissan is headquartered in Japan, has an alliance with France's Renault, and conducts business on every continent. English is the firm's official language.

Fair uses a variety of media to share information within the organization, ranging from e-mail, video conferencing, and satellite television to more traditional newsletters, meetings, and memos. Before selecting any medium, however, she carefully plans what she wants to achieve. "First, you have to think about your objective, the audiences you are targeting, and your communication strategies," she says. "Then you think about the tactics. Every situation or initiative may require a different approach."

Several times each year, Fair serves as moderator for internal "town hall meetings," during which senior executives provide updates on key issues and answer questions from employees. Rotating from North American headquarters to different regional sites, these meetings reach all U.S., Canadian, and Mexican facilities via live satellite feeds and encourage audience participation. "Often, we field questions in advance from the employee base," Fair notes. "We also take e-mailed questions during the meeting." If time runs out, questions are answered in the company's internal *Dateline* newsletter and posted on their intranet.

One of Fair's biggest challenges has been handling communication related to the Nissan Revival Plan, an aggressive three-year strategy calling for massive organizational changes to restore the company's profitability, slash its costs, reduce its debt by half, and promote growth. Not only did Nissan need internal support to achieve its ambitious goals, but it also needed to explain the plan—an unusual one for a Japanese firm—to industry media, financial analysts, share-

holders, and other outsiders. "The only way to galvanize the employee base and get the message to external audiences was to get the communication function involved at the start," Fair explains. "The key was developing clear, consistent messages to be communicated internally and externally." Fair therefore limits the number of points in each message and repeats the major ideas in more than one message to increase audience understanding and retention.

To find out whether audiences understand the Nissan Revival Plan messages, Fair conducts twice-yearly global employee surveys and annual surveys of business leaders and media representatives. She also asks local facilities to circulate questionnaires following specific company announcements. "We ask, 'Did your employees understand the key messages?' " she says. "How do they feel about it? Are they on board? Is there a more effective tool we should be using for communication?" Monitoring this feedback helps Fair and her team analyze audience response and keep Nissan's communication on track in the race that never ends.

"The key was developing clear, consistent messages to be communicated internally and externally."

■ Communicating in Organizations

CO1. Describe the components of communication.

The margin note above shows which communication objective is being addressed in this text.

Communication is necessary if an organization is to achieve its goals.

■ See Slide 1.1.

■ A chapter overview appears in the *Instructor's Resource Manual.*

These designers from Bruce Mau Design Studios in Toronto are engaging in both nonverbal communication (such as body movement, voice qualities, and use of space) and verbal communication (speaking, listening, reading, and writing).

Real people in real organizations are highlighted in these photos, most of which are taken from magazines and newspapers.

Walk through the halls of a contemporary organization—no matter whether it's a small start-up entrepreneurial firm, a Fortune 500 global giant, a state government office, or a not-for-profit organization—and what do you see? You will see managers and other employees reading reports, drafting e-mail messages, attending meetings, conducting interviews, talking on the telephone, conferring with subordinates, holding business lunches, reading mail, dictating correspondence, and making presentations. In short, you see people *communicating.*

An organization is a group of people working together to achieve a common goal, and communication is a vital part of that process. Indeed, communication must have occurred before a common goal could even be established. And a group of people working together must interact; that is, they must *communicate* their needs, thoughts, plans, expertise, and so on. Communication is the means by which information is shared, activities are coordinated, and decision making is enhanced.

Understanding how communication works in business and how to communicate competently within an organization will help you participate more effectively in every aspect of business. Consider these recent research findings:[1]

■ Research by the National Association of Colleges and Employers (NACE) identified the top ten characteristics employers seek in job candidates. Number 1 was communication skills, followed by motivation/initiative and teamwork skills.

■ A survey of 224 recent business graduates ranked communication as the most important area of knowledge both for securing employment after graduation and for advancement and promotion once on the job.

■ A survey of 6,000 people conducted by *Young Executive* magazine found that the most annoying habit of American bosses was poor communication.

■ A survey of 200 corporate vice presidents reported they spend the equivalent of nearly three months a year writing correspondence and reports.

■ A survey of 1,000 white- and blue-collar workers found that the most frequent cause of workplace resentment and misunderstandings is poor communication.

■ A survey of Fortune 500 human resource directors found that (a) reading and following directions, (b) listening and following directions, and (c) communication are the most essential skills for the contemporary workplace.

■ Eighty percent of the managers at 402 firms surveyed nationwide said that most of their employees need to improve their writing skills, up from 65 percent the previous year. But only 21 percent of the firms offered training in writing skills.

Note also from Communication Snapshot 1 that the lack of competent written communication skills is the number one source of dissatisfaction that employers have about their employees.

Clearly, good communication skills are crucial to your success in the organization. Competent writing and speaking skills will help you get hired, perform well, and earn promotions. If you decide to go into business for yourself, writing and speaking skills will help you obtain venture capital, promote your product, and manage your employees. These same skills will also help you achieve your personal and social goals.

It is no wonder then that, according to Mark H. McCormack, chairman of International Management Group, and best-selling author of *What They Don't Teach You at Harvard Business School,* "People's written communications are probably more revealing than any other single item in the workplace."[2]

■ For more on good communication skills, see the supplemental lecture/discussion notes in the *Instructor's Resource Manual.*

communication snapshot 1

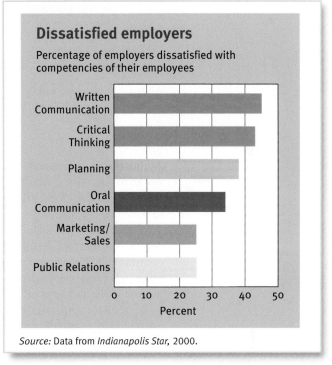

Dissatisfied employers

Percentage of employers dissatisfied with competencies of their employees

Source: Data from *Indianapolis Star,* 2000.

Snapshots—one in each chapter—provide statistical insight into the communication habits of people.

■ The Components of Communication

Because communication is such a vital part of the organizational structure, our study of communication begins with an analysis of its components. **Communication** is the process of sending and receiving messages—sometimes through spoken or written words and sometimes through such nonverbal means as facial expressions, gestures, and voice qualities. Thus, if someone communicates the following message to you and you receive it, communication will have taken place. However, only if you understand Chinese will the communication have been successful.*

Communication is the sending and receiving of verbal and nonverbal messages.

*Illustrated above is the Chinese word for *crisis,* which is composed of the words *danger* and *opportunity,* perhaps an inspirational reminder to always remain hopeful.

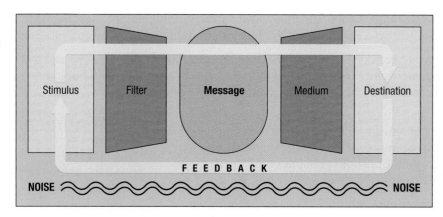

figure1.1

The Components of Communication

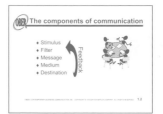

■ See Slide 1.2.

■ See Slide 1.3.

As illustrated in Figure 1.1, the communication model consists of five components: the stimulus, filter, message, medium, and destination. Ideally, the process ends with feedback to the sender, although feedback is not necessary for communication to have taken place.

To illustrate the model, let us follow the case of Dave Kaplan, a chemical engineer at Industrial Chemical, Inc. (We'll become quite familiar with Dave and his company in the coming chapters.) In 2000, in the process of working on another project, Dave developed Ultra Light, a flat, electroluminescent sheet of material that serves as a light source. Dave could see the enormous business opportunity offered by a paper-thin light fixture such as Ultra Light, which was bendable and could be produced in a variety of shapes and sizes.

The market for lighting is vast, and Dave, even though at the time an engineer and not a businessman, felt the sting of inventing a device that had great potential but that belonged to somebody else (Industrial Chemical, Inc.). He was disappointed in IC's eventual decision not to manufacture and market this product. As we learn what happened to Dave Kaplan after IC's decision, we'll examine the components of communication, one at a time.

Incident	Communication Component
Dave receives a memorandum from the head of R&D.	Dave receives a *stimulus*.
He interprets the memo to mean that IC has no interest in his invention.	He *filters* the stimulus.
He decides to relay this information to his brother.	He forms a *message*.
He telephones Marc.	He selects a *medium*.
His brother receives the call.	The message reaches its *destination*.
Marc listens and gives Dave his reaction.	Marc provides *feedback*.

The Stimulus

In order for communication to take place, there first must be a **stimulus,** an event that creates within an individual the need to communicate. This stimulus can be internal or external. An internal stimulus is simply an idea that forms within your mind. External stimuli come to you through your sensory organs—your eyes, ears, nose, mouth, and skin. A stimulus for communicating in business might be an e-mail message you just read, a bit of gossip you heard over lunch, or even the hot air generated by an overworked heating system (or colleague!).

You respond to the stimulus by formulating a message: a **verbal message** (written or spoken words), a **nonverbal message** (nonwritten and nonspoken signals), or some combination of the two. For Dave Kaplan, the stimulus for communication was a memorandum he received from the head of the research and development (R&D) department informing him that IC was not interested in developing Ultra Light but would, instead, sell the patent to some company that was interested.

Step 1: A stimulus creates a need to communicate.

■ According to playwright George Bernard Shaw, "The greatest problem in communication is the illusion that it has been accomplished."

The Filter

If everyone had the same perception of events, your job of communicating would be easier; you could assume that your perception of reality was accurate and that others would understand your motives and intent. Instead, each person has a unique perception of reality, based on his or her individual experiences, culture, emotions at the moment, personality, knowledge, socioeconomic status, and a host of other variables. These variables act as a **filter** in shaping everyone's unique impressions of reality.

Once your brain receives a message, it begins to interpret the stimulus to derive meaning from it so that you will know how to respond or whether any response is even necessary.

The memo Dave received from R&D simply reinforced what he had come to expect at his company, which showed little interest in exploiting unexpected discoveries such as Ultra Light. Dave's long involvement in the research that had led to this product caused him to assume a protective, almost paternalistic, interest in its future. Besides, after so many years in the lab, Dave was ready for a new challenge. These factors, then, acted as a filter through which Dave interpreted the memo and formulated his response—a phone call to his brother in Chicago.

At the time of Dave's call, Marc Kaplan was sitting alone in his office at a Chicago advertising agency sampling different brands of cheese pizza (see the photo to the right). As a marketing manager in charge of a new pizza account, he was preoccupied with finding a competitive edge for his client's product, and his perception of Dave's message was filtered by his current situation.

To hear his scientist brother, the MIT graduate who all his life had preferred to pursue solitary scholarly research, suddenly erupting over the phone with the idea of starting a

Step 2: Our knowledge, experience, and viewpoints act as a filter to help us interpret (decode) the stimulus.

The brain attempts to make sense of the stimulus.

An example of communication at work.

Let's form a company, Marc.

This is my brother? I don't believe this.

business contradicted Marc's lifelong preconceptions about Dave and acted as a strong filter resisting Dave's urgent message. Furthermore, Marc's emotional and physical frame of reference—hunkered down as he was over several cheese pizzas—did not put him in a receptive mood for a grand scheme that would take tens of thousands of dollars and many years of hard work. But Marc's background—his economic status, his education, and his current job—added another point of view, in this case a highly favorable filter for taking in Dave's message.

If Dave is good enough at communicating his message, he might be able to persuade Marc to join him in buying the Ultra Light patent from IC and starting a business of their own.

The Message

Step 3: We formulate (encode) a verbal or nonverbal response to the stimulus.

Dave's message to Marc was, "Let's form our own company." The extent to which any communication effort achieves its desired goal depends on how well you construct the **message** (the information to be communicated). Success at communicating depends not only on the purpose and content of the message but also on how skillful you are at communicating, how well you know your **audience** (the person or persons with whom you're communicating), and how much you hold in common with your audience. As a scientist, Dave Kaplan did not have an extensive business vocabulary. Nor did he have much practice at oral business presentations and the careful pacing and selective reinforcement required in such circumstances. In effect, Dave was attempting to make an oral business proposal, unfortunately without much technique or skill.

"You're crazy, Dave. You don't know what you're talking about." This initial response from Marc made it clear to Dave that his message wasn't getting through. But what Dave lacked in skill, he made up for in knowing his audience (his kid brother) backward and forward.

"You're chicken, Marc" had always gotten Marc's attention and interest in the past, and it worked again. Dave kept challenging Marc, something he knew Marc couldn't resist, and kept reminding him of their common ground: all the happy adventures they had shared as kids and adults.

The Medium

Step 4: We select the form of the message (medium).

Once the sender has encoded a message, the next step in the process is to transmit that message to the receiver. At this point, the sender must choose the **medium,** that is, the means of transmitting the message. Oral messages might be transmitted through a staff meeting, personal conference, telephone conversation, voice mail, or even such informal means as the company grapevine. Written messages might be transmitted through a memorandum, a report, a brochure, a bulletin board notice, e-mail, a company newsletter, or an addition to the policies and procedures manual. And nonverbal messages might be transmitted through facial expressions, gestures, or body movement. (See Spotlight 1, "The Medium Is the Message," on page 10.)

Because Dave is in the process of talking with Marc over the phone, his medium is a telephone conversation. You should be aware that the most commonly used forms of communication are not necessarily the most effective ones. The International Association of Business Communicators (IABC) recently surveyed nearly 1,000 organizations about their communication practices. As shown in Figure 1.2, although e-mail was found to be the most frequently used medium of communication, it was not considered the most effective medium.[3]

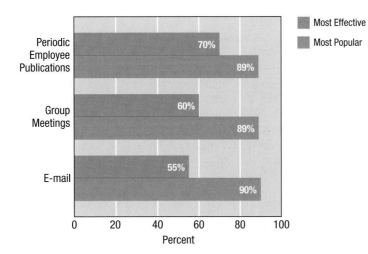

figure 1.2

Effectiveness Versus Popularity of Communication Media

The Destination

The message is transmitted and then enters the sensory environment of the receiver, at which point control passes from the sender to the receiver. Once the message reaches its destination, there is no guarantee that communication will actually occur. We are constantly bombarded with stimuli, and our sensory organs pick up only part of them. Even assuming your receiver does perceive your message, you have no assurance that it will be interpreted (filtered) as you intended. Your transmitted message then becomes the source, or stimulus, for the next communication episode, and the process begins anew.

> *Step 5: The message reaches its destination and, if successful, is perceived accurately by the receiver.*

After Dave's enthusiastic, one-hour phone call, Marc promised to consider the venture seriously. Marc's response provided **feedback** (reaction to a message) to Dave on how accurately his own message had been received. In time, it led to many more versions of the communication process, both written and oral, before the two brothers founded Urban Systems, a small "start-up" company whose primary product is Ultra Light. The company employs 178 people at its corporate headquarters in Ann Arbor, Michigan, and at a completely automated manufacturing plant in Charlotte, North Carolina.

The Dynamic Nature of Communication

From our look at the components of communication and the model presented in Figure 1.1 on page 6, you might erroneously conclude that communication is a linear, static process—flowing in an orderly fashion from one stage to the next—and that you can easily separate the communicators into senders and receivers. That is not at all the case.

> *Communication is not a linear, static process.*

Two or more people often send and receive messages simultaneously. At the same time you are receiving one message, you may be sending another. For example, the look on your face as you are receiving a message may be sending a new message to the sender that you either understand, agree with, or are baffled by the message being sent. And the feedback thus given may prompt the sender to modify his or her intended message.

Thus, artificially "freezing" the action in order to examine each step of the communication process separately causes us to lose some of the dynamic richness of that process in terms of both its verbal and nonverbal components.

The Medium Is the Message

According to critic Marshall McLuhan, the medium you use to express your message not only identifies the form of the message but also becomes a part of the message itself. How do you determine which medium will be most effective for your message? And exactly how does the medium affect the message you send?

Situation A: Telephone

Assume that your travel plans for two weeks from now just changed and you find that you'll have to stay overnight in Detroit instead of continuing on to Kansas City. You decide to use the evening to wine and dine a good customer in nearby Grosse Pointe Woods. Which medium should you use to invite her and her spouse to dinner?

The simplest and fastest thing to do, of course, is to pick up the phone and call your customer. But because you're both busy people (isn't everyone, these days?), you should be prepared to leave a voice mail message, if necessary:

Voice Mail

Hi, Marge. Stan Petrie here from Eastern Container Corporation. It's 2:30 p.m. on Monday, October 1. I just found out that I'm going to be in town Wednesday night, October 17, and hope you and Casper can be my guests for dinner at the Midtown Club. If you can come, let's plan to meet in the lobby at 7 p.m. Please give me a call back at 282-555-8221 to let me know if you can join me. I look forward to seeing you. Bye.

Notice how your choice of telephone communication affected the content of your message. First, because some answering machines and voice-message systems don't record the time, you included the time and date of your call. Also, recognizing that some systems have limited capacity, you cut out the small talk and left a concise, to-the-point message (after all, you don't want to get disconnected midsentence). You were also considerate enough to provide your phone number, which also encourages a prompt callback.

Because you were leaving a voice message, you were able to use certain nonverbal clues—such as enthusiasm and warmth in your tone of voice—to help convey a friendly message and encourage this important customer to accept your invitation. As you can see, oral messages generally assume a more informal tone than do written messages.

Situation B: E-mail

Uh, oh. You just realized that (1) Marge and Casper might not know where the Midtown Club is, and (2) they have young children and will need to leave some emergency location information with their sitter. Phone messages work best for one-way calls or for requests that require a short, simple response. They do not work well for detailed messages because the listener must listen and try to take notes at the same time.

Instead of phoning, you decide to send Marge an e-mail:

E-mail

Hi, Marge:
I will be in town on Wednesday, October 17, and invite you and Casper to be my guests for dinner at the Midtown Club (2378 Schuylkill Road; Phone: 313-555-8766).

If you can join me, let's plan to meet in the lobby at 7 p.m. We should be finished with dinner by 9:30 p.m.

Boxed features called Spotlights illustrate how business communication is affected by three contemporary issues: international, technology, and ethics.

Urban Systems: A Continuing Case Study

As we join Urban Systems (US), Dave and Marc's company has annual sales in the $30 million range, with a net profit last year of $1.4 million. It is considered a progressive company by the investment community, with skillful management and healthy earnings potential. The local community considers US to be a good corporate citizen; it is nonpolluting, and its officers are active in community affairs.

It will be good to visit with you and Casper again.
Stan Petrie
Eastern Container Corporation
282-555-8221
spetrie@ecc.com

One advantage of e-mail (of any written communication, in fact) is that you can revise your message before sending it—to make it more effective. Also, the recipient can save or print the message if desired, thereby providing documentation. Another advantage is that responding is simple; the recipient can simply click the Reply button and either accept or decline your invitation. Note also that because your phone number is included in your "signature," you don't need to include it in the body of the e-mail itself.

Situation C: Letter

Now assume a different scenario. For some reason, Marge has not placed an order with Eastern Container Corporation in more than a month, and you want to gently broach this subject with her to find out why. Given the fact that she may be embarrassed at not swinging any business your way lately, Marge might be reluctant to accept your invitation and might need some "incentive" to join you.

Wanting to make a favorable impression on this good customer and realizing that e-mail is not always free from prying eyes, you decide to invite her to dinner in a letter. (After all, the dinner is still two weeks away, so you have time to go the "snail mail" route.)

Business Letter

Dear Marge:
Your company's feedback earlier this spring helped

---

us redesign our series of corrugated shipping cartons, and I'd like to thank you in person.

Would you and Casper be my guests for dinner at the Midtown Club on Wednesday, October 17? The club is located at 2378 Schuylkill Road (at the intersection of Schuylkill and Main); its phone number is 313-555-8766. If you can join me, let's plan to meet in the lobby at 7 p.m. We should be finished with dinner by 9:30 p.m.

It will be good to see you again—and also to let you in on a few "surprises" we discovered along the way to redesigning these cartons.
Sincerely,

Notice how the medium affects the message in this version. First, in the transmitted document, the message will be formatted in regular business letter format and on letterhead stationery, which will give it a more formal appearance. Second, note the differences in the organization of the message—for example, the persuasive opening and the "teaser" at the end. Finally, because space is not at a premium, you can include more information in a business letter than is advisable in voice mail and e-mail messages (remembering, however, that conciseness is a virtue in any form of communication).

The overall tone of the business letter also differs from that of the voice-mail message. To illustrate the differences, read the voice-mail message aloud; then read the business letter aloud. You will immediately note the difference in the naturalness of each message for its intended medium. The medium is the message—at least, in part.

Sometimes in your communications, you have a choice as to which medium to use (of course, sometimes you do not). Competent communicators ensure that both the medium and the message itself help them achieve their communication objective.

You will be seeing more of the Kaplan brothers and Urban Systems in the chapters ahead, as communication within the organization serves as an ongoing case study for each of the major areas of business communication—from this basic model of communication all the way through to the final chapter. You'll have the opportunity to get to know the people in the company and watch from the inside as they handle every type of business communication in concrete terms. Right now,

An Urban Systems continuing case problem is at the end of each chapter.

you can learn more of the background of Urban Systems by reading the Appendix to Chapter 1 (beginning on page 36), which contains an overview of the company's history, products, financial data, and all-too-human personnel.

■ Verbal Communication

CO2. Identify the common forms of written and oral communication.

It is the ability to communicate by using words that separates human beings from the rest of the animal kingdom. Our verbal ability also enables us to learn from the past—to benefit from the experience of others.

Oral Communication

Verbal messages are composed of words—either written or spoken.

Oral communication is one of the most common functions in business. Consider, for example, how limiting it would be if a manager could not attend meetings, ask questions of colleagues, make presentations, appraise performance, handle customer complaints, or give instructions.

Oral communication is different from written communication in that it allows more ways to get a message across to others. You can clear up any questions immediately; use nonverbal clues; provide additional information; and use pauses, emphasis, and voice tone to stress certain points.

According to research, these are the most annoying voice qualities, listed in decreasing order of annoyance:[4]

Whining, complaining, or nagging tone	44%
High-pitched, squeaky voice	16%
Mumbling	11%
Talking very fast	5%
Weak, wimpy voice	4%
Flat, monotonous tone	4%

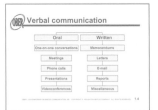

■ See Slide 1.4.

■ Here is one business consultant's view of the present state of affairs regarding oral communication in business: "Samson of biblical fame killed 10,000 Philistines with the jawbone of an ass. Similar destruction occurs on a daily basis with the same weapon." (Dianna Booher, *Communicating with Confidence*, New York: McGraw-Hill, 1994, p. x.)

For oral communication to be effective, a second communication skill—listening—is also required. No matter how well crafted the content and delivery of an oral presentation, it cannot achieve its goal if the intended audience does not have effective listening skills. Some research has found that nearly 60 percent of all communication problems in business are caused by poor listening.[5]

Written Communication

Writing is more difficult than speaking because you have to get your message correct the first time; you do not have the advantage of immediate feedback or nonverbal clues such as facial expressions to help you achieve your objective. Examples of typical written communication in industry include the following:

- *E-mail (electronic mail):* **E-mail** (see Figure 1.3) is a message transmitted electronically over a computer network. Often, in the contemporary office, e-mail has replaced traditional memorandums and, in many cases, letters.

- *Website:* A **website** comprises one or more pages of related information that is posted on the World Wide Web and is accessed via the Internet; the main page of a website is called its "home page."

- *Memorandums:* A **memorandum** is a written message sent to someone working in the same organization.

- *Letters:* A **letter** is a written message sent to someone outside the organization.

- *Reports:* A **report** is an orderly and objective presentation of information that assists in decision making and problem solving. Examples of common business reports include policies and procedures, status reports, financial reports, personnel evaluations, and computer printouts.

- *Miscellaneous:* Other examples of written communication include contracts, sales literature, newsletters, and bulletin board notices.

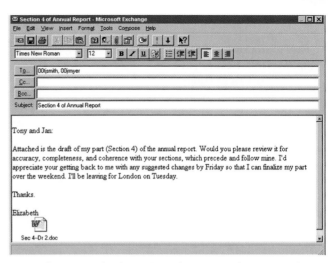

(Screen shot reprinted with permission from Microsoft Corporation)

figure**1.3**

Example of E-mail

Most oral communication is temporary; written communication is permanent.

Writing is crucial to the modern organization because it serves as the major source of documentation. A speech may make a striking impression, but a memorandum leaves a permanent record for others to refer to in the future in case memory fails or a dispute arises.

For written messages to achieve their goals, they must, of course, be read. The skill of efficient reading is becoming more important in today's technological society. The abundance of widespread computing and word processing capabilities, along with the proliferation of convenient and economical photocopying and faxing, has created more paperwork rather than less. It is estimated that the typical manager reads about a million words every week.[6] Thus, information overload is one of the unfortunate by-products of our times (see Spotlight 2, "Overcoming Information Anxiety," on page 15). These and other implications of technology on business communication are discussed throughout this text.

■ Directions of Communication

For an organization to be successful, communication must flow freely through formal and informal channels.

CO3. Explain the directions that make up the formal communication network.

The Formal Communication Network

Within the organization, information may be transmitted from superiors to subordinates (downward communication), from subordinates to superiors (upward communication), among people at the same level on the organizational chart (horizontal communication), and among people in different departments within the organization (cross-channel communication). These four types of communication make up the organization's **formal communication network.** We'll use part of Urban Systems' organizational chart, shown in Figure 1.4, to illustrate the directions of communication. (See page 37 in the Appendix to Chapter 1 for a more complete chart.)

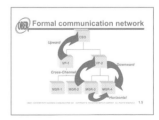

■ See Slide 1.5.

figure1.4

figure1.4

Part of the Formal Communication Network at Urban Systems

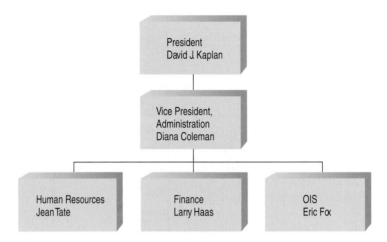

Downward Communication   In most organizations the largest number of vertical communications move downward—from someone of higher authority to someone of lower authority. For example, at Urban Systems (Figure 1.4), Dave Kaplan sends an e-mail message to Diana Coleman about a computer report; she, in turn, confers with Eric Fox. Through written and oral channels, information regarding job performance, policies and procedures, day-to-day operations, and other organizational information is communicated.

Higher-level management communicates with lower-level employees through such means as e-mail, memorandums, conferences, telephone conversations, company newsletters, policy manuals, and videotapes. One of the problems with written downward communication is that management may assume that what is sent downward is received and understood. Unfortunately, that is not always the case. If you're the boss, you should also recognize that your downward messages will receive more attention, faster responses, and more approval than messages coming from peers or superiors. The fact that those in subordinate positions seek your goodwill does not necessarily mean that your ideas are of higher quality or that they are communicated more effectively.

The free flow of communication upward helps prevent management isolation.

Upward Communication   Upward communication is the flow of information from lower-level employees to upper-level employees. In Figure 1.4, for example, Jean Tate sends a monthly status report to the president regarding human resource actions for the month, and Diana responds to Dave's memo regarding the computer report. Upward communication can take the form of e-mail, memorandums, conferences, reports, suggestion systems, or union publications, among others.

Upward communication is important because it provides higher management with the information needed for decision making. It also cultivates employee loyalty by giving employees an opportunity to be heard, to air their grievances, and to offer suggestions. Finally, upward communication provides the feedback necessary to let supervisors know whether subordinates received and understood messages that were sent downward.

Horizontal Communication   Horizontal communication is the flow of information among peers within the same work unit. For example, the administration divi-

Overcoming Information Anxiety

Executives, like nearly everyone else in this information-laden society, are being bombarded by more data than they can absorb. According to Richard Wurman, author of *Information Anxiety*, to function in business, we are being forced to assimilate a body of knowledge that is expanding by the minute.

For example, consider these statistics:

- The total amount of unique information generated worldwide each single year is about 1.5 exabytes (one exabyte is 1 followed by 18 zeroes). Stored on floppy disks, this amount of information would stack 2 million miles high.

- About 9,600 periodicals are published in the United States each year.

- Office workers spend 60 percent of their days processing documents.

- It is estimated that one weekday edition of each day's *New York Times* contains more information than the average person in seventeenth-century England was likely to come across in an entire lifetime.

Wurman believes it's a myth that the more choices you have, the more freedom you enjoy. More choices simply produce more anxiety. So as you decrease the number of choices, you decrease the fear of having made the wrong one.

The Black Hole

Trying to process all this information can induce "information anxiety"—apprehension about the ever-widening gap between what we understand and what we think we should understand. In other words, it is the black hole between data and knowledge. Here are some symptoms of information anxiety as Wurman describes them:

- Nodding your head knowingly when someone mentions a book, artist, or news story that you have actually never heard of.

- Feeling guilty about that ever-higher stack of periodicals waiting to be read.

- Feeling depressed because you don't know what all the buttons on your VCR do.

Wurman believes that "the System" is at fault—too many people are putting out too much data.

Nobody Knows It All

The first step in overcoming information anxiety is to accept that there is much you won't ever understand. Let your ignorance be an inspiration to learn, not something to conceal. Wurman recommends standing in front of a mirror and practicing, "Could you repeat that?" or "I'm not sure I understand" instead of pretending to understand what you do not.

Other suggestions include the following:

- Separate what you are really interested in from what you merely think you should be interested in.

- Minimize the time you spend reading or watching news that isn't relevant to your life.

- Reduce your pile of office reading.

If all else fails, heed Wurman's conclusion: "Most information is useless. Give yourself permission to dismiss it."[7]

---

sion holds a weekly staff meeting at which the three managers (Jean, Larry, and Eric) exchange information about the status of their operations.

Horizontal communication is important to help coordinate work assignments, share information on plans and activities, negotiate differences, and develop interpersonal support, thereby creating a more cohesive work unit. The more that individuals or departments within an organization must interact with each other to accomplish their objectives, the more frequent and intense will be the horizontal communication.

The most common form of horizontal communication is the committee meeting, where most coordination, sharing of information, and problem solving take place. Intense competition for scarce resources, lack of trust among coworkers, or concerns about job security or promotions can sometimes create barriers to the free flow of horizontal information.

Cross-Channel Communication   Cross-channel communication is the exchange of information among employees in different work units who are neither subordinate nor superior to one another. For example, each year a payroll clerk in Jean Tate's department sends out a request to all company employees for updated information about the number of exemptions they claim on their tax forms.

Staff specialists use cross-channel communications frequently because their responsibilities typically involve many departments within the organization. Because they lack line authority to direct those with whom they communicate, they must often rely on their persuasive skills, as, for instance, when the human resources department encourages employees to complete a job-satisfaction questionnaire.

The Informal Communication Network

CO4. Describe the characteristics of the grapevine.

The informal communication network (grapevine) transmits information through nonofficial channels within the organization.

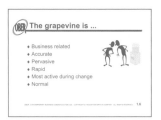

■ See Slide 1.6.

The **informal communication network** (or the *grapevine*, as it is called) is the transmission of information through nonofficial channels within the organization. Carpooling to work, waiting to use the photocopier, jogging at noon, eating in the cafeteria, or chatting at a local PTA meeting—wherever workers come together, they are likely to hear and pass on information about possible happenings in the organization. Employees often say that the grapevine is their most frequent source of information on company plans and performance. In one survey of 451 executives, 91 percent reported that employees typically use the grapevine for information on company "bad news" such as layoffs and takeovers. Office politics was cited as a grapevine topic by 73 percent, whereas only 41 percent said their employees turned to the grapevine for "good news." Another survey found that 39 percent of the managers thought that business matters were the most common subject discussed at the office water cooler—and 17 percent admitted they didn't have a clue.[8]

These are the common characteristics of the grapevine:[9]

■ Most of the information passed along the grapevine (about 80 percent) is business related, and most of it (75 to 95 percent) is accurate.

■ The grapevine is pervasive. It exists at all levels in the organization—from the corporate boardroom to the assembly line.

■ Information moves rapidly along the grapevine.

■ The grapevine is most active when change is taking place and when one's need to know or level of fear is highest—during layoffs, plant closings, acquisitions, mergers, and the like.

■ The grapevine is a normal, often vital, part of every organization.

Rather than trying to eliminate the grapevine (a futile effort), competent managers accept its existence and pay attention to it. They act promptly to counteract false rumors. Most of all, they use the formal communication network (including meetings, memos, newsletters, and bulletin boards) to ensure that all news—positive and negative—gets out to employees as quickly and as completely as possible. The free flow of information within the organization not only stops rumors, but is also simply good business.

■ Barriers to Communication

Considering the complex nature of the communication process, your messages may not always be received exactly as you intended. As a matter of fact, sometimes your messages will not be received at all; at other times, they will be received incompletely or inaccurately. Some of the obstacles to effective and efficient communication are verbal; others are nonverbal. As illustrated in Figure 1.5, these barriers can create an impenetrable "brick wall" that makes effective communication impossible.

The informal communication network is important in helping an organization achieve its objectives. Obongo, a California tech start-up company, sponsors a monthly potluck lunch for its multicultural management team.

Verbal Barriers

Verbal barriers are related to what you write or say. They include inadequate knowledge or vocabulary, differences in interpretation, language differences, inappropriate use of expressions, overabstraction and ambiguity, and polarization.

Inadequate Knowledge or Vocabulary   Before you can even begin to think about how you will communicate an idea, you must, first of all, *have* the idea; that is, you must have sufficient knowledge about the topic to know what you want to say. Regardless of your level of technical expertise, this may not be as simple as it sounds. Assume, for example, that you are Larry Haas, manager of the finance department at Urban Systems. Dave Kaplan, president of the company, has asked you to evaluate an investment opportunity. You've completed all the necessary research and are now ready to write your report. Or are you?

Have you analyzed your audience? Do you know how much the president knows about the investment so that you'll know how much background information to include? Do you know how familiar Dave is with investment terminology? Can you safely use abbreviations like *NPV* and *RRR*, or will you have to spell out and perhaps define *net present value* and *required rate of return*? Do you know whether the president would prefer to have your conclusions at the beginning of the report, followed by your analysis, or at the end? What tone should the report take? The answers to such questions will be important if you are to achieve your objective in writing the report.

Differences in Interpretation   Sometimes senders and receivers attribute different meanings to the same word or attribute the same meaning to different words. When this happens, miscommunication can occur.

CO5. **Identify the major verbal and nonverbal barriers to communication.**

You must know enough about both your topic and your audience to express yourself precisely and appropriately.

■ See Slide 1.7.

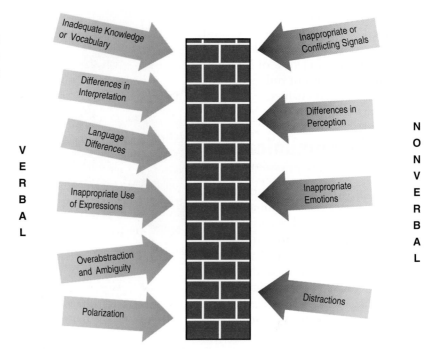

figure1.5
Verbal and Nonverbal Barriers to Communication

A word's denotation defines its meaning; its connotation indicates our associations with the word.

■ Ask students to write down their own reactions to each of these words. Then tabulate the results and discuss.

Every word has both a denotative and a connotative meaning. **Denotation** refers to the literal, dictionary meaning of a word. **Connotation** refers to the subjective, emotional meaning that you attach to a word. For example, the denotative meaning of the word *plastic* is "a synthetic material that can be easily molded into different forms." For some people, the word also has a negative connotative meaning—"cheap or artificial substitute." For other people, the word means a credit card, as in "He used plastic to pay the bill."

Most of the interpretation problems occur because of the personal reactions engendered by the connotative meaning of a word. Do you have a positive, neutral, or negative reaction to the terms *broad, bad, aggressive, hard-hitting, workaholic, corporate raider, head-hunter, golden parachute, or wasted*? Are your reactions likely to be the same as everyone else's? The problem with some terms is not only that people assign different meanings to the term but also that the term itself might cause such an emotional reaction that the receiver is "turned off" to any further communication with the sender.

Language Differences   In an ideal world, all managers would know the language of each culture with which they deal. International businesspeople often say that you can buy in your native language anywhere in the world, but you can sell only in the language of the local community. Most of the correspondence between U.S. or Canadian firms and foreign firms is in English; in other cases, the services of a qualified interpreter (for oral communication) or translator (for written communication) may be available. But even with such services, problems can occur. Consider, for example, the following blunders:[10]

■ In Brazil, where Portuguese is spoken, a U.S. airline advertised that its Boeing 747s had "rendezvous lounges," without realizing that rendezvous in Portuguese implies prostitution.

- In China, Kentucky Fried Chicken's slogan "Finger-lickin' good" was translated "So good you suck your fingers."

- In Puerto Rico, General Motors had difficulties advertising Chevrolet's Nova model because the name sounds like the Spanish phrase "No va," which means "It doesn't go."

To ensure that the intended meaning is not lost during translation, important documents should first be translated into the second language and then re-translated into English. Be aware, however, that communication difficulties can arise even among native English speakers. For example, a British advertisement for Electrolux vacuum cleaners displayed the headline "Nothing Sucks Like An Electrolux." Copywriters in the United States and Canada would never use this wording!

Inappropriate Use of Expressions Expressions are groups of words whose intended meanings are different from their literal interpretations. Examples include slang, jargon, and euphemisms.

- **Slang** is an expression, often short-lived, that is identified with a specific group of people. Business, of course, has its own slang, such as *24/7, bandwidth, hard-ball, strategic fit,* and *window of opportunity*. Teenagers, construction workers, immigrants, knowledge professionals, and just about every other subgroup you can imagine all have their own sets of slang. Using appropriate slang in everyday speech presents no problem; it conveys precise information and may indicate group membership. Problems arise, however, when the sender uses slang that the receiver doesn't understand. Using slang when communicating with someone whose native language is not English can cause misunderstandings. Slang that sends a negative nonverbal message about the sender can also be a source of problems.

- **Jargon** is the technical terminology used within specialized groups; it has sometimes been called "the pros' prose." Technology, for example, has spawned a whole new vocabulary. Do you know the meaning of these common computer terms?

applet	FAQ	JPEG	plug'n'play
blog	flame	killer app	ROFL
BRB	hacker	locked up	spam
BTW	HTML	patch	worm
CU	IMO	PDA	WYSIWYG
e-commerce			

As with slang, the problem is not in using jargon—jargon provides a very precise and efficient way of communicating with those familiar with it. The problem comes either in using jargon with someone who doesn't understand it or in using jargon in an effort to impress others.

- **Euphemisms** are inoffensive expressions used in place of words that may offend or suggest something unpleasant. Sensitive writers and speakers use euphemisms occasionally, especially to describe bodily functions. How many ways, for example, can you think of to say that someone has died?

Slang, jargon, and euphemisms all have important roles to play in business communication—so long as they're used with appropriate people and in appropriate

■ "A word is not a crystal, transparent and unchanged; it is the skin of a living thought and may vary greatly in color and content according to the circumstances and time in which it is used." (Oliver Wendell Holmes, Jr.)

The use of slang, jargon, and euphemisms is sometimes appropriate and sometimes inappropriate.

■ Ask your students to think of synonyms for *die*. Then write them on the board. What are the connotations of each?

ASK Ober

Your textbook author encourages students and teachers to e-mail him about the text and business communication (e-mail: askober@ober.net). Ask Ober shows a sample of these e-mails and his answers. Letters and their responses have been edited for length and clarity.

contexts. They can, however, prove to be barriers to effective communication when used to impress, when used too often, or when used in inappropriate settings.

The word transportation *is abstract; the word automobile is* concrete.

Overabstraction and Ambiguity   An **abstract word** identifies an idea or a feeling instead of a concrete object. For example, *communication* is an abstract word, whereas *memorandum* is a **concrete word,** a word that identifies something that can be seen or touched. Abstract words are necessary in order to communicate about things you cannot see or touch. However, communication problems result when you use too many abstract words or when you use too high a level of abstraction. The higher the level of abstraction, the more difficult it is for the receiver to visualize exactly what the sender has in mind. For example, which sentence communicates more information: "I acquired an asset at the store" or "I bought a laser printer at Best Buy"?

Similar communication problems result from the overuse of ambiguous terms such as *a few, some, several,* and *far away,* which have too broad a meaning for use in much business communication.

Thinking in terms of all or nothing limits our choices.

Polarization   At times, some people act as though every situation is divided into two opposite and distinct poles, with no allowance for a middle ground. Of course, there are some true dichotomies. You are either human or nonhuman, and your company either will or will not make a profit this year. But most aspects of life involve more than two alternatives.

For example, you might assume that a speaker either is telling the truth or is lying. In fact, what the speaker actually says may be true, but by selectively omitting some important information, he or she may be giving an inaccurate impression. Is the speaker telling the truth or not? Most likely, the answer lies somewhere in between. Likewise, you are not necessarily either tall or short, rich or poor, smart or dumb. Competent communicators avoid inappropriate either/or logic and instead make the effort to search for middle-ground words when such language best describes a situation.

Incidentally, remember that what you do *not* say can also produce barriers to communication. Suppose, for example, that you congratulate only one of the three people who took part in making a company presentation. How would the other two presenters feel—even though you said nothing negative about their performance? Or suppose you tell one of them, "You really did an outstanding job this time." The presenter's reaction might be, "What was wrong with my performance last time?" (And how about this announcement from the author's seven-year-old son one day after school: "Hey, Dad, guess what? I didn't get my name on the board today." What's the implication?)

What you do not say may also communicate a message.

Nonverbal Barriers

Not all communication problems are related to what you write or say. Some are related to how you act. Nonverbal barriers to communication include inappropriate or conflicting signals, differences in perception, inappropriate emotions, and distractions.

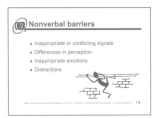

■ See Slide 1.8.

Inappropriate or Conflicting Signals   Suppose a well-qualified applicant for an administrative assistant position submits a résumé with a typographical error, or an accountant's personal office is in such disorder that she can't find the papers she needs for a meeting with a client. When verbal and nonverbal signals conflict, the receiver tends to put more faith in the nonverbal signals because nonverbal messages are more difficult to manipulate than verbal messages.

When we say one thing— for example, that we are pleased to meet someone—but our actions, posture, or expression suggests something contradictory, others will usually believe what we do rather than what we say.

Many nonverbal signals vary from culture to culture. Remember also that the United States itself is a multicultural country: a banker from Boston, an art shop owner from San Francisco, and a farmer from North Dakota are likely to both use and interpret nonverbal signals in quite different ways. What is appropriate in one context might not be appropriate in another.

Communication competence requires that you communicate nonverbal messages that are consistent with your verbal messages and that are appropriate for the context.

Differences in Perception   Even when they hear the same speech or read the same document, people of different ages, socioeconomic backgrounds, cultures, and so forth often form very different perceptions. We discussed earlier the mental filter by which each communication source is interpreted. Because each person is unique, with unique experiences, knowledge, and viewpoints, each person forms a different opinion about what he or she reads and hears.

Some people tend automatically to believe certain people and to distrust other people. For example, when reading an e-mail from the company president, one employee may be so intimidated by the president that he or she accepts everything the president says, whereas another employee may have such negative feelings about the president that he or she believes nothing the president says.

It is generally more effective to depend on logic instead of emotions when communicating.

Inappropriate Emotions   In most cases, a moderate level of emotional involvement intensifies the communication and makes it more personal. However, too much emotional involvement can be an obstacle to communication. For example, excessive anger can create such an emotionally charged environment that reasonable discussion is not possible. Likewise, prejudice (automatically rejecting certain people or ideas), stereotyping (placing individuals into categories), and boredom all hinder effective communication. Such emotions tend to create a blocked mind that is closed to new ideas, rejecting or ignoring information that is contrary to one's prevailing belief.

■ Noise is likely to become more of a problem in the future. The high cost of office space means that more people will be sharing smaller areas. Issues such as privacy and telephone etiquette (tone of voice, volume) will have to be addressed.

Distractions   Any environmental or competing element that restricts one's ability to concentrate on the communication task hinders effective communication. Such distractions are called **noise.** Examples of *environmental* noise are poor acoustics, extreme temperature, uncomfortable seating, body odor, poor telephone connections, and illegible photocopies. Examples of *competing* noise are other important business to attend to, too many meetings, and too many reports to read.

Competent communicators make the effort to write and speak clearly and consistently and try to avoid or minimize any verbal or nonverbal barriers that might cause misunderstandings.

■ Ethics and Communication

CO6. Explain the legal and ethical dimensions of communicating.

Each of us has a personal code of **ethics,** or rules of conduct, that might go beyond legal rules to tell us how to act when the law is silent. When composing a business proposal, drafting a sales letter, writing a human resources policy, or recruiting a candidate for a job, we make conscious decisions regarding what information to include and what information to exclude from our messages. For the information that is included, we make conscious decisions about how to phrase the language, how much to emphasize each point, and how to organize the message. Such decisions have legal and ethical dimensions—both for you as the writer and for the organization.

Defamation

Oral defamation is slander. *Written defamation is* libel.

Any false and malicious statement that is communicated to others and that injures a person's good name or reputation may constitute **defamation.** Defamation in a temporary form such as in oral communication is called **slander;** defamation in a permanent form such as in writing or on a videotape is called **libel.** The three major conditions for proving defamation are that the statement be false, be communicated to others, and be harmful to a person's good name or reputation. Thus, telling Joe Smith to his face that he is a liar and a crook does not constitute defamation (slander) unless a third person hears the remarks. In addition, truth is generally an acceptable defense to a charge of defamation.

Competent communicators use objective language and verifiable information when communicating about others. For example, instead of saying, "Mr. Baker is a poor credit risk," they might say, "Mr. Baker was at least ten days late in making his payments to us four times during the past six months."

Invasion of Privacy

Any unreasonable intrusion into the private life of another person or denial of a person's right to be left alone may constitute an **invasion of privacy.** Thus, using someone's name or photograph in a sales promotion without that person's permission may be an invasion of privacy. Of particular concern today are the vast amounts of employee and customer information being maintained in corporate databases. The proliferation of microcomputers, networks, and electronic mail makes it possible to access large amounts of data about employees and customers easily.

Various state and federal laws protect the individual's right to privacy. The federal government defines *right to privacy* as "the right of individuals to participate in decisions regarding the collection, use, and disclosure of information personally identifiable to that individual."[11] Thus, someone's right to privacy may be violated if his or her records are read by someone not authorized to examine them or who has no compelling business reason for examining them.

Competent communicators ensure that they do not misuse information about others in their communications and that their communications are available only to people who legitimately need such information.

■ See Slide 1.9.

The right to privacy is the individual's right to be left alone.

Fraud and Misrepresentation

A deliberate misrepresentation of the truth for the purpose of inducing someone to give up something of value is called **fraud.** Fraud can occur either when one party actually makes a deliberately false statement (called *active fraud*) or when one party deliberately conceals some information that he or she is required to reveal (*passive fraud*).

To be fraudulent, the statements must involve facts. Opinions and persuasive arguments or exaggerated claims about a product (called *sales puffery*) do not constitute fraud even if they turn out to be false. For example, "The Celeste is the only American-made car that comes with leather seats as standard equipment" is a statement of fact, which, if incorrect, might constitute fraud. However, "The Celeste is the most luxurious car in America" is an opinion; even if most car buyers did not agree with the statement, it would still not be considered fraud.

You should also recognize that a statement of opinion, even if it is not fraudulent, might still be unethical. For example, advertising that "The Celeste is the most luxurious car in America" might not be fraudulent; but it would be highly unethical if, in fact, you did not believe that to be the case.

Misrepresentation is a false statement that is made innocently with no intent to deceive the other party. If misrepresentation is proved, the contract or agreement may be rescinded. If fraud is proved, the contract or agreement may be rescinded, and the offended party may collect monetary compensation.

Competent communicators are aware of the relevant laws and ensure that their oral and written messages are accurate, in terms of what is communicated *and* what is left uncommunicated.

■ Investment banker Michael Milken earned as much as $550 million in a single year, but because of his unethical and illegal business practices, his firm, Drexel Burnham Lambert, was heavily fined by the federal government. The company was forced eventually into bankruptcy, and Milken was imprisoned.

■ For more on legal considerations, see the supplemental lecture/ discussion notes in the *Instructor's Resource Manual.*

Other Ethical Considerations

Sometimes being legally right is not sufficient justification for our actions (see Spotlight 3, "How Would You Respond?," on page 24). Many corporations have

How Would You Respond?

How would you react to each of the following minicases on business ethics developed by Kirk Hanson, a senior lecturer at the Stanford University Graduate School of Business and corporate ethics consultant? Formulate your responses before reading the suggested solutions.

Situations

1. You are about to take a job with Almost Perfect, Inc. You like everything you have learned about the company except the reputation the firm has for long working hours. You have a young family and are committed to spending time with them. What role should the hours have in your decision?

2. You have been on the job for four days. Your boss hands you a report she hasn't had time to complete. "Just copy the numbers off last month's report," she says. "Nobody at headquarters ever really reads these." What do you do?

3. A new engineer who has just joined your group drops by your office and hands you a file stamped with the name of his former employer. "I thought you'd like to have a look at their list of key customers," he says. What do you do?

4. Despite a strongly worded company policy prohibiting gratuities from suppliers, you know your boss in the purchasing department is taking weeklong vacations paid for by a key vendor. What do you do?[12]

Suggested Solutions

1. Turn down the job or negotiate openly for more reasonable hours. You will never be satisfied if you take a job that sets up a constant value conflict. Be willing to pay the price for a good family life.

2. Offer to collect the real data for the report. Everyone is tested in the first weeks by coworkers who favor short-cuts or small ethical compromises. Establish your values; insist on getting the real data if push comes to shove.

3. Give him back the folder unread and tell him, "We don't do things like that around here." Watch him carefully. If he wasn't faithful to his obligations to his former employer, he won't be faithful to you.

4. Report him to a higher authority in the company, but be sure you have some proof before you do. He has violated such a clear standard that it is unlikely he can be persuaded to stop. Ask the higher authority to protect you from retaliation.

A message can be true and still be unethical.

developed their own codes of ethics to govern employee behavior. For the business communicator, the matter of ethics governs not only one's behavior but also one's communication of that behavior. In other words, how we use language involves ethical choices.

When you have doubts about the ethical propriety of your writing, ask yourself these questions:

1. Is this message true?
2. Does it exaggerate?
3. Does it withhold or obscure information that should be communicated?
4. Does it promise something that cannot be delivered?
5. Does it betray a confidence?
6. Does it play unduly on the fears of the reader?
7. Does it reflect the wishes of the organization?

Competent communicators use their knowledge of communication to achieve their goals while acting in an ethical manner.

■ Introducing the 3Ps (Problem, Process, Product) Model

Every chapter in this text concludes with a 3Ps model designed to illustrate important communication concepts covered in the chapter (see the following section).

These short case studies of typical communication assignments include the *problem*, the *process*, and the *product* (the 3Ps). The *problem* defines the situation and discusses the need for a particular communication task. The *process* is a series of questions that provides step-by-step guidance for accomplishing the specific communication task. Finally, the *product* is the result—the finished document.

The 3Ps model provides a practical demonstration of a particular type of communication, shown close up so that you can see the *process* of writing, not just the results. This process helps you focus on one aspect of writing at a time. Use the 3Ps steps regularly in your own writing so that your written communications will be easier to produce and more effective in their results.

Pay particular attention to the questions in the Process section and ask yourself similar questions as you compose your own messages. Finally, read through the finished document and note any changes made from the draft sentences composed in the Process section.

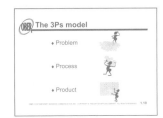

DAFFY DEFINITIONS	*word*wise

Readers of the *New York Times* and *Washington Post* were asked to provide fresh definitions for old words. A sampling of their submissions:

Abdicate:	To give up all hope of ever having a flat stomach
Alphabet:	The most aggressive bet on the table
Approbation:	A fear of early release from prison
Coffee:	A person who is coughed upon
Defibrillator:	A lie detector
Ineffable:	A guaranteed Grade-A term paper

The 3Ps model guides you step-by-step through a typical writing assignment by posing and answering relevant questions about each aspect of the message.

■ For more on the 3Ps model, see the supplemental lecture/discussion notes in the *Instructor's Resource Manual.*

The 3Ps model
- ◆ Problem
- ◆ Process
- ◆ Product

■ See Slide 1.10.

Communication ethics is a primary concern for most businesses. IBM's chief privacy officer, Harriet Pearson, deals with such issues as instant access, massive databases, regulations, and lawsuits.

The **3Ps**

Problem, Process, Product

WRITING AN ETHICAL STATEMENT

Problem

Assume the role of Jason, a quality control engineer for an automobile manufacturer. You are responsible for testing a new airbag design. Your company is eager to install the new airbags in next year's models because two competitors have similar airbags on the market. However, your tests of the new design have not been completely successful. All of the airbags tested inflated on impact, but 10 airbags out of every 100 tested inflated only 60 percent. These partially inflated airbags would still protect passengers from most of a collision impact, but the passengers might receive more injuries than they would with fully inflated bags.

Before reporting the test results, you tell your supervisor that you would like to run more tests to make sure that the airbags are reliable and safe. But your supervisor explains that the company executives are eager to get the airbags on the market and want the results in a few days. You now feel pressured to certify that the airbags are safe (and indeed, they all inflated—at least partially).[13]

Process

1. What is the problem you are facing?

   I must decide exactly how I will phrase the certification sentence in my report.

2. What would be the ideal solution to this problem?

   I would be given additional time to conduct enough tests to assure myself that the airbags are reliable and safe.

3. Why can't the ideal solution be recommended?

   The company is pressuring me to certify the airbags now because two competitors have already introduced similar airbags.

4. Brainstorm possible certification statements that you might make.

   - All the airbags inflated.
   - None of the airbags failed to inflate.
   - Ninety percent of the airbags inflated fully; the rest inflated only 60 percent.

5. How will you determine which is the best statement? In other words, what criteria will you use to evaluate the statements?

   - Would the statement be in the best interests of the company?

- ■ Would the statement be in the best interests of the public?
- ■ Would the statement be in my own best interests?

6. Now evaluate each alternative in terms of these criteria.

All the airbags inflated.

This statement is true and is a positive statement that will probably satisfy management. However, it overstates the success of the tests and is somewhat misleading in what it omits—that 10 percent of the airbags inflated only partially. I may be harming potential users by giving them a false sense of security; in addition, I may be leaving the company open to lawsuits resulting from failure of airbags to inflate fully.

None of the airbags failed to inflate.

Again, this statement is true but omits important information the consumer needs. In addition, it is a negative statement, which will not please management.

Ninety percent of the airbags inflated fully; the rest inflated only 60 percent.

This statement provides the most accurate assessment of the test results. It emphasizes the positive and does state that some problems exist. The most serious risk with this alternative is that it could delay the release of the new design on the market. If this happens, my job might be at risk. In addition, it doesn't interpret the meaning of the partially inflated airbags.

7. Using what you've discovered about each alternative, construct the certification statement you will include in your report to management.

Product

Results of my testing of the new airbag design indicate that 90 percent of the airbags inflate fully on impact; the remaining 10 percent inflate 60 percent, which is sufficient to protect passengers from most of a collision impact.

■ A parallel BusCom Online Teaching Center is available for instructors using this text. Here you will find a monthly newsletter with additional teaching tips and hot-off-the-press current event items, lecture and supplemental discussion notes, additional application exercises and cases, PowerPoint slides, and a forum for idea exchange. Call your Houghton Mifflin representative for the free password to this important resource.

co1. Identify the components of communication.

co2. Identify the common forms of written and oral communication.

co3. Explain the directions that make up the formal communication network.

co4. Describe the characteristics of the grapevine.

co5. Identify the major verbal and nonverbal barriers to communication.

co6. Explain the legal and ethical dimensions of communicating.

Visit the **BusCom Online Learning Center** (at http://college.hmco.com) to find several resources that will help you succeed in this course. See our ACE interactive self-tests to assess your knowledge of chapter content and to review and reinforce basic language arts skills. Here you will also be able to learn more about the Internet, locate business information, get help with writing problems, and learn more about employment communication and available jobs and employers.

■ Summary

The communication process begins with a stimulus. On the basis of your unique knowledge, experience, and viewpoints, you filter, or interpret, the stimulus and formulate the message you wish to communicate. The next step is to select a medium of transmission for the message. Finally, the message reaches its destination. If it is successful, the receiver perceives it as a source for communication and provides appropriate feedback to you.

Verbal communication includes oral (speaking and listening) and written (writing and reading) communication. Common forms of written communication in business include e-mail messages, websites, memorandums, letters, and reports.

The organization's formal communication network consists of downward communication from superiors to subordinates, upward communication from subordinates to superiors, horizontal communication among people at the same level, and cross-channel communication among people in different departments within the organization.

The informal communication network (also called the grapevine) consists of information transmitted through nonofficial channels. Rather than try to eliminate it, managers should accept its existence and pay attention to it.

Sometimes barriers are present that interfere with effective communication. Examples of verbal barriers are inadequate knowledge or vocabulary, differences in interpretation, language differences, inappropriate use of expressions, overabstraction and ambiguity, and polarization. Examples of nonverbal barriers are inappropriate or conflicting signals, differences in perception, inappropriate emotions, and distractions.

Regardless of the size and type of organization, every business writer faces ethical questions when communicating orally and in writing. Legal questions arise with regard to defamation, invasion of privacy, and fraud or misrepresentation. In choosing what information to convey, and which words and sentences to use, we make ethical choices—moral decisions about what is right, even when no question of law is involved.

■ See Slide 1.11.

■ Key Terms

You should now be able to define the following terms in your own words and give an original example of each:

abstract word (20)   communication (5)

audience (8)   concrete word (20)

connotation (18)

defamation (22)

denotation (18)

e-mail (12)

ethics (22)

euphemism (19)

feedback (9)

filter (7)

formal communication network (13)

fraud (23)

informal communication network (16)

invasion of privacy (22)

jargon (19)

letter (13)

libel (22)

medium (8)

memorandum (13)

message (8)

misrepresentation (23)

noise (22)

nonverbal message (7)

report (13)

slander (22)

slang (19)

stimulus (7)

verbal message (7)

website (12)

- jargon
- letter
- libel
- medium
- memorandum
- message
- misrepresentation
- noise
- nonverbal message
- report
- slander
- slang
- stimulus
- verbal message
- website

■ See Slide 1.12.

■ Consider treating this list as an end-of-chapter exercise for students to define and give an example of each term.

■ Exercises

1 **Nissan North America, Inc. Revisited**   By regularly asking for feedback from employees, media representatives, business leaders, and others, Debra Sanchez Fair is able to gauge whether her audiences have received and understood the messages sent by Nissan North America. If changes are necessary, she and her staff decide whether to switch to another medium, repeat key points for reinforcement, or entirely change the message content. Fair knows that good communication starts with a clear sense of purpose and a thorough knowledge of the audience.

The first Exercise in each chapter relates back to An Insider's Perspective. Exercises also contain continuing examples used throughout the chapters.

■ Suggestions and sample solutions for exercises appear in the *Instructor's Resource Manual.*

Problem

You are in charge of dealer relations for Nissan North America. At the end of the workday, you receive a call from an angry dealer in the Midwest who yells about being repeatedly disconnected during calls to Nissan's Tokyo headquarters. Over and over, this dealer screams about the rude treatment he says he has received when trying to talk with people in Nissan's Japanese headquarters. You doubt any employees would be rude on purpose, yet it is your job to ensure smooth relations with dealers.

Process

a. What is the problem you are facing in this situation?
b. What verbal and nonverbal barriers to communication seem to be operating here?
c. What options do you see for resolving this problem?
d. What criteria can you use to determine the option that will best solve this problem?
e. Using these criteria, evaluate your options and identify the best one.

Product

What opening statement can you make to the dealer as a way of implementing the option you have selected as the best solution to this problem?

CO1. Describe the components of communication.

CO2. Identify the common forms of written and oral communication.

■ See Handout 1.1.

CO3. Explain the directions that make up the formal communication network.

2 Communication Process   Use an incident from a recent television program to illustrate each of the five components of the communication process. Identify any communication barriers that you observed.

3 Communication Components   Working with a partner, identify the five components of communication in the following situation:

> Alice Liston has had a dream of going to State College. She has worked hard to maintain a 3.95 GPA and has a very high ACT score. Because her family is not in a position to pay her tuition, Alice applied for an academic scholarship to State College. Two weeks later Alice receives a letter from the scholarship committee. She nervously reads the letter and then runs to her bedroom to e-mail her best friend letting her know that she had received a full-ride scholarship to State College. Her friend reads the e-mail message two hours later.

After identifying the five components in this scenario, working in pairs, prepare your own communication scenario and identify the five components of communication for it.

4 Internet Exercise   This chapter discussed how e-mail messages are replacing traditional memorandums and letters in the contemporary office. But are e-mail messages sent or received by managers and employees really private? Using Internet search tools such as Google.com, search such word combinations as *e-mail (or email) + privacy* to investigate the issue of e-mail privacy at work. Why are companies concerned about employee use of e-mail? What are they doing to monitor e-mail messages? How are employees reacting to this situation? Share your findings in a brief classroom presentation; be sure to include your views about whether companies should be allowed to monitor e-mail messages by employees.

5 Communication Directions   Think of an organization to which you belong or a business with which you are familiar. Provide a specific illustration of each of the four directions in the formal communication network. Then develop an organizational chart similar to the one in Figure 1.4 on page 14.

6 Communicating at Urban Systems   Using the organizational chart from the Appendix to Chapter 1 (page 37), determine the direction (downward, upward, horizontal, or cross-channel) and the formality (formal or informal) being used in each of the following situations:

a. David J. Kaplan sends an e-mail message to Paul Yu regarding a recent drop in sales.
b. Mary Lyons talks to Larry Haas by telephone about financing for some new manufacturing equipment.
c. O. J. Drew visits with C. B. Odom over lunch about possible changes on the production line.
d. Ann Stetsky meets with Marc Kaplan to review their upcoming presentation to the company's employees.
e. Wendy Janish e-mails O. J. Drew asking questions about the latest Ultra Light product to help her prepare the new advertising campaign.

   f. Luis Diaz talks with Thomas Mercado while playing golf about adding a new storage facility.

   g. Marc Kaplan gets a voice-mail message from Thomas Mercado asking him for information about a presentation to David J. Kaplan.

   h. Diana Coleman receives a report from Jean Tate outlining the new hiring policy

   i. Eric Fox calls Mary Lyons at home to ask her about the layoff rumors.

7 **Grapevine**   Read a journal article about the company grapevine. Then write a one-page summary of the article. Proofread for content and language errors and revise as needed. Staple a photocopy of the article to your summary and submit both to your instructor.

co4. Describe the characteristics of the grapevine.

8 **The Digital Grapevine**   The international airline Swissair has an excellent safety record, but its management knows that accidents can occur at any time. As a result, Swissair has developed a plan to guide the company's communication response to emergencies. The purpose is to ensure that employees, media representatives, and other audiences have fast and convenient access to accurate information. As part of this plan, the airline is always ready to post a special webpage with crisis contacts and other details. The company had to put its plan into effect not long ago when a Swissair jet crashed near Nova Scotia. Immediately after the crash, management posted a webpage with facts about the accident and created a prominent link to the page from the airline's home page at http://www.swissair.com so the public—and Swissair employees—could get up-to-the-minute news.

   Now Swissair has hired you to evaluate its management of the digital grapevine and to suggest additional ways of improving internal communication during emergencies. With what types of emergencies should Swissair be concerned? What kind of information would employees need during these crises? How do you recommend that Swissair use the Internet to provide its employees with accurate, updated information during such emergencies? Prepare a brief memorandum to management, summarizing your recommendations.

9 **Slanguage**   Sign on to Google at http://www.google.com or some other search engine and enter the search term *slang*. You will find hundreds of sources of slang for different audiences, including college slang, drug-related slang, biker slang, and playground slang, as well as slang from different countries.

   Identify five common slang expressions from five different audiences of communicators. Were you able to find any instance of different audiences using different slang expressions to communicate the same concept? Write a one-page double-spaced report of your findings and conclusions.

10 **Communication Barriers**   Chapter 1 listed six verbal communication barriers and four nonverbal communication barriers. Which category of communication barriers—verbal or nonverbal—do you believe is easier to overcome? Why? Share your thoughts with the rest of the class.

co5. Identify the major verbal and nonverbal barriers to communication.

11 **Diversity** "I'll never understand our people in Pakistan," Eileen said. "I wrote our local agent over there, who's supposedly a financial wizard, this note: 'If your firm wants to play ball with us, we'll need the straight scoop. What's your bottom-line price on the STX model with all the bells and whistles? Also, if you pull out all the stops, can we get delivery by Xmas?' And you know what he did? He wrote me back a long letter, inquiring about my health and my family, but never answering my questions! If they don't get on the ball, I'm going to recommend that we stop doing business with them." From a communication standpoint, what is happening here? What advice can you give Eileen? Rewrite her message to the Pakistani agent to make it more effective.

CO6. Explain the legal and ethical dimensions of communicating.

12 **Code of Ethics** Working with several classmates, develop a code of ethics for this class. Share your code of ethics with the other groups in the class. Based on the items presented to the class, as a class, select a code of ethics that all class members can abide by for the semester.

13 **You Are Invited** Recently, two million people opened their mailboxes to find what they thought was a wedding invitation. It was the same size as a wedding invitation, was printed on pale-gray card stock, had the words *RSVP* in silver on the envelope, and was sent using a regular postage stamp. Only after opening the envelope did readers discover that the message was an "invitation" to subscribe to Verizon Online high-speed Internet service.

You've probably received mail like this, because companies have found these come-ons effective. Do you think it is ethical for companies to use gimmicks like this to induce customers to read their sales letters? If so, which gimmicks are acceptable and which are not? Would a sales message contained in an envelope that was made to look like an official government communication be ethical?

Write a one-page double-spaced report giving your view of this practice. Use logic, rather than emotionalism, to discuss why you think as you do.

■ See Handout 1.2.

14 **Legal** Sam was thinking of hiring Olivia Mason for an open sales territory. Knowing she had previously worked at Kentron, he called his friend there, Barry Kelley, to ask about her performance. "She's very smart, but I wouldn't hire her again, Sam," Barry said. "She's a little lazy. Sometimes she wouldn't begin making her calls until late morning or even after lunch. And she was also sloppy with her paperwork. I assume she's honest, but I never could get her to file receipts for all her expenses. Of course, she was going through a messy divorce then, so maybe that affected her job performance." Sam thanked his friend and notified Olivia that she was not being hired for the job.

If Olivia learned of Kelley's comments, would she have the basis for a legal suit? If so, what type and on what grounds? How could Kelley have reworded his comments to convey the information in a businesslike, ethical manner?

15 **Ethics** You are the office manager of the Natural-Disaster Recovery Team for People Helping People. After testing several new word processing programs, you wrote a memo to your supervisor requesting the purchase of 15 copies of Microsoft Word XP so that each member of your office staff would have a copy. You have just received your memo back from your supervisor with this handwritten note attached to it:

I'm tired of purchasing software and then not having it do what it says it will do. Let's order one copy of the program first and make copies for all your staff. If in two months everyone is still happy with the program, I'll buy 14 more copies to make us legitimate. After all, we have to be careful with the funds donated to our organization.

How do you respond?

16 **Sign of the Times**   You work part-time at a busy pawnshop in central San Antonio. A number of neighborhood stores have been burglarized in recent years, and the owner wants criminals to think twice before they break into his pawn shop. After thinking about the situation, he posts this sign in the window one night: "$10,000 reward offered to any officer of the law shooting and killing any person attempting to rob this property."

When you come to work the next morning and see the sign, your first thought is that it will probably be an effective deterrent. As the day goes on, however, you begin to have doubts about the ethics of posting such a sign. Although you don't know of any law that would apply to this situation, you're not sure that your boss is doing the right thing. You decide to speak to him when he returns to lock up that evening. In preparation for this discussion, list the points you might make to convince the boss to take the sign down. Next, list the points in favor of leaving the sign up. If you were in charge, what would you do? Explain your answer in a brief report to the class.

Urban Systems Sees the Light

continuing case 1

Marc Kaplan asked Dave to approve the following draft sales letter, which Marc wanted to mail out next month to the 4,200 members of the Office Furniture Dealers' Association (OFDA) as the kickoff campaign for Urban Systems' Ultra Light Strips. After reading the letter twice, Dave had still not approved it. Something about the tone of the letter bothered him.

Dear Manager:

Would you like us to come visit you in jail?

Now, it's true that you probably won't be put in jail for requiring your computer operators to sit in front of a monitor eight hours a day, but you just might get slapped with a lawsuit from a disgruntled employee who complains of back problems or failing eyesight. One pregnant employee even won damages by blaming her miscarriage on emotional stress caused by too many hours sitting at her computer! And two studies published this past year that warn of dangers from long periods of working at a computer don't help the situation any.

Each chapter ends with a case study on Urban Systems. By solving these cases, students will encounter communication problems typical to the workplace.

■ Possible solutions to the Continuing Case are described in the *Instructor's Resource Manual.*

Dave Kaplan edits a sales memo his brother, Marc, drafted for potential customers.

■ See Slide 1.13.

■ See Handout 1.3.

Before going to your lawyer, come to US—to Urban Systems—for the answer to your problems. We have recently patented a new strip lighting system for modular furniture that will throw precisely the right amount of soft light around the monitor. With Ultra Light Strips, your operators won't have to put up with glare from their monitors, they won't have to position themselves in a certain way just to read the monitor, and they won't have shadows falling on their copy holders. As a result, they will be happier as well as more productive.

And if wiring is in place, just about anyone can install Ultra Light Strips. Just order the lengths you need—from 1 foot to 20 feet long. They are completely flexible, so that you can easily bend them around your modular furniture. And because they attach with Velcro strips, you can move them around and reuse them as your needs change.

We're really the only game in town when it comes to flexible task lighting. For example, the Mod Light by GME produces 200 foot-candles—far too much light to provide the needed contrast between the screen and surrounding light; your operators will soon begin to make careless errors from visual fatigue. And the Light Mite from Tedesco has long had a reputation for poor reliability. In addition, both GME and Tedesco produce their light fixtures abroad, while Ultra Light Strips are 100 percent American-made! With Ultra Light Strips lighting the way, your operators' increased productivity will easily cover the cost of these strips within the first six months of use. Crush the competition. And avoid those costly legal battles. Call us toll-free at 1-800-555-2883 for a free on-site demonstration. We can also show you the many other uses of Ultra Light that will save your company money.

Sincerely,
Marc Kaplan
Vice President, Marketing

Critical Thinking

1. What is your reaction to this letter? Is the letter effective? Is it ethical? Explain.

2. If this letter represented your only knowledge of Urban Systems, what would be your opinion of the company? In other words, what kind of corporate image does the letter portray?

3. Without actually rewriting the letter, what revisions can you suggest for giving Marc's letter a more ethical tone?

LABtest 1

Retype the following e-mail message from Dave, inserting any needed commas according to the comma rules introduced in LAB (Language Arts Basics) 2 on page 576.

McCormick Place in Chicago ,(PLACE) Illinois , has been chosen to host the largest ,(ADJ) most comprehensive lighting exhibit and conference ever held in the United States. This conference ,(NONR) which is known as the International Lighting Expo , will be held on June 14–16 ,(DATE) 2006 , and is

5 expected to draw more than a thousand participants. "This will be the first such conference ever held in the United States ,(QUOT) " noted the program chair Dave Kaplan ,(QUOT) "and we also intend for it to be the best."

Exhibitors are invited to enter their best new lighting products

10 for judging in the "Best of Show" competition ,(IND) and all lighting companies are invited to compete for the "Energy Miser" awards. Entries for each award will be evaluated by an international panel of lighting experts ,(IND) and will be awarded at the closing session of the three-day conference.

15 The purpose of this message ,(DIR AD) Ms. Allison , is to inquire whether your company would be interested in supplying a speaker for one of the sessions. Although your company would be responsible for all expenses ,(INTRO) we will supply a coordinator ,(SER) overhead projector , and screen for each session. We can ,(TRAN) in addition , provide other reasonable

20 accommodations if arrangements are made in advance. If you would be interested in participating ,(INTRO) please call me at 555-1038 to discuss the details of your sponsorship of this important industry event.

■ See Slide 1.14.

■ See Slide 1.15.

■ See Slide 1.16.

Urban Systems, Inc.

URBAN SYSTEMS

The Company

Urban Systems, Inc. (US) is a small "start-up" company whose primary product is Ultra Light, a new, paper-thin light source that promises to revolutionize the illumination industry. The company employs 178 people at its corporate headquarters in Ann Arbor, Michigan, and in a completely automated manufacturing plant in Charlotte, North Carolina. It is incorporated under the laws of the state of Michigan, with all stock privately held by the founders and their families.

Urban Systems has annual sales in the $30 million range, with a net profit last year of $1.4 million. It is considered a progressive company by the investment community, with good management and good earnings potential. The local community considers US to be a good corporate citizen; it is a nonpolluting firm, and its officers are active in the local chamber of commerce and in community affairs.

Urban Systems headquarters in Ann Arbor, Michigan.

The Product

Ultra Light is a flat, electroluminescent sheet of material that serves as a light source. It is capable of replacing most fluorescent, neon, and incandescent light fixtures. Physically, Ultra Light is a paper-thin sheet of chemically treated material laminated between thin layers of clear plastic. In effect, it is a credit-card-thin light fixture that is bendable and that can be produced in a variety of shapes and sizes. Operated by either battery or wall current, it generates a bright white or colored light.

Ultra Light is cost-competitive with other, more conventional lighting, and its life expectancy is measured in years. All of this, combined with the appeal of its very thin profile, battery operation ("use it anywhere"), the evenly distributed light it produces, and the way it can conform to a variety of physical shapes, makes Ultra Light a new product with a lot of potential.

Company History

US was founded in 2001 by two brothers, David and Marc Kaplan. Dave was a chemical engineer at Industrial Chemical, Inc., when he developed the basic concept of Ultra Light while working on another project. Because IC was not interested in pursuing the manufacturing and marketing of this product, Dave bought all rights to Ultra Light from IC and patented it in 2000. Then he and his younger brother Marc, formerly a marketing manager for an advertising agency in Chicago, started Urban Systems in an empty warehouse in Midland, Michigan.

The company received start-up funds through personal investments of $50,000 by Dave Kaplan and $35,000 by Marc and a $68,500 five-year loan from the United States Small Business Administration. Because of Marc's advertising background, the company's five-year business plan focused on marketing Ultra Light initially for advertising purposes—to illuminate signs, point-of-purchase displays, and the like. Later, as the company became better established in the marketplace, plans were to expand into industrial, office, and consumer applications. Hence, a company name—Urban Systems—was selected that was broad enough to encompass a variety of products.

After a somewhat uneven start, US had become profitable by the end of its fourth year of operations and had outgrown its original building. The company recently built an 11,000-square-foot facility in an attractive office park in Ann Arbor, Michigan, to house its administrative, marketing, and R&D functions. The company also moved its manufacturing operations to Charlotte, North Carolina, in a leased facility. The manufacturing facility is completely automated, with state-of-the-art robotics, just-in-time inventory control, and a progressive union-management agreement. The latest three-year labor contract expires next year.

Personnel

A partial organization chart for Urban Systems is shown in Figure 1. Each corporate position and the person currently occupying that position are described below.

Board of Directors   The board comprises David J. Kaplan, chair; Marc Kaplan, vice-chair; Judith Klehr Kaplan (David Kaplan's wife), secretary/treasurer; Thomas V. Robertson, general counsel; and Eileen Jennings (vice president of U.S. National Bank of Michigan). As required by the articles of incorporation, the board meets quarterly at company headquarters.

President
David J. Kaplan

Dave Kaplan, age 46, is a professional engineer-turned-manager. He graduated with honors from the Massachusetts Institute of Technology with a degree in chemical engineering. Upon graduation from MIT, he began working as a chemical engineer in the polymer division at Industrial Chemical, where he worked until 2001 when he started US. During his time at IC, he attended graduate school part-time at Central Michigan University, where he received his MBA degree in 1989. Although he was offered numerous management positions at IC, he elected to continue working as a chemical engineer. His work resulted in numerous profitable patents for IC, and he was considered a highly respected member of the scientific staff.

figure1   **Urban Systems Organizational Chart**

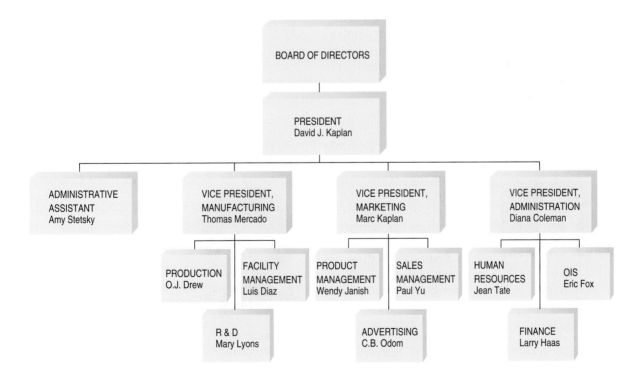

Dave has published numerous articles in scholarly journals, has presented papers in his area of specialty at several international conferences, and has served as president of the Michigan Society of Chemical Engineers.

Although he manages his new company effectively, Dave will tell you that some of his happiest times were working in the lab at IC—pursuing some esoteric research project alone and at his own pace. He will also tell you that the aspects of managing Urban Systems that he dislikes the most are attending the incessant meetings and having to manage and be responsible for the work of others. At US, Dave is considered a perfectionist and a workaholic. Although not an especially warm person, he is highly respected by his staff.

Administrative
Assistant
Amy Stetsky

Amy Stetsky, or "Stetsky" as she is called by nearly everyone who knows her, was one of the first people hired by Dave Kaplan. She is 32 years old, has an associate's degree in office systems, and recently earned the Certified Administrative Professional (CAP) designation as a result of passing an intensive exam administered by the International Association of Administrative Professionals (IAAP). She is highly respected and well liked by everyone in the organization.

Vice President,
Manufacturing
Thomas Mercado

Thomas Mercado knows the production business from top to bottom. He is 47 years old and has been with the company from the beginning, having been hired away from a similar job at Steelcase Corporation. Tom has earned the respect of both Dave and his subordinates, including the engineers in the R&D unit.

Tom gives his staff wide latitude in running their units. He supports them, even when they make mistakes. He does insist, however, on being kept informed at every step of the way. He is a very direct type of person—you always know where you stand with him. If any of his subordinates have some bad news to convey, they know he wants to know immediately and directly—with no beating around the bush.

Although he gets along well with both Dave and his subordinates, he and Marc Kaplan have had several run-ins during the past five years. Privately, he would tell you that he believes Marc is a "lightweight" who is not particularly effective in marketing the firm's products. Tom is especially upset that Marc has shot down several new product ideas proposed by Tom's R&D staff.

Vice President,
Marketing
Marc Kaplan

People who know both Dave and Marc Kaplan cannot believe they are brothers. Marc, age 42, is the complete opposite of Dave. He is warm and outgoing, with a wide circle of friends both in and out of business. His extensive network of personal and professional contacts has resulted in numerous large and lucrative orders for the firm.

Marc depends heavily on his three managers, especially for in-house operations. He spends a great deal of time away from the office—entertaining customers and prospective customers, attending conventions where US exhibits its products, and making the rounds of golf tournaments and after-hours cocktail parties.

Marc is aware of Tom's feelings about him but brushes them aside as normal jealousy. He believes that if he could get Tom to go on a golf outing with him a few times, things could be patched up. As it is, although their relationship is somewhat strained, it is not affecting either's ability to do his job.

Vice President,
Administration
Diana Coleman

Age 38, Diana Coleman has a master of science degree in management information systems from Stanford University. She was promoted to her present position only last year, having served as manager of the Office and Information Systems (OIS) unit at Urban Systems for four years prior to that.

Diana is an ardent feminist. She is also very involved in politics and worked extensively in the unsuccessful campaign of Walter K. Mason, the Liberal Party candidate for governor of Michigan last year.

Diana manages the division that houses both the human resources function and the office function; the office function employs a large number of clerical and secretarial workers (all of whom are female). When Dave Kaplan offered her the promotion to vice president, Diana informed him that one of her goals would be to institute policies that would upgrade the role of women within the company. Although she gets along well with Tom Mer-cado, she resents Marc Kaplan's sometimes condescending attitude toward her and what she considers his chauvinistic attitude toward many of the females on his staff.

Financial Data

By year's end, assets for Urban Systems totaled $23.2 million, with net income of $1.4 million. Earnings per share for the current year were $1.08; and a dividend of $0.64 per share was paid on the 1.3 million outstanding shares (all of which are held by the two Kaplan families).

2

Work-Team Communication

After you have finished this chapter, you should be able to

1. **Communicate effectively in small groups.**

2. **Explain the meaning and importance of nonverbal messages.**

3. **Communicate effectively with diverse populations both within the United States and internationally.**

4. **Listen effectively in business situations.**

5. **Use effective techniques for conducting business by telephone.**

6. **Plan, conduct, and participate in a business meeting.**

7. **Use a professional demeanor and appropriate behavior to maintain effective working relationships.**

Entrepreneur Gilbert C. Morrell Jr. didn't need work-team communication for the first nine years of his company's existence because he *was* the company. He started Nucon in 1982 to provide nuclear consulting services to utilities and gradually expanded into temporary staffing, engineering, and training services. Today Nucon has more than 500 full- and part-time employees, and although Morrell spends much of his time working with clients, he puts a high priority on certain internal meetings.

"I run the senior management meetings, where the department heads and I discuss the company's basic vision, goals and objectives, and current issues," says Morrell. "But when I attend interdepartmental meetings, I let the department heads run the meeting, and I try not to dominate. Sometimes I'm there for support, sometimes I'm there to be sure employees know that the topic is important."

If Morrell disagrees with an idea proposed in a meeting, he can be convinced to change his mind "if the argument is sound or if it reflects information I don't have. I am willing to listen because there may be something I don't know that may persuade me." No so with ideas that go against Nucon Group's core values. In these situations, the CEO says, "I will respectfully listen to the other person's point and then explain why we won't follow that course of action." When turning down an idea, he often buffers his refusal with additional information to help the meeting's participants understand his position.

As the head of a multimillion-dollar corporation, Morrell needs to remember the names and affiliations of hundreds of business contacts. "I don't forget a face, but I sometimes have trouble remembering what people do even if I know their names," he explains. Therefore, when he is first introduced to a new customer or supplier, he offers his business card and asks for the other person's card. Later he takes a few minutes to jot notes about the circumstances of the meeting and Nucon's business relationship with this new contact.

Meetings, e-mail messages, faxes, and letters all have their place in Morrell's workday. However, he says, "I don't like to use e-mail for issues that are specific and significant. For immediate attention on a time-sensitive issue, I prefer the good old telephone." Because he is constantly on the go, visiting with clients or checking out facilities, he is never without his cell phone. In his view, telephone communication offers "instant gratification."

"I am willing to listen because there may be something I don't know that may persuade me."

■ Communicating in Work Teams

CO1. Communicate effectively in small groups.

■ See Slide 2.1.

■ A chapter overview appears in the *Instructor's Resource Manual.*

> *If the group is too large, members may begin to form cliques, or subgroups.*

A **team** is a group of individuals who depend on one another to accomplish a common objective. Teams are often superior to individuals because they can accomplish more work, are more creative, have more information available to them, and offer more interpersonal communication dynamics. There is a synergy at work in which the group's total output exceeds the sum of each individual's contribution.

A recent study carried out at three universities—Purdue, Indiana, and Ohio State—compared the performance of virtual teams (whose members had not met but communicated only by speakerphone) and traditional in-person teams. The researchers found that virtual teams were more productive at brainstorming, whereas face-to-face teams were more productive in tasks where they had to negotiate and reach a decision.[1]

On the other hand, teams can waste time, accomplish little work, and create an environment in which interpersonal conflict can rage. As anyone who has ever worked in a group can attest, there is also the danger of *social loafing,* the psychological term for avoiding individual responsibility in a group setting.

Two to seven members seems to be the most appropriate size range for most effective work teams. Small-team research indicates that five is an ideal size for many teams.[2] Smaller teams often do not have enough diversity of skills and interests to function effectively as a team, whereas larger teams may lack healthy team interaction because just a few people may dominate the discussions.

The Variables of Group Communication

Three factors—conflict, conformity, and consensus—greatly affect the efficiency with which a team operates and the amount of enjoyment members derive from it.

■ See Slide 2.2.

> *Debate* issues, *not* personalities.

Conflict   Managers who demonstrate skill in resolving workplace conflicts are seen as effective leaders—which, in turn, enhances their advancement potential.[3] Conflict is a greatly misunderstood facet of group communication. Many group leaders work hard to avoid conflict because they think it detracts from a group's goals. Their attitude is that a group experiencing conflict is not running smoothly and is destined to fail.

In fact, conflict is what group meetings are all about. One purpose of collaborating on a project is to ensure that various viewpoints are heard so that agreement as to the most appropriate course of action can emerge. Groups can use conflict productively to generate and test ideas before they are implemented. Rather than indicating that a meeting is disorderly, the presence of conflict indicates that members are actively discussing the issues. If a group does not exhibit conflict by debating ideas or questioning others, there is very little reason for it to exist. The members may as well be working individually.

Conflict, then, is the essence of group interaction. Competent communicators use conflict as a means to determine what is and what is not an acceptable idea or solution. Note, however, that the conflict we are talking about involves debate about *issues,* not about *personalities.* Interpersonal conflict can, indeed, have serious negative consequences for work teams.

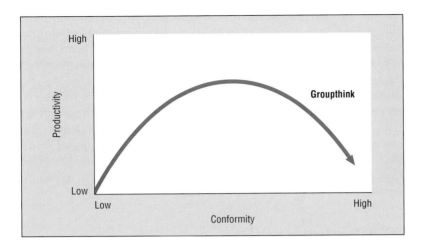

figure**2.1**

Effect of Excessive Conformity on a Group's Productivity

Conformity Conformity is agreement with regard to ideas, rules, or principles. Members may be encouraged to disagree about the definition of a problem or possible solutions, but certain fundamental issues—such as how the group should operate—should be agreed to by everyone.

Although group conformity and group cohesiveness are necessary for successful small-group communication, too much cohesiveness can result in what has been termed **groupthink**, the barrier to communication that results from an overemphasis on unity, which stifles opposing ideas and the free flow of information (see Figure 2.1).[4]

The pressure to conform can become so great that negative information and contrary opinions are never even brought out into the open and discussed. Thus, the group loses the advantage of hearing and considering various perspectives. In effective work-team communication, conflicts, different opinions, and questions are considered an inevitable and essential part of the collaborative process.

Consensus Consensus means reaching a decision that best reflects the thinking of all team members. It is finding a solution that is acceptable enough that all members can support it (perhaps, though, with reservations) and that no member actively opposes it. Consensus is not necessarily a unanimous vote, or even a majority vote. In a majority vote, only the majority are happy with the end result; people in the minority may have to accept something they don't like at all.

Not every decision, of course, needs to have the support of every member; to push for consensus on every matter would require a tremendous investment of time and energy. The group should decide ahead of time when to push for consensus—for example, when reaching decisions that have a major effect on the direction of the project or the conduct of the team.

Consensus does not mean a unanimous vote—or even necessarily a majority vote.

Initial Group Goals

It is difficult to work effectively as a team if the team members do not know one another well and are not aware of each member's strengths and weaknesses, styles of working, experiences, attitudes, and the like. Thus, the first task of most new teams is to get to know one another. For small teams to function effectively, not only the

The group's first task is to get to know one another.

■ See Slide 2.3.

task dimension but also the social dimension must be considered. Some amount of "small talk" about family, friends, current happenings, and the like before and after the meetings is natural and helps to establish a supportive and open environment. You want to be able to compliment each other without embarrassment and to disagree without fear.

Too often, decisions just "happen" in a team; members may go along with what they think everyone else wants. Teams should therefore discuss how they will make decisions and should develop operating rules. They should talk about what would be legitimate reasons for missing a meeting, establish a procedure for informing others of an absence beforehand and of keeping the absent member informed of what was accomplished at the meeting, and decide what being "on time" means. In short, they should develop "norms" for the team.

Giving Constructive Feedback

Giving and receiving feedback should be a part of every team's culture.

The single most important skill to have in working through any problem is the ability to give constructive feedback. There are proven methods for giving and receiving criticism that work equally well for giving and receiving praise.[5]

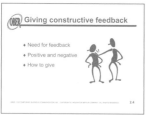

■ See Slide 2.4.

Acknowledge the Need for Feedback   Feedback is vital; it is the only way to find out what needs to be improved and should be an overall part of the team's culture. Thus, your team must agree that giving and receiving feedback is an acceptable part of how you will improve the way you work together. This way, no one will be surprised when he or she receives feedback.

Give Both Positive and Negative Feedback   Many people take good work for granted and give feedback only when there are problems. Unfortunately, this habit is counterproductive. People are far more likely to pay attention to your complaints if they have also received your compliments.

■ See Slide 2.5.

Learn How to Give Feedback   Use these guidelines for compliments as well as complaints:

1. *Be descriptive.* Relate objectively what you saw or what you heard. Give specific examples: the more recent, the better.
2. *Avoid using labels.* Words like *undependable, unprofessional, irresponsible,* and *lazy* are labels that we attach to behaviors. Instead, describe the behaviors and drop the labels.
3. *Don't exaggerate.* Be exact. To say, "You're always late for meetings" is probably untrue and therefore unfair.
4. *Speak for yourself.* Don't refer to absent, anonymous people ("A lot of people here don't like it when you . . .").
5. *Use "I" statements.* This is perhaps the most important guideline. For example, instead of saying, "You are frequently late for meetings," say, "I feel annoyed when you are late for meetings." "I" statements create an adult/peer relationship (see Figure 2.2).

"I" statements tell specifically how someone's behavior affects you.

Conflict Resolution

Most conflicts in groups can be anticipated or prevented if a group spends time developing itself into a team, getting to know one another, establishing ground rules, discussing norms for group behavior, and the like. However, no matter how much planning is done or how conscientiously team members work, conflicts occasionally show up.

One of the worst tactics to take is to accept problems blindly. Problems rarely disappear on their own. However, you should neither overreact nor underreact to group problems. Some behaviors are only fleeting disruptions and can be ignored. Others are chronic and disruptive and must be resolved.

Think of each problem as a group problem. Groups should avoid the temptation to defuse conflicts by making a scapegoat of one member—for example, "We'd

React to problems appropriately, consider them "group" problems, and have realistic expectations about the group process.

Lucent puts its managers through a paper-plane management exercise to foster team building, increase intraoffice communications, and improve client relations. The same exercise has been used by Motorola and NASA.

figure**2.2**

Using "I" Statements When Giving Feedback

Sequence	Explanation
1. "When you . . ."	Start with a "When you . . ." statement that describes the behavior without judgment, exaggeration, labeling, attribution, or motives. Just state the facts as specifically as possible.
2. "I feel . . ."	Tell how the behavior affects you. If you need more than a word or two to describe the feeling, it's probably just some variation of joy, sorrow, anger, or fear.
3. "Because I . . ."	Now say why you are affected that way. Describe the connection between the facts you observed and the feelings they provoke in you.
4. (Pause for discussion)	Let the other person respond.
5. "I would like . . ."	Describe the change you want the other person to consider . . .
6. "Because . . ."	. . . and why you think the change will help alleviate the problem.
7. "What do you think?"	Listen to the other person's response. Be prepared to discuss options and compromise on a solution.

How the feedback will work:

When you [do this], I feel [this way], because [of such and such]. What I would like you to consider is [doing X], because I think it will accomplish [Y]. What do you think?

Example:

"When you are late for meetings, I get angry because I think it is wasting the time of all the other team members and we are never able to get through our agenda items. I would like you to consider finding some way of planning your schedule that lets you get to these meetings on time. That way we can be more productive at the meetings, and we can all keep to our tight schedules."

Source: From Peter R. Scholtes, *The Team Handbook,* 2d ed., Madison, WI: Joiner Associates, 1996, pp. 6–27. Copyright © 1996 Joiner Associates Inc. Reprinted with permission.

A S K Ober

Dear Dr. Ober:

In Chapter 5, you state that the "you" attitude should be used except when conveying negative information. Yet, in Chapter 2, when you talk about giving effective feedback, you say to start with a "When you . . ." statement. Isn't this contradictory if you're giving negative feedback? Instead of saying, "When you do not have your part of the plan drafted at the time we agreed upon . . ." wouldn't it be better to say, "When all parts of the plan are not drafted at the time we agreed upon . . ."?

—Lisa M.

Dear Lisa:

This sequence ("When you . . . , I feel . . .") is effective for both positive and negative feedback and is recommended by *The Team Handbook*, which is excerpted in Chapter 2, "Work-Team Communication." The reason that "you" can be used effectively here is that the behavior is simply being factually described—without including any accusations, labeling, or other emotional baggage. The alternative wording you suggest would, of course, also be effective so long as the listener/reader recognized whose negative behavior was being pointed out.

—Scot

E-mail your questions and comments to askober@ober.net.

---

be finished with this report now if Sam had done his part; you never can depend on him." Rarely is one person solely responsible for the success or failure of a group effort. Examine each problem in light of what the group does to encourage or allow the behavior and what the group can do differently to encourage more constructive behavior. Because every member's role is a function of both his or her own personality and the group's personality, the group should consider how to help every person contribute more to the collaborative efforts.

Finally, be realistic. Don't assume responsibility for the happiness of others. You are responsible for behaving ethically and for treating other group members with respect, but the purpose of the group is not to develop lifelong friendships or to solve other people's time-management or personal problems.

Competent communicators welcome all contributions from group members, regardless of whether the members agree or disagree with their own views. They evaluate each contribution objectively and respond in a nonthreatening manner, with comments that are factual, constructive, and goal-oriented. If the atmosphere becomes tense, they make a light comment, laugh, compliment, recall previous incidents, or take other helpful actions to restore harmony and move the group forward. If interpersonal conflict appears to be developing into a more or less permanent part of the group interactions, the group should put the topic of conflict on its agenda and then devote sufficient meeting time to discussing and working through the conflict.

Team Writing

Writing as part of a team is a common task in contemporary organizations.

The increasing complexity of the workplace makes it difficult for any one person to have either the time or the expertise to be able to identify and solve many of the problems that arise and prepare written responses. This situation especially applies to long or complex documents. The differing talents, skills, and perspectives of several individuals are often needed in a joint effort to analyze a given situation and generate proposals or recommendations. Thus, team writing is becoming quite prevalent in organizations.

In addition to the general team-building guidelines discussed in the previous section, writing teams should follow these strategies.

Develop a work schedule—and stick to it.

Assign Tasks and Develop a Schedule   Start by determining the goals of the project and identifying the reader. Determine the components of the project, the research needed, and the date when each aspect needs to be completed. Then divide the tasks equitably, based on each member's needs, interests, expertise, and commitment to the project.

Meet Regularly   Schedule regular meetings through-out the project to pool ideas, keep track of new developments, assess progress, avoid overlap and omissions, and, if necessary, renegotiate the workload and redefine tasks. As soon as you have finished gathering data, meet as a group to develop an outline for the finished project. This outline should show the sequence of major and subordinate topics in the document. Beware of a "data-dump," in which every bit of information gathered is dumped into the final document. Not *all* of the information that you collect may need to be included in the report.

Draft the Document   The goal at this stage is not to prepare a finished product but to draft all of the content. You have two options:

- *Assign parts to different members.* Having each member write a different part of the document provides an equitable distribution of the work and may produce a draft more quickly. You must ensure, however, that each member is writing in his or her area of expertise and that all have agreed on such style issues as the degree of formality, direct versus indirect organization, and use of preview and summary.

- *Assign one person to draft the entire document.* Assigning one member (presumably the most talented writer) to draft the entire document helps guarantee a more consistent writing style and lessens the risk of serious omissions or duplication. You must, however, provide sufficient guidance to the writer and allow ample time for one person to complete the entire writing task.

ROCKING THE BOAT   *word*wise

Actual names of recreational boats recorded by the Boat Owners Association of the United States:

A Loan Again
Codfather
Dot Calm
Forget Me Knot
Jamaica-Me-Crazy
Keel-Joy
Pier Pressure
Rudder Chaos
Sail Bad the Sinner
Sail-La-Vie
Sloop Du Jour
Yachta, Yachta, Yachta

■ See Slide 2.6.

Harvard University's law school runs a two-day seminar for CEOs entitled "Managing the Difficult Business Communication." Instead of trying to avoid conflict, the best companies learn to harness it to spur creativity.

Ensure that the final group document "speaks with one voice"—that is, that it is coherent and unified.

■ See Slide 2.7.

Do not neglect the final step of proofreading.

Concentrate on group goals rather than individual goals.

■ See Slide 2.8.

One common pitfall in team writing is the failure to achieve a single "voice" in the project. Regardless of who prepares each individual part of the report, the final report must look and sound as though it were prepared by one writer. Think of the report as a single document, rather than as a collection of parts. Organize and present the data so that the report comes across as coherent and unified.

Provide Helpful Feedback on Team Writing   Commenting on the writing of peers can be helpful both to you and to the colleague whose writing you're reviewing. As you respond to the writing of others, you practice techniques that will help you react more effectively to your own writing. As a writer, you benefit from the viewpoints of multiple audiences and from learning what does or doesn't work in your writing. In a team environment, peer comments create more active involvement and can help foster a sense of community within the team.

When reviewing a colleague's writing, follow the guidelines presented in Checklist 1, "Commenting on Peer Writing," on page 49.

Revise the Draft   Be sure to allow enough time for editing the draft. This task is best accomplished by providing each member with a copy of the entire draft beforehand (to allow time for reading and making notes) and then meeting as a group to review each section for errors in content, gaps or repetition, and effective writing style.

Decide who will be responsible for making the changes to each section, how the document will be formatted, and who will be responsible for proofreading the final document. Typically, one person (preferably not the typist) will be assigned to review the final draft for consistency and correctness in content, style, and format.

The Ethical Dimension of Work-Team Communication

Accepting membership on a team implies acceptance of certain standards of ethical behavior. One of the most basic of these standards is to put the good of the team ahead of personal gain. Team members should set aside private agendas in their team actions and avoid advocating positions that might benefit them personally but that would not be best for the team.

Team members also have an ethical responsibility to respect the integrity and emotional needs of one another. Everyone's ideas should be treated with respect, and no action should be taken that results in a loss of self-esteem for a member.

Finally, each member has an ethical responsibility to promote the team's welfare—by contributing his or her best efforts to the team's mission and by refraining from destructive gossip, domination of meetings, and other counterproductive actions.

■ Nonverbal Communication

CO2. Explain the meaning and importance of nonverbal messages.

Not all the communication that occurs on work teams, or on the job in general, is spoken, heard, written, or read—that is, verbal. According to management expert Peter Drucker, "The most important thing in communication is to hear what isn't

✔checklist1

Commenting on Peer Writing

✔ Read first for meaning; that is, comment on the large issues first—issues such as the paper's focus, organization, appropriateness for the intended audience, and overall clarity.

✔ Assume the role of reader—not instructor. Your job is to help the writer, not to grade the assignment.

✔ Point out sections that you liked, as well as those you disliked, explaining specifically why you thought they were effective or ineffective (not "I liked this part" but "You did a good job of explaining this difficult concept").

✔ Prefer "I" language (not "You need to make this clearer" but "I was confused here").

✔ Comment helpfully—but sparingly. There is no need to point out the same misspelling a dozen times.

✔ Emphasize the *writer* when giving positive feedback: for example, "I'm glad you were able to get the most current figures from the company's home page." And emphasize the *text* (rather than the writer) when giving negative feedback: for example, "This argument would be more persuasive for me if it contained the most current figures."

✔ Avoid taking over the text. Accept the fact that it is someone else's writing—not your own. Make constructive suggestions, but avoid making decisions or demands.

being said."[6] A nonverbal message is any message that is not written or spoken. The nonverbal message may accompany a verbal message (smiling as you greet a colleague), or it may occur alone (selecting the back seat when entering the conference room for a staff meeting). Nonverbal messages are typically more spontaneous than verbal messages, but that does not mean that they are any less important. One study has shown that only 7 percent of the meaning communicated by most messages comes from the verbal portion, with the remaining 93 percent being conveyed nonverbally.[7]

The six most common types of nonverbal communication in business are discussed in the following sections.

Body Movement

By far, the most expressive part of your body is your face—especially your eyes. Research shows that receivers tend to be quite consistent in their reading of facial expressions. In fact, many of these expressions have the same meaning across different cultures.[8] Eye contact and eye movements tell you a lot about a person, although—as we shall see later—maintaining eye contact with the person to whom you're speaking is not perceived as important (or even polite) in some cultures.

Gestures are hand and upper-body movements that add important information to face-to-face interactions. As the game of charades proves, you can communicate quite a bit without using oral or written signals. More typically, gestures are used to help illustrate and reinforce your verbal message.

Nonverbal messages are unwritten and unspoken.

■ See Handout 2.1.

Cultures differ in the importance they attach to eye contact.

■ See Slide 2.9.

■ Gestures that are routine in the United States may have a very different significance in other cultures. In *Blunders in International Business,* David A. Ricks reports that an American worker inadvertently offended his Korean boss when he beckoned him with a crooked finger, a gesture Koreans consider quite rude.

Body stance (posture, placement of arms and legs, distribution of weight, and the like) is another form of nonverbal communication. For example, leaning slightly toward the person with whom you're communicating would probably be taken as a sign of interest and involvement in the interaction. On the other hand, leaning back with arms folded across the chest might be taken (and intended) as a sign of boredom or defiance.

One interesting example of research into the use of gestures occurred when a Chicago psychiatrist studied former President Clinton's videotaped grand jury testimony about his relationship with Monica Lewinsky. Dr. Alan Hirsch found that the president touched his nose once every four minutes when he gave answers that later were shown to be false. By contrast, he did not touch his nose at all when he gave truthful answers.[9]

Physical Appearance

Our culture places great value on physical appearance. Television, newspapers, and magazines are filled with advertisements for personal-care products, and the ads typically feature attractive users of these products. Attractive people tend to be seen as more intelligent, more likable, and more persuasive than unattractive people; in addition, they earn more money.[10]

Your appearance is particularly important for making a good first impression. Although you may not be able to change some of your physical features, understanding the importance of good grooming and physical appearance can help you to emphasize your strong points. Also, your clothing, jewelry, office and home furnishings, and automobile provide information about your values, taste, heritage, conformity, status, age, sexuality, and group identification.

Elsie Cross Associates runs a three-day retreat for work-team members to raise awareness, examine racial and gender bias, and seek ways to change. According to Cross, "there is anger, shouting, and sometimes tears" at these workshops, but the goal is always constructive feedback and change. (Note the body language of each participant.)

Voice Qualities

No one speaks in a monotone. To illustrate, read the following sentence aloud, each time emphasizing the italicized word. Note how the meaning changes with each reading.

Your tone of voice can emphasize or subordinate the verbal message—or even contradict it.

- *You* were late. (*Answers the question "Who was late?"*)

- You *were* late. (*Responds to the other person's denial of being late.*)

- You were *late*. (*Emphasizes how late the person was.*)

Voice qualities such as volume, speed, pitch, tone, and accent carry both intentional and unintentional messages. For example, when you are nervous, you tend to speak faster and at a higher pitch than normal. People who constantly speak too softly risk being interrupted or ignored, whereas people who constantly speak too loudly are often seen as being pushy or insecure.

A significant number of voice qualities are universal across all human cultures. For example, around the world, adults use higher-pitched voices to speak to children, in greetings, and during courtship. Also, in almost every language, speakers use a rising intonation to ask a question.[11]

Time

How do you feel when you're late for an appointment? When others are late? The meaning given to time varies greatly by culture, with Americans and Canadians being much more time-conscious than members of South American or Middle Eastern cultures.

The meaning we attach to time depends on our culture, our status, and the specific situation.

Time is related not only to culture but also to one's status within the organization. You would be much less likely to keep a superior waiting for an appointment than you would a subordinate. Time is also situation-specific. Although you normally might not worry about being five minutes late for a staff meeting, you would probably arrive early if you were the first presenter.

Touch

Touch is the first sense we develop, acquired even before birth. Some touches, such as those made by a physician during an examination, are purely physical; others, such as a handshake, are a friendly sign of willingness to communicate; and still others indicate intimacy.

■ The first scientific study of nonverbal communication was published in 1872 by Charles Darwin in *The Expression of the Emotions in Man and Animals*.

The importance of touching behavior varies widely by culture. One international study found that in typical social exchanges, people from San Juan, Puerto Rico, touched an average of 180 times an hour, those in Paris touched 110 times per hour, those in Gainesville, Florida, touched 2 times per hour, and those in London touched not at all.[12]

Although touching is a very important form of business communication, it is one that most people do not know how to use appropriately and effectively. The person who never touches anyone in a business setting may be seen as cold and standoffish, whereas the person who touches too frequently may cause the receiver to feel apprehensive and uncomfortable.

Space and Territory

Different types of communication occur at different distances.

When you are on a crowded elevator, you probably look at the floor indicator, at advertisements, at your feet, or just straight ahead. Most people in our culture are uncomfortable in such close proximity to strangers. Psychologists have identified four zones within which people in our culture interact.[13]

1. *Intimate Zone:* From physical contact to about 18 inches is where all your body movements occur; this is the area in which you move throughout the day. It is an area normally reserved for close, intimate interactions. Business associates typically enter this space infrequently and only briefly—perhaps to shake hands or pat someone on the back.

■ Police interrogators are taught to intrude well inside the personal zone when questioning suspects, as a means of intentionally creating discomfort.

2. *Personal Zone:* This zone, extending from 18 inches to about 4 feet, is where conversation with close friends and colleagues takes place. Unlike interaction in the intimate zone, normal talking is frequent in the personal zone. Some, but not a great deal of, business interaction occurs here; for example, business lunches typically occur in this zone.
3. *Social Zone:* From 4 feet to 12 feet, the social zone is where most business exchanges occur. Informal business conferences and staff meetings occur within this space.
4. *Public Zone:* The public zone extends from 12 feet to as far as the eye can see and the ear can hear. It is the most formal zone, and the least significant interactions occur here. Because of the great distance, communication in the public zone is often one way, as from a speaker to a large audience.

■ See Slide 2.10.

Competent communicators recognize their own personal space needs and the needs of others. When communicating with people who prefer more or less space, the competent communicator makes the adjustments necessary to facilitate reaching his or her objective.

■ Communicating in a Diverse Environment

CO3. Communicate effectively with diverse populations both within the United States and internationally.

Paying attention to the needs of others means that we recognize and accept diversity. When we talk about diversity, we mean cultural differences not only within the U.S and Canadian work force but also in the worldwide marketplace. The dominant role that the United States plays in the global economy does not mean that international business matters are handled "the American way." Some years ago a book called *The Ugly American* condemned Americans abroad for their "Let 'em do it our way or not at all" attitude. As Al Ries, chairman of Trout & Ries Advertising Inc., once pointed out, "A company that keeps its eye on Tom, Dick, and Harry is going to miss Pierre, Hans, and Yoshiko."[14]

International business would not be possible without international communication.

When we talk about culture, we mean the customary traits, attitudes, and behaviors of a group of people. **Ethnocentrism** is the belief that one's own cultural group is superior. Such an attitude hinders communication, understanding, and goodwill between trading partners. An attitude of arrogance is not only counterproductive but also unrealistic, considering that the U.S. population represents less than 5 percent of the world population. Moreover, of the world's countries, the United States is currently fourth in population and is expected to drop to eighth place by the year 2050.[15]

Another fact of life in international business is that comparatively few Americans speak a foreign language. Although English is the major language for conducting business worldwide, it would be naive to assume that it is the other person's responsibility to learn English.

Diversity will have profound effects on our lives and will pose a growing challenge for managers (see, for example, Communication Snapshot 2, "Who Interacts Daily with a Non-English Speaker?" and Spotlight 4, "Internationally Yours," on page 54). The following discussion provides useful guidance for communicating with people from different cultures—both internationally as well as domestically. Although it is helpful to be aware of cultural differences, competent communicators recognize that each member of a culture is an individual, with individual needs, perceptions, and experiences, and should be treated as such.

Cultural Differences

Cultures differ widely in the traits they value. For example, as shown in Table 2.1 on page 55, international cultures differ widely in their emphasis on individualism, long-term orientation, time orientation, power distance, uncertainty avoidance, formality, materialism, and context-sensitivity. (You should be aware, of course, that just as you are learning the international way of communicating, other cultures are learning the American way of communicating. At some point, perhaps one universal way of communicating will emerge—but don't hold your breath!)

Each person interprets events through his or her mental filter, and that filter is based on the receiver's unique knowledge, experiences, and viewpoints. For example, the language of time is as different among cultures as the language of words. Americans, Canadians, Germans, and Japanese are very time-conscious and very precise about appointments; Latin American and Middle Eastern cultures tend to be more casual about time. For example, if your Mexican host tells you that he or she will meet with you at three, it's most likely *más o menos* (Spanish for "more or less").

Businesspeople in both Asian and Latin American countries tend to favor long negotiations and slow deliberations. They exchange pleasantries at some length before getting down to business. Likewise, many non-Western cultures use the silent intervals for contemplation, whereas businesspeople from the United States and Canada tend to have little tolerance for silence in business negotiations. As a result, Americans and Canadians may rush in and offer compromises and counterproposals that would have been unnecessary if they had shown more patience.

Body language, especially gestures and eye contact, also varies among cultures. For example, our sign for "okay"—forming a circle with our forefinger and thumb—means "zero" in France, "money" in Japan, and a vulgarity in Brazil (see Figure 2.3 on page 56). Americans and Canadians consider eye contact important. In Asian and many Latin American countries, however, looking a partner full in the eye is considered an irritating sign of ill breeding.

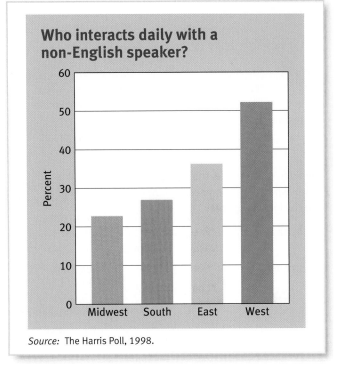

communication snapshot 2

Who interacts daily with a non-English speaker?

Source: The Harris Poll, 1998.

Cultures differ not only in their verbal language but also in their nonverbal language. Very few nonverbal messages have universal meanings.

Companies receiving most of their sales from abroad

Company	% of Sales
Gillette	65
Colgate	65
IBM	59
NCR	59
Coca-Cola	54
Dow Chemical	54
Xerox	54
Caterpillar	53
Hewlett-Packard	53

■ See Slide 2.11.

■ According to an old joke, What do you call someone who speaks three languages? *Trilingual.* What do you call someone who speaks two languages? *Bilingual.* What do you call someone who speaks one language? *American.*

spotlight4
ACROSS CULTURES

Internationally Yours

Most of the correspondence between U.S. or Canadian firms and foreign firms takes place in English. Even when the language is the same, however, different meanings can result.

Losing Something in the Translation

Consider, for example, the miscommunication that occurred when these phrases were translated from English into the local language:

American English:	"The Electrolux is the strongest vacuum available."
British English:	"Nothing sucks like an Electrolux."
English:	"Come alive with Pepsi."
Thai:	"Bring your ancestors back from the dead with Pepsi."
English:	"I'm just tickled to death to be here."
Russian:	"Scratch me until I die."

Très Chic: Communicating Continentally

When communicating with international business colleagues, customers, venture capitalists, and other important audiences, you will often find not only language differences but also other differences in usage and style.

Phone Numbers   Continental (European) style calls for the use of periods rather than hyphens or parentheses to separate parts of a phone number: for example, 317.555.1086 rather than 317-555-1086 or (317) 555-1086. Dot-style telephone numbers seem to be gaining popularity in the United States, where they are sometimes viewed as classier and more elegant.

Spelling and Word Choice   The British (and current and former British colonies, such as Canada) use these spellings: *authorise, behaviour, centre, cheque, labour, legalise, organisation, practise, programme,* and *theatre,* among others. Unless your spelling checker uses a British dictionary, it will probably reject those spellings. The British also use *holiday* instead of *vacation; lift* instead of *elevator;* and *underground* instead of *subway.*

Punctuation   Americans put periods inside closing quotation marks, whereas the British place them outside. Also, British usage calls for single quotation marks where American usage calls for double quotation marks. Thus, Americans would type "I see." The British would type 'I see'. Also, British and Continental style omits periods after *Dr., Mr., Ms.,* and other courtesy titles, as well as after *Jr.* and *Sr.*

Decimals   Americans and the British use a period to indicate a decimal point (1.57 percent), whereas some countries (including France) use a comma instead (1,57 percent).

Dates   American writers use a month/day/year format (such as May 15, 2006, or 05/15/06). Outside the United States, a day/month/year format is the norm (15 May 2006, or 15-05-06). The influential International Organization for Standardization, a 130-nation federation dedicated to global uniformity, has issued ISO 8601, which requires putting the year first, month second, and day last (2006-06-15). Because so many companies seek ISO approval to simplify international trade, this year-month-day style will likely become more prevalent everywhere.

Touching behavior is very culture-specific. Many Asians do not like to be touched, except for a brief handshake in greeting. However, handshakes in much of Europe tend to last much longer than in the United States and Canada, and Europeans tend to shake hands every time they see each other, perhaps several times a day. Germans typically use a firm grip and one shake; Asians typically grasp the other's hand delicately and shake only briefly. In much of Europe, men often kiss each other upon greeting; unless an American or Canadian businessperson is aware of this custom, he or she might react inappropriately.

table2.1

Cultural Values

Value	High	Low
Individualism: Cultures in which people see themselves first as individuals and believe that their own interests take priority.	*United States* Canada Great Britain Australia Netherlands	Japan Taiwan Mexico Greece Hong Kong
Long-Term Orientation: Cultures that maintain a long-term perspective.	*United States* Canada	Pacific Rim countries
Time Orientation: Cultures that perceive time as a scarce resource and that tend to be impatient.	*United States*	Pacific Rim and Middle Eastern countries
Power Distance: Cultures in which management decisions are made by the boss simply because he or she is the boss.	France Spain Japan Mexico Brazil	*United States* Israel Germany Ireland
Uncertainty Avoidance: Cultures in which people want predictable and certain futures.	Israel Japan Italy Argentina	*United States* Canada Australia Singapore
Formality: Cultures that attach considerable importance to tradition, ceremony, social rules, and rank.	Latin American countries	*United States* Canada Scandinavian countries
Materialism: Cultures that emphasize assertiveness and the acquisition of money and material objects.	Japan Austria Italy	Scandinavian countries
Context Sensitivity: Cultures that emphasize the surrounding circumstances (or context), make extensive use of body language, and take the time to build relationships and establish trust.	Asian, Hispanic, and African countries	Northern European countries

Source: From *Human Relations* by A. J. DuBrin. © 1997. Adapted by permission of Prentice-Hall, Inc. Upper Saddle River, NJ.

Our feelings about space are partly an outgrowth of our culture and partly a result of geography and economics. For example, Americans and Canadians are used to wide-open spaces and tend to move about expansively, using hand and arm motions for emphasis. But in Japan, which has much smaller living and working spaces, such abrupt and extensive body movements are not typical. Likewise, Americans and Canadians tend to sit face to face so that they can maintain eye contact, whereas the Chinese and Japanese (to whom eye contact is not as important) tend to sit side by side during negotiations.

When in doubt about how to act, follow the lead of your host.

figure 2.3
Same Sign, Different Meanings

OK sign
France: you're a zero; **Japan:** please give me coins; **Brazil:** an obscene gesture; **Mediterranean countries:** an obscene gesture

Thumbs-up
Australia: up yours; **Germany:** the number one; **Japan:** the number five; **Saudi Arabia:** I'm winning; **Ghana:** an insult; **Malaysia:** the thumb is used to point rather than the finger

Thumbs-down
Most countries: something is wrong or bad

Thumb and forefinger
Most countries: money; **France:** something is perfect; **Mediterranean:** a vulgar gesture

Open palm
Greece: an insult dating to ancient times; **West Africa:** You have five fathers, an insult akin to calling someone a bastard

Source: Atlanta Committee for Olympic Games, by Sam Ward, *USA Today.* Taken from Ben Brown, "Atlanta Out to Mind Its Manners," *USA Today,* March 14, 1996, p. 7c. Copyright © 1996 *USA Today.* Reprinted with permission.

IBM's corporate work force diversity staff, headed by Ted Childs (top center), helps make sure that downsizing doesn't mean homogenization of the employee pool.

Also, the sense of personal space differs among cultures. In the United States and Canada, most business exchanges occur at about 5 feet, within the so-called social zone discussed earlier. However, both in the Middle East and in Latin American countries, this distance is too far. Businesspeople there tend to stand close enough to feel your breath as you speak. Most Americans and Canadians tend to back away unconsciously from such close contact.

Finally, social behavior is very culture-dependent. For example, in the Japanese culture, the matter of who bows first upon meeting, how deeply the person bows, and how long the bow is held is very dependent upon one's status.

Competent communicators become familiar with such role-related behavior and also learn the customs regarding giving (and accepting) gifts, exchanging business cards, the degree of formality expected, and the accepted means of entertaining and being entertained.

Group-Oriented Behavior

As shown earlier in Table 2.1 on page 55, the business environment in a capitalistic society such as the United States and Canada places great value on the contributions of the individual toward the success of the organization. Individual effort is often stressed more than group effort, and a competitive atmosphere prevails. In other cultures, however, originality and independence of judgment are not valued as highly as teamwork. The Japanese say, "A nail standing out will be hammered down." Thus, the Japanese go to great lengths to reach decisions through consensus, wherein every participating member, not just a majority, is able to agree.

Closely related to the concept of group-oriented behavior is the notion of "saving face." The desire to save face simply means that neither party in a given interaction should suffer embarrassment. Human relationships are highly valued in Japanese cultures and are embodied in the concept of *wa,* or the Japanese pursuit of harmony. This concept makes it difficult for the Japanese to say "no" to a request because it would be impolite. They are very reluctant to offend others—even if they unintentionally mislead them instead. Thus, a "yes" to a Japanese might mean "Yes, I understand you" rather than "Yes, I agree." Latin Americans also tend to avoid an outright "no" in their business dealings, preferring instead a milder, less explicit, response. In intercultural communications, one has to read between the lines, because what is left unsaid or unwritten may be just as important as what *is* said or written.

Expect negotiations to take longer when unanimous agreement rather than majority rule is the norm.

Strategies for Communicating Across Cultures

When communicating with people from different cultures, whether abroad or at home, use the following strategies.

■ The Microsoft Encarta online encyclopedia takes international communication to a new level by using "different facts for different folks." For example, in the U.S. version of Encarta, Microsoft gives credit for inventing the telephone to Alexander Graham Bell. In the Italian version, however, the credit goes to Antonio Meucci. (*Wall Street Journal,* June 25, 1999, p. A1.)

Maintain Formality   Compared to the traditional U.S. and Canadian cultures, most other cultures value and respect a much more formal approach to business dealings. Call others by their titles and family names unless specifically asked to do otherwise. By both verbal and nonverbal clues, convey an attitude of propriety and decorum. Most other cultures do not equate formality with coldness.

Show Respect   Withhold judgment, accepting the premise that attitudes held by an entire culture are probably based on sound reasoning. Listen carefully to what is being communicated, trying to understand the other person's feelings. Learn about your host country—its geography, form of government, largest cities, culture, current events, and the like.

Showing respect is probably the easiest strategy to exhibit—and one of the most important.

Communicate Clearly   To ensure that your oral and written messages are understood, follow these guidelines:

- Avoid slang, jargon, and other figures of speech. Expressions such as "They'll eat that up" or "out in left field" are likely to confuse even a fluent English speaker.

- Be specific and illustrate your points with concrete examples.

- Provide and solicit feedback; summarize frequently; provide a written summary of the points covered in a meeting; ask your counterpart to paraphrase what has been said; encourage questions.

- Use a variety of media: handouts (distributed before the meeting to allow time for reading), audiovisual aids, models, and the like.

- Avoid attempts at humor; humor is likely to be lost on your counterpart.

- Speak plainly and slowly (but not so slowly as to appear condescending), choosing your words carefully.

■ See Slide 2.12.

■ For more on diversity and communication, see the supplemental lecture/discussion notes in the *Instructor's Resource Manual.*

"GENTLEMEN, THERE'S BEEN SOME CRITICISM FROM SOME QUARTERS ABOUT THE SUPPOSED LACK OF DIVERSITY IN THE TOP RANKS OF THIS COMPANY."

Value Diversity   Those who view diversity among employees as a source of richness and strength for the organization can help bring a wide range of benefits to their organization. Whether you happen to belong to the majority culture or to one of the minority cultures where you work, you will share your work and leisure hours with people different from yourself—people who have values, mannerisms, and speech habits different from your own. This statement is true today, and it will be even truer in the future. The same strategies apply whether the cultural differences exist at home or abroad.

Cultural diversity provides a rich environment for solving problems and for expanding horizons.

A person who is knowledgeable about, and comfortable with, different cultures is a more effective manager because he or she can avoid misunderstandings and tap into the greater variety of viewpoints that a diverse culture provides. In addition, such understanding provides personal satisfaction.

Diversity Within the United States

Perhaps, up to this point, you have been inferring that you must leave the United States and Canada to encounter cultures different from your own. Nothing could be further from the truth. In fact, the term *minority* is becoming something of a misnomer. For example, the white population in the United States will decline from a total of 80 percent of the population in 1980 to a bare majority (less than 53 percent) in 2050.[16]

It is true, of course, that we are members of many cultures other than an ethnic culture, such as sex and age group. Although the sexual makeup of the U.S. population has remained about 50-50 for the past 150 years, the median age of the population has been steadily growing:[17]

- 1850: 19 years
- 1900: 23 years
- 1950: 30 years
- 2000: 36 years

Race Manners: The Color of Speech

Bruce A. Jacobs

Speech is a high-stakes ethnic code, a set of clues we use to make instant decisions about strangers. We screen each other's language like soldiers on patrol in a combat zone or a scouting party from the starship *Enterprise*. You see a youngish black man in a store? You make him, in your mind's eye, walk the walk and talk the talk, even if he is a medical student from Shaker Heights. You talk to someone on the phone who speaks standard English? She's white. It's automatic.

Language is loaded. Every black standard-English speaker has stories of making business arrangements on the phone and then—surprise!—getting a different response in person. Hurt feelings, and sometimes lawsuits, result. It goes further. Middle-class African Americans who speak mainstream English are sometimes seen as Uncle Toms by other blacks, who may view the very act of such speech as "giving in" to the coercion of white society.

Language, like artillery, carries a charge. And we aim it, however unintentionally, at one another's heads. When we make assumptions about one another on subways and in stores and in offices, much more is at stake than mere speech.

While linguists continue to debate the nature of Ebonics (most agree it is a dialect), the fact remains that it is a form of nonstandard English in a nation in which standard English is the rule. We do children no favors by assigning official status to a vernacular when what they really need, beyond their everyday speech, is mastery of the language of the marketplace.

Black or white, you can appreciate the history, depth, and beauty of black English while insisting on fluency in standard English. If you are white, understand that use of black English says no more and no less about the speaker's character than your speech says about yours. If you are black, understand that the same applies to standard English.

Ethnic Jokes

Black jokes. Jewish jokes. Polish jokes. They are awful. They are demeaning. They are racist and divisive. They are unforgivable. And in just the right context and the right company, some of them are funny.

While we may be more than willing to laugh at ourselves in the warmth of safe company, we are *not* willing to fling wide the doors and invite others to laugh at us. We know that what might be a wicked little joke in our own self-protective hands is, in the hands of someone who does not mean well, a weapon. You could call this two-sided attitude toward jokes hypocrisy. I call it survival.

The Black Ambassador

It is a title conferred every day upon individual African Americans without their permission: "Ambassador for Black People Everywhere." It bestows the responsibility upon black people, anytime and anywhere, to enlighten well-intentioned nonblacks about the black point of view—as in, "Why do so many black people feel that—?" or, "What is black people's opinion of—?" From the questioner's standpoint, this is all perfectly innocent; when you have few or no black friends and little understanding of black life, you open whatever windows you can. And who better to ask for help than an African American?

But that's the problem. You are asking *an* African American: one person, with one set of experiences, one heart, and one brain. Here he or she is, minding his or her own business on the bus or at work, and suddenly he or she is asked to step in for millions of black folk. The temptation is to snap, "Why are you asking *me*?"

Look, it's not wrong for a well-meaning white person to seek out a black person's opinion. It's wrong, though, to treat that opinion as anything other than one person's view. The unspoken assumption behind a what-do-black-people-think interrogation ("One black opinion is the same as any other, so I'll ask you") is aggravating beyond belief. Imagine the gall of, say, a foreigner asking a white American "how white people feel" about antipoverty programs. *Which* white people?

Forget entirely about gaining any kind of broad knowledge about black folk from talking with one or two people. There are no shortcuts. If you want to know what one black friend thinks about something, ask him or her. If you want to know what a lot of black people think, ask a lot of black people.

To paraphrase Judith Martin (otherwise known as Miss Manners), the purpose of manners is to help people to be as comfortable as possible in one another's company. If we will invest in manners for the sake of an enjoyable dinner, surely we will do so for the sake of our survival. See you at the table.[22]

■ McDonald's offers restaurant management programs and summer corporate internships for minority college students. *Black Enterprise* magazine rated Xerox as one of the best places for blacks to work. Hewlett-Packard lets female applicants know that as an employer, it was rated highly by *Working Woman* magazine.

Men and women often communicate differently.

Perhaps the second thing we should realize is that ethnicity is not a characteristic limited to people of color; white Americans are ethnic, too. Every ethnic and racial group in the world—all six billion of us—has its own physical and cultural characteristics. Of course, every person within an ethnic group has his or her own individual characteristics as well.

Is it any wonder, then, that communicating about ethnic and racial matters is so hazardous? Yet we have no choice. We must learn to communicate comfortably and honestly with one another. If we use the wrong terminology, make an unwarranted assumption, or present only one side of the story, our readers or listeners will let us know soon enough. In Spotlight 6, "Race Manners: The Color of Speech," on page 61, writer Bruce A. Jacobs highlights possible flashpoints in communications between white Americans and black Americans. Do you agree or disagree with his analysis? Why?

Gender Issues in Communication Gender roles consist of the learned behavior associated with being male or female. Certain differences typically exist in male/female communication patterns:[23]

1. Women communicate largely to build rapport; men communicate primarily to preserve independence and status by displaying knowledge and skill.
2. Men prefer to work out their problems by themselves, whereas women prefer to talk out solutions with another person.
3. Women are more likely to compliment the work of a coworker; men are more likely to be critical.
4. Men tend to interrupt to dominate a conversation or to change the subject; women tend to interrupt to agree with or to support what another person is saying.
5. Men tend to be more directive in their conversation, whereas women emphasize politeness.
6. Men are more interested than women in calling attention to their own accomplishments.
7. Men tend to dominate discussions during meetings.
8. Men tend to internalize successes ("That's one of my strengths") and to externalize failures ("We should have been given more time"). Women tend to externalize successes ("I was lucky") and to internalize failures ("I'm just not good at that").
9. In the workplace, men speak differently to other men than they do to women, and women speak differently to other women than they do to men.
10. Even when gender is not readily apparent in online communication, men and women have recognizably different styles in posting to the Internet.

Recognize that these differences often (but not always) do exist (see Figure 2.5). Thus, women should not take it personally if a male coworker fails to praise their work; he may simply be engaging in gender-typical behavior. If a male manager feels that a female colleague is more interested in relating to others in the group and seeking consensus than in solving the problem, she may simply be engaging in gender-typical behavior.

Competent communicators seek to understand and adapt to these differences. According to Alice Sargeant, author of *The Androgynous Manager,*

> Men and women should learn from one another without abandoning successful traits they already possess. Men can learn to be more collaborative and intuitive, yet remain result-oriented. Women need not give up being nurturing in order to learn to be comfortable with power and conflict.[24]

Communicating with People with Disabilities Since the Americans with Disabilities Act (ADA) was passed, more physically disabled individuals than ever before have been able to enter the workplace. The act protects approximately 43 million U.S. citizens who have physical or mental impairments that significantly limit a major life activity. It guarantees that persons with disabilities who are qualified to perform the essential functions of a job, with or without reasonable accommodation, will not be discriminated against in hiring and promotion in most public and private organizations.

Relate versus **Debate**
Rapport versus **Report**
Cooperation versus **Competition**

figure**2.5**
Goals of Gender Communication
Do you know women and men who defy these gender stereotypes?

But competent communicators go beyond the legal requirements. Depending on each individual situation, some reasonable changes in the way you communicate will be appreciated. For example, when being introduced to someone who uses a wheelchair, bend over slightly to be closer to eye level. If the person is able to extend his or her hand for a handshake, offer your hand. For lengthy conversations, sit down so that you are both eye to eye. People who use wheelchairs may see their wheelchairs as extensions of their personal space, so avoid touching or leaning on their wheelchair.

Most hearing-impaired people use a combination of hearing and lip reading. Face the person to whom you're speaking, and speak a bit slower (but not louder) than usual. When talking with a person who is blind, deal in words rather than in gestures or glances. As you approach him or her, make your presence known; if in a group, address the person by name so that he or she will know to whom you are talking. Identify yourself and use your normal voice and speed.

Everyone needs help at one time or another. If someone with a disability looks as if he or she needs assistance, ask whether help is wanted and follow the person's wishes. But resist the temptation to take too much care of an individual with a disability. Don't be annoying or patronizing.

Always, everywhere, avoid using language like "Are you deaf?," "He's a little slow," or "What are you, blind?" Such language is disrespectful to those with physical or cognitive disabilities; in fact, such language is disrespectful to everyone.

When making presentations, consider the needs of those with disabilities—in terms of seating, handouts and other visual aids, and the like. As always when communicating, the best advice is to know your audience. Also, see the "unseen." Recognize that some disabilities are invisible. Be alert and sensitive to colleagues who

Making reasonable accommodations for workers with disabilities is a normal part of the contemporary workplace.

may have allergies or other sensitivities, unseen physical disabilities, addictions, or other life-threatening (or even fatal) conditions.

Accept accommodations as a normal part of the workplace. We all need accommodations of some sort, not necessarily a wheelchair but perhaps a standard office chair that needs adjustment for users of different height. Embrace the idea that accommodating coworkers, customers, and guests with disabilities is a normal function of the workplace. In short, show that you are a team player who values social inclusion.

Most important, relax. Insofar as possible, forget about the disability, and treat the person as you would anyone else. That person was hired because of the contribution he or she could make to the organization—not because of the disability.

■ Listening

CO4. **Listen effectively in business situations.**

There is a difference between hearing and listening.

Whether across continents or across a conference table, effective communication requires both sending and receiving messages—both transmission and reception. Whether you are making a formal presentation to 500 people or conversing with one person over lunch, your efforts will be in vain if your audience does not listen.

Listening involves much more than just hearing. You can hear and not listen (just as you can listen and not understand). Hearing is simply perceiving sound; sound waves strike the eardrum, sending impulses to the brain. Hearing is a passive process, whereas listening is an active process. When you *perceive* a sound, you're merely aware of it; you don't necessarily comprehend it. When you *listen*, you interpret and assign meaning to the sounds.

Consider the automobile you drive. When the car is operating normally, even though you *hear* the sound of the engine as you're driving, you're barely aware of it; you tend to tune it out. But the minute the engine begins to make a strange sound—not necessarily louder or harsher, but just *different*—you immediately tune back in, listening intently to try to discern the nature of the problem. You *heard* the normal hum of the engine but *listened* to the strange noise.

The Problem of Poor Listening Skills

Although listening is the communication skill we use the most frequently, most people have not been taught how to listen effectively.

Listening is the communication skill we use the most. White-collar workers typically devote at least 40 percent of their workday to listening. Yet immediately after hearing a ten-minute oral presentation, the average person retains only 50 percent of the information. Forty-eight hours later, only 25 percent of what was heard can be recalled.[25] Thus, listening is probably the least developed of the four verbal communication skills (writing, reading, speaking, and listening).

One of the major causes of poor listening is that most people have simply not been taught how to listen well. Think back to your early years in school. How much class time was devoted to teaching you to read and write? How many opportunities were you given to read aloud, participate in plays, or speak before a group? Chances are that reading, writing, and perhaps speaking were heavily stressed in your education. But how much formal training have you had in listening? If you're typical, the answer is "Not much."

Another factor that contributes to poor listening skill is the disparity between the speed at which we normally speak and the speed at which our brains can process data. We can think faster than we can speak—about four times faster, as a matter of fact. Thus, when listening to others, our minds begin to wander, and we lose our ability to concentrate on what is being said.

Here are some results of ineffective listening:

- Instructions not being followed
- Equipment broken from misuse
- Sales lost
- Feelings hurt
- Morale lowered
- Productivity decreased
- Rumors started
- Health risks increased

Still, poor listening skills are not as readily apparent as poor speaking or writing skills. It's easy to spot a poor speaker or writer but much more difficult to spot a poor listener because a poor listener can fake attention. In fact, the poor listener may not even be aware of this weakness. He or she may mistake hearing for listening.

The poor listener may not be aware of his or her weakness.

Keys to Better Listening

The good news is that you can improve your listening skills. Tests at the University of Minnesota show that individuals who receive training in listening improve their listening skills by 25 percent to 42 percent.[26] To learn to listen more effectively, whether you're involved in a one-on-one dialogue or are part of a mass audience, give the speaker your undivided attention, stay open-minded, avoid interrupting, and involve yourself in the communication.

■ See Slide 2.14.

Give the Speaker Your Undivided Attention   During a business presentation, a member of the audience may hear certain familiar themes, think, "Oh no, not that again," and proceed to tune the speaker out. Or during a conference with a subordinate, an executive may make or take phone calls, doodle, play around with a pen or pencil, or do other distracting things that give the speaker the impression that what he or she has to say is unimportant or uninteresting.

Physical distractions are the easiest to eliminate. Simply shutting the door or asking your assistant to hold all calls will eliminate many interruptions during personal conferences. If you're in a meeting where the environment is noisy, the temperature too cold or hot, or the chairs uncomfortable, try to tune out the distractions rather than the speaker. Learn to ignore those annoyances over which you have no control and to concentrate instead on the speaker and what he or she is saying.

Physical distractions are easier to eliminate than mental distractions.

Mental distractions are more difficult to eliminate. But with practice and effort, you can discipline yourself, for example, to temporarily forget about your fatigue or to put competing thoughts out of your mind so that you can give the speaker your attention.

Just as it is important for the speaker to maintain eye contact with the whole audience, it is also important for the *listener* to maintain eye contact with the speaker. Doing so sends the message that you're interested in what the speaker has to say, and the speaker will be more likely to open up to you and provide the information you need.

Pay more attention to what the speaker says than to how he or she says it.

We talk about giving the speaker your undivided attention. Actually, it would be more accurate to say that you give the speaker's *comments* your undivided attention; that is, you should focus on the content of the talk and not be overly concerned about how the talk is delivered. It is true, of course, that nonverbal clues do provide important information. However, do not be put off by the fact that the speaker may have dressed inappropriately, spoken too fast or in an unfamiliar accent, or appeared nervous. Almost always, *what* is said is more important than how it is said.

Likewise, avoid dismissing a topic simply because it is uninteresting or is presented in an uninteresting manner. "Boring" does not mean unimportant. Some information that may be boring or difficult to follow may in fact prove to be quite useful to you and thus be well worth your effort to give it your full attention.

Stay Open-Minded   Regardless of whom you're listening to or what the topic is, keep your emotions in check. Listen objectively and empathetically. Be willing to accept new information and new points of view, regardless of whether they mesh with your existing beliefs. Concentrate on the content of the message rather than on its source.

Keeping an open mind results in a win/win situation.

Don't look at the situation as a win/lose proposition; that is, don't consider that the speaker wins and you lose if you concede the merits of his or her position. Instead, think of it as a win/win situation: the speaker wins by convincing you of the merits of his or her position, and you win by gaining new information and insights that will help you perform your duties more effectively.

Maintain neutrality as long as possible, and don't jump to conclusions too quickly. Instead, try to understand *why* the speaker is arguing a particular point of view and what facts or experience convinced the speaker to adopt this position. When you assume this empathetic frame of reference, you will likely find that you neither completely agree with nor completely disagree with every point the speaker makes. This ability to evaluate the message objectively will help you gain the most from the exchange.

Interrupting a speaker creates a barrier to effective communication.

Don't Interrupt   Perhaps because of time pressures, we sometimes get impatient. As soon as we've figured out what a person is going to say, we tend to interrupt to finish the sentence for the speaker; this practice is especially a problem when listening to a slow speaker. Or as soon as we can think of a counterargument, we tend to rush right in—regardless of whether the speaker has finished or even paused for a breath.

Such interruptions have many negative consequences. First, they are rude. Second, instead of speeding up the exchange, such interruptions actually tend to drag it out because they often interfere with the speaker's train of thought, causing backtracking. The most serious negative consequence, however, is the nonverbal message such an interruption sends: "I have the right to interrupt you because what I have to say is more important than what you have to say!" Is it any wonder, then, that such a message hinders effective communication?

There is a difference between listening and simply waiting to speak. Even if you're too polite to interrupt, don't simply lie in wait for the first available opportunity to barge in with your version of the truth. If you're constantly planning what you'll say next, you can hardly listen attentively to what the other person is saying.

Americans tend to have low tolerance for silence. Yet waiting a moment or two after someone has finished before you respond has several positive effects—especially in an emotional exchange. It gives the person speaking a chance to elaborate on his or her remarks, thereby drawing out further insights. It also helps create a quieter, calmer, more respectful atmosphere, one that is more conducive to solving the problem at hand.

Involve Yourself   As we have said, hearing is passive whereas listening is active. You should be *doing* something while the other person is speaking (and we don't mean doodling, staring out the window, or planning your afternoon activities).

Much of what you should be doing is mental. Summarize to yourself what the speaker is saying; create what the experts call an *internal paraphrase* of the speaker's comments. We can process information much faster than the speaker can present it, so use that extra time for active listening—ensuring that you really are hearing not only what the person is saying but the motives and implications as well.

Some listeners find it helpful to jot down points, translating their mental notes into written notes. If you do so, keep your notes brief; don't become so busy writing down the facts that you miss the message. Concentrate on the main ideas; if you get them, you'll be more likely to remember the supporting details later. Recognize also that even if a detail or two of the speaker's message might be inaccurate or irrelevant, the major points may still be valid. Evaluate the validity of the overall argument; don't get bogged down in trivia.

Be selfish in your listening. Constantly ask yourself, How does this point affect *me*? How can I use this information to further my goals or to help myself perform my job more effectively? Personalizing the information will help you to concentrate more easily and to weigh the evidence more objectively—even if the topic is difficult to follow or uninteresting and even if the speaker has some annoying mannerisms or an unpleasant personality.

Encourage the speaker by letting him or her know that you're actively involved in the exchange. Maintain eye contact, nod in agreement, lean forward, utter encouraging phrases such as "Uh huh" or "I see." In a conversation, ensure that your mental paraphrases are on target by summarizing aloud for the speaker what you think you're hearing. You can give such feedback as "So you believe . . . , is that true?" or "Do you mean that . . . ?" This in turn enables the speaker to clarify remarks, add new information, or clear up any misconceptions. Further, it tells the speaker that you're paying attention to the exchange.

> *Involve yourself mentally in what the speaker is saying.*

> ■ You can, however, listen too carefully. With today's cubicle office environments, corporate etiquette consultants have noted an increase in the habit of "dipping"—that is, butting in on conversations overheard behind an office cubicle.

■ Communicating by Telephone

Consider these statistics regarding telephone communication:[27]

- There is an average of more than one phone per person in the United States.

- AT&T processes more than 75 million calls every single day.

- The average length of phone calls is 6 minutes for local calls and 10 minutes for long-distance calls.

- Americans make more than 6.3 billion international calls every year (with an average cost of 34 cents per minute).

- More than 50 percent of Americans (143 million people) own a cell phone.

No wonder, then, that communicating effectively by telephone is a critical managerial skill, one that becomes increasingly important as the need for instantaneous information increases. Your telephone demeanor may be taken by the caller as the attitude of the entire organization. Every time the phone rings, your organization's future is on the line.

> CO5. **Use effective techniques for conducting business by telephone.**

Your Telephone Voice

Because the person to whom you're speaking has no visual clues to augment the auditory clues, a voice that is raspy, hoarse, shrill, loud, or weak can make you sound angry, excited, depressed, or bored—even when you aren't. Therefore, try to control your voice and project a friendly, competent, enthusiastic image to the other party.

Sit or stand tall and greet the caller with a smile.

To make your voice as clear as possible, sit or stand tall and avoid chewing gum or eating while talking. If your head is tilted sideways to cradle the phone between your head and shoulder, your throat is strained and your words may sound unclear.

Greet the telephone caller with a smile—just as you would greet someone in person. Your voice sounds more pleasant when you're smiling. An experiment was once conducted in which telephone salespeople were instructed to smile when they talked to their customers on one day and to scowl on the next. The salespeople sold almost twice as much on the days they were smiling.[28]

When the phone rings, pause, shift gears mentally, smile, and then answer the phone. Some firms even attach a sticker to the phone to remind employees to smile. "Smile," the sticker says, "it might be the boss calling."

Your Telephone Technique

Although every office worker will answer phones, the people who answer the firm's main number are vital to the firm's public image. These people must be trained and highly qualified—not the newest or least informed workers, as is often the case. These people's contacts with customers can have more impact on the organization's public image than the best advertising and promotional campaign.

Always answer the phone by the second or third ring. Regardless of how busy you are, you do not want to give the impression that your company doesn't care about its callers. Answer clearly and slowly, giving the company's name. Remember that even if you give the same greeting 50 times a day, your callers probably hear it only once. Make sure they can understand it.

Give the caller your undivided attention.

Be a good listener. Just as you would never continue writing or reading while someone speaks to you in person, do not engage in such distracting activities during phone calls. Pay attention especially to getting names correct and use the person's name during the conversation to personalize the message.

As with most other communication forms, emphasize positive language. Instead of saying, "I don't know," say, "Let me check and call you right back." Instead of "you'll have to . . . ," say, "We'll be happy to handle that if you'll just . . ."

It is estimated that 70 percent of all business calls are placed on hold at some time during the conversation and that the average American business executive spends over 60 hours on hold every year.[29] If you must put a caller on hold, always ask, "May I put you on hold?" and then give the caller an opportunity to respond. Long-distance callers may prefer to call back rather than to be put on hold. When you get back on the line, do not appear rushed or exasperated. Give the patient caller your complete attention.

Voice Mail

Whether you love it or hate it, voice mail (for example, "Press 1 to leave a message or press 2 to speak to an operator") is here to stay. Although some callers find voice mail impersonal and irritating, most are grateful for the opportunity to leave a message when they're unable to reach their party.

Before you even make a call, recognize that you might have to leave a message, so plan your message beforehand. Be polite and get to the point quickly. Clearly define the purpose of the call and the desired action and always give your phone number—even if the caller has it on file. The calls that get returned the fastest are those that are easiest to make.

If you have voice mail on your own phone, follow these guidelines:

Plan what message you will leave before you make the call.

- Never use voice mail as a substitute for answering your phone when you are available. Your customers, suppliers, and fellow workers deserve more consideration than that.

- Record your outgoing message in your own voice and keep it short. Here is an example: "Hello, this is John Smith. Please leave me a message and I'll get back to you as quickly as I can. Thank you." Change your message when you will be away from the office for an extended period of time.

- Check your messages at least daily and return calls promptly. Callers assume that you've received their messages and may interpret a lack of response as rudeness.

Telephone Tag

The telephone would be a much more efficient instrument if we could be assured of reaching our party each time we call. Instead, we're often forced to play an unproductive game of telephone tag, in which Party A calls Party B, is unable to reach her, and leaves a message. Party B then returns A's call, is unable to reach him, and leaves a message. And the process continues until the connection is finally made or until one party gives up in frustration.

Only 17 percent of business callers reach their intended party on the first try, 26 percent by the second try, and 47 percent by the third try. Thus, it takes the majority of business callers at least three tries to reach their intended party.[30]

To avoid telephone tag, plan the timing of your calls. Try to schedule them at times when you're most likely to reach the person. Also, announce when you're returning a call. If you're returning someone's call and get a secretary on the line, begin by saying you're returning the boss's call. This will clue the secretary that the boss wants to speak to you.

If necessary, find out what time would be best to call back or whether someone else in the organization can help. Finally, know when to call it quits. If you haven't reached your intended party after numerous attempts, it is unlikely that further attempts will be successful. When all else fails, stop calling and write a letter or use e-mail.

Cell Phones and Paging Devices

Nothing is more disconcerting than to have your business presentation interrupted by the ringing of someone's handheld cell phone or the beeping of someone's pager. In public locations where conversation is expected (such as in airline terminals), using a cell phone or answering a page is appropriate. However, at formal meetings, restaurants, movies, and social occasions, you should either turn off your device or switch to the "silent-alert" mode (typically either a light or a vibrating device).

Turn your cell phone off during social occasions.

When calling someone on a cell phone, get down to business quickly; both you and the recipient are paying by-the-minute charges for using the phone. And when driving, remember that safety comes first. Do not make (or answer) a call while maneuvering in difficult traffic.

■ Business Meetings

CO6. Plan, conduct, and participate in a business meeting.

Effective managers know how to run and participate in business meetings.

■ Humorist Robert Orben has commented, "Sometimes I get the feeling that the two biggest problems in America today are making ends meet—and making meetings end."

Much of the listening you'll do in the workplace will be in the context of business meetings. Meetings serve a wide variety of purposes in the organization. They keep members informed of events related to carrying out their duties; they provide a forum for soliciting input, solving problems, and making decisions; and they promote unity and cohesiveness among the members through social interaction.

Considering these important purposes, it is not surprising that as many as 20 million meetings take place each day in the United States. The average executive spends 25 percent to 70 percent of his or her day in meetings (an average of three hours per day, according to research by MCI WorldCom Conferencing)—and considers about a third of them to be unproductive. No wonder, then, many managers complain that "meetingitis" has become a national plague in American business. (Someone once described a meeting as an occasion for a group of people to keep minutes and waste hours.) The typical American business meeting is a staff meeting held in a company conference room for just under two hours, with no written agenda distributed in advance.[31]

The ability to conduct and participate in meetings is a crucial managerial skill. One survey of more than 2,000 business leaders showed that executives who run a meeting well are perceived to be better managers by both their superiors and their peers.[32]

To use meetings as an effective managerial tool, you need to know not only how to run them but also when to call them and how to follow up afterward. Like so many decisions you will have to make about communication, your choices will be guided by what you hope to accomplish.

Planning the Meeting

■ See Slide 2.15.

When you add up the hourly salaries and fringe benefits of those planning and attending a meeting, the cost can be considerable. Managers must make sure they're getting their money's worth from a meeting, and that requires careful planning: identifying the purpose and determining whether a meeting is really necessary, preparing an agenda, deciding who should attend, and planning the logistics.

Identifying Your Purpose   The first step is always to determine your purpose. The more specific you can be, the better results you will get. A purpose such as "to discuss how to make our marketing representatives more effective" is vague and therefore not as helpful as "to decide whether to purchase cellular phones for our marketing representatives." The more focused your purpose, the easier it will be to select a means of accomplishing that purpose.

Determine whether a meeting is the best way to accomplish your goal.

Determining Whether a Meeting Is Necessary   Sometimes meetings are not the most efficient means of communication. For example, a short memo or e-mail message is more efficient than a face-to-face meeting to communicate routine information. Similarly, it doesn't make sense to use the weekly staff meeting of ten people to hold a long discussion involving only one or two of the members. A phone call or smaller meeting would accomplish that task more quickly and at less cost.

However, alternative means of conveying or securing information often present their own problems. Some people don't read written messages carefully, or they interpret them differently. Time is lost in transmitting and responding to written messages. And information may be garbled as it moves from person to person and from level to level.

Preparing an Agenda Once you've established your specific purpose, you need to consider in more detail what topics the meeting will cover and in what order. This list of topics, or **agenda**, will accomplish two things: (1) it will help you prepare for the meeting by showing what background information you'll need, and (2) it will help you run the meeting by keeping you focused on your plan.

Knowing what topics will be discussed will also help those attending the meeting to plan for the meeting effectively—reviewing needed documents, bringing pertinent records, deciding what questions need to be raised, and the like. The survey of 2,000 business leaders mentioned earlier revealed that three-fourths of the managers consider agendas to be essential for efficient meetings; yet nearly half the meetings they attend are *not* accompanied by written agendas.[33]

Formal, recurring business meetings might follow an agenda like this one; of course, not every meeting will contain all these elements:

1. Call to order
2. Roll call (if necessary)
3. Reading and approval of minutes of previous meeting (if necessary)
4. Reports of officers and standing committees
5. Reports of special committees
6. Old business
7. New business
8. Announcements
9. Program
10. Adjournment

Each item to be covered under these headings should be identified, including the speaker (if other than the chair); for example:

7. New business
   a. Review of December 3 press conference
   b. Recommendation for annual charitable contribution
   c. Status of remodeling—Jan Fischer

Deciding Who Should Attend A great number of ad hoc meetings take place each business day for the purpose of solving a specific problem. If you must decide who will attend a particular meeting, your first concern is how the participants relate to your purpose. Who will make the decision? Who will implement the decision? Who can provide needed background information? On the one hand, you want to include all who can contribute to solving the problem; on the other hand, you want to keep the meeting to a manageable number of people.

Consider also how the potential group members differ in status within the organization, in knowledge about the issue, in communication skills, and in personal relationships. The greater the differences, the more difficult it will be to involve everyone in a genuine discussion aimed at solving the problem.

Don't underestimate the impact of potential group members' hidden agendas. If any member's personal goals for the meeting differ from the group goals, conflicts can arise, and the quality of the resulting decisions can be impaired. Meeting separately with some of the important participants ahead of time might help

An agenda helps focus the attention of both the leader and the participants.

Everyone at the meetings should have a specific reason for being there.

to identify sources of potential dissension and provide clues for dealing with them.

Membership in recurring meetings (such as a committee meeting) is relatively fixed. Even for these meetings, the planner must decide whether outsiders should be invited to observe, participate, or simply be available as resource people.

Plan carefully the physical arrangement of the meeting room.

Determining Logistics   It would be unwise to schedule a meeting that requires extensive discussion and creative problem solving at the end of the workday, when members may be exhausted emotionally and physically. Likewise, it would be counterproductive to schedule a three-hour meeting in a room equipped with uncushioned folding chairs, poor lighting, and extreme temperatures.

Instead, facilitate group problem solving by making intelligent choices about the timing and location of the meeting, room arrangements, types of audiovisual equipment, and the like. Doing so will increase the likelihood of achieving the goals of the meeting.

With regard to seating arrangements, the most important tip is to make the decision *consciously;* that is, if you have a choice, use the arrangement that best fits your purpose (see Figure 2.6):

- The rectangular arrangement is most commonly used for formal meetings, with the chairperson sitting at the head of the table, farthest from the door.

- The circular arrangement is more informal and encourages an equal sharing of information and leadership functions.

figure 2.6

Meeting Room Setups

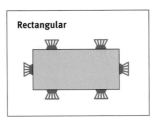
Rectangular

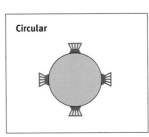
Circular

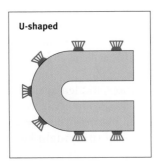
U-shaped

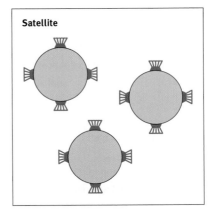
Satellite

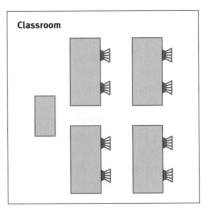
Classroom

- For larger meetings, a U-shaped setup is desirable because it allows each attendee to see all other meeting participants.

- A satellite arrangement is often useful for training sessions or when participants are to be divided into groups. This arrangement allows the chair to move freely around the room, addressing each group separately.

- A classroom arrangement is appropriate when most of the information is one way—from the leader to the audience; but even in this setup, the leader should encourage interaction among group members.

Conducting the Meeting

Planning for a meeting goes a long way toward ensuring its success, but the manager's job is by no means over when the meeting begins. A manager must be a leader during the meeting, keeping the group focused on the point and encouraging participation.

Punctuality   Unless a high-level member or one whose input is vital to the business at hand is tardy, make it a habit to begin every meeting on time. Doing so will send a powerful nonverbal message to chronic late arrivers that business will be conducted and decisions made whether or not they're present.

If you wait for latecomers, you send the message to those who *were* punctual that they wasted their time by being prompt. As a result, they will probably arrive late for subsequent meetings. And the habitual late arrivers will then begin arriving even later! Avoid this vicious cycle by beginning (and ending) at the appointed times.

An efficient leader begins and ends each meeting on time.

Following the Agenda   One key to a focused meeting is to follow the agenda. At formal meetings you will be expected to discuss all items on the published agenda and no items not on the agenda. The less formal the meeting, the more flexibility you have in allowing new topics to be introduced. It's always possible that new information that has a bearing on your problem may arise. To prevent discussion simply because you didn't include the item on your agenda would make it more difficult for you to achieve your purpose. But as leader of the meeting, you must make certain that new topics are directly relevant.

Leading the Meeting   Begin the meeting with a statement of your purpose and an overview of the agenda. As the meeting progresses, keep track of time. Don't let the discussion get bogged down in details.

Preventing people from talking too much or digressing from the topic requires tact. Comments like "I see your point, and that relates to what we were just discussing" can keep you on track without offending the speaker. You'll also need to encourage the participation of the quieter members of the group with comments like "Juan, how does this look from the perspective of your department?"

At the end of the meeting, summarize for everyone what the meeting has accomplished. What was decided? What are the next steps? Review any assignments and make sure that everyone understands his or her responsibilities.

Determine which problem-solving strategy is appropriate.

During the meeting, someone—either an assistant, the leader, or someone the leader designates—should record what happens. That person must report objectively and not impose his or her own biases.

figure 2.7   Parliamentary Procedure for Business Meetings

To Do This:	You Say This:	Interrupt the speaker?	Need a second?	Debatable?	Amendable?	Vote needed?
Main Motion *(A main motion brings an action before the group. It may be made only when no other motion is pending and must be made by one person and seconded by another person before it can be discussed.)*						
Make a main motion	*I move that . . .*	Yes	Yes	Yes	Yes	Maj
Secondary Motion *(A secondary motion may be made and considered while a main motion is pending and must be acted on before the main motion can be considered further.)*						
Amend a motion.	*I move to amend by . . .*	No	Yes	Yes	Yes	Maj
Take a recess.	*I move that we take a . . . recess.*	No	Yes	No	Yes	Maj
Adjourn.	*I move that we adjourn.*	No	Yes	No	No	Maj
Appeal a chair's ruling.	*I appeal the decision of the chair.*	Yes	Yes	Yes	No	Maj
Ask a question.	*I rise to a point of information.*	Yes	No	No	No	None
Point out a rule violation.	*I rise to a point of order.*	Yes	No	No	No	None
Suspend a rule of the group.	*I move to suspend the rule . . .*	No	Yes	No	No	$2/3$
Raise a point of parliamentary procedure.	*I rise to a parliamentary inquiry.*	Yes	No	No	No	None
Require that the agenda be followed.	*I call for orders of the day.*	Yes	No	No	No	None
State a request affecting one's rights.	*I rise to a question of privilege.*	Yes	No	No	No	None
Call for a secret ballot.	*I move the vote be taken by ballot.*	No	Yes	No	Yes	Maj
Call for a public standing or show-of-hands vote.	*I call for a division.*	Yes	No	No	No	None
Close debate.	*I move the previous question.*	No	Yes	No	No	$2/3$
Close nominations.	*I move to close nominations.*	No	Yes	No	Yes	$2/3$
Consider parts of a motion separately.	*I move to divide the question.*	No	Yes	No	Yes	$2/3$
Lay the pending motion aside temporarily. (The purpose is to enable the group to consider a more urgent matter that has arisen. If the tabled motion is not taken from the table by the next regularly scheduled meeting, the motion dies.)	*I move to lay the question on the table.*	No	Yes	No	No	Maj
Postpone to a certain time. (The purpose is to defer action until a later date—for example, when more information has been gathered.)	*I move to postpone the question until . . .*	No	Yes	Yes	Yes	Maj
Postpone indefinitely. (The purpose is to avoid taking action on the motion, thereby killing it.)	*I move to postpone the question indefinitely.*	No	Yes	Yes	No	Maj
Refer a motion to a committee.	*I move to refer the question to . . .*	No	Yes	Yes	Yes	Maj
Motion That Brings a Question Again Before the Group *(A motion that brings a question again before the group enables the group to reconsider an action voted on earlier.)*						
Reconsider a previously passed motion. (The motion must be made at the same meeting as the original vote and must be made by someone from the majority side of the original vote.)	*I move to reconsider the vote on . . .*	No	Yes	Yes	No	Maj
Revoke an action taken at a previous meeting.	*I move to rescind the motion relating to . . . adopted at the . . . meeting.*	No	Yes	Yes	Yes	$2/3$*
*Requires a two-thirds vote if no prior notice has been given, a majority vote if prior notice has been given.						
Take from the table. (*See* "Lay the pending motion aside temporarily" above.)	*I move to take the question from the table.*	No	Yes	No	No	Maj

Notes

1. Special rules adopted by the group take precedence over *Robert's Rules of Order*.
2. A majority of the entire membership constitutes a quorum (the minimum number of members who must be present to transact business).
3. A vote is not required to approve the minutes of the previous meeting. Meeting minutes are simply accepted as read and/or distributed, or they are accepted as corrected.
4. A vote is not required to accept a committee report. However, committee recommendations that require action must be voted on. Motions made on behalf of the committee do not require a second.
5. After a motion has been made and seconded, the chair repeats the motion before calling for discussion and again before calling for the vote.

Parliamentary Procedure   Every group needs to adopt rules that permit the orderly transactions of business in meetings. The larger the group and the more important its mission, the more important it is to establish written rules of order (called **parliamentary procedure**). Imagine, for example, the chaos that could result if a meeting did not follow the basic rule that only one person may have the floor and speak at a time!

The basic principle of parliamentary procedure is that the minority shall be heard but that the majority shall prevail. The reference guide for parliamentary procedure—the authority used by governments, associations, and business organizations the world over—is *Robert's Rules of Order*.[34] The rationale for using parliamentary procedure is given in the preface of that classic:

> The application of parliamentary law is the best method yet devised to enable assemblies of any size, with due regard for every member's opinion, to arrive at the general will on a maximum number of questions of varying complexity in a minimum time and under all kinds of internal climate ranging from total harmony to hardened or impassioned division of opinion.[35]

Robert's Rules of Order was written in 1896 by Gen. Henry M. Robert, a U.S. Army officer who was active in many civic and educational organizations; it has been revised periodically since then. The current edition contains more than 650 pages of rules and procedures; those that are most helpful for running the typical business meeting are summarized in Figure 2.7 on page 74.

Knowledge of basic parliamentary procedure is a strategic communication skill for managers. Anyone who runs a business meeting, whether at work or in connection with a professional, civic, or social organization, would do well to become familiar with the basic requirements of conducting meetings in a parliamentary manner.

Following Up the Meeting

Routine meetings may require only a short memorandum or e-mail as a follow-up to what was decided. Formal meetings or meetings where controversial ideas were discussed may require a more formal summary.

Minutes are an official record of the proceedings; they summarize what was discussed and what decisions were made. Generally, they should emphasize what was *done* at the meeting, not what was *said* by the members. Minutes may, however, present an intelligent summary of the points of view expressed on a particular issue, without names attached, followed by the decision made. Avoid presenting minutes that are either so short they lack the "flavor" of what transpired or so long they tend to be ignored.

The first paragraph of minutes should identify the type of meeting (regular or special); the meeting date, time, and place; the presiding officer; the names of those present (or absent) if customary; and the fact that the minutes of the previous meeting were read and approved.

The body of the minutes should contain a separate paragraph for each topic. According to parliamentary procedure, the name of the maker of a motion, but not the seconder, should be entered in the minutes. The precise wording of motions, exactly as voted on, should also appear in minutes. It is often helpful to use the same subheadings as in the agenda. A sample portion of the minutes of a business meeting follows:

In parliamentary procedure, the minority is heard and the majority prevails.

This 61-word sentence is probably as good an example as you're likely to find of a long sentence that communicates its message clearly and concisely.

■ See Handout 2.2.

Formal meetings require formal minutes of what took place.

The minutes should be accurate, objective, and complete.

Review of December 3 Press Conference

A videotape of the December 3 press conference conducted by Donita Doyle was viewed and discussed. Roger Eggland's motion that "Donita Doyle be commended for the professional and ethical manner in which she presented the company's view at the December 3 press conference" was adopted unanimously without debate.

Recommendation for Annual Charitable Contribution

Tinrah Porisupatani moved "that American Chemical donate $15,000 to a worthwhile charity operating in Essex County." Linda Peters moved to amend the motion by inserting the words "an amount not exceeding" after the word "donate." On a motion by Todd Chandler, the motion to make a donation, with the pending amendment, was referred for further study to the Social Responsibility Committee with instructions to recommend a specific amount and charity and report at the next meeting.

The last paragraph of the minutes should state the time of adjournment and, if appropriate, the time set for the next meeting. The minutes should be signed by the person preparing them. If someone other than the chair prepares the minutes, the minutes should be read and approved by the chair before being distributed.

Guidelines for conducting business meetings are summarized in Checklist 2, "Business Meetings" (see page 77), and minutes of a meeting are shown in Model 1, "Minutes of a Meeting" (see pages 78–79).

■ Business Etiquette

CO7. Use a professional demeanor and appropriate behavior to maintain effective working relationships.

Learn what is considered appropriate behavior in your organization.

■ See Slide 2.16.

Business etiquette is the practice of polite and appropriate behavior in the business setting. It dictates what behaviors are proper and under what circumstances; thus, business etiquette is really concerned with interaction between people—not meaningless ritual.

Each organization has its own rules about what is and is not considered fitting in terms of dress, ways of addressing superiors, importance of punctuality, and the like. In addition, every country and every culture has its own rules. Generally, these rules are not written down but must be learned informally or through observation. Executives who follow correct business etiquette are more confident and appear more in charge; and the higher you advance in your career, the more important such behavior will become.

Business etiquette differs in many ways from social etiquette. The manager who enumerates all his or her accomplishments to the superior during a performance appraisal is simply being savvy; the manager who does so during a social engagement is being boorish. You must be sensitive to what is appropriate under any given circumstances.

Good manners are good business; they communicate a strong positive message about you as a person. As Mark Twain once observed about etiquette, "Always do right: you will please some people and astonish the rest."

✔checklist 2

Business Meetings

Planning the Meeting

✔ Identify the purpose of the meeting.

✔ Prepare an agenda for distribution to the participants.

✔ Decide who should attend the meeting.

✔ Determine the logistics of the meeting—timing, location, room and seating arrangements, and types of audiovisual equipment needed.

✔ Assign someone (even if it is yourself) the task of taking notes during the meeting. These notes should be objective, accurate, and complete.

Conducting the Meeting

✔ Encourage punctuality by beginning and ending the meeting on time.

✔ Begin each meeting by stating the purpose of the meeting and reviewing the agenda.

✔ Establish ground rules that permit the orderly transaction of business. Many organizations follow parliamentary procedure.

✔ Control the discussion to ensure that it is relevant, that a few members do not monopolize the discussion, and that all members have an opportunity to be heard.

✔ At the end of the meeting, summarize what was decided, what the next steps are, and what each member's responsibilities are.

Following Up the Meeting

✔ If the meeting was routine and informal, follow it up with a memorandum or e-mail summarizing the major points of the meeting. For more formal meetings, prepare and distribute minutes.

Meeting and Greeting

The important point to remember about making introductions is simply to *make them.* The format you use is less important than the fact that you avoid the awkwardness of requiring two people to introduce themselves.

The basic rule for introductions is to present the lower-ranking person to the higher-ranking person, regardless of age or gender: "Mr. CEO, this is my new assistant." If the persons you're introducing are equal in rank, mention the older one first, mention the guest first, or (traditionally) mention the woman first.

The format for an introduction might be like this: "Helen, I'd like you to meet Carl Byrum. Carl just began working here as a junior account manager. Carl, this is Helen Smith, our vice president." Or in a social situation, you might just say, "Rosa, this is Gene Stauffer. Gene, Rosa Bennett." The appropriate response to an introduction is "How do you do, Gene?" Regardless of the gender of the two people being introduced, either may initiate the handshake—a gesture of welcome.

To help remember the name of someone you've met, make a point of using his or her name when shaking hands. And using the person's name again at least once during the conversation will help fix that name in your mind. If you cannot remember someone's name, when the person approaches you, simply extend your

■ See Handout 2.3.

Use a person's name in the conversation to help remember it.

model1

MINUTES OF A MEETING

Reports the events in the order in which they occurred.

Provides headings to aid readability.

Provides only enough detail to give an indication of what took place.

Provides exact wording of the motions made and indicates the action taken. Unless policy dictates, it is not necessary to identify the seconder of a motion or to provide a tally of the vote taken.

1

COMPUTER USE COMMITTEE
Minutes of the Regular Meeting
May 18, 20—

2   Members Present: S. Lindsey (Chair), L. Anderson-White, F. Griffin, T. King (Secretary), Z. Petropoulou, G. Ullom, J. West, K. Wolff

Shannon Lindsey called the meeting to order at 8:35 a.m. The minutes of the April 14 meeting were approved with the correction that Frank Griffin be recorded as present.

REPORT OF THE BUDGET SUBCOMMITTEE

Zoe Petropoulou reported that the Corporate Executive Council had approved an additional $58,000 for subcommittee allocation for hardware purchases through September 30, 20—. The subcommittee plans to send out RFPs by the end of the month and to make allocation recommendations to CUC at the June meeting. Zoe also distributed a handout (Appendix A) showing the current-year hardware and software allocations through May 1.

OLD BUSINESS

None.

NEW BUSINESS

Standardization of Web Page Development Software. Jenny West moved that "beginning September 1, 20—, CUC approve expenditures for web page development software only for Microsoft FrontPage 2003." She summarized the coordination, training, and site-maintenance problems that are now being encountered as a result of individual webmasters using different programs and answered questions from the floor. Gina Ullom moved to amend the motion by inserting the words "or later version" after "FrontPage 2003." The amendment passed, and the amended motion was adopted after debate.

Grammar and Mechanics Notes

1 Unless a different format is traditional, use regular report format for meeting minutes.

2 Identify the meeting attendees, listing the chair first followed by others in either alphabetic or position order.

model1

2

Speech-Recognition Software. Shannon Lindsey reported that she had received numerous requests for information or recommendations for purchasing speech-recognition software and asked for committee input. Extensive discussion followed concerning the cost, the amount of training required, accuracy, resulting noise level for carrel workers, and the overall implications of such software for touch-typing skills. The motion by Lisa Anderson-White that "the chair appoint a task force to study the issue and report back at the next meeting" passed. The chair appointed Lisa Anderson-White and Frank Griffin to the task force.

ANNOUNCEMENTS

Shannon Lindsey made the following announcements:

- She has received three positive comments and no negative feedback from her March 15 memo to department heads announcing the new repair and maintenance policy.

3

- She has been asked to represent CUC at the June 18 long-range planning meeting of the Corporate Executive Council to answer questions about planned hardware and software expenditures for the next three years.
- Anthem Computer Services has asked permission to make a 30-minute presentation to CUC. In accordance with committee policy, she rejected the request.

ADJOURNMENT

The meeting was adjourned at 10:40 a.m. The next regular meeting is scheduled for 8:30 a.m. on June 20.

4   Respectfully submitted,

Terry King

Terry King, Secretary

Enc: Appendix A: Hardware and Software Allocations
c: Department Heads
       Director of Purchasing
       Corporate Executive Council

Announces the date and time of the next meeting. (Provide the location only if it differs from the regular meeting site.)

Grammar and Mechanics Notes

3 Use parallel language for enumerated or bulleted items.

4 Format the closing parts in a manner similar to that found in a business letter.

hand and say your name. The other person will typically respond by shaking your hand and also giving his or her name.

Whenever you greet an acquaintance whom you've met only once some time ago, introduce yourself and immediately follow it with some information to help the other person remember, unless he or she immediately recognizes you—for example, "Hello, Mr. Wise, I'm Eileen Wagoner. We met at the Grahams' party last month."

Today, most American businesspeople have business cards, although the protocol for exchanging them isn't as strict here as it is in some other countries. In business settings, you should present your card at the end of the encounter—as a way of establishing that you're interested in continuing the relationship. Never present your card during a meal (wait until it is over), and never offer your card at any time during a social function.

Dining

The restaurant you select for a business meal reflects on you and your organization. Choose one where the food is of top quality and the service dependable. In general, the more important your guest, the more exclusive the restaurant. If a maitre d' (headwaiter) seats you and your guest, your guest should precede you to the table. If you're seating yourselves, take the lead in locating an appropriate table. Give your guest the preferred seat, facing the window with an attractive view or facing the dining room if you're seated next to the wall.

Here are some additional tips to follow for a successful and enjoyable business meal:

- The guests wait until the host unfolds the napkin and places it in the lap before doing the same. Do not begin eating until the host takes the first bite of food.

- If you're the host, to signal the waiter that you're ready to order, close your menu and lay it on the table. To get the server's attention, say "Excuse me" when

Exchange business cards at the end of a business encounter.

■ Deloitte & Touche, an accounting and consulting firm, added a business etiquette seminar to its employee leadership-training program. About half of the company's new hires are recent college graduates and "tend to be ill-at-ease in social settings," says human resources director Bill Bagley. (Salina Khan, "'When in Rome': Wise in Biz Travel," *USA Today,* May 18, 1999, p. 7E.)

Massachusetts Institute of Technology runs a "charm school" the Friday before each spring semester begins. It attracts 1,000 students each year. Here, MIT students learn to tie a knot correctly.

figure2.8

Table Setting

Use silverware from the outside and work your way in. Remember: glass to the right; pass to the right.

he or she is nearby, or catch the server's eye and quietly signal for him or her to come to the table, or ask a nearby server to ask yours to come to your table. The host's order is generally taken last.

- If you leave the table during the meal, leave your napkin on your chair. At the end of the meal, place the napkin, unfolded, on the table.

- When using silverware, start from the outside. As shown in Figure 2.8, your glass is the one at the right of your place setting. When passing food or condiments, pass to the right, offering items to someone else before you serve yourself.

- Don't put your elbows on the table while eating, although you may do so between courses.

- Place the knife across the top edge of the plate, with the cutting edge toward you, when it is not being used. To signal the waiter that you are through with your plate, place your knife and fork diagonally across the middle of the plate.

- Spoon soup away from you. Avoid salting food before tasting it; if asked to pass the salt or pepper, pass both together.

- The person who issues the invitation is expected to pay the bill. In most parts of the country, the usual tip for standard service is 15 percent to 20 percent of the food and bar bill and 10 percent of the cost of the wine. An appropriate tip for the cloakroom attendant is $.50–$.75 per coat, or $1 in an expensive restaurant. If you use valet parking, tip the attendant $1–$2 after your car is brought to the door.

- Send a thank-you note immediately after the meal. Be sure to write more than a token note, mentioning something special about the décor, the food, the service, the company of the people with whom you dined, or your satisfaction with the business discussed.

Giving Gifts

Avoid giving gifts that are extravagant or personal or that might be perceived as a bribe.

Giving gifts to suppliers, customers, or workers within one's own organization is typical at many firms, especially in December during the holiday period. Although such gifts are often deeply appreciated, you must be sensitive in terms of whom you give a gift to and the type of gift you select. Most people would consider a gift appropriate if it meets these four criteria:

- *It is an impersonal gift.* Gifts that can be used in the office or in connection with one's work are nearly always appropriate.

- *It is for past favors.* Gifts should be used to thank someone for past favors, business, or performance—*not* to create obligations for the future. A gift to a prospective customer who has never ordered from you before might be interpreted as a bribe.

- *It is given to everyone in similar circumstances.* Singling out one person for a gift and ignoring others in similar positions would not only embarrass the one selected but also create bad feelings among those who were ignored.

- *It is not extravagant.* A very expensive gift might make the recipient uneasy, create a sense of obligation, and call into question your motives for giving.

Give appropriate gifts on appropriate occasions.

Although it is often the custom for a superior to give a subordinate a gift, especially one's assistant, it is less usual for the subordinate to give a personal gift to a superior. More likely, coworkers will contribute to a joint gift for the boss, again selecting one that is neither too expensive nor too personal. As always, follow local customs when giving gifts to international colleagues (see Spotlight 7, "Gift Giving–Japanese Style," on page 83).

Dressing Appropriately

Different positions, different companies, and different parts of the country and world have different dress codes—some stated explicitly in the company manual, others communicated indirectly via corporate culture. In the absence of other information, you should choose well-tailored, clean, conservative clothing for the workplace.

Dress-down days (like "Casual Fridays") have gained popularity in U.S. business. A Gallup poll found that 57 percent of U.S. companies now allow casual dress at least once a week.[36] The adoption of these casual days has caused some confusion about what exactly is considered appropriate. These guidelines for "business casual" from Levi Strauss & Co.[37] should prove helpful:

Business casual does not mean sloppy.

1. Aim for a classic but understated look when selecting casual business wear. Pick clothing that is comfortable yet communicates a professional attitude. Subtle, quality accessories (such as belts, jewelry, and scarves) coordinated with an outfit can show attention to important details.
2. Combine business wardrobe items with casual attire—for example, a button-down shirt with khakis and loafers, with either a more colorful tie or scarf or just a sport coat or sweater. Ask, "Am I successfully representing myself and my company?"

Gift Giving—Japanese Style

When conducting business in Japan, there are few occasions when giving a gift is not considered appropriate. There are two occasions, however, when gift giving is mandatory—for the Japanese as well as for those doing business with the Japanese. These two occasions are *O-chugen,* which falls in midsummer, and *O-seibo,* at year's end. *O-seibo,* which can only be compared with Christmas, is an especially important gift-giving occasion, with more than $10 billion spent on gifts during this one season.

What to Give

As incongruous as it might sound, your best bet in selecting a gift for your Japanese colleague is to "Buy American." Your best choices for gifts are items that either are not easily available in Japan or are quite expensive there. Anything with a prominent American label might be appropriate. Brand names such as Gucci, Ralph Lauren, and L. L. Bean are understood and valued in Japan.

Regional gifts are always popular—such as Vermont maple syrup, mugs with your city name, university sweatshirts, baseball caps from famous teams, and even subscriptions to popular American magazines. Food selections are also appropriate—including such items as fruit and preserves, cheese, beef, and wine and spirits (especially bourbon, which is a uniquely American product).

Make sure that whatever items you choose are of the highest quality, but never ostentatious. Tact is the key to successful gift giving: nothing too large and extravagant or too small and cheap. Take your cue from your Japanese colleagues. And remember that hierarchical relationships are important. Never give the same gift (or an equally priced gift) to people at different levels in the same organization.

How to Give

The presentation of the gift may be as important as the gift itself. The gift should be wrapped attractively in top-quality gift wrap (not white, which signifies death), and it is customary to transport the gift in a neat paper bag (so as not to call attention to the fact that you're bringing a gift).

When presenting the gift, extend it to the recipient with both hands (a sign of respect and humility), while making a self-deprecating comment such as "This is really nothing at all." It is customary for the recipient to then put aside the gift and not open it in the presence of the giver.

When you give a gift to a Japanese colleague, you can expect to receive one of similar value in the near future. Similarly, if you receive a gift, you will be expected to reciprocate. The Japanese (and many other Asian societies) value relationships highly, and giving gifts is one way of maintaining relationships.[38]

3. Casual does not mean sloppy. Clothing should be clean, pressed or wrinkle-free, and without holes or frayed areas. Like suits and tailored clothing, casual business wear lasts longer and looks better with special care.

4. Keep the focus on work quality. Anything worn to the gym or beach (or to clean the garage) should be left at home. Avoid clothing that is too revealing or tight-fitting. Trendy or "high-fashion" clothing may communicate a whimsical or pretentious attitude that is not suitable for most offices. T-shirts are probably not a good idea. Keep clothing colors muted and coordinated to help create a professional appearance.

■ A *Wall Street Journal* article noted the trend may be passing. Sales of both men's and women's suits are now increasing after years of sales decline. (*Wall Street Journal,* April 6, 2001, p. B.1.)

A 13-square-mile area in southern Los Angeles County is among the most linguisitically varied areas in the country. Thirty-nine of the 40 most commonly spoken languages are spoken there. At a minimall there, a Vietnamese restaurant shares space with an acupuncture center, an Indian clothing shop, and a Farmers Insurance office.

5. Pay attention to the fit of your clothing. Pants should break just above the shoe, sleeves should reach the base of the hand and show just a bit of the cuff when a jacket is worn, and shirt collars should button comfortably without pinching or leaving gaps. Also, if a tie is worn, its tip should reach just below the bottom of the belt buckle.

6. Shoes matter. Leather shoes are generally preferable, but if athletic shoes are allowed, make sure they are clean, subtle in design, and scuff-free. Leather shoes look best when polished and in good repair. For most offices, open-toed sandals and beach thongs are not appropriate.

7. Take the day's schedule into account when dressing. If a meeting with visitors is scheduled, dress more traditionally or check to see if casual dress might be appropriate.

8. When in doubt, leave it out. Casual clothing should make the employee and coworkers work more comfortably. Ask the manager ahead of time if you have any questions.

Around the Office

Follow the golden rule in your dealings with others at work.

Many situations that occur every day in the typical office call for common courtesy. The basis for appropriate behavior is always the golden rule: "Treat others as you yourself would like to be treated."

Cubicle Courtesy   An estimated 40 million people in today's work force spend their work hours in a cubicle.[39] Because cubicles provide so little privacy, cubicle courtesy is especially important. Always knock or ask permission before entering someone's cubicle, and never wander into someone's unoccupied cubicle without permission. Never shout a comment to someone in the next cubicle. If it's too hard to walk over, call instead. Do not leave valuables in your cubicle unattended. Avoid talking on the phone or to visitors too loudly, and avoid strong perfumes or colognes. Finally, honor the occupant's privacy by not staring at his or her computer screen or listening to private conversations.

Drinking Coffee   If there is a container provided to pay for the coffee, do so every time you take a cup; don't force others to treat you to a cup of coffee. Also, take your turn making the coffee and cleaning the pot if that task is performed by the group. Although in most offices it is acceptable to drink coffee or some other beverage while working, some offices have an unwritten rule against snacking at one's desk. Regardless, never eat while talking to someone in person or on the telephone.

Smoking   Many offices prohibit smoking anywhere on the premises. If you smoke, follow the rules strictly. Smoking in public anywhere is increasingly considered bad manners, not to mention a health hazard.

Using the Copier or Fax Machine   If you're using the copier or fax machine for a large job, and someone approaches with a small job, let that person go ahead of you. Also, be sure to refill the paper holder after completing a job, and reset the copier machine counter after using it. (The next user, intending to make one copy, will not appreciate having to wait for—and pay for—100 copies instead, simply because you failed to reset the counter.)

The **3Ps**
Problem, Process, Product

A PLAN FOR A BUSINESS MEETING

You are Dieter Ullsperger, director of employee relations for the city of Eau Claire, Wisconsin. The city manager has asked your department to develop a policy statement regarding the solicitation of funds from employees during work hours for employee weddings, retirements, anniversaries, and the like.

Despite the good intentions of such efforts, the city manager questions whether they put undue pressure on some employees and take unreasonable time from official duties. You have already gathered secondary data regarding this matter and have spoken with your counterparts in Jacksonville, Florida; Milwaukee, Wisconsin; and Memphis, Tennessee. You are now ready to begin planning a first draft of the policy statement.

Process

1. What is the purpose of your task?

   To prepare a policy statement on soliciting funds from employees during office hours.

2. Is a meeting needed?

   Because this policy will affect every employee in city government, it should be developed on the basis of input from representatives of the work force. Therefore, a planning meeting is desirable.

3. What will be the agenda?

   My first reaction is that the meeting agenda is to write the new policy. I recognize, however, that it is not reasonable for a policy statement to be written during a meeting. Thus, the real agenda is to develop the broad outlines for the policy. The policy will be planned collaboratively; drafted individually; reviewed collaboratively; and finally, revised individually.

4. Who should attend the meeting?

   Because I want to ensure broad consensus on this policy, I'll ask the union stewards of our two unions to attend. (I'll represent management.) I'll also ask the city attorney to attend to ensure that our policy is legal. Finally, I'll ask Lyn Paterson in Transportation to attend; she is a veteran city employee who is well respected among her peers and has served as the unofficial social chairperson for numerous fundraising events over the past several years. I'll telephone each of those people to ask for his or her voluntary participation in this project.

5. What about logistics?

> Because I want the meeting to be informal, we'll hold it in the small conference room downstairs, which has an oval table. The only audiovisual equipment I'll need is a chalkboard to display any ideas we might have. I'll ask my assistant to take minutes. Since I was not given a specific deadline, I'll delay the meeting for three weeks because two retirement parties are already scheduled in the meantime.

Product

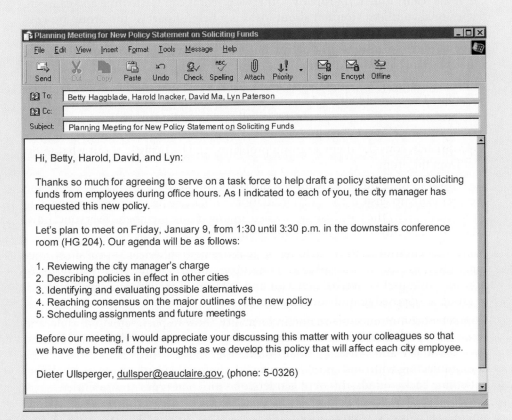

Planning Meeting for New Policy Statement on Soliciting Funds

File   Edit   View   Insert   Format   Tools   Message   Help

Send   Cut   Copy   Paste   Undo   Check   Spelling   Attach   Priority   Sign   Encrypt   Offline

To: Betty Haggblade, Harold Inacker, David Ma, Lyn Paterson

Cc:

Subject: Planning Meeting for New Policy Statement on Soliciting Funds

Hi, Betty, Harold, David, and Lyn:

Thanks so much for agreeing to serve on a task force to help draft a policy statement on soliciting funds from employees during office hours. As I indicated to each of you, the city manager has requested this new policy.

Let's plan to meet on Friday, January 9, from 1:30 until 3:30 p.m. in the downstairs conference room (HG 204). Our agenda will be as follows:

1. Reviewing the city manager's charge
2. Describing policies in effect in other cities
3. Identifying and evaluating possible alternatives
4. Reaching consensus on the major outlines of the new policy
5. Scheduling assignments and future meetings

Before our meeting, I would appreciate your discussing this matter with your colleagues so that we have the benefit of their thoughts as we develop this policy that will affect each city employee.

Dieter Ullsperger, dullsper@eauclaire.gov, (phone: 5-0326)

Visit the **BusCom Online Learning Center** (at http://college.hmco.com) for additional resources to help you with this course and with your future career.

■ Summary

Teams can accomplish more and better-quality work in less time than individuals can *if* the teams function properly. Otherwise, teams can waste time and cause interpersonal conflicts. Conflict about ideas is a helpful part of the group process, whereas interpersonal conflicts are detrimental. An appropriate emphasis on consensus and conformity is productive, but too much emphasis can lead to groupthink, wherein legitimate differences of opinion are not even discussed.

co1. Communicate effectively in small groups.

At the beginning, group members should get to know one another and set operating rules. They should also acknowledge the need for positive and negative feedback and know how to give productive feedback, including providing helpful feedback on team writing. When problems arise, group members should react to them appropriately, consider them as group problems, and be realistic about what to expect from the group.

For group writing projects, team members should develop a work schedule and meet regularly to ensure proper coordination. Either one person can be assigned to write the draft, or the parts can be divided among group members. Everyone, however, should be involved in revising the draft.

co2. Explain the meaning and importance of nonverbal messages.

Nonverbal communication includes body movement, physical appearance, voice qualities, time, touch, and space and territory. Cultures differ greatly in terms of how they interpret nonverbal behavior and in terms of the importance they attach to group as opposed to individual behavior.

co3. Communicate effectively with diverse populations both within the United States and internationally.

Competent communicators maintain formality, show respect, remain flexible, and write and speak clearly when communicating with people of different cultures. Even if you live and work in a small community in the United States, you will be communicating with, and should learn to be comfortable with, people with different ethnic backgrounds, different genders, and different types of disabilities.

co4. Listen effectively in business situations.

Listening is the most used but least developed of the verbal communication skills. Whether listening to a formal presentation or conversing with one or two people, you can learn to listen more effectively by giving the speaker your undivided attention, staying open-minded about the speaker and the topic, avoiding interrupting the speaker, and involving yourself actively in the communication.

co5. Use effective techniques for conducting business by telephone.

When communicating by telephone, give the person to whom you're speaking your undivided attention, speak clearly, listen carefully, and treat the other party with courtesy. Take positive steps to avoid the inconvenience of not being able to reach your party (telephone tag) and use voice mail appropriately. Use cell phones and paging devices only in public places, and practice courtesy when using a speakerphone for conference calls.

co6. Plan, conduct, and participate in a business meeting.

Planning a business meeting requires determining your purpose and deciding whether a meeting is the most efficient way of accomplishing that purpose. You must then determine your agenda, decide who should attend, and plan such logistics as timing, location, and room arrangements.

When conducting a meeting, begin with a statement of your purpose and agenda. Then follow the agenda, keeping things moving along. Control those who talk too much, and encourage those who talk too little. Use whatever strategies seem appropriate for solving problems and managing conflicts. At the end of the meeting, send a follow-up memo if needed or distribute minutes of the meeting.

Business etiquette is a guide to help people behave appropriately in business situations. To be effective in business, learn how to make introductions, conduct business lunches, give suitable gifts, dress appropriately, and maintain good working relationships around the office. Good manners are good business.

co7. Use a professional demeanor and appropriate behavior to maintain effective working relationships.

■ Key Terms

You should now be able to define the following terms in your own words and give an original example of each.

agenda (71)

business etiquette (76)

ethnocentrism (52)

groupthink (43)

minutes (75)

parliamentary procedure (75)

team (42)

■ See Slide 2.17.

■ Consider treating this list as an end-of-chapter exercise for students to define and give an example of each term.

Exercises

① **The 3Ps (Problem, Process, and Product) Model: Communication Applications at the Nucon Group**   As you saw in the chapter-opening profile, Gilbert C. Morrell, Jr. prefers to personally conduct all senior management meetings devoted to high-level issues such as company goals. However, he attends but does not lead certain interdepartmental meetings. This allows the department heads and their staff members to fully explore problems and alternatives, and, with his input, decide on appropriate solutions.

Problem: Imagine that you are a special assistant to Morrell. He has called a senior management meeting for October 19 to discuss next year's corporate goals and to assess the changing competitive situation. You have been asked to prepare a brief e-mail message asking participants for their suggestions about specific topics for the agenda.

Process:

a. What is the purpose of this meeting, and is a meeting even necessary?
b. Why would Morrell ask participants for suggestions about the agenda in advance of the actual meeting?
c. What information should you include in this message?

Product: Write a subject line for your e-mail message and list two points you should make in the body of the message.

■ Suggestions and sample solutions for exercises appear in the *Instructor's Resource Manual.*

co1. Communicate effectively in small groups.

2 **Work Rules in Practice** Interview a business executive and have him or her explain how work teams are used in his or her organization. Try to find out if teams are used, how often teams are used, how the teams are usually formed, how successful the team process is, what problems come up in team settings, and anything else you think would be meaningful regarding the use of teams in business. Prepare a short report of your findings.

3 **Work-Team Communications** Think of the last team or group setting in which you were involved. Briefly describe for the class (in two or three minutes) the purpose of the group, how the group was formed, how well or (not so well) the group functioned, and if ground rules were established before working on the project. Describe how the variables of group communication—conflict, conformity, and consensus—were or were not incorporated. Was groupthink an issue? Did the group struggle with any problems related to gender, culture, or ethnicity? What was the group's decisions, and did the decisions work effectively?

4 **Providing Feedback** Everyone had agreed to have his or her part of the five-year marketing plan drafted by the time your team met today. What would be an appropriate response to each of the following incidents at today's meeting? Where appropriate, use the steps shown in Figure 2.2, "Using 'I' Statements When Giving Feedback," on page 45, to compose your response.

a. Fred did not have his part ready (although this is the first time he has been late).
b. Thales did not have his part ready (the third time this year he has missed a deadline).
c. Anita not only had her part completed but also had sketched out an attractive design for formatting the final document.
d. Sunggong was 45 minutes late for the meeting because his car had skidded into a ditch as a result of last night's snowstorm.
e. Elvira left a message that she would have to miss the meeting because she was working on another report, one due tomorrow.

co2. Explain the meaning and importance of nonverbal messages.

5 **Entrepreneurship** Marty Chernov, owner of a small salvage yard employing 18 people, has an appointment with John Garrison Boyd IV, vice president of Metropolitan Bank, to discuss his application for a $35,000 business loan. What helpful guidelines can you give Marty regarding his nonverbal behavior at the conference?

6 **Face to Face** More than any other body part, our faces reveal our emotions, opinions, and moods. For each of the following facial parts, provide as many examples as you can of the expression and the emotion or mood it can express, either voluntarily or unconsciously. (For example, showing our tongue expresses dislike or disagreement.) (a) nose, (b) lips, (c) eyebrows, (d) tongue, (e) eyelids, (f) eyes, (g) forehead.

7 **Diversity** Assume that you are a supervisor in a firm where one-third of the work force is Hispanic, about evenly divided between Mexican Americans and

Cuban Americans. All are either U.S. citizens or legal residents. Because both groups speak Spanish as their native language, can you assume that both groups have similar cultures? Do some research (including Internet research) on both groups in terms of their typical educational backgrounds, political beliefs, job experiences, and the like. Organize your findings into a two-page report (typed, double-spaced).

co3. Communicate effectively with diverse populations both within the United States and internationally.

8 **Diversity**   As a manager, how would you respond to each of the following situations? What kind of helpful advice can you give to each party?

a. Alton gets angry when several of the people he works with talk among themselves in their native language. He suspects they are talking and laughing about him. As a result, he tends to avoid them and to complain about them to others.

b. Jason, a slightly built office worker, feels intimidated when talking to his supervisor, a much larger man who is of a different racial background. As a result, he often is unable to negotiate effectively.

c. Raisa is embarrassed when she must talk to Roger, a subordinate who suffered major facial disfigurement when a grenade exploded in Vietnam. She doesn't know how to look at him. As a result, she tends to avoid meeting with him face to face.

d. Sheila, the only female manager on staff, gets incensed whenever her colleague Alex apologizes to her after using profanity during a meeting. First, she tells him, he shouldn't be using profanity at all. Second, if he does, he should not apologize just to her for using it.

e. When Jim arrived as the only male real-estate agent in a small office, it was made clear to him that he would have to get his own coffee and clean up after himself—just like everyone else. Yet whenever the FedEx truck delivers a heavy carton, the women always ask him to lift the package.

9 **International**   Joe arrived 15 minutes late for his appointment with Itaru Nakamura, sales manager for a small manufacturer to which Joe's firm hoped to sell parts. "Sorry to be late," he apologized, "but you know how the local drivers are. At any rate, since I'm late, let's get right down to brass tacks." Joe began to pace back and forth in the small office. "The way I see it, if you and I can come to some agreement this afternoon, we'll be able to get the rest to agree. After all, who knows more about this than you and I?" Joe sat down opposite his colleague and looked him straight in the eye. "So what do you say? Can we agree on the basics and let our assistants hammer out the details?" His colleague was silent for a few moments, then said, "Yes." Discuss Joe's intercultural skills. Specifically, what did he do wrong? What did Nakamura's response probably mean?

10 **International Communication**   Working with a teammate, select a foreign country. Using two or more Internet sites, outline various cultural differences of the selected country that might impact international business dealings. Look for differences regarding customs, use of space, hand gestures, time orientation, social behavior, the manner in which business is conducted, and other business-related issues. Prepare an outline of your findings, and submit it and the Internet sources to your instructor.

co4. Listen effectively in business situations.

11 Listening   Your instructor will assign you a television show to watch this week—a news program, talk show, or documentary. Using the listening techniques you learned in this chapter, take notes on the important points covered in the presentation. Listen for the major themes, not the details. Write a one-page memo to your instructor summarizing the important information you heard. Should every student's paper contain basically the same information? Explain your answer.

12 Serial Communication   Divide into groups of four students each: A, B, C, and D. Within each group have A and B leave the room. Then have C read aloud the one-page report that he or she prepared for Exercise 11 at a normal reading rate and without repeating any of the data while D takes notes. Have A rejoin the group and take notes while D reads the notes taken of C's oral report. Then have B rejoin the group and take notes while A reads the notes taken of D's oral notes. Finally, have D reread aloud his or her original report and B reread aloud his or her notes. How much of the original story was lost in the respective transmissions? How much was added to the original story? Think of some ways the accuracy could have been improved during each transmission. Write up your results in a typed e-mail to your instructor.

co5. Use effective techniques for conducting business by telephone.

■ See Slide 2.18.

13 Communicating by Telephone   Role-play the situation described below. Record the conversations for later evaluation. While two students are role-playing, the others in the class should be making notes of what went well and what might have been improved. To help simulate a telephone environment, have the two student actors sit back to back so that they cannot see each other or the other class members.

Situation: You are Chris Renshaw, administrative assistant for Ronald Krugel, the marketing manager at Kraft Enterprises. Terry Plachta, an important customer whom you've never met, calls your boss with a complaint that an item ordered two weeks ago does not work as advertised. Your boss won't be back in the office until tomorrow afternoon.

14 Evaluating Telephone Communications   Telephone two organizations in your area. Your purpose is to speak to the director of human resources to learn how much time he or she spends in meetings each week and to get an evaluation of the effectiveness of these meetings. Call at least three times if you're not successful the first time. Leave a message if necessary. Keep a log of each person with whom you speak at each organization and evaluate the effectiveness of that person's telephone communication skills. Finally, write a summary of what you learned about meetings in that organization. Submit both your log and your summary to your instructor.

■ See Slide 2.19.

15 Leaving Effective Telephone Messages   Assume that on your third try (see Exercise 14) you were still unsuccessful in reaching the director of human resources by telephone. Instead you got a recording asking you to leave a message of no more than 30 seconds. Compose the message you would leave.

co6. Plan, conduct, and participate in a business meeting.

16 Communication in Meetings   Attend a departmental meeting, a faculty senate meeting, a city council meeting, a school of business meeting, a student government meeting, a business meeting or some other meeting. Identify such variables as the following:

- Purpose of the meeting
- Role of an agenda
- Members present and their punctuality
- Layout of the room
- Person presiding
- Use of parliamentary procedure
- Outcomes of the meeting

Take minutes of the meeting, answer all of the questions listed in this exercise, and submit both to your instructor.

17 Planning a Business Meeting   Assume that you are a dean at your institution, which does not celebrate Martin Luther King Jr.'s birthday with a paid holiday. You are seeking the support of the college's four other deans for making the third Monday in January a holiday for all college employees and students. Will a meeting best serve your purpose? Why or why not? What alternatives are there for resolving the issue? Assuming you decide to call a meeting, prepare a memorandum including the agenda to send to the other deans. Submit both your memo and your responses to the questions to your instructor.

18 Conducting a Meeting   Divide into groups of five, with each person assuming the role of a dean at your institution (see Exercise 17). Draw straws to determine who will be the dean calling the meeting, and use this person's agenda. Conduct a 15- to 20-minute meeting. Following the meeting, evaluate its effectiveness. Did you achieve your objective? Explain your answer.

19 Using Business Etiquette   Assume that you're the dean of your college. Think of three people to whom it would be appropriate to give a gift during December holidays and three people to whom it would not be appropriate to give a gift. Identify the individuals and their positions, and give reasons for your decisions. For the three people to whom you *would* give, suggest an appropriate gift and a recommended price range.

co7. Use a professional demeanor and appropriate behavior to maintain effective working relationships.

20 Pleased to Meet You   Assume the role of Marc Kaplan at Urban Systems, Inc. (see the Appendix to Chapter 1 on page 36). You are expecting Ms. Sonia Muñoz, an important potential client from Atlanta, for a business meeting at 10 a.m., accompanied by Mr. Gunnar Burns, her personal assistant. You've met both of them once before. During the course of the day, make the following introductions:

a. Sonia Muñoz and Amy Stetsky
b. Amy Stetsky and Gunnar Burns
c. Gunnar Burns and Diana Coleman
d. Gunnar Burns and Dave Kaplan

■ Possible solutions to the Continuing Case are described in the *Instructor's Resource Manual.*

■ See Handout 2.4.

continuing
case 2

Don't Let the Smoke Get in Your Eyes

Outside on a smoke break, Marc Kaplan ground his cigarette into the ashtray in the lovely covered courtyard that Urban Systems maintained for its employees. "Won't those save-the-earth people ever be satisfied?" he thought. For some years now, US had enforced a policy of no smoking anywhere within the building—including private offices. Now Diana had just sent a memo to Dave Kaplan asking that the no-smoking policy be extended to outside areas owned by the company as well. This policy would mean that smokers would have to journey across a busy intersection to the small municipal park across the street to light up.

Diana cited health dangers, reduced air quality, rights of nonsmokers, and damage to company property. Marc knew he could cite some arguments also: the rights of smokers, the unfairness of imposing new restrictions that were not in place when employees were hired, the reduced productivity due to increased time spent on outside smoking breaks, and the fact that other health-related productivity hazards (such as gross obesity) were not banned. He felt he could enlist the support of O. J. Drew and Wendy Janish—the other two smokers in the management offices. Tom Mercado, an ex-smoker, was an unknown.

At any rate, Dave Kaplan had decided to hold a special meeting of the executive committee, made up of him and the three vice presidents, the following week to discuss and resolve the issue. Parliamentary procedure is followed at these meetings.

Oral and Written Communication Projects

1. Assume the role of Dave Kaplan. Compose a memo to the executive committee announcing the meeting and outlining the agenda.

2. Have four members play the roles of Dave and the three vice presidents; Dave conducts the meeting. The other class members should listen actively, take

At the executive committee meeting, Marc presents his reasons for not extending the no-smoking policy.

notes, and be prepared to discuss the events afterward. Each observer should also serve as the secretary and submit a set of minutes for the meeting.

Critical Thinking

3. After role-playing, discuss the situation. How did each actor feel? Was anyone arguing a position with which he or she didn't really agree? Was correct parliamentary procedure followed? Was the meeting successful? Did anyone win? Lose?

LABtest 2

Dave Kaplan prepared a draft of the monthly column that he writes for *Home Remodeling*. Retype the following passage, inserting any needed punctuation according to the punctuation rules introduced in LAB 3 on page 583.

Rita Gonzales of Santa Fe, New Mexico, wants to know this :(EXP)

"(QUOT) I've heard that replacing my old fashioned bulbs with compact -(ADJ)

fluorescents will save $50 per bulb and reduce global warming.

Will this type of bulb create that drab, corpselike appearance in

5   everybodys home? '(PRO) "(QUOT)

The answer is that modern fluorescent bulbs produce

excellent color quality rather than the drab bluish hue of older

ones. I use them exclusively in my own home no one has checked ;(NO CONJ)

my pulse lately to see if I am still breathing. To quote Jim

10 Dulley in Cut Those Bills, published in the Dallas Morning "(TITLE) " (TITLE)

News, You can lose the blues and still cut costs. "(QUOT) " (QUOT)

There are decorative globe, bullet, candelabra, and bent -(ADJ)

tube designs and recessed, task, and spot lighting will focus ,(COMMA)

15 the light where you need it. Fluorescent lightings main '(SING)

advantage is its economy. Fifty five dollars is the typical -(NUM)

annual savings on homeowners utility bills. '(PLUR)

For more information, contact the Industry Conservation

Council at 317-555-8016 and ask for George Mandrake, energy

analyst Betty Bow, economist or Bob Onwood, staff analyst. ;(SER) ;(SER)

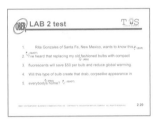

■ See Slide 2.20.

■ See Slide 2.21.

■ See Slide 2.22.

3

Communication Technology

After you have finished this chapter, you should be able to

1. **Identify the major sources of electronic information.**

2. **Browse and search the World Wide Web.**

3. **Evaluate the quality of the electronic data you gather.**

4. **Share electronic information.**

magine giving 600,000 engineers access to information about 20,000 products or answering questions about orders placed by 30,000 companies. Scott Roller faces these kinds of communication challenges every day as Internet Marketing Director at Texas Instruments (TI), which makes high-tech products such as communications chips. He is responsible for the content and functionality of the TI.com website, where engineers working for corporate customers can research the specifications of TI's chips. He also oversees several password-protected extranets for sharing proprietary information such as product delivery dates with customers, partners, and distributors.

One of Roller's top priorities is making TI.com as user-friendly as possible for engineers, the primary audience. For example, engineers who are familiar with TI chips can quickly search the site either by product name or part number. Once they locate the appropriate page, they can dig deeper to obtain more product details. What happens when an engineer needs help determining which TI chips are suitable for certain situations and projects? "This is the harder challenge," notes Roller. "A customer may come to TI.com with a power-supply problem such as, 'I have an input voltage of 12 volts and I need to regulate it down to a 3.3-volt supply and a 1.8-volt supply that can drive 1 amp of current. Help me out.'" In response, Roller and his team have created online tools that enable

an insider's
perspective

SCOTT ROLLER
Internet Marketing Director,
Texas Instruments
(Dallas, Texas)

engineers to enter their specific requirements and instantly view a list of recommended products.

In addition, Roller spends considerable time browsing the Internet to spot trends, keep an eye on what competitors are doing, and stay abreast of relevant industry news. Knowing that some information may be fact and some may be opinion, he carefully evaluates what he finds online. "First and foremost is the credibility of the source," he says. Even when information is from a credible source, Roller adds, "I still take it with a grain of salt. Before I implement anything, I confirm by checking several different sources to be sure that the information makes sense."

Because TI operates globally, Roller relies on e-mail to keep conversations going with colleagues in other offices. "I find it particularly useful when working with our teams overseas," he explains. "For example, when I'm home in the evening, I can send an e-mail message to a colleague in Shanghai"—which is 13 hours ahead of TI's headquarters in Dallas—"and after a good dialogue, we'll have an issue resolved within 20 minutes."

"Before I implement anything, I confirm by checking several different sources to be sure that the information makes sense."

■ See Slide 3.1.

■ A chapter overview appears in the *Instructor's Resource Manual*.

■ According to former vice presidential candidate Geraldine Ferraro, "It was not long ago that people thought that semiconductors were part-time orchestra leaders and microchips were very, very small snack foods."

One of the most pressing strategic questions facing e-commerce sites in the struggle to become profitable is how to turn browsers into buyers. Alissa Kozuh, editor of Nordstrom.com, analyzes the words that people put into the site's search engine every month (all 45,000 of them) to understand what customers are looking for.

■ Our Need to Know—Now!

Consider the following situations, all typical of those occurring thousands of times every day:

■ The removable hard disk drive Janice purchased and installed six months ago has just crashed. She needs to contact the company to determine whether the disk drive is still under warranty and, if so, how she can get it repaired or replaced.

■ Chris's boss, the director of human resources, asks her to make a hotel reservation for January 15–18 at a hotel in downtown San Francisco that charges between $200 and $250 per night.

■ Kim's company is trying to get ISO 2000 certification to expand its operations into central Europe. She wonders what is involved in securing such certification and what the advantages and disadvantages of certification are.

■ Marc has just read an article in the *Wall Street Journal* about Auto-by-Tel, an online automobile buying service. He wonders if it would be a profitable company in which to invest his $8,500 Keogh account.

■ As part of Raúl's term paper in European art history, he needs to include a color photograph of the *Mona Lisa*.

■ You've finally finished cramming for tomorrow's accounting exam and are ready to relax for a bit. What movies are on TV tonight?

As these situations illustrate, our need for information is insatiable and unrelenting. Today, information is a mass commodity—not a scarce resource. The secret to dealing with this phenomenon is being able to access and make use of that information. As painful as it might be to contemplate, much (if not most) of your education is going to be obsolete within a few years. You will have a lifelong need to update your skills, secure relevant, accurate information, and share that information with others.

To the rescue comes the **Internet,** a worldwide collection of computers in university labs, business offices, and government centers—all interconnected, all filled with massive amounts of information, and all accessible for free (or nearly so) to anyone with an Internet account (which includes almost all college students). The ability to access this information stored in thousands of computers worldwide and to chat with anyone around the globe at any hour of the day bestows tremendous power on anyone who knows how to retrieve, evaluate, and share that information.

Before you can communicate, you must, first of all, have something important to communicate. Thus, it makes sense for us to learn how to access and share information now—before we learn about specific communication strategies. This chapter shows you how to use different forms of technology to communicate more easily, more efficiently, and more effectively.

Contemporary managers need up-to-date information—and they need it now! Learn how to secure the information you need—whether it is a phone number, statistic, or research report.

■ Accessing Electronic Information

An entire knowledge industry has evolved in which organizations store huge amounts of statistical, financial, and bibliographic information in the memory banks of their mainframe computers or on compact discs and then make this information available to users worldwide for a fee.

An **electronic database** is a computer-searchable collection of information on a general subject area, such as business, education, or psychology. Electronic databases are fast; you can typically collect more data electronically in a half hour than would be possible in an entire day of conventional library research. They are available either on CD-ROM or online via computer network or telephone hookup.

In addition, electronic databases are typically more current than printed databases; most are updated weekly or monthly. Also, each contains several years' worth of citations, whereas manual indexes require searching through individual annual volumes and monthly supplements. Finally, electronic databases are extremely flexible. You can use different search terms, combine them, and modify your search at every step. (See Spotlight 8, "The Paperless Office?," on page 100, for an update on the future of paper documents.)

Although you may never write another academic report after graduating from college, you *will* continue to need to locate information—for business, political, or personal reasons. Computer-assisted information retrieval has now become so widely available, economical, and easy to use that it has emerged as a powerful tool for helping managers solve problems and make decisions.

CO1. Identify the major sources of electronic information.

You can conduct a comprehensive search for data without ever leaving your office, via online computer searching.

Much of the information we need is too new to be available in printed form.

■ The Internet

As we noted earlier, the Internet is a vast information system that connects millions of computers worldwide, allowing them to exchange all types of information and to conduct many types of business transactions, such as online banking and shopping. Some of you may even be taking this course (or another course) via distance learning on the Internet (see Spotlight 9, "So You're a Distance Learning Student").

Chances are that the very information you need is stored somewhere on the Internet. You have to learn how to access it.

The Paperless Office?

Twenty years ago, the concept of the "paperless office" inspired visions of desks uncluttered by stacks of memos, empty and no-longer-needed file cabinets, and in-baskets being converted into desktop planters. The prediction of a paperless office was based on the belief that offices would eventually store all information on some type of electronic medium, which would then be filed, retrieved, and disseminated at will. The advantage of this type of system is that electronic storage, retrieval, and dissemination are faster and less expensive than manual paper methods.

Paper Consumption Is Growing

Reality proved somewhat different from this vision, however. Paper consumption tripled from 1940 to 1980 and tripled again from 1980 to 1990. Today the average person interacts with 1,800 pounds of the white stuff each year. Offices today use more than 6.4 million tons of paper per year. In fact, the corporate use of paper is growing at a rate twice that of the growth in the gross national product.

The increasing use of paper also has environmental implications. Despite recent advances in paper manufacture and the creation of tree farms (called pulp plantations), the paper industry remains one of the most energy-intensive manufacturing processes in the country. Paper-making consumes vast amounts of water and creates air and water pollution.

Technology Is Part of the Problem

In short, the paperless office has not yet become reality, and probably never will. Part of the problem is technology itself: according to recent research, about three-fourths (74 percent) of all documents created on the computer are printed out—at least once.

Consider the Internet, for example. With millions of sources of information now at their fingertips, users typically print out promising sources as their first action—*just in case* they might need them in the future. (It has always been true that the vast majority of papers filed never see the light of day again.)

In addition, the number of fax machines—the one true global communications standard—has increased 22-fold over the last decade. Also, laser and ink-jet printers make it easy to print out drafts for editing. Add to that factor the increase in the use (and speed) of laser copiers, which has shot up 12-fold in the past decade, and you begin to get the picture.

In short, instead of reducing paperwork, paperwork has now merely become automated. That is, instead of typists typing one sheet at a time, word processors now crank documents out of printers like bullets from a machine gun.

The Function of Paper Is Changing

The reason that paper has not disappeared from the landscape is that it is so convenient and portable. Paper documents are easy to read and can be taken and used anywhere—regardless of whether a computer is accessible. The *purpose* of paper, however, is changing; that is, paper as *storage* is giving way to paper as *interface.* Paper serves as an interface when we print documents to be read and not merely to be filed, and when we print out documents on demand and then discard them when done.

In summary, the paperless office is a myth. Technology isn't eliminating paper documents any more than typewriters eliminated the need for pencils. Instead of doing away with paper documents, technology is simply making them "prettier" and more accessible. As Raul Fernandez, president of Proxicom, an Internet consulting company in Reston, Virginia, puts it, "I wouldn't bet against something that's been used for 4,500 years."[1]

Although numerous types of resources are available on the Internet, our interest here is in two main types: discussion resources (consisting primarily of mailing lists and newsgroups) and reference resources (consisting primarily of the World Wide Web). Almost all students are online, and as shown in Communication Snapshot 3 on page 102, two-thirds of all American adults currently have an online connection.

So You're a Distance Learning Student

Instead of traveling to a physical classroom, you've decided to bring this business communication course into your home or office, using technologies such as the Internet, videotape, videoconferencing, audiotape, or even low-tech "snail mail." But what does it take to be a *successful* distance learning student? Daniel Granger, director of distance learning at University College, Minnesota, stresses that distance learning "requires a pretty well-motivated student—that is, a student who is able to manage his or her own time, and set deadlines for him- or herself." In short, the first success factor is to be willing and able to work independently.

Set a Schedule

Just as you would follow a set schedule for coming to class and submitting assignments in a regular classroom, you should establish a routine for your distance learning activities. If you're taking a Web-based course, for instance, you should log on at regular intervals to download information from the instructor, join online discussions and critique assignments, read messages from other classmates, and upload assignments. In between online sessions, make time to study the assigned material and complete the related exercises. Be disciplined about managing your time to ensure that you can juggle all of your commitments.

Stay Motivated

The second success factor is to maintain your motivation throughout the entire business communication course. This issue can be quite a challenge, given your other work and personal obligations that may pop up from day to day. Nevertheless, by focusing on your goals, you can set the right priorities and develop the drive to follow through. Look at it this way: when distance learning is one of your top priorities, every class-related task you complete moves you one step closer to your short-term goal of completing the course and your longer-term goals of personal and professional improvement—and it gives you the satisfaction of a job well done.

Get Involved

The third success factor is an ability to overcome the isolation of distance learning by interacting with your instructor and classmates. It's not enough to read all of the assignments and submit your homework on time; to get the most out of the course, you'll need to stay in close contact with your instructor as well as with other students. Let the instructor know if you're having technical problems with the mechanics of distance learning, have questions about course content, or want feedback about a specific aspect of your work. To hone your teamwork skills, seek out opportunities to collaborate with your classmates. In this way, you'll not only be able to learn from their insights, but also get more practice in group problem solving.

Sharpen Your Writing Skills

The fourth success factor is an ability to thoughtfully express yourself in writing. Take the time to think through every class-related message before you send it. Remember, misunderstandings can easily result when messages are just words on a screen. So choose your words carefully and focus on ideas, not people. Remember that your unseen classmates and instructor—like you—deserve to be treated with respect.[2]

Internet Resources

Discussion groups on the Internet allow you to participate in interactive, ongoing discussions on a particular topic with people all over the world.

A **mailing list** is a discussion group in which messages are sent directly to members via e-mail. On the Internet, these mailing lists are called *listservs*. To become a member, you must first subscribe to the list (typically by sending an e-mail message

Mailing-list messages are sent directly to you as e-mail.

communication snapshot 3

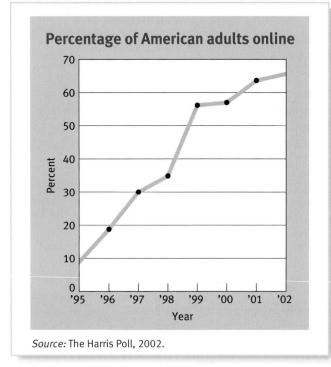

Percentage of American adults online

Source: The Harris Poll, 2002.

You must log on to a newsgroup to read the new messages.

■ See Slide 3.2.

CO2. Browse and search the World Wide Web.

to the listserver). From then on, any messages posted to the list are automatically sent to your e-mail address. Listservs are usually created to enable members to exchange information and views about a particular topic. Your instructor, for example, may create a mailing list for your class. Any message posted to that mailing list either by the instructor or by one of the students will then be sent to (and presumably read by) all members of the class. Such a list would be discontinued at the end of the school term. Some more-or-less permanent mailing lists provide searchable archive files that contain all of the old messages.

A **newsgroup** is a discussion group in which messages (called *articles*) are posted at the newsgroup site. Anyone can connect to the site via an Internet *usenet* connection as frequently as desired to read any newly posted articles. Newsgroups differ from mailing lists in that newsgroup members have to "visit" the newsgroup site to see any new messages, whereas new messages are automatically sent as e-mail to mailing-list members. The news administrator determines how long old articles remain archived (and, therefore, available for searching).

Figure 3.1 shows a typical e-mail message posted from a listserv (top) and a newsgroup article (bottom).

The fastest-growing segment of the Internet (and the resource that is of most interest to us) is the **World Wide Web** (also known as WWW or simply the Web). Web documents, called *pages,* can contain text, graphics, sound, and video, all written in *hypertext.* Hypertext links in the document enable the reader to explore as much or as little of a document as desired. Clicking on a hypertext link instantly opens that document. Users access this type of information by using a software program known as a *Web browser,* the most popular of which are Microsoft Internet Explorer and Netscape Navigator.

Browsing and Searching the World Wide Web

Nobody "owns" the Internet; that is, there is no one governing authority that can make rules and impose order. Thus, it should not surprise you that the massive amount of information available on the Internet is not neatly and logically organized for easy search and retrieval. One "Internaut" describes the situation this way:

> Imagine yourself having a key to the door of a large library. Unfortunately, everyone else has a key also. Everyone has free access to put anything they want in the library, wherever they want to put it. To make matters worse, there is no librarian, there is no card catalog, no computerized index, no map, and no reference staff; so after people deposit materials, there is no structure to help others locate them. The Internet is like that library—a disorganized chaotic repository of information.[3]

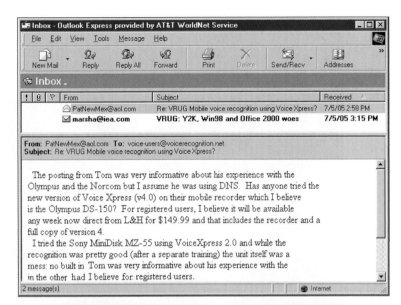

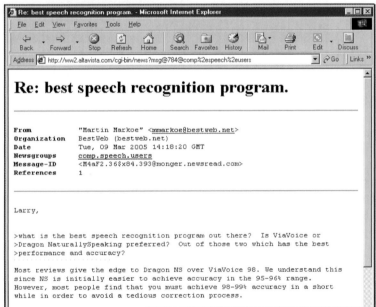

figure 3.1

Listserv E-mail Posting (top) and Newsgroup Posting (bottom)

Fortunately, a variety of search sites are available on the Internet to make accessing Internet resources if not painless, at least more pleasant and productive. Basically, these sites fall into two categories—*directories* for browsing the Internet and *indexes* for searching for specific information.

Browsing the Internet   Web directories are hyperlinked lists of websites, hierarchically organized into topical categories and subcategories. Clicking your way through these lists will lead you to website links for the subject you're investigating. Use these directories when you need to find common information that can be easily classified. If you aren't looking for something very specific, try moving down

When browsing, you can go deeper and deeper into a subject, gradually narrowing your focus.

General Motors, Ford, and Daimler-Chrysler recently teamed up to form Covisint, a supply chain based entirely on the Web that handles up to half a trillion dollars in annual purchases from 8,000 individual suppliers. Here, Deborah Burton, manager of procurement, follows the proceedings of a recent online auction to secure the cheapest cost for a windshield-wiper blade.

■ See Slide 3.3.

Some "metasearch" indexes (such as Metacrawler) search through numerous individual search sites. Because they are locating more resources, these searches naturally take much longer than using an individual search site.

Take the time to learn basic Boolean logic; it will save you time and enhance the efficiency of your searches.

through the general categories listed to reach a more specific category (in computer language, to "drill down"). In this way, you can narrow your search.

Searching the Internet   Web indexes are massive, computer-generated databases containing information on millions of webpages and usenet newsgroup articles. By entering keywords or phrases, you can retrieve lists of webpages that contain your search term. The lists are created by *Web crawlers* (also called *robots* or *spiders*), software programs that roam the Web, looking for new sites by following links from page to page. Once your query executes, the Web search site displays the list of hits as a page containing the URLs (Universal Resource Locators, or Internet addresses) that are hyperlinked.

The success of your Internet search will depend on how skillfully you choose your keywords (or *search terms*). Remember that the computer makes a very literal search; it will find exactly what you ask for—and nothing more. If you use the search term *secretaries*, many search indexes will not find citations for the words *secretary* or *secretarial*. Some indexes have a feature known as *truncation,* which allows you to search for the root of a term. Thus, a search for *secre* would retrieve *secret, secretarial, secretaries, secretary, secretion,* and so on. You would then choose the entries appropriate for your purpose.

One of the most common mistakes people make is to use too few keywords in their searches or to use the wrong kinds of keywords. (Too many hits is just as unhelpful as too few hits.) Generally, try to identify three or four keywords—and use nouns. The only time you generally need to use adjectives or adverbs is if the term itself contains one—such as *World Wide Web* (and don't forget to put phrases in quotation marks).

Most indexes also allow the use of logical search operators (called *Boolean logic*) in the keywords. There are four basic search operators—AND, OR, NOT, and NEAR—and as you can see, they are always typed in all capitals. The operators broaden or narrow searches as follows:

- AND identifies sources that contain both term 1 AND term 2; AND decreases the number of hits.

- OR identifies sources that contain either term 1 OR term 2; OR increases the number of hits.

- NOT excludes sources that contain the NOT term; NOT decreases the number of hits.

- NEAR identifies sources in which the two terms are within a given distance from each other; NEAR decreases the number of hits.

Placing quotation marks around a phrase requires the exact matching of a phrase. As in algebra, the operations inside parentheses are performed first, and most search engines read command lines from left to right. Thus, the search term *"heavy metal"* would eliminate the flagging of websites devoted to metals and ores, whereas *"metal" NOT "heavy metal"* would find *only* those sites devoted to metals and ores. Study carefully Spotlight 10, "Browsing and Searching the World Wide Web," on pages 106–109, which illustrates step-by-step the process of browsing and searching the Web—in this case, searching for information about speech-recognition computer programs.

Evaluating the Quality of Electronic Information

Anyone with access to the Internet can post pretty much anything that he or she wants online. There is no law, regulation, or Internet policy that states that the information posted on the Internet has to be true, objective, intelligent, or politically correct (recall that there is no central authority for managing the Internet).

According to Donald T. Hawkins, editor-in-chief of *Information Science Abstracts*,[4]

> Information does not gain or lose credibility simply by virtue of its format (print or electronic). However, because of the ephemeral, dynamic, and fluid nature of the Web and the lack of a review process, one must be much more cautious when evaluating information obtained from it than when evaluating information obtained from a peer-reviewed or scholarly journal.
>
> More stringent evaluation criteria should be used for Web-based sources than for print sources. Methods of evaluating print sources have evolved over many years and have stood the test of time. The Web . . . is constantly evolving.

The range of informational quality on the Net is enormous. Information posted by governmental and educational institutions (typically, those sites that end in ".gov" or ".edu") is most often comprehensive, accurate, and up-to-date. Most pages sponsored by commercial organizations (typically, those sites that end in ".com") are also of high quality, as long as you recognize the profit incentive for these pages. Personal home pages and those sponsored by advocacy

■ See Slide 3.4.

■ See Slide 3.5.

CO3. Evaluate the quality of the electronic data you gather.

Don't believe everything you read!

A S K **Ober**

Dear Dr. Ober:

I am writing about an Internet reference in Chapter 3, Exercise 12. The case was based on an article by Don McAuliffe, "Provident Tries to Make Banking More Friendly." The website given to access this article was http://www.crmdaily.com/perl/printer/12613. I cannot get this URL to work.

—Laurie B.

Dear Laurie:

I've just spent a considerable amount of time searching online and, unfortunately, the article by Don McAuliffe is apparently no longer available on the Internet. That is, of course, one of the frustrations about using Internet sources as reference notes, but sometimes, as in this case, it was unavoidable because the information was simply not available elsewhere.

—Scot

E-mail your questions and comments to askober@ober.net.

Browsing and Searching the World Wide Web

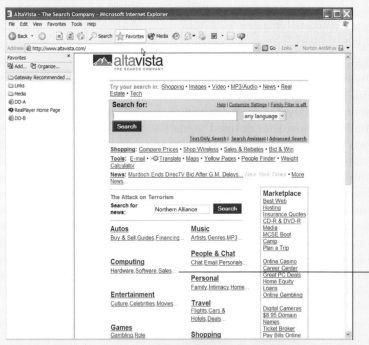

Jean Tate needs information about speech-recognition software programs and logs on to the AltaVista site on the Internet (at http://www.altavista.com). She has a choice of *browsing* the Web using the AltaVista categories or *searching* the Web using the Search For window. Because she isn't sure what she is looking for, Jean decides to browse and "drill down" through the categories listed. She clicks on *Software*.

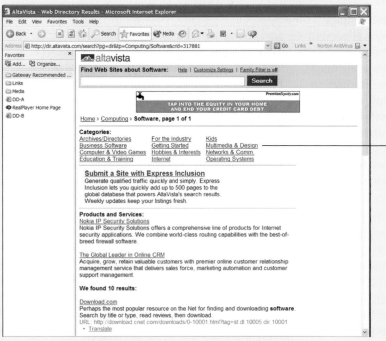

A list of subcategories, all related to software, appears. Jean clicks on *Multimedia & Design*.

The AltaVista screen shots on pages 106–109 are reproduced with permission of Yahoo! Inc. ©2004 by Yahoo! Inc. YAHOO! and the YAHOO! logo are trademarks of Yahoo! Inc.

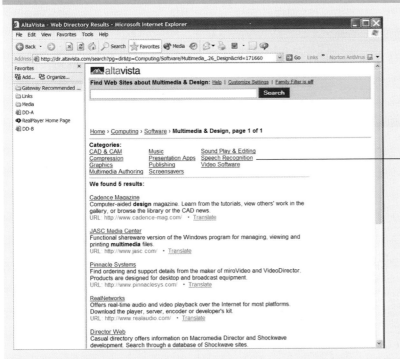

Note how AltaVista keeps track of each level of information. You can click on any level to return to that level and browse another category. Jean has now found the topic she is looking for and clicks on *Speech Recognition*.

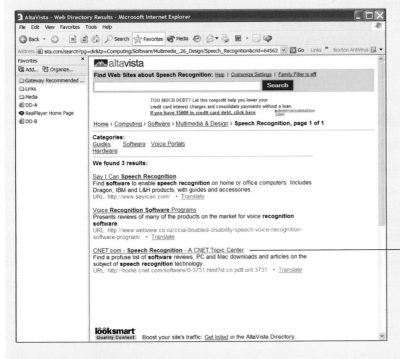

After scanning the resulting list of possible sources, Jean clicks on the third one.

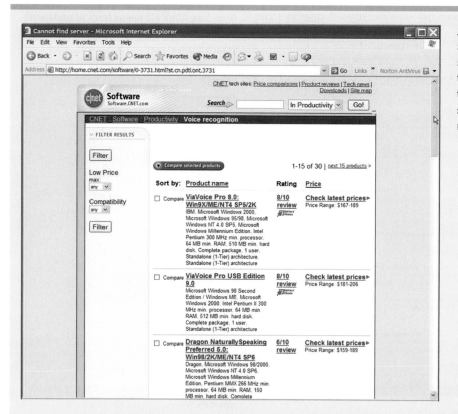

Jean can explore any of the 30 sites identified, print them out, save them, or press the Back button to return to the list of sources to select another one. Instead, she clicks on the Home button to return to AltaVista's home page.

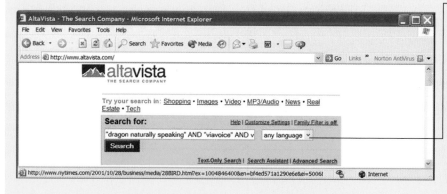

Now switching from a browsing to a searching mode, Jean types the names in the Search window of three popular speech-recognition software programs. Note that she encloses each title in quotation marks to ensure that it is read as a phrase. Note also that she includes the Boolean operator AND, which means that the identified sites must include all three terms. In addition, Jean types the terms in all lowercase letters, which tells AltaVista to search for all cases of the terms—all uppercase, sentence case, lowercase, or some combination.

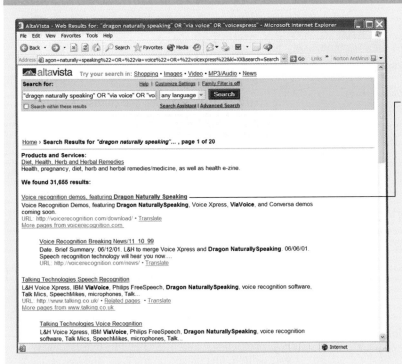

AltaVista locates 31,655 sites that contain the software titles. The titles are listed in relevancy rank order, with AltaVista's best estimate of the most useful sites appearing at the top of the list. Jean clicks on the first site.

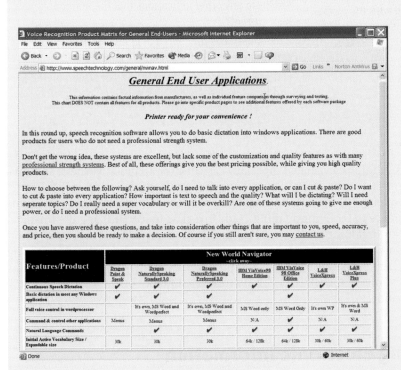

This site contains a very useful table comparing the most popular voice recognition software programs. Jean continues her exploration, saving and printing out whatever sites she wants to study further.

✓checklist 3

Evaluating the Quality of Internet Resources[5]

Criterion 1: Authority

✓ Is it clear who sponsors the page and what the sponsor's purpose in maintaining the page is?

✓ Is it clear who wrote the material and what the author's qualifications for writing on this topic are?

✓ Is there a way of verifying the legitimacy of the page's sponsor; that is, is there a phone number or postal address to contact for more information?

✓ If the material is protected by copyright, is the name of the copyright holder given?

Criterion 2: Accuracy

✓ Are the sources for any factual information clearly listed so they can be verified in another source?

✓ Has the sponsor provided a link to outside sources (such as product reviews or reports filed with the SEC) that can be used to verify the sponsor's claims?

✓ Is the information free of grammatical, spelling, and other typographical errors? (These kinds of errors not only indicate a lack of quality control but can actually produce inaccuracies in information.)

✓ Are statistical data in graphs and charts clearly labeled and easy to read?

✓ Does anyone monitor the accuracy of the information being published?

Criterion 3: Objectivity

✓ For any given piece of information, is the sponsor's motivation for providing it clear?

✓ Is the information content clearly separated from any advertising or opinion content?

✓ Is the point of view of the sponsor presented in a clear manner, with well-supported arguments?

Criterion 4: Currentness

✓ Are there dates on the page to indicate when the page was written, first placed on the Web, and last revised?

✓ Are there any other indications that the material is kept current?

✓ If the material is presented in graphs or charts, is it clearly stated when the data was gathered?

✓ Is there evidence that the page has been completed and is not still in the process of being developed?

■ See Handout 3.1.

co**4.** **Share electronic information.**

organizations should be evaluated especially carefully for accuracy, fairness, and coverage. The same is true for usenet newsgroups and mailing lists.

The consequences of making decisions based on invalid data can range from minor inconvenience to receiving a failing grade in a class to jeopardizing the financial viability of your organization. You are responsible for the quality of the information you include in your correspondence, reports, and presentations. Avoid accepting something as fact just because you saw it on the Net. Evaluate your sources critically, using the questions in Checklist 3, "Evaluating the Quality of Internet Resources" (above), as a guide.

■ Sharing Electronic Information

Technology helps us not only access information but also share it with others. You will often incorporate the information you access electronically into your own electronic communications—correspondence, reports, phone calls, and the like (we cover business presentations in Chapters 13 and 14)—using a variety of technological innovations.

E-mail

In e-mail (electronic mail), messages are composed, transmitted, and usually read on computer screens. Today, e-mail has replaced the telephone as the preferred medium to communicate in business. There are nearly a billion e-mail addresses assigned in the world. Consumers comprise 60 percent of the e-mail accounts, equivalent to 1 address for every 13 people on the planet.[6]

E-mail has, in fact, become so popular that it can be time-consuming to read and answer. Another problem relates to the fact that e-mail is typically written "on the fly"—composed and sent while keyboarding. Writers therefore sometimes tend to ignore effective writing principles. According to Charles McGoon, e-mail may be

"Didn't you get my e-mail?"

> desensitizing us to egregious grammatical gaffes. . . . Would you write a printed memo to your boss with typos in it? To what earthly purpose? How can someone on the other end of an e-mail message know that you're really an intelligent person?[7]

Competent communicators follow the guidelines shown in Checklist 4, "Effective E-mail Practices," on page 112, to ensure that their e-mail messages achieve their objectives.

Groupware

Groupware is a form of software that automates information sharing between two or more remote users and enables them to communicate electronically and coordinate their efforts easily.

One form of groupware—a *group-authoring system*—enhances the process of collaborative writing by enabling different people to comment with ease on one another's writing. This type of program keeps an "edit trail" of changes made, who made them, and when. Because group members can comment on both the original draft and other members' comments and can raise and answer questions, such programs can reduce the need for time-consuming face-to-face meetings. Today, in fact, most word processing software can function quite effectively as groupware for editing team writing projects (see Spotlight 11, "Using Microsoft Word to Edit a Team Document," on pages 113–115).

No matter what type of software you use to coordinate writing projects, follow these guidelines:

■ Assign someone the role of manager of the document to keep the discussion on track and to edit comments as needed.

■ Determine beforehand how often each participant should check for changes.

■ Instead of *caveat emptor* ("let the buyer beware"), Web users should follow *caveat lector* ("let the reader beware").

■ See Slides 3.6 and 3.7.

■ See Slide 3.8.

✔checklist 4

Effective E-mail Practices

Format

✔ **Use short lines and short paragraphs (especially the first and last paragraphs).** They are much easier to read. Avoid formatting a long message as one solid paragraph.

✔ **Don't shout.** Use all-capital letters only for emphasis or to substitute for italicized text (such as book titles). Do NOT type your entire message in all capitals. It is a text-based form of *shouting* at your reader and is considered rude (not to mention being more difficult to read).

✔ **Proofread your message before sending.** Don't let the speed and convenience of e-mail lull you into being careless. Although an occasional typo or other surface error will probably be overlooked by the reader, excessive errors or sloppy language creates an unprofessional image of the sender.

Content

✔ **Choose your recipients carefully.** Don't send a message to an entire mailing list (for example, the whole department) if it applies to only one or two people.

✔ **Use a descriptive subject line.** Most e-mail programs allow the reader to preview all new messages by date received, sender, and subject, so the wording of the subject line may determine not only *when* but even *if* a message is read. Use a brief, but descriptive, subject line.

✔ **Greet your recipient.** Downplay the seeming impersonality of computerized mail by starting your message with a friendly salutation, such as "Hi, Amos" or "Dear Mr. Fisher."

✔ **Insert previous messages appropriately.** Most e-mail programs allow you to insert the original message into your reply. Use this feature judiciously. Occasionally, it may be helpful for the reader to see his or her entire message replayed. More often, however, you can save the reader time by establishing the context of the original message in your reply—for example, "Here is my opinion of the AlphaBat system that you asked for in your May 28 e-mail."

✔ **Use a direct style of writing.** Put your major idea in the first sentence or two. If the message is so sensitive or emotionally laden that a more indirect organization would be appropriate, you should reconsider whether e-mail is the most effective medium for the message.

✔ **Think twice; write once.** Because it is so easy to respond immediately to a message, you might be tempted to let your emotions take over. Such behavior is called "flaming" and should be avoided. Always assume the message you send will never be destroyed.

✔ **Provide an appropriate closing.** Some e-mail programs identify only the e-mail address (for example, "70511.753@aol.com") in the message header. Don't take a chance that your reader won't recognize you. Include your name, e-mail address, and any other appropriate identifying information at the end of your message. Most e-mail programs can automatically insert a "signature" containing this information at the end of every message.

- Minimize clutter by encouraging the use of e-mail or other communication channels for one-on-one communication. Provide everyone with e-mail addresses and phone numbers of all participants.

- If you're an inexperienced user, copy the newest file before making your comments—to simplify reverting to the original if you later change your mind.

spotlight11
ON TECHNOLOGY

Using Microsoft Word to Edit a Team Document

Once upon a time, to edit a group report you would first print out several copies of the report and distribute them to your team members. The team, in turn, would hand-write their comments on their copies and send them back to you. Finally, you'd manually collate the copies, make whatever changes were necessary, and print out a final copy of the report.

Today, anyone with access to a computer and e-mail can easily coordinate team efforts and collaborate electronically. In fact, you can accomplish group editing simply by using a word processing program such as Microsoft Word.

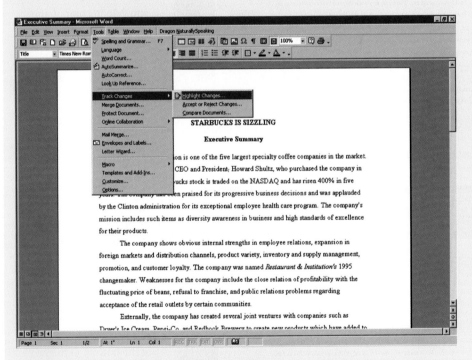

Assume, for example, that your team is conducting a company analysis of the popular Starbucks coffee shops. As the designated writer for the team, you create the draft of your document. Then, to keep track of changes that others make to the document, from the Word menu bar, you select Tools, Track Changes, Highlight Changes (see screen A). You then send your two other team members—Lanying Zhao and Sandy Overton—the document as an e-mail attachment and ask for their comments.

Screen A: With Microsoft Word, you can easily keep track of any changes made to your document.

Teleconferencing and Videoconferencing

A **teleconference** (that is, a telephone conference call) is a meeting of three or more people, at least some of whom are in different locations, who communicate via telephone. The primary advantage of teleconferences is that they save time and money because participants do not have to leave their offices. As in all telephone communications, however, this medium limits the amount of nonverbal cues available to the participants.

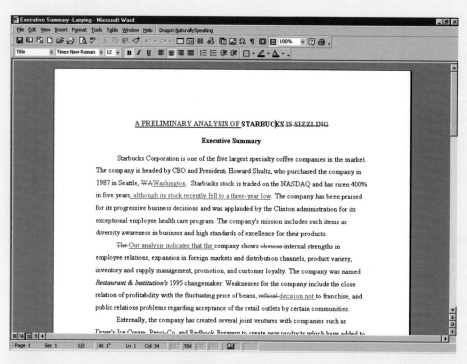

Screen B: Microsoft Word automatically underlines inserted text and strikes through deleted text.

Lanying prefers to do line-by-line editing, so she first makes a copy of the report (saving the original in case she later changes her mind) in Microsoft Word and then makes her changes on the document itself. Because the document has been saved with Track Changes enabled, Lanying's proposed changes show up in color on the screen. In screen B, for example, she proposes changing the report title from "Starbucks Is Sizzling" to "A Preliminary Analysis of Starbucks."

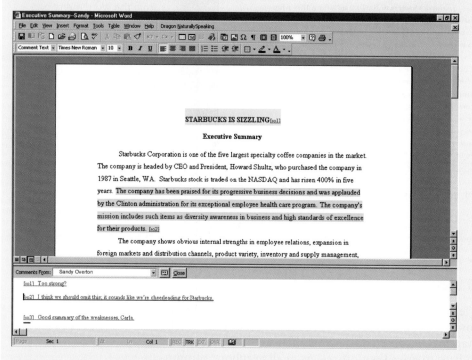

Screen C: In Microsoft Word, it's a simple task for a team member to add comments and questions to the original document.

Sandy receives the same draft of the report; he prefers to comment on the text rather than make line-by-line changes. He highlights the text he wants to comment on and then selects Comment from the Insert menu. A comment window opens at the bottom of the screen where he can type in his comments. In screen C, for example, Sandy has highlighted the last two sentences in the first paragraph and makes this comment: "I think we should omit this; it sounds like we're cheerleading for Starbucks."

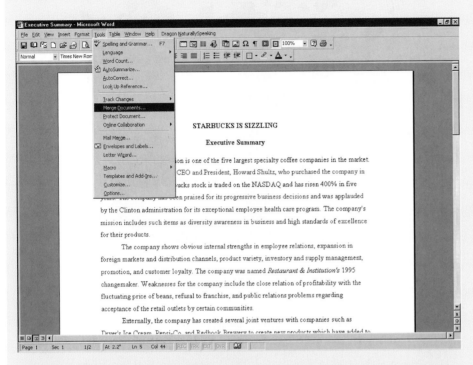

Screen D: As the designated writer for the team, you can easily produce a final document by merging the comments and suggested changes from all team members.

When Lanying and Sandy are finished, they e-mail their annotated documents back to you. As the designated writer, you must decide which of their changes to accept or reject. You begin by opening your original document and then merging both sets of annotations into your document. To do so, you select Tools, Merge Documents from the menu (see screen D).

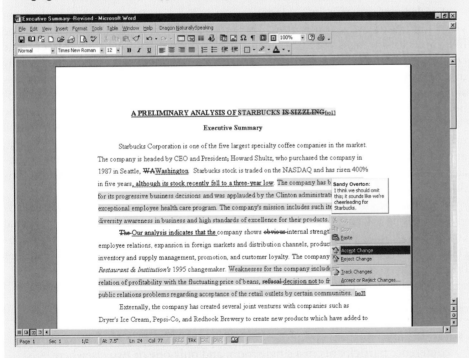

Screen E: Each team member's comments and proposed changes are shown in a different color for you to accept or reject.

The merged document (screen E) shows your original material along with comments and changes suggested by Lanying and Sandy. Because Lanying made her changes on the document itself, it's easy to follow her changes. To see Sandy's comments, you pause the mouse over the highlighted text so that his comments appear on screen. For every suggested change, you can accept or reject the revisions by right-clicking while pausing the mouse over the comment.

Despite the failure of many large dot-com start-ups, a surprising number of small web start-ups, called mini-dots, are surviving by sticking to niches they know well and using Net resources, from e-mail to customer-sharing arrangements. According to Aron Benon, founder of Florist.com, "Today, the Internet is what the telephone was when it was invented—a way to further our reach."

A **videoconference** is an interactive meeting between two or more people using video linkups at two or more sites. The audio and video signals that transmit the live voices and images may be transmitted through telephone lines, direct cable connections, microwave, or satellite. Videoconferencing has grown tremendously in recent years, spurred by the increasing cost of travel, more affordable transmission rates, and the advent of more effective hardware. As with other distant technologies, however, participants may miss some nonverbal cues and may prefer the personal chemistry that develops more easily in face-to-face meetings. Also, some users are uncomfortable in front of a camera and worry about how they look, act, and sound. These self-conscious feelings are likely to diminish, however, as managers become more familiar with the medium and develop more experience in conducting business this way.

Using a small webcam, you can hold your own videoconference directly from your computer.

Personal one-on-one videoconferencing is becoming popular as people take advantage of the advent of inexpensive personal webcameras attached to personal computers. This technology allows two people to conduct an on-the-spot videoconference using nothing more than their personal computers and Internet hookup.

Follow these guidelines when conducting a teleconference or videoconference:

- Plan ahead. Prepare a detailed agenda and follow it.

- Involve all participants frequently during the call. Try to avoid having most conference participants in a single room and only one or two elsewhere.

- Speak normally. There's no need to shout—or to drum your fingers on the table, play with your pen, or make other distracting sounds.

- Be prepared. Provide participants with copies of the agendas, handouts, other visual aids, and the like ahead of time. Follow up with meeting minutes.

- In a teleconference, encourage folks to position themselves near the phone when talking, but avoid noisily sliding the phone around the table. Always address individuals by name to assure their attention, and ask participants to identify themselves before speaking.

- In a videoconference, when you want to speak, introduce yourself; then wait until the camera is focused on you before beginning to speak. (High-end videocameras are able to automatically focus on the person speaking.)

- Prepare any graphics with video in mind. Wait until the camera focuses on your visual aid before discussing it, and make sure that your visual aids are simple, with readable fonts.

- Avoid sudden movements. Current technology cannot handle as many frames per second in videoconferences as television can. Maintain a quiet posture, avoid moving around unnecessarily, and limit unnecessary gestures. Rely more on your voice than your hands.

> ## *word*wise
>
> **REQUIRED READING**
>
> Actual book titles published within the past ten years, according to *Bookseller* magazine.
>
> - *The Flat-Footed Flies of Europe*
> - *Fancy Coffins to Make Yourself*
> - *Tea Bag Folding*
> - *The Art and Craft of Pounding Flowers*
> - *Lightweight Sandwich Construction*

A Word of Caution

As we have seen, our need for up-to-date and accurate information is insatiable, and technology helps satisfy this need. One downside of this technology is a fragmenting of society as our number of shared experiences diminishes in the resulting glut of information. Says David Shenk, author of *Data Smog, Surviving the Information Glut*[8]:

> Technically, we possess an unprecedented amount of information; however, what is commonly known has dwindled to a smaller and smaller percentage every year. This should be a sobering realization for a democratic nation, a society that must share information in order to remain a union.

Also, according to historian Daniel Boorstin, "Every advance in the history of communications has brought us in closer touch with people far away from us, but at the expense of insulating us from those nearest to us."[9]

Competent communicators use technology to full advantage to accomplish their communication goals but are mindful of the need for shared personal interactions as well. In short, they practice both high-tech *and* high-touch communication.

EVALUATING THE QUALITY OF INTERNET DATA

Problem

Assume the role of Jean Tate, director of human resources at Urban Systems. You are concerned that one of the data-entry operators at your company has been diagnosed with carpal tunnel syndrome, a neuromuscular disorder of the tendons and tissue in the wrists caused by repeated hand motions. As illustrated in Spotlight 10 on pages 106–109, you have been researching the possibility of purchasing speech-recognition software for data-entry operators so that they can dictate their data into a microphone and have it automatically appear on the computer screen, without the need for keyboarding.

You have decided to field-test two speech-recognition programs and to purchase a high-quality microphone (better than the generic headset included with the software packages). To start your research, you have visited the Internet once again and identified the three sites shown in the accompanying figures. Now you need to evaluate the quality of the information contained in these sites to see whether the information can be used to help you make a decision.

Company Home Page

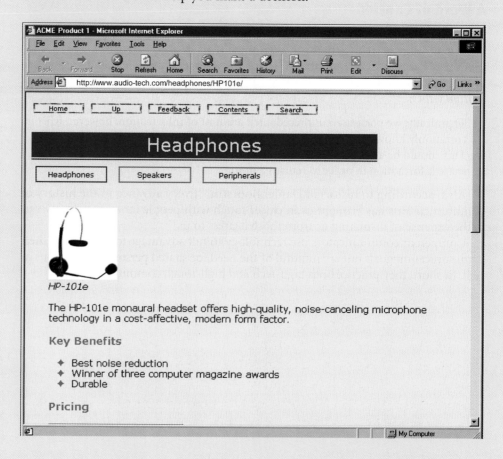

118

Newsgroup Message

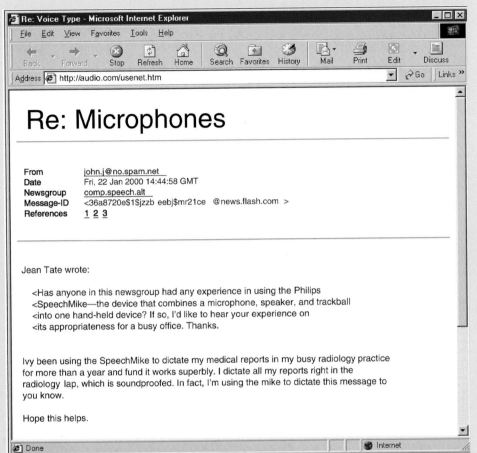

Personal Home Page

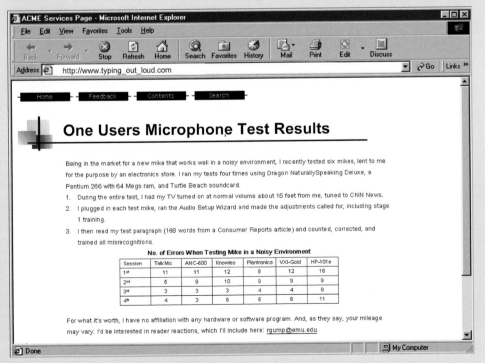

Process

1. Using the guidelines discussed in Checklist 3 on page 110, evaluate the strengths and weaknesses of the home page of Audio-Tech, a retailer of audio equipment.

   - It is clear who sponsors the site.
   - The content is free from most grammar and usage errors (note, however, the misspelling of the word *effective* in the first paragraph).
   - Because the company is trying to sell its products, the data is probably up to date.
   - The site is well designed and easy to read and navigate.
   - No evidence is presented to back up the claims of "best noise reduction" and "durable."
   - The site provides no links to verify the magazine awards received by the product.

2. Evaluate the strengths and weaknesses of the newsgroup message.

   - From the header information, it is easy to identify the sponsor of the site and the date of the message.
   - The writer copied enough (and only enough) of the original message to place his comments in perspective.
   - Although the information probably represents the writer's objective thinking, it is irrelevant for us because our intended use is in a busy (and noisy) business office.
   - The message is full of errors—presumably caused by the speech-recognition software and microphone being used to record the message (which actually contradicts the writer's written message).

3. Evaluate the strengths and weaknesses of the personal home page.

   - The site is well designed and easy to read and navigate.
   - Although not shown on the screen capture, the site clearly identifies the sponsor, date of the last update, and contact information.
   - The content is free from most grammar and usage errors (note, however, the missing apostrophe in the word *users* in the title).
   - The content provides specific and helpful details about the test conditions and the results obtained.
   - The last paragraph lends credibility to the test results.
   - The content doesn't indicate when the test was conducted; thus I don't know whether the hardware and software used are the latest versions.

Product

After conducting my preliminary investigation, I have decided not to purchase either product. The HP-101e microphone was the least accurate of the six mikes tested, and our data-entry operators who have carpal tunnel syndrome may be uncomfortable using a handheld mike for long periods of data entry. I'll continue researching the issue before making a purchase decision.

Visit the **BusCom Online Learning Center** (http://college.hmco.com) for additional resources to help you with this course and with your future career.

■ Summary

co1. Identify the major sources of electronic information.

Our need for information is insatiable and unrelenting. Much of the information we need can be located on an as-needed basis from electronic sources—including CD-ROMs and online information services. Increasingly, however, we are turning to the discussion and reference resources of the Internet and tapping into the massive amount of information located in its networked computers around the world. Mailing lists and newsgroups are discussion resources on the Internet that allow you to participate in interactive, ongoing discussions on a particular topic. Reference resources on the Internet include the World Wide Web, which contains pages of text, graphics, sound, and video, with hyperlinks that enable the reader to instantly jump to related topics.

co2. Browse and search the World Wide Web.

Electronic information can be located by using directories for browsing the Internet and indexes for searching for specific information. Use directories when the information you are seeking can be easily classified; otherwise, use one (or more) of the search engines. Use logical search operators (such as AND, OR, NOT, and NEAR) and phrases to make your search more efficient and productive.

co3. Evaluate the quality of the electronic data you gather.

Because the quality of the information on the Internet varies tremendously, you should seriously evaluate the information you receive before deciding whether to use it. Evaluate all information in terms of the authority of the writer and sponsoring organization and the accuracy, objectivity, and currentness of the content.

co4. Share electronic information.

Today, e-mail is the preferred medium of communicating in business. Competent communicators ensure that they use appropriate formats (especially a descriptive subject line) and content for their e-mail messages. They also make appropriate use of other emerging technologies, including groupware, teleconferencing, and videoconferencing.

■ See Slide 3.9.

■ Consider treating this list as an end-of-chapter exercise for students to define and give an example of each term.

■ Key Terms

You should now be able to define the following terms in your own words and give an original example of each.

electronic database (99)   newsgroup (102)

groupware (111)   teleconference (113)

Internet (99)   videoconference (116)

mailing list (101)   World Wide Web (102)

■ Exercises

1 **The 3Ps (Problem, Process, and Product) Model: Communication Applications at Texas Instruments**   Thinking about how to harness Internet technology to give customers the best possible service keeps Scott Roller busy. He and his colleagues at Texas Instruments use e-mail constantly and find it especially valuable for staying in contact with their counterparts overseas. As an experienced user of the Internet, Roller is well aware of the need to evaluate downloaded information before he relies on it for any decisions or refers to it in internal documents and messages.

Problem

Assume that you are starting a summer internship with Texas Instruments. Your first assignment is to look for online sources of information about the projected growth in Internet usage during the next few years. This information will be used to help estimate the increased visitor volume that the company might expect on its TI.com website so that Roller can plan for additional networking equipment and personnel. Search the Internet for two or three credible sources of this information and then prepare to draft an e-mail message telling Roller the results of your search.

■ Suggestions and sample solutions for exercises appear in the *Instructor's Resource Manual.*

Process

a. Why do you need to check the credibility of your Internet sources before drafting your message to Roller?
b. Will you use discussion resources or reference resources (or both) in your search? Why?
c. What sources do you find when you conduct the search, and how do you know these sources are credible?
d. What do you need to tell Roller about each source you have located?

Product

Write a descriptive subject line for your e-mail message and list the main points you will make in this message.

2 Technology in Business   Working with a classmate, interview two to four businesspeople. Ask them about the role technology plays in their business operations. Summarize your findings and e-mail the results to your instructor. Find answers to the following questions:

CO1. Identify the major sources of electronic information.

a. What kind of technologies do they routinely use on the job?
b. How has technology impacted their job?
c. What do they enjoy most about using technology?
d. What do they dislike about technology?
e. How often do they use technology?
f. What technology do they use the most?
g. What advantages or disadvantages do they see regarding their use of technology?
h. Has technology made them more effective in the workplace, or has it just made it faster to get things done?

3 The Invisible Web   Much information stored on the Web cannot be identified through normal search engines. The reason is that such information is stored in databases that cannot be accessed directly or is stored in a format (such as Adobe's PDF files) that cannot be indexed by Web crawlers. Using your favorite search engine, do a search for "invisible web" (don't forget the quotation marks), and study some of the sources you identify. Based on your research, what strategies can you use to access this "invisible" information? Try out some of them and analyze their effectiveness. Create an example of a research problem where you would not be successful using traditional search engines, and then explain step-by-step how you were able to access this information using some of the strategies you've uncovered. Write up your findings in a one- or two-page double-spaced report.

CO2. Browse and search the World Wide Web.

4 **Communication Technology**   Select which communication technology, if any, would be best for delivering messages in the following situations, and explain why.

a. A departmental meeting will be held on Friday at 2 p.m. in the conference room.
b. A worker needs to be notified that he or she is going to be laid off.
c. Plant managers located throughout North America need to be trained on a new operation.
d. A salesperson needs to ask a potential customer in the same city about meeting for lunch to discuss a new product.
e. A salesperson needs to get a contract signed by his or her supervisor and returned quickly.
f. The CEO needs to let all employees know some major changes in the company's dress code
g. The vice president is traveling to Mongolia in February and needs to know what the weather will be like.
h. The marketing manager wants to let all of his or her customers throughout the United States know about an upcoming sale.

5 **Searching the Internet**   Recall the six situations on page 98 that require the collection of information. Locate and download at least one article on the Internet that would help you answer each question. Then prepare a short report to your instructor describing how you collected your data—for example, the search sites you used, the keywords you used, and the amount of information you found. Include a photocopy of each Internet article as an appendix to your report.

6 **Locating Specific Information**   You have been asked to determine the feasibility of opening a frozen yogurt store in Greenville, North Carolina. Answer the following questions, using the latest figures available. Provide a citation for each source.

a. What were the number of establishments and the total sales last year for TCBY, a frozen yogurt franchise?
b. What is the population of Greenville, North Carolina? What percentage of this population is between the ages of 18 and 24?
c. What is the per capita income of residents of Greenville?
d. What is the name and address of the president of TCBY, a frozen yogurt franchise?
e. What is the climate of Greenville, North Carolina?
f. How many students are enrolled at East Carolina University?
g. What is the market outlook for frozen yogurt stores nationwide?
h. What is the most current journal or newspaper article you can find on this topic?

7 Who uses the Internet?   Although Internet usage has become commonplace in the business world, finding credible sources for tracking who is using the Internet—and how—can be difficult. Visit the Cyberatlas site (**http://cyberatlas .internet.com**) and follow the link to the Big Picture. Examine some of the statistics describing trends in Web traffic, e-mail usage, and Web shopping. What sources are cited for these statistics? Select one of the sources and evaluate its quality using the questions in Checklist 3 on page 110. Based on your analysis, do you consider this source to be authoritative, accurate, objective, and current? Be prepared to explain and support your evaluation during a class discussion.

8 The Quality of Internet Resources   Select two Internet resources and evaluate them based on the four criteria—authority, accuracy, objectivity, and currentness—from Checklist 3 on page 110. Submit copies of the resources and a brief summary of their quality to your instructor.

CO3. Evaluate the quality of the electronic data you gather.

9 Questionable Internet Resources   Pick a business-related topic. Do research for the topic on the Internet using the four basic search operators—AND, OR, NOT, and NEAR. Try to find misinformation regarding the topic. Make a copy of the questionable information and discuss why you believe the information is unreliable.

10 Effective E-mail Practices   Evaluate the following e-mail message in terms of the guidelines provided in Checklist 4 (see page 112). Specifically, what would you change to make it more effective? Should this message have been sent as an e-mail message in the first place? Discuss.

CO4. Share electronic information.

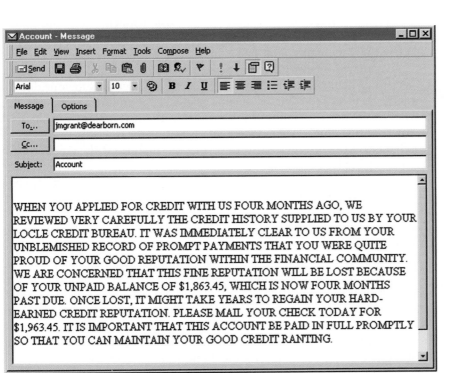

■ See Slide 3.10.

■ Did your students catch the misspelling of the last word in the body?

11 **Revising an E-mail Message**   Revise the e-mail message shown on page 125, following the e-mail guidelines in Checklist 4 on page 112. List at the bottom of your message the specific practices of effective e-mails that you were able to follow in your communication.

12 **The Downside of Technology**   As noted above in the section entitled "A Word of Caution," historian Daniel Boorstin believes that "every advance in the history of communications has brought us in closer touch with people far away from us, but at the expense of insulating us from those nearest to us." Explain what this means and give some evidence in support of this statement in a classroom discussion.

■ See Slide 3.11.

13 **Teleconferencing**   Your instructor will divide you into teams with three members. Hold a short team meeting with this brief agenda: introduce yourselves (if necessary), exchange phone numbers and e-mail addresses, elect a team leader, and decide on a convenient time to have a conference call. The purpose of the conference call is to (a) discuss any disadvantages you can identify of using the Web and (b) agree on the three most serious disadvantages of Web use. You will then assign each team member to write a one-half-page discussion of one of the three factors. Do *not* discuss the project at all during your brief team meeting. All discussions will be held during the teleconference and, later, using e-mail. The team leader will place the conference call, tape-record the call, and lead the discussion.

■ See Slide 3.12.

14 **Revising a Team Document Electronically**   Send your one-half-page discussion (see Exercise 13) as an e-mail attachment to your other two team members. When you receive their drafts, open the attachments in a word processing program, turn on Track Changes, make whatever changes you feel would improve the documents, and then e-mail them back to the appropriate writers. Copy yourself on every e-mail you send and print out the copy when you receive it. When you receive your team members' revisions to your document, merge their revised copies with your original copy and make whatever changes you feel are needed. Continue this process, with the team leader in charge, until you have one unified team document discussing the three disadvantages of our reliance on the Internet. Submit to your instructor: (a) the tape recording of your conference call, along with the short report you prepared as a result of the call; and (b) the final team report, including copies of all e-mail messages as an appendix to the report.

15 **Videoconferencing—Long-Distance Diagnosis**   Dr. Pamela Prescott, assistant professor of internal medicine and endocrinology at UC Davis Medical Center in Sacramento, California, has asked you to sit in on a videoconference in which she will examine an older patient located 70 miles away from the Center. UC Davis is on the cutting edge of a trend toward videoconference consultations in which medical specialists like Dr. Prescott talk with and view patients and medical personnel in outlying facilities. You are a communication expert advising UC Davis on how to make such videoconferences more productive while remaining sensitive to a patient's needs and concerns.

As the videoconference proceeds, you learn that the patient's thyroid gland was removed 18 months ago. Dr. Prescott tells her elderly patient that, based on laboratory tests, she suspects that cancer is still present in an adjacent area. You notice that the patient's face flushes with color and she becomes more fidgety after hearing the news. After the videoconference, Prescott admits that breaking bad news is easier if she is in the same room with the patient, not miles away.

Now you have to step back and think about the communication aspects of medical videoconferences. Draft a list of the benefits and limitations of medical videoconferencing. For each limitation, identify one or two possible solutions. Write a memo about your views and ways to overcome the limitations. Alternatively, if your instructor prefers, prepare a two-minute presentation summarizing your ideas. Source: Based on information in Kathy Robertson, "Tele-Doc," *Sacramento Business Journal*, December 4, 2000, http://sacramento.bcentral.com/sacramento/stories/2000/12/04/focus1.html.

continuing
case 3

Internet Scavenger Hunt

Well, they had their little meeting about extending the no-smoking policy (see Continuing Case 2, page 93). Not surprisingly, Dave ended the meeting by asking Diana and Marc to submit memos outlining their arguments for and against a smoking ban at Urban Systems.

Diana and Marc both had the same idea—jump on the Internet and locate some good sources. As a starting point, Diana thought that the American Cancer Society would probably have some useful information if she could figure out how to reach that organization. Marc expected that the tobacco companies might provide some support; he also had heard about a tobacco research institute sponsored by the tobacco companies. Both assumed they'd be able to find articles, editorials, or research studies to give them the ammunition they needed to persuade Dave.

■ A suggested solution to the continuing case can be found in the *Instructor's Resource Manual*.

Written Communication Projects

1. Locate at least two newsgroup articles to support Diana's position and two to support Marc's position.

2. Locate at least three World Wide Web articles to support each position.

3. Locate a mailing address and phone number for the American Cancer Society.

Marc searches the Internet to locate credible evidence to support his position.

Critical Thinking

4. Evaluate each resource you located in terms of the criteria provided in Checklist 3 on page 110. Would you be confident using data from all of the sources in your memo to your boss? Why or why not?

5. Judging from just the electronic information you've uncovered, which of the two sides do you think has the stronger argument? Why?

LABtest 3

■ See Slide 3.13.

■ See Slide 3.14.

Retype the following e-mail message from Dave, correcting any grammar errors according to the rules introduced in LAB 4 on page 591.

Urban Systems ~~have~~ *has (AGR—CO NAME)* just introduced *WiteLite,* an ultraviolet filtered, full-spectrum light source that combats Seasonal Affective Disorder (SAD), a type of depression caused by the decrease of daylight during the fall and winter months. Marc Kaplan

5   of Urban Systems announced the new product yesterday and disclosed that the disorder affects ~~himself~~ *him (CASE—REF)* and ten million other Americans.

The winter months can leave people starving for daylight. With just ten hours of sunlight possible each day for residents in the northern half of the ~~country. The~~ *country, the (FRAG)* darkness can become overwhelming

10   for some ~~people, it~~ *people. It (RUN-ON)* can drive them to clinical depression.

The symptoms of the disorder ~~isn't~~ all that different from *aren't (AGR—INT WD)*

clinical depression, except that they are seasonal. Although

depression is the ~~more~~ serious symptom, other symptoms include *most (MOD)*

lethargy, a desire to sleep longer, diminished libido, seasonal

15 weight gain, social withdrawal, mood changes, and anxiety.

A possible symptom students might suffer is a severe change in

their grades during winter months. If a student ~~was~~ to flunk ~~their~~ *were (AGR—MOOD)*   *his or her (AGR—GEN)*

classes in winter when ~~they normally get~~ high grades at other times *he or she normally gets (AGR—GEN)*

of the year, SAD may be playing a part. Students, in fact, are the

20 type of sufferers ~~whom~~ are least likely to seek treatment. *who (CASE—NOM)*

The main treatment for the disorder is straightforward. Either

light therapy or more hours of direct sunlight ~~is~~ needed to *are (AGR—SUB-VB)*

alleviate the symptoms. Experts warn that there ~~is~~ numerous dangers *are (AGR—SUB-EXPL)*

involved in self-diagnosis. None of the serious symptoms ~~is~~ likely *are (AGR—PRO)*

25 to be treated successfully without professional help. Mr. Kaplan

indicated that questions about *WiteLite* can be addressed to

Urban Systems or to ~~he~~ directly at 313-555-6080. *him (CASE—OBJ)*

■ See Slide 3.15.

■ See Slide 3.16.

■ See Slide 3.17.

■ See Handout 3.3.

4

Writing with Style: Individual Elements

communication
OBJECTIVES

After you have finished this chapter, you should be able to

1. Write clearly.

2. Prefer short, simple words.

3. Write with vigor.

4. Write concisely.

5. Prefer positive language.

6. Use a variety of sentence types.

7. Use active and passive voice appropriately.

No matter who manages to stay in the ring—or who lands outside—Gary Davis uses positive language to describe the situation. He is vice president of corporate communications for World Wrestling Entertainment (WWE), which arranges more than 300 professional wrestling events every year in the United States, Europe, Asia, and Australia. Wrestling fans follow the action through the WWE's popular *SmackDown!* and *Raw* television programs and its magazines, videos, and DVDs. Davis's role is to communicate with a diverse international audience of media representatives, investors, advertisers, business partners, government officials, and community groups.

Most of the written messages Davis sends are business letters, full-length news releases, and news alerts—brief e-mail messages about a particular issue or development. On occasion, he prepares special oral or video presentations for specific external audiences. Whether drafting a routine announcement or explaining the company's response to an unexpected problem, the WWE executive emphasizes that "the key is to write as if the glass is half full. If you do that, your message will come out positive." To make his meaning clear, Davis is especially careful to avoid overusing negative words and to eliminate double negatives. "Someone might write something like 'He did not think it would not work,'" he says, "when the real meaning is, 'He thought it would work.'"

Another way Davis helps audiences grasp his meaning is by writing simply and concisely. "Although it is very easy to overwrite, to say too much, to be too flowery, this

an insider's perspective

GARY DAVIS
Vice President of
Corporate Communications,
World Wrestling
Entertainment (Stamford, CT)

obscures what you're trying to say," he notes. "From a business communication stand-point, less is more." Once he has developed a sentence or paragraph that concisely and accurately makes a certain point, he reuses this language, customized as appropri-ate, when writing about that topic in future messages.

Demonstrating the power of concrete, positive language in the service of an impor-tant ideal, Davis recently wrote a letter showcasing the SmackDown Your Vote! initiative, supported by the WWE and a dozen partner groups. The let-ter, released to the me-dia, quoted WWE stars talking about registering young voters and encour-aging them to become poll workers. "We wanted to create a document that would put our wrestlers in front of the public in a different light," says Davis. "This letter is as much about the impor-tance of the message as it is about the fact that our talent and our company are associated with putting this to-gether." The result: hundreds of thousands of young voters are becoming involved in the election process—and the WWE is enhancing its credibility with key audiences.

"From a business communication standpoint, less is more."

■ See the Reference Manual at the end of the text for a review of Language Arts Basics (LAB):
1. Parts of speech
2. Commas
3. Other punctuation
4. Grammar
5. Mechanics
6. Correct word usage

■ A chapter overview appears in the *Instructor's Resource Manual.*

Your writing can be error-free and still lack style, but it cannot have style unless it is error-free.

Style refers to the effectiveness of the words, sentences, paragraphs, and overall tone of your message.

■ What Do We Mean by *Style*?

If you study the six LAB (Language Arts Basics) exercises in the Reference Manual at the end of this book, you will know how to express yourself *correctly* in most business writing situations; that is, you will know how to avoid major errors in grammar, spelling, punctuation, and word usage. But a technically correct message may still not achieve its objective. For example, consider the following paragraph:

NOT: During the preceding year just past, Oxford Industries operated at a financial deficit. It closed three plants. It laid off many employees. The company's president was recently named Iowa Small Business Executive of the Year. Oxford is now endeavoring to ascertain the causes of its financial exigency. The company president said that . . .

This paragraph has no grammatical, mechanical, or usage errors. But it is not clear, vigorous, or coherent. For example:

■ Consider the phrase "preceding year just past." *Preceding* means "just past," so why use both terms?

■ In the second sentence, was closing the three plants the *cause* or the *result* of the financial deficit?

■ What is the point of the sentence about the president?

■ If you were speaking instead of writing, would you really say "endeavoring to ascertain," or would you use simpler language, like "trying to find out"?

■ Finally, there are no transitions, or bridges, between the sentences; as a result, they don't flow smoothly.

Although the paragraph is technically correct, it lacks **style.** By style, we mean the way in which an idea is expressed (not its *substance*). Style consists of the particular words the writer uses and the manner in which those words are combined into sentences, paragraphs, and complete messages.

Now compare the first-draft paragraph above with this revised version:

BUT: Last year Oxford Industries lost money and, as a result, closed three plants and laid off 200 employees. Now the company is trying to determine the causes of its problems. In an explanation to stockholders, Oxford's president, who was recently named Iowa Small Business Executive of the Year, said that . . .

The revised version is more direct and readable. It clarifies relationships among the sentences. It uses concise, familiar language. It presents ideas in logical order. In short, it has *style.* Chapters 4 and 5 discuss the principles of effective writing style for business, illustrated in Figure 4.1. Apply these principles of style as you write the letters, memos, e-mails, and reports that are assigned in later chapters.

While writing the first draft of a message, you should be more concerned with content than with style. Your major objective should be to get your ideas down in some form, without worrying about style and mechanics. (**Mechanics** are elements

Writing with style:
Individual elements

- Write clearly.
- Prefer short, simple words.
- Write with vigor.
- Write concisely.
- Prefer positive language.
- Use a variety of sentence types.
- Use active and passive voice appropriately.

4.1

■ See Slide 4.1.

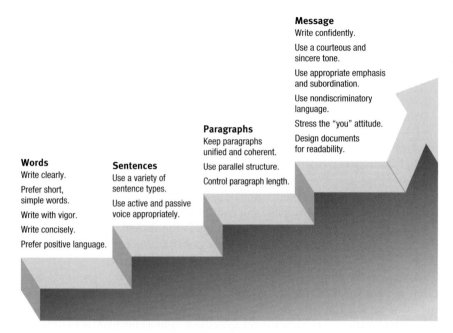

Message
Write confidently.

Use a courteous and
sincere tone.

Use appropriate emphasis
and subordination.

Use nondiscriminatory
language.

Stress the "you" attitude.

Design documents
for readability.

Paragraphs
Keep paragraphs
unified and coherent.

Use parallel structure.

Control paragraph length.

Sentences
Use a variety of
sentence types.

Use active and passive
voice appropriately.

Words
Write clearly.

Prefer short,
simple words.

Write with vigor.

Write concisely.

Prefer positive language.

figure 4.1
**Steps to an Effective
Writing Style**

in communication that show up only in written form, including spelling, punctuation, abbreviations, capitalization, number expression, and word division.)

The more familiar you are with basic stylistic principles, the easier it will be to write your first draft and the less editing you will need to do later. So studying these principles first makes your writing process more efficient. You will then return to these principles when revising your writing to make sure that you have followed each guideline.

Mechanics refers to how an idea is expressed in writing.

■ Choosing the Right Words

Individual words are our basic units of writing, the bricks with which we build meaningful messages. All writers have access to the same words. The care with which we select and combine words can make the difference between a message that achieves its objective and one that does not. Discussed below are five principles of word choice to help you write more effectively.

Clarity

The basic guideline for writing, the one that must be present for the other principles to have meaning, is to write clearly—to write messages the reader can understand, depend on, and act on. You can achieve clarity by making your message accurate, by using familiar words, and by avoiding dangling expressions and unnecessary jargon.

co1. **Write clearly.**

Be Accurate   A writer's credibility is perhaps his or her most important asset, and credibility depends greatly on the accuracy of the message. If by carelessness, lack of preparation, or a desire to manipulate, a writer misleads the reader, the damage is immediate and long-lasting. A reader who has been fooled once may not trust the writer again.

Accuracy is the most important attribute in business writing. It involves more than freedom from errors.

■ "When I use a word, it means just what I choose it to mean—neither more nor less."—Humpty Dumpty in Lewis Carroll's *Through the Looking Glass.*

Accuracy can take many forms. The most basic is the truthful presentation of facts and figures. But accuracy involves much more. For example, consider the following sentence from a memo to a firm's financial backers:

> The executive committee of Mitchell Financial Services met on Thursday, May 28, to determine how to resolve the distribution fiasco.

Suppose, on checking, the reader learns that May 28 fell on a Wednesday this year—not on a Thursday. Immediately, the reader may suspect everything else in the message. The reader's thinking might be, "If the writer made this error that I *did* catch, how many errors that I *didn't* catch are lurking there?"

Now consider more subtle shades of truth. The sentence implies that the committee met, perhaps in an emergency session, for the *sole* purpose of resolving the distribution fiasco. But suppose this matter was only one of five agenda items being discussed at a regularly scheduled meeting. Is the statement still accurate? Suppose the actual agenda listed the topic as "Discussion of Recent Distribution Problems." Is *fiasco* the same as *problems*?

Ethical communicators make sure the overall tone of their message is accurate.

The accuracy of a message, then, depends on what is said, how it is said, and what is left unsaid. Competent writers assess the ethical dimensions of their writing and use integrity, fairness, and good judgment to make sure their communication is ethical. Closely related to accuracy is completeness. A message that lacks important information may create inaccurate impressions. A message is complete when it contains all the information the reader needs—no more and no less—to react appropriately.

As a start, answer the five Ws: Tell the reader *who, what, when, where,* and *why.* Leaving out any of this information may result either in decisions based on incomplete information or in extra follow-up correspondence to gather the needed information.

Use language that you and your reader understand.

Use Familiar Words Your message must be understood before someone can act on it. So you must use words that are both familiar to you (so that you will not misuse the word) and familiar to your readers.

Marilyn vos Savant (identified by the *Guinness Book of World Records* as the smartest person alive) once asked her readers what the following paragraph meant:

> When promulgating your esoteric cogitations or articulating your superficial sentimentalities and amicable philosophical and psychological observations, beware of platitudinous ponderosity. Let your verbal evaporations have lucidity, intelligibility, and veracious vivacity without rodomontade or thespian bombast. Sedulously avoid all polysyllabic profundity, pompous propensity, and sophomoric vacuity.[1]

Her translation: Don't use big words!

A true story illustrates this point. A young soldier, serving in Vietnam as a typist for a general, received a report he thought the general should see. Believing that "for your edification" meant "for your information" (it actually means "for your *improvement*"), the typist wrote "Sir: For your edification" on the report and sent it to the general. Back came the general's reply: "Private: First, look up the word *edification.* Then see me for *your* edification!"

Don't assume that only long words cause confusion. Consider the following sentences:

NOT: Rejecting *ruth*, the candidate would *limn* about how he *fain* would be the *birr* to *moil* for the *ruck* if the nation's *weal* were ensured.

BUT: Rejecting pity, the candidate would describe how he gladly would be the driving
force to work hard for the great masses if
the nation's prosperity were ensured.

The seven short italicized words in the first version
would probably be understandable only to a crossword
puzzle addict (or a speller at the National Spelling Bee,
from whose website the words came). Most readers,
however, would understand the second version.

Long words are sometimes useful in business communication, of course, and should be used when appropriate. The larger your vocabulary and the more
you know about your reader, the better equipped you
will be to choose and use correctly those words that
are familiar to your reader.

EVER WONDER?   *word* **wise**

Why *phonetic* isn't spelled the way it is pronounced?
Why *abbreviated* is such a long word?
Why doctors call what they do *practice*?
Why the person who invests all your money is called a
broker?
Why the time of day with the slowest traffic is called
rush hour?
Why, if flying is so safe, they call the airport the
terminal?

Avoid Dangling Expressions   A **dangling expression** is any part of a sentence
that doesn't logically fit in with the rest of the sentence. Its relationship with the
other parts of the sentence is unclear; it *dangles.* The two most common types of
dangling expressions are misplaced modifiers and unclear antecedents.

To correct dangling expressions, (1) make the subject of the sentence the doer
of the action expressed in the introductory clause; (2) move the expression closer
to the word that it modifies; (3) make sure that the specific word to which a pronoun refers (its *antecedent*) is clear; or (4) otherwise revise the sentence.

NOT: After reading the proposal, a few problems occurred to me. *(As written,
the sentence implies that "a few problems" read the proposal.)*

BUT: After reading the proposal, I noted a few problems.

NOT: Dr. Ellis gave a presentation on the use of drugs in our auditorium. *(Are
drugs being used in the auditorium?)*

BUT: Dr. Ellis gave a presentation in our auditorium on the use of drugs.

NOT: Robin explained the proposal to Joy, but she was not happy with it.
(Who was not happy—Robin or Joy?)

BUT: Robin explained the proposal to Joy, but Joy was not happy with it.

■ Gary Blake and Robert W.
Bly, in *The Elements of
Business Writing,* point out
the need for clarity in writing.
Read the following sentence:
"It is advisable to purchase
stocks when their prices are
depressed and to sell them at
the top of the market." Now
compare it to: "Buy low and
sell high."—Bernard Baruch.

OBER Avoid dangling expressions.

• Abraham Lincoln wrote the Gettysburg Address
  while traveling to Gettysburg on the back of an
  envelope.
• I had been driving for about 40 years when I fell
  asleep at the wheel and had an accident.
• Two cars were reported stolen by the Groveton
  police yesterday.
• "Dr. Ruth to talk about sex with newspaper
  editors."

4.2

■ See Slide 4.2.

Avoid Unnecessary Jargon   Jargon is technical vocabulary used within a special
group. Every field has its own specialized words, and jargon offers a precise and efficient way of communicating with people in the same field. But problems arise
when jargon is used to communicate with someone who does not understand it.
For example, to a banker the term CD means a "certificate of deposit," but to a
stereo buff or computer user it means a "compact disc." Even familiar words can be
confusing when given a specialized meaning.

Does the field of business communication have jargon? It does—just look at the
Key Terms list at the end of each chapter. The word *jargon* itself might be considered communication jargon. In this text, such terms are first defined and then
used to make communication precise and efficient. Competent writers use specialized vocabulary to communicate with specialists who understand it. And they avoid
using it when their readers are not specialists.

*Jargon is sometimes
appropriate and sometimes
inappropriate.*

DILBERT

Short, Simple Words

CO2. Prefer short, simple words.

■ See Handout 4.1, page 1.

■ See Handout 4.1, page 2.

More than 70 percent of the words in Lincoln's Gettysburg Address (190 out of 267) are only one syllable long.

Short and simple words are more likely to be understood, less likely to be misused, and less likely to distract the reader. Literary authors often write to *impress;* they select words to achieve a specific reader reaction, such as amusement, excitement, or anger. Business writers, on the other hand, write to *express;* they want to achieve *comprehension.* They want their readers to focus on their information, not on how they convey their information. Using short, simple words helps achieve this goal.

> **NOT:** To recapitulate, our utilization of adulterated water precipitated the interminable delays.

> **BUT:** In short, our use of impure water caused the endless delays.

It is true, of course, that often no short, simple word is available to convey the precise shade of meaning you want. For example, there is no one-syllable replacement for *ethnocentrism* (the belief that one's own cultural group is superior), a concept introduced in Chapter 2. Our guideline is not to use *only* short and simple words but to *prefer* short and simple words. (As Mark Twain, who was paid by the word for his writing, noted, "I never write *metropolis* for seven cents because I can get the same price for *city.* I never write *policeman* because I can get the same money for *cop.*")

One analysis of more than 2,500 actual documents typed in industry found that more than half of all word occurrences in these documents contained four or fewer characters and just one syllable. As shown in Communication Snapshot 4, the average word used in business writing contains five characters.[2]

Here are some examples of needlessly long words, gleaned from various business documents, with their preferred shorter substitutes shown in parentheses:

ascertain (learn)	indispensable (vital)	substantial (large)
endeavor (try)	initiate (start)	termination (end)
enumerate (list)	modification (change)	utilization (use)
fluctuate (vary)	recapitulate (review)	

You need not strike these long words totally from your written or spoken vocabulary; any one of these words, used in a clear sentence, would be acceptable. The problem is that a writer may tend to fill his or her writing with very long words when simpler ones could be used. Use long words in moderation.

You've probably heard the advice "Write as you speak." Although not universally true, such advice is pretty close to the mark. Of course, if your conversation is peppered with redundancies, jargon, and clichés, you would not want to put such weaknesses on paper. But typical conversation uses mostly short, simple words—

the kind you *do* want to put on paper. Don't assume that the bigger the words, the bigger the intellect. In fact, you need a large vocabulary and a well-developed word sense to select the best word. And more often than not, that word is short and simple. Write to express—not to impress.

> *Write to express—not to impress.*

Vigor in Writing

Vigorous language is specific and concrete. Limp language is filled with clichés, slang, and buzz words. Vigorous writing holds your reader's interest. But if your reader isn't even interested enough to read your message, your writing can't possibly achieve its objective. A second reason for writing with vigor has to do with language itself. Vigorous writing lends vigor to the ideas presented. A good idea looks even better dressed in vigorous language, and a weak idea looks even weaker dressed in limp language.

CO3. Write with vigor.

■ See Slide 4.3.

Use Specific, Concrete Language   In Chapter 1, we discussed the communication barriers caused by overabstraction and ambiguity. When possible, choose *specific* words—words that have a definite, unambiguous meaning. Likewise, choose *concrete* words—words that bring a definite picture to your reader's mind.

■ See Slide 4.4.

NOT: The vehicle broke down several times recently.

BUT: The delivery van broke down three times last week.

In the first version, what does the reader imagine when he or she reads the word *vehicle*—a golf cart? automobile? boat? space shuttle? Likewise, how many times is *several*—two? three? fifteen? What is *recently*? The revised version tells precisely what happened.

Sometimes we do not need such specific information. For example, in "The president answered *several* questions from the audience and then adjourned the meeting," the specific number of questions is probably not important. But in most business situations, you should watch out for words like *several, recently, a number of, substantial, a few,* and *a lot of.* You may need to be more exact.

Likewise, use the most concrete word that is appropriate; give the reader a specific mental picture of what you mean. That is, learn to talk in pictures:

NOT: The vice president was bored by the presentation.

BUT: The vice president kept yawning and looking at her watch.

Bored is an abstract concept. "Yawning and looking at her watch" paints a vivid picture.

Be sure that your terms convey as much meaning as the reader needs to react appropriately. Watch out for terms like *emotional meeting* (anger or gratitude?), *bright color* (red or yellow?), *new equipment* (postage meter or cash register?), and *change in price* (increase or decrease?).

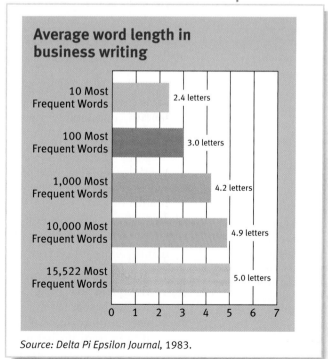

communication snapshot **4**

Average word length in business writing

10 Most Frequent Words	2.4 letters
100 Most Frequent Words	3.0 letters
1,000 Most Frequent Words	4.2 letters
10,000 Most Frequent Words	4.9 letters
15,522 Most Frequent Words	5.0 letters

Source: Delta Pi Epsilon Journal, 1983.

Nowhere is the use of specific, concrete language more important than in personal ads and job applications. Craig Newmark, shown here, runs a website, Craigslist, where twenty- and thirty-somethings search for jobs, homes, and love. The list has become so popular that a movie, *24 Hours on Craigslist.org,* has been made about the 23,000 San Francisco residents who post their ads on the list.

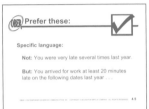

■ See Slide 4.5.

■ See Slide 4.6.

Concrete words present a vivid picture.

Businesses realize the value of using specific, concrete language that paints a picture. You should, too.

Avoid Clichés, Slang, and Buzz Words   A **cliché** is an expression that has become monotonous through overuse. It lacks freshness and originality and may also send the unintended message that the writer couldn't be bothered to choose language geared specifically to the reader.

NOT: Enclosed please find an application form that you should return at your earliest convenience.

BUT: Please return the enclosed application form before May 15.

Picture a person finding "thank you for your recent letter" in all 15 letters he or she reads that day. How sincere and original does it sound?

Here are some examples of other expressions that have become overused (even in other countries; see Spotlight 12, "Same Rules the World Over," on page 139) and that therefore sound trite and boring. Avoid them in your writing.

According to our records	It goes without saying that
Company policy requires	Needless to say
Do not hesitate to	Our records indicate that
For your information	Please be advised that
If I can be of further help	Take this opportunity to
If you have any other questions	Under separate cover

spotlight12
ACROSS CULTURES

Same Rules the World Over

The strategies for writing effective business messages discussed in this chapter are universal. The passage below, from a business communication text for Chinese business executives, recommends substituting concise phrases for long, empty ones.[3]

"简洁"是有客观标准的。虽然西方国家的作者之间在怎样用词才算"简洁"方面还是有争论的，不过他们的一些看法还是有一定参考价值的。现把他们所做的某些词句的"不简洁"与"简洁"的比较列在下面供参考：

不 简 洁   **简 洁**

Wordy	Concise	Wordy	Concise
enclosed herewith	enclosed	under separate cover	separately
enclosed you will find	enclosed is	a long period of time	a long time
please be advised that	(four wasted words)	continuous and uninterrupted	continuous (or: uninterrupted)
please don't hesitate to call upon us	please write us	during the year of 1971	during 1971
please feel free to write	please write	endorse on the back of this check	endorse this check
prior to	before		
this is to advise you	(five wasted words)	for a price of $300	for $300

As noted earlier, slang is an expression, often short-lived, that is identified with a specific group of people. If you understand each word in an expression but still don't understand what it means in context, chances are you're having trouble with a slang expression. For example, read the following sentence:

It turns my stomach the way you can break your neck and beat your brains out around here, and they still stab you in the back.

To anyone unfamiliar with American slang (a nonnative speaker, perhaps), this sentence might seem to be about the body because it refers to the stomach, neck, brains, and back. The real meaning, of course, is something like this:

I am really upset that this company ignores hard work and loyalty when making personnel decisions.

Avoid slang in most business writing, for several reasons. First, it is informal, and much business writing, although not formal, is still *businesslike* and calls for standard word usage. Second, slang is short-lived. A slang phrase used today may not be in use—and thus may not be familiar—in three years, when your letter is retrieved from the files for reference. Third, slang is identified with a specific group of people, and others in the general population may not understand the intended meaning. For these reasons, avoid terms like these in most business writing:

can of worms	knock it off	security blanket
chew out	once-over	use your noodle
go for broke	pay through the nose	wiped out
hate one's guts	play up to	zonked out

■ For an extended discussion of international issues, see "Communicating in a Diverse Environment" in Chapter 2, pages 52–64.

■ The Lord's Prayer contains 66 words and the Gettysburg Address contains 267 words, but a recent government regulation on the sale of cabbage contains 26,911 words. (*National Review*, January 1996, p. 81.).

Clichés and buzz words go in and out of style too quickly to serve as effective components of written business communication.

A **buzz word** is an important-sounding expression used mainly to impress other people. Because buzz words are so often used by government officials and high-ranking businesspeople—people whose comments are "newsworthy"—these expressions get much media attention. They become instant clichés and then go out of fashion just as quickly. At either end of their short life span, they cause communication problems. If an expression is currently being used by everyone, it sounds monotonous, lacking originality. If it is no longer being used by anyone, readers may not understand the intended meaning. Here are examples of recent "in" expressions:

action plan	multitasking	pushing the envelope
bandwidth	on the same page	repurposing
bottom line	out of the loop	value-added
heads up	paradigm	
mission-critical	proactive	

Be especially careful of turning nouns and other types of words into verbs by adding *-ize*. Such words as *agendize, prioritize, strategize, unionize,* and *operationalize* quickly become tiresome.

Conciseness

CO4. Write concisely.

Businesspeople are busy people. The information revolution has created more paperwork, giving businesspeople access to more data. Having more data to analyze (but presumably not being able to read any faster or having more time in which to do so), managers want information presented in the fewest possible words. To achieve conciseness, make every word count. Avoid redundancy, wordy expressions, hidden verbs and nouns, and other "space-eaters."

■ A university creative writing class was asked to write a concise essay containing these elements: (a) religion, (b) royalty, (c) sex, and (d) mystery. The winning essay read: "My God," said the Queen, "I'm pregnant. I wonder who the father is!"

Avoid Redundancy　　A **redundancy** is the unnecessary repetition of an idea that has already been expressed or intimated. Eliminating the repetition contributes to conciseness.

■ See Slide 4.7.

> **NOT:**　Signing both copies of the lease is a necessary requirement.
>
> **BUT:**　Signing both copies of the lease is necessary.

> **NOT:**　Combine the ingredients together.
>
> **BUT:**　Combine the ingredients.

Redundancy and repetition are not the same.

A *requirement* is by definition *necessary,* so only one of the words is needed. And to *combine* means to bring *together,* so using both words is redundant. Don't confuse redundancy and repetition. Repetition—using the same word more than once—is occasionally effective for emphasis (as we will discuss in the next chapter). Redundancy, however, serves no purpose and should always be avoided.

Some redundancies are humorous, as in the classic Samuel Goldwyn comment, "Anybody who goes to a psychiatrist ought to have his head examined," or the sign in a jewelry store window, "Ears pierced while you wait." Most redundancies, however, are simply *verbiage*—excess words that consume time and space. Avoid them. (See Figure 4.2.)

Make every word count.

Do not use the unnecessary word *together* after such words as *assemble, combine, cooperate, gather, join, merge,* or *mix.* Do not use the unnecessary word *new* before

figure4.2

Avoid Unnecessary Words

new beginner	assemble together	connect up
new discovery	combine together	divide up
new fad	cooperate together	eat up
new innovation	gather together	lift up
new progress	mix together	rest up

such words as *beginner, discovery, fad, innovation,* or *progress.* And do not use the unnecessary word *up* after such words as *connect, divide, eat, lift, mix,* and *rest.* Also avoid the following common redundancies (use the words in parentheses instead):

advance planning (planning)
any and all (any *or* all)
basic fundamentals (basics *or* fundamentals)
repeat again (repeat)
over again (over)
past history (history)
plan ahead (plan)

but nevertheless (but *or* nevertheless)
each and every (each *or* every)
free gift (gift)
sum total (sum *or* total)
true facts (facts)
when and if (when *or* if)

Another type of redundancy to avoid is needlessly adding a noun to an abbreviation that already stands for that noun. For example, you should not write *ATM machine* because ATM stands for "automated teller machine." Similarly, avoid *PIN number, SALT talks, HIV virus, OPEC countries,* and *RSVP requested.*

Avoid Wordy Expressions   Although wordy expressions are not necessarily writing errors (as redundancies are), they do slow the pace of the communication and should be avoided. For example, try substituting one word for a phrase whenever possible.

NOT: In view of the fact that the model failed twice during the time that we tested it, we are at this point in time searching for other options.

BUT: Because the model failed twice when we tested it, we are now searching for other options.

The original sentence contains 28 words; the revised sentence, 16. You've "saved" 12 words. In his delightful book, *Revising Business Prose,* Richard Lanham speaks of the "lard factor": the percentage of words saved by "getting rid of the lard" in a sentence. In this case,

$$28 - 16 = 12; 12 \div 28 = 43 \text{ percent}$$

Thus, 43 percent of the original sentence was "lard," which fattened the sentence without providing any "nutrition." Lanham suggests, "Think of a lard factor (LF) of ⅓ to ½ as normal and don't stop revising until you've removed it."[4]

Here are examples of other wordy phrases and their preferred one-word substitutes in parentheses:

are of the opinion that (believe)
due to the fact that (because)
for the purpose of (for *or* to)
in order to (to)

in the event that (if)
pertaining to (about)
with regard to (about)

■ See Slide 4.8.

Use the fewest number of words that will achieve your objective.

■ Thomas Jefferson once observed that "the most valuable of all talents is that of never using two words when one will do."

■ See Slide 4.9.

Changing verbs to nouns produces weak, uninteresting sentences.

Avoid Hidden Verbs and Subjects   A hidden verb is a verb that has been changed into a noun form, thereby weakening the action. Verbs are *action* words and should convey the main action in the sentence. They provide interest and forward movement. Consider this example:

NOT: Carl made an announcement that he will give consideration to our request.

BUT: Carl announced that he will consider our request.

What is the real action? It is not that Carl *made* something or that he will *give* something. The real action is hiding in the nouns: Carl *announced* and will *consider*. These two verb forms, then, should be the main verbs in the sentence. Notice that the revised sentence is much more direct—and four words shorter (LF = 33 percent). Here are some other actions that should be conveyed by verbs instead of being hidden in nouns:

arrived at the conclusion (concluded)	has a requirement for (requires)
came to an agreement (agreed)	held a meeting (met)
gave a demonstration of (demonstrated)	made a payment (paid)
performed an analysis of (analyzed)	gave an explanation (explained)

■ See Slide 4.10.

A pronoun in an expletive does not stand for any noun.

Like verbs, subjects play a prominent role in a sentence and should stand out, rather than being obscured by an expletive beginning. An **expletive** is an expression such as *there is* or *it is* that begins a clause or sentence and for which the pronoun has no antecedent. Because the topic of a sentence beginning with an expletive is not immediately clear, you should use such sentences sparingly in business writing. Avoiding expletives also contributes to conciseness.

NOT: There was no indication that it is necessary to include John in the meeting.

BUT: No one indicated that John should be included in the meeting.

Imply or Condense   Sometimes you do not need to explicitly state certain information; you can imply it instead. In other situations, you can use adjectives and adverbs instead of clauses to convey the needed information in a more concise format.

NOT: We have received your recent letter and are happy to provide the data you requested.

BUT: We are happy to provide the data you recently requested.

NOT: This brochure, which is available free of charge, will answer your questions.

■ See Handout 4.2.

BUT: This free brochure will answer your questions.

Positive Language

co5. Prefer positive language.

Words that create a positive image are more likely to help you achieve your objective than are negative words. For example, you are more likely to persuade someone to do as you ask if you stress the advantages of doing so rather than the disadvantages of not doing so. Positive language also builds goodwill for you and your organization and often gives more information than negative language. Note the differences in tone and amount of information given in the following pairs of sentences:

NOT: The briefcase is not made of cheap imitation leather.

BUT: The briefcase is made of 100 percent belt leather for years of durable service.

NOT: We cannot ship your merchandise until we receive your check.

BUT: As soon as we receive your check, we will ship your merchandise.

NOT: I do not yet have any work experience.

BUT: My two terms as secretary of the Management Club taught me the importance of accurate recordkeeping and gave me experience in working as part of a team.

■ See Slide 4.11.

Expressions like *cannot* and *will not* are not the only ones that convey negative messages. Other words, like *mistake, damage, failure, refuse,* and *deny,* also carry negative connotations and should be avoided when possible.

Avoid negative-sounding words.

NOT: Failure to follow the directions may cause the blender to malfunction.

BUT: Following the directions will ensure many years of carefree service from your blender.

NOT: We apologize for this error.

BUT: We appreciate your calling this matter to our attention.

NOT: We close at 7 p.m. on Fridays.

BUT: We're open until 7 p.m. on Fridays to give you time to shop after work.

■ Negative language also often has the opposite effect of that which is intended. As an example, tell students, "Do not think of elephants." What does everyone think of?

When you're given only 15 minutes to convince venture capitalists to invest $8 million in your small start-up high-tech company, you must make sure every single word of your presentation counts. Krishna Subramanian, CEO of Kovair, was successful in her presentation to 300 investors at a Silicon Valley forum.

The subjunctive mood sounds more hopeful than an outright refusal.

Sometimes you can avoid negative language by switching to the subjunctive mood, which uses words like *wish, if,* and *would* to refer to conditions that are impossible or improbable. Such language softens the impact of the negative message, making it more palatable to the reader. Here are two examples:

NOT: I cannot speak at your November meeting.

BUT: I wish it were possible for me to speak at your November meeting.

NOT: I cannot release the names of our clients.

BUT: Releasing the names of our clients would violate their right to privacy.

In short, stress what *is* true and what *can* be done rather than what is not true and what cannot be done. This is not to say that negative language has no place in business writing. Negative language is strong and emphatic, and sometimes you will want to use it. But unless the situation clearly calls for negative language, you are more likely to achieve your objective and to build goodwill for yourself and your organization by stressing the positive.

Because words are the building blocks for your message, choose them with care. Using short, simple words; writing with clarity, vigor, and conciseness; and using positive language will help you construct effective sentences and paragraphs. If you are one of the many students learning business communication for whom English is a second language, see Spotlight 13, "So You're an ESL Speaker," on page 145.

■ See Slide 4.12.

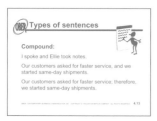

■ See Slide 4.13.

CO6. Use a variety of sentence types.

Use a simple sentence for emphasis and variety.

■ Writing Effective Sentences

A sentence has a subject and predicate and expresses at least one complete thought. Beyond these attributes, however, sentences vary widely in style, length, and effect. They are also very flexible; writers can move sentence parts around, add and delete information, and substitute words to express different ideas and emphasize different points. To build effective sentences, use a variety of sentence types, and use active and passive voice appropriately.

Types of Sentence

There are four basic sentence types—simple, compound, complex, and compound-complex—all of which are appropriate for business writing.

Simple Sentence   A **simple sentence** contains one independent clause (that is, a clause that can stand alone as a complete thought). Because it presents a single idea and is usually short, a simple sentence is often used for emphasis. Although a simple sentence contains only one independent clause, it may have a compound subject or compound verb (or both). All of the following sentences are simple.

I quit.

Individual Retirement Accounts are a safe option.

Both Individual Retirement Accounts and Simplified Employee Pension Plans are safe and convenient options as retirement investments for the entrepreneur.

spotlight13
ACROSS CULTURES

So You're an ESL Speaker

If English is your second language, speak up! One of the best ways to become proficient in English—or any other language that is not your native tongue—is to practice by speaking it as often as possible. Take advantage of the many opportunities you'll have during this business communication course to engage in conversation with your classmates and the instructor and to make oral presentations. As you practice, speak slowly, enunciate each word clearly and distinctly, and pay attention to your phrasing for proper emphasis.

During this course, you'll also be able to improve your English by reading the book and other written materials, by working on written assignments, and by listening to native English speakers in class. When you're reading and encounter an unfamiliar word, first try to determine its meaning from the context. Then you can confirm your guess by checking the definition in a good ESL dictionary, such as *English as a Second Language Dictionary*.

When you're writing an assignment, take time to study the samples in the text. What words are used in the samples of proper usage? How long are the sentences, and how are they combined to form paragraphs? How do the samples of proper usage differ from the samples of poor usage? These contrasts can help you avoid common mistakes as you become more proficient in English.

Always proofread your written work carefully and, as a final check, ask a native English speaker to read it and point out any errors so that you can correct them before submitting your assignment.

When you're speaking with a classmate who uses an English word that you don't know, politely ask about the word's meaning. This exercise is a good way to enlarge your vocabulary while learning about contemporary usage. Whenever possible, look for opportunities to interact with students who are native English speakers by participating in class discussions and personal conversations, joining a school club or another student activity, or organizing a study group. You'll learn English more quickly if you hear it spoken by native speakers and practice formulating a response in formal and informal settings.

Some schools offer additional support to their ESL students, so ask whether your school has any ESL programs or can provide a tutor for one-on-one assistance with assignments.

Don't be discouraged if you read, write, or speak English slowly at first. As your comprehension improves, you'll be able to increase your speed and communicate with less effort. Meanwhile, be sure to recognize and celebrate even your smallest gains—because small steps forward, over time, can add up to giant leaps in learning.[5]

Compound Sentence   A **compound sentence** contains two or more independent clauses. Because each clause presents a complete idea, each idea receives *equal* emphasis. (If the two ideas are not closely related, they should be presented in two separate sentences.) Here are three compound sentences:

> Stacey listened, but I nodded.

> Morris Technologies made a major acquisition last year, and it turned out to be a disaster.

> Westmoreland Mines moved its headquarters to Prescott in 1984; however, it stayed there only five years and then moved back to Globe.

Use a compound sentence to show coordinate (equal) relationships.

Complex Sentence   A **complex sentence** contains one independent clause and at least one dependent clause. For example, in the first sentence below, "The scanner will save valuable input time" is an independent clause because it makes sense by itself. "Although it cost $235" is a dependent clause because it does not make sense by itself.

Use a complex sentence to express subordinate relationships.

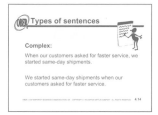

■ See Slide 4.14.

■ See Slide 4.15.

Although it cost $235, the scanner will save valuable input time.

George Bosley, who is the new CEO at Hubbell, made the decision.

I will be moving to Austin when I assume my new position.

The dependent clause provides additional, but *subordinate,* information related to the independent clause.

Compound-Complex Sentence   A **compound-complex sentence** contains *two or more* independent clauses and *one or more* dependent clauses.

I wanted to write the report myself, but I soon realized that I needed the advice of our legal department. *(two independent clauses and one dependent clause)*

If I can, I'll do it; if I cannot, I'll ask Sheila to do it. *(two independent clauses and two dependent clauses)*

Sentence Variety   Using a variety of sentence patterns and sentence lengths helps keep your writing interesting. Note how simplistic and choppy too many short sentences can be and how boring and difficult too many long sentences can be.

Too Choppy:

Golden Nugget will not purchase the Claridge Hotel. The hotel is 60 years old. The asking price was $110 million. It was not considered too high. Golden Nugget had wanted some commitments from New Jersey regulators. The regulators were unwilling to provide such commitments. Some observers believe the refusal was not the real reason for the decision. They blame the weak Atlantic City economy for the cancellation. Golden Nugget purchased the Stake House in Las Vegas in 2000. It lost money on that purchase. It does not want to repeat its mistake in Atlantic City.
(Average sentence length = 8 words)

Too Difficult:

Golden Nugget will not purchase the Claridge Hotel, which is 60 years old, for an asking price of $110 million, which was not considered too high, because the company had wanted some commitments from New Jersey regulators, and the regulators were unwilling to provide such commitments. Some observers believe the refusal was not the real reason for the decision but rather that the weak Atlantic City economy was responsible for the cancellation; and since Golden Nugget purchased the Stake House in Las Vegas in 2000 and lost money on that purchase, it does not want to repeat its mistake in Atlantic City.
(Average sentence length = 50 words)

Use a variety of sentence patterns and lengths.

The sentences in these paragraphs should be revised to show relationships between ideas more clearly, to keep readers interested, and to improve readability. Use simple sentences for emphasis and variety, compound sentences for coordinate (equal) relationships, and complex sentences for subordinate relationships.

More Variety:

Golden Nugget will not purchase the 60-year-old Claridge Hotel, even though the $110 million asking price was not considered too high. The company had wanted some commitments from New Jersey regulators, which the regulators were unwilling to provide. However, some observers blame the cancellation on the weak Atlantic City economy. Golden Nugget lost money on its 2000 purchase of the Stake House in Las Vegas, and it does not want to repeat its mistake in Atlantic City. *(Average sentence length 5–20 words)*

The first two sentences in the revision are complex, the third sentence is simple, and the last sentence is compound. The lengths of the four sentences range from 12 to 27 words. To write effective sentences, use different sentence patterns and lengths. Most sentences in good business writing range from 16 to 22 words.

Active and Passive Voice

Voice is the aspect of a verb that shows whether the subject of the sentence acts or is acted on. In the **active voice**, the subject *performs* the action expressed by the verb. In the **passive voice**, the subject *receives* the action expressed by the verb.

CO7. Use active and passive voice appropriately.

ACTIVE:	Best Buy offers a full refund on all orders.
PASSIVE:	A full refund on all orders is offered by Best Buy.
ACTIVE:	Shoemacher & Doerr audited the books in 2005.
PASSIVE:	The books were audited in 2005 by Shoemacher & Doerr.

Passive sentences add some form of the verb *to be* to the main verb, so passive sentences are always somewhat longer than active sentences. In the first set of sentences just given, for example, compare *offers* in the active sentence with *is offered by* in the passive sentence.

In active sentences, the subject is the doer of the action; in passive sentences, the subject is the receiver of the action. And because the subject gets more emphasis than other nouns in a sentence, active sentences emphasize the doer, and passive sentences emphasize the receiver, of the action. In the second set of sentences, either version could be considered correct, depending on whether the writer wanted to emphasize *Shoemacher & Doerr* or *the books*.

Use active sentences most of the time in business writing, just as you naturally use active sentences in most of your conversations. Note that verb *voice* (active or passive) has nothing to do with verb *tense*, which shows the time of the action. As the following sentences show, the action in both active and passive sentences can occur in the past, present, or future.

■ See Slide 4.16.

In active sentences, the subject performs the action; in passive sentences, the subject receives the action.

NOT:	A very logical argument was presented by Hal. *(Passive voice, past tense)*
BUT:	Hal presented a very logical argument. *(Active voice, past tense)*
NOT:	An 18 percent increase will be reported by the eastern region. *(Passive voice, future tense)*
BUT:	The eastern region will report an 18 percent increase. *(Active voice, future tense)*

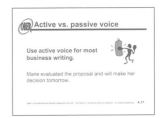

■ See Slide 4.17.

Passive sentences are generally more effective than active sentences for conveying negative information.

Passive sentences are most appropriate when you want to emphasize the *receiver* of the action, when the person doing the action is either unknown or unimportant, or when you want to be tactful in conveying negative information. All the following sentences are appropriately stated in the passive voice:

> Protective legislation was blamed for the drop in imports. *(Emphasizes the receiver of the action)*

> Transportation to the construction site will be provided. *(The doer of the action not important)*

> Several complaints have been received regarding the new policy. *(Tactfully conveys negative news)*

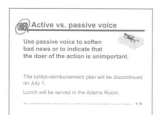

See Slide 4.18.

 A S K **Ober**

Dear Dr. Ober:

I am currently a student at Baker College and am very interested in a business mentioned often in your text. I would like some further information on Urban Systems and an address and phone number where I would be able to reach them. Do they have a website?

—Michelle

Dear Michelle:

Urban Systems is a completely fictional company that I "created" to illustrate important business communication concepts. It is, however, a composite of the many small companies I've consulted with over the past 25 years, and the situations depicted in the case problems are all typical of those encountered in small companies operating in the contemporary business environment. The people in the photographs that accompany these end-of-chapter case studies are just actors.

—Scot

E-mail your questions and comments to askober@ober.net.

Words, sentences, and paragraphs are all building blocks of communication. You have seen how using a variety of sentence types and using active and passive voice appropriately can help make your sentences more effective. In the next chapter, we will combine these sentences to form logical paragraphs and complete messages.

WRITING A CONCISE MESSAGE

You are Lyn Poe, administrative assistant for the Office and Information Systems Department at Midstate College. You have drafted the following announcement that you intend to post to the university computer network bulletin board (the line numbers are shown for editing purposes only). You now wish to make the announcement as concise as possible—not only to make it more effective but also to have it take up less space (bandwidth) on the computer network.

Administrative Professionals Workshop Scheduled for April 21

Wednesday, April 22, is Administrative Professionals Day, which is a	1
part of the larger observance that is known as Administrative Professionals	2
Week®, which spans April 19–25. Businesses have observed Administrative	3
Professionals Week® or its predecessor annually since 1952 to recognize secre-	4
taries and other administrative professionals, upon whose skills, loyalty, and	5
efficiency the functions of business and government offices depend.	6
In keeping with this occasion, the Office and Information Systems	7
Department of Midstate College makes an announcement of its 11th	8
Annual Administrative Professionals Workshop on Tuesday, April 21,	9
between 8:30 a.m. and 3 p.m. at the New Theatre Restaurant in	10
downtown Portland.	11
Dr. Lee Stafford will begin our workshop by speaking on "How to	12
Manage Conflict, Criticism, and Anger." Stafford motivates and educates	13
people to be the best they can be, but nevertheless he likes to have a	14
good time doing it. His humor-filled presentations are packed with	15
practical information that promotes positive change. He is a licensed	16
psychologist, holds a Ph.D. in motivation, and has more than 30 years of	17
experience in speaking, consulting, and training.	18
Conflict is a hard thing to like. However, whether it involves a	19
client with an overdue bill or an office quarrel with a coworker,	20
conflict is an integral part of the working world. Stafford helps his	21
clients learn that there is value to conflict. He will make a	22
presentation of techniques to handle and give criticism without	23
offense, deal with anger, and respond to hostility from others.	24
Stafford's second presentation is "Life on the High Wire: Balancing	25
Work, Family, and Play." Society has raised the ante on what it takes	26
to be a "normal" human being. There are ever-increasing demands to be,	27
do, and own more and more. Today, for the first time in our history, we	28
talk openly about burnout. Stafford will hold a discussion of the	29
successful balancing of work, family, and play.	30
Our closing session will feature Tom Graves, a professional magician	31
for more than 20 years. Graves was first influenced by watching various	32

33 magicians and ventriloquists on the *Ed Sullivan Show*. He will give a
34 demonstration of puppetry, mental telepathy, expert close-up magic,
35 comedy, juggling, and balloon-animal sculpture. It would appear that
36 Graves's talents are the most unique in the world. Drawings for free
37 gifts will be held following his performance.
38   There is a cost for this all-day workshop in the amount of $125 per
39 participant. For registration or more information, call 555-7821 or
40 visit our website at www.workshop.msc.edu.

Process

1. The fourth guideline in this chapter discusses four techniques for writing more concisely. Review your draft. Do you have any redundant phrases that can be eliminated?

   Oops! I see two redundancies: In line 36 I'll change "most unique" to "unique" and in lines 36–37 I'll change "free gifts" to "gifts."

2. Does your document contain any wordy expressions?

   Yes—and I can simply delete both: "It would appear that" in line 35 and "in the amount" in line 38.

3. How about hidden verbs?

   Ouch!—four of them. Here's what I'll do:

   ■ Line 8: Shorten "makes an announcement of" to "announces."
   ■ Lines 22–23: Shorten "make a presentation of" to "present."
   ■ Line 29: Shorten "hold a discussion of" to "discuss."
   ■ Lines 33–34: Shorten "give a demonstration of" to "demonstrate."

4. Any hidden nouns?

   Actually, my draft contains two hidden nouns, but I want to change only one: In line 38, I'll change "There is a cost for this all-day workshop" to "This all-day workshop costs." In line 27, I want to keep "There are ever-increasing demands to." It sounds natural, and because the announcement contains no other expletive beginnings, I think it's okay.

5. Now reread the draft to see if you can shorten other phrases either by implying them instead of stating them outright or by condensing them.

   The very first sentence contains two—"which is" and "that is"; and I can simply omit both of them.

Product   Here is the final version of the announcement, which, incidentally, contains 32 fewer words, making it more concise—and more economical.

**ADMINISTRATIVE PROFESSIONALS WORKSHOP
SCHEDULED FOR APRIL 21**

Wednesday, April 22, is Administrative Professionals Day, part of the larger observance known as Administrative Professionals Week®, which spans April 19–25.

Businesses and secretaries have observed this week annually since 1952 to recognize the secretary and other administrative professionals, upon whose skills, loyalty, and efficiency the functions of business and government offices depend.

In keeping with this occasion, the Office and Information Systems Department of Midstate College announces its 11th Annual Administrative Professionals Workshop on Tuesday, April 21, between 8:30 a.m. and 3 p.m. at the New Theatre Restaurant in downtown Portland.

Dr. Lee Stafford will begin our workshop by speaking on "How to Manage Conflict, Criticism, and Anger." Stafford motivates and educates people to be the best they can be, and he likes to have a good time doing it. His humor-filled presentations are packed with practical information that promotes positive change. He is a licensed psychologist, holds a Ph.D. in motivation, and has more than 30 years of experience in speaking, consulting, and training.

Conflict is a hard thing to like. However, whether it involves a client with an overdue bill or an office quarrel with a coworker, conflict is an integral part of the working world. Stafford helps his clients learn that there is value to conflict.

He will present techniques to handle and give criticism without offense, deal with anger, and respond to hostility from others.

Stafford's second presentation is "Life on the High Wire: Balancing Work, Family, and Play." Society has raised the ante on what it takes to be a "normal" human being. There are ever-increasing demands to be, do, and own more and more. Today, for the first time in our history, we talk openly about burnout. Stafford will discuss the successful balancing of work, family, and play.

Our closing session will feature Tom Graves, a professional magician for more than 20 years. Graves was first influenced by watching various magicians and ventriloquists on the *Ed Sullivan Show.* He will demonstrate puppetry, mental telepathy, expert close-up magic, comedy, juggling, and balloon-animal sculpture. Graves's talents are unique. Drawings for gifts will be held following his performance.

The total cost for this all-day workshop is $125 per participant. For registration or to receive more information, call 555-7821 or visit our website at www.workshop.msc.edu.

Visit the **BusCom Online Learning Center (http://college.hmco.com)** for additional resources to help you with this course and with your future career.

■ Summary

Achieve clarity by making your message accurate, by using familiar words, and by avoiding dangling expressions and unnecessary jargon.

Write to express—not to impress. Short, simple words are more likely to be understood, less likely to be misused, and less likely to distract the reader. Prefer longer words only if they express your idea more clearly.

Use specific, concrete language and avoid clichés, slang, and buzz words. Be especially careful of turning nouns and other types of words into verbs by adding *-ize* (such as *operationalize* or *strategize*).

To achieve conciseness, make every word count. Avoid redundancy, wordy expressions, hidden verbs and subjects, and other "space-eaters." Sometimes it is not necessary to explicitly state certain information; instead, it can be implied. In other situations, the use of adjectives or adverbs instead of clauses can convey the needed information in a more concise format.

Stress what is true and what can be done rather than what is not true or what cannot be done. Words that create a positive image are more likely to help you achieve your communication objective than will negative words.

Because it presents a single idea and is usually short, prefer simple sentences for emphasis. Prefer compound sentences to communicate two or more ideas of equal importance. When communicating two or more ideas of unequal importance, prefer complex sentences and place the subordinate idea in the dependent clause. A compound-complex sentence contains two or more independent clauses and one or more dependent clauses.

Use active voice to emphasize the doer of the action and passive voice to emphasize the receiver of the action.

co1. Write clearly.

co2. Prefer short, simple words.

co3. Write with vigor.

co4. Write concisely.

co5. Prefer positive language.

co6. Use a variety of sentence types.

co7. Use active and passive voice appropriately.

■ Key Terms

You should be able to define the following terms in your own words and give an original example of each.

active voice (147)

buzz word (140)

cliché (138)

complex sentence (145)

compound-complex sentence (146)

compound sentence (145)

dangling expression (135)

expletive (142)

mechanics (132)

passive voice (147)

redundancy (140)

simple sentence (144)

style (132)

■ See Slide 4.19.

■ Consider treating this list as an end-of-chapter exercise for students to define and give an example of each term.

■ Exercises

■ Suggestions and sample solutions for exercises appear in the *Instructor's Resource Manual*.

1 **The 3Ps (Problem, Process, and Product) Model: Communication Applications at World Wrestling Entertainment**   Gary Davis makes every word count as he writes letters, news releases, and e-mail news alerts for a diverse international audience. He also develops oral and video presentations to keep external audiences updated about certain issues. Knowing that some of his messages reach many thousands of people, Davis uses simple, positive, and concise wording to clarify his meaning.

Problem

Imagine that you are helping Davis write a news release announcing a special series of appearances supporting the SmackDown Your Vote! program. Several World Wrestling Entertainment stars will be traveling to five college campuses to encourage voter registration among students who are at least 18 years old. This news release will be sent to the five campus newspapers as well as to newspapers and radio stations in the surrounding towns. Think about how you can use words, sentences, and paragraphs to explain the program, publicize these appearances, and encourage student attendance.

Process

a. What do you want to accomplish with this news release?
b. Who are your primary and secondary audiences?
c. What should you know about these audiences before you start to write?
d. Would you use any negative language in this news release? Why or why not?
e. Would you use any passive voice in this news release? Why or why not?

Product

Write a concise headline for this news release and identify three specific points you should include in the body.

CO1. Write clearly.

2 **Clear Writing**   Rewrite the following message to make sure it uses familiar words, avoids dangling expressions, and avoids unnecessary jargon. Add details as needed to make the message complete.

A family plans carefully, invests cautiously, and spends wisely; then suddenly it faces pecuniary disaster because the old man is hospitalized by an out-of-the-blue illness. As a patron of Valley Insurance Company, this supplemental hospital protection is indispensable for your family's welfare. Not only will the new-fangled Group Hospital Supplement Insurance Plan help them meet their needs, but it is also as plain as the nose on your face that it is affordable as well.

As one of our cherished customers, we guarantee your acceptance. You cannot be turned down. For only pennies a day, you can ensure your financial safekeeping.

3 Jargon   Revise this paragraph to get rid of jargon and to make the passage appropriate for a first-year college student who has never taken a communication or business course.

> Regardless of the medium selected, noise may be encountered after the communication stimulus enters the receiver's filter. Such a problem occurs in both the formal and the informal communication networks. Workers experiencing ethnocentrism may have special problems with language connotations.

4 Dangling Expressions   Revise these sentences to eliminate dangling expressions.

a. As a young child, his father took him on business trips to London and Paris.
b. The Federal Reserve banks maintain excellent relations with the major financial institutions, but they are still not doing as much as they had expected.
c. As a community of business academicians, excellent teaching is our top priority.
d. Driving through Chicago in the fog, the street signs were hard to read.
e. To become law, the senator must sign the bill by the end of the session.
f. Falling from the tree limb, the boy's lip was cut open.
g. Walking down the street, the crowded van drove right by the two children.
h. Trying to close the deal, the bonus offer was presented to the customers.
i. While drilling a hole to bring in the 220 wiring, a crack was created in the wall.
j. After attending the meeting, the minutes were prepared by the secretary.

5 Checking Out Checking Accounts   When Michael Sherman, founder of Sherman Assembly Systems in San Antonio, Texas, learned that one of his employees had been robbed after cashing a paycheck, he became concerned. Sherman Assembly makes electronic cable equipment, and some of its manufacturing employees are former welfare recipients who have little experience with financial institutions. Digging deeper, Sherman learned that many of these employees used check-cashing services on payday because they didn't understand how bank accounts worked. He decided to educate his employees by arranging for a local bank manager to visit the factory, explain how checking accounts work, and help employees fill out applications for special low-minimum-balance accounts.

As Sherman's assistant, you have volunteered to write an announcement about the bank manager's visit, explaining in simple and straightforward terms how employees will benefit from using checking accounts. Follow this chapter's principles of style as you draft this brief memo, making up any details you need to complete this assignment, such as the bank name, the manager's name, and the time and date of the visit.

■ See Slide 4.20.

co2. **Prefer short, simple words.**

6 Simple Language   Revise this paragraph to make it more understandable.

> The consultant demonstrated how our aggregate remuneration might be ameliorated by modifications in our propensities to utilize credit for compensating for services. She also endeavored to ascertain which of our characteristics were analogous to those of other entities for which she had fabricated solutions. She recommended we commence to initiate innumerable modifications in our procedures to increase cash flow, which she considers indispensable for facilitating increased corporate health.

7 Specific and Concrete Words   Revise this paragraph to use more specific, concrete language.

To stimulate sales, Mallmart is lowering prices substantially on its line of consumer items. Sometime soon, it will close most of its stores for several days to provide store personnel time to change prices. Markdowns will range from very little on its line of laundry equipment to a great deal on certain sporting equipment. Mallmart plans to rely on advertising to let people know of these price reductions. In particular, it is considering using a popular television star to publicize the new pricing strategy.

CO3. Write with vigor.

8 Clichés, Slang, and Buzz Words   Make this paragraph more vigorous by eliminating clichés, slang, and buzz words.

At that point in time the corporate brass were under the gun; they decided to bite the bullet and let the chips fall where they may. They hired a head honcho with some street smarts who would be able to interface with the investment community. Financewise, the new top dog couldn't be beat. He was hard as nails and developed a scenario that would have the company back on its feet within six months. Now it was up to the team players to operationalize his plans.

CO4. Write concisely.

9 Conciseness   Revise the following paragraphs to make them more concise.

a. In spite of the fact that Fox Inc. denied wrongdoing, it agreed to a settlement of the patent suit for a price of $6.3 million. Industry sources were surprised at the outcome because of the fact that the original patent had depreciated in value. In addition to the above, Fox also made an agreement to refrain from the manufacture of similar computers for a period of five years in length. It appears that with the exception of Emerson's new introductions, innovations in workstations will be few in number during the next few years.

b. First and foremost, Alan Greenspan is a pragmatist. The favorable advantage of that approach is that he is able to reach a consensus of opinion on most matters. He will announce his latest agreements at a news conference at 3 p.m. in the afternoon.

10 Wordy Expressions   Revise the following sentences to eliminate wordy phrases by substituting a single word wherever possible.

a. Push the red button in the event that you see any smoke rising from the cooking surface.

b. More than 40 percent of the people polled are of the opinion that government spending should be reduced.

c. Please send me more information pertaining to your new line of pesticides.

d. Due to the fact that two of the three highway lanes were closed for repairs, I was nearly 20 minutes late for my appointment.

11 Hidden Verbs   Revise the following sentences to eliminate hidden verbs and convey the appropriate action.

a. After much deliberation, the group came to a decision about how to make a response to the lawsuit.

b. Although Hugh wanted to offer an explanation of his actions, his boss refused to listen.

c. Nationwide Call Systems is performing an analysis of our calling patterns to determine how we can save money on long-distance telephone calls.

12 Hidden Subjects   Rewrite the following sentences to eliminate the hidden subjects.

a. There are four principles of marketing that we need to consider.
b. It is a good time to invest in the stock market.
c. The new manager said it is not his duty to complete the weekly report.
d. There are several new assignments that should be made.
e. It is our intent to complete the project by Friday at 3 p.m.
f. If you are confused about the assignment, there are some diagrams that you should review.
g. It is going to be much better having this procedure in place.
h. There is a possible solution to this problem that we haven't considered.

13 Positive Language   Revise the following paragraph to eliminate negative language.

CO5. **Prefer positive language.**

> We cannot issue a full refund at this time because you did not enclose a receipt or an authorized estimate. I'm sorry that we will have to delay your reimbursement. We are not like those insurance companies that promise you anything but then disappear when you have a claim. When we receive your receipt or estimate, we will not hold up your check. Our refusal to issue reimbursement without proper supporting evidence means that we do not have to charge you outlandish premiums for your automobile insurance.

14 Positive Impressions   Revise the following signs often seen in stores:

a. "No shirt, no shoes, no service."
b. "American Express cards not accepted."
c. "No returns without receipts."
d. "No smoking."
e. "No dogs allowed."

15 Internet Exercise   This chapter emphasized the use of positive, concise language in business messages—but are messages about legislative actions and proposals reported this way? To find out, go to Thomas at http://thomas.loc.gov/, the Library of Congress website that posts information about House and Senate actions and proposals. At the Thomas home page, select "Congressional Record" and then "This Congress, by Date." Follow the "House" link on the most recent issue to the table of contents, then click on the link to the first article. Do you see negative language in this article? If so, in what context is it used? Is the language concise or wordy? Choose one of the paragraphs or items mentioned in this article and rewrite it using positive, concise language.

CO6. Use a variety of sentence types.

16 **Sentence Categories** Identify what type of sentence—simple, compound, complex, or compound-complex—each of the following sentences is. Internal punctuation has been omitted to avoid giving hints.

a. Walking down the street with my sister I saw two men dressed in dark suits running out of the bank.
b. Hillary went to see the new branch manager but the manager had gone to lunch.
c. See the coach and turn in your gear.
d. When you have finished your homework please clean your room.
e. You will have 12 hours to complete the job.
f. Allen had gone to see his brother in Kansas so he was not able to speak at the conference.
g. We will take the test on Monday although you should be ready by Friday.
h. If you want I will call her but if I don't call she will not come.
i. I will try to get the project finished and shipped to you by tomorrow.
j. The fifth order arrives today it should be the last one.

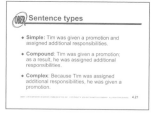

■ See Slide 4.21.

17 **Sentence Types** For each of the following lettered items, write a simple, a compound, and a complex sentence that incorporates both items of information. For the complex sentences, emphasize the first idea in each item.

a. Tim was given a promotion/Tim was assigned additional duties.
b. Eileen is our corporate counsel/Eileen will write the letter on our behalf.

18 **Sentence Variety** Working in groups of three, rewrite the following paragraph by varying sentence types and sentence lengths to keep the writing interesting.

Smartfood was founded by Ann Withey, Andrew Martin, and Ken Meyers in 1984. The product was the first snack food to combine white cheddar cheese and popcorn. Ann Withey perfected the Smartfood recipe in her home kitchen after much trial and error. Smartfood sales were reportedly only $35,000 in 1985. During that time, the product was available only in New England. By 1988, sales had soared to $10 million. This attracted the attention of Frito-Lay. The snack-food giant bought Smartfood in 1989 for $15 million. Since the purchase, Frito-Lay has not tampered with the popular Smartfood formula. It has used its marketing expertise to keep sales growing, despite the growing number of challengers crowding the cheesy popcorn market.[6]

19 **Sentence Length** Write a long sentence (40 to 50 words) that attempts to make sense. Then revise the sentence so that it contains 10 or fewer words. Finally, rewrite the sentence so that it contains 16 to 22 words. Which sentence is the most effective? Why?

20 **Variety in Sentences**   Write a 250-word paper on any topic in Chapter 4 using only simple sentences (one independent clause). Then, rewrite the paper using the same information but using simple, compound, and complex sentences. Explain why you decided to use each type of sentence in the second version. Submit both versions and your explanation to your instructor.

21 **Active and Passive Voice**   For each of the following sentences, first identify whether the sentence is active or passive. Then, if necessary, revise the sentence to use the more effective verb voice.

CO7. **Use active and passive voice appropriately.**

a. We will begin using the new plant in 2005, and the old plant will be converted into a warehouse.
b. A very effective sales letter was written by Paul Mendleson. The letter will be mailed next week.
c. You failed to verify the figures on the quarterly report. As a result, $5,500 was lost by the company.

continuing
case 4

URBAN
SYSTEMS

Stetsky Corrects the Boss

Well, Amy Stetsky opened Dave Kaplan's Microsoft Word document on her computer and prepared to edit the hard copy she had printed. It was the first draft of a speech that Dave had written and e-mailed to her. He was going to deliver the speech next month at a meeting of the Ann Arbor chapter of the Organizational Systems Research Association. Here's what Stetsky read:

■ A suggested solution to the Continuing Case can be found in the *Instructor's Resource Manual*.

Extensive research shows that lighting has a direct affect on worker productivity and job satisfaction. Lighting that is of appropriate quantity and quality provides efficient comfortable illumination and a safe work environment. They also help to develop a feeling of visual comfort and an aesthetically attractive work area. Which increases job satisfaction.

Appropriate lighting makes the task more visible thus increasing both the speed and the accuracy of the work performed. Inadequate amounts of light causes poor workmanship inaccurate work and lowered production. For example one study conducted by the general industrial corporation showed that when illumination was temporarily reduced by no more than five percent the output of word processing operators decreased by twelve percent. In addition the accuracy of all the operators each of who were paid according to the number of correct lines they produced decreased by eight percentage.

An other study at the interstate national bank showed that errors in processing checks decreased by forty percent when lighting was increased. The productivity of the cash register clerks at a large outlet of united food marts was reduced by twenty eight percent when they were forced to work in reduced lighting for three

As she types, Stetsky routinely edits Dave's memos and speeches for style, grammar, and mechanics.

weeks because of store remodeling. According to the researchers they also spoke with several clerks whom complained about headaches and eyestrain and customers whom complained about slow lines and errors in register receipts.

As a result of such vision research forward looking facilities managers human development personnel and labor unions are all beginning to monitor carefully the quality and quantity of illumination by which employees preform their jobs. Farthermore they are looking to technology to bring more flexibility more efficiency and to provide higher quality illumination for the seeing environment. In short they are looking at light in a new light!

Critical Thinking

1. How effective would this speech section be if it were delivered exactly as written?

Writing Project

2. With Dave's permission, Stetsky routinely edits his documents, correcting minor grammar and usage errors. As she edits, she corrects punctuation, capitalization, spelling, and word division. In short, Stetsky is a professional, and her work reflects it. Assuming the role of Stetsky, transcribe the original dictation in double-spaced format (leaving one blank line between each line of type and indenting each paragraph). Make whatever changes are needed to correct errors in grammar, mechanics, punctuation, and usage. (If necessary, refer to the LABs in the Reference Manual at the back of the text.)

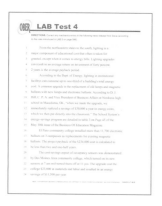

■ See Handout 4.3.

LABtest 4

Retype the following press release from Urban Systems, correcting any mechanical errors (including misspellings) according to the rules introduced in LAB 5 on page 596.

From the northeastern states to the ~~south~~, *South (COMPASS POINT)* lighting is a

major component of educational costs that often is taken for

granted, except when it comes to energy bills. Lighting upgrades

can result in an average return on investment of ~~forty~~ *40 (MEASUREMENT)* percent.

5   ~~2~~ *Two (FIRST WORD OF SENTENCE)* years is the average payback period.

According to the ~~Dept.~~ *Department (SPELLED OUT)* of Energy, lighting in institutional

~~facilitys~~ *facilities (SPELLING)* can consume up to one-third of a building's total energy

cost. A common upgrade is the ~~replacment~~ *replacement (SPELLING)* of old lamps and magnetic

ballasts with new lamps and electronic ballasts. According to D. J.

10   Hill, ~~C. P. A.~~ *CPA (NO PERIODS)* and ~~Vice President of Business Affairs~~ *vice president of business affairs (TITLE AFTER NAME)* at Nordonia

~~high school~~ *High School (PROPER NOUN)* in Macedonia, ~~Oh.~~, *Ohio (SPELL OUT)* "~~when~~ *When (FIRST WORD OF SENTENCE)* we made the upgrade, we

immediately realized a savings of $30,000 a year in energy costs,

which we then put directly into the classroom." The ~~School System's~~ *school system's (COMMON NOUN)*

energy-savings programs are detailed in ~~table 3 on Page 45~~ *Table 3 on page 45 (NOUN PLUS NUMBER)* of the

15   May ~~10th~~ *10 (MONTH PRECEDES DAY)* issue of ~~the Business Of Education Magazine~~. *the Business of Education Magazine (TITLE)*

El Paso ~~community college~~ *Community College (PROPER NOUN)* installed more than 11,700 electronic

ballasts on ~~3~~ ~~campusses~~ *three (BELOW 10) campuses (SPELLING)* as replacements for existing magnetic

ballasts. The projected payback of the $234,000 cost is calculated to

be less than ~~two and one-half~~ *2 1/2 (or 2 ½) (MIXED NUMBER)* years.

20   The cost-savings aspect of occupancy sensors was demonstrated

by Des Moines Area ~~community college~~, *Community College (PROPER NOUN)* which turned on its new

sensors at 7 ~~am~~ *a.m. (MEASUREMENT)* and turned them off at 11 ~~pm~~. *p.m. (MEASUREMENT)* The upgrade cost the

college $23,800 in ~~materiels~~ *materials (SPELLING)* and labor and resulted in an energy

savings of $11,500 per year.

■ See Slide 4.22.

■ See Slide 4.23.

■ See Slide 4.24.

■ See Slide 4.25.

■ See Slide 4.26.

Writing with Style:
Overall Tone and Readability

Written communication is vital in Bobbie Kroman's world. Every day she receives up to 100 e-mail messages in her role as general manager of Barnes & Noble's College Division, overseeing six college bookstores around New York City. She reserves letters for more formal situations, such as officially documenting contracts, proposals, and business negotiations or responding to customer complaints.

Kroman always writes with the reader in mind. "I put myself into the reader's shoes and think, 'If I were getting this message, how would I want to be spoken to? How would I want to be addressed and treated? What would I want to know right away?' I adjust my language, style, and level of sophistication for each reader," she says. When responding to customer complaints, she starts her message with a few conciliatory sentences, even if she believes the complaint is unreasonable. Then she gets to the point, spelling out in detail what she plans to do.

an insider's
perspective

BOBBIE KROMAN
General Manager, College Division, Barnes & Noble
(New York, NY)

She takes particular care with the tone of her e-mails and letters to international business contacts. For example, Kroman used highly formal, courteous language when answering the letters of a Brazilian customer. Because he never used her first name during their 18-month correspondence, she avoided using his first name in the salutation.

When Kroman wants to call attention to an idea, she uses italics and different fonts for emphasis. She also uses shorter paragraphs to make related ideas stand out and subordinates secondary information in parenthetical phrases. When using repetition for emphasis, she says, "I never use the same words twice. I express the idea at the beginning and reiterate, using different language at the end."

Recently Kroman had to write a letter to resolve a six-month dispute with a supplier. First she had a staff member call the supplier to clarify the facts of the situation. Next, she and her staff brainstormed about what Barnes & Noble could do and should do to solve the problem. With this preparation, Kroman sat down and drafted a tactful two-page letter.

Her opening paragraph restated the dispute; her next three paragraphs summarized each side's actions during the previous months. Only in her fourth paragraph did Kroman actually lay out her proposal for resolving the problem, followed by a fifth paragraph suggesting how to clear up several minor issues. Her final paragraph established a deadline for receiving a response. Two days later, the supplier agreed to the proposal. The letter worked, Kroman says, because "it said all the key things the reader needed to know to make an immediate decision."

"I always write with the reader in mind."

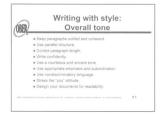

■ See Slide 5.1.

Use a new paragraph to signal a change in direction.

CO1. Keep paragraphs unified and coherent.

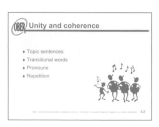

■ See Slide 5.2.

■ Developing Logical Paragraphs

A paragraph is a group of related sentences that focus on one main idea. The main idea is often identified in the first sentence of the paragraph, which is then known as a *topic sentence.* The body of the paragraph supports this main idea by giving more information, analysis, or examples. A paragraph is typically part of a longer message, although one paragraph can contain the entire message, especially in such informal communications as memorandums and e-mail.

Paragraphs organize the topic into manageable units of information for the reader. Readers need a cue to tell them when they have finished a topic so they can pause and refocus their attention on the next topic. To serve this purpose, paragraphs must be unified and coherent, be stated in parallel structure, and be of an appropriate length.

Keeping Paragraphs Unified and Coherent

Although closely related, unity and coherence are not the same. A paragraph has *unity* when all its parts work together to develop a single idea consistently and logically. A paragraph has *coherence* when each sentence links smoothly to the sentences before and after it.

Unity   A unified paragraph gives information that is directly related to the topic, presents this information in a logical order, and omits irrelevant details. The following excerpt is a middle paragraph in a memorandum arguing against the proposal that Collins, a baby-food manufacturer, should expand into producing food for adults:

NOT: [1] We cannot focus our attention on both ends of the age spectrum. [2] In a recent survey, two-thirds of the under-35 age group named Collins as the first company that came to mind for the category "baby-food products." [3] For more than 50 years we have spent millions of dollars annually to identify our company as the baby-food company, and market research shows that we have been successful. [4] Last year, we introduced Peas 'N Pears, our most successful baby-food introduction ever. [5] To now seek to position ourselves as a producer of food for adults would simply be incongruous. [6] Our well-defined image in the marketplace would make producing food for adults risky.

Before reading further, rearrange these sentences to make the sequence of ideas more logical. As written, the paragraph lacks unity. You may decide that the overall topic of the paragraph is Collins's well-defined image as a baby-food producer. So Sentence 6 would be the best topic sentence. You might also decide that Sentence 4 brings in extra information that weakens paragraph unity and should be left out. The most unified paragraph, then, would be Sentences 6, 3, 2, 5, and 1, as shown here:

BUT: Our well-defined image in the marketplace would make producing food for adults risky. For more than 50 years we have spent millions of dollars annually to identify our company as the baby-food company, and market research shows that we have been successful. In a recent survey, two-thirds of the under-35 age group named Collins as the first company that came to mind for the category "baby-food products." To now seek to position ourselves as a producer of food for adults would simply be incongruous. We cannot focus our attention on both ends of the age spectrum.

A topic sentence is especially helpful in a long paragraph. It usually appears at the beginning of a paragraph. This position helps the writer focus on the topic, so the paragraph will have unity. And it lets the reader know immediately what the topic is.

> *The topic sentence usually goes at the beginning of the paragraph.*

Coherence   A coherent paragraph weaves sentences together so that the discussion is integrated. The reader never needs to pause to puzzle out the relationships or reread to get the intended meaning. The major ways to achieve coherence are to use transitional words and pronouns, to repeat key words and ideas, and to use parallel structure.

Transitional words help the reader see relationships between sentences. Such words may be as simple as *first* and other indicators of sequence.

> *Coherence is achieved by using transitional words, pronouns, repetition, and parallelism.*

> Ten years ago, Collins tried to overcome market resistance to its new line of baby clothes. <u>First</u>, it mounted a multimillion-dollar ad campaign featuring the Mason quintuplets. <u>Next</u>, it sponsored a Collins Baby look-alike contest. <u>Then</u> it sponsored two network specials featuring Dr. Benjamin Spock. <u>Finally</u>, it brought in the Madison Avenue firm of Morgan & Modine to broaden its image.

The words *first, next, then,* and *finally* clearly signal step-by-step movement. Now note the following logical transitions, aided by connecting words:

> I recognize, <u>however</u>, that Collins cannot thrive on baby food alone. <u>To begin with</u>, since we already control 73 percent of the market, further gains will be difficult. <u>What's more</u>, the current baby boom is slowing. <u>Therefore</u>, we must expand our product line.

Transitional words act as road signs, indicating where the message is headed and letting the reader know what to expect. Here are some commonly used transitional expressions grouped by the relationships they express:

■ See Handout 5.1.

Relationship	*Transitional Expressions*
addition	also, besides, furthermore, in addition, moreover, too
cause and effect	as a result, because, consequently, hence, so, therefore, thus
comparison	in the same way, likewise, similarly
contrast	although, but, however, in contrast, nevertheless, on the other hand, still, yet
illustration	for example, for instance, in other words, to illustrate
sequence	first, second, third, then, next, finally
summary/conclusion	at last, finally, in conclusion, therefore, to summarize
time	meanwhile, next, since, soon, then

A second way to achieve coherence is to use pronouns. Because pronouns stand for words already named, using pronouns binds sentences and ideas together. The pronouns are underlined here:

> If Collins branches out with additional food products, one possibility would be a fruit snack for youngsters. Funny Fruits were tested in Columbus last summer, and

<u>they</u> were a big hit. Roger Johnson, national marketing manager, says <u>he</u> hopes to build new food categories into a $200 million business. <u>He</u> is also exploring the possibility of acquiring other established name brands. <u>These</u> acquired brands would let Collins expand faster than if <u>it</u> had to develop a new product of <u>its</u> own.

Purposeful repetition aids coherence; avoid needless repetition.

A third way to achieve coherence is to repeat key words. In a misguided attempt to appear interesting, writers sometimes use different terms for the same idea. For example, in discussing a proposed merger, a writer may at different points use *merger, combination, union, association,* and *syndicate.* Or a writer may use the words *administrator, manager, supervisor,* and *executive* all to refer to the same person. Such "elegant variation" only confuses the reader, who has no way of knowing whether the writer is referring to the same concept or to slightly different variations of that concept. Avoid needless repetition, but use purposeful repetition to link ideas and thus promote paragraph coherence. Here is a good example:

> Collins has taken several <u>steps</u> recently to enhance profits and project a stronger leadership position. One of these <u>steps</u> is streamlining operations. Collins's line of children's clothes was <u>unprofitable</u>, so it discontinued the line. Its four produce farms were likewise <u>unprofitable</u>, so it hired an outside professional <u>team</u> to manage them. This <u>team</u> eventually recommended selling the farms.

Ensure paragraph unity by developing only one topic per paragraph and by presenting the information in logical order. Ensure paragraph coherence by using transitional words and pronouns and by repeating key words.

Parallel Structure

CO2. Use parallel structure.

The term **parallelism** means using similar grammatical structure for similar ideas—that is, matching adjectives with adjectives, nouns with nouns, infinitives with infinitives, and so on. Much widely quoted writing uses parallelism—for example, Julius Caesar's "I came, I saw, I conquered" and Abraham Lincoln's "government of the people, by the people, and for the people." Parallel structure smoothly links ideas and adds a pleasing rhythm to sentences and paragraphs, thereby enhancing coherence.

Parallelism refers to consistency.

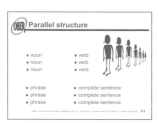

■ See Slide 5.3.

NOT: The new dispatcher is competent and a fast worker.

BUT: The new dispatcher is competent and fast.

NOT: The new grade of paper is lightweight, nonporous, and it is inexpensive.

BUT: The new grade of paper is lightweight, nonporous, and inexpensive.

NOT: The training program will cover

1. Vacation and sick leaves
2. How to resolve grievances
3. Managing your workstation

BUT: The training program will cover

1. Vacation and sick leaves
2. Grievance resolution
3. Workstation management

NOT: One management consultant recommended either selling the children's furniture division or its conversion into a children's toy division.

BUT: One management consultant recommended either selling the children's furniture division or converting it into a children's toy division.

NOT: Gladys is not only proficient in word processing but also in desktop publishing.

BUT: Gladys is proficient not only in word processing but also in desktop publishing.

In the last two sets of sentences above, note that correlative conjunctions (such as *both/and, either/or,* and *not only/but also*) must be followed by words in parallel form. Be especially careful to use parallel structure in report headings that have equal weight and in numbered and bulleted lists.

Paragraph Length

How long should a paragraph of business writing be? As with other considerations, the needs of the reader, rather than the convenience of the writer, should determine the answer. Paragraphs should help the reader by signaling a new idea as well as by providing a physical break. Long blocks of unbroken text look boring and needlessly complex. And they may unintentionally obscure an important idea buried in the middle (see Figure 5.1). On the other hand, a series of extremely short paragraphs can weaken coherence by obscuring underlying relationships.

Essentially, there are no fixed rules for paragraph length, and occasionally one- or ten-sentence paragraphs might be effective. However, most paragraphs of good business writers fall into the 60- to 80-word range—long enough for a topic sentence and three or four supporting sentences.

A paragraph is both a logical unit and a visual unit. It is logical in that it discusses only one topic. It is visual in that the end of the paragraph signals readers to pause and digest the information (or, perhaps, just to rest). Although a single paragraph should never discuss more than one major topic, complex topics may need to be divided into several paragraphs. Your purpose and the needs of your reader should ultimately determine paragraph length.

CO3. **Control paragraph length.**

Excessively long paragraphs look boring and difficult.

■ Creating an Appropriate Tone

Having chosen the right words to construct effective sentences and then having combined these sentences into logical paragraphs, we now examine the tone of the complete message—the complete letter, memorandum, report, or the like. **Tone** in writing refers to the writer's attitude toward both the reader and the subject of the message. The overall tone of your written message affects your reader just as your tone of voice affects your listener in everyday exchanges. You also, of course, want to ensure the appropriateness of the overall tone of your electronic messages (see Spotlight 14, "Netiquette").

The business writer should strive for an overall tone that is confident, courteous, and sincere; that uses emphasis and subordination appropriately; that contains nondiscriminatory language; that stresses the "you" attitude; and that is enhanced by effective design. (Style Principles 1–7 were presented in Chapter 4.)

■ A chapter overview appears in the *Instructor's Resource Manual.*

figure5.1

The Effect of Paragraph Length on Readability

Books & More
623 Northfield Road
Detroit, MI 48200
313.555.3000

MEMO TO: Max Dillion, Sales Manager
FROM: Richard J. Hayes
DATE: February 25, 20--
SUBJECT: New-Venture Proposal

The purpose of this memorandum is to propose the purchase or lease of a van to be used as a mobile bookstore. We could then use this van to generate sales in the outlying towns and villages throughout the state. We have been aware for quite some time that many small towns around the state do not have adequate bookstore facilities, but the economics of the situation are such that we would not be able to open a comprehensive branch and operate it profitably. However, we could afford to stock a van with books and operate it for a few days at a time in various small towns throughout the state. As you are probably aware, the laws of this state would permit us to acquire a statewide business license fairly easily and inexpensively. With the proper advance advertising, we should be able to generate much interest in this endeavor. It seems to me that this idea has much merit because of the flexibility it offers us. For example, we could tailor the length of our stay with the size of the town and the amount of business generated. In addition, we could tailor our inventory to the needs and interests of the particular locales. We might spend a day or two at a retirement community, where we would stock books on hobbies, fiction, gardening, and investments. The next week we might visit a town that is celebrating an anniversary, and we would stock books relating to state events and history. In addition, when various organizations are holding conventions in the state, we might make arrangements to park the van at a convenient spot at the convention center and feature books of interest to the particular group attending. The driver of the van would act as the salesperson, and we would, of course, have copies of our complete catalog so that mail orders could be taken as well. Please let me have your reactions to this proposal. If you wish, I can explore the matter further and generate cost and sales estimates.

jmc

Books & More
623 Northfield Road
Detroit, MI 48200
313.555.3000

MEMO TO: Max Dillion, Sales Manager
FROM: Richard J. Hayes
DATE: February 25, 20--
SUBJECT: New-Venture Proposal

The purpose of this memorandum is to propose the purchase or lease of a van to be used as a mobile bookstore. We could then use this van to generate sales in the outlying towns and villages throughout the state.

We have been aware for quite some time that many small towns around the state do not have adequate bookstore facilities, but the economics of the situation are such that we would not be able to open a comprehensive branch and operate it profitably. However, we could afford to stock a van with books and operate it for a few days at a time in various small towns throughout the state. As you are probably aware, the laws of this state would permit us to acquire a statewide business license fairly easily and inexpensively.

With the proper advance advertising, we should be able to generate much interest in this endeavor. It seems to me that this idea has much merit because of the flexibility it offers us. For example, we could tailor the length of our stay with the size of the town and the amount of business generated. In addition, we could tailor our inventory to the needs and interests of the particular locales.

We might spend a day or two at a retirement community, where we would stock books on hobbies, fiction, gardening, and investments. The next week we might visit a town that is celebrating an anniversary, and we would stock books relating to state events and history. In addition, when various organizations are holding conventions in the state, we might make arrangements to park the van at a convenient spot at the convention center and feature books of interest to the particular group attending.

The driver of the van would act as the salesperson, and we would, of course, have copies of our complete catalog so that mail orders could be taken as well. Please let me have your reactions to this proposal. If you wish, I can explore the matter further and generate cost and sales estimates.

jmc

These two memorandums contain identical information. Which is more inviting to read?

CO4. Write confidently.

Write confidently.

Not: I trust this schedule change will satisfy your needs.

But: This schedule change will enable you to remain at home each morning until your child leaves for school.

■ See Slide 5.4

But not *too* confidently.

Not: I know you will like our new delivery schedule.

But: Our new delivery schedule will assure same-day service for all of your clients.

■ See Slide 5.5.

Writing with Confidence

Your message should convey the confident attitude that you have done a competent job of communicating and that your reader will do as you ask or will accept your decision. If you believe that your explanation is complete, that your request is reasonable, or that your decision is based on sound logic, you are likely to write with confidence. Such confidence has a persuasive effect on your audience. Avoid using language that makes you sound unsure of yourself. Be especially wary of beginning sentences with "I hope," "If you agree," and similar self-conscious terms.

NOT: If you'd like to take advantage of this offer, call our toll-free number.

BUT: To take advantage of this offer, call our toll-free number.

NOT: I hope that you will agree that my qualifications match your job needs.

BUT: My qualifications match your job needs in the following respects.

In some situations, the best strategy is simply to omit information. For example, you should not provide the reader with excuses for denying your request, suggest that something might go wrong, or intimate that the reader might not be satisfied.

spotlight14
ON TECHNOLOGY

Netiquette

"Netiquette" is network etiquette—a professional code of behavior for electronic communication. In other words, netiquette is a set of guidelines for behaving properly online. Follow these five guidelines to become (and remain) a welcomed member of the electronic community:

1. Remember that you're communicating with another human being.

Because of the lack of nonverbal clues, it's easy to misinterpret the other person's meaning. Remember that the recipient has feelings more or less like your own. Stand up for yourself and your beliefs but be sensitive to other people's feelings. Never write something to someone on e-mail or in a discussion group that you would not say to that person in a face-to-face encounter. Avoid sending heated messages (called "flaming") even if you're provoked. As many users have learned to their dismay, e-mail can be misaddressed or forwarded—sometimes with devastating consequences.

2. Behave ethically.

Standards of online behavior are simply *different from*—but not lower than—those for personal behavior. Five of the "Ten Commandments for Computer Ethics," developed by the Computer Ethics Institute, concern the legal and ethical dimensions of electronic communication:

> Thou shalt not use a computer to steal.
> Thou shalt not use a computer to bear false witness.
> Thou shalt not use or copy software for which you have not paid.
> Thou shalt not use other people's computer resources without authorization.
> Thou shalt not appropriate other people's intellectual output.

Respect other people's privacy. Don't read other people's e-mail, and get permission before copying or forwarding someone's message to another party. Similarly, don't copy another's artwork (including cartoons, clip-art, or music) without securing permission.

3. Lurk before you leap.

When you enter a discussion group that's new to you, take time to look around. Read the messages for a few days to get a sense of how the people who are already there act. Then go ahead and participate. Read the FAQs (Frequently Asked Questions). Ensure the accuracy (and relevance) of anything you post. Bad information spreads like wildfire on the Internet.

After familiarizing yourself with a newsgroup, don't be afraid to share your knowledge and experiences. The Internet was founded because scientists wanted to share information, and gradually the rest of us got in on the act. So do your part to be helpful and to expand knowledge. That's why the Internet is called a *community*.

4. Respect other people's time and bandwidth.

When you send a message via e-mail or a discussion group, you're taking up other people's time. Therefore, make sure the time they spend reading your message is time well spent. You're also taking up bandwidth—the information-carrying capacity of the telephone lines or networks used to transmit your message. Don't copy more people than necessary in an e-mail note, and don't include a copy of the original message in your reply unless necessary.

Despite the information superhighway's super speed, be patient. Don't expect instant responses to all your questions. Remember that a project that may be of extreme importance to you might be of less concern to others. If you can find the answers yourself with a little electronic digging, don't expect others to do it for you.

5. Be tolerant of other people's mistakes.

Electronic communication can be a scary place for novices, and we were all network newbies once. So when someone makes a mistake—whether it's a spelling error, a stupid question, an irrelevant comment, or an unnecessarily long answer—be kind. If you want to be helpful, point out errors by a private e-mail message, not by public posting to a newsgroup. Give people the benefit of the doubt.

In short, netiquette, like good manners in all other situations, is based on adherence to the golden rule: Do unto others as you would have them do unto you. Communicate with others as you would like them to communicate with you.[1]

■ See Slide 5.6.

■ See Slide 5.7.

Modest confidence is the best tactic.

NOT: I know you are a busy person, but we would really enjoy hearing you speak.

BUT: The fact that you are involved in so many different enterprises makes your views on small business all the more relevant for our audience.

NOT: Let us know if you experience any other problems.

BUT: Your GrassMaster lawn mower should now give you many years of trouble-free service.

A word of caution: Do not appear *overconfident*; that is, avoid sounding presumptuous or arrogant. Be especially wary of using such strong phrases as "I know that" and "I am sure you will agree that."

NOT: I'm sure you'll agree our offer is reasonable.

BUT: This solution should enable you to collect the data you need while still protecting the privacy of our clients.

Competent communicators are *confident* communicators. They write with conviction, yet they avoid appearing to be pushy or presumptuous.

spotlight15
ON TECHNOLOGY

Electronic Punctuation Tones Up E-mail

Although e-mail is a form of written communication, sometimes its immediacy and intimacy make it more like a phone conversation than an exchange of letters or memos. But the rich nonverbal cues that are such an important and natural part of conversations (pauses, voice tone, emphasis, and the like) are missing in e-mail exchanges. Without some device to indicate tone of voice, misunderstandings might result and might lead to an abrupt or even angry response. Such a response, called "flaming," can weaken your ability to accomplish your objective.

Shortcuts are sometimes used to convey emotions. For example, typing ‹grin› or just ‹g› softens the effect of a sarcastic remark and lets the reader know you're joking. Commonly used abbreviations in e-mail include IMHO (in my humble opinion), FWIW (for what it's worth), and BTW (by the way).

Do not, however, carry abbreviations to the extreme, as in the following message:

AFAIK, I'll BRB. FWIW, TTYL. BTW, be careful, IYKWIMAITYD.

Translation:

As far as I know, I'll be right back. For what it's worth, I'll talk to you later. By the way, be careful, if you know what I mean (and I think you do).

Another form of shorthand is the *smiley* or *emoticon*, which is a simple icon used to convey humor and other emotions. Common examples are :-) and :-(. When you tilt your head to the left, you can see that the colon represents the eyes and the hyphen represents the nose of a happy or sad face. Here are other examples of smileys (tilt your head to the left to get their meanings):

:´-(	I'm crying
:-X	My lips are sealed.
´:-)	I accidentally shaved off one eyebrow.
0:-)	I'm an angel.
}:-›	I'm a devil.
*‹†:-)	I'm Santa Claus.
=:-)	I'm a punk rocker.
:-)))	I'm overweight.

Although smileys are not appropriate for most business e-mail, occasionally they might lend just the right human touch to a particular message.[2]

Courtesy and Sincerity

A tone of courtesy and sincerity builds goodwill for you and your organization and increases the likelihood that your message will achieve its objective. For example, lecturing the reader or filling a letter with **platitudes** (trite, obvious statements) implies a condescending attitude. Likewise, readers are likely to find offensive such expressions as "you failed to," "we find it difficult to believe that," "you surely don't expect," or "your complaint."

NOT: Companies like ours cannot survive unless our customers pay their bills on time.

BUT: By paying your bill before May 30, you will maintain your excellent credit history with our firm.

NOT: You sent your complaint to the wrong department. We don't handle shipping problems.

BUT: We have forwarded your letter to the shipping department. You should be hearing from them within the week.

Your reader is sophisticated enough to know when you're being sincere. To achieve a sincere tone, avoid exaggeration (especially using too many modifiers or too strong modifiers), obvious flattery, and expressions of surprise or disbelief.

NOT: Your satisfaction means more to us than making a profit, and we shall work night and day to see that we earn it.

BUT: We value your goodwill and have taken these specific steps to ensure your satisfaction.

NOT: I'm surprised you would question your raise, considering your overall performance last year.

BUT: Your raise was based on an objective evaluation of your performance last year.

Competent communicators use both verbal and nonverbal signals to convey courtesy and sincerity (see Spotlight 15, "Electronic Punctuation Tones Up E-mail," on page 170). However, it is difficult to fake these attitudes. The best way to achieve the desired tone is to truly assume a courteous and sincere outlook toward your reader.

CO5. **Use a courteous and sincere tone.**

A platitude *is a statement so obvious that including it in a message would insult the reader.*

Use a courteous and sincere tone.

Not: Our No. 1 concern is to protect the environment when we build our addition at Morse Lake.

But: We have taken three specific steps to protect the environment when we build our addition at Morse Lake.

■ See Slide 5.8.

Obvious flattery and exaggeration sound insincere.

Use a courteous and sincere tone.

Not: I can't believe you expect me to accept this offer.

But: This offer would be more attractive if it included a six-month trial period.

■ See Slide 5.9.

No one understands the importance of a courteous and sincere tone better than Ali Kasikci, general manager of the Peninsula Beverly Hills hotel, the only hotel in Southern California to win both the Mobil Travel Guide Five-Star Award and the AAA Five-Diamond Award.

Emphasis and Subordination

CO6. Use appropriate emphasis and subordination.

Not all ideas are created equal. Some are more important and more persuasive than others. Assume, for example, that you have been asked to evaluate and compare the Copy Cat and the Repro 100 photocopiers and then to write a memo report recommending one for purchase. Assume that the two brands are alike in all important respects except these:

Feature	Copy Cat	Repro 100
Speed (copies per minute)	15	10
Cost	$2,750	$2,100
Enlargement/Reduction?	Yes	No

Let your reader know which ideas you consider most important.

As you can see, the Copy Cat has greater speed and more features. Thus, a casual observer might think you should recommend the Copy Cat on the basis of its additional advantages. Suppose, however, that most of your photocopying involves fewer than five copies of each original, all of them full-sized. Under these conditions, you might conclude that the Repro 100's lower cost outweighs the Copy Cat's higher speed and additional features; you therefore decide to recommend purchasing the Repro 100. If you want your recommendation to be credible, you must make sure your reader views the relative importance of each feature the same way you do. To do so, use appropriate emphasis and subordination techniques.

Techniques of Emphasis   To emphasize an idea, use any of the following strategies (to subordinate an idea, simply use the opposite strategy):

To subordinate an idea, put it in the dependent clause.

1. Put the idea in a short, simple sentence. However, if you need a complex sentence to convey the needed information, put the more important idea in the independent clause. (The ideas communicated in each independent clause of a *compound* sentence receive *equal* emphasis.)

   SIMPLE: The Repro 100 is the better photocopier for our purposes.

   COMPLEX: Although the Copy Cat is faster, 98 percent of our copying requires fewer than five copies per original. *(Emphasizes the fact that speed is not a crucial consideration for us.)*

■ See Slide 5.10.

2. Place the major idea first or last. The first paragraph of a message receives the most emphasis, the last paragraph receives less emphasis, and the middle paragraphs receive the least emphasis. Similarly, the middle sentences within a paragraph receive less emphasis than the first sentence in a paragraph.

   The first criterion examined was cost. The Copy Cat sells for $2,750 and the Repro 100 sells for $2,100, or 24 percent less than the cost of the Copy Cat.

■ See Slide 5.11.

3. Make the noun you want to emphasize the subject of the sentence. In other words, use active voice to emphasize the doer of the action and passive voice to emphasize the receiver.

ACTIVE: The Repro 100 costs 24 percent less than the Copy Cat. *(Emphasizes the Repro 100 rather than the Copy Cat.)*

PASSIVE: The relative costs of the two models were compared first. *(Emphasizes the relative costs rather than the two models.)*

■ See Slide 5.12.

4. Devote more space to the idea.

> The two models were judged according to three criteria: cost, speed, and enlargement/reduction capabilities. Total cost is an important consideration for our firm because of the large number of copiers we use and our large volume of copying. Last year our firm used 358 photocopiers and duplicated more than 6.5 million pages. Thus, regardless of the speed or features of a particular model, if it is too expensive to operate, it will not serve our purposes.

5. Use language that directly implies importance, such as "most important," "major," or "primary."

> The most important factor for us is cost.

(In contrast, use terms such as "least important" or "a minor point" to subordinate an idea.)

6. Use repetition (within reason).

> However, the Copy Cat is expensive—expensive to purchase and expensive to operate.

7. Use mechanical means (within reason)—enumeration, italics, solid capitals, second color, indenting from left and right margins, or other elements of design—to emphasize key ideas.

> But the most important criterion is cost, and the Repro 100 costs 24 percent **less** than the Copy Cat.

■ Winston Churchill used an excellent example of effective repetition in his speech to the House of Commons on May 13, 1940: "We shall fight on the beaches, we shall fight on the landing grounds, we shall fight in the fields and in the streets, we shall fight in the hills; we shall never surrender."

The Ethical Dimension   In using emphasis and subordination, your goal is to ensure a common frame of reference between you and your reader; you want your reader to see how important you consider each idea to be. Your goal is *not* to mislead the reader. For example, if you believe that the Repro 100 is the *slightly* better choice, you would certainly not want to intentionally mislead your reader into concluding that it is *clearly* the better choice. Such a tactic would be not only unethical but also unwise. Use sound business judgment and a sense of fair play to help yourself achieve your communication objectives.

Use language that expresses your honest evaluation; do not mislead the reader.

Making Language Nondiscriminatory

Nondiscriminatory language treats everyone equally, making no unwarranted assumptions about any group of people. Using nondiscriminatory language is smart business because (a) it is the ethical thing to do and (b) we risk offending others if we do otherwise. Consider the types of bias in this report:

co7. **Use nondiscriminatory language.**

Be sensitive to your readers' feelings.

> The finishing plant was the scene of a confrontation today when two ladies from the morning shift accused a foreman of sexual harassment. Marta Maria Valdez, a Hispanic inspector, and Margaret Sawyer, an assembly-line worker, accused

Mr. Engerrand of making suggestive comments. Mr. Engerrand, who is 62 years old and an epileptic, denied the charges and said he thought the girls were trying to cheat the company with their demand for a cash award.

Were you able to identify the following instances of bias or discriminatory language?

- The women were referred to as *ladies* and *girls,* although it is unlikely that the men in the company are referred to as *gentlemen* and *boys.*

- The term *foreman* (and all other *-man* occupational titles) has a sexist connotation.

- The two women were identified by their first and last names, without a personal title, whereas the man was identified by a personal title and last name only.

- Valdez's ethnicity, Engerrand's age, and Engerrand's disability were identified, although they were irrelevant to the situation.

Competent communicators make sure that their writing is free of sexist language and free of bias based on such factors as race, ethnicity, religion, age, sexual orientation, and disability.

Sexist Language   It makes no business sense to exclude or perhaps offend half the population by using sexist language. To avoid sexism in your writing, follow these strategies:

1. Use neutral job titles that do not imply that a job is held by only men or only women.

Instead of	*Use*
chairman	chair, chairperson
foreman	supervisor
salesman	sales representative
woman lawyer	lawyer
workman	worker, employee

2. Avoid words and phrases that unnecessarily imply gender.

Instead of	*Use*
best man for the job	best person for the job
executives and their wives	executives and their spouses
housewife	homemaker
manmade	artificial, manufactured
manpower	human resources, personnel

Use language that implies equality.

When making the table arrangements for the president's luncheon, be sure to seat Arlene Kelly next to Mr. Jameson, our new African-American salesman from Philadelphia. Also, remember that Mr. Little is confined to a wheelchair and should be seated on the main level. The other executives and their wives may be seated in any order.

■ See Slide 5.13.

■ Other sexist terms to avoid are *policeman, clergyman, fireman, mailman, stewardess, statesman,* and *handyman.* Instead, use *police officer, member of the clergy, firefighter, letter carrier, flight attendant, diplomat,* and *janitor* or *custodian.*

3. Avoid demeaning or stereotypical terms.

Instead of	*Use*
My girl will handle it.	My assistant will handle it.
Watch your language around the ladies.	Watch your language.
Housewives like our long hours.	Our customers like our long hours.
He was a real jock.	He enjoyed all types of sports.
Each nurse supplies her own uniforms.	Nurses supply their own uniforms.

■ See Slide 5.14.

4. Use parallel language.

Instead of	*Use*
Joe, a broker, and his wife, a beautiful brunette	Joe, a broker, and his wife, Mary, a lawyer (*or* homemaker)
Ms. Wyllie and William Poe	Ms. Wyllie and Mr. Poe
man and wife	husband and wife

5. Use appropriate personal titles and salutations.

   ■ If a woman has a professional title, use it (Dr. Martha Ralston, the Rev. Deborah Connell).

   ■ Follow a woman's preference in being addressed as *Miss, Mrs.,* or *Ms.*

   ■ If a woman's marital status or her preference is unknown, use *Ms.*

   ■ If you do not know the reader's gender, use a nonsexist salutation (Dear Investor:, Dear Friend:, Dear Customer:, Dear Policyholder:).

   ■ Alternatively, you may use the full name in the salutation (Dear Chris Andrews:, Dear Terry Brooks:).

6. Whether it is appropriate to use *he* or *his* as generic pronouns in referring to men or women (for example, "Each manager must evaluate *his* subordinates annually") is currently a matter of some debate. Proponents argue that its use is based on tradition and on the fact that no genderless alternative pronoun exists. Opponents argue that its use appears to exclude females. Although many businesspeople would not be offended by such use, some would be. The conservative approach is to avoid such usage whenever possible by adopting any of these strategies:

   ■ Use plural nouns and pronouns.

      All managers must evaluate their subordinates annually.

ASK Ober

Dear Dr. Ober:

I am an instructor at Upper Iowa University. In Chapter 5, Exercise 12, you have this sentence for correction: "Both Dr. Fernandez and his assistant, Andrea Lee-McNeill, attended the new-product seminar." I corrected this and went over it in class stating that the correct answer was to state, "Dr. Fernandez and his assistant, Ms. Lee-McNeill, attended the new-product seminar." Several of my students questioned this and said that since "Dr." is an earned title and "Ms." is not, the original sentence was correct. They thought that identifying the sex of Ms. Lee-McNeill but not of Dr. Fernandez wasn't appropriate.

—Lori S.

Dear Lori:

This is more a matter of style and comfort than a matter of correctness. I personally would treat both names the same, regardless of sex. Thus, any of the following would be acceptable:

Dr. Fernandez and her (or his) assistant, Ms. Lee-McNeill

Dr. Jane (or John) Fernandez and her (or his) assistant, Ms. Andrea Lee-McNeill

Jane (or John) Fernandez and her (or his) assistant, Andrea Lee-McNeill.

Thanks for writing.

—Scot

E-mail your questions and comments to askober@ober.net.

- *But not:* Each manager must evaluate **their** subordinates annually.
- Use second-person pronouns *(you, your)*.

  You must evaluate your subordinates annually.
- Revise the sentence.

  Each manager must evaluate subordinates annually.
- Use *his or her* (sparingly).

  Each manager must evaluate his or her subordinates annually.

> Excessive use of the term *he or she* or *his or hers* sounds awkward.

> Mention group membership only if it is clearly relevant.

Other Discriminatory Language   We are all members of different groups, each of which may have different customs, values, and attitudes. If you think of your readers as individuals, rather than as stereotypical members of some particular group, you will avoid bias when communicating about race, ethnic background, religion, age, sexual orientation, and disabilities. Group membership should be mentioned only if it is clearly pertinent. As noted in Communication Snapshot 5, there is a perception in this country that a substantial number of Americans are discriminated against.

NOT: Richard McKenna, noted black legislator, supported our position.

BUT: Richard McKenna, noted legislator, supported our position.

NOT: Because of rising interest rates, he welshed on the deal.

BUT: Because of rising interest rates, he backed out of the deal.

NOT: Anita Voyles performed the job well for her age.

BUT: Anita Voyles performed the job well.

NOT: Patricia Barbour's lesbianism has not affected her job performance.

BUT: Patricia Barbour's job performance has been exemplary.

Competent communicators avoid the appearance of ageism in their writing. According to Michael W. Melvill (shown in the photo), he may be considered old at age 63, but he recently became the first person to pilot a rocket ship into space in a privately funded venture. He points out that many of the early jets were tested by relatively old pilots, whose experience and memory more than made up for youthful energy and reflexes.

NOT: Mary, an epileptic, had no trouble passing the medical examination.

BUT: Mary, who has epilepsy, had no trouble passing the medical examination.
(When the impairment is relevant, separate the impairment from the person.)

The "You" Attitude

Are you more interested in how well *you* perform in your courses or in how well your classmates perform? When you hear a television commercial, are you more interested in how the product will benefit *you* or in how your purchase of the product will benefit the sponsor? If you're like most people reading or hearing a message, your conscious or unconscious reaction is likely to be "What's in it for *me*?" Knowing that this is true provides you with a powerful strategy for structuring your messages to maximize their impact: stress the "you" attitude, not the "me" attitude.

The **"you" attitude** emphasizes what the *receiver* (the listener or the reader) wants to know and how he or she will be affected by the message. It requires developing *empathy*—the ability to project yourself into another person's position and to understand that person's situation, feelings, motives, and needs. To avoid sounding selfish and uninterested, focus on the reader—adopt the "you" attitude.

CO8. Stress the "you" attitude.

Answer the reader's unspoken question, "What's in it for me?"

■ See Slide 5.15.

NOT: I am shipping your order this afternoon.

BUT: Your order should arrive by Friday.

NOT: We will be open on Sundays from 1 to 5 p.m., beginning May 15.

BUT: You will be able to shop on Sundays from 1 to 5 p.m., beginning May 15.

Receiver Benefits   An important component of the "you" attitude is the concept of **receiver benefits**—emphasizing how the *receiver* (the reader or the listener) will benefit from doing as you ask. Sometimes, especially when asking a favor or refusing a request, the best we can do is to show how *someone* (not necessarily the reader) will benefit. But whenever possible, we should show how someone *other than ourselves* benefits from our request or from our decision.

NOT: We cannot afford to purchase an ad in your organization's directory.

BUT: Advertising exclusively on television allows us to offer consumers like you the lowest prices on their cosmetics.

NOT: Our decorative fireplace has an oak mantel and is portable.

BUT: Whether entertaining in your living room or den, you can still enjoy the ambience of a blazing fire because our decorative fireplace is portable. Simply take it with you from room to room.

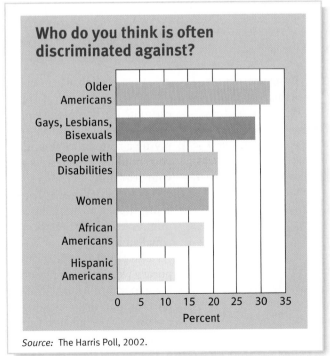

communication snapshot 5

Who do you think is often discriminated against?

Source: The Harris Poll, 2002.

■ See Slide 5.16.

In some situations you do not want to focus attention on the reader.

■ Richard Lauchman, in *Plain Style*, says, "A good writer works hard so that the reader won't have to."

■ See Handout 5.2.

co9. Design documents for readability.

Although readability formulas are helpful, other factors are also important.

Note that the revised sentences, which stress reader benefits, are longer than the original sentences—because they contain *more information*. Yet they are not verbose; that is, they do not contain unnecessary words. You can add information and still write concisely.

Exceptions   Stressing the "you" attitude focuses the attention on the reader, which is right where the attention should be—most of the time. In some situations, however, you may want to avoid focusing on the reader; these situations all involve conveying negative information. When you refuse someone's request, disagree with someone, or talk about someone's mistakes or shortcomings, avoid connecting the reader too closely with the negative information. In such situations, avoid second-person pronouns (*you* and *your*), and use passive sentences or other subordinating techniques to stress the receiver of the action rather than the doer.

NOT: You should have included more supporting evidence in your presentation.

BUT: Including more supporting evidence would have made the presentation more convincing.

NOT: You failed to return the merchandise within the 10-day period.

BUT: We are happy to give a full refund on all merchandise that is returned within 10 days.

Note that neither of the revised sentences contains the word *you*. Thus, each helps to separate the reader from the negative information, making the message more tactful and palatable.

■ Effective Page Design

The term **readability** refers to the ease of understanding a passage based on its style of writing and physical appearance. Various readability formulas are available that estimate the complexity of a passage on the basis of an analysis of such factors as sentence length, number of syllables per word, and word frequency. Although applying a readability formula is helpful in judging the readability of your message, you should use the results as a guide only. You could, for example, artificially change your readability score by using shorter sentences and shorter words. But sometimes a longer word is more precise and more familiar than a shorter word. Likewise, lowering the score by using all short sentences (for example, all simple sentences) might obscure the relationships among ideas because then all ideas would receive equal emphasis.

The physical appearance of your document also affects its readability. Contemporary word processing software makes it easy for writers to *design* their documents for maximum impact and effectiveness. Although the product is always more important than the packaging, there is no denying that an attractively formatted document, with legible type and plenty of white space, will help you achieve your communication objectives.

Consider the following design guidelines, which are illustrated in Spotlight 16, "Designing Documents," on page 180. Both versions of the Spotlight report contain the same information. Compare the typed version with the designed version for impact and readability.

Keep It Simple   The most important guideline is to use a simple, clean, and consistent design. It would be distracting, for example, to use many different type styles and sizes in the same document. Instead, select one serif typeface (*serifs* are the small strokes at the tops and bottoms of characters, such as the "feet" at the bottom of a *T*; sans serif typefaces have no such ornamental strokes) for the body of your report and one sans serif typeface for headings and subheadings. One popular combination is Times Roman for body type and Arial (or Helvetica) for special treatments such as headings, subheadings, and captions for figures.

This is an example of Times Roman in 10-point type. Because the serifs aid in readability, Times Roman is a good choice for the body of your report.

This is an example of Helvetica in 10-point type. Because it contrasts nicely with Times Roman, Helvetica is a good choice for headings.

Similarly, it would be distracting if a reader is accustomed to seeing lists arranged in a certain format but then encounters a list formatted differently. The reader would have to pause to figure out what is different, and why. Make sure that whatever decisions you initially make about margins, spacing, headings, and the like are followed consistently throughout your report.

Use White Space to Advantage   Use generous top, bottom, and side margins to make your document inviting to read. Consider white space (the blank sections of the document) as part of your overall design. In general, the more white space, the better. Break up long paragraphs into shorter ones, and leave generous space before and after headings. Separate lengthy areas of text with subheadings. Subheadings not only break up solid blocks of type but also enhance readability by periodically providing signals for the reader.

Select a Suitable Line Length and Type Size   Line length can have a major effect on the readability of a document. Lines that are too short weaken coherence because they needlessly disrupt the normal horizontal pattern of reading. Lines that are too long cause readers to lose their place when they return to the beginning of the next line. In general, use a line no shorter than 25 characters and no longer than 75 characters for business documents. Although one column is standard for business reports, any business document can also be typed in two or three columns on a standard-sized page.

For the body of most business reports, select a type size between 10 points (elite size) and 12 points (pica size); 1 point equals 1/72 of an inch. Proportionately larger type should be used for headings and subheadings.

I'M WARNING YOU   *word***wise**

Actual product labels:

On a portable stroller: "Caution: Remove infant before folding for storage."
On a package of fireplace logs: "Caution: Risk of fire."
On a dessert box: "Product will be particularly hot after heating."
On a hair dryer: "Do not use while sleeping."
On a musical birthday candle: "Do not use soft wax as earplugs."

Use a simple, consistent design.

■ See Slide 5.17.

The empty space on a page also communicates.

■ See Slide 5.18.

Designing Documents

STAFF EMPLOYEES' EVALUATION OF THE BENEFIT PROGRAM AT ATLANTIC STATE UNIVERSITY

Employee benefits ar
important form of em
nonprofit organizati
of Commerce survey,
roll costs, averaging
1997, p. 183). Thus,
zation's benefit pro
evaluated.

To ensure that the b
sity's 2,500 staff
possible, David Rigg
this report on Janua

Purpose and Scope

Specifically, the f
in this study: What
Atlantic State Unive
this question, the f

1. How knowledgeab
   program?
2. What are the em
   benefits now av
3. What benefits,
   added to the pr

This study attempted
Whether the preferen
in the scope of the

Procedures

A list of the 2,489
fits was generated f

Plain Version

**Staff Employees' Evaluation
of the Benefit Program
at Atlantic State University**

EMPLOYEE BENEFITS ARE a rapidly growing and an increasingly important form of employee compensation for both profit and nonprofit organizations. According to a recent U.S. Chamber of Commerce survey, benefits now constitute 37% of all payroll costs, averaging $9,732 yearly for each employee (Berelson, 1997, p. 183). Thus, on the basis of cost alone, an organization's benefit program must be carefully monitored and evaluated.

To ensure that the benefit program for Atlantic State University's 2,500 staff personnel is operating as effectively as possible, David Riggins, director of personnel, authorized this report on January 21, 2002.

**Purpose
and
Scope**

Specifically, the following problem statement was addressed in this study: What are the opinions of staff employees at Atlantic State University regarding their benefits? To answer this question, the following subproblems were addressed:

• How knowledgeable are the employees about the benefit program?
• What are the employees' opinions of the value of the benefits now available?
• What benefits, if any, would the employees like to have added to the program?

This study attempted to determine employee preferences only. Whether the preferences are economically feasible is not within the scope of the study.

Procedures

A list of the 2,489 staff employees who are eligible for benefits was generated from the January 21 payroll run. By means of a 10% systematic sample, 250 employees were selected for the survey. On February 11, each of the selected employees was sent via campus mail the cover letter and questionnaire shown in Appendixes A and B. A total of 206 employees completed questionnaires, for a response rate of 82%.

In addition to the questionnaire data, personal interviews were held with Lois White, compensation specialist at ASU; Roger Ray, chair of the Staff Personnel Committee at ASU; and Lewis Rigby, director of the State Personnel Board. The primary data provided by the survey and personal interviews was then analyzed

Designed Version

Determine an Appropriate Justification Format   All text lines in the body of your document should be left-justified; that is, they should all begin at the left margin. However, the end of each line may be either right-justified (sometimes called *full justification*) or ragged right. In general, a justified line presents a clean, formal look, whereas a ragged-right line gives an informal, casual appearance.

Use full justification for a formal appearance and an uneven right margin for an informal appearance.

This is an example of a justified column, which produces even left and right margins. You should have the hyphenation feature of your word processor turned on when justifying lines.	This is an example of a column with a ragged-right margin—that is, one where the lines end unevenly. Ragged-right lines provide a more interesting, casual appearance.

Format Paragraphs Correctly   Designed documents use only single spacing. New paragraphs are indicated either by leaving a blank line before the paragraph or by indenting the first line. Do not, however, both indent *and* leave a blank line; that would be too much. Even when paragraphs are indented, designed documents typically do not indent the first line of a paragraph that immediately follows a heading or subheading; it is obvious that what follows a heading is a new paragraph.

Writers sometimes use various techniques at the start of a document to engage the reader immediately: beginning the first word of the document with an extra-large, decorative letter; typing the first three or four words in solid capitals; or setting the first paragraph in larger type than the rest of the document. The purpose of such techniques is to make the copy attractive and inviting to read.

■ According to Mary A. De Vries in *Internationally Yours,* you should *over*punctuate your international letters, even though the trend in domestic correspondence is to *under*punctuate. This trend has been encouraged in part because less punctuation means fewer keystrokes in production and hence faster preparation. But it's not always a timesaver in international correspondence, particularly if a misunderstood message has to be clarified later.

Emphasize Words and Ideas Appropriately   On a typewriter, underlining and solid capitals were about the only way to emphasize a word or idea. Designed documents, however, have a variety of techniques readily available—larger type size, boldface lettering, and italic type, for example. Any of these techniques is preferable to underlining and solid capitals. Solid capitals are appropriate only for very short headings. Unlike lowercase letters, capital letters are all the same size and are therefore more difficult to read. Nonstandard type styles, such as outline or shadow type, are inappropriate in business documents; they provide visual clutter and are distracting.

Use special emphasis techniques sparingly.

Use boldface for strong emphasis and italic for medium emphasis in the body of a document. Both boldface and italic type, along with a larger type size, may be used for headings and subheadings; just be sure your main headings stand out more than your subheadings. When headings are displayed prominently, they may be typed in upper- and lowercase letters or with only the first word and proper names in uppercase. Any of the following three styles would be appropriate for a heading:

Opinions of Present Benefits
Opinions of Present Benefits
Opinions of present benefits

Format Lists for Readability   Because lists or enumerations are surrounded by white space, with each item by itself on a separate line, they tend to stand out more than when the same material is presented in narrative form. You have the choice of using either numbered lists or bulleted lists. Number your lists when *sequence* is important ("Here are the five steps for requesting temporary help") or when the list is long and numbering will help when referring to a specific point. When sequence is not important and the list is short, use bullets (small squares or circles) to call attention to each item. Keep the bullets small and close to the items to which they re-

Use numbered lists when order is important; otherwise, use bulleted lists.

late. For both numbered and bulleted lists, either a first-line-indented style or a hanging style may be used. Both of the following lists are formatted appropriately:

To begin using Dragon NaturallySpeaking, follow these steps:

1. Double-click the NatSpeak icon on the desktop.
2. If you wish to dictate directly into your word processing program, open that program.
3. Connect your microphone to the computer.
4. Begin dictating directly into the microphone, speaking in a normal voice and enunciating clearly. The text you dictate will appear in the active window.

Each typeface can vary in a number of important ways:

- Posture: Roman (vertical) and italic (oblique)
- Weight: Hairline, thin, light, book, regular, medium, demibold, bold, heavy, black, and ultra
- Width: Condensed, regular, and expanded
- Size: Text (all type sizes up to 12 points) and display (type sizes larger than 12 points)

■ Serif type is more *readable* and is best for text; sans serif type is more *legible* and is best used for headlines. Unless you have a design background, never combine more than two typefaces on the same page. Never combine two serif fonts or two sans serif fonts on the same page.

Use graphics only when they help you achieve your report objectives.

Use Graphics—In Moderation   When used in moderation, graphics can add interest and aid comprehension:

Central Airlines has been designated as the official carrier for this year's international conference in London. To receive a 15 percent discount off most coach fares, call 225-555-2525 and use this event number: XJ-1056. The reduced fares are available for one week before and one week after the conference.

This is especially the case when using charts and tables.

In addition, writers today can use files of computerized drawings, called *clipart*, that can be electronically inserted into their documents. To be effective, such clipart must be used sparingly and be well drawn, relevant, and in proper scale. Unless you are certain that a particular piece of clipart will help you tell your story more effectively, save clipart for more informal communications such as company newsletters and advertising documents. Most business reports should have a dignified, businesslike appearance.

Horizontal and vertical lines (called *rules*), another graphic device, can also be used in moderation to separate different elements of the document. Horizontal rules can be narrow or wide; vertical rules (sometimes used to separate columns) should be very narrow. If horizontal rules are used at the top and bottom of a page, the top rule is generally wider than the bottom.

■ Effective Business Writing

■ According to Marty Stuckey in *The Basics of Business Writing,* the person who receives your document will decide in approximately four seconds whether to read what took you hours, perhaps days, to write.

Writing style goes beyond *correctness*. Although a document that contains many grammatical, mechanical, or usage errors could hardly be considered effective, a document that contains no such errors might still be ineffective because it lacks style. Style involves choosing the right words, writing effective sentences, develop-

✓checklist 5

Writing with Style

Words

✓ *Write clearly.* Be accurate and complete; use familiar words; avoid dangling expressions and unnecessary jargon.

✓ *Prefer short, simple words.* They are less likely to be misused by the writer and more likely to be understood by the reader.

✓ *Write with vigor.* Use specific, concrete language; avoid clichés, slang, and buzz words.

✓ *Write concisely.* Avoid redundancy, wordy expressions, and hidden subjects and verbs.

✓ *Prefer positive language.* Stress what you *can* do or what *is* true rather than what you cannot do or what is not true.

Sentences

✓ *Use a variety of sentence types.* Use simple sentences for emphasis and variety, compound sentences for coordinate relationships, complex sentences for subordinate relationships, and compound-complex sentences for both coordinate and subordinate relationships. Most sentences should range from 16 to 22 words.

✓ *Use active and passive voice appropriately.* Use active voice in general and to emphasize the doer of the action; use passive voice to emphasize the receiver.

Paragraphs

✓ *Keep paragraphs unified and coherent.* Develop a single idea consistently and logically; use transitional words, pronouns, and repetition when appropriate.

✓ *Use parallel structure.* Match adjectives with adjectives, nouns with nouns, infinitives with infinitives, and so on.

✓ *Control paragraph length.* Use a variety of lengths, although most paragraphs should range from 60 to 80 words.

Overall Tone

✓ *Write confidently.* Avoid sounding self-conscious (by overusing such phrases as "I think" and "I hope"), but also avoid sounding arrogant or presumptuous.

✓ *Use a courteous and sincere tone.* Avoid platitudes, exaggeration, obvious flattery, and expressions of surprise or disbelief.

✓ *Use appropriate emphasis and subordination.* Emphasize and subordinate through the use of sentence structure, position, verb voice, amount of space, language, repetition, and mechanical means.

✓ *Use nondiscriminatory language.* Avoid bias about gender, race, ethnic background, religion, age, sexual orientation, and disabilities.

✓ *Stress the "you" attitude.* Emphasize what the receiver wants to know and how the receiver will be affected by the message; stress reader benefits.

✓ *Design your documents for readability.* Write at an appropriate level of difficulty so that your readers can understand the passage; design your documents so that they are attractive and easy to comprehend.

ing logical paragraphs, and setting an appropriate overall tone. Checklist 5 summarizes the 16 principles discussed in Chapters 4 and 5.

These principles will help you communicate your ideas clearly and effectively. They provide a solid foundation for the higher-order communication skills you will be developing in the following chapters. At first, you may find it somewhat difficult and time-consuming to constantly assess your writing according to these criteria. Their importance, however, merits the effort. Soon you will find that you are applying these principles automatically as you compose and revise messages.

■ See Handout 5.3.

The 3Ps
Problem, Process, Product

WRITING AN UNBIASED MESSAGE

Problem

As chair of the employee grievance committee, you must approve the minutes of each meeting before they are distributed. Following is the draft of a paragraph from the minutes that the committee secretary has forwarded for your approval:

> Mr. Timmerman argued that the 62-year-old Kathy Bevier should be replaced because she doesn't dress appropriately for her seamstress position in the alteration department. However, the human resources director, who is female, countered that we don't pay any of the girls in the alteration department well enough for them to buy appropriate attire. Mr. Timmerman did acknowledge that the seamstress performs her job well, considering her age and the fact that she suffers from arthritis. He added that he just wished she would dress more businesslike instead of wearing the colorful clothes and makeup that reflect her immigrant background.

Process

1. List any examples of gender bias contained in this paragraph.
   - "Mr. Timmerman" versus "Kathy Bevier"
   - "seamstress"
   - "who is female"
   - "any of the girls"

2. Are there examples of age bias?
   - "62-year-old"
   - "considering her age"

3. Are there instances of other discriminatory biases that you would want to correct?
   - Disability bias: "suffers from arthritis"
   - Nationality bias: "colorful clothes and makeup that reflect her immigrant background"

Ralph Timmerman argued that Kathy Bevier should be replaced because she doesn't dress appropriately for her sewing position in the alteration department. However, the human resources director countered that we don't pay these employees well enough for them to buy appropriate attire. Timmerman acknowledged that Bevier performs her job well. He added that he just wished she would dress more businesslike.

 Visit the **BusCom Online Learning Center** (http://college.hmco.com) for additional resources to help you with this course and with your future career.

■ Summary

Your paragraphs should be unified and coherent. Develop only one topic per paragraph, and use transitional words, pronouns, and repetition to move smoothly from one idea to the next.

co1. Keep paragraphs unified and coherent.

Express similar ideas in similar grammatical structure. For example, match adjectives with adjectives, nouns with nouns, infinitives with infinitives, and so on. Be especially careful to use parallel structure in report headings and in numbered lists.

co2. Use parallel structure.

Although paragraphs of various lengths are desirable, most should range from 60 to 80 words. To help the reader follow your logic, avoid very long paragraphs and avoid strings of very short paragraphs.

co3. Control paragraph length.

Your message should convey the attitude that you have done a competent job of communicating and that your reader will do as you ask or will accept your decision. Avoid, however, sounding presumptuous or arrogant.

co4. Write confidently.

Use a tone of courtesy and sincerity to build goodwill and to help you achieve your objectives. Avoid lecturing the reader or using platitudes.

co5. Use a courteous and sincere tone.

Not all ideas are equally important, so use techniques of emphasis and subordination to develop a common frame of reference between writer and reader. To emphasize an

co6. Use appropriate emphasis and subordination.

idea, put the idea in a short, simple sentence; place the major idea first or last; make the noun you want to emphasize the subject of the sentence; devote more space to the idea; use language that directly implies importance; or use mechanical means.

CO7. Use nondiscriminatory language.

CO8. Stress the "you" attitude.

CO9. Design documents for readability.

Use nondiscriminatory language in your writing by treating everyone equally and by not making unwarranted assumptions about any group of people.

Keep the emphasis on the reader—stressing what the reader needs to know and how the reader will be affected by the message.

Use the design techniques introduced on pages 178–182 of this chapter to make your messages physically attractive, inviting to read, and easy to understand.

■ See Slide 5.19.

■ Consider treating this list as an end-of-chapter exercise for students to define and give an example of each term.

■ Key Terms

You should now be able to define the following terms in your own words and give an original example of each.

nondiscriminatory language (173)	receiver benefits (177)
parallelism (166)	tone (167)
platitude (171)	"you" attitude (177)
readability (178)	

■ Suggestions and sample solutions for exercises appear in the *Instructor's Resource Manual.*

■ Exercises

1 The 3Ps (Problem, Process, and Product) Model: Communication Applications at Barnes & Noble, College Division Bobbie Kroman relies heavily on written communication to keep relations with suppliers and customers running smoothly. Although she uses e-mail for routine messages, she prefers the formality of a letter for proposals and for responses to customer complaints. When writing to business contacts in other countries, she uses a courteous tone and emphasizes the main point by restating it in different words at the beginning and the end of her letter.

Problem

Kroman has asked you, the manager of a New York–area Barnes & Noble college bookstore, to answer a Brazilian customer's inquiry about delivery schedules for international orders. The customer wants to compare the time needed to receive orders by air and by ship. Your research shows that orders sent by ship can arrive up to six weeks later than orders sent by air. However, you also want this customer to know that sending an order by air can cost up to 70 percent more than sending it by ship.

Process

a. Why are you writing this letter?
b. What do you need to know about your audience?
c. How can you stress the "you" attitude in your letter?

Product

Draft your letter; consider what points you will cover and in what order.

2 **Paragraph Unity and Coherence**   From the following sentences, select the best topic sentence; then list the other sentences in an appropriate order.

co1. Keep paragraphs unified and coherent.

a. Businesses will spend $150 billion a year on goods and services marketed by telephone.
b. The telephone is becoming one of the nation's chief timesavers.
c. Telephones save time, save money, and establish goodwill.
d. Telephones can sell an idea, service, or product.
e. Telephones can be used to answer questions, clear up confusion, and produce immediate responses.
f. More and more business is being conducted by telephone.
g. The telephone is on its way to becoming a number one marketing tool.

3 **Transitions**   Insert logical transitions in the blanks to give the following paragraph coherence:

Columbia is widening its lead over Kraft in the computer-magazine war. _____ its revenues increased 27 percent last year, whereas Kraft's increased only 16 percent. _____ its audited paid circulation increased to 600,000, compared to 450,000 for Kraft. _____ Kraft was able to increase both the ad rate and the number of ad pages last year. One note of worry _____ is Kraft's decision to shut down its independent testing laboratory. Some industry leaders believe much of Kraft's success has been due to its reliable product reviews. _____ Columbia has just announced an agreement whereby Stanford University's world-famous engineering school will perform product testing for Columbia.

4 **Parallelism**   Determine whether the following sentences use parallel structure. Revise sentences as needed to make the structure parallel.

co2. Use parallel structure.

a. The store is planning to install a new cash-register system that is easier to operate, easier to repair, and cheaper to maintain than the current system.
b. According to the survey, most employees prefer either holding the employee cafeteria open later or its hours to be kept the same.
c. The quarterback is expert not only in calling plays but also in throwing passes.
d. Our career-guidance book will cover

  - Writing résumés

  - Application letters

  - Techniques for interviewing

CO3. Control paragraph length.

5 **Paragraph Length**   Read the following paragraph and determine how it might be divided into two or more shorter paragraphs to help the reader follow the complex topic being discussed.

> Transforming a manuscript into a published book requires several steps. After the author submits the manuscript, the copy editor makes any needed grammatical or spelling changes. The author reviews these changes to be sure that they haven't altered the meaning of any sentences or sections. Then the publisher sends the manuscript out for typesetting. Next, the author proofreads the typeset galleys and gives the publisher a list of any corrections. These corrections are incorporated into the page proofs, which show how the pages will look when printed. The author and publisher review these page proofs for any errors. Only after all corrections have been made does the book get published. From start to finish, this process can take as long as a year.

6 **Writing Like You Mean It**   Revise the paragraph to create a more confident tone.

> If you believe my proposal has merit, I hope that you will allocate $50,000 for a pilot study. It's possible that this pilot study will bear out my profit estimates so that we can proceed on a permanent basis. Even though you have several other worthwhile projects to consider for funding, I know you will agree the proposal should be funded prior to January 1. Please call me before the end of the week to tell me that you've accepted my proposal.

CO4. Write confidently.

7 **Writing Confidently**   Revise the following sentences to convey an appropriately confident attitude.

  a. Can you think of any reason not to buy a wristwatch for dressy occasions?
  b. I hope you agree that my offer provides good value for the money.
  c. Of course, I am confident that my offer provides good value for the money.
  d. You might try to find a few minutes to visit our gallery on your next visit to galleries in this area.

CO5. Use a courteous and sincere tone.

■ See Slide 5.20.

8 **Being Courteous and Sincere**   Revise this passage to avoid platitudes, obvious flattery, and exaggeration.

> You, our loyal and dedicated employees, have always been the most qualified and the most industrious in the industry. Because of your faithful and dependable service, I was quite surprised to learn yesterday that an organizational meeting for union representation was recently held here. You must realize that a company like ours cannot survive unless we hold labor costs down. I cannot believe that you don't appreciate the many benefits of working at Allied. We will immediately have to declare bankruptcy if a union is voted in. Please don't be fooled by empty rhetoric.

9. Evaluating Writing Style   As a college student with a potentially bright future, you no doubt frequently receive letters from credit-card companies, department stores, insurance firms, and the like, soliciting your business. Select a letter that you or a colleague has received, and analyze it for courtesy and sincerity. Does it follow the guidelines discussed in this chapter? What is your overall reaction to the letter? Write a statement of evaluation.

10. Evaluating Job Candidates   Assume that you have evaluated two candidates for the position of sales assistant. This is what you have learned:

a. Carl Barteolli has more sales experience.
b. Elizabeth Larson has more appropriate formal training (college degree in marketing, attendance at several three-week sales seminars, and the like).
c. Elizabeth Larson's personality appears to mesh more closely with the prevailing corporate attitudes at your firm.

CO6. Use appropriate emphasis and subordination.

■ See Slide 5.21.

You must write a memo to Robert Underwood, the vice president, recommending one of these candidates. First, assume that personality is the most important criterion and write a memo recommending Elizabeth Larson. Second, assume that experience is the most important criterion and write a memo recommending Carl Barteolli. Use appropriate emphasis and subordination in each message. You may make up any reasonable information needed to complete the assignment.

11. Using Techniques of Emphasis   Revise each sentence by applying the indicated technique of emphasis. In each case, emphasize the problems of cold weather.

a. Use one complex sentence.

Outdoor workers in White Butte, North Dakota, have to battle severe winter conditions. However, outdoor workers in Atlanta, Georgia, face mild winter conditions.

b. Choose the noun you want to emphasize as the subject of the sentence.

Telephone and utility repair personnel who work outdoors have to cope with dangerous working conditions created by subzero temperatures.

c. Use language that directly implies importance.

Outdoor workers generally face a range of weather conditions, but frigid temperatures can pose particularly severe problems.

d. Use repetition.

Utilities in the northern states frequently remind outdoor workers about the cold-weather dangers of frostbite and hypothermia.

CO7. Use nondiscriminatory language.

12 **Using Nondiscriminatory Language**   Revise the following sentences to eliminate discriminatory language.

a. The mayor opened contract talks with the union representing local policemen.
b. While the salesmen are at the convention, their wives will be treated to a tour of the city's landmarks.
c. Our company gives each foreman the day off on his birthday.
d. Our public relations director, Heather Marshall, will ask her young secretary, Bonita Carwell, to take notes during the president's speech.
e. Neither Rev. Batista nor his secretary, Doris Hawkins, had met the new family.

13 **Sexist Language**   Identify at least one nonsexist word for each of the following words: *businessman, policeman, fireman, manhole cover, waitress, stewardess, mankind, male nurse, repairman,* and *mailman.*

CO8. Stress the "you" attitude.

14 **Positive Tone and "You" Attitude**   Rewrite the following sentences to reflect a more positive tone or "you" attitude.

a. You made three mistakes on your report.
b. You failed to submit the correct information.
c. If you don't get this project finished soon, your days here are numbered.
d. We want to thank you for your help with the project.
e. We will not repair your car until we get your authorization.
f. You cannot be selected without signing the enclosed form.
g. I appreciate your feedback on this project.
h. We value your business with our company.
i. We saw your article in the school newspaper.
j. We do not sell that product in the extra large size.

■ See Slide 5.22.

15 **Stressing the "You" Attitude**   Revise the following paragraph to make the reader the center of attention.

We are happy to announce that we are offering for sale an empty parcel of land at the corner of Mission and High Streets. We will be selling this parcel for $89,500, with a minimum down payment of $22,500. We have had the lot rezoned M-2 for student housing. We originally purchased this lot because of its proximity to the university and had planned to erect student housing, but our investment plans have changed. We still feel that our lot would make a profitable site for up to three 12-unit buildings.

■ See Slide 5.23.

16 **Reader Benefits**   Revise the following sentences to emphasize reader benefits.

a. We have been in the business of repairing sewing machines for more than 40 years.
b. We need donations so we can expand the free-food program in this community.

   c. Company policy requires us to impose a 2 percent late charge when customers don't pay their bills on time.

   d. Although the refund department is open from 9 a.m. to 5 p.m., it is closed from 1 p.m. to 2 p.m. so our employees can take their lunch breaks.

17 **Readability Level**   Select a passage of at least 500 words from a textbook used in another class. Rewrite the passage using the principles outlined in Chapters 4 and 5. Discuss the changes you made and the reasons you made them. Submit the copy and your revised version to your instructor for evaluation.

18 **Document Readability**   Working with a partner, write a summary of Principle 9—Design Your Documents for Readability. Incorporate at least four of the design techniques presented in this section as you prepare the document. Present the document to your instructor for evaluation.

CO**9.** **Design documents for readability.**

19 **Document Design**   Working in groups of three, reformat the press release shown in LAB Test 5 to incorporate the elements of effective document design discussed in this chapter. You may edit the document as needed as long as you do not change the basic information.

continuing case 5

Drew Drafts a Drab Memo

Here is a first-draft memo written by O. J. Drew to Tom Mercado:

■ A suggested solution to the Continuing Case can be found in the *Instructor's Resource Manual.*

MEMO TO: Thomas Mercado, vice president, manufacturing
FROM: O. J. Drew, production manager
DATE: October 13, 20—
SUBJECT: Charlotte Expansion

As you will remember, when we opened our Charlotte plant, we made plans to increase capacity within three years. We're now approaching the end of our third year, and even though sales are increasing, I suggest we delay any expansion plans for another two years.

To begin with, interest rates are heading up across the board. Last week, North Carolina National Bank and Wachovia Bank both raised their prime rates quite a bit. This is the highest it has been in several years. Other big banks are likely to follow with similar increases. Both NCNB and Wachovia financed our initial efforts in Charlotte—at a lower rate. The *Wall Street Journal* predicts that interest rates will remain high for at least the next 18 months. A second reason for my suggestion is that present capacity is sufficient to support our present level of sales. If sales continue to grow substantially, we will continue to have sufficient capacity for three more years. We can increase production for minimal plant cost by simply adding a third shift. Adding a third shift will lower per-unit costs and enable us to convert numerous part-time positions to full-time positions, with a corresponding savings in fringe benefits. Finally, our union contract expires next year. Although our plant is automated, we still employ 95 unionized workers. These men's wage demands are high, and we will simply not be able to afford an expansion. I predict getting a reasonable union contract this time will be a hard nut to crack. In addition, Diana believes that if a strike is at all possible, we won't even be using the capacity we presently have—let alone expanded capacity.

For these reasons, I recommend we delay any expansion plans for another two years at least. I hope you will agree with me. Luis Diaz does; and if you desire, we can produce a formal report of our recommendation for you to present to the board. Let me know if you have any questions.

juv

Critical Thinking

1. In terms of what you know about Tom Mercado (see Appendix to Chapter 1 on page 36), assess the readability of this memo for its intended audience. What factors not measured by readability formulas affect the readability of this memo?

Writing Projects

2. Analyze each paragraph, using Checklist 5 on page 183 as the basis for your analysis. What effective and ineffective techniques has Drew used?

3. List each transitional expression that was used in the second paragraph to achieve coherence. Does the paragraph have unity? Explain.

4. Revise this memorandum, making whatever changes are necessary to increase its effectiveness. You may make up any needed facts as long as they are reasonable.

■ See Handout 5.4.

■ See Slide 5.24.

Thomas depends on specific and accurate information to successfully manage the manufacturing operations at Urban Systems.

LABtest 5

Retype the following press release from Dave, correcting any word-usage problems according to the rules introduced in LAB 6 on page 603.

could've

After a hundred years, you ~~could of~~ assumed that there would be

nothing new to say about the flashlight. With a bulb, batteries,

its

and tube, ~~it's~~ function hasn't changed much. However, you should

infer

not ~~imply~~ that the flashlight itself hasn't changed.

5   Today's flashlights are smaller and lighter than the one in-

Regardless

vented in 1898. ~~Irregardless~~ of the fact that it hasn't changed

different from

much in function, its form is now ~~different than~~ earlier versions.

Surely   *lies*

~~Sure~~, part of the flashlight's evolution ~~lays~~ in commercialism,

but it also stems from childhood memories. You can't repeat these

complement

10   memories, but you can create new ones to ~~compliment~~ them. Some of

imminent

the new flashlights are already on the market; others are ~~eminent~~.

whose

Remember the watch ~~who's~~ tiny built-in flashlight lets you tell

the time in the dark? The next generation is a nightlight and

you're

clock, in case ~~your~~ really interested in the time when you visit

15   the john.

principle

In ~~principal~~, a bendable flashlight is a traditional flashlight,

but it also fastens to the forehead or hangs over your neck so

lose

that you don't ~~loose~~ your place when reading. A musical version

anyone

lets ~~any one~~ keep two of life's necessities at hand.

20   Finally, there is a flashlight designed to combat Seasonal

affects

Affective Disorder, in which insufficient light ~~effects~~ a person's

personality; it turns your entire pillow into a reading lamp.

■ See Slide 5.25.

■ See Slide 5.26.

■ See Slide 5.27.

■ See Slide 5.28.

■ See Slide 5.29.

6

The Process of Writing

communication
OBJECTIVES

After you have finished this chapter, you should be able to

1. Specify the purpose of your message and analyze your audience.

2. Compose a first draft of your message.

3. Revise for content, style, and correctness.

4. Arrange your document in a standard format.

5. Proofread your document for content, typographical, and format errors.

Editing for a global audience that moves on with each mouse click, Noel McCarthy knows that all the articles he posts must be clear, concise, and compelling. McCarthy is editor-in-chief of *Executive Perspectives,* the free monthly online business magazine of the international accounting and consulting firm PriceWaterhouseCoopers (PwC). Although PwC's 120,000 employees are welcomed to browse the online magazine, its primary readership is a broad external audience of executives and managers in client companies, media firms, government agencies, and higher education.

Every month, McCarthy and his editors read 150 business and economics publications to select six articles for the "Digest" section of the magazine. Then, he says, "we whittle them down to their core arguments and add introductory paragraphs," along with links to the original article for readers who want more information. For the "International Briefings" section, staff members edit local business updates submitted by PwC correspondents in offices around the world. Again, brevity and clarity are top priority.

For the monthly "Re: Business" section of *Executive Perspectives,* McCarthy polishes four original articles submitted by PwC partners, managers, and directors. Recent articles have examined business conditions in Russia, China, and Cyprus as well as corporate governance, privacy, cyber-crime, money laundering, and the rodeo business. "We edit for grammar and style, yet we work hard to preserve the writer's individual voice because we don't want to put our audience to sleep by producing bland, corporate gobbledy-

an insider's
perspective

NOEL McCARTHY
Editor-in-Chief,
PriceWaterhouseCoopers,
Executive Perspectives
(New York, NY)

gook," notes the editor-in-chief. "We look to major magazines like *Time* and *Newsweek* as our benchmarks of excellence."

When editing articles, McCarthy minimizes jargon and avoids what he calls "acronymese"—too many acronyms. His readers recognize common regulatory acronyms such as SEC (for Securities and Exchange Commission), but other acronyms can seem like a secret language for the initiated. McCarthy pays particular attention to the organization of information. "I check that each point is explained clearly and carefully," he says, "and that we don't leave out any step in the chain of logic."

No matter how many times he reads an article on the screen, McCarthy finds he misses something if he doesn't proofread on the printed page. In addition, "I like to have at least two or three sets of eyes read my writing." Then a professional proofreader reads every article and flags any errors for correction before the editors finalize that month's issue of *Executive Perspectives*. Proofreading doesn't end even when new articles are posted on the first of the month. Early the next morning, McCarthy says, "everybody is reading everybody else's writing, just to be sure."

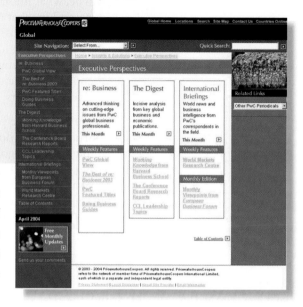

"Brevity and clarity are top priority."

The writing process consists of planning, drafting, revising, formatting, and proofreading.

There is no single "best" writing process. In fact, all good writers develop their own process that suits their own ways of tackling a problem. But one way or another, competent communicators typically perform the following five steps when faced with a business situation that calls for a written response (see Figure 6.1):

1. *Planning:* Determining what the purpose of the message is, who the reader will be, what information you need to give the reader to achieve your purpose, and in what order to present the information.
2. *Drafting:* Composing a first draft of the message.
3. *Revising:* Editing for content, style, and correctness.
4. *Formatting:* Arranging the document in an appropriate layout.
5. *Proofreading:* Reviewing the document to check for content, typographical, and format errors.

The amount of time you devote to each step depends on the complexity, length, and importance of the document. Not all steps may be needed for all writing tasks. For example, you may go through all the steps if you are writing a business plan to get funding for a small business but not if you are answering an e-mail message inviting you to a meeting. Nevertheless, these steps are a good starting point for completing a writing assignment—either in class or on the job.

The process of writing

- Specify the purpose of your message and analyze your audience.
- Compose a first draft of your message.
- Revise for content, style, and correctness.
- Arrange documents in a standard format.
- Proofread your document for content, typographical, and format errors.

6.1

■ See Slide 6.1.

■ A chapter overview appears in the *Instructor's Resource Manual.*

CO1. Specify the purpose of your message and analyze your audience.

■ Planning

Planning, the first step in writing, involves making conscious decisions about the purpose, audience, content, and organization of the message.

figure6.1

The Five Steps in the Writing Process

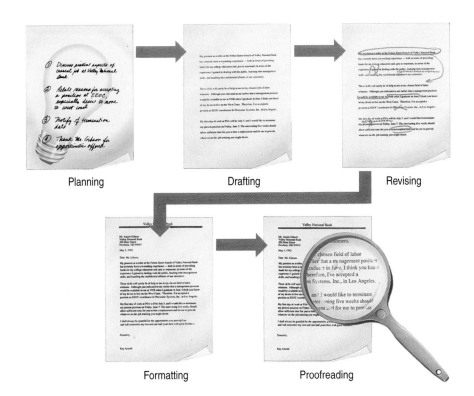

Planning   Drafting   Revising

Formatting   Proofreading

Purpose

The first decision relates to the purpose of the message. If you don't know why you're writing the message (that is, if you don't know what you hope to accomplish), then later you'll have no way of knowing whether you've achieved your goal. In the end, what matters is not how well crafted your message was or how attractive it looked on the page; what matters is whether you achieved your communication objective. If you did, your communication was successful; if you did not, it was not.

Most writers find it easier to start with a general purpose and then refine the general purpose into a specific one. The specific purpose should indicate the response desired from the reader.

Assume, for example, that you are a marketing manager at Seaside Resorts, a chain of small hotels along the California, Oregon, and Washington coasts. You have noted that many of the larger hotel chains have instituted "frequent-stay" plans, which reward repeat customers with free lodging, travel, or merchandise. You want to write a message recommending a similar plan for your small hotel. Your general purpose might be this:

General Purpose: To describe the benefits of a
                frequent-stay plan at
                Seaside Resorts.

Such a goal is a good starting point, but it is not specific enough. To begin with, it doesn't identify the intended audience. Are you writing a memo to the vice president of marketing recommending this plan, or are you writing a letter to frequent business travelers recommending that they enroll in this plan? Assume, for the moment, that you're writing to the marketing vice president. What is she supposed to *do* as a result of reading your memo? Do you want her to simply understand what you've written? agree with you? commit resources for further research? agree to implement the plan immediately? How will you know if your message achieves its objective? Perhaps you decide that your specific purpose is this:

Specific Purpose: To persuade Cynthia to approve
                the development and implementation of a frequent-stay plan for
                a 12-month test period in Seaside's three Oregon resorts.

The West Wing **creator and writer Aaron Sorkin completes the writing process week after week for 17 million viewers. "I just want to survive one episode at a time,"** he said, **"so I'm trying to write better—and faster."**

The purpose should be specific enough to serve as a yardstick for judging the success of the message.

A S K Ober

Dear Dr. Ober:

Tell me the truth. Do you use the five steps in the writing process that you describe in Chapter 6 every time you write something? Do you always sit down and (a) plan what you're going to say, (b) draft your message, (c) revise it, (d) format it, and then (e) proofread it?

—Don B.

Dear Don:

The short answer is no, I do not always follow the five steps. For example, in responding to your memo, I'm composing at the keyboard. Although I may backspace and revise a phrase (I just did it: I had written "revise a sentence" and then changed it to "revise a phrase"), I did not outline what I wanted to say, nor did I worry about formatting.

As I try to make clear when discussing the process of writing in Chapter 6, using these five steps is a good starting point for completing a writing assignment—either in class or on the job. I should add that the one step I never neglect—even in dashing off a quick e-mail—is the last step. I always proofread what I've written before hitting the Send button.

—Scot

E-mail your questions and comments to askober@ober.net.

■ See Slide 6.2.

A clearly stated purpose helps you avoid including irrelevant and distracting information.

■ See Slide 6.3.

■ See Slide 6.4.

Now you have a purpose that's specific enough to guide you as you write the memo and to permit you to judge, in time, whether your message achieved its goal.

In another situation, your general purpose might be to resolve a problem regarding a shipment of damaged merchandise, and your specific purpose might be to persuade the manufacturer to replace the damaged shipment at no cost to you within 10 days. Or your general purpose might be to refuse a customer's claim, and your specific purpose might be to convince the customer that your refusal is reasonable and to maintain the customer's goodwill.

Having a clear-cut statement of purpose lets you focus on the content and organization, eliminating any distracting information and incorporating all relevant information.

Audience Analysis

To maximize the effectiveness of your message, you should perform an **audience analysis;** that is, you should identify the interests, needs, and personality of your receiver. Recall our discussion of mental filters in Chapter 1. Each person perceives a message differently because of his or her unique mental filter. Thus, we need to determine the level of detail, the language to be used, and the overall tone by answering the pertinent questions about audience discussed in the following sections (see Figure 6.2).

Who Is the Primary Audience?   For most correspondence, the audience is one person, which simplifies the writing task immensely. It is much easier to personalize a message addressed to one individual than a message addressed to many individuals. Sometimes, however, you will have more than one audience. In this case, you need to identify your **primary audience** (the person whose cooperation is crucial if your message is to achieve its objectives) and then your **secondary audience** (others who will also read and be affected by your message). If you can satisfy no one else, try to satisfy the needs of the primary decision maker. If possible, also satisfy the needs of any secondary audience.

figure6.2

Questions for Audience Analysis

Make your audience the "star" of your message.

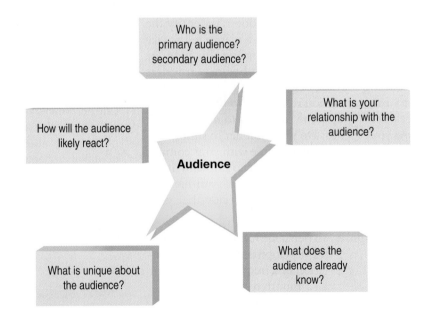

If, for example, you're presenting a proposal that must be approved by the general manager but that will also require the cooperation of your colleagues in other departments, the general manager is the primary audience and your colleagues are the secondary audience. Gear your message—its content, organization, and tone—mainly to the needs of the general manager. Most often (but not always), the primary audience will be the highest-level person to whom you're addressing your communication.

What Is Your Relationship with the Audience?

Does your audience know you? If not, you will first have to establish your credibility by assuming a reasonable tone and giving enough evidence to support your claims. Are you writing to someone inside or outside the organization? If outside, your message will often be a little more formal and will contain more background information and less jargon than if you are writing to someone inside the organization.

Your relationship with the reader determines the tone and content of your message.

What is your status in the organization in relation to your audience? Communications to your superiors are obviously vital to your success in the organization. Such communications are typically a little more formal, less authoritarian in tone, and more information-filled than communications to peers or subordinates. In addition, such messages are typically "front-loaded"—that is, they use a direct organizational style and present the major idea in the first paragraph. Study your superior's own messages to get a sense of his or her preferred style and diction, and adapt your own message accordingly.

Most communications to your superiors will probably be organized in a direct style.

When you communicate with subordinates, be polite but not patronizing. Try to instill a sense of collaboration and of corporate ownership of your proposal. When praising or criticizing, be specific; and criticize the action—not the person. As always, praise in public but criticize in private.

How Will the Audience React?

If the reader's initial reaction to both you and your topic is likely to be *positive,* your job is relatively easy. You can use a direct approach—beginning with the most important information (for example, your conclusions or recommendations) and then supplying the needed details. If the reader's initial reaction is likely to be *neutral,* you may want to use the first few lines of the message to get the reader's attention and convince him or her that what you have to say is important and that your reasoning is sound. Make sure your message is short and easy to read and that any requested action is easy to take.

Suppose, however, that you expect your reader's reaction—either to your topic or to you personally—to be *negative.* Here you have a real sales job to do. If the reader shows a personal dislike of you, your best strategy is to call on external evidence and expert opinion to bolster your position. Show that others, people whom the reader is likely to know and respect, share your opinions. Use courteous, conservative language, and suggest ways the reader can cooperate without appearing to "give in"—perhaps by reminding the reader that new circumstances and new information call for new strategies.

If the expected reader reaction is negative, present lots of evidence and expert testimony.

If you anticipate that your reader will oppose your proposal, your best strategy is to supply extra evidence. Instead of one example, give two or three. Instead of quoting one external source, quote several. Begin with the areas of agreement, stress reader benefits, and try to anticipate and answer any objections the reader might have. Through logic, evidence, and tone, build your case for the reasonableness of your position.

Determine how much information the reader needs.

What Does the Audience Already Know?

Understanding the audience's present grasp of the topic is crucial to making decisions about content and writing style. You must decide how much background information is necessary, whether the use of jargon is acceptable, and what readability level is appropriate. If you are writing to multiple audiences, gear the amount of detail to the level of understanding of the key decision maker (the primary audience). In general, it is better to provide too much rather than too little information.

What Is Unique About the Audience?

The success or failure of a message often depends on little things—the extra touches that say to the reader, "You're important, and I've taken the time to learn some things about you."

What can you learn about the personal interests or demographic characteristics of your audience that you can build into your message? Is the reader a "take-charge" kind of person who would prefer to have important information up front—regardless of whether the news is good or bad? What level of formality is expected? Would the reader be flattered or be put off by the use of his or her first name in the salutation? Have good things or bad things happened recently at work or at home that may affect the reader's receptivity to your message?

Competent communicators analyze their audience and then use this information to structure the content, organization, and tone of their messages.

■ See Handout 6.1.

Make the reader feel important by personalizing the content.

Example of Audience Analysis

To illustrate the crucial role that audience analysis plays in communication, let's consider three different scenarios for the memo to the marketing vice president requesting a pilot test of a frequent-stay incentive program.

First, assume that Cynthia Haney, vice president of marketing and your immediate superior, will be the only reader of your memo; that is, she has the authority to approve or reject your proposal. Ms. Haney is an old hand in the hotel business, having had 20 years of managerial experience, and she respects your judgment. She has made it clear that she likes directness in writing and wants the important information up front—so that she can get the major ideas first and then skim the rest of the communication as necessary. The first paragraph of your memo to her might then use a direct approach, as follows:

Some readers like a direct approach, regardless of the purpose of the message.

> The purpose of this memo is to recommend implementing a frequent-stay plan for a 12-month test period in our three Oregon resorts. This recommendation is based on a review of the policies of our competitors and on an analysis of the costs and benefits of instituting such a program. The pertinent data is presented below.

In the next scenario, assume that Haney assumed her position at Seaside Resorts just six months ago and that she is still "learning the ropes" of the hospitality industry. Up to this point, your relationship with her has been cordial, although she is probably not very familiar with your work. That being the case, the first paragraph of your memo might use an indirect approach, in which you discuss your procedures and present the evidence before making a recommendation.

> The attached *Wall Street Journal* article discusses four small hotel resorts that have started frequent-stay plans. The purpose of this memo is to describe such plans and analyze their costs and benefits. Then I will recommend what action Seaside might take in this regard.

In a third scenario, suppose that instead of having confidence in your skills, Haney has given some indication that she *doesn't* yet completely trust your judgment. You might then be wise to add a second paragraph to establish your credibility.

Establish credibility by showing the basis for your recommendations.

> To gather the needed data, I studied published reports prepared by the Hotel and Restaurant Association. Then, I interviewed the person in charge of frequent-stay programs at three hotels. Finally, Dr. Kenneth Lowe, professor of hospitality services at Southern Cal, reviewed and commented on my first draft. Thus, this proposal is based on a large body of data collected over two months.

As can be seen, the type of information you include in your message, the amount, and the organization reflect what you know (or can learn) about your audience.

The Role of Persuasion in Communicating

Any business communication—no matter how routine—involves more than just information dumping. You must select and organize the information with a specific audience and purpose in mind. In a real sense, persuasion is a major purpose of any communication. Whether your goal is to sell, to motivate, to convey bad news, or simply to inform, your ability to persuade ultimately determines the degree of success or failure that you will achieve. Your motivations may vary from greed to altruism, and your methods may vary from overt to subtle, but in the end you seek to direct others' behavior toward a desired course of action or point of view.

Every document you write seeks to persuade—through credibility, emotion, or logic.

Persuasion, of course, is not *coercion*—far from it. In some cases, people may be forced to do something, but they can't be forced to believe something. They must be persuaded in ways that are agreeable to them. The word *persuade,* in fact, stems from a Latin root that means *agreeable.*

In his work *Rhetoric,* Aristotle identified three methods by which people can be persuaded:

- *Ethos,* an appeal based on credibility

- *Pathos,* an appeal based on emotion

- *Logos,* an appeal based on logic

These methods remain as relevant today as they were when Aristotle wrote about them more than two thousand years ago.

Angela Talavera, right, is a special prosecutor in Ciudad Juárez, Mexico. Here, she uses the persuasive methods of ethos (credibility) and pathos (emotion) to win the confidence of the mother of a missing girl.

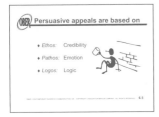

■ See Slide 6.5.

Ethos   Ethos is an ethical appeal based on who you are and how your audience perceives you. Advertisers use this type of appeal frequently—for example, in celebrity endorsements. Your audience must believe that you know what you are talking about. Sometimes your credibility comes from your audience's prior knowledge and experience in dealing with you; at other times, you must first establish your credibility with your audience before they will buy your message. To grasp the importance of credibility, assume that you just heard that a giant meteor would crash onto Earth in 24 hours. How would your reaction differ if this announcement came from the Psychic Hot Line versus Stephen Hawking?

Competent communicators know their audience—and ensure that their audience knows them.

Pathos   Pathos appeals to an audience's emotions. You might, for example, use examples or what-if situations to make an audience happy, sad, or scared. You are probably familiar, for example, with the American Express commercials highlighting the problems faced by customers who lost their credit cards while vacationing abroad. The message: "To avoid this type of stress and fraud, always carry American Express."

Competent communicators are careful in their use of emotional appeals, however, recognizing that such appeals can be overused and that audiences may assume that you're appealing to emotions because you're short on objective, logical reasons.

Which is more persuasive—a fact, an inference, or an opinion?

Logos   For most business communication situations, logic is the most effective form of persuasion—facts, inferences, and opinion. Aristotle defined the three aspects of logic this way:

- *fact:* that which is indisputably true

- *inference:* that which is probably true

- *opinion:* that which is possibly true

The more factual data you can bring to bear on your position, the more likely you are to persuade. Nevertheless, inferences that can be drawn based on available data and opinion (especially expert opinion) are also persuasive.

Competent communicators tend to rely on logical appeals and ensure that the facts, inferences, and expert opinion they use have relevance—both to their position and to their audience.

Content

Once you have determined the purpose of your message and identified the needs and interests of your audience, the next step is to decide what information to include. For simple messages, such as routine e-mail, this step presents few problems. However, many communication tasks require numerous decisions about what to include. How much background information is needed? What statistical data best supports the conclusions? Is expert opinion needed? Would examples, anecdotes, or graphics aid comprehension? Will research be necessary, or do you have what you need at hand?

Do not start writing until you have planned what you want to say.

The trick is to include enough information so that you don't lose or confuse the reader, yet avoid including irrelevant material that wastes the reader's time and obscures the important data. Different writers use different methods for identifying what information is needed. Some simply jot down notes on the points they plan to cover. For all but the simplest communications, the one thing you should *not* do is to start drafting immediately, deciding as you write what information to include. Instead, start with at least a rudimentary outline of your message—whether it's in your head, in a well-developed typed outline, or in the form of notes on a piece of scratch paper.

One useful strategy is **brainstorming**—jotting down ideas, facts, possible leads, and anything else you think might be helpful in constructing your message. Aim for quantity, not quality. Don't evaluate your output until you've run out of ideas. Then begin to refine, delete, combine, and otherwise revise your ideas to form the basis for your message.

Another possible strategy is **mind mapping** (also called *clustering*), a process that avoids the step-by-step limitations of lists. Instead, you write the purpose of your message in the middle of a page and circle it. Then, as you think of possible points to add, write them down and link them by a line either to the main purpose or to another point. As you think of other details, add them where you think they might fit. This visual outline offers flexibility and encourages free thinking. Figure 6.3 shows an example of mind mapping for our frequent-stay memo.

DRESSED FOR SUCCESS	*word* **wise**

A lawyer wears a suit to work. Here's what other people wear:

Electrician:	Shorts
Boxer:	Socks
Golfer:	T-shirt
Psychiatrist:	Slip
Painter:	Coat
Firefighter:	Hose

■ According to Sonja Sakovich, president of a San Francisco consulting firm, mind mapping works because brains usually don't produce ideas in a linear way. Sakovich has introduced firms such as AT&T and Pacific Bell to mind mapping. At AT&T, systems analysts use mind mapping to clearly illustrate software and information needs.

Organization

The final step in the planning process is to establish the **organization** of the message—that is, to determine in what order to discuss each topic. After you have brainstormed or mapped out your ideas around a main idea, you need to organize them into an outline that you can use to draft your message into its most effective form.

Classification (grouping related ideas) is the first step in organizing your message. Once you've grouped related ideas, you then need to differentiate between the major and minor points so that you can line up minor ideas and evidence to support the major ideas.

The most effective sequence for the major ideas often depends on the reaction you expect from your audience. If you expect a positive response, you may want to use a direct approach, in which the conclusion or major idea is presented first, followed by the reasons. If you expect a negative response, you may decide to use an indirect approach, in which the reasons are presented first and the conclusion after.

Because of the importance of the sequence in which topics are discussed, the recommended organization of each specific type of communication is discussed in detail in the chapters that follow. (See also Chapter 4's coverage of paragraph unity, coherence, and length—all of which are important elements of organization.)

To maintain good human relations, base your organization on the expected reader reaction.

■ Drafting

Having now finished planning, you are finally ready to begin **drafting**—that is, composing a preliminary version of a message. The success of this second stage of the process depends on the attention you gave to the first stage. The warning given earlier bears repeating: Don't begin writing too soon. Some people believe they have weak writing skills; when faced with a writing task, their first impulse is therefore to jump in and get it over with as quickly as possible. Avoid the rush. Follow each of the

co2. Compose a first draft of your message.

figure 6.3

A Sample Mind Map

five steps of the writing process to ease the journey and improve the product. As shown in Communication Snapshot 6, the quality of the writing is enhanced when writers not only plan what they want to write but also jot down notes to guide them.

Do not combine drafting and revising. They involve two separate skills and two separate mindsets.

Probably the most important thing to remember about drafting is to just let go—let your ideas flow as quickly as possible onto paper or computer screen, without worrying about style, correctness, or format. Separate the drafting stage from the revising stage. Although some people revise as they create, most find it easier to first get their ideas down on paper in rough-draft form, then revise. It's much easier to polish a page full of writing than a page full of *nothing*. As one writing authority has noted,

> Writing is art. Rewriting is craft. Mix the two at your peril. If you let your inner editor (who, according to popular theory, lives in the left side of your brain) into the process too early, it's liable to overpower your artist, blocking your creative flow.[1]

So avoid moving from author to editor too quickly. Your first draft is just that—a *draft*. Don't expect perfection, and don't strive for it. Concentrate, instead, on recording in narrative form all the points you identified in the planning stage. When you have finished and then begin to revise, you will likely discover that a surprising amount of your first draft is usable and will be included in your final draft.

If a report is due in five weeks, some managers (and students) spend four weeks worrying about the task and one week (or even one long weekend) actually writing the report. Similarly, when given 45 minutes to write a letter or memo, some people spend 35 minutes anxiously staring at a blank page or blank screen and 10 minutes actually writing. These people are experiencing **writer's block**—the inability to focus on the writing process and to draft a message. The causes of writer's block are typically one or more of the following:

- *Procrastination:* Putting off what we dislike doing.

- *Impatience:* Growing tired of the naturally slow pace of the writing process.

- *Perfectionism:* Believing that our draft must be perfect the first time.

These factors naturally interfere with creativity and concentration. In addition, they undermine the writer's self-image and make him or her even more reluctant to tackle the next writing task. The treatment for writer's block lies in the strategies discussed in the following paragraphs.

1. **Choose the right environment.** The ability to concentrate on the task at hand is one of the most important components of effective writing. The best environment may *not* be the same desk where you normally do your other work. Even if you can turn off the phones and shut the door to visitors, silent distractions can bother you—a notation on your calendar reminding you of an important upcoming event, notes about a current project, even a photograph of a loved one. Many people write best in a library-type environment, with a low noise level, relative anonymity, and the space to spread out notes and other resources on a large table. Others find a computer room conducive to thinking and writing, with its low level of constant background noise and the presence of other people similarly engaged.

2. **Schedule a reasonable block of time.** If the writing task is short, you can block out enough time to plan, draft, and revise the entire message at one sitting. If the task is long or complex, however, schedule blocks of no more than two hours or so. After all, writing is hard work. When your time is up or your work completed, give yourself a reward—take a break or get a snack.

3. **State your purpose in writing.** Having identified your specific purpose during the planning phase, write it at the top of your blank page or tack it on the bulletin board in front of you. Keep it visible so that it will be uppermost in your consciousness as you compose.

Employ the power of positive thinking: You can write an effective message!

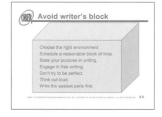

■ See Slide 6.6.

■ Poet Louise Glück on writer's block: "I question the assumption behind writer's block, which is that one should be writing all the time . . . at times we simply have nothing to say. Then we need to get back in the world and put more life into ourselves." Business writers, however, usually have a built-in purpose for writing something.

communication snapshot 6

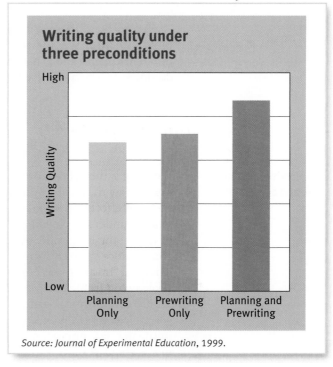

Writing quality under three preconditions

Source: Journal of Experimental Education, 1999.

*"I wish you would make up your mind, Mr. Dickens.
Was it the best of times or was it the worst of times?
It could scarcely have been both."*

4. **Engage in free writing.** Review your purpose and your audience. Then, as a means of releasing your pent-up ideas and getting past the block, begin **free writing;** that is, write continuously for five to ten minutes, literally without stopping. Although free writing is typically considered a predrafting technique, it can also be quite useful for helping writers "unblock" their ideas.

   While free writing, don't look back and don't stop writing. If you cannot think of anything to say, simply keep repeating the last word or keep writing some sentence such as, "I'll think of something soon." Resist the temptation to evaluate what you've written. At the end of five or ten minutes, take a breather, stretch and relax, read what you've written, and then start again, if necessary.

5. **Avoid the perfectionism syndrome.** Remember that the product you're producing now is a *draft*—not a final document. Don't worry about style, coherence, spelling or punctuation errors, and the like. The artist in you must create something before the editor can refine it.

6. **Think out loud.** Some people are more skilled at *speaking* their thoughts than at writing them. Picture yourself telling a colleague what you're writing about, and explain aloud the ideas you're trying to get across. Hearing your ideas will help sharpen and focus them.

7. **Write the easiest parts first.** The opening paragraph of a letter or memo is often the most difficult one to compose. If that is the case, skip it and begin in the middle. In a report, the procedures section may be easier to write than the recommendations. Getting *something* down on paper will give you a sense of accomplishment, and your writing may generate ideas for other sections.

> *You need not write the parts of a message in the order in which they will finally appear. Begin with the easiest parts.*

Try each of these strategies for avoiding writer's block at least once; then build into your writing routine those strategies that work best for you. Just as different athletes and artists use different strategies for accomplishing their goals, so do different writers. There is no one best way, so choose what is effective for you.

■ See Slide 6.7.

CO3. Revise for content, style, and correctness.

■ Revising

Revising is the process of modifying a document to increase its effectiveness. Having the raw material—your first draft—in front of you, you can now refine it into the most effective document possible, considering its importance and the time constraints under which you are working. If possible, put your draft away for a period of time—the longer the better. Leaving time between creation and revision helps you distance yourself from your writing. If you revise immediately, the memory of what you "meant to say" rather than what you actually wrote may be so strong that it keeps you from spotting weaknesses in logic or diction.

If you're a typical writer, you will have made numerous minor revisions even as you were composing; however, as noted earlier, you should save the major revisions until later. For important writing projects, you will probably want to solicit comments about your draft from colleagues as part of the revision process.

■ See Slide 6.8.

Although we have discussed revising as the third step of the writing process, in fact it involves several steps. Most writers revise first for content, then for style, and finally for correctness. All types of revision are most efficiently done from a typed copy of the draft rather than from a handwritten copy.

Revising for Content

After an appropriate time interval, first reread your purpose statement and then the entire draft to get an overview of your message. Ask yourself such questions as these:

Ensure that all needed information—and only needed information—is included.

- Is the content appropriate for the purpose I've identified?

- Will the purpose of the message be clear to the reader?

- Have I been sensitive to the needs of the reader?

- Is all the information necessary?

- Is any needed information missing?

- Is the order of presentation of the points effective?

Although it is natural to have a certain pride of authorship in your draft document, don't be afraid to make whatever changes you think will strengthen your document—even if it means striking out whole sections and starting again from scratch. The aim is to produce a revised document in which you can have even more pride.

For Portland, Oregon, ad agency Wieden+Kennedy, promoting a creative environment in which to create advertising copy is a necessity. They even provide a rooftop hammock to help copy writers generate ideas and even draft their copy.

Revising for Style

Next, read each paragraph again (aloud, if possible), using the 16 criteria contained in Checklist 5 on page 183 as the basis for your evaluation. Reading aloud gives you a feel for the rhythm and flow of your writing. Long sentences that made sense as you wrote them may leave you out of breath when you read them aloud.

"I'm unbelievably nit-picky about every word. I could never turn something in until I've dealt with every semicolon five times."
—Dave Barry

If time permits and the importance of the document merits it, try reading your message aloud to friends or colleagues, or have them read your revised draft. Ask them what is clear or unclear. Can they identify the purpose of your message? What kind of image do they get of the writer just from reading the message? Adhering to Checklist 5 and securing feedback from colleagues will help you identify areas of your message that need revision.

Revising for Correctness

The final phase of revising is **editing**, the process of ensuring that writing conforms to standard English. Editing involves checking for correctness—that is, identifying problems with grammar, spelling, punctuation, and word usage. You may want to use your word processor's grammar checker as a starting point for editing (see Spotlight 17, "Use You're Grammar Check Her—Four What Its Worth," on pages 210–211). Editing should follow revision because there is no need to correct minor errors in passages that may later be revised or deleted. Writers who fail to check for grammar, mechanical, and usage errors risk losing credibility with their reader. Such errors may distract the reader, delay comprehension, cause misunderstandings, and reflect negatively on the writer's abilities.

All three types of revision—for content, style, and correctness—can be accomplished most efficiently on a computer.

■ See Slides 6.9. and 6.10.

CO4. Arrange your document in a standard format.

■ See Slide 6.11.

■ See Slide 6.12.

■ Formatting

Letters are external documents sent to people outside the organization; *memos* are internal documents sent to people inside the same organization as the writer. Today, most traditional memos have been replaced by e-mail; and, in fact, many letters are now sent as e-mail attachments rather than through the mail. E-mail and reports may be either internal or external. No one format for any type of business document is universally accepted as standard; a fair amount of variation is common in industry. Detailed guidelines for the most common formatting standards are presented in the Reference Manual at the back of this text.

To some extent, technology is changing formatting standards. For example, although formatting is traditionally the next-to-last step in the writing process, you may in fact make some formatting decisions at the planning or drafting stages. For example, your word processing program has probably been set with default side margins of 1 to 1¼ inches, which are appropriate for most documents.

In addition, e-mail messages all look like memorandums—whether they are sent to someone inside or outside the organization. They typically contain *To:, From:, Date:,* and *Subject:* lines just as memos do, and they do not contain an inside address as is typical in letters. The important point is to use the format that is appropriate for each specific message.

Regardless of who actually types your documents, *you* are the one who signs and submits them, so *you* must accept responsibility for not only the content but also the mechanics, format, and appearance of your documents. In addition, executives now keyboard many of their own documents—without the help of an assistant.

Another advantage of standard formatting is simply that it is more efficient. Formatting documents the same way each time means that you do not need to make individual layout decisions for every document. Thus, a standard format not only saves time but also gives a consistent appearance to the organization's documents.

Finally, readers *expect* to find certain information in certain positions in a document. If the information is not there, the reader is unnecessarily distracted. For all these reasons, you should become familiar with the standard conventions for formatting documents.

■ See Slide 6.13.

Take personal responsibility for all aspects of a message that goes out under your name.

■ Proofreading

Proofreading is the final quality-control check for your document. Remember that a reader may not know whether an incorrect word resulted from a simple typo or from the writer's ignorance of correct usage. And even one such error can have adverse effects (see Figure 6.4). Being *almost perfect* is not good enough; for example, if your telephone directory were only 99 percent perfect, each page would contain about four wrong numbers! And imagine the embarrassment of the tax preparer who submitted supporting statements for a client's tax return that contained this direction: "Please reference *Lie 12* on Schedule C." (Would a computer's spelling checker have caught this error?) Or how about the newspaper ad that Continental Airlines ran in the *Boston Herald,* in which the company advertised one-way fares from Boston to Los Angeles for $48? The actual one-way fare was *$148.* That typographical error cost Continental $4 million, because it sold 20,000 round-trip tickets at a loss of $200 each.[2]

Don't depend on having an assistant catch and correct every mistake; become a "super blooper snooper" yourself. It's your reputation that is at stake. Take responsibility for ensuring the accuracy of your communications, just as you take responsibility for your other managerial tasks. Proofread for content, typographical, and format errors.

■ *Content Errors:* First, read through your document quickly, checking for content errors. Was any material omitted unintentionally? Unfortunately, writers who use word processing to move, delete, and insert material sometimes omit passages unintentionally or duplicate the same passage in two different places in the document. In short, check to be sure that your document *makes sense.*

■ *Typographical Errors:* Next, read through your document slowly, checking for typographical errors. Watch especially for errors that form a new word— for example, "I took the figures *form* last month's

co5. Proofread your document for content, typographical, and format errors.

Typographical errors may send a negative nonverbal message about the writer.

figure6.4

The Need for Competent Proofreading Skills

If 99.9% accuracy is acceptable to you, then

Every hour:

- 18,300 pieces of mail will be mishandled.
- 22,000 checks will be credited to the wrong bank accounts.
- 72,000 phone calls will be misplaced by telecommunication services.

Every day:

- 12 newborn babies will be given to the wrong parents.
- 107 incorrect medical procedures will be performed.

Every year:

- 2.5 million books will be shipped with the wrong cover.
- 20,000 incorrect drug prescriptions will be written.

Not to mention that:

- 315 entries in *Webster's Third New International Dictionary of the English Language* will be misspelled.

spotlight17
ON TECHNOLOGY

Use You're Grammar Check Her—Four What Its Worth

Most of us can use all the help we can get when it comes to writing, and that's where grammar checkers come in. These tools, which are now standard features of most word processing programs, identify spelling and typographical problems as well as possible examples of awkward writing, clichés and jargon, passive voice, mismatched punctuation marks, and the like. They then propose alternatives that you can accept, reject, or mark for subsequent fixing.

Grammar checkers compare words and phrases in a document with built-in lists of words and phrases. Some even go beyond the compare-and-mark function by using artificial intelligence to identify incorrectly used homonyms such as *there, their,* and *they're.*

In addition to flagging possible spelling, grammar, and style problems, many programs identify such common punctuation problems as placing a comma after (instead of before) a quotation mark or leaving two spaces between words. Finally, many programs provide a word count and readability grade level.

How well do such programs work? Some of the suggestions identified are close to nitpicking. Typically, a large percentage of the words and phrases that are flagged as possible errors are, in fact, used appropriately; conversely, other more serious errors or stylistic problems are not identified.

Let's apply Microsoft Word's grammar and spelling checker to the first draft of the student-written passage in The 3Ps (Problem, Process, and Product) model exercise on page 216. Here is the draft:

1   The Entrepreneurial Association of Baker College (EABC) shares your
2   interest in increasing the number of scholarships available to business majors.
3   We recently voted to establish an annual $1000 scholarship for a jr. or sr. student
4   majoring in Entrepreneurship. To fund this scholarship, we propose selling
5   doughnuts and coffee in the main lobby from 7:30–10:30 A.M. daily. All of the
6   profits will be earmarked for the Scholarship fund. A secondary benifit of this
7   project is that it will provide practical work experience for our club members. We
8   will purchase out own supplies and equipment, and keep careful records. When
9   they are not in use, the supplies and equipment will be stored in the office of
10 Professor Grant Edwards, our Sponsor. DPMA follows similar procedures with
11 it's fund raising project of selling computer disks in the main lobby.
12 We need your approval of this scholarship project in time for us to begin in
13 January. This project also provides a convenient service for faculty, staff, and
14 students.

■ A real-life incident illustrates the need for proofreading: To apologize for an argument, a husband sent his wife some flowers and told the florist the card should read, "I'm sorry. I love you." However, when the flowers arrived, the card read, "I'm sorry I love you."

reports." Such errors are difficult to spot. Also be on the lookout for repeated or omitted words. Double-check all proper names and all figures, using the original source if possible. Professional proofreaders find that writers often overlook errors in the titles and headings of reports, in the opening and closing parts of letters and memos, and in the last paragraph of all types of documents.

Spelling Alerts

The spelling checker correctly identified the one misspelling in the passage ("benifit" in line 6) and suggested the correct spelling "benefit." Not surprisingly, the checker also identified the abbreviation "DPMA" in line 10 (actually, the abbreviation is correct) and incorrectly suggested "DAMP" instead.

Grammar Alerts

The grammar checker correctly identified the misused "it's" in line 11 and suggested the correct form "its." However, it incorrectly identified the sentence in lines 8 to 10 ("When they are not in use, the supplies and equipment will be stored in the office of Professor Grant Edwards, our Sponsor") as a sentence fragment when, in fact, it is a complete sentence.

In addition, the grammar checker flagged the sentence "All of the profits will be earmarked for the Scholarship fund" in lines 5 and 6 as being in the passive voice and suggested that it be changed to the active voice. On closer inspection, however, the sentence is more effectively stated in the passive voice because the receiver of the action "the profits" is more important than the doer "EABC." You want your grammar checker to provide this kind of alert so that you can make a case-by-case decision as to whether your original wording is more effective or should be changed.

Errors Not Identified

More important, however, are the errors that the checker did *not* identify:

- Line 3: "jr. or sr." should be spelled out: "junior or senior" and "Entrepreneurship" should not be capitalized.
- Line 3: "$1000" should be formatted as "$1,000."
- Line 5: "from 7:30–10:30 A.M." should be reformatted as "from 7:30 to 10:30 a.m."
- Line 6: "Scholarship fund" should be "scholarship fund."
- Line 8: "out" should be "our"; in addition, the comma should be omitted after the word "equipment."
- Line 10: "Sponsor" should be lowercase.
- Line 11: "fund raising" should be hyphenated: "fund-raising."

Finally, the grammar checker did not identify that the opening paragraph is 164 words long, much longer than the 60 to 80 words recommended for a typical paragraph in business writing.

Results of Relying on the Computer Grammar and Spelling Checker

In summary, applying the grammar and spelling checker in Microsoft Word gave these results:

- Identified 18 percent (2 of 11) of the actual errors, missing 82 percent of the errors.
- Identified 3 "errors" that were, in fact, correct.
- Missed 1 stylistic error (excessively long first paragraph).

Would you (or your instructor—or your boss) consider these results acceptable?

- *Format Errors:* Visually inspect the document for appropriate format. Are all the parts included and in the correct position? What will be the receiver's first impression before reading the document? Does the document look attractive on the page? Do not consider the proofreading stage complete until you are able to read through the entire document without making any changes. There is always the possibility that in correcting one error you inadvertently introduced another.

✔checklist6

The Writing Process

Planning

✔ Determine the purpose of the message.
- Make it as specific as possible.
- Identify the type of response desired from the reader.

✔ Analyze the audience.
- Identify the audience and your relationship with this person.
- Determine how the audience will probably react.
- Determine how much the audience already knows about the topic.
- Determine what is unique about the audience.

✔ Determine what information to include in the message, given its purpose and your analysis of the audience.

✔ Organize the information.
- Prefer a direct approach for routine and good-news messages and for most messages to superiors: present the major idea first, followed by supporting details.
- Prefer an indirect approach for persuasive and bad-news messages written to someone other than your superior: present the reasons first, followed by the major idea.

Drafting

✔ Choose a productive work environment and schedule a reasonable block of time to devote to the drafting phase.

✔ Let your ideas flow as quickly as possible, without worrying about style, correctness, or format.

✔ Do not expect a perfect first draft; avoid the urge to revise at this stage.

✔ If possible, leave a time gap between writing and revising the draft.

Revising

✔ Revise for content: determine whether all information is necessary, whether any needed information has been omitted, and whether the content has been presented in an appropriate sequence.

✔ Revise for style: follow the guidelines in Checklist 5 (see page 183).

✔ Revise for correctness: use correct grammar, mechanics, punctuation, and word choice (see the Reference Manual).

Formatting

✔ Format the document according to commonly used standards (see the Reference Manual).

Proofreading

✔ Proofread for content errors, typographical errors, and format errors.

■ See Handout 6.2.

The 3Ps
Problem, Process, Product

A SIMPLE MEMO

Today is December 3, 20—, and you are Alice R. Stengren, president of the Entrepreneurial Association of Baker College. *EABC* is the newest of the six student organizations in the school of business and has 38 members. It was formed two years ago when the department of management instituted a major in entrepreneurship.

The association recently voted to institute an annual $1,000 EABC scholarship. The scholarship will be awarded on the basis of merit to a junior or senior business student majoring in entrepreneurship at Baker College. Funds for the scholarship will be raised by selling coffee and doughnuts each day from 7:30 to 10:30 a.m. in the main lobby of the building. Write a memo to Dean Richard Wilhite, asking permission to start this fund-raising project in January.

1. What is the purpose of your memo?

   To convince the dean to let EABC sell coffee and doughnuts in the main lobby from 7:30 to 10:30 a.m. daily, beginning in January.

2. Describe your primary audience.

   Dean Richard Wilhite:

   - Former president of Wilhite Energy Systems (started the company—an entrepreneur himself)
   - 46 years old; has been business dean at Baker for six years (very familiar with the school and college)
   - Nationally known labor expert
   - Holds tenure in the department of management (which offers an entrepreneurship major)
   - Has spoken about the need to increase scholarships
   - Devotes a great deal of time to lobbying the legislature and raising funds (recognizes the need for fund-raising)
   - Doesn't know me personally but is familiar with EABC

3. Is there a secondary audience for your memo? If so, describe.

   No secondary audience.

4. Considering your purpose, what information should you include in the memo? (Either brainstorm and jot down the topics you might cover or construct a mind map.)

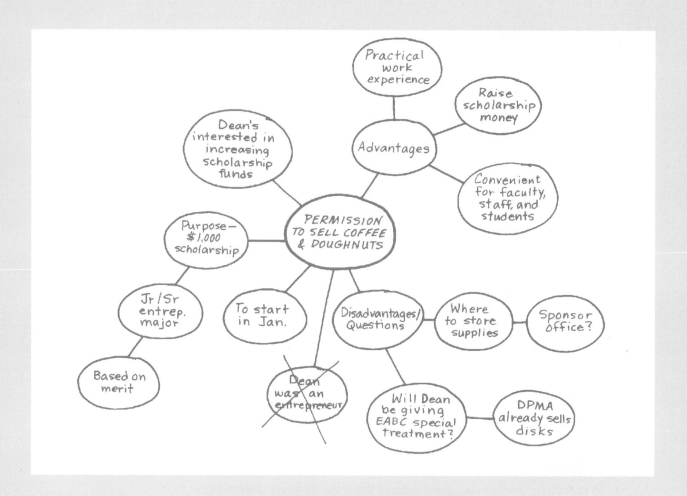

5. Jot down the major topics in the order in which you'll discuss them.

   a. Dean's interest in increasing scholarships
   b. Introduce scholarship and our fund-raising proposal
   c. Practical work experience that members will get
   d. Possible drawbacks (where to store supplies; special treatment for EABC)
   e. Other needed details
   f. Close—convenient for faculty, staff, students

6. Using the rough outline developed in Step 5, write your first draft. Concentrate on getting the needed information down. Do not worry about grammar, spelling, punctuation, transitions, unity, and the like at this stage.

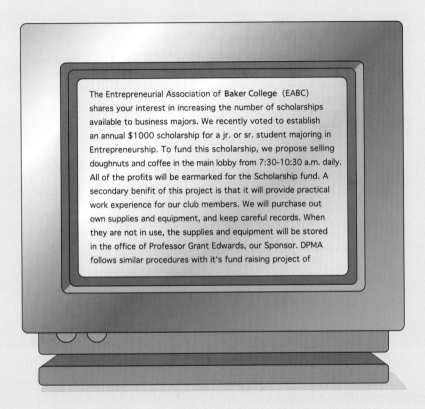

The Entrepreneurial Association of **Baker College** (EABC) shares your interest in increasing the number of scholarships available to business majors. We recently voted to establish an annual $1000 scholarship for a jr. or sr. student majoring in Entrepreneurship. To fund this scholarship, we propose selling doughnuts and coffee in the main lobby from 7:30-10:30 a.m. daily. All of the profits will be earmarked for the Scholarship fund. A secondary benifit of this project is that it will provide practical work experience for our club members. We will purchase out own supplies and equipment, and keep careful records. When they are not in use, the supplies and equipment will be stored in the office of Professor Grant Edwards, our Sponsor. DPMA follows similar procedures with it's fund raising project of

7. Print your draft and revise it for content, style, and correctness. (See the revised draft on page 216.)

8. How will you transmit this message; that is, what format will you use?

    I could, of course, send the dean an e-mail message. Given the importance of this request, however, I'll format it as a memo on our college's letterhead. That way the request will look more professional, and the dean will have a printed copy for review.

9. Format your revised draft, using a standard memo style. Then proofread.

Product

The Entrepreneurial Association of Baker College (EABC) shares your interest in increasing the number of scholarships available to business majors. *Toward that end,* We recently voted to establish an annual $1,000 scholarship for a jr. or sr. student majoring in ~~E~~ntrepreneurship. To fund this scholarship, we propose selling doughnuts and coffee in the main lobby from 7:30 *to* 10:30 A.M. daily. All ~~of the~~ profits will be earmarked for the ~~S~~cholarship fund. A secondary ben~~e~~fit of this project is that it will provide practical work experience for our club members. We will purchase ~~our~~ *our* own supplies and equipment, and keep careful records. When ~~they are~~ not in use, the supplies and equipment will be stored in the office of Professor Grant Edwards, our ~~S~~ponsor. DPMA follows similar procedures with it's fund-raising project of selling computer disks in the main lobby.

We look forward to receiving
~~We need~~ your approval of this ~~scholarship~~ *fund-raising* project in time for us to begin in January. ~~This project also provides~~ a convenient service for faculty, staff, and students. *In addition to raising new scholarship money and providing work experience for our members, we will also be providing*

Revised Draft

Baker College
1020 South Washington
Owosso, Michigan 48867-4400
Telephone (989) 729-3300
Fax (989) 729-3411

MEMO TO: Dean Richard Wilhite

FROM: Alice R. Stengren, President   *ARS*
Entrepreneurial Association of Baker College

DATE: December 3, 20—

SUBJECT: Establishment of EABC Scholarship

The Entrepreneurial Association of Baker College (EABC) shares your interest in increasing the number of scholarships available to business majors. Toward that end, we recently voted to establish an annual $1,000 scholarship for a junior or senior student majoring in entrepreneurship. To fund this scholarship, we propose selling doughnuts and coffee in the main lobby from 7:30 to 10:30 a.m. daily. All profits will be earmarked for the scholarship fund.

A secondary benefit of this project is that it will provide practical work experience for our club members. We will purchase our own supplies and equipment and keep careful records. When not in use, the supplies and equipment will be stored in the office of Professor Grant Edwards, our sponsor. The Data Processing Management Association follows similar procedures with its fund-raising project of selling computer disks in the main lobby.

We look forward to receiving your approval of this fund-raising project in time for us to begin in January. In addition to raising new scholarship money and providing work experience for our members, we will also be providing a convenient service for faculty, staff, and students.

Baker College / Auburn Hills • Cadillac • Cass City • Flint • Fremont • Jackson • Mount Clemens • Muskegon • Owosso • Port Huron
Regionally Accredited by North Central Association of Colleges and Schools Commission on Institutions of Higher Education / Member, Association of Independent Colleges and Universities of Michigan

Finally, after planning, drafting, revising, formatting, and proofreading your document, transmit it—confident and satisfied that you've taken all reasonable steps to ensure that it achieves its objectives. The steps in the writing process are summarized in Checklist 6.

Visit the **BusCom Online Learning Center** (at http://college.hmco.com) for additional resources to help you with this course and with your future career.

■ Summary

CO1. Specify the purpose of your message and analyze your audience.

Before writing, identify the purpose of your intended message. Carefully analyze your audience (or audiences) and determine what information to include. Determine whether a direct or indirect organizational plan will help you achieve your goals better.

CO2. Compose a first draft of your message.

Select an appropriate environment for drafting, and schedule enough time. Concentrate on getting the information down, without worrying about style, correctness, or format. Leave a time gap between writing and revising the draft.

CO3. Revise for content, style, and correctness.

Revise first for content—to determine whether all the needed information (and no unneeded information) have been included. Then revise for style, ensuring that the manner in which you present your ideas is effective. Finally, revise for correctness, being sure to avoid any errors in grammar, mechanics, punctuation, and word choice.

CO4. Arrange your document in a standard format.

Use a generally accepted format for your letters, memos, e-mail, and reports to provide efficiency for the writer, readability for the receiver, and a consistent appearance for the organization's documents.

CO5. Proofread your document for content, typographical, and format errors.

Read through your document to ensure that the document makes sense. Be on the lookout for typos. Finally, visually inspect the document for appropriate format.

■ Key Terms

■ Consider treating this list as an end-of-chapter exercise for students to define and give an example of each term.

You should now be able to define the following terms in your own words and give an original example of each.

■ See Slide 6.14.

audience analysis (198)

brainstorming (203)

drafting (203)

editing (208)

free writing (206)

mind mapping (203)

organization (203)

primary audience (198)

revising (207)

secondary audience (198)

writer's block (205)

■ Exercises

■ Suggestions and sample solutions for exercises appear in the *Instructor's Resource Manual*.

1 The 3Ps (Problem, Process, and Product) Model: Communication Applications at PriceWaterhouseCoopers' *Executive Perspectives*   Noel McCarthy follows all five steps in the writing process when he prepares and edits articles for his company's *Executive Perspectives* online magazine. He takes particular care with proofreading because he is writing for a global audience of thousands. When proofreading, he likes to print out his articles, mark any changes, and then revise the documents on the screen. Only after two colleagues and a professional proofreader have proofed an article does it appear on the magazine website.

Problem

As the editor of the "International Briefings" section, you receive dozens of update articles monthly from PwC correspondents located in different countries. Although your length guidelines are somewhat flexible, you know your busy readers appreciate articles that get to the point quickly. When an article is too long or ineffectively organized, you revise it, clear the edited version with the correspondent, and get it ready for posting. You have just edited an article by tax specialist Simone Dumont, your correspondent in France, and you are sending her the revised version for one last look. You want her to understand and accept your editing so she will continue submitting articles. At the same time, you want to be sure that your revisions haven't inadvertently changed the meaning of her content. Prepare an e-mail message to accompany the revised article.

Process

a. What is the specific purpose of your e-mail message?
b. Describe your audience.
c. Is pathos or logos most appropriate for this message?
d. What topics should you include in this message?
e. What phrase will you write on the subject line of your e-mail message?

Product

Using your knowledge of the writing process, prepare a one-page e-mail message, making up any reasonable data needed to complete this assignment.

2 The 3Ps (Problem, Process, and Product) Model: A Simple Memo

Problem

According to a story you read in the student newspaper this morning (May 25), the president of your university has proposed to the board of trustees that beginning next year, every employee must pay the same price for his or her contribution to the university's health-insurance plan—regardless of whether the employee is single, married without children, or married with children.

You are single and do not feel it is fair that single employees will be required to pay the same premium for health insurance as married employees pay for family coverage. As president of the Campus Singles Club, an organization made up of single staff and faculty members at the university, write to the president, objecting to this proposal.

Process

a. What is the purpose of your memo?
b. Describe your primary audience.
c. Is there a secondary audience for your memo? If so, describe it.
d. Brainstorm for a few moments, jotting down all the points you might cover in your memo.
e. Review the points you've jotted down and then list all the points you will cover—in the order in which you will cover them.
f. Using this rough outline, compose a first draft. For now, don't worry about style, grammar, and mechanics.
g. Print out your draft and revise it for content, style, and accuracy.

Product

Format your revised draft, using plain paper and a standard memo format. Then proofread and submit to your instructor both your memo and your responses to the preceding questions. If requested to do so, submit both documents as an e-mail message to your instructor.

CO1. Specify the purpose of your message and analyze your audience.

3 Communication Purpose   Compose a specific goal for each of the following.

a. A memo to a professor asking him to change a grade.
b. A letter to MasterCard about an incorrect charge.
c. A letter to the president of a local bank thanking her for speaking at your student organization meeting.
d. A memo of reprimand to a subordinate for leaving the warehouse unlocked overnight.

4 Communication Purpose and Reader Response   For each of the following communication tasks, indicate the specific purpose and the desired response.

a. A letter to a state senator about a proposed state surcharge on college tuition.
b. A memo to your payroll department head about an incorrect paycheck.
c. A letter to the college newspaper discussing the quality of the cafeteria food in recent months.
d. A memo to your assistant asking about the status of an overdue report.

5 Audience Analysis   Assume you must write an e-mail message to your current business communication professor, asking him or her to let you take your final examination one week early so that you can attend your cousin's wedding.

a. Perform an audience analysis of your professor. List everything you know about this professor that might help you compose a more effective message.
b. Write two good opening sentences for this message, the first one assuming that you are an A student who has missed class only once this term and the second assuming you are a C student who has missed class six times this term.

6 Audience Analysis Revisited   Now assume the role of the professor (see Exercise 5) who must reply to the request of the student with the C grade who has missed class six times. You'll tell the student that you are not willing to schedule an early exam.

a. Perform an audience analysis of yourself (as the student). What do you know about yourself that would help the professor write an effective message?
b. Should the professor use a direct or an indirect organization? Why?
c. Write the first sentence of the professor's message.

7 Audience Reaction   Read the following situations and decide what the audience reaction would be and whether a direct or indirect organizational plan would be better. Explain your answers.

a. As the manager of a small retail clothing store, you are preparing a memo to let the employees know they are getting a 50-cent-per-hour raise.
b. As the assistant manager of a hotel, you are writing to a customer letting her know that the jewelry she left in her room when she departed has not been found.
c. As a newly hired advertising director, you are e-mailing the president of the company requesting a 10 percent increase in your advertising budget.

d. You are writing a letter to customers announcing a new product that will be available in the store starting next month.

8 **Ethos, Pathos, and Logos**   You and a partner are working for an advertising firm. You have recently landed the account for a national tire company. You know about three appeals for persuasion: ethos, pathos, and logos. You decide to write three television commercials for the tire company—each using one of these appeals. Explain how you might use each appeal in a television commercial for tires. Turn the assignment in to your instructor for evaluation.

9 **Group Brainstorming**   Working in groups of three or four, come up with as many uses for a brick as you can. Make a list of all the suggestions and then share your list with the other groups in the class. How does your list compare to the other groups? How many new ideas did the other groups come up with that your group hadn't thought of? How big was the combined list?

10 **Free Writing**   As office manager for station WFYI (the nonprofit National Public Radio affiliate in Indianapolis), you want to buy a scanner to use with the three computers in your office. The scanner would let you input graphics (charts and pictures) into your computer documents and enter data without having to rekeyboard it. A scanner operates like a photocopier: you feed a copy of a picture or a page of text into the machine, and the picture or text then appears on your computer screen, where it can be used by your word processing or other software programs.

co2. Compose a first draft of your message.

You must write a memo, the goal of which is to convince the general manager to let you buy a scanner and related software for $425. Think about ways you could use this equipment. Then free write for 10 to 15 minutes without stopping and without worrying about the quality of what you're writing. (You may first want to reread the discussion of free writing on page 206 of this chapter.) Now examine what you have written. If you were actually going to write the memo, how much of your output could you use after revision?

11 **Mind Mapping (Clustering)**   Assume you must write a two-page, double-spaced abstract of the important points of this chapter. *Without reviewing the chapter,* prepare a mind map of the points you might want to cover.

12 **Organizing**   Prepare a rough outline for the abstract, using the mind map as your guide. List the major and minor points you will cover and the order in which you will cover them. (You do not have to follow your mind map precisely; it's only for guidance.)

13 **Brainstorming, Organizing, and Drafting**   Assume you are going to write a letter to your state senator about a proposed 6 percent increase in college tuition fees next year.

a. Determine a specific purpose of your letter.
b. Brainstorm at least six facts, ideas, and questions you might want to raise in your letter.
c. Determine an effective sequence of the points you decide to include in the letter.
d. Type the specific purpose at the top of a blank page.

e. Write the easiest part of the letter first. With which part did you start? Why?

f. Continue to draft the remaining sections of the letter.

g. Did you use every fact, question, or idea on your list? Explain your choices.

CO3. Revise for content, style, and correctness.

14 **Revising for Style**   What type of position would you like immediately upon graduation? With what type of organization and in what part of the country would you like to work? Where do you expect to be in terms of your career five years from now?

Write a one-page paper on this topic. Have a partner read your paper aloud and then give you feedback on how the paper sounds. What is clear? What is not? Does it flow smoothly? What changes should be made? Then make any changes you feel are necessary. Then follow the same process with your partner's paper. Submit both papers with corrections noted to your instructor for feedback.

15 **Revising**   Bring in a one-page composition you have written in the past—an essay exam response, business letter, or the like. Make sure your name is *not* on the paper. Exchange papers among several colleagues (so that you are not revising the paper of the person who is revising yours) and complete the following revision tasks.

a. Read the paper once, revising for content. Make sure that all needed information is included, no unneeded information is included, and the information is presented in a logical sequence.

b. Read the paper a second time, revising for style. Make sure that the words, sentences, paragraphs, and overall tone are appropriate.

c. Read the paper a third time, revising for correctness. Make sure that grammar, mechanics, punctuation, and word choice are error-free.

Return the paper to the writer. Then, using the revisions of your paper as a guide only (after all, *you* are the author), prepare a final version of the page. Submit both the marked-up version and the final version of your paper to your instructor.

CO4. Arrange your document in a standard format.

16 **Work-team Communication**   You will work in groups of four for this assignment. Assume that a large shopping center is next to your campus and many day students park there for free while attending classes. The shopping center management is considering closing this lot to student use, citing the need for additional space for customer parking. The four members of your group represent four student organizations (a sorority, a fraternity, a business student organization, and a campus service organization), which have decided to write a joint letter to the manager of the shopping center, trying to convince him to maintain the status quo.

Following the five-step process outlined in this chapter, compose a one-page letter to the manager. Brainstorm to generate ideas for the content of the letter; have each member of the group call out possible points to include while one person writes down all the ideas. Don't evaluate any of the ideas until you have worked for 10 to 15 minutes. Then discuss each point listed and decide which ones to include and in what order.

Format your letter in block style. Address it to Mr. Martin Uthe, Executive Manager, Fairview Shopping Center, P.O. Box 1083, DeKalb, IL 60115. Type an envelope, sign and fold the letter, and insert it into the envelope before submitting it to your instructor.

17 Proofreading   Assume that you are Michael Land and you wrote and typed the following letter. Proofread the letter, using the line numbers to indicate the position of each error. Proofread for content, typographical errors, and format. For each error, indicate by a *yes* or *no* whether the error would have been identified by a computer's spelling checker. (*Hint:* Can you find 30 content, typographical, or format errors?)

1   April 31 2005

2   Mr. Thomas Johnson, Manger

3   JoAnn @ Friends, Inc.

4   1323 Charleston Avenue

5   Minneapolis, MI 55402

6   Dear Mr. Thomas:

7   As a writing consultant, I have often aksed aud-

8   iences to locate all teh errors in this letter.

9   I am allways surprized if the find all the errors.

10   The result being that we all need more practical

11   advise in how to proof read.

12   To aviod these types of error, you must ensure that

13   that you review your documents carefully. I have

14   preparred the enclosed exercises for each of you

15   to in your efforts at JoAnne & Freinds, Inc.

16   Would you be willing to try this out on you own

17   workers and let me know the results.

18   Sincerly Yours

19   Mr. Michael Land,

20   Writing Consultant

CO5. Proofread your document for content, typographical, and format errors.

■ See Handout 6.3.

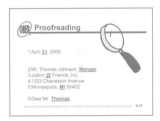

■ See Slides 6.15–16.17.

18 Organizing Messages—Eyeing Discount Contact Lens Sales   Your boss, Jonathon Coon, has his eye on a better way to retail disposable contact lenses. Coon is CEO of 1-800 Contacts, a discounter that sells disposable contact lenses online and by phone. Although his firm's annual revenues exceed $100 million, Coon has difficulty buying directly from lens manufacturers, which generally prefer to sell through optometrists. In fact, despite the rise of 1-800 Contacts and competing operations, the optometry industry still accounts for 70 percent of all contact lens retail sales. The issue is so contentious that 32 states have filed antitrust lawsuits against certain manufacturers, optometrists, and the American Optometric Association. Howard Braverman, the association's president, has been reported as saying that his organization doesn't pressure manufacturers to restrict sales to optometrists.

Coon asks you, his executive assistant, to write an e-mail to one of CNN's business reporters. Coon wants to call attention to his company's difficulties in buying directly, present information showing that consumers could save a significant amount on contact lens purchases if they were able to buy many brands from discounters such as 1-800 Contacts, and encourage the reporter to cover the story on the air. Should you use a direct or indirect approach to organize this information? Why? Draft a first paragraph for this e-mail, based on your organization strategy.

continuing
case 6

■ A possible solution to the Continuing Case is described in the *Instructor's Resource Manual*.

■ See Handout 6.4.

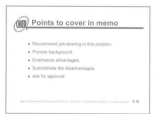

■ See Slide 6.18.

Two Heads Are Better Than One

Last year the Office Information Systems (OIS) Department installed a voice-mail system. One of the features of this system is that users can now call over the telephone and dictate their correspondence and reports. All executives and R&D engineers below the rank of vice president use the system. Three full-time transcriptionists in the OIS department then transcribe the dictation using word processing software. Turnaround time is typically less than five hours.

Yesterday, Angela Harper, one of the three transcriptionists, told department head Eric Fox that she really wants to be able to spend more time with her three-year-old. She asked about the possibility of job-sharing. She has a friend, Li Ying Yu, who has had extensive experience as a transcriptionist and who would also like to work half-time. Angela could work from 8 a.m. until noon daily, and Li Ying could work from 1 until 5 p.m. daily. Eric has had difficulty finding workers; he does not want to lose Angela.

On the plus side, if he accepts Angela's plan, he will have two highly qualified employees. If one employee is sick, the other might be willing to cover for her. Two employees working only half a day would probably be more productive than one employee working the entire day, and any deficiencies in one employee might be compensated for by the other (for example, if one employee is better at handling technical vocabulary, such dictation could be saved for her). On the negative side is the fact that there might be some coordination problems (especially in the beginning), and fringe benefits will be increased somewhat (he estimates about 15 percent).

Eric decides to write a memo to Diana Coleman recommending job-sharing for this one position. Because job-sharing would be a new company policy, he knows that his memo will ultimately be forwarded to Dave Kaplan for his reaction.

Angela Harper, a transcriptionist at Urban Systems, asked about the possibility of job-sharing as a means of spending more time at home with her three-year-old daughter. Contemporary organizations must address such worker-friendly issues as job-sharing, telecommuting, and on-site child care.

Critical Thinking

1. Assume the role of Eric Fox. What is the specific goal of your memo?

2. Who are the primary and secondary audiences for this memo? What do you know about the primary audience that will help you write a more effective memo?

Writing Projects

3. List the points you should cover in the memo—in order.

4. Write a draft of the memo. (You may make up any needed information, as long as it is reasonable.)

5. Revise the draft.

6. Format the memo, proofread, and submit.

■ See Slide 6.19.

■ See Slide 6.20.

LABtest 6

Retype the following letter to the editor from Dave, inserting any needed commas according to the comma rules introduced in LAB 2 on page 576.

(DATE)   *(NONR)*

Your lead editorial on May 19 2005 lamented light pollution

which limits our views of the night sky. As a person who loves the
(INTRO)

profound beauty of the night sky I thank you for spreading the word

about the loss of this precious environmental resource.
                    (TRAN)   *(PLACE)*

5   A retired lighting engineer however from Louisville Kentucky

disputed many of the points you made. He stated that streetlights

were not the problem and that the average streetlight is designed to
                                                            (INTRO)

put 95 percent of its light on the street. While the best ones do they are

a small minority. Many spill a quarter or more of their light horizontally

10   and upward.

The ultimate goals of lighting are security and visibility.
                                      (IND)

More light does not necessarily aid these goals and it can actually

defeat them if the lighting is of poor quality.
                        (QUOT)

James Thurber stated "There are two kinds of light: the glow

15   that illumines and the glare that obscures." We can preserve the
            (SER)   *(SER)*

beauty of the night sky enhance our security and reduce our energy
                        (DIR AD)

costs. Fellow lighting engineers I challenge you to apply the crea-
    (ADJ)

tive dedicated energies of our profession to solving this problem.

■ See Slide 6.21.

■ See Slide 6.22.

■ See Handout 6.5

7

Routine Messages

communication
OBJECTIVES

After you have finished this chapter, you should be able to

1. **Compose a routine request.**

2. **Compose a routine reply.**

3. **Compose a routine claim letter.**

4. **Compose a routine adjustment letter.**

5. **Compose a goodwill message.**

Writing letters on behalf of her bunny mascot takes up a good portion of entrepreneur Ann Withey's time. Withey is cofounder of Annie's Homegrown, a $10 million business that makes packaged all-natural macaroni and cheese products. The company is Withey's second business venture, started after she and a partner sold their first business, Smartfood Popcorn, to Frito-Lay for $15 million in 1989. These days, she lives with her family on an organic farm in Connecticut and, in between weekly visits to the company's Massachusetts office, stays in contact with employees via phone, fax, and e-mail.

an insider's
perspective

ANN WITHEY
Cofounder, Annie's
Homegrown

Competing against corporate giants, Withey has built her business through social responsibility and folksy communication, seeking to connect with customers on a more personal level. That's why every package carries information about social causes along with a chatty letter signed "Annie" and a drawing of Bernie, the "Rabbit of Approval." "One of the things that attracts people to our products is that Annie is real and not a made-up Madison Avenue icon," Withey explains. (Bernie is real, too; his niece, Scout, recently succeeded him as company mascot.)

While another staff member handles e-mail messages, Withey responds to roughly 1,500 letters every month. Most are requests for free information about one of the causes promoted on product packages, such as a listing of scholarships or a "Be Green" bumper sticker. Although these items are routine requests, "90 percent of the

226

time, people add a positive line or two saying 'we love your pasta,'" she says. In response, Withey sends a form letter headed "Dear Friend," which opens with an expression of sincere appreciation for the reader's support and loyalty. The letter refers to the enclosed information, again thanks the reader, and closes with Bernie's picture next to Withey's signature. Making the most of every customer contact, this routine reply also includes an order form, a coupon, and information about related products and community donations.

Out of this avalanche of correspondence, about 20 letters every week require a customized response. Withey handwrites these letters, tailoring the content for each reader. "A lot of kids write about their pets and ask me about Bernie," she says. "I keep my letters light, answering their questions and explaining that Scout has taken over for Bernie. I always mention their pet's name and say how flattered I am that they took the time to let me know how much they like our products."

Withey also handwrites letters to parents who rave about the taste and convenience of her products. "Before I write, I try to envision that person sitting at the kitchen table writing to me," she says. "This helps me plan a genuine, unique letter that addresses each person's concerns." She first thanks the reader for his or her support, then picks out a specific detail from the original letter that she can discuss in her response. Finally, she closes on a friendly note by thanking the reader for "bringing a smile to my face." Withey's highly personal approach to communication reflects her overall business philosophy: "I'm a customer, too, and I treat people the way I would want to be treated."

"Before I write, I try to envision that person. . . . This helps me plan a genuine, unique letter that addresses each person's concerns."

■ A chapter overview appears in the *Instructor's Resource Manual.*

Routine messages

- Compose a routine request.
- Compose a routine reply.
- Compose a routine claim letter.
- Compose a routine adjustment letter.
- Compose a goodwill message.

■ See Slide 7.1.

The direct style presents the major idea first, followed by needed details.

Use an indirect plan when you present negative news or anticipate reader resistance.

■ Planning the Routine Message

Most of the typical manager's correspondence consists of communicating about routine matters. For example, a small-business owner asks for a catalog and credit application from a potential supplier; a manager at a large corporation sends a memo notifying employees of a change in policy; a consumer notifies a company that an ordered product arrived in damaged condition; or a government agency responds to a request for a brochure.

Although routine, such messages are of interest to the reader because the information the message contains is necessary for day-to-day operations. For example, although no company is pleased when a customer is dissatisfied with one of its products, the company *is* interested in learning about such situations so that it can correct the problem and prevent its recurrence.

When the purpose of a message is to convey routine information and our analysis of the audience indicates that the reader will probably be interested in its contents, we use a **direct organizational plan.** The main idea is stated first, followed by any needed explanation, then a friendly closing, as illustrated in Figure 7.1.

The advantage of using a direct organizational plan for routine correspondence is that it puts the major news first—where it stands out and gets the most attention. This saves the reader time because he or she can quickly see what the message is about by scanning the first sentence or two. The **indirect organizational plan,** in which the reasons are presented before the major idea, is often used for persuasive and bad-news messages and is covered in subsequent chapters.

You may transmit your message as an interoffice memorandum (written to someone in the same organization), a letter (written to someone outside the organization), or an e-mail message (written to anyone in the world with computer e-mail capabil-

figure 7.1

A Typical Routine E-mail Message

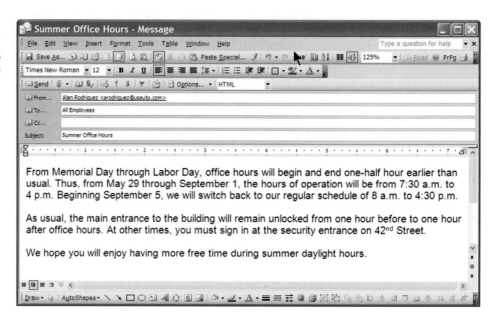

ity). (See Communication Snapshot 7 for research showing how long it takes businesses to respond to e-mail queries.) Still, the principles of effective business writing discussed in Chapters 4–6 apply, regardless of the medium used to transmit the message. Always include a descriptive subject line—regardless of the medium used.

Before learning how to write routine messages, you should know that many times a written message is not the most effective means of achieving your objective. Often a quick phone call or a walk down the hall to a colleague's office will work faster and at less expense than a written message. However, when you need a permanent record of your message (or of the reader's response to your message) or when the topic requires elaboration, a written message is more effective.

Determine first of all whether a written message is needed.

For example, if you want to confirm that the staff meeting starts at 10 a.m. tomorrow, you would probably telephone a colleague. However, if you want to confirm that a colleague has agreed to share the cost of a new advertising campaign, you would probably want to have this information on file in a written memo or e-mail.

Of course, not all messages are routine, as we will see in the following chapters. Messages that the reader is likely to resist require persuasion and are discussed in Chapter 8, and messages that contain bad news are discussed in Chapter 9.

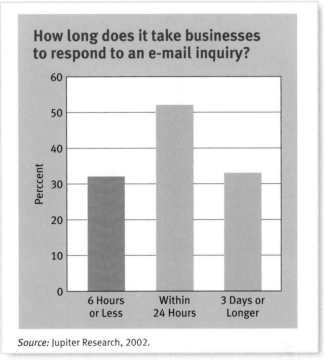

communication snapshot 7

How long does it take businesses to respond to an e-mail inquiry?

Source: Jupiter Research, 2002.

■ Routine Requests

A request is routine if you anticipate that the reader will readily do as you ask without having to be persuaded. For example, a request for specific information about an organization's product is routine because all organizations appreciate the opportunity to promote their products. However, a request for free samples of a company's product to distribute at your store's anniversary sale might not be routine because the company might have concluded that such promotion efforts are not cost-effective; thus, you would have to *persuade* the reader to grant the request.

co1. Compose a routine request.

Major Idea First

When making a routine request, present the major idea—your request—clearly and directly in the first sentence or two (see, however, Spotlight 18, "When in Rome . . . ," on page 231). You may use a direct question, a statement, or a polite request to present the main idea. A polite request is a statement that is phrased as a question out of courtesy but takes a period instead of a question mark, such as "May I please have your answer by May 3." Use a polite request when you expect the reader to respond by *acting* rather than by actually giving a yes-or-no answer. Always pose your request clearly and politely, and give any background information needed to set the stage. All of the following are effective routine requests:

Use a direct question, polite request, or statement to present your request.

Direct Question: Does Black & Decker offer educational discounts for public institutions making quantity purchases of tools? Blair Junior High School will soon be replacing approximately 50 portable electric drills used by our industrial technology students.

Statement: Please let me know how I might invest in your deferred money-market fund. As an American currently working in Bangkok, Thailand, I cannot easily take advantage of your automatic monthly deposit plan.

Polite Request: Would you please answer several questions about the work performance of Janice Henry. She has applied for the position of industrial safety officer at Inland Steel and has given your name as a reference.

Decide in advance how much detail you are seeking. If you need only a one-sentence reply, it would be unfair to word your request in such a way as to prompt the writer to provide a three-page answer. Define clearly the type of response you want and phrase your request to elicit that response.

NOT: Please explain the features of your Interact word processing program.

BUT: Does your Interact word processing program automatically number lines and paragraphs?

Do not ask more questions than are necessary. Make the questions easy to answer.

Remember that you are imposing on the goodwill of the reader. Ask as few questions as possible—and never for any information that you can reasonably get on your own. If many questions *are* necessary, number them; most readers will answer questions in the order in which you pose them and will thus be less likely to skip one unintentionally. Yes-or-no questions or short-answer questions are easy for the reader to answer; but when you need more information, use open-ended questions.

Arrange your questions in logical order (for example, order of importance, chronological order, or simple-to-complex order), word each question clearly and objectively (to avoid bias), and limit the content to one topic per question. If appropriate, assure the reader that the information provided will be treated confidentially.

Explanation and Details

Explain why you're making the request.

Most of the time you will need to give additional explanation or details about your initial request. Include any needed background information (such as the reason for

spotlight18
ACROSS CULTURES

When in Rome . . .

The direct organizational style is suggested for each type of message presented in this chapter. This style can be summarized in five words: *Present the major idea immediately.* American business executives have little time and patience for needless formalities and "beating around the bush."

Such is not always the case, however, when writing to someone whose culture and experiences are quite different from your own. Businesspeople in some countries may find letters written in the direct style too harsh and abrupt, lacking in courtesy. You should therefore adapt your writing style to the expectations of the reader.

For example, an American manufacturer sent a form sales letter to many domestic and foreign retail stores

inviting inquiries about stocking its line of fishing tackle. Note the differences in two of the responses the manufacturer received, shown below.

The moral is simple. Write as your receiver expects you to write. Take a cue from his or her own writing. If the letters you receive from an international associate are written in a direct style, you may safely respond in a similar style. However, if the letters you receive are similar to the Chinese response below, you might try a more formal, less direct style when responding. Although you would not want to *adopt* the reader's style, you might need to *adapt* your own style, on the basis of your analysis of the audience.

Would you please send me a sample of the fishing tackle you advertised in your October 3 letter, along with price and shipping information. As a long-time retailer of fishing tackle, I would be especially interested in any items you might have for fly fishing.

Since the trout season starts in six weeks, I would appreciate having this information as soon as possible.

American Request

It was with great pleasure that we received your letter dated 3 October. We send our deepest respects and wish to inform you that Yoon Sung Fishing Tackle Company, Ltd., has been selling fishing items for 38 years.

We would be pleased to consider your merchandise. May we ask you to please send us samples, price, and shipping information. It will be a great pleasure to conduct business with your company.

Chinese Request

---

asking) either immediately before or after making the request. For example, suppose you received the polite request given earlier asking about Janice Henry's job performance. Unless you were also told that the request came from a potential employer and that Janice Henry had given your name as a reference, you might be reluctant to provide such confidential information.

Or assume that you're writing to a former employer or professor asking for a letter of recommendation. You might need to give some background about yourself to jog the reader's memory. Or you might need to justify or expand on your request. Put yourself in the reader's position. What information would you need to answer the request accurately and completely?

A reader is more likely to cooperate if you can show how he or she will benefit from agreeing to your request. In fact, it is often the communication of such benefits that makes the message routine rather than persuasive.

■ See Slide 7.2.

If possible, show how others benefit from your receiving the requested information.

Will you please help us serve you better by answering several questions about your banking needs. We're building a branch bank in your neighborhood and would like to make it as convenient for you as possible.

In general, you should identify reader benefits when they may not be obvious to the reader, but you need not belabor the point if such benefits are obvious. For example, a memo asking employees to recycle their paper and plastic trash would probably not need to discuss the value of recycling, since most readers would already be familiar with the advantages of recycling.

Friendly Closing

Close on a friendly note.

In your final paragraph, assume a friendly tone. Close by expressing appreciation for the assistance to be provided (but without seeming to take the recipient's cooperation for granted), by stating and justifying any deadlines, or by offering to reciprocate. Make your ending friendly, positive, and original, as illustrated by the following examples:

> Please let me know if I can return the favor.

> We appreciate your providing this information, which will help us make a fairer evaluation of Janice Henry's qualifications for this position.

> May I please have the product information by October 1, when I place my Christmas wholesale orders? That way, I will be able to include Kodak products in my holiday sales.

Figure 7.2 on page 234 illustrates how *not* to write an effective routine request. Model 2 (page 235), a revised version of the ineffective example, illustrates the guidelines discussed previously for writing an effective routine request.

■ See Slides 7.3 and 7.4.

■ Routine Replies

CO2. Compose a routine reply.

Routine replies provide the information requested in the original message or otherwise comply with the writer's request. Like the original request letters, they are organized in a direct organizational style, putting the "good news"—the fact that you're responding favorably—up front.

Respond promptly so that the information will arrive in time to be used.

Probably one of the most important guidelines to follow is to answer promptly. If a potential customer asks for product information, ensure that the information ar-

CATHY   **by Cathy Guisewite**

rives before the customer must make a purchase decision. Otherwise, the time it took you to respond will have been wasted. Also, delaying a response might send the unintentional nonverbal message that you do not want to comply with the writer's request.

Your response should be courteous. If you appear to be acting grudgingly, you will probably lose any goodwill that a gracious response might have earned for you or your organization.

NOT: Although we do not generally provide the type of information you requested, we have decided to do so in this case.

BUT: We are happy to provide the information you requested.

Grant the request or give the requested information early in the message. Doing so not only saves the reader's time but also puts him or her in a good state of mind immediately. Although the reader may be pleased to hear "We have received your letter of June 26," such news is not nearly so eagerly received as telling the reader "I would be pleased to speak at your Engineering Society meeting on August 8; thanks for thinking of me." Put the good news up front—where it will receive the most emphasis.

Be sure to answer all the questions asked or implied, using objective and clearly understood language. Although it is often helpful to provide additional information or suggestions, you should never fail to at least address all the questions asked—even if your answer is not what the reader hopes to hear. Questions are usually answered in the order in which they were asked, but consider rearranging them if a different order makes more sense.

The reader will probably be in a positive mood as the result of your letter, and you may consider either including some sales promotion if appropriate or building goodwill by implying such characteristics about your organization as public spiritedness, quality products, social responsibility, or concern for employees. To be effective, sales promotion and goodwill appeals should be subtle; avoid exaggeration and do not devote too much space to such efforts.

Often the writer's questions have been asked by others many times before; in such a situation, a form letter may be the most appropriate way to respond. A **form letter** is a letter with standardized wording that is sent to different people. With word processing, it is often difficult to tell the difference between a form letter and a personal letter. If a stockholder wrote asking why your company conducted business in Cuba, a personal reply would probably be called for. However, if a potential stockholder wrote asking for a copy of your latest annual report, you might simply send an annual report, along with a form letter such as the following:

We are happy to send you our latest annual report. Also enclosed is a copy of a recent profile of Dennison Industries contained in the June issue of *Fortune* magazine.

As you study our annual report, note the diversity of our product offerings—from men's clothing to massive earth movers. This diversity is one of the reasons we have shown a profit for each of the past 57 years. Our 5-, 10-, and 15-year income statements are shown on page 8 of the enclosed report.

WORDS WORTH *word*wise

The longest word you can spell without repeating a letter: *Uncopyrightable.* It uses 15 of the 26 letters.
The longest word with just one vowel: *strengths*
The word with the longest definition in most dictionaries: *set.* In the *Oxford English Dictionary,* the verb *set* has over 430 meanings consisting of approximately 60,000 words.
The longest common word without an *a, e, i, o,* or *u*: *rhythms*.
The only two common words with six consonants in a row: *catchphrase* and *latchstring*.
Beijing has three dotted letters in a row. So does *Fiji* and *hijinks*.

■ See Slide 7.5.

■ See Slides 7.6. and 7.7.

Consider using form letters for answering frequent requests.

figure7.2

Ineffective Example of a Routine Request

Uses a subject line that is too general to be helpful. (It is not even clear to the reader whether you're providing or requesting product information.)

Begins in an indirect, roundabout manner and introduces irrelevant background information.

Embeds the requests for information in the middle of a long paragraph.

Closes with a cliché, without providing any incentive for responding.

Provides incomplete sender identification.

Refer to any enclosures in your letter to make sure they are read.

■ Sincerely,

Rhoda Stern

Rhoda Stern

rac
Enclosure

Use positive language to create a positive impression.

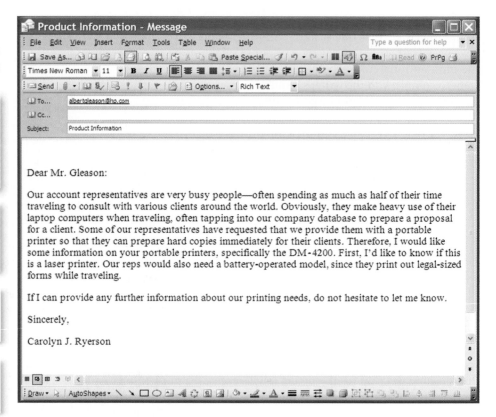

Dennison Industries stock is traded on the New York Stock Exchange, listed under "DenIn." Simply call your local broker to join the 275,000 other satisfied investors in Dennison Industries common stock.

In the body of your message, refer to any enclosure and then add an enclosure notation at the bottom of the letter. Referring to a specific page of an enclosed brochure or to a particular paragraph of an enclosed document helps ensure that such enclosures will be read.

Close your letter on a positive, friendly note. Avoid such clichés as "If you have additional questions, please don't hesitate to let me know." Use original wording, personalized especially for the reader.

Model 3 on page 238 is a routine reply to the request shown in Model 2 on page 235. The original request asked three questions about the printer, and the answers are as follows:

1. No, the DM-4200 is not a laser printer.
2. No, it is not battery operated.
3. Yes, it does accept legal-sized paper.

As you can see, only one of the three questions can be answered with an un- qualified "yes," and that is the question the respondent chose to lead off with. Positive language helps soften the impact of the negative responses to the other three questions. Also, reader benefits are stressed throughout the letter. Instead of

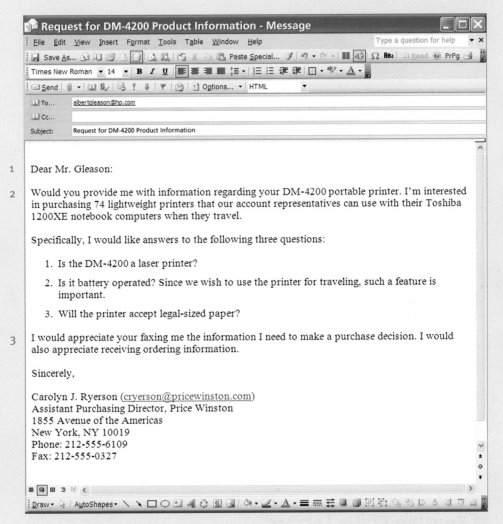

ROUTINE REQUEST

This message is from a potential customer to a manufacturer.

Presents the request in the first sentence, followed by the reason for asking.

Enumerates questions for emphasis and clarity; makes questions easy to answer.

Expresses appreciation, hints at a reader benefit.

Text of the email message:

Dear Mr. Gleason:

Would you provide me with information regarding your DM-4200 portable printer. I'm interested in purchasing 74 lightweight printers that our account representatives can use with their Toshiba 1200XE notebook computers when they travel.

Specifically, I would like answers to the following three questions:

1. Is the DM-4200 a laser printer?
2. Is it battery operated? Since we wish to use the printer for traveling, such a feature is important.
3. Will the printer accept legal-sized paper?

I would appreciate your faxing me the information I need to make a purchase decision. I would also appreciate receiving ordering information.

Sincerely,

Carolyn J. Ryerson (cryerson@pricewinston.com)
Assistant Purchasing Director, Price Winston
1855 Avenue of the Americas
New York, NY 10019
Phone: 212-555-6109
Fax: 212-555-0327

Grammar and Mechanics Notes

1 Format e-mail messages for easy readability—and always proofread before sending.

2 *your DM-4200 portable printer.:* Use a period after a polite request.

3 *I would appreciate your faxing:* Use the possessive form of a pronoun *(your)* before a gerund *(faxing)*.

When Wayne Inouye took over as CEO of faltering consumer-PC maker eMachines, Inc., he decided that to understand how to fix the company, he would respond to calls from irate customers personally. His customer focus began when he sold guitars.

■ See Handout 7.1.

just describing the features, the writer shows how the features can benefit the reader.

Checklist 7 summarizes the points you should consider when writing and responding to routine requests. Use this checklist as a guide in structuring your message and in evaluating the effectiveness of your first draft. In addition, when composing messages that have legal implications, follow the strategies provided in Spotlight 19, "Messages with Legal Implications," on page 239.

■ Routine Claim Letters

CO3. Compose a routine claim letter.

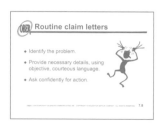

■ See Slide 7.8.

A **claim letter** is written by the buyer to the seller, seeking some type of action to correct a problem with the seller's product or service. The purchaser may be an individual or an organization. A claim letter differs from a simple complaint letter in that it requests some type of adjustment (such as repairing or replacing the product). As a matter of fact, many complaint letters would probably be more successful if they carried an implied claim that the writer wanted some adjustment to be made as a result of poor service, unfair practices, or the like. The desired adjustment might be nothing more than an explanation or apology, but the mere fact that you request some direct action will increase your chances of getting a satisfactory response.

A claim letter can be considered routine if you can reasonably anticipate that the reader will comply with your request. If, for example, you ordered a shipment of shoes for your store that were advertised at $23.50 each and the wholesaler charged you $32.50 instead, you would write a routine claim letter, asking the seller to correct the error. But suppose the wholesaler marked the price down to

✔checklist7

Routine Requests and Replies

Routine Requests

✔ Present the major request in the first sentence or two, preceded or followed by reasons for making the request.

✔ Provide any needed explanation or details.

✔ Phrase each question so that it is clear, is easy to answer, and covers only one topic. Ask as few questions as possible, but if several questions are necessary, number them and arrange them in logical order.

✔ If appropriate, incorporate reader benefits and promise confidentiality.

✔ Close on a friendly note by expressing appreciation, justifying any necessary deadlines, offering to reciprocate, or otherwise making your ending personal and original.

Routine Replies

✔ Answer promptly and graciously.

✔ Grant the request or begin giving the requested information in the first sentence or two.

✔ Address all questions asked or implied; include additional information or suggestions if that would be helpful.

✔ Include subtle sales promotion if appropriate.

✔ Consider developing a form letter for frequent requests.

✔ Refer to any items you enclose with the letter, and insert an enclosure notation at the bottom.

✔ Close on a positive and friendly note, and use original wording.

$19.50 two days after you placed your order. Then instead of writing a routine claim letter, you might want to write a persuasive letter, trying to convince the wholesaler to give you the lower price. (Persuasive letters are discussed in the next chapter.)

Contemporary corporate culture places a premium on product quality and customer service, and most companies make a genuine effort to settle claims from customers. They want to know if their customers are dissatisfied with their products so that they can correct the situation. A dissatisfied customer may not only refuse to purchase additional products from the offending company but may also tell others about the bad experience. One study of consumers showed that the typical dissatisfied customer tells 9–13 other people about the incident and that each of them, in turn, tells four or five more people. The typical satisfied customer, on the other hand, recommends the product or service to four or five other people.[1]

Write your claim letter promptly—as soon as you've identified a problem. Delaying unnecessarily might not only push you past the warranty date but also raise suspicions about the validity of your claim; the more recent the purchase, the more valid your claim will appear.

Although some consumer advocates suggest addressing your claim letter to the company president, business courtesy argues for first giving the company's order department or customer relations department an opportunity to solve the problem.

■ See Slides 7.9. and 7.10.

model3

ROUTINE REPLY

This letter responds to the request in Model 2 on page 235.

Begins by answering the "yes" question first.

Answers all questions, using positive language and pointing out the benefits of each feature.

Uses paragraphs instead of enumeration to answer each question because each answer requires elaboration.

Gives important purchase information; closes on a forward-looking note.

September 12, 20—

Ms. Carolyn J. Ryerson
Assistant Purchasing Director
Price Winston
1855 Avenue of the Americas
New York, NY 10019

Di–Mark
320 Industrial Avenue
Palo Alto, CA 94300
TEL 650.555.1200

Dear Ms. Ryerson:

Subject: Information You Requested About the DM-4200

Yes, our popular DM-4200 printer does accept legal-sized paper. Its 15-inch carriage will enable your representatives to print out complex spreadsheets while on the road. Of course, it also adjusts easily to fit standard $8\frac{1}{2} \times 11$-inch paper.

1   For quiet operation and easy portability, the Di-Mark uses ink-jet printing on plain paper. This technology provides nearly the same quality output as a laser printer at less than half the cost.

Although many travelers use their computers on a plane or in their automobiles, they typically wait until reaching their destination to print out their
2   documents. Thus, the DM uses AC power only, thereby reducing its weight by nearly a pound. The extra-long 12-foot power cable will let you power-up your printer easily no matter where the electrical outlet is hidden.

3   To take the DM-4200 for a test drive, call your local Best Buy at 800-555-2189. They will show you how to increase your productivity while increasing your luggage weight by only 4 pounds.

Sincerely yours,

Albert Gleason

Albert Gleason, Sales Manager

juc
4   By Fax

Grammar and Mechanics Notes

1 *ink-jet printing:* Hyphenate a compound adjective before a noun.

2 *its:* Do not confuse *its* (the possessive pronoun) with *it's* (the contraction for "it is").

3 *a test drive,:* Place a comma after an introductory expression.

4 *By Fax:* For reference purposes, include a delivery notation if appropriate.

spotlight19
ON LAW AND ETHICS

Messages with Legal Implications

All written messages carry certain legal implications. For example, if you knowingly write something false about a company that results in damages to that company's reputation or financial well-being, you are guilty of libel. Therefore, in all messages ensure that your information is accurate and that your message does not violate any federal or state laws.

Some types of messages have special legal implications. Follow these guidelines when writing letters of recommendation, letters rejecting a job applicant, and memos containing personnel evaluations.

Writing a Letter of Recommendation

1. Be fair—to yourself, to the prospective employer, to the applicant whom you're recommending, and to the other applicants for the same position.

2. Begin by giving the name of the applicant, the position for which the applicant is applying, and the nature and length of your relationship with the applicant.

3. Label the information "confidential," and state that you were asked to provide this information.

4. Discuss only job-related traits and behaviors, be as objective as possible, and support your statements with specific examples.

5. If writing a recommendation for a specific position, answer all questions asked and gear your comments to the applicant's qualifications for the particular job.

6. Present any negative information in such a way that the reader will perceive it with the same degree of importance that you do.

7. Close by giving an overall summary of your evaluation.

Rejecting a Job Applicant

1. Keep the letter short; the candidate is anxious to learn whether your decision is "yes" or "no."

2. Provide a short, supportive buffer, perhaps mentioning some specific positive comment about the candidate's résumé or interview.

3. Indicate that another candidate was chosen (not that the reader was *not* chosen), and briefly explain why.

4. Close on an off-the-topic note, perhaps thanking the reader for applying or extending best wishes.

Writing a Personnel Evaluation

1. Be fair—to yourself, to the employee, and to the organization.

2. Discuss only job-related behaviors and traits.

3. Document any praise or criticism with specific examples. Avoid exaggeration—either positive or negative.

4. Ensure that any negative information receives only the appropriate amount of emphasis.

5. Emphasize the improvement aspect of the evaluation; that is, state specifically what steps should be taken to improve performance.

6. Close with an overall summary of your evaluation or with a friendly, forward-looking comment.

Such departments are designed to handle these problems most efficiently; and their employees are the most knowledgeable about specific company policies and procedures, warranty information, and the like. Only if your claim is not settled satisfactorily at this level should you then appeal to a higher level of management in the company.

Although you may be frustrated or angry as a result of the situation, remember that the person to whom you're writing was not *personally* responsible for your problem. Be courteous and avoid emotional language. Assume that the company is

Assume a courteous tone; avoid emotionalism.

reasonable and will do as you reasonably ask. Avoid any hint of anger, sarcasm, threat, or exaggeration. A reader who becomes angry as a result of the strong language in your claim letter will be less likely to do as you ask. Instead, using factual and unemotional language, begin your routine claim letter directly, telling exactly what the problem is.

NOT: You should be ashamed at your dishonest advertising for the videotape *Safety Is Job One.*

BUT: The videotape *Safety Is Job One* that I rented for $125 from your company last week lived up to our expectations in every way but one.

NOT: I am disgusted at the way United Express cheated me out of $12.50 last week. What a rip-off!

BUT: An overnight letter that I mailed on December 3 did not arrive the next day, as promised by United Express.

Provide needed details.

After you have identified the problem, begin your explanation. Provide as much background information as necessary—dates, model numbers, amounts, photocopies of canceled checks or correspondence, and the like. Use a confident tone and logic (rather than emotion) to present your case. Write in an impersonal style, avoiding the use of "you" pronouns so as not to link your reader too closely to the negative news.

NOT: I delivered this letter to you sometime in the early afternoon on December 3. Although you promised to deliver it by 3 p.m. the next day, you failed to do so.

BUT: As shown on the enclosed copy of my receipt, I delivered this letter to United Express at 3:30 p.m. on December 3. According to the sign displayed in the office, any package received by 4 p.m. is guaranteed to arrive by 3 p.m. the following business day.

If possible, mention something positive about the product.

Tell exactly what went wrong and how you were inconvenienced. If it is true and relevant, mention something positive about the company or its products to make your letter appear reasonable.

According to the enclosed arrival receipt, my letter was not delivered until 8:30 a.m. on December 5. Because the letter contained material needed for a dinner meeting on December 4, it arrived too late to be of any use. This is not the type of on-time service I've routinely received from United Express during the eight years I've been using your delivery system.

Finally, tell what type of adjustment you expect. Do you want the company to replace the product, repair it, issue a refund, simply apologize, or what? End the letter on a confident note.

I would appreciate your refunding my $12.50, thereby reestablishing my confidence in United Express.

In some situations, you may not know what type of adjustment is reasonable; then, you would leave it up to the reader to suggest an appropriate course of action.

■ McDonald's, USAirways, FedEx, and Clairol are just a few of the many companies that see customers' complaints as a way to improve service. Their policies are to respond positively to customers' claims by answering their letters and offering gift certificates or replacement merchandise.

This might be the situation when you suffered no monetary loss but simply wish to avoid an unpleasant situation in the future (such as discourteous service, long lines, or ordering the wrong model because of having received incomplete or misleading information).

Please let me know how I might avoid this problem in the future.

Model 4 on the following page illustrates a routine claim letter about a defective product, asking for a specific remedy.

Mandy Kwong, a pharmacy department manager, uses appropriate body language, facial expressions, and direct eye contact to win the confidence of her customers at a CVS pharmacy in Rockville, Maryland.

■ Routine Adjustment Letters

An **adjustment letter** is written to inform a customer of the action taken in response to the customer's claim letter. Few people bother to write a claim letter unless they have a real problem, so most claims that companies receive are legitimate and are adjusted according to the individual situation. If the action taken is what the customer asked for or expected, a routine adjustment letter using the direct organizational plan would be written.

You should note that *anyone* in an organization may be called upon to write claim and adjustment letters—not just those working in sales or customer service. For example, an accounting manager may send (and receive) a letter complaining of poor service from an employee.

CO4. Compose a routine adjustment letter.

An adjustment letter responds to a claim letter.

Overall Tone

A claim represents a possible loss of goodwill and confidence in your organization or its products. Because the customer is upset, the overall tone of your adjustment letter is crucial. Since you have already decided to honor the claim, your best strategy is to adopt a gracious, trusting tone. Give your customer the benefit of the doubt. It does not make sense to adopt a grudging or resentful tone and risk losing whatever goodwill you might have gained from granting the adjustment.

Adopt a gracious, confident tone for your adjustment letters.

Avoid using negative language when describing the basis for the claim.

NOT: Although our engineers do not understand how this problem could have occurred if the directions had been followed, we are nevertheless willing to repair your generator free of charge.

BUT: We are happy to repair your generator free of charge. Within ten days, a factory representative will call you to schedule a convenient time to make the repair.

Your overall tone should show confidence both in the reader's honesty and in the essential worth of your own organization and its products. To the extent

Routine adjustment letters

- Respond promptly, giving the good news up front.
- Briefly explain what went wrong and how you fixed the problem.
- Reestablish the customer's confidence.
- Close on a confident, forward-looking note.

7.11

■ See Slide 7.11.

model4

**ROUTINE CLAIM—
REMEDY SPECIFIED**

*This claim letter is about a
defective product.*

**Identifies the problem imme-
diately and tells how the
writer was inconvenienced.**

**Provides the needed details
in a nonemotional, busi-
nesslike manner.**

**Identifies and justifies the
specific remedy requested.**

Closes on a confident note.

 **OTIS CANDY COMPANY**   BOX 302, EDEN, NC 27932, 919-555-4822, FAX: 919-555-4831, WWW.OTISCANDY.COM

April 14, 20—

1 Customer Relations Representative
Sir Speedy, Inc.
26722 Plaza Drive
Mission Viejo, CA 92690-9077

Dear Customer Relations Representative:

Subject: Poor Quality of Photocopying

The poor quality of the 13-page full-color handout you duplicated for me on April 8 made the handouts unsuitable for use in my recent presentation. As a result, I had to use black-and-white copies duplicated in-house instead.

2 As you can see from the enclosed handout, the colors often run together and the type is fuzzy. The photocopying is not equivalent in quality to that illustrated in
3 Sir Speedy's advertisement on page 154 of the April issue of *Business Management*.

I have already given the presentation for which these handouts were made, so re-duplicating them would not solve the problem. Because I have not yet paid your Invoice 4073 for $438.75, would you please cancel this charge.

4 I know that despite one's best efforts, mistakes will occasionally happen, and I am confident that you will correct this problem promptly.

Sincerely,

Claire D. Scriven

Claire D. Scriven
Marketing Manager

ric
Enclosure

Grammar and Mechanics Notes

1 If an addressee's name is unknown, you may use a title in both the inside address and the salutation.

2 *run together and:* Do not insert any punctuation before the *and* separating the two independent clauses because the second clause, "the type is fuzzy," is so short.

3 April issue of *Business Management:* Italicize magazine titles.

4 *occasionally:* Note that this word has two *c*'s and one *s*.

possible, use neutral or positive language in referring to the claim (for example, write "the situation" instead of "your complaint"). Also avoid appearing to doubt the reader. Instead of saying "you claim that," use more neutral wording, such as "you state that."

Finally, respond promptly. Your customer is already upset; the longer this anger remains, the more difficult it will be to overcome.

Good News First

Nothing that you are likely to tell the reader will be more welcomed than the fact that you are granting the claim, so put this news up front—in the very first sentence if possible. The details and background information will come later, as illustrated by the following examples:

> A new copy of the *American World Dictionary* is on its way to your office, and I assure you that no pages are missing from this copy. I checked it myself!

> The enclosed $17.50 check reimburses you for your company's delayed overnight letter. Thank you for bringing this matter to my attention.

> Thanks to you, we have undertaken a new training program for our housekeeping staff. Please use the enclosed coupon for two nights' free stay at the Ambassador to see for yourself the difference your letter has made.

It is often appropriate to thank the reader for giving you an opportunity to resolve the situation, but what about apologizing? An apology, which tends to emphasize the negative aspects of the situation, is generally not advised for small, routine claims that are promptly resolved to the customer's satisfaction. Instead, emphasize the positive aspects and look forward to future transactions. If, however, the customer has been severely inconvenienced or embarrassed and the company is clearly at fault, a sincere apology would be in order. In such a situation, first give the good news and then apologize in a businesslike manner; avoid repeating the apology in the closing lines.

> I have contracted with a local mason to rebuild your home's brick walkway, which our driver damaged on February 23. I am truly sorry for the inconvenience this situation has caused you and am grateful for your understanding.

Explanation

After presenting the "good news," you must educate your reader as to why the problem occurred and, if appropriate, what steps you've taken to make sure it doesn't recur. Explain the situation in sufficient detail to be believable, but don't belabor the reason for the problem. Emphasize the fact that you stand behind your products. Avoid using negative language, don't pass the buck, and don't hide behind a "mistakes-will-happen" attitude.

> Let me explain what happened. On December 4, the plane that had your letter in its cargo bay could not land at O'Hare Airport because of a snowstorm and was diverted to Detroit. Although our Detroit personnel worked overtime to reload the mail onto a delivery truck, which was then driven to Chicago, the shipment did not arrive until early on December 5.

It is appropriate to apologize for serious problems.

Explain specifically, but briefly, what went wrong.

■ See Slides 7.12 and 7.13.

Use resale to reassure the customer of the worth of your products.

Because the reader's faith in your products has been shaken, you also have a sales job to do. You must build into your letter **resale**—that is, information that reestablishes the customer's confidence in the product purchased or in the company that sells the product. To be believable, do *not* promise that the problem will never happen again; that's unrealistic. Do, however, use specific language, including facts and figures when possible.

NOT: We can assure you that this situation will not happen again.

BUT: Fortunately, such incidents are rare. For example, even considering bad weather, airline strikes, and the like, United Express has maintained an on-time delivery record of 97.6 percent during the past 12 months. No other delivery service even comes close to this record.

If the customer is at fault, explain in tactful, impersonal language how to avoid such problems in the future.

Sometimes you may decide to honor a claim even when the customer is at fault—perhaps because the writer has been a good customer for many years or represents important potential business. In such situations, your beginning paragraph should still convey the good news that you're honoring the claim, but you might temper the enthusiasm a bit. And in the explanatory paragraphs, you would tactfully communicate to the reader the facts surrounding the case—that the reader is at fault, the product was misused, the warranty has expired, or whatever the situation requires.

On the one hand, it is necessary to inform the reader of the circumstances so that he or she won't keep repeating the problem. On the other hand, if you do so in an insulting manner, you will lose the reader's goodwill. Instead, use impersonal, tactful language, taking special pains not to lecture the reader or sound condescending. For example, in the second paragraph that follows, note that the pronoun *you* is not used at all when explaining the misuse of the equipment.

■ Responding positively to a customer's complaint can turn anger into brand loyalty, according to Technical Assistance Research Programs, Inc. (TARP). TARP suggests that a customer whose complaints have been satisfied will more likely purchase products in the future than a customer who never complained.

Because we value your friendship, we are pleased to repair your Braniff 250 copier free of charge. Our maintenance technician tells me that she took care of the problem on September 15.

Your machine's register indicated that 9,832 copies had been made since the copier was installed on July 18. The Braniff 250 is designed for low-level office use—fewer than 1,500 copies per month. If you find that you will continue to experience high-volume usage, I suggest trading up to the Braniff 300, which will easily handle your needs. We will gladly offer you $1,300 as a trade-in allowance.

Positive, Forward-Looking Closing

Do not mention the claim in the closing. Instead, look to the future.

End your letter on a positive note. Do not refer to the problem again, do not apologize again, do not suggest the possibility of future problems, and do not imply that the reader might still be upset. Instead, use strategies that imply a continuing relationship with the customer, such as a comment about the satisfaction the reader will receive from the repaired product or improved service or appreciation for the reader's interest in your products.

Include sales promotion only if you are confident that your adjustment has restored the customer's confidence in your product or service; otherwise, it might backfire. If used, sales promotion should be subtle and should involve a new product or accessory rather than promoting a new or improved model of what the reader has already bought.

NOT: Again, I apologize for the delay in delivering your letter. If you experience such problems again, please don't hesitate to write.

BUT: We have enjoyed serving your delivery needs for the past eight years, Ms. Clarke, and look forward to many more years of service.

OR: If you're the type of person who has frequent crash deadlines, Ms. Clarke, you will probably be interested in our eight-hour delivery service. It is described in the enclosed brochure.

■ For other examples of adjustment letters, see the *Instructor's Resource Manual.*

Model 5 on the following page illustrates an adjustment letter, and Checklist 8 on page 247 summarizes the guidelines for writing routine claim and adjustment letters.

■ Goodwill Messages

A **goodwill message** is one that is sent strictly out of a sense of kindness and friendliness. Examples include messages conveying congratulations, appreciation, and sympathy. These messages achieve their goodwill objective precisely because they have no true business objective. To include even subtle sales promotion in such messages would defeat their purpose. Recipients are quick to see through such efforts. Letters that include sales promotion or resale are *sales* letters, as might be expected, and are covered elsewhere in this text.

That is not to say, however, that business advantages do not accrue from such efforts. People naturally like to deal with businesses and with people who are friendly and who take the time to comment on noteworthy occasions. The point is that such business advantages are strictly incidental to the real purpose of extending a friendly gesture.

Often the gesture could be accomplished by telephoning instead of by writing—especially for minor occasions. But a written message, either in place of or in addition to the phone call, is more thoughtful, more appreciated, and more permanent. And because it requires extra effort and the recipient will receive fewer of them, a written message is much more meaningful than a telephone message.

CO5. Compose a goodwill message.

General Guidelines

To ensure that your goodwill messages achieve their desired effect, follow these five guidelines:

1. *Be prompt.* Too often, people consider writing a goodwill message but then put it off until it is too late. The most meaningful messages are those received while the reason for them is still fresh in the reader's mind.
2. *Be direct.* State the major idea in the first sentence or two, even for sympathy notes; since the reader already knows the bad news, you don't need to shelter him or her from it.

Five guidelines for goodwill messages: be prompt, direct, sincere, specific, and brief.

model 5

ADJUSTMENT LETTER

This adjustment letter responds to the claim letter in Model 4 on page 242.

Tells immediately that the adjustment is being made; thanks the reader.

Explains briefly, but specifically, what happened.

Looks forward to a continuing relationship with the customer; does not mention the problem again.

Sir Speedy, Inc.   April 22, 20—

1   Ms. Claire D. Scriven
Marketing Manager
Otis Candy Company
Box 302
Eden, NC 27932

Dear Ms. Scriven:

Subject: Cancellation of Invoice 4073

2   Sir Speedy is, of course, happy to cancel the $438.75 charge for Invoice 4073. I appreciate your taking the time to write and send us a sample handout.

3   Upon receiving your letter, I immediately sent your handout to our quality-control personnel for closer examination. They agreed that the handouts should have been redone before they left our facilities. We have now revised our procedures to ensure that before each order is shipped, it is inspected by someone other than the person preparing it.

CORPORATE OFFICES

26722 Plaza Drive

P.O. Box 9077

Mission Viejo, CA 92690-9077

Tel: (949) 348-5000

Fax: (949) 348-5010

www.sirspeedy.com

To better serve the media needs of our corporate customers, we are installing the Xerox DocuCenter 480 copier, the most sophisticated industrial color copier system available. Thus, when you send us your next order, you'll see that your handouts are of even higher quality than those in the *Business Management* advertisement that impressed you.

Sincerely yours,

David Foster

David Foster
Customer Relations

Grammar and Mechanics Notes

1 Type the position title either on the same line as the person's name or, as here, on a line by itself.

2 *Invoice 4073:* Capitalize a noun that precedes a number.

3 *personnel:* Do not confuse *personnel* (employees) with *personal* (private).

✓checklist 8

Routine Claim and Adjustment Letters

Routine Claim Letters

✓ Write your claim letter promptly—as soon as you've identified a problem.

✓ Strive for an overall tone of courtesy and confidence. If true and relevant, mention something positive about the company or its products somewhere in the letter.

✓ Begin the letter directly, identifying the problem immediately.

✓ Provide as much detail as necessary. Using impersonal language, tell specifically what went wrong and how you were inconvenienced.

✓ If appropriate, tell what type of adjustment you expect—replacement, repair, refund, or apology. End on a confident note.

Routine Adjustment Letters

✓ Respond promptly; your customer is already upset.

✓ Begin the letter directly, telling the reader immediately what adjustment is being made.

✓ Adopt a courteous tone. Use neutral or positive language throughout.

✓ If appropriate, thank the reader for writing, and apologize if the customer has been severely inconvenienced or embarrassed because of your company's actions.

✓ In a forthright manner, explain the reason for the problem in sufficient detail to be believable, but don't belabor the point. If appropriate, briefly tell what steps you've taken to prevent a recurrence of the problem.

✓ Provide information that reestablishes your customer's confidence in the product or your company. Be specific enough to be believable.

✓ If the customer was at fault, explain in impersonal and tactful language the facts surrounding the case.

✓ Close on a positive note, implying customer satisfaction and the expectation of a continuing relationship.

3. *Be sincere.* Avoid language that is too flowery or too strong. Use a conversational tone, as if you were speaking to the person directly, and focus on the reader—not on yourself. Take special care to spell names correctly and to make sure your facts are accurate.

4. *Be specific.* If you're thanking or complimenting someone, mention a specific incident or anecdote. Personalize your message to avoid having it sound like a form letter.

5. *Be brief.* You don't need two pages (or, likely, even one full page) to get your point across. Often a personal note card is more appropriate than full-sized business stationery. Because they are considered personal notes, goodwill messages do not require a subject line (unless, of course, they are sent via e-mail).

■ See Handout 7.2.

Congratulatory Messages

Congratulatory notes should be sent for major business achievements—receiving a promotion, announcing a retirement, winning an award, opening a new branch, celebrating an anniversary, and the like. Such notes are also appropriate for personal milestones—engagements, weddings, births, graduations, and other note-worthy occasions. Congratulatory notes should be written both to employees within the company and to customers, suppliers, and others outside the firm with whom you have a relationship.

> Congratulations, Tom, on your election to the presidency of the United Way of Alberta County. I was happy to see the announcement in this morning's newspaper and to learn of your plans for the upcoming campaign.
>
> Best wishes for a successful fund drive. This important community effort surely deserves everyone's full support.

■ For another example of a goodwill letter (a congratulatory letter on a promotion), see the *Instructor's Resource Manual.*

Thank-You Notes

Thank-you notes are expected in some situations; they are unexpected (and therefore much appreciated) in others.

A note of thanks or appreciation is often valued more than a monetary reward. A handwritten thank-you note is especially appreciated today, when people routinely receive so many "personalized" computer-generated messages. A handwritten note assures the reader that you are offering sincere and genuine thanks, rather than simply sending out a form letter. And if you take the trouble to send a photocopy of your note to the person's supervisor, the recipient will be twice blessed.

Thank-you notes (either typed or handwritten) should be sent whenever someone does you a favor—gives you a gift, writes a letter of recommendation for you, comes to your support unexpectedly, gives a speech or appears on a panel, and so on. Don't forget that customers and suppliers like to be recognized as well. Unexpected thank-you notes are often the most appreciated—to the salesperson, instructor, administrative assistant, copy center operator, restaurant server, receptionist, or anyone else who provided service beyond the call of duty.

■ See Slides 7.14 and 7.15.

> Thank you so much, Alice, for serving on the panel of suppliers for our new-employee orientation program. Your comments on scheduling problems and your suggestions for alleviating them were especially helpful. They provided the kind of information that only an experienced pro like you could give.
>
> I think you could tell from the comments and many questions that your remarks were well received by our new employees. We certainly appreciate your professional contributions.

Sympathy Notes

Begin by expressing sympathy, offer some personal memory of the deceased, and close by offering comfort.

Expressions of sympathy or condolence to a person who has experienced pain, grief, or misfortune are especially difficult to write but are also especially appreciated. People who have experienced serious health problems, a severe business setback, or the death of a loved one need to know that others are thinking of them and that they are not alone.

Some of the most difficult messages to write are those expressing sympathy over someone's death. These notes should be handwritten, when possible. They should not avoid mentioning the death, but they need not dwell on it. Most sympathy notes are short. Begin with an expression of sympathy, mention some specific quality or personal reminiscence about the deceased, and then close with an expression of comfort and affection. An offer to help, if genuine, would be appropriate (see Model 6 on the next page).

1  Ralston Purina Company

April 3, 20—

2 Dear Ralph,

I was deeply saddened to learn of Jane's sudden death. It was certainly a great shock to her many friends and colleagues.

Jane had a well-earned reputation here for her top-notch negotiating skills and for her endearing sense of humor. She was an accomplished manager and a good friend, and I shall miss her greatly.

3 If I can help smooth the way in your dealings with our human resources office, I would be honored to help. Please call me on my private line (555-1036) if there is anything I can do.

Affectionately,

Bob

Checkerboard Square
St. Louis, Missouri 63164-0001

G85F-95A8

GOODWILL MESSAGE

This goodwill message expresses sympathy to the husband of a coworker who died.

Begins with an expression of sympathy.

Mentions some specific quality or personal reminiscence.

Closes with a genuine offer of help.

Grammar and Mechanics Notes

1 Use either company letterhead or personal stationery for sympathy notes.

2 Insert a comma (instead of a colon) after the salutation of a personal letter.

3 Handwrite the sympathy note, if possible.

A ROUTINE ADJUSTMENT LETTER

You are Kathryn Smith, a correspondent in the customer service department of Dillard's Department Store. This morning (May 25, 20—), you received the following letter from Mrs. Henrietta Daniels, an angry customer:

Dear Customer Service Manager:

I am really upset at the poor-quality shades that you sell. Two months ago I purchased two pairs of your pleated fabric shades in Wedgewood Blue at $35.99 each for my two bathroom windows. A copy of my $74.32 bill is enclosed.

Was this an effective claim letter? Why or why not?

The color has already begun to fade from these shades. I couldn't believe it when I checked and found that they now look tie-dyed! That is not the look I wish for my home.

Since these shades did not provide the type of wear that I paid for, please refund my $74.32.

Sincerely,

You take Mrs. Daniels' itemized bill down to the sales floor and find the model of shades she purchased. You can only conclude that Mrs. Daniels' home has large bathroom windows because the only size this particular shade comes in is 64 inches long by 32 inches wide. And printed right on the tag attached to the shade is this caution: "Warning: The imported fabric in this shade makes it unsuitable for use in areas of high humidity." Clearly, these shades were not made for bathroom use. You call up Mrs. Daniels' account on your computer and find that she has been a loyal customer for many years. You decide, therefore, to refund her $74.32, even though she misused the product. Write the adjustment letter (Mrs. Henrietta Daniels, 117 Pine Forest Drive, Atlanta, GA 30345).

1. What is the purpose of your letter?

   To refund Mrs. Daniels' money, tactfully explain that you were not at fault, and retain her goodwill.

2. Describe your audience.

   - An important customer
   - Angry at you at the present time
   - Now believes your product is of poor quality
   - May be the type of person who doesn't read instructions carefully

3. List in the appropriate order the topics you'll discuss.

   a. Give the refund.

   b. Explain that the shades weren't intended for bathroom use.

   c. Promote your cotton and polyester bathroom curtains.

4. Write a gracious opening sentence for your letter that tells Mrs. Daniels you're refunding the $74.32. Be warm and positive in granting her request. Remember, however, that she was at fault; therefore, do not be overly enthusiastic.

   You have been a valued and faithful customer of ours for several years, Mrs. Daniels, and we are therefore refunding your $74.32.

5. Write the sentence that explains how the shades were misused. Use tactful, neutral, and impersonal language, avoiding the use of second-person pronouns (*you* and *your*).

   As the tag attached to the shades explains, the fine imported woven material used in these shades reflects sunlight without fading but will not withstand the high humidity typical of bathrooms.

6. Now write your closing paragraph, in which you promote your cotton and polyester bathroom curtains.

   For the elegant look and durable service you want in your bathroom, please consider the cotton and polyester bathroom curtains shown in the enclosed brochure. They come in Wedgewood Blue and can be custom-ordered in the exact size you desire.

Product

Dillard's, Inc.
1600 Cantrell Road – P.O. Box 486 – Little Rock, Arkansas 72203
Telephone: 501-376-5200   Fax: 501-376-5917

May 25, 20—

Mrs. Henrietta Daniels
117 Pine Forest Drive
Atlanta, GA 30345

Dear Mrs. Daniels:

Subject: Your Refund Request for $74.32

You have been a valued customer of ours for several years, and we are, therefore, refunding your $74.32. A check for that amount is enclosed. You can simply return the blue shades to our customer service window the next time that you stop by Dillard's.

As the tag attached to the shades explains, the fine imported woven material used in these shades reflects sunlight without fading but will not withstand the high humidity typically found in bathrooms. However, when these shades are used on windows in living rooms, dining rooms, and bedrooms, they will provide many years of beautiful and carefree service.

For the elegant look and durable service you want in your bathroom, please consider the cotton and polyester bathroom curtain shown in the enclosed brochure. They come in Wedgewood Blue and can be custom-ordered in the exact size you require. Please come in and let us show them to you.

Sincerely,

Kathryn Smith

Kathryn Smith
Customer Service Department

jmr
Enclosures

Visit the **BusCom Online Learning Center** (at http://college.hmco.com) for additional resources to help you with this course and with your future career.

■ Summary

When composing a routine request, present the major request early, along with reasons for making the request. Word your questions so that they are clear and easy to answer. Finally, close on a friendly note.

Answer routine requests promptly and graciously. Grant the request early in the letter and answer all questions asked. Close on a positive and friendly note, and use original language.

Write claim letters promptly, begin the letter directly, and tell specifically what went wrong and what resolution you're seeking. Throughout, strive for an overall tone of courtesy and confidence. End on a confident note.

Answer claim letters promptly, use neutral or positive language, and adopt a courteous tone. Begin the letter directly, telling immediately what adjustment is being made. Provide information that reestablishes your customer's confidence in the product, and close on a positive note.

Write goodwill messages to express congratulations, appreciation, or sympathy. Write promptly, using a direct pattern, and be sincere, specific, and brief.

CO1. Compose a routine request.

CO2. Compose a routine reply.

CO3. Compose a routine claim letter.

CO4. Compose a routine adjustment letter.

CO5. Compose a goodwill message.

■ Key Terms

You should now be able to define the following terms in your own words and give an original example of each.

adjustment letter (241)

claim letter (236)

direct organizational plan (228)

form letter (235)

goodwill message (245)

indirect organizational plan (228)

resale (244)

■ See Slide 7.16.

■ Consider treating this list as an end-of-chapter exercise for students to define and give an example of each term.

■ Suggestions and sample solutions for exercises appear in the *Instructor's Resource Manual.*

■ Exercises

1 **Annie's Homegrown Revisited**   Most of the 1,500 letters to which Ann Withey responds every month are routine requests for free information offered by Annie's Homegrown; the remainder are letters with specific comments on the product or the company mascot, which require a more personalized response. Because her goal is to strengthen relationships with customers, Withey uses an upbeat tone, expresses appreciation for the customer's loyalty, and carefully tailors each letter to the reader's interests.

Problem

As Ann Withey's executive assistant, you are writing a letter in response to a customer's request for information about your firm's position on environmental protection. The customer, Jeff Biancolo, is a long-time fan of your products and is particularly interested in the company's recycling efforts. In addition to addressing his specific concerns, you plan to include a copy of the company's preprinted statement of support for environmental initiatives.

Process

a. What is the purpose of your letter?
b. Describe your audience.
c. List in order the topics to be discussed.
d. Write an opening paragraph, letting Mr. Biancolo know the purpose of the letter and conveying the firm's strong commitment to environmental protection.
e. Write a sentence referring to the preprinted statement you are enclosing with the letter.
f. Write a closing paragraph thanking Mr. Biancolo for his interest in, and loyalty to, the company.

Product

Using your knowledge of routine messages, write this letter to Jeff Biancolo (287 Mandalay Road, Bartlett, TN 38101).

■ See Handout 7.3.

2 The 3Ps (Problem, Process, and Product) Model: A Claim Letter for a Defective Product

Problem

You are J. R. McCord, purchasing agent for People's Energy Company. On February 3, you ordered a box of four laser cartridges for your Sampson Model 25 printers at $69.35 each, plus $6.85 shipping and handling—total price of $284.25. The catalog description for this cartridge (Part No. 02-8R01656) stated, "Fits Epson and Xerox printers and most compatibles." Since the Sampson is advertised as a Xerox clone printer, you assumed the cartridges would fit. When the order arrived, you discovered that the cartridges didn't fit your Sampson. Although the cartridge is the same shape, it is about $1/4$ inch thicker and won't seat properly on the spindles.

You believe that your supplier's misleading advertising caused you to order the wrong model cartridge. You'd like the company to either refund the $284.25 you paid on its Invoice 95-076 or replace the cartridges with ones that do work with your printers. You'll be happy to return all four cartridges if the company will give you instructions for doing so.

Write your routine claim letter.

Process

a. What is the purpose of your letter?
b. Describe your audience.
c. Write the first sentence of your letter, in which you identify the problem. Strive for an overall tone of courtesy and confidence.
d. Using impersonal language, write the middle section of the letter, in which you tell specifically what went wrong and how you were inconvenienced by the problem.
e. Write the last paragraph of the letter, in which you identify the type of adjustment you expect and also perhaps mention some positive aspect of the company or its products.

Product

Revise, format, and proofread your letter, which should be addressed to the Customer Service Department of Nationwide Office Supply, located at 2640 Kerper Boulevard in Dubuque, IA 52001. Submit to your instructor both your responses to the process questions and your final letter.

3 **Routine Request—Product Information**   Luis St. Jean is a famous design house in France with annual sales of $1.2 billion in clothing, perfume, scarves, and other designer items. Each year it prepares more than 150 original designs for its seasonal collections. As head buyer for Cindy's, an upscale women's clothing store at Mall of America in Minneapolis, you think you might like to begin offering LSJ's line of perfume. You need to know more about pricing, types of perfume offered, minimum ordering quantities, marketing assistance provided by LSJ, and the like. You'd also like to know if you can have exclusive marketing rights to LSJ perfumes in the Minneapolis area and whether you would have to carry LSJ's complete line (you don't think the most expensive perfumes would be big sellers).

Write to Mr. Henri Vixier, License Supervisor, Luis St. Jean, 90513 Cergy, Pointoise Cedex, France, seeking answers to your questions.

co1. **Compose a routine request.**

4 **Routine Request—Membership Information**   Although your part-time job is only temporary while you finish college, your boss wants you to gain more experience in public speaking and has suggested that you join Toastmasters International, an organization devoted to helping its members practice and improve their public-speaking skills. You are interested in determining whether your town has a local chapter and, if so, the time and place of meetings, the amount of annual dues, and the like.

Locate the Toastmasters International homepage on the Internet and find an e-mail address. Compose an e-mail message, asking several specific pertinent questions. E-mail a copy of your message to your instructor. Follow your instructor's direction regarding whether to mail your message to Toastmasters.

5 **Routine Request—Letter of Recommendation**   As part of your application papers for a one-semester internship at American Express, you are asked to include a letter of recommendation from one of your business professors. You made a good grade in MGT 382: Wage and Salary Administration, which you took three semesters ago from Dr. Dennis Thavinet in the management department at your institution. You liked the course so well that you missed class only twice (for good reasons). Although you were not one of the most vocal members in class, Dr. Thavinet did commend you for your group project. American Express (at 1850 East Camelback Road, Phoenix, AZ 85017) wants to know especially about your ability to work well with others.

Compose (but do not send) an e-mail message to Dr. Thavinet (djthavinet@marsu.edu), asking for a letter of recommendation. You would like him to respond within one week.

■ See Handout 7.4.

6 **Routine Request—Product Information**   Choose an advertisement from a newspaper or magazine for a product or service about which you have some interest. The ad probably does not have sufficient space to provide all the information you need to make an intelligent purchase decision. Write to the company (if necessary, locate its address using one of the directories available in your library or on the Internet), asking at least three questions about the product. Be sure to mention where you learned about the product. Try to encourage a prompt response.

Attach a copy of the ad to your letter and submit both to your instructor. Your instructor may ask you to mail the letter so that the class can later compare the types of responses received from different companies.

7 **Internet Exercise**   Websites often provide an easy, preaddressed form for visitors to use when submitting e-mail messages, and Gateway Computer is no exception. Visit Gateway's website (at http://www.gateway.com) and follow the links to "Contact Us" on the right side of the page. Then follow the "E-mail Customer Service" link at the right of the page to see how to contact the company by e-mail. The dean wants to know how the PCs are shipped to the school, how much shipping costs are, and how students can buy on credit. Draft a routine request for this information that you can paste into Gateway's preaddressed e-mail form.

8 **Routine Request—Seeking Day-Care Space**   Allegheny Child Care Academy operates 33 day-care centers in Philadelphia, Pittsburgh, Detroit, and other urban areas, serving the children of welfare-to-work parents. Because Allegheny benefits from government subsidies, the children receive academic instruction, lunches and dinners, and exercise, and the parents pay affordable rates. Many parents either walk their children to the center or arrive by public transportation, so Allegheny's CEO, David Henry, is always on the lookout for facilities it can rent in centrally located, inner-city neighborhoods.

Henry has hired you as Allegheny's director of real estate and facilities. Because the firm is planning to expand its operations in Cleveland, Ohio, and Oakland, California, you decide to write national real estate firms requesting information about potential rental properties. Your first letter will go to Forest City Enterprises, Inc. (Terminal Tower, Suite 1100, 50 Public Square, Cleveland, OH 44113-2203), which develops and manages commercial properties across the country. What is the major idea you want to express in your letter? How much detail will you need from Forest City? Will you need to explain your request or add any details? How should you close this letter? Using your knowledge of routine requests, draft this message (make up any details you need).

CO2. Compose a routine reply.

9 **Routine Reply—Fashion Show**   You are Yolanda Davis, a fashion design professor at the University of Nevada. You have one of the best fashion design programs in the western United States. You have received a letter from Greg Bunker, a fashion merchandizing teacher at Churchill County High School in Fallon, Nevada.

Greg has asked about the possibility of having a regional fashion show prior to the state fashion show in May. The high school in Fallon is not well suited for the competition, so Greg is wondering if you would be willing to host seven high schools from northern Nevada at your campus in Reno. Greg believes that most of the schools would be bringing between 10 and 15 students to the competition. They want to hold the contest on Friday, March 12, 20—. They would like to begin at 9 a.m. and hope to be finished by noon.

You are excited to host the high school students because you think it will be good exposure for UNR. You can host the schools on that day. You have made arrangements for several classrooms from 9 a.m. to noon. Schools should have their students at the Pace Building, Room 145, to register. Registration is from

8:00 to 8:30 a.m. You will need to charge the schools $50 each to cover your expenses.

Write a letter to Greg letting him know the good news and the details of the event. His address is Greg Bunker, Fashion Merchandising Instructor, Churchill County High School, 665 South Maine Street, Fallon, Nevada 89406.

10 **Routine Reply—Comedian on Board**   You are the director of entertainment for a cruise ship, the *Sea Princess*. You are always looking for new acts to book on your cruises. Yesterday, you received a letter from Barbara Greensburg, manager of Houston Entertainment Inc., who requested that you book one of her clients, Herman Thayer.

Herman is a young comedian from Houston who has appeared in local comedy clubs in Houston and the surrounding area. He has received great reviews for these shows. Herman also recently finished a college campus tour, which, according to Barbara, was very successful.

Barbara is now trying to get Herman a "gig" for a few weeks in May. You have made a few calls to promoters in Houston and found that Herman is very good. You would like to meet with him and Barbara to discuss the possibility of having him perform on some of your cruises.

Write a letter to Barbara inviting her and Herman to come to Mobile, Alabama, on March 15 for a visit. If things work out, you have two cruises that you could book him on during the month of May. Barbara's address is P.O. Box 4790, Houston, TX 77590.

11 **Routine Response—Product Information**   As the business manager for Maison Richard, a 200-seat restaurant in Seattle, you received an inquiry from Chris Shearing, 1926 Second Avenue, Seattle, WA 98101. She had several questions about the meat and fish served in your restaurant. Here are her questions and the answers:

a. *Are the cattle from which your beef comes allowed to roam freely on an open range instead of being fattened in cramped feedlots?* No, allowing free-roaming would increase the muscle tissue in the beef, making it less tender.

b. *Are the cattle fed antibiotics and hormones?* Yes, to ensure a healthy animal and to promote faster growth.

c. *Do your trout come from lakes and streams?* No, they're farm-grown, which is more economical and results in less disease.

Ms. Shearing is a well-known animal-rights activist, and you want to present your case as positively as possible to avoid the loss of her goodwill and any negative publicity that might result. Respond to her letter, supplying whatever other appropriate information you feel is reasonable.

■ See Handout 7.5.

12 **Routine Response—Form Letter**   You are the executive producer for *The Sherry Show,* a popular syndicated morning talk show on public television featuring Sherry Baker as host. The show features interviews and panel discussions on a wide variety of current topics.

Because Sherry takes questions and comments from the audience, it is important to have a full house each day. When the show started two years ago, you had trouble filling the 150-seat studio. Now, however, you get more ticket requests than you can accommodate. Anyone wanting a ticket must write at least four months ahead and can request no more than four tickets (which are free). The show tapes from 9:30 until 11 a.m. Monday through Friday each week. Tickets are for reserved seats, but any seats not occupied by 9 a.m. are released on a first-come, first-served basis. Studio doors close promptly at 9:15 each morning and do not reopen until the show ends at 11 a.m. Children under age 12 are not admitted.

Write a form letter telling people how to order tickets and conveying other needed information. The letter will be sent to anyone who requests ticket information.

13 Work-Team Communication—Routine Response   You are a member of the Presidents' Council, an organization made up of the presidents of each student organization on campus. You just received a memorandum from Dr. Robin H. Hill, dean of students, wanting to know what types of social projects the student organizations on campus have been engaged in during the past year. The dean must report to the board of trustees on the important role played by student organizations—both in the life of the university and community and in the development of student leadership and social skills. She wants to include such information as student-run programs on drug and alcohol abuse, community service, and fundraising.

Working in groups of four, identify and summarize the types of social projects that student organizations at your institution have completed this year. Then organize and synthesize your findings into a one-page memo to Dr. Hill. After writing your first draft, have each member review and comment on the draft. Then revise as needed and submit. Use only factual data for this assignment.

CO3. Compose a routine claim letter.

14 Routine Claim—Pump Order Mix Up   Assume the role of Uriah Castleton, purchasing agent for Western Electric in Gilbert, Arizona. You recently placed an order (Purchase Order No. 44-0987) for 12 Model 2500 air conditioning pumps (Part No. 2500-89712) from ACE Supply Inc. in Phoenix.

When the pumps arrived, you noticed you had received more than 12 pumps, and they were not Model 2500. ACE had accidentally sent 25 Model 1200 pumps. Although you could sell the Model 1200 pumps, you already have plenty of them in stock. What you really need is the Model 2500 pumps.

Write a letter to Brent Sewell, the shipping manager at ACE Supply Inc., requesting that they ship the 12 Model 2500 pumps quickly because you only have three more left in stock. Also ask what his plans are for your returning the 25 Model 1200 pumps. Enclose a copy of your purchase order. The address for ACE Supply is P.O. Box 2238, Phoenix, Arizona 85012.

15 Claim Letter—Inaccurate Reporting   As the marketing manager for ReSolve, a basic computer spreadsheet program for Windows, you were pleased that your product was reviewed in the current issue of *Computing Trends*. The review praised your product for its "lightning-fast speed and convenient user interface." You were not pleased, however, that your product was downgraded because it lacked high-level graphics capability. The reviewer compared ReSolve with full-featured spreadsheet programs costing, on average, $200 more than your program. No wonder, then, that your program rated a 6.6 out of 10, coming in third out of the five programs reviewed. If your program had been compared with similar low-level programs, you feel certain that ReSolve would have easily come out on top.

Although you do not want to get the magazine upset with your company (Software Entrepreneurs, Inc.), you do feel that it should compare apples with apples and should conduct another review of your program. Write to Roberta J. Horton, the magazine's review editor, at 200 Public Square in Cleveland, OH 44114, and tell her so.

16 Claim Letter—Poor Service As the owner of Parker Central, a small plumbing business, you try to instill in all your employees a customer-first attitude. Therefore, you were quite put off by your own treatment yesterday (July 13) at the hands of the receptionist at Englehard Investment Service (231 East 50 Street, Indianapolis, IN 46205). You showed up 20 minutes early for your 2:30 p.m. appointment with Jack Nutley, an investment counselor with the firm. You were meeting with him for the first time to discuss setting up a Simplified Employee Pension (SEP) plan for your 20 employees.

To begin with, the receptionist ignored you for at least five minutes until she finished the last paragraph of a document she was typing. Then, after finding out whom you wanted to see, she did not even call Jack's office to announce your arrival until 2:30 p.m. Finally, you learned that Jack had just become ill and had to go to the doctor. So you wasted half an afternoon and were also insulted by the receptionist's rude treatment.

You decide to write to Jack Nutley about the receptionist's office behavior. Your claim is for better service in the future. You want him to know that if you are going to continue to be treated in such a manner, you have no interest in doing business with his firm. Write the claim letter.

17 Routine Claim—No More Level Billing Your employer, Clearwater Fisheries, imports and bones fish for resale to hotels and food markets. When you were hired as office manager two years ago, you suggested that the Chicago company avoid the surprise of unusually high monthly utility bills by requesting year-round level billing. With this system, the utility (Chicago Power and Light) divides the total year's anticipated energy usage by 12 so that each month's bill is approximately the same. This arrangement worked well until April. Then Clearwater started working with Anergen Corp., a local firm that transforms biodegradable materials—such as fish bones and fat—into energy. Because Anergen now uses Clearwater's by-products to produce electricity and natural gas, you called the utility in early April and asked to switch back to monthly billing.

When you opened the May invoice this morning, you noticed that the utility was still using level billing. The usage detail reflected far lower consumption of both electricity and gas, as you expected, but the bill was for the same amount as in April. You decide to bring this matter to the attention of Chicago Power and Light's customer service department (at 4500 Lake Drive, Chicago, IL 60617).

18 Routine Adjustment—Something Is Fishy Assume the role of Fredrick Samuelson, operator of Samuelson's Catering Service. You recently catered a holiday luncheon for Jones, Wilson, and Associates, a law firm in Albuquerque.

You worked with Karen Ahmed-Ashton, one of the administrative assistants, on the details of the meal. Karen had ordered salmon for the entrée. However, your supplier was unable to provide enough fresh salmon to serve the 250-plus guests who were invited to the luncheon. You became aware of the shortage of salmon at the last minute, so you made a decision to substitute halibut for the salmon. You were unable to get in touch with Karen before the luncheon to clear the substitution.

The luncheon was well received by the 265 people who attended. You received many compliments on the quality of the food. You billed Karen $18.95 per person for the meal—the same price you would have charged for the salmon. Now, three days later you receive a letter from Karen asking that $2 per plate be deducted because you substituted halibut for the salmon.

You value the company's business, and the substitution was made without her approval, so you decide to make the adjustment. Write to Karen explaining the reason for the substitution. Enclose a check for $530. Add other details to complete the letter. Send the letter to Ms. Karen Ahmed-Ashton, Administrative Assistant, Jones, Wilson, and Associates, 350 West Cotton Tree Lane, Albuquerque, New Mexico 87201.

CO4. Compose a routine adjustment letter.

(19) **Adjustment Letter—Company at Fault**   Assume the role of customer service representative at Nationwide Office Supply (see Exercise 2). You've received Mr. McCord's letter (People's Energy Company, Wheatley Road, Old Westbury, NY 11568). You've done some background investigation and have learned that what the customer said is true—the Sampson Model 25 *is* a Xerox clone and your catalog does state that this cartridge fits Xerox printers and most compatibles. The problem came about because the Model 25, Sampson's newest model, was introduced shortly after your catalog went to press. This model's spindle is slightly shorter than previous Sampson models.

Unfortunately, you do not carry in your inventory a cartridge that will fit the Sampson Model 25. The customer should return the case COD, marking on the address label "Return Authorization 95-076R." In the meantime, you've authorized a refund of $284.25; Mr. McCord should receive the check within 10 days. Convey this information to Mr. McCord.

(20) **Adjustment Letter—Customer at Fault**   Assume the role of customer service representative at Nationwide Office Supply (see Exercises 2 and 19). You've done some background investigation and have learned that Mr. McCord was somewhat mistaken in stating that the Sampson Model 25 is a Xerox clone. What Sampson advertises instead is that the Model 25 uses the same character set as Xerox printers; this means that all fonts available from Xerox can also be downloaded to the Model 25. Sampson neither states nor implies that Xerox-compatible cartridges or other supplies will fit its machines.

Because the customer made an innocent mistake and you will be able to resell the unused cartridges, you decide to honor his claim anyway. He should return the case prepaid, marking on the address label "Return Authorization 95-076R." In the meantime, you're shipping him four cartridges (Part No. 02-9R32732) that *will* work on the Model 25; he can expect to receive them within 10 days. You're also enclosing your summer catalog.

(21) **Adjustment Letter—Form Letter**   As the new review editor at *Computing Trends* (see Exercise 15), you've already come to expect that whenever products are panned in your magazine, you can expect a negative reaction from the developers. You're happy to hear from them, however, because they sometimes bring to light additional information that your readers will find helpful. Unless the review contained a factual error, your policy is to publish the letters in the

"Feedback" column in a future issue. (In this particular instance, you compared ReSolve with the full-featured spreadsheets because that is exactly how Software Entrepreneurs, Inc., advertises the program.)

You review most major software products once yearly in your state-of-the-art computer labs, using criteria established by your readers. Write a form letter that you can send to product developers who write to complain about the review of their products, giving them this information.

22 **Adjustment Letter—Form Letter**   Assume the role of fulfillment representative at Paperbacks by Post, a book club that automatically mails members a selected paperback every month unless they send back a postcard declining the shipment. Although the system works well most of the time, occasionally a member receives a book even after returning the refusal postcard. In such cases, your company asks the member to take the parcel to the post office, which will return it at company expense. You also cancel the invoice and send the member a discount coupon toward future selections.

Write a form letter that you can send to members who complain about receiving an unwanted shipment. Advise them to act promptly, posting returns no later than two weeks after receipt.

23 **Goodwill Message—Great Teacher, Honored Guest**   As mayor of Seaside, Oregon, you want to congratulate Elizabeth Mortensen for being named Elementary Teacher of the Year for the state of Oregon. Elizabeth has been teaching at the local elementary school for 15 years and has been one of the best teachers in the fourth grade for all of those years.

CO5. **Compose a goodwill message.**

She has developed innovative teaching methods for teaching science and math and has also introduced some new safety programs for the children at the school. She has made a big difference in the lives of many young people in your community. You want to recognize her many contributions to the town's young people by having her as the guest of honor at the Seaside Recognition Dinner in June.

Write a letter congratulating Ms. Mortensen on her Teacher-of-the-Year award and invite her to attend the recognition dinner as the guest of honor.

24 **Goodwill Letter—Appreciation**   Think of a recent speech you have heard and enjoyed—perhaps by a speaker at a student organization meeting, a speaker sponsored by your institution, a guest speaker in class, or some similar presentation. If necessary, do some research to locate a correct mailing address for this person. Then write this person a letter of appreciation, letting him or her know how much you enjoyed and benefited from his or her remarks. (If you have not heard a speech you enjoyed lately, write a former professor, expressing appreciation for what you learned in class.) Use only actual data for this assignment.

continuing case7

The Case of the Missing Briefcase

It was Friday afternoon and Paul Yu was determined to take care of all pending correspondence before leaving for the weekend. On Tuesday, he had received a memo from Maurice Potts, an Urban Systems sales representative, that said in part:

■ A suggested solution to the Continuing Case can be found in the *Instructor's Resource Manual.*

■ See Handout 7.6.

■ See Handout 7.7.

Last week I made a sales presentation to Albany Electronics and carried two briefcases with me—my regular case plus a second case filled with handouts and brochures.

At the conclusion of my presentation, I distributed the handouts and brochures, picked up my regular briefcase and left—completely forgetting about my second case. When I discovered the following morning what had happened, I immediately called Albany Electronics, but it has been unable to locate the missing case.

This leather briefcase was two months old and cost $287.50 (see the attached sales slip). Since the Urban Systems policy manual states that employees will be reimbursed for all reasonable costs of carrying out their assigned duties, may I please be reimbursed for the $287.50 lost briefcase.

Paul had been thinking about this situation all week; he had even discussed it with Marc Kaplan, but Marc told him to make whatever decision he thought reasonable. On the one hand, Maurice is a good sales representative, and the policy manual does contain the exact sentence Maurice quoted. On the other hand, Paul does not feel that US should be responsible for such obvious mistakes as this; assuming responsibility for such mistakes would not only be expensive but also might encourage padded expense accounts.

Finally, Paul decides to do two things. First, he'll write a memo to the sales staff, interpreting more fully company policy. Policy 14.2 is entitled *Reimbursement of Expenses,* and Paragraph 14.2.b states, "With the approval of their supervisors, employees will be reimbursed for all reasonable costs of carrying out their assigned duties." Paul wants the sales staff to know that in the future he intends to interpret this policy to mean that any personal property that is stolen will be reimbursed at its present value (not its replacement value) if reasonable care has been taken to secure such property, if the incident is reported within three days, and if the value of the property can be determined. Lost or damaged personal property will normally not be reimbursed, no matter what the reason. Any sales representative may, of course, appeal Paul's decisions to the vice president of marketing.

Second, because the present policy may not have been sufficiently clear, Paul will write a memo to Maurice and agree to reimburse him $287.50 for the briefcase. He'll also enclose a copy of the new policy memo he is sending out to the sales staff.

After losing his second briefcase, Maurice Potts holds fast to his remaining case. He believes he should be reimbursed for the $287.50 cost of the briefcase he left behind.

Critical Thinking

1. How reasonable was Maurice Potts's claim? Was the intent of the policy clear? Should Paul have reimbursed him? Why or why not?
2. How reasonable is Paul's interpretation of the company policy?

Writing Projects

3. Compose the two documents that Paul intends to write: the memo to the sales staff and the memo to Maurice Potts. Format them in an appropriate style.

LABtest 7

Retype the following press release from Urban Systems, correcting any punctuation problems according to the rules introduced in LAB 3 on page 583.

Tivoli Industries *(PLUR)* new illuminated step lights are designed to illuminate and define step edges with a soft, glowing light. Their nonskid surface assures a secure footing while providing necessary illumination for stairways.

5   The LampPaks *(SING)* cardboard container is designed for shipping spent fluorescent tubes from the end user back to an authorized hazardous waste *- (ADJ)* disposal company. The product was introduced for one reason: *(EXP)* The Environmental Protection Agency now requires that everyones *(SING)* fluorescent tubes be disposed of in accordance with

10   the Resource Conservation and Recovery Act. The LampPak can hold up to 64 standard tubes; *(NO CONJ)* a package for tubes smaller than one- *(NUM)* half foot is also available. The cartons are shipped flat, thereby saving on shipping costs and storage space.

    Bruck has introduced the Shou (which means "long life" *(TERM)*), a

15   lighting system with specially designed fixtures that feature curves and flowing shapes. According to a recent article in In- *(TITLE)* dustrial Interior Design, "The unity *(QUOT)* of handcrafted cased glass . . . *(OMI)* creates ambient illumination that complements contemporary interior designs." *(QUOT)*

20   Finally, Verilux, a 40 *- (ADJ) -* year old fluorescent manufacturer has developed a sunlight simulator used by people with seasonal affective disorder, commonly known as the "winter blues." *(TERM)* The light is a self-contained tube that produces flicker *- (ADJ)* free light with almost no UV radiation or electromagnetic field.

■ See Slides 7.17–7.21.

8

Persuasive Messages

communication
OBJECTIVES

After you have finished this chapter, you should be able to

1. Compose a persuasive message promoting an idea.

2. Compose a persuasive message requesting a favor.

3. Compose a persuasive claim.

4. Compose a sales letter.

As a sales representative for the Memphis-based industrial packaging distributor Wurzburg, Inc., Patrick Vijiarungam can provide everything that a manufacturer needs to pack items so shipments arrive at their destinations safely—boxes, filler, even foam spacers to protect odd-shaped parts. "When I write a persuasive letter," he says, "I use both emotional and logical appeals." The audience for his persuasive letters includes purchasing agents, project engineers, and plant managers.

Because this audience may ignore sales letters sent as an initial contact, Vijiarungam usually calls to discuss general needs and to set up a meeting. "Although it is not always easier, it is better to reach someone by phone first," he observes. "Some larger corporations want an introductory letter, but whether that letter is read or absorbed is something else. Purchasing agents can be so inundated by sales letters that I prefer the personal touch of a phone call to make an impression and get their attention."

After the sales call, Vijiarungam uses the opening of his follow-up sales letter to show appreciation for the reader's time and interest. He briefly reminds the reader about their meeting. Next, he addresses the reader's problem and suggests how his company can solve it.

an insider's
perspective

PATRICK VIJIARUNGAM
Sales Representative,
Wurzburg, Inc.
(Memphis, Tennessee)

Using a logical appeal, Vijiarungam touches on specific product benefits, as well as availability, delivery schedules, and prices. His more subtle emotional appeal becomes the letter's central theme. "Wurzburg has been in business for almost a hundred years," he says. "Our reputation as a knowledgeable and honorable company is a key selling point." While he does not try to translate the company's good reputation into dollars and cents, he knows readers find it significant and persuasive. To motivate action, he closes by mentioning a possible schedule for the project or offering his company's technical expertise for other problems.

Vijiarungam sees objections—to pricing, for example—as opportunities to "turn the situation around and come out a hero to the customer." Not long ago, he learned that a long-time customer was considering a competitor's bids. In response, Vijiarungam drafted a persuasive letter thanking the customer for his business and reiterating Wurzburg's commitment to service and quality. He outlined pricing ideas for current and future orders and then thanked the customer for involving Wurzburg in the competitive comparison. The letter worked: "Our prices were not as low as the competitor's prices, but because of our previous relationship and the fact that we have actually done everything we said we would do, the customer decided to stay with us."

"When I write a persuasive letter, I use both emotional and logical appeals."

Persuasion is necessary when the other person initially resists your efforts.

■ Planning the Persuasive Message

Persuasion is the process of motivating someone to take a specific action or to support a particular idea. Persuasion motivates someone to believe something or to do something that he or she would not otherwise have done. Every day many people try to persuade you to do certain things or to believe certain ideas. Likewise, you have many opportunities to persuade others each day.

As a businessperson, you will also need to persuade others to do as you want. You may need to persuade a superior to adopt a certain proposal, a supplier to refund the purchase price of a defective product, or a potential customer to buy your product or service. In a sense, *all* business communication involves persuasion. Even if your primary purpose is to inform, you still want your reader to accept your perspective and to believe the information you present.

The essence of persuasion is overcoming initial resistance. The reader may resist your efforts for any number of reasons. Your proposal may require the reader to spend time or money—at the very least, you're asking for his or her time to *read* your message. Or the reader may have had bad experiences in the past with similar requests or may hold opinions that predispose him or her against your request.

Your job in writing a persuasive message, then, is to talk your readers into something, to convince them that your point of view is the most appropriate one. You'll have the best chance of succeeding if you tailor your message to your audience, provide your readers with reasons they will find convincing, and anticipate and deflect or disarm their objections. Such tailor-made writing requires careful planning; you need to define your purpose clearly and analyze your audience.

Purpose

Decide specifically what you want the reader to do as a result of your message.

The purpose of a persuasive message is to motivate the reader to agree with you or to do as you ask. Unless you are clear about the specific results you wish to achieve, you won't be able to plan an effective strategy that will achieve your goals.

Suppose, for example, you want to convince your superior to adopt a complex proposal. The purpose of your memo might be to persuade your superior to either (1) adopt your proposal, (2) approve a pilot test of the proposal, or (3) schedule a meeting where you can present your proposal in person and answer any questions. Achieving any one of these three goals may require a different strategy. Similarly, if you're writing a sales letter, you must determine whether your purpose is to actually make a sale, to get the reader to request more information, or to schedule a sales call. Again, your specific goal determines your strategy.

Knowing your purpose lets you know what kind of information to include in your persuasive message. "Knowledge is power" and never is this saying truer than when writing persuasive messages. To write effectively about an idea or product, you must know the idea or product intimately. If you're promoting an idea, consider all of the ramifications of your proposal.

- Are there competing proposals that should be considered?
- What are the implications for the organization (and for you) if your proposal is adopted and it *fails?*
- How does your proposal fit in with the existing plans and direction of the organization?

If you're promoting a product, how is the product made, marketed, operated, and maintained? You also need to learn this same information about your competi-

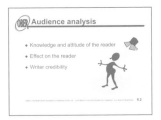

tion's products so you can determine the major differences between yours and theirs.

Audience Analysis

The more you're able to promote the features of your idea or product as satisfying a *specific* need of your audience, the more persuasive your message will be. Suppose, for example, you're promoting a line of men's shoes; you should stress different features, depending on your audience.

Young executive: stylish . . . comes in various shades of black and brown . . . a perfect accessory to your business wardrobe

Mid-career executive: perfect detailing . . . 12-hour comfort . . . stays sharp-looking through days of travel

Retired executive: economical . . . comfortable . . . a no-nonsense type of shoe

The point to remember is to know your audience and to personalize your message to best meet its needs and interests. Use the "you" attitude to achieve the results you want. When sending a form letter to perhaps thousands of readers, your approach cannot, of necessity, be as personal. Nevertheless, you should still strive to make the approach as personal as possible.

Knowledge and Attitude of the Reader   What does the reader already know about the topic? Determining this will tell you how much background information you should include. What is the reader's predisposition toward the topic? If it is negative, then where one or two reasons might ordinarily suffice, you will need to give more. Initial resistance also calls for more objective, verifiable evidence than if the reader were initially neutral. You also need to learn *why* the reader is resistant so that you can tailor your arguments to overcome those specific objections.

"I can't tell you what a pleasure and a privilege it is to teach such a bright-looking group of individuals."

As subjects watch a series of commercials, researchers at the Brain Sciences Institute in Melbourne, Australia, monitor a dozen different regions of the brain to see if they are forming emotional attachments to products.

Show how your reader will be affected by your proposal.

Effect on the Reader   How will your proposal affect the reader? If the reader is being asked to commit resources (time or money), discuss the rewards for doing so. If the reader is being asked to endorse some proposal, provide enough specific information to enable the reader to make an informed decision. The reader wants to know "What's in it for me?" *You* are already convinced of the wisdom of your proposal. Your job is to let the reader know the benefits of doing as you ask.

To be persuasive, you must present *specific, believable* evidence. However, one of the worst mistakes you could make would be to simply describe the features of the product or list the advantages of doing as you ask. Instead, put yourself in the reader's place. Discuss how the reader will benefit from your proposal. Emphasize the *reader* rather than the product or idea you're promoting.

NOT: The San Diego Accounting Society would like you to speak to us on the topic of expensing versus capitalizing 401-C assets.

BUT: Speaking to the San Diego Accounting Society would enable you to present your firm's views on the controversial topic of expensing versus capitalizing 401-C assets.

Sometimes your readers won't benefit *directly* from doing as you ask. If you are trying to entice your employees to contribute to the United Way, for example, it would be difficult to discuss direct reader benefits. In such situations, discuss the *indirect* benefits of reader participation; for example, show how someone other than you, the solicitor of the funds, will benefit.

> Your contribution will enable inner-city youngsters, many of whom have never even been outside the city of Columbus, to see pandas living and thriving in their natural habitat.

Writer Credibility   What is your credibility with the reader? The more trustworthy you are, the more trustworthy your message will appear. Credibility comes from many sources. You may be perceived as being credible by virtue of the position you hold or by virtue of being a well-known authority (see, for example, Communication Snapshot 8). Or you may achieve credibility for your proposal by supplying convincing evidence, such as facts and statistics that can be verified.

Suppose, for example, you have worked in an advertising production department and have extensive experience with color reproduction. If you are writing a memo to a colleague suggesting that certain photos will not reproduce clearly and should therefore be replaced, you probably don't need to explain your expertise. Your colleague is likely to believe you. But if you are writing a letter to the photographer, who does not know you, you would probably want to discuss past incidents that lead you to conclude the photos should be replaced.

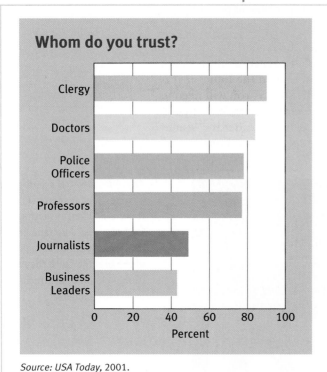

communication snapshot 8

Whom do you trust?

Source: USA Today, 2001.

A reader who trusts you is more likely to trust your message.

■ Organizing a Persuasive Request

A persuasive request seeks to motivate the reader to accept your idea (rather than to buy your product). The purpose of your message and your knowledge of the reader will help determine the content of your message and the sequence in which you discuss each topic.

Determining How to Start the Message

In the past, it was common practice to organize *all* persuasive messages by using an indirect organizational plan—presenting the rationale first, followed by the major idea (the request for action)—and this plan is still used for many persuasive messages. However, writers today should determine which organizational plan (direct or indirect) will help them better achieve their objectives.

Direct Plan—Present the Major Idea First.   Most superiors prefer to have messages from their subordinates organized in the direct style introduced in Chapter 7. Thus, when writing persuasive messages that travel up the organization, you should generally present the main idea (your recommendation) first, followed by the supporting evidence. The direct organizational plan saves time and immediately satisfies the reader's curiosity about your purpose. To get readers to accept your proposal when using the direct plan, present your recommendation along with the criteria or brief rationale in the first paragraph.

Prefer the direct plan when writing persuasive messages to your superior.

> **NOT:**   I recommend we hold our Pittsburgh sales meeting at the Mark-Congress Hotel.
>
> **BUT:**   I have evaluated three hotels as possible meeting sites for our Pittsburgh sales conference and recommend we meet at the Mark-Congress Hotel. As discussed below, the Mark-Congress is centrally located, has the best meeting facilities, and is moderately priced.

In general, prefer the direct organizational plan for persuasive messages when any of the following conditions apply:

- You are writing to superiors within the organization.

- Your audience is predisposed to listen objectively to your request.

- The proposal does not require strong persuasion (that is, there are no major obstacles present).

- The proposal is long or complex (a reader may become impatient if your main point is buried in a long report).

- You know that your reader prefers the direct approach.

■ See Slide 8.3.

Indirect Plan—Gain the Reader's Attention First   Unfortunately, many times your readers will initially resist your suggestions. Your job then is to explain the merits of your proposal and show how the reader will benefit from doing as you ask. Because a reluctant reader is more likely to agree to an idea *after* he or she understands its merits, your plan of organization is to convince the reader before asking for action.

■ See Slide 8.4.

Hans and Ivan Hageman started a school that gives at-risk black and Hispanic kids a fair shot at a future. They spend much of their time trying to persuade potential donors to support the Harlem school.

Thus, you should use the indirect organizational plan when writing to subordinates, when strong persuasion is needed, or when you know that your reader prefers the indirect plan. When using the indirect plan, you delay asking for action until after you've presented your reasons.

A subject line that does not disclose your recommendation should be used in persuasive letters. Don't announce your purpose immediately, but rather, lead up to it gradually.

NOT: SUBJECT: Proposal to Sell the Roper Division (too specific)

NOT: SUBJECT: Proposal (too general)

BUT: SUBJECT: Analysis of Roper Division Profitability

The first test of a good opening sentence in a persuasive request is whether it is interesting enough to catch and keep the reader's attention. It won't matter how much evidence you have marshaled to support your case if the recipient does not bother to continue reading carefully after the first sentence.

A **rhetorical question** is often effective as an opening sentence. A rhetorical question is asked strictly to get the reader thinking about the topic of your message; a literal answer is not expected. Of course, questions with obvious answers are not effective motivators for further reading and, in fact, may insult the reader's intelligence. Similarly, yes-or-no questions rarely make good lead-ins because pondering an answer doesn't require much thought.

NOT: How would you like to save our department $7,500 yearly?

BUT: What do you think the labor costs are for changing just one light bulb? $10? $25? More?

NOT: Did you know that the Hartford Community Fund is more than 75 years old?

BUT: What do Paul Newman and the Hartford Community Fund have in common?

Sometimes an unusual fact or unexpected statement will draw the reader into the message. At other times, you might want to select some statement about which the reader and writer will agree—to immediately establish some common ground.

Our company spent more money on janitorial service last year than on research and development.

■ See Slides 8.5 and 8.6.

A five-year-old boy taught me an important lesson last week.

Automotive News calls your 6-year/60,000-mile warranty the best in the business. (opening for a persuasive claim letter)

Your opening statement must also be relevant to the purpose of your message. If it is too far off the topic or misleads the reader, you risk losing goodwill, and the reader may simply stop reading. At the very least, the reader will feel confused or deceived, making persuasion more difficult.

The opening statement must be relevant.

Keep your opening statement short. Often an opening paragraph of just one sentence will make the message inviting to read. Few readers have the patience to wade through a long introduction to figure out the purpose of the message. In summary, make the opening for a persuasive message written in the indirect organizational plan interesting, relevant, and short. The purpose is to make sure your reader gets to the body of your message.

Creating Interest and Justifying Your Request

Regardless of whether your opening is written in a direct or indirect style, you must now begin the process of convincing the reader that your request is reasonable. This process may require several paragraphs of discussion, depending on how much evidence will be needed to convince the reader. Because it takes more space to state *why* something should be done than simply to state *that* it should be done, persuasive requests are typically longer than other types of messages.

Provide convincing evidence and use a reasonable tone.

To convince your readers, you must be objective, specific, logical, and reasonable. Avoid emotionalism, obvious flattery, insincerity, and exaggeration. Let your evidence carry the weight of your argument.

NOT: Locating our plant in Suffolk instead of in Norfolk would result in considerable savings.

BUT: Locating our plant in Suffolk instead of in Norfolk would result in annual savings of nearly $175,000, as shown in Table 3.

NOT: Why should it take a thousand phone calls to convince your computer to credit my account for $38.50?

BUT: Even after five phone calls over the past three weeks, I find that $38.50 has still not been credited to my account.

■ See Slides 8.7 and 8.8.

The type of evidence you present depends, of course, on the circumstances. The usual types of evidence are these:

■ *Facts and statistics: Facts* are objective statements whose truth can be verified; *statistics* are facts consisting of numbers. Both must be relevant and accurate. For example, statistics that were accurate five years ago may no longer be accurate today. Avoid, however, overwhelming the reader with statistical data. Instead, highlight a few key statistics—for emphasis.

■ *Expert opinion:* Testimony from authorities on the topic might be presented if their input is relevant and, if necessary, you can supply the experts' credentials. Expert opinion is especially persuasive to readers who don't recognize you as an authority on the subject.

■ *Examples:* Specific cases or incidents used to illustrate the point under discussion should be relevant, representative, and complete.

Present the benefits (either direct or indirect) that will accompany the adoption of your proposal, and provide enough background and objective evidence to enable the reader to make an informed decision.

Dealing with Obstacles

■ See Slide 8.9.

Ignoring any obvious obstacles to granting your request would provide the reader a ready excuse to refuse your request. Assume, for example, that you're trying to persuade a supplier to provide an in-store demonstrator of the firm's products—even though you know it's against the supplier's company policy to do so. If you ignore this factor, you're simply inviting the reader to respond that company policy prohibits granting your request. Instead, your strategy should be to show that *even considering such an obstacle,* your request is still reasonable, perhaps as follows:

> Last year we sold 356 of your Golden Microwave ovens. We believe the extensive publicity our sale will generate justifies your temporarily setting aside company policy and providing an in-store demonstrator. The ease of use and the actual cooked results that your representative will be able to display are sure to increase the sales of your microwaves.

Note the reader benefits in the last sentence.

If you're asking someone to speak to a professional organization but are unable to provide an honorarium, emphasize the free publicity the speaker will receive and the impact that the speaker's remarks will have on the audience. If you're asking for confidential information, discuss how you will treat it as such. If you're asking for a large donation, explain how payment can be made on the installment plan or by payroll deduction and point out the tax-deductible feature of the donation. (See Spotlight 20, "How Can You Collect Money That Is Due You?," on page 273, for guidelines on asking for money that is due you.)

Subordinate your discussion of major obstacles.

Even though you must address the major obstacles, do *not* emphasize them. Subordinate this discussion by devoting relatively little space to it, by dealing with obstacles in the same sentence as a reader benefit, or by putting the discussion in the middle of a paragraph. Regardless of how you do it, show the reader that you're aware of the obvious obstacles and that despite them, your proposal still has merit.

Motivating Action

■ See Slide 8.10.

Although your request has been stated (direct organizational plan) or implied (indirect organizational plan) earlier, give a direct statement of the request late in the message—after most of the background information and reader benefits have been thoroughly covered. Make the specific action that you want clear and easy to take. For example, if the reader agrees to do as you ask, how is he or she to let you know? Will a phone call suffice, or is a written reply necessary? If a phone call is adequate, have you provided a phone number? If you're asking for a favor that requires a written response, have you included a stamped, addressed envelope?

How Can You Collect Money That Is Due You?

The primary purpose of collection messages is to collect past-due accounts. The secondary purpose is to retain the debtor's goodwill. The collection process usually begins with the mailing of the monthly statement, and the vast majority of accounts are paid by the due date. For those that are not, companies often use a four-stage series of messages: reminder, inquiry, appeal, and ultimatum (more than one message may be sent at any one of these stages).

For All Collection Letters

1. Ensure that the information is accurate and that your message follows all federal and state laws regarding collection practices.

2. Adopt a tone of reasonableness and helpfulness; avoid anger.

3. Send letters promptly and—if payment doesn't result—at systematic intervals so the debt is never out of the reader's mind.

4. In every letter include the reader's account number, the amount owed, and a prepaid envelope.

Reminder Stage

1. Assume the reader has simply overlooked paying.

2. Avoid embarrassing the customer by sending a personal letter. Instead, send a second copy of the bill or an impersonal form letter.

Inquiry Stage

1. Assume the reader is deliberately not paying because of some unusual circumstance.

2. Send a short, personalized letter, written in the direct pattern.

3. Remind the reader that payment is late, ask why the account hasn't been paid, and solicit either payment or a plan for payment.

4. Don't provide excuses and don't suggest that the reader has merely overlooked payment.

Appeal Stage

1. Assume the reader must be persuaded to pay.

2. Write a persuasive letter—in the indirect pattern.

3. Select one central appeal to use and stress it throughout the letter. The most effective appeals (in increasing order of forcefulness) are resale, fair play, pride, self-interest, and fear.

4. Make the opening attention-getter interesting, short, and related to the central appeal.

5. In the middle section, continue to stress the central appeal, using reader benefits and positive language to motivate payment.

6. Close by directly asking for payment, combining your request with another reader benefit.

Ultimatum Stage

1. Assume the reader has no intention of paying.

2. Write in a direct pattern; at this point, maintaining goodwill is less important than securing payment.

3. In a polite and businesslike manner, explain exactly what you intend to do if the bill is not paid. Review the efforts you've already made to collect.

4. Give the reader one last opportunity to pay, setting a specific deadline.

Ask for the desired action in a confident tone. If your request or proposal is reasonable, there is no need to apologize, and you surely do not want to supply the reader with excuses for refusing. Take whatever steps you can to ensure a prompt reply.

Note the indirect benefit implied.

NOT: I know you're a busy person, but I would appreciate your completing this questionnaire.

BUT: So that this information will be available for the financial managers attending our fall conference, I would appreciate your returning the questionnaire by May 15.

NOT: If you agree this proposal is worthwhile, please let me know by June 1.

Note the motivation for a prompt reply.

BUT: To enable us to have this plan in place before the opening of our new branch on June 1, simply initial this memo and return it to me.

Checklist 9 on page 275 summarizes guidelines to use in writing persuasive requests. Although you will not be able to use all these suggestions in each persuasive request, you should use them as an overall framework for structuring your persuasive message.

■ See Handout 8.1.

CO1. Compose a persuasive message promoting an idea.

CO2. Compose a persuasive message requesting a favor.

■ Common Types of Persuasive Requests

In many ways, writing a persuasive request is more difficult than writing a sales letter because reader benefits are not always so obvious in persuasive requests. This section provides specific strategies and examples for selling an idea, requesting a favor, and writing a persuasive claim letter.

Selling an Idea

You will have many opportunities to use your education and experience to help solve problems faced by your organization. On the job you will frequently write messages proposing one alternative over another, suggesting a new procedure, or in some other way recommending some course of action. Organize such messages logically, showing what the problem is, how you intend to solve the problem, and why your solution is sound. Write in an objective style and provide evidence to support your claims.

The memo in Model 7 on page 276 illustrates the selling of an idea. In this case, a marketing supervisor for an auto-parts supplier is asking the vice president to reassign parking spaces to give preference to those employees driving American-made cars. Because the memo is written to his superior, the writer uses a direct organizational style.

Requesting a Favor

It has often been said that the wheels of industry are greased with favors. The giving and receiving of favors makes success more likely and makes life in general more agreeable.

A request for a favor differs from a routine request in that routine requests are granted almost automatically, whereas favors require persuasion. For example,

✓checklist 9

Persuasive Requests

Determine How to Start the Message

✓ **Direct Plan**—Use a direct organizational plan when writing to superiors, when your audience is predisposed to listen objectively to your request, when the proposal does not require strong persuasion, when the proposal is long or complex, or when you know your reader prefers the direct approach. Present the recommendation, along with the criteria or brief rationale, in the first paragraph.

✓ **Indirect Plan**—Use an indirect organizational plan when writing to subordinates, when strong persuasion is needed, or when you know your reader prefers the indirect approach. Start by gaining the reader's attention.

■ Make the first sentence motivate the reader to continue reading. Use, for example, a rhetorical question, unusual fact, unexpected statement, or common-ground statement.

■ Keep the opening paragraph short (often just one sentence), relevant to the message, and, when appropriate, related to a reader benefit.

Create Interest and Justify Your Request

✓ Devote the major part of your message to justifying your request. Give enough background and evidence to enable the reader to make an informed decision.

✓ Use facts and statistics, expert opinion, and examples to support your proposal. Ensure that the evidence is accurate, relevant, representative, and complete.

✓ Use an objective, logical, reasonable, and sincere tone. Avoid obvious flattery, emotionalism, and exaggeration.

✓ Present the evidence in terms of either direct or indirect reader benefits.

Minimize Obstacles

✓ Do not ignore obstacles or any negative aspects of your request. Instead, show that even considering them, your request is still reasonable.

✓ Subordinate the discussion of obstacles by position and amount of space devoted to the topic.

Ask Confidently for Action

✓ State (or restate) the specific request late in the message—after most of the benefits have been discussed.

✓ Make the desired action clear and easy for the reader to take, use a confident tone, do not apologize, and do not supply excuses.

✓ End on a forward-looking note, continuing to stress reader benefits.

---

asking a colleague to trade places with you on the program for the monthly managers' meeting might be considered a routine request. Asking the same colleague to prepare and give your presentation for you would more likely be a favor, requiring some persuasion.

Although friends and close colleagues often do each other favors as a matter of course, many times in business the granting of a favor might not be so automatic—especially if you don't know the person to whom you're writing. In such situations, you will want to begin your request with an attention-getter and stress the reader benefits from granting the favor.

Discuss at least one reader benefit before making your request. Explain why the favor is being asked and continue to show how the reader (or someone else) will

■ For more on the different types of appeals, see the *Instructor's Resource Manual.*

Favors require persuasion because the reader gets nothing tangible in return.

model7

PERSUASIVE REQUEST —SELLING AN IDEA

This persuasive memo uses the direct plan because the memo travels up the organization.

Begins by introducing the recommendation, along with a brief rationale.

Provides a smooth transition to the necessary background information. Cites statistics and external testimony for credibility.

Repeats the recommendation after presenting most of the rationale.

Neutralizes an obvious obstacle.

Closes on a positive, confident note; motivates prompt action.

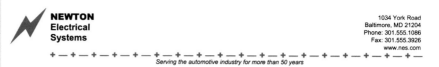

**NEWTON
Electrical
Systems**

1034 York Road
Baltimore, MD 21204
Phone: 301.555.1086
Fax: 301.555.3926
www.nes.com

Serving the automotive industry for more than 50 years

1 **MEMO TO:**   Elliott Lamborn, Vice President

  FROM: Jenson J. Peterson, Marketing Supervisor jjp

  DATE: April 3, 20—

  SUBJECT: Proposal to Reassign Employee Parking Lots

As one way of showing our support for the Ford Motor Company, which accounts for nearly half of our annual sales, I propose that the close-in employee parking lots around our headquarters be restricted to use by owners of Ford vehicles.

During their frequent visits to our headquarters, Ford personnel must pass the em-
2 ployee parking lot. When they do, they will see that approximately 70 percent of our employees drive vehicles manufactured by competitors of Ford. In fact, a Ford purchasing agent asked me last week, "How can you expect us to support you if you don't support us?"

The purpose of this memo, then, is to seek approval to have our close-in employee parking lot restricted to use by Ford vehicles. The maintenance department estimates that it will need four weeks and about $500 to make the needed signs.

Our labor contract requires union approval of any changes in working conditions. However, Sally Marsh, our shop steward, has told me that she would be willing to consider this matter—especially if similar restrictions are imposed on the executive parking lot.

3 Since our next managers' meeting is on May 8-10, I look forward to being able to announce the new plan to them. By approving this change, Newton will be sending a powerful positive message to our visitors: Our employees believe in the products we sell.

JJP

Grammar and Mechanics Notes

1 Because of its more readable format, writers often prefer a standard memo format for persuasive messages—even when e-mail is available. Often, the memo is sent as an attachment to an e-mail message.

2 *70 percent:* Use figures and the word "percent" in business correspondence.

3 *managers' meeting:* Place the apostrophe *after* the *s* to form the possessive of a plural noun (*managers*).

benefit from the favor. Keep a positive, confident tone throughout, and make the action clear and easy to take.

Often the favor is requested because the reader is an expert on some topic. If that is the case, you may legitimately make a complimentary remark about the reader. Make sure, however, that your compliment sounds sincere. Readers are rightfully suspicious, for example, when they read in a form letter that they have been specifically chosen to participate in some project. ("Me and how many thousands of others?" they might wonder.) On the other hand, such a compliment in a letter that is obviously personally typed and signed has much more credibility.

The most important factor to remember in asking for a favor has to do with the favor itself rather than with the writing process. Keep your request reasonable. Don't ask someone else to do something that you can or should do for yourself.

Figure 8.1 on page 278 illustrates how *not* to write an effective persuasive request. Model 8 on page 279, a revised version of the ineffective example, illustrates the guidelines discussed previously for writing an effective persuasive request. The reader and writer do not know each other, which makes persuasion a little more challenging and which calls for an indirect organizational plan. Reader benefits (the opportunity to promote the reader's firm and the flattering prospect of being the center of attention) are included.

> **AROUND THE WORLD**   *word***wise**
>
> - The word *taxi* is spelled the same way in nine languages: English, French, Danish, Dutch, German, Swedish, Spanish, Norwegian, and Portuguese.
> - The only countries in the world with just one syllable in their names are Chad, France, Greece, and Spain.
> - United Arab Emirates is the longest name of a country consisting of alternating vowels and consonants.
> - Pikes Peak is spelled without an apostrophe by Colorado state law.
> - *Q* is the only letter that does not occur in the names of the 50 U.S. states.
> - There are more English speakers in China than in the United States.

For a sincere tone, make any complimentary comments unique to the reader.

Writing a Persuasive Claim

As discussed in Chapter 7, most claim letters are routine letters and should be written using a direct plan of organization—stating the problem early in the letter. Because it is to the company's benefit to keep its customers happy, most reasonable claims are settled to the customer's satisfaction. Therefore, persuasion is not ordinarily necessary.

Suppose, however, that you wrote a routine claim letter and the company, for some reason, denied your claim. If you still feel that your original claim is legitimate, you might then write a *persuasive* claim letter—using all the techniques discussed earlier in this chapter for writing persuasive requests. Or assume that your new photocopier broke three days after the warranty period expired. The company is not legally obligated to honor your claim, but you may decide to try to persuade it to do so anyway.

Showing anger in your persuasive claim letter is counterproductive, even if the company turns down your original claim. The goal of your letter is not to vent your anger but to solve a problem. And that is more likely to happen when a calm atmosphere prevails.

As in a routine claim letter, you will need to explain in sufficient detail precisely what the problem is, how it came about, and how you want the reader to solve the problem. Use a calm, objective, courteous tone, avoiding anger and exaggeration. Although similar in some respects to a routine claim letter, the persuasive claim differs in two important ways: it has an attention-getting opening and it presents more evidence.

co3. Compose a persuasive claim.

■ For a discussion on persuading someone to give to charity and persuading someone to grant credit, see the supplemental lecture/discussion notes in the *Instructor's Resource Manual*.

Avoid showing anger.

figure8.1

An Ineffective Persuasive Request

Uses a subject line that is too specific

Begins by directly asking for the favor, using me-attitude language.

Omits important information (such as: Who will be attending the conference? How many attendees? How long will the presentation be?). Identifies the obstacle in a selfish manner—without including any reasons to minimize the obstacle.

Gives a deadline for answering—without providing any rationale.

Closes with a cliché.

January 15, 20—

Ms. Tanya Porrat, Editor
Autoimmune Diseases Monthly
1800 Ten Hills Road, Suite B
Boston, MA 02145

Dear Ms. Porrat

Subject: Request for You to Speak at the Multiple Sclerosis Congress

I have a favor to ask—a rather large one, I'm afraid. Having served as editor of a professional journal myself, I know how busy editors are, but I was wondering if you would be willing to fly to Washington, DC, on April 25 and speak at the closing banquet of our annual Multiple Sclerosis Congress.

The problem, of course, is that as a nonprofit association, we cannot afford to pay you an honorarium. I trust that this won't be a problem for you. We would, however, be willing to reimburse you for air travel and hotel accommodations.

Our conference attendants would benefit tremendously from your vast knowledge of multiple sclerosis, so we're really hoping you'll say yes. Just let me know your decision by March 3 in case we have to make other arrangements.

Please call me if you have any questions.

Cordially

May Lyon

May Lyon, Banquet Chair

National Multiple Sclerosis Society
733 Third Avenue
New York, NY 10017-3288

Tel 212 986 3240
1 800 FIGHT MS
Fax 212 986 7981
E-Mail: nat@nmss.org
www.nmss.org

January 21, 20—

1 Ms. Tanya Porrat, Editor
Autoimmune Diseases Monthly
1800 Ten Hills Road, Suite B
Boston, MA 02145

Dear Ms. Porrat

Subject: Program Planning for the Multiple Sclerosis Congress

2 "The average person has about 1 chance in 1,000 of developing MS." That comment of yours in a recent interview in the *Boston Globe* made me sit up and think.

Your knack for exploring little-known facts like that would certainly be of keen interest to those attending our annual congress in Washington, DC, on April 23-25. As the keynote speaker at the banquet at the Mayflower Hotel on April 25, you would be able to present your ideas on current initiatives to the 200 people present. You would, of course, be our guest for the banquet, which begins at 7 p.m. Your 45-minute presentation would begin at about 8:30 p.m.

We will reimburse you for air travel and hotel accommodations. Although our nonprofit association is unable to offer an honorarium, we do offer you an opportunity to introduce your journal and to present your ideas to representatives of major autoimmune groups in the country.

3 We'd like to announce your presentation in our next newsletter, which goes to press on March 3. Won't you please call to let me know you can come. We'll have a large, enthusiastic audience of medical researchers waiting to hear you.

Cordially

May Lyon

May Lyon, Banquet Chair

4

The National MS Society...One thing people with MS can count on.

---

model8

PERSUASIVE REQUEST—ASKING A FAVOR

This persuasive request uses the indirect plan because the writer does not know the reader personally and because strong persuasion is needed.

Opens by quoting the reader, thus complimenting her.

Intimates the request; provides the necessary background information.

Subordinates a potential obstacle by putting it in the dependent clause of a sentence.

Closes with a restatement of a reader benefit.

Grammar and Mechanics Notes

1 To increase readability, do not italicize publication titles in addresses.

2 *Boston Globe:* Italicize the titles of separately published works, such as newspapers, magazines, and books.

3 *you can come.:* Use a period after a courteous request.

4 Do not include reference initials if the letter writer also types the letter.

Attention-Getting Opening   Recall that you begin a routine claim letter by stating the problem. This type of opening would not be wise for a persuasive claim, because the reader may conclude the claim is unreasonable until he or she reads your rationale.

NOT: Would you please repair my Minolta 203 copier without charge, even though the 90-day warranty expired last week.

BUT: We took a chance and lost! We bet that the Minolta 203 we purchased from you 96 days ago would prove to be as reliable as the other ten Minoltas our firm uses.

■ Research shows that 95 percent of dissatisfied customers don't bother to complain to the company in question, which makes the 5 percent who do complain a valuable source of information about what the company can do to improve its product or service. A reasonable complaint letter, then, is likely to elicit a reasonable response from any company interested in its customers' satisfaction.

The original opening is counterproductive, providing a ready excuse for denying the claim. The revised version holds off making the request until enough background information has been provided. Note also the personal relationship the writer is beginning to establish with the reader in the revised version—disclosing not only that the company owns ten other Minolta copiers but also that the other copiers have all been very reliable. Such an understanding tone will make the reader more likely to grant the request.

In a courteous manner, provide complete details.

More Evidence   Because your claim either is nonroutine or has been rejected once, you will need to present as much convincing evidence as possible. Explain fully the basis for your claim; then request a specific adjustment.

Model 9 on page 281 illustrates these guidelines for writing a persuasive claim letter.

■ Writing a Sales Letter

CO4. **Compose a sales letter.**

The heart of most business is sales—selling a product or service. Much of a company's sales effort is accomplished through the writing of effective sales letters—either individual letters for individual sales or form letters for large-scale sales.

In large companies, the writing of sales letters is centered in the advertising department and is a highly specialized task performed by advertising copywriters and marketing consultants. Within a few years after graduation, however, a growing number of college students opt to own their own businesses. These start-up companies are typically quite small, with only a few employees.

Small-business owners often write their own sales letters.

In such a situation, the company must mount an aggressive sales effort to develop business, but the company is typically too small to hire a full-time copywriter or marketing consultant. Thus, the owner usually ends up writing these sales letters, which are vital to the ongoing health of the firm. So no matter where you intend to work, the chances are that at some point you will need to write sales letters.

The indirect organizational plan is used for sales letters. It is sometimes called the *AIDA* plan, because you first gain the reader's *attention,* then create *interest* in and *desire* for the benefits of your product, and finally motivate *action.*

model9

PERSUASIVE CLAIM

June 18, 20—

Customer Service Supervisor
Northern Airlines
P.O. Box 619616
Dallas/Fort Worth Airport, TX 75261-9616

Dear Customer Services Supervisor:

1   I think you will agree that a relaxing 90-minute flight on Northern Airlines is more enjoyable than a grueling six-hour automobile trip. Yet, on June 2, my wife and I found ourselves doing just that—driving from Saginaw, Michigan, to Indianapolis—in the middle of the night and in the company of three tired children.

2   We had made reservations on American Flight 126 a month earlier. When we arrived at the airport, we were told that Flight 126 had been canceled. Your gate agent (Ms. Nixon) had graciously rebooked us on the next available flight, leaving at 9:45 the next morning.

Since the purpose of our trip was to attend a family wedding on June 3, we had no choice but to cancel our rebooked flight and to drive to Indianapolis instead. When we tried to turn in our tickets for a refund, Ms. Nixon informed us that because the flight had been canceled due to inclement weather, she would be unable to credit my American Express charge card.

3   As a frequent flier on Northern, I've often experienced the "Welcome Aboard!" feeling that is the basis for your current advertising; and I believe you will want to extend that same taken-care-of feeling to your ticket operations as well. Please credit my American Express charge card (No. 4102 817 171) for the $680 cost of the five tickets, thus putting out the welcome mat again for my family.

Sincerely,

Oliver J. Arbin

Oliver J. Arbin
4   518 Thompson Street
Saginaw, MI 48607

This persuasive claim letter uses the indirect plan: the writer does not personally know the reader and thus cannot expect the favor to be granted automatically.

Begins on a warm and relevant note.

Provides a smooth transition from the opening sentence.

Provides the necessary background information.

Tells exactly what the problem is in a neutral, courteous tone.

Provides a rationale for granting the claim; asks confidently for specific action; mentions the reader benefit of keeping a satisfied customer.

Grammar and Mechanics Notes

1 *just that—driving:* To insert a dash, type two hyphens (--) with no space before or after. The word processing program automatically converts two hyphens into a printed dash.

2 *rebooked:* Write most *re-* words solid—without a hyphen.

3 *taken-care-of feeling:* Hyphenate a compound adjective that comes before a noun.

4 For personal business letters on plain paper, type your address below your name.

Selecting a Central Selling Theme

Your first step is to become thoroughly familiar with your product, its competition, and your intended audience. Then, you must select a **central selling theme** for your letter. Most products have numerous features that you will want to introduce and discuss. For your letter to make a real impact, however, you need to have a single theme running through your letter—a major reader benefit that you introduce early and emphasize throughout the letter. One noted copywriting consultant calls this principle a basic law of direct-mail advertising and labels it $E^2 = 0$, meaning that when you try to emphasize *everything*, you end up emphasizing *nothing*.[1]

It would be unrealistic to expect your reader to remember five different features that you mention about your product. In any case, you have only a short time to make a lasting impression on your reader. Use that time wisely to emphasize what you think is the most compelling benefit from owning your product. Two means of achieving this emphasis are *position* and *repetition*. Introduce your central selling theme early (in the opening sentence if possible), and keep referring to it throughout the letter.

Gaining the Reader's Attention

Review the earlier section on gaining the reader's attention when writing persuasive requests.

A reply to a request for product information from a potential customer is called a **solicited sales letter**. An **unsolicited sales letter**, on the other hand, is a letter promoting a firm's products that is mailed to potential customers who have not expressed any interest in the product. (Unsolicited sales letters are also called *prospecting letters.* Some recipients, of course, call them *junk mail.*)

Because most sales letters are unsolicited, you have only a line or two in which to grab the reader's attention. Unless a sales letter is addressed to the reader personally and is obviously not a form letter, the reader is likely to just skim it—either out of curiosity or because the opening sentence was especially intriguing.

Most readers will scan the opening even of a form letter, perhaps just to learn what product is being promoted. If you can capture their attention in these first few lines, they may continue reading. Otherwise, all your efforts will have been wasted. The following types of opening sentences have proven effective for sales letters.

Technique	Example
Rhetorical question	What is the difference between extravagance and luxury? (*promoting a high-priced car*)
Thought-provoking statement	Most of what we had to say about business this morning was unprintable! (*promoting an early morning television news program*)
Unusual fact	If your family is typical, you will wash one ton of laundry this year. (*promoting a laundry detergent*)

A S K Ober

Dear Dr. Ober:

Would you be kind enough to show me how to approach the case "Selling a Service—Small Business" that is included in the chapter on persuasive messages. Thank you.

—*Paula W.*

Dear Paula:

Your instructor probably would not want me to provide individual help on this case, but take a look at the 3Ps exercise on pages 289–291 within the chapter. If you answer these seven questions for the exercise you're working on, you'll be well on your way to drafting an effective response.

—Scot

E-mail your questions and comments to askober@ober.net.

Current event	The new Arrow assembly plant will bring 1,700 new families to White Rock within three years. (*promoting a real estate company*)
Anecdote	During six years of college, the one experience that helped me the most did not even occur in the class-room. (*promoting a weekly business magazine*)
Direct challenge	Drop the enclosed Pointer pen on the floor, writing tip first, and then sign your name with it. (*promoting a no-blot ballpoint pen*)

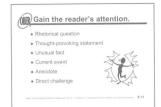

■ See Slide 8.11.

As in persuasive requests, the opening of a sales letter should be interesting, short, and original. When possible, incorporate the central selling theme into your opening; and avoid irrelevant, obvious, or timeworn statements.

> *Many attention-getting openings consist of a one-sentence paragraph.*

If you have received an inquiry from a potential customer about your product, you know that the person is already at least mildly interested in the product. Therefore, when you write solicited sales letters, an attention-getting opening is not as crucial. In such a situation, you might begin by expressing appreciation for the customer's inquiry and then start introducing the central selling theme.

Creating Interest and Building Desire

If your opening sentence is directly related to your product, the transition to the discussion of features and reader benefits will be smooth and logical. Make sure that the first sentence of the following paragraph relates directly to the idea introduced in your opening sentence. Unrelated ideas will make the reader pause and feel puzzled.

Interpreting Features The major part of your letter (typically, several paragraphs) will probably be devoted to creating interest and building desire for your product. You should not only describe the product and its features but, more important, *interpret* these features by showing specifically how each will benefit the reader. Make the reader—not the product—the subject of most of your sentences.

> *Devote several paragraphs to interpreting the product's features.*

Marketers refer to the benefit a user receives from a product or service as the **derived benefit**. As Charles Revson, founder of the Revlon cosmetics company, once said, "In our factory we make lipstick; in our advertising we sell hope."[2]

NOT: The JT Laser II prints at the speed of ten pages per minute.

BUT: After pressing the print key, you'll barely have time to reach over and retrieve the page from the bin. The JT Laser II's print speed of ten pages per minute is twice that of the typical printer.

NOT: Masco binoculars zoom from 3 to 12 power.

BUT: With Masco binoculars, you can look a ruby-throated hummingbird squarely in the eye at 300 feet and see it blink.

■ See Slides 8.12 and 8.13.

Although emphasizing the derived benefit rather than product features is generally the preferred strategy, two situations call for emphasizing product features instead: when promoting a product to experts and when promoting expensive equipment. For example, if the car you're promoting to sports car enthusiasts achieves a maximum torque of 138 ft-lb at 3,000 rpm or produces 145 hp at 5,500 rpm, tell the reader that. You would sound condescending trying to interpret to such experts what this means.

Using Vivid Language   Use action verbs when talking about the product's features and benefits. Within reason, use colorful adjectives and adverbs, being careful, however, to avoid a hard-sell approach. Finally, to convey a dynamic image, use positive language, stressing what your product *is,* rather than what it is *not.*

> **NOT:** The paper tray is designed to hold 200 sheets.
>
> **BUT:** The paper tray holds 200 sheets—enough to last the busy executive a full week without reloading.
>
> **NOT:** The Terminator snowblower is not one of those lightweight models.
>
> **BUT:** The Terminator's 4.5 hp engine is 50 percent more powerful than the standard 3.0 hp engine used in most snowblowers.

Maintain credibility by providing specific facts and figures.

Using Objective, Ethical Language   To be convincing, you must present specific, objective evidence. Simply saying that a product is great is not enough. You must provide evidence to show *why* or *how* the product is great. Here is where you'll use all the data you gathered before you started to write. Avoid generalities, unsupported superlatives and claims, and too many or too strong adjectives and adverbs.

> **NOT:** At $595, the Sherwood moped is the best buy on the market.
>
> **BUT:** The May 2004 *Independent Consumer* rated the $595 Sherwood moped the year's best buy.

Positive statements by independent agencies lend powerful support.

> **NOT:** We know you will enjoy the convenience of our Bread Baker.
>
> **BUT:** Our Bread Baker comes with one feature we don't think you'll ever use: a 30-day, no-questions-asked return policy.

Although the law allows you to promote your product aggressively, there are certain legal and ethical constraints under which you will want to operate. The guidelines provided in Spotlight 21, "What May You Say in a Sales Letter?," on page 285, apply to U.S. law and customs. When operating in the international environment, you should follow local laws and customs.

Focus on the one feature that sets your product apart.

Focusing on the Central Selling Theme   The recurring theme of your letter should be the one feature that sets your product apart from the competition. If your reader remembers nothing else about your product, this one feature is what you want him or her to remember. Whenever possible, unify the features under one umbrella theme—whether the theme is convenience, ease of use, flexibility, price, or some other distinguishing characteristic around which you can build your case.

Discussing and fully interpreting these features may take a considerable amount of space, and some readers may be unwilling to read through a long sales letter.

spotlight21
ON LAW AND ETHICS

What May You Say in a Sales Letter?

May I say that our product is the best on the market?
Yes. You may legally express an opinion about your product; this is called *puffery*. You may not, however, make a claim that can be proven false, such as saying that your product is cheaper than a competing product when, in fact, your product is not cheaper.

The typist mistakenly typed the price of our product as $19.95, instead of the correct price of $29.95. Do I have to sell it for $19.95?
No. You are not legally responsible for an honest mistake, as long as your intent was not to deceive the buyer.

May I include a sample of my product with my letter and require the reader to either send payment or return the product at my expense?
No. Readers do not have to pay for or return any unordered goods. They may legally treat them as a gift from you.

I want to send a sales letter promoting our rock music to high school students. May I legally accept orders from minors?
Yes. You may accept their orders, and if you do, you are legally bound to honor the contract. However, until they reach the age of adulthood (18 years in some states and 21 years in others), minors may legally cancel a contract and return the merchandise to you.

In my showroom, I want to sell the furniture that has small nicks and scratches on it. If I state in my sales letter that all sales are final and sale items are marked "as is," do I have to issue refunds to anyone who complains?
No. By using the term "as is," you tell the consumer that you are not promising new merchandise.

Without my knowledge, my assistant wrote a letter in which she promised a customer a 10 percent price break; such a price reduction is clearly against store policy. Do we have to honor my assistant's price?
Yes. Your assistant was acting as your agent, and her promise is legally binding on your firm.

However, those who do will be more motivated to respond favorably. The test of an effective sales letter is the number of sales it generates—*not* the number of people who read the letter.

Mentioning Price   If price is your central selling theme, introduce it early and emphasize it often. In most cases, however, price is not the central selling theme and should therefore be subordinated. Introduce the price late in the message, after most of the advantages of owning the product have been discussed. To subordinate price, state it in a long complex or compound sentence, perhaps in a sentence that also mentions a reader benefit.

> You'll consider the $250 cost of this spreadsheet seminar repaid in full the very next time your boss asks you to revise the quarterly sales budget—on a Friday afternoon!

Use techniques of subordination when mentioning price.

Sometimes it is helpful to present the price in terms of small units—for example, showing how subscribing to a weekly magazine costs less than $1 per week, rather than $50 per year. Or compare the price to that of a familiar object—"about what you'd pay for your morning newspaper or cup of coffee."

Referring to Enclosures   Sometimes, some of the features of a product or service are best displayed in a brochure that you can enclose with the sales letter. Subordinate your reference to the enclosure, and refer to some specific item in the enclosure to increase the likelihood of its being read.

NOT: I have enclosed a sales brochure on this product.

BUT: Note the porcelain robin's detailed coloring on the actual-size photograph on page 2 of the enclosed brochure.

NOT: I have enclosed an order blank for your convenience.

BUT: Use the enclosed order blank to send us your order today. Within three weeks, you will be enjoying this museum-quality sculpture in your own home.

Motivating Action

■ For an additional 3Ps model sample for a persuasive request, see the Supplementary Teaching Materials in the *Instructor's Resource Manual.*

Although the purpose of your letter should be apparent right from the start, delay making your specific request until late in the letter—after you have created interest and built desire for the product. Then state the specific action you want.

If the desired action is an actual sale, make the action easy to take by including a toll-free number, enclosing an order blank, accepting credit cards, and the like. For high-priced items, it would be unreasonable to expect to make an actual sale by mail. Probably no one has read a sales letter promoting a new automobile and then phoned in an order for the car. For such items, your goal is to get the reader to take just a small step toward purchasing—sending for more information, stopping by the dealer for a demonstration, or asking a sales representative to call. Again, make the step easy for the reader to take.

Provide an incentive for prompt action by, for example, offering a gift to the first 100 people who respond or stressing the need to buy early while there is still a good selection, before the holiday rush, or during the three-day sale. Make your push for action *gently,* however. Any tactic that smacks of high-pressure selling at this point is likely to increase reader resistance.

Use confident language when asking for action, avoiding such hesitant phrases as "If you want to save money" or "I hope you agree that this product will save you time." When asking the reader to part with money, it is always a good idea to mention a reader benefit in the same sentence.

Push confidently, but gently, for prompt action.

NOT: Hurry! Hurry! Hurry! These sale prices won't be in effect long.

NOT: If you agree that this ice cream maker will make your summers more enjoyable, you can place your order by telephone.

BUT: To have your Jiffy Ice Cream Maker available for use during the upcoming July 4 weekend, simply call our toll-free number today.

Consider putting an important marketing point in a postscript (P.S.). Some marketing studies have shown that a postscript notation is the most-often-read part of a sales letter.[3] It can be as long or as short as needed, but it should contain new and interesting information.

■ See Handout 8.2.

✓checklist 10

Sales Letters

Prepare

✓ Learn as much as possible about the product, the competition, and the audience.

✓ Select a central selling theme—your product's most distinguishing feature.

Gain the Reader's Attention

✓ Make your opening brief, interesting, and original. Avoid obvious, misleading, and irrelevant statements.

✓ Use any of these openings: rhetorical question, thought-provoking statement, unusual fact, current event, anecdote, direct challenge, or some similar attention-getting device.

✓ Introduce (or at least lead up to) the central selling theme in the opening.

✓ If the letter is in response to a customer inquiry, begin by expressing appreciation for the inquiry and then introduce the central selling theme.

Create Interest and Build Desire

✓ Make the introduction of the product follow naturally from the attention-getter.

✓ *Interpret* the features of the product; instead of just describing the features, show how the reader will benefit from each feature. Let the reader picture owning, using, and enjoying the product.

✓ Use action-packed, positive, and objective language. Provide convincing evidence to support your claims—specific facts and figures, independent product reviews, endorsements, and so on.

✓ Continue to stress the central selling theme throughout.

✓ Subordinate price (unless price is the central selling theme). State price in small terms, in a long sentence, or in a sentence that also talks about benefits.

Motivate Action

✓ Make the desired action clear and easy to take.

✓ Ask confidently, avoiding the hesitant "If you'd like to" or "I hope you agree that."

✓ Encourage prompt action (but avoid a hard-sell approach).

✓ End your letter with a reminder of a reader benefit.

P.S. If you stop in for a demonstration before May 1, you'll walk out with a free box of color transparencies (retail value $21.95)—just for trying Up Front, the new presentation software program by Acme Products.

These guidelines for writing an effective sales letter are illustrated in Model 10 on page 288 and summarized in Checklist 10 above. As always, the test of the effectiveness of a message is whether it achieves its goal. Use whatever information you have available (especially in terms of audience analysis) to help your letter achieve its goal.

model10

SALES LETTER

Starts with a rhetorical question.

Introduces need for safety and security as the central selling theme.

Presents specific evidence and discusses it in terms of reader benefits.

Emphasizes *you* instead of the product in most sentences.

Subordinates price in a long sentence that also discusses benefits.

Makes the desired action clear and easy to take; ends with a reader benefit.

2455 Paces Ferry Road, N.W. • Atlanta, GA 30339-4024
(770) 433-8211

1

2   Dear Homeowner:

Do you view your home as an investment or as your castle? Is it primarily a tax write-off or a place of refuge?

Most of us view our homes as places where we can feel safe from outside intrusions. Thus, we feel threatened by government statistics showing that 5.3 percent of all U.S. households were burglarized last year. How can we protect ourselves?

Today, there's a simple and dependable alarm that protects up to 2,500 square feet. Just plug in the Safescan Home Alarm System and turn the key. You then have 30 seconds to leave and 15 seconds to switch off the alarm once you return.

3   Worried that your dog might trigger the alarm? Safescan screens out normal sounds like crying babies, outside traffic, and rain. But hostile noises like breaking glass and splintering wood trigger the alarm. The 105-decibel siren is loud enough to alert neighbors and to drive away even the most determined burglar.

What if a smart burglar disconnects the electricity to your home or pulls the plug? Built-in batteries assure that Safescan operates through power failures, and batteries recharge automatically. Best of all, installation is easy. Simply mount the 4-pound unit on a wall, and plug it in. Nothing could be faster. Finally, there is a $259 home alarm that you can trust; and the one-year warranty and ten-day return policy ensure your complete satisfaction.

Last year, 3.2 million burglaries occurred in the United States, but you can now tip the odds back in your favor. To order the Safescan Home Alarm System, stop by your nearest Home Depot. Within minutes, Safescan can be guarding your home, giving you peace of mind.

Sincerely yours,

Jeffrey Parret

Jeffrey Parret
National Sales Manager

Grammar and Mechanics Notes

1 In general, omit the date and inside address in form sales letters. Subject lines are also frequently omitted.

2 *Dear Homeowner:* Note the generic salutation.

3 *crying babies, outside traffic, and:* Separate items in a series by commas.

The 3Ps
Problem, Process, Product

A SALES LETTER

Problem

You are the proprietor of Lee's Consumer Products, a small retail store located in the Fiesta Mall in Mesa, Arizona. You have recently become the exclusive dealer for Voice Note, a digital recorder that allows you to record messages to yourself rather than scribbling them on scraps of paper.

The recorder is $2\frac{1}{2} \times 1 \times \frac{1}{2}$ inches, weighs 3 ounces, and is made in Japan from sturdy plastic. It records messages that are a maximum of 60 seconds long and holds 30 minutes of dictation. A lock button prevents recording over a message. After the message has been played back, the chip automatically resets for use the next time. The Voice Note is operated by pressing the Record button and speaking. It runs on two AAA batteries that are included and comes with a 90-day warranty and a 30-day full-refund policy.

To field-test this product, you decide to try a local direct-mail campaign directed at the business community. You purchase a mailing list containing the names and addresses of the 800 members of the Phoenix Athletic Club, a downtown facility used by businesspeople for lunch, after-work socializing, exercise, and social affairs. The club has racquetball and tennis courts, an indoor pool, and exercise rooms. Its yearly membership fee is $3,000. You decide to send these 800 members a form letter promoting the Voice Note for $29. You'll include your local phone number (555-2394) for placing credit-card orders by phone, or the readers may stop by the store to purchase the recorder in person.

Process

1. Describe your audience.

   - Businessmen and -women
   - Active (sports and exercise facilities)
   - Upscale (can afford $3,000 annual membership)
   - Probably very busy professionally and socially

2. What will be your central selling theme?

   Convenience/portability is the unique benefit of Voice Note.

3. Write an attention-getter that is original, interesting, and short; that is reader-oriented; that relates to the product; and, if possible, that introduces the central selling theme.

   You're driving home on the freeway in bumper-to-bumper traffic when the solution to a nagging problem facing you at work suddenly pops into your head. But by the time you get home 30 minutes later, your good idea has vanished.

4. Jot down the features you might discuss and the reader benefits associated with each feature.

Size is 2½ × 1 × ½ inches, weighs 3 ounces: *smaller and lighter than a microcassette recorder; fits in shirt pocket or purse; easy to use on the go.*

Records 60-second messages—a maximum of 30 minutes' worth: *room enough for most "to-do" messages—30 different reminders.*

Press Record button and then speak; lock function prevents overrecording: *easy to use, even in car; not a lot of buttons to fiddle with.*

Powered by two AAA batteries (included): *real portability.*

5. Write the sentence that mentions price. (Since price is not the central selling theme, it should be subordinated.)

The Voice Note's price of $29 is less than you'd pay for a bulky microcassette recorder that is much less convenient for on-the-go use.

6. What action are you seeking from the reader?

To purchase the Voice Note.

7. How can you motivate prompt action?

Make the action easy to take; offer warranty and guarantee satisfaction; stress that the sooner you buy, the sooner you'll enjoy using it.

Product

Lee's Consumer Products
Fiesta Mall • 1200 Dobson Road • Mesa, Arizona 85201
TEL: 480-555-2394 • www.leesconsumerproducts.com

Dear Club Member:

You leave the Phoenix Athletic Club and are heading home on the freeway in bumper-to-bumper traffic when the solution to a nagging problem at work pops into your head. But by the time you get home, your good idea has vanished.

Next time, carry Voice Note, the 3-ounce digital recorder that allows you to record reminders to yourself on the go. Now you can "jot" down your ideas as soon as they occur. As you know, inspiration often strikes far from a pad and pencil!

Much smaller than a microcassette (2 ½ x 1 x ½ inches), Voice Note slips into your shirt pocket or purse. And there aren't a lot of buttons to fiddle with. Just press Record and speak. A lock prevents overrecording your earlier messages.

You can record up to 30 different messages of 60 seconds each—"to do" messages like "Call Richard about the Apple computer contract" or "Place order for 200 shares of SRP stock" or even "Pick up Jenny from soccer practice at 5:30." After playback, the tape automatically resets for immediate use.

For true portability, the Voice Note is powered by two AAA batteries (included). Your satisfaction is guaranteed by our 90-day warranty and 30-day refund policy. The Voice Note's price of $29 is less than you'd pay for a bulky microcassette recorder that is much less convenient for on-the-go use. For credit-card orders, simply call us at 555-2394. Or stop by our retail store at Fiesta Mall for a personal demonstration.

The next time you need to pick up a quart of milk on the way home, make a Voice Note. You won't come home empty-handed.

Sincerely,

Richard E. Lee

Richard E. Lee

Visit the **BusCom Online Learning Center** (at http://college.hmco.com) for additional resources to help you with this course and with your future career.

■ Summary

co1. Compose a persuasive message promoting an idea.

When writing to superiors, use a direct writing style, giving the proposal or recommendation, along with the criteria or a brief rationale, in the first paragraph. For most other persuasive messages, prefer an indirect writing style. First gain the reader's attention by using an opening paragraph that is relevant, interesting, and short. For persuasive requests promoting an idea, devote the majority of the message to discussing the merits of your proposal and showing specifically how your proposal meets some need of the reader. Provide evidence that is accurate, relevant, representative, and complete. Discuss and minimize any obstacles to your proposal.

co2. Compose a persuasive message requesting a favor.

Begin your request with an attention-getter and stress the reader benefits from granting the favor. Discuss at least one reader benefit before making your request, and show how someone other than you will benefit from the favor. Keep a positive tone throughout, and make the action clear and easy to take.

co3. Compose a persuasive claim.

Write persuasive claims in the indirect organization, beginning with an attention-getting opening. Use a calm, objective, courteous tone, avoiding anger and exaggeration. Explain in detail the problem, and provide objective evidence to persuade the reader to grant the claim.

co4. Compose a sales letter.

For sales letters, introduce a central selling theme early and build on it throughout the message. Devote most of the message to showing how the reader will specifically benefit from owning the product. Subordinate the price, unless price is the central selling theme.

■ Key Terms

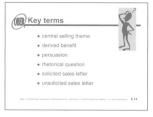

■ See Slide 8.14.

■ Consider treating this list as an end-of-chapter exercise for students to define and give an example of each term.

You should now be able to define the following terms in your own words and give an original example of each.

central selling theme (282)	rhetorical question (270)
derived benefit (283)	solicited sales letter (282)
persuasion (266)	unsolicited sales letter (282)

■ Exercises

1 **The 3Ps (Problem, Process, and Product) Model: Communication Applications at Wurzburg, Inc.**   Before Patrick Vijiarungam begins writing to any potential customer, he calls to make a personal connection and meets with the manufacturer to learn more about its packaging needs. Then he drafts a follow-up sales letter suggesting specific products to solve the company's packaging problems and reiterating Wurzburg's good reputation. By establishing credibility, emphasizing reader benefits, and showing appreciation, Vijiarungam makes a persuasive case for doing business with Wurzburg.

Problem

You are a sales trainee with Wurzburg. After going with Patrick Vijiarungam to visit a potential customer, you have to draft your first sales letter. You found out that the manufacturer ships laser printer toner cartridges from its distribution center in Memphis to stores across the country. The manufacturer wants to prevent the cartridges from being damaged in transit (by having a few of the delicate parts jostled out of alignment or denting the plastic housing, for example). You know that Wurzburg can design sturdy corrugated boxes for shipping and cardboard spacers to secure the cartridges inside the boxes.

Process

a. Describe your audience.
b. Should you use a direct or indirect organizational plan for this letter? Why?
c. What points should you include in the body of your letter?
d. Write an opening that is attention-getting, relevant, and introduces your central selling theme.
e. What action do you want the audience to take?
f. Write a closing paragraph to motivate your audience to take the desired action.

Product

Using your knowledge of persuasive messages, draft this sales letter, inventing any reasonable data needed to complete this assignment.

2 **The 3Ps (Problem, Process, and Product) Model: A Persuasive Message—Selling an Idea**

Problem

You are O. B. Presley, a sales representative for Midland Medical Supplies. Like most of the other 38 Midland reps, you are on the road three or four days a week, promoting your products to hospitals, clinics, and physicians in private practice. Three years ago, Midland purchased 8-pound laptop computers for all sales reps. These computers simplified your job immensely, especially in terms of filing call reports. Each evening in your hotel room, you keyboard the report, showing to whom you spoke, their experiences with your products, what features they'd like to see changed, and the like. You then submit these reports, along with actual orders, electronically to headquarters via the computer's built-in modem.

■ Suggestions and sample solutions for exercises appear in the *Instructor's Resource Manual.*

■ See Handout 8.3.

CO1. **Compose a persuasive message promoting an idea.**

■ An additional 3Ps model activity on persuasive requests appears in the Supplementary Teaching Materials section in the *Instructor's Resource Manual.*

It occurs to you that you could be more productive by replacing your bulky laptop with a notebook computer and built-in portable printer. That way, whenever a customer wanted a specification sheet for a new product, you could electronically retrieve the information from the company's mainframe computer and print it out on the spot for the customer. You're sure you'd get additional sales as a result.

The specific system you're interested in is the Canon NoteJet, a Pentium-based notebook computer that has a built-in modem and ink-jet printer. The entire system weighs just 7.7 pounds and sells for $1,899 with 256MB of RAM and a 10GB hard-disk drive. The only problem is that you don't know what to do with your present laptop computer. There's not much demand for used laptops, especially for three-year-old 8-pounders. Still, you think notebooks would be a good investment for all sales reps. Send a memo to Charles J. Redding, national sales manager, trying to sell him on the idea.

Process

a. Describe your audience.
b. Should you use a direct or indirect organizational plan? Why?
c. Write the opening sentence of your memo.
d. List the reasons you might discuss for your proposal—including any reader benefits associated with each reason.
e. What is an obstacle that might prevent you from achieving your objective?
f. Write a sentence that addresses this obstacle (subordinate this discussion).
g. Write the last paragraph of your memo, in which you state (or restate) your request. Make the action easy for the reader to take, ask confidently, and end on a forward-looking note.

Product

Draft, revise, format, and proofread your memo. Then submit both your responses to the process questions and your revised memo to your instructor.

■ See Handout 8.4.

3 Routine Request—Helping a Friend   You are the plant manager of the Monterey Manufacturing Company in Pearl River, Louisiana. You manufacture automotive ball bearings. Currently you have 125 employees. One of your employees, Francis Benoit, has been diagnosed with lung cancer.

Francis is well known and well liked at the plant, but his illness has kept him out of work for over two months, and he has exhausted all of his sick leave. His doctor believes he will probably be out of work for at least three more months. You want to encourage your employees to donate sick leave time to Francis. Employees can donate up to five days sick leave each. No one is required to participate, but anyone who can should give at least a few hours of sick leave.

To donate sick leave time to Francis, employees must fill out a form in the Human Resource Management department. Forms must be submitted before the end of the month for accounting purposes. Any unused hours and days will return to those who have donated on a proportional basis.

Write a memo to be posted in the break room encouraging the employees to donate time to Francis.

4 Gold Doesn't Always Glitter   For the last few years your union has been negotiating an incentive bonus plan for the employees at the Fremont Gold Extraction plant in Fairbanks, Alaska. The plan was designed to compensate employees based on their productivity and would be given as a bonus at the end of the year based on the company's profitability.

Finally you, as the union representative, got the company to agree to the plan. At first the plan appeared a success. Projections showed that some employees would earn bonuses of up to $5,000. The production rates had increased dramatically, and everyone seemed to be happy with the arrangement.

Now in the second half of the year, because of the increased production, the price of gold is taking a "nose dive." Although the plan seemed like a good idea, it needs to be reworked. You know the workers are expecting bonuses, but you want them to vote to rescind the plan. Not getting the bonus this year will hurt, but they need to have a plan that will consistently reward them for their efforts.

Write a memo to the employees persuading them to vote to rescind the negotiated incentive bonus plan. The vote will be from 6 to 8 p.m. in the union hall on Tuesday, September 1, 20—.

5 **Watch What You Say!**   Is it just you or is profanity now being used everywhere— even in the workplace? Although you're no prude, as the store manager for DVDs Plus, you want to avoid creating a hostile work environment and also ensure that your employees project a positive image for the organization (and for themselves). Write a memo to your sales staff encouraging them to clean up their language.

6 **Building Internship Programs**   Students in your construction management program are struggling to find good-paying jobs after graduation. You are determined to resolve the issue. You have seen effective internship programs offered in other schools, and you believe that an internship program would be a great way for your students who are approaching graduation to get some very valuable hands-on experience in their chosen fields.

You also believe that some of the construction firms in the area could benefit from the innovative techniques your students are learning in the classroom. The internship would help students get their foot in the door. Your experience with internships has been that once the student works with a company and the company spends time training the student, the company is more likely to hire him or her later on.

You are proposing a program that would allow your students to get a 12-week paid internship with local construction companies. The first two weeks of the internship would give the student an overview of the company's operation. For the last ten weeks, the student would receive specialized training in a particular area. Students would be paid one half of the rate of an entry-level employee.

As the job placement director of your school in rural Mississippi, write a letter to Cleo S. Johnson, the owner of Johnson and Sons Construction, at 980 Yellow Jack Drive, Starkville, Mississippi 39759. Persuade him to accept an intern from your school for a 12-week assignment.

7 **Selling an Idea—Indirect Organizational Plan**   Refer to Exercise 2. Assume that you (O. B. Presley) are relatively new on the job and have not yet earned the trust of the national sales manager. In addition, you know that Redding is not a big fan of technology. Therefore, you decide to write your memo using an indirect organizational plan. Write the memo.

8 **Selling an Idea—Oversized Dressing Rooms**   You are Robert Kilcline, a merchandising manager at Nordstrom, Inc., a fine clothing store in Seattle.

Your firm has decided to open a new store in Fashion Square Mall, an upscale department store on the north side. Retail space is quite expensive in this mall (nearly 50 percent more expensive than at your other locations), so Nordstrom facility engineers are trying to make every inch of space count.

Despite the costs, you feel that to be competitive in this mall, you will have to offer superior customer service. You already offer a no-questions-asked return policy, abundant inventory to ensure a complete selection of sizes and colors, and a harpist who performs on the main floor from 11 a.m. until 2 p.m. daily. But you think that the new store should also have oversized dressing rooms—ones large enough to hold a comfortable chair, garment rack, and adjustable three-sided mirrors. You want your customers to be able to make their selections in comfort.

You estimate that adding the furnishings and additional 20 square feet per dressing room in the new store will add $18,500 to the construction costs, plus $155 to the monthly lease. Present your ideas in a memo to your boss, Rebecca Chavez, executive vice president.

9 **Internet Exercise**   Many businesses—on and off the Internet—use persuasive messages for both sales and nonsales purposes. Consider the situation at DoubleClick, a company that places advertisements for clients on various websites. Visit the firm's site (at http://www.doubleclick.com) and follow the link to review its privacy policy, especially the section about cookies and how to opt out. Then find and follow the link that discusses how consumers can opt out of DoubleClick's customized advertising program. Now assume the role of DoubleClick's webmaster. Draft an e-mail message intended to persuade consumers to reverse their opt-out decisions and continue allowing DoubleClick to send them customized advertising messages.

co2. Compose a persuasive message requesting a favor.

10 **Conference Speaker**   You are planning a conference for your professional organization. A good friend from your college days at UCLA, Virginia Jackson, is a highly regarded motivational speaker. You want to get her to be the keynote speaker for your annual conference, which will be held in Palm Springs, California, on Friday, October 22, 20—. You would not be able to pay her normal speaking fee of $2,000, but you could cover her airfare and lodging.

Although you were quite close in college, you have not visited in several years. The last time you did speak to her, she indicated that she would enjoy getting together with you and some other friends in the area. You could arrange to have her fly to Palm Springs on Thursday and leave on Sunday morning. Her speech would be from 10 to 11 a.m. on Friday. You and some of her other friends could spend time on Thursday and Saturday renewing old acquaintances.

Write a letter to Virginia at 1250 Whitney Lane in Saxapahaw, NC 27340, inviting to come to California to visit and be the keynote speaker at the conference.

11 **Requesting a Favor—Field Trip**   You are David Pearson, owner and manager of Jack 'n Jill Preschool. During the next few weeks, you will be discussing food and nutrition with the youngsters; and you want to end the unit by having the children walk to the nearby Salad Haven, take a tour of the kitchens, and then make their own salads for lunch from the restaurant's popular salad bar. Of course, each family would pay for its child's meal. In fact, to help make the visit easier, you'll collect the money beforehand and pay the cashier for everyone at once. You will ask several parents to come with you to help supervise the 23 children, ages three through five, although they will probably need some extra help from the salad-bar attendants. You can come any day during the week of October 10–14. State regulations require that the children eat lunch between 11 a.m. and 12:30 p.m. Write to Donna Jo Luse (Manager, Salad Haven, 28 Grenvale Road, Westminster, MD 21157) asking for permission to make the field trip.

■ See Handout 8.5.

12 Requesting a Favor—Celebrity Donation   Coming out of the movie theater after watching the Academy Award–winning movie *Rocky Mountain Adventure*, starring Robert Forte, you suddenly have an idea. As executive director of the Wilderness Fund, you've been searching for an unusual raffle prize for your upcoming fundraiser. You wonder whether you could persuade Robert Forte to donate some item used in this popular movie (perhaps a stage prop or costume item) for the raffle. The Wilderness Fund is an 8,000-member nonprofit agency dedicated to preserving forest lands—the very type of lands photographed so beautifully in Forte's latest movie. Write to the actor at Century Studios, 590 North Vermont Avenue, Los Angeles, CA 90004.

13 Persuasive Request—Sidestepping a Digital Ban   The dean of your college recently read a news article describing how students can use pagers, cell phones, and handheld computers to share answers during classroom exams. According to the article, one-third of students in a recent survey said they've cheated during tests, and half said they've cheated on written assignments. As a result, the dean issued a statement forbidding students from having or using electronic handheld devices in class when working on tests and projects.

Your sister is about to give birth to twins, and you've pleaded with your instructors to relax the ban on cell phones for the next three weeks so that you can take the call if it comes during a test. The instructors, however, need the dean's permission to make such an exception. Now you must submit a written request for the dean's consideration. Should you use the direct or indirect plan? Why? How can you justify your request? What obstacles can you anticipate—and how can you overcome them? Based on your knowledge of persuasive requests, write a letter to the dean (making up the details for this assignment).

14 Writing a Persuasive Claim—Azaleas   You are Vera Malcolm, the facilities manager for Public Service Company of Arkansas. In preparation for the recent dedication of your new hydroelectric plant, you spruced up the grounds near the viewing stand. As part of the stage decorations, you ordered ten potted azaleas at $28.50 each (plus $10.50 shipping) from Jackson-Parsons Nurseries (410 Wick Avenue, Youngstown, OH 44555) on February 3. The bushes were guaranteed to arrive in show condition—ready to burst into bloom within three days—or your money would be cheerfully refunded.

The plants arrived in healthy condition but were in their final days (perhaps hours) of flowering—certainly in no shape to display at the dedication. You decided, instead, to plant the azaleas as part of your permanent landscaping. Because the plants arrived only three days before the dedication, you had to purchase substitute azaleas from the local florist—at a much higher price.

CO3. Compose a persuasive claim.

In fact, you ended up paying $436 for the florist plants—$140.50 more than the Jackson-Parsons price. You feel that the nursery was responsible for your having to incur the additional expenditure. Write a letter asking Jackson-Parsons to reimburse your company for the $140.50.

15 **Writing a Persuasive Claim—Fans in the Stands**   Assume the role of the ticket manager for the Provo Angels Rookie League baseball team. You are looking for sponsors to be featured at your minor league baseball games. You also want to put fans in the stands and get youngsters interested in baseball.

You are planning a promotion that will allow local merchants to purchase tickets that would be donated to underprivileged children. The promotion involves businesses donating $500 worth of tickets (100 tickets) in exchange for being the featured sponsor at one of the Angels games. The company donating the tickets would be featured during the seventh-inning stretch. The children who received the tickets would also be featured and would receive a visit from Charlie the Wonder Pooch—the Angels' mascot.

This promotion would be good for the children, it would be good for your fan base, and it would be good for the businesses that would get some good publicity. Write a letter to the president of Allred's Sporting Goods, John N. Allred, encouraging him to be a featured sponsor at one of your games in August. His address is 4215 North Lake Creek Road, Heber City, UT 84032.

16 **Writing a Persuasive Claim—Ripped Suit**   After a hurried taxi ride from La-Guardia Airport to the Marriott Marquis Hotel on May 15, you barely made it to your 2 p.m. appointment. You did not realize until you sat down at the conference table that you had ripped the pants of your $450 suit on an exposed spring in the taxi seat. The next day, your tailor tells you there is no way to repair the rip invisibly, so the suit is, in effect, now useless. Since you've owned the suit for a year, you don't expect the taxi company to reimburse you for $450, but you do think reimbursement of $200 is reasonable. From your taxi receipt, you learn that you took Taxi 1145 belonging to Empire State Taxi (50 West 77th Street, New York, NY 10024). Since this is a personal claim, write your letter on plain paper, using your own return address.

17 **Writing a Persuasive Claim—Lemon SUV**   As the new owner of a sports utility vehicle, you were expecting to head into the backcountry for some camping and fishing trips. You purchased the SUV three months ago from Howard Williams, the owner of Big Willie's Auto. You paid $10,500 for the two-year-old SUV. Mr. Williams offered you a 12-month, 12,000-mile extended warranty for $1,000, which you decided to purchase.

When you purchased the vehicle, it had 38,645 miles on the odometer; now it shows only 40,012 miles. You have driven it fewer than 1,500 miles. It has been in the shop on two occasions in the three months. The first time you took it off-road, you had problems and had to have it towed back to town. The problem seems to be with the vehicle's transmission. So far, Mr. Williams has paid for the towing, $50, and transmission repair bills of $587.50; but you are getting tired of the continual problems with this "lemon."

Although the warranty does not cover the installation of a new transmission, you want Mr. Williams to pay for one. You have a friend who will install a new one for only $850—other shops have quoted $1,800 to do the job. This will give you some peace of mind and eliminate the every-other-month trip to the repair shop. This would also restore your confidence in Mr. Williams as a fair businessperson. This will also help him because at the current rate, he will probably pay more for transmission repairs under the warranty than the $1,150. Your friend will guarantee the new transmission for 24 months, so Mr. Williams would be off the hook for transmission repairs.

Write to Mr. Williams at Big Willie's Auto, 385 Bishop Road, Lawton, OK 73501, persuading him to pay the $850 for installation of a new transmission.

18 Selling a Product—Work Boots As sales manager for Industrial Footwear, Inc., send a form sales letter advertising your Durham work boot to 3,000 members of Local 147 of the Building Trades Union. Local 147 is made up primarily of construction workers on high-rise buildings in Houston.

CO4. **Compose a sales letter.**

The Durham is an 8-inch, waterproof, insulated boot, made of oil-tanned cowhide. It exceeds the guidelines for steel-toe protection issued by the American National Standards Institute (ANSI). The Durham has an all-rubber heel that provides firm footing, and its steel shanks provide additional support for arches and heels. It comes in whole sizes 7–13 in black or brown at a price of $79, plus $4.50 shipping. The price is guaranteed for the next 30 days. There is a one-year, no-questions-asked warranty.

Select a suitable salutation for your form letter and omit the date and inside address. The purpose of the letter is to motivate readers to order the boots by using the enclosed order blank or by calling your toll-free order number, 800-555-2993.

19 Writing a Solicited Sales Letter—Real Estate As a Realtor in the local franchise of National Home Sales, you receive a letter from Ms. Edith Willis (667 Rising Hills Drive, Xenia, OH 45385). Her letter states, in part,

> I am a single mother of two young children who is being transferred to your town and wish to purchase a three-bedroom condominium in a nice area in the price range of $100,000 to $125,000. I would be able to make a maximum down payment of $25,000. Would you please write me, letting me know whether you have any property available that would fit my needs.

Although the housing market in your small town is tight, you do have a condominium available that might suit her needs. It has three bedrooms plus a finished basement, is air-conditioned (important in your part of the country), and is four years old. The neighborhood elementary school is considered the best in town; the only drawback is that the condominium is next door to a large but attractive apartment building. The home is listed for $119,900.

Send Ms. Willis a photograph and fact sheet on the listing. The purpose of your letter is to encourage her to phone you at 602-555-3459 to make an appointment to visit your office so that you can personally show her this and perhaps other properties you have available.

20 Work-team Communication—Pushing Snacks Assume the role of Randy Escobedo, vice president of marketing for Krisbee Snax, a midsized snack food manufacturer in the Northeast. Your company is introducing a new snack food. The snack food industry is very competitive; and you believe your best chance to introduce the new product, Krisbee Korns, is to get grocery stores to feature the tasty, low-fat snacks on their end-of-aisle displays. Your company has a good reputation for quality snacks, and this new product promises to be a top seller. However, most grocery stores reserve the end-of-aisle display space for the bigger food companies in the industry.

You are willing to offer a sizeable discount (50 percent) in the price you charge retailers for the new product in exchange for this prime location in their stores during the month of November. Retailers who feature your new product can purchase 26 oz. bags of Krisbee Korns for only $1.25—half the normal selling price. These bags have a suggested-retail price for $3.99, so the mark up would be more than 200 percent. In addition to this promotional allowance, you also plan a big advertising campaign for this new product, which should increase their sales even more.

Write a letter to Ms. Betty Eagleston, corporate buyer for the Allen's Food grocery store chain, persuading her to feature Krisbee Korns on the end-of-aisle displays in Allen's Food stores during the month of November. Write to her at the corporate headquarters located at 4815 Crane Creek Road in Avondale, WV 24811.

21 Selling a Service—Small Business   While studying for your bar exams, you decide to start a part-time business delivering singing telegrams throughout the Atlanta metropolitan area. For a flat fee of $150, you'll personally deliver a greeting card and sing any song (in good taste) of the customer's choice—using either the actual wording of the song or special lyrics composed by the customer. You promote your company (Musical Messages) for birthdays, anniversaries, graduations, promotions, and other special occasions.

Send a form letter to a random sample of Atlanta's residents, promoting your service. The purpose of your letter is to persuade the reader to call you at 404-555-9831 to order a singing telegram. Orders must be prepaid (no credit cards), and you require seven days' notice.

22 Form Letter—Selling for Charity   As the director of fundraising for the Buckeye Bread Basket, a Cleveland charity that buys food for people in need, you are starting a new program. You plan to sell holiday greeting cards to raise money for your annual Thanksgiving Day dinner. This year, more than 400 needy people (including singles and families) are expected to attend the dinner. An Ohio artist created the original watercolor scene on the cards, which come in boxes of 10, with green envelopes. People who buy the cards are able to take a tax deduction for their donations; the money from the sale of a single box can feed a family of four on Thanksgiving.

Write a form letter that will persuade people to order your cards. The price is $12 per box, plus $1 postage and handling, and orders can be placed using the enclosed form and return envelope.

23 Writing a Sales Letter—Making Dough from Organic Bread   You are a marketing consultant hired by Todd's Organic Garden Breads, which makes a variety of healthy, whole-wheat, eight-grain, sunflower-seed, and poppy-seed breads. Todd Lleras, who founded the southern Florida bakery after a successful career as a model, learned the business under the direction of a master baker. Although his fresh, organic breads retail for about 30 percent more than ordinary breads, Lleras has seen a steady rise in demand for his products. You believe that consumers and store executives alike are attracted by the company's colorful packaging and promotions, which feature the photogenic founder and his infant daughter.

Lleras originally sold his breads through small health-food outlets, but then was able to get his breads onto the shelves of Wild Oats and other health-food supermarkets. Now the company is moving into a larger baking facility and needs to expand its sales to mainstream supermarkets and gourmet specialty shops. You've done some research and believe that the breads would sell well at Dean & Deluca, a gourmet food retailer that operates upscale stores, cafés, and a catalog division. Lleras asks you to draft a sales letter on his behalf to Dean & Deluca's president, John B. Richards (at 560 Broadway, New York, NY 10012). What central selling theme will you use? How will you capture the reader's attention in this unsolicited letter? What features and benefits will you emphasize? How will you motivate action? Write this letter, using your knowledge of persuasive messages and supplying any specifics you need to complete this assignment.

continuing
case 8

Flying High at Urban Systems

Diana, Jean, and Larry were analyzing the quarterly expense report. "Look at line item 415," Diana said. "Air-travel expenses have increased 28 percent from last year. Is there any room for savings there?"

"Jean and I were discussing that earlier," Larry said. "I think we should begin requiring our people to join all the frequent-flyer programs so that after they fly 20,000 to 30,000 miles on

■ A suggested solution to the Continuing Case can be found in the *Instructor's Resource Manual.*

Should Urban Systems or its traveling employees receive the benefit of frequent-flyer miles earned while traveling on company business?

any one airline, they get a free ticket. Then we should require them to use that free ticket the next time they have to take a business trip for us."

"I disagree," Jean said. "To begin with, there's no easy way to enforce the requirement. Who's going to keep track of how many miles each person flies on each airline and when a free flight coupon is due that person? It would make us appear to be Big Brother, looking over their shoulders all the time.

"In addition, our people put in long hours on the road. If they can get a free ticket and occasionally are able to take their spouses along with them, what's the big deal? They're happier and probably end up doing a better job for us."

"Still," Larry countered, "company resources were used to purchase the original tickets, so logically the free tickets belong to the company. And why should our people who travel get free tickets, compliments of the company, when those who don't travel do not get free tickets?"

Jean was ready with a counterargument, but Diana put an end to the discussion: "Both of you think about the matter some more and let me have a memo by next week giving me your position. Then I'll decide."

Critical Thinking

1. Jot down all the reasons you can think of for and against Larry's proposition—including any reasons that might not have been discussed at the meeting. What are the benefits associated with each reason? Has this topic been covered on the Internet?

Writing Projects

2. Assume the role of Larry. Write a memo to Diana trying to persuade her to begin requiring employees to use their frequent-flyer miles toward business travel. Knowing that Jean will be writing a memo arguing the opposing viewpoint—that employees should be able to use their free airline tickets for personal use—try to counteract her possible arguments.

3. Now assume the role of Jean. Write a memo to Diana arguing for the status quo. Try to anticipate and counteract Larry's likely arguments.

OBER Critical thinking

FOR Larry's proposal:

- Using free tickets from frequent-flyer programs would save the company money.
- All employees should be entitled to the same fringe benefits.
- Nontraveling employees might experience lowered morale.
- Company money was used to buy the tickets, so logically the free tickets belong to the company.

8.15

OBER Critical thinking

AGAINST Larry's proposal:

- There is no easy way to enforce the requirement.
- Additional personnel would be needed to monitor the process, which would be expensive in itself.
- The morale of employees who do travel is improved if occasionally they can travel with family members.
- Employees who are happy with their job benefits are more highly motivated.

8.16

■ See Slides 8.15 and 8.16.

LABtest 8

Retype the following news item, correcting any grammar errors according to the rules introduced in LAB 4 on page 591.

With 14,000 professionals registered, Lightfair Interna-

tional has won its bet that Las Vegas would be a good location

for its trade show for architectural lighting. Not only is Vegas

one of the top trade show cities in the ~~world. But~~ *world, but* (FRAG) its streets

5   simply shimmer with billions of bright lights. This show is the

~~biggest~~ *bigger* (MOD) of the two international lighting shows planned this

year. In fact, if it ~~wasn't~~ *weren't* (AGR—SUBJ) for the competing smaller regional

shows, this would be the largest lighting show ever held.

The conference program at this and similar shows ~~offer~~ *offers* (AGR—INT WD)

10   light designers and architects a chance to earn continuing educa-

tion credits. None of the sessions ~~are~~ *is* (AGR—PRO) to be repeated, and nei-

ther tape recorders nor videotaping ~~are~~ *is* (AGR—SUB → VB) allowed in any session.

One highlight of the show is a presentation by Luc Lafor-

tune, lighting director for the Cirque du ~~Soleil, Lightfair~~ *Soleil. Lightfair* (RUN-ON) also

15   has organized a group trip to see the Cirque du Soleil's perma-

nent Las Vegas show. Lafortune is always a lively speaker; and at

last year's show, it was ~~him~~ *he* (CASE—NOM) who provided a look at the chal-

lenges of lighting the dangerous feats of circus performers.

There ~~are~~ *is* (AGR—EXPL), for the first time, one session featuring light-

20   ing designers who will address the issues of adapting theatrical

fixtures for permanent installations. Walt Disney Imagineering is

also providing a look at lighting for ~~their~~ *its* (AGR—CO NAME) themed environments.

Lighting designers Charles Stone from London and Rogier

Heide from Amsterdam ~~takes~~ *take* (AGR—GEN) a look into the crystal ball of lighting

25   for a preview of the future. Stone and ~~him~~ *he* (CASE—NOM) will also answer audi-

ence questions. Finally, the great Paul Gregory himself talks

about project management in a global market.

■ See Slides 8.17–8.20.

■ See Handout 8.6.

Bad-News Messages

After you have finished this chapter, you should be able to

1. **Compose a message that rejects an idea.**

2. **Compose a message that refuses a favor.**

3. **Compose a message that refuses a claim.**

4. **Compose an announcement that conveys bad news.**

Open disclosure is the way Howard High deals with messages about potential problems. High is strategic communications manager for Intel, the global leader in making microprocessors for personal computers. As a company spokesperson, he shares information about the $21 billion company and its products with reporters from U.S. and foreign business publications. Intel products are definitely high-tech; they're also high-profile, thanks to the "Intel Inside" brand-building campaign that has established the company's worldwide reputation for quality.

As Intel adds innovative features and more processing power to new chips, it faces the challenge of managing public perceptions and expectations of product performance to prevent disappointment. This endeavor is where insightful audience analysis and open disclosure pay off. "Chip products are extremely complex," comments High. "Although our chips are becoming better and better, we try to communicate to the buying public that there are limitations, so that people do not expect absolute perfection."

For example, if a chip's actual performance differs from the original specifications, Intel notes the differences on an "errata list" that is circulated to dealers and computer users through the World Wide Web and other sources. Not everyone wants to study the technical details, but Intel provides complete information so that those who are interested can find out what they need to know. "We didn't do this in the past," explains High, "but now we realize that making this information available takes away the

an insider's perspective

HOWARD HIGH
Strategic Communications
Manager, Intel Corporation
(Santa Clara, California)

potential for a negative reaction. We would rather err on the side of being open and truthful so people don't ask, 'Why didn't you tell us about this problem? Why did you keep this a secret?' "

When he has to communicate a bad-news message about a problem that may affect a large number of customers, High will take additional steps to publicize the issue. "We would probably involve a senior-level manager as the spokesperson or the quoted source in the news release and, if necessary, hold an audioconfer-ence call with reporters to explain the situation," he says. He also arranges for speedy replies to customers who write or e-mail the com-pany to express their concerns.

Intel's customer-focused communication policy was influenced by the 1994 media coverage of a technical problem with the original Pentium pro-cessor chip. After the chip was introduced, internal analysis showed that it had a floating-point error problem. Believing that the flaw would affect few customers, Intel fixed the problem but did not publicize it. Then a col-lege professor doing sophisticated mathematical calculations found and discussed the problem with colleagues via the Internet. Business re-porters who read the Internet messages called Intel and were told that the problem had been fixed and that newer versions of the chip would soon be available. Then a television reporter picked up the story, which sparked widespread media interest. Initially, Intel announced that it would selectively re-place the chips, based on the company's determination of how each customer was using his or her computer. However, a firestorm of customer protests convinced Intel to change its policy, and within 30 days, it had a global process for providing free replacement chips on request.

This experience gave Intel new insights into handling bad-news messages. "As a company, we learned how to change the way we manage this kind of communication," High observes. "Now we really understand the importance of looking at these issues from our customers' perspective."

"We would rather err on the side of being open and truthful so people don't ask, 'Why didn't you tell us about this problem?' "

■ See Slide 9.1.

■ A chapter overview appears in the *Instructor's Resource Manual.*

Your objectives are to convey the bad news and retain the reader's goodwill.

■ Planning the Bad-News Message

At some point in our lives we have all probably been both the senders and the recipients of bad news. And just as most people find it difficult to accept bad news, they also find it difficult to convey bad news. Therefore, like persuasive messages, bad-news messages require careful planning. According to Andrew Grove, a founder of Intel Corporation, "The worse the news, the more effort that should go into communicating it."

How you write your messages won't change the news you have to convey, but it may determine whether your reader accepts your decision as reasonable—or goes away mad. As noted in Chapter 6, every letter can be considered a persuasive letter. This idea is especially true for bad-news letters, where you must persuade the reader of the reasonableness of your decision. Note, for example, the persuasive tone of the bad-news message written by Gary Larson, creator of "The Far Side" comic strip, shown in Spotlight 22, "Whose Idea Was This?," on page 308.

Your purpose in writing a bad-news message is twofold: first, to say "no" or to convey bad news, and second, to retain the reader's goodwill. To accomplish these goals, you must communicate your message politely, clearly, and firmly. And you must show the reader that you've seriously considered the request but that as a matter of fairness and good business practice, you must deny the request.

Sometimes you can achieve your purpose better with a phone call or personal visit than with a written message. A phone call is often appropriate when the reader will not be personally disappointed in the outcome, and a personal visit is often called for when you are giving a subordinate negative news of considerable consequence. Frequently, though, a written message is most appropriate because it lets you control more carefully the wording, sequence, and pace of the ideas presented. In addition, it provides a permanent record of what was communicated. As shown in Communication Snapshot 9, most business respondents to one survey felt that Fridays are the best day for communicating bad news.

Interestingly, according to a research study reported in *Information Systems Research Journal,* delivering bad news by e-mail rather than in person or by phone helps ensure a more accurate and complete message.[1] The authors hypothesize that the reason is what has been called "the Mum Effect"—that is, because communicating bad news is difficult, the messenger often delays, distorts, or incompletely communicates the needed information. Because of the greater anonymity of e-mail, messengers may be more forthcoming when they can deliver an unpopular message via e-mail.

communication snapshot 9

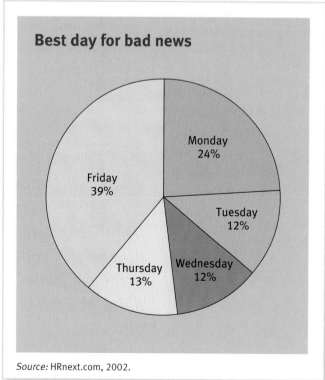

Best day for bad news

Monday 24%

Tuesday 12%

Wednesday 12%

Thursday 13%

Friday 39%

Source: HRnext.com, 2002.

Organizing to Suit Your Audience

The reader's needs, expectations, and personality—as well as the writer's relationship with the reader—will largely determine the content and organization of a bad-news message. Thus you need to put yourself in the place of the reader.

To decide whether to use the direct or the indirect plan for refusing a request, check the sender's original message. If the original message was written in the direct style, the sender may have considered it a routine request, and you would be safe in answering in the direct style. If the original message was written in the indirect style, the sender probably considered it a persuasive request, and you should consider answering in the indirect style. (However, messages written to one's superior are typically written in the direct style, regardless of whether the reader considers the original request routine or persuasive.)

For example, an e-mail message telling employees that the company cafeteria will be closed for one day to permit installation of new equipment can be written directly and in a paragraph or two. A message telling employees that the company cafeteria will be closed permanently and that employees will now have to go outside for lunch (and pay higher prices) would require more explanation and should probably be written in the indirect style.

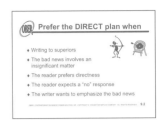

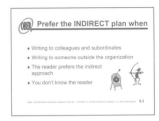

■ See Slides 9.2 and 9.3.

Direct Plan—Present the Bad News Immediately

As discussed in Chapter 7, many requests are routine; the writer simply wants a yes-or-no decision and wants to hear it in a direct manner. Similarly, if an announcement of bad news is not likely to generate an emotional response from the reader, you should use a direct approach. The direct plan for bad-news messages is basically the same plan used for routine messages discussed in Chapter 7: present the major idea (the bad news) up front. To help readers accept your decision when using the direct plan, present a brief rationale along with the bad news in the first paragraph.

NOT: The annual company picnic originally scheduled for August 3 at Riverside Park has been canceled.

BUT: Because ongoing construction at Riverside Park might present safety hazards to our employees and their families, the annual company picnic originally scheduled for August 3 has been canceled.

As usual, state the message in language as positive as possible, while still maintaining honesty.

NOT: Our departmental compliance report will be late next month. (*too blunt*)

NOT: I am pleased to announce that our departmental compliance report will be submitted on March 15. (*too positive*)

BUT: The extra time required to resolve the

Being forthright and upfront about bad news is generally the best tactic. Many observers feel that if Martha Stewart had simply admitted the details of her phone call with stockbroker Peter Bacanovic, the entire incident would never have made the headlines nor have had the serious repercussions it is now having on her company, Martha Stewart Living Omnimedia.

spotlight22
ON LAW AND ETHICS

Whose Idea Was This?

Gary Larson is a syndicated cartoonist whose "The Far Side" cartoon strip has been published in more than 17 languages and has appeared in 1,900 newspapers worldwide. When Larson found that his cartoons were being displayed and distributed (illegally) on numerous Web sites, he knew he had to do something. Not only were he and his publishers losing money from the unauthorized distribution of his artwork, but Larson had also lost control of where and how his creative work appeared.

Of course, Larson could have simply had his lawyers issue a "cease-and-desist" order to the Net offenders. Because he wanted a more personal touch, however, he set about composing a letter that sought to persuade his fans to stop distributing his work without permission. The letter that he ultimately sent was thus both a persuasive letter and a bad-news letter. Here is his letter in its entirety. Judge for yourself how effective it is:[2]

> To Whom It May Concern:
>
> I'm walking a fine line here. On the one hand, I confess to finding it quite flattering that some of my fans have created Web sites displaying and/or distributing my work on the Internet, and on the other, I'm struggling to find the words that convincingly but sensitively persuade these "Far Side" enthusiasts to "cease and desist" before they have to read these words from some lawyer.
>
> What impact this unauthorized use has had (and is having) in tangible terms is, naturally, of great concern to my publishers and therefore to me—but it's not the focus of this letter. My effort here is to try and speak to the intangible impact, the emotional cost to me personally, of seeing my work collected, digitized, and offered up in cyberspace beyond my control.
>
> Years ago, I was having lunch one day with the cartoonist Richard Guindon, and the subject came up of how neither one of us ever solicited or accepted ideas from others. But until Richard summed it up quite neatly, I never really understood my own aversion to doing this: "It's like having someone else write in your diary," he said. And how true that statement rang with me. In effect, we drew cartoons that we hoped would be entertaining or, at the very least, not boring; but regardless, they would always come from an intensely personal, and therefore original, perspective.
>
> To attempt to be "funny" is a very scary, risk-laden proposition. (Ask any stand-up comic who has ever

---

■ "Mr. Corleone is a man who insists on hearing bad news at once."
—Mario Puzo, *The Godfather*

Baton Rouge refinery problem means that our departmental compliance report will be submitted on March 15 rather than on March 1.

Then follow with any needed explanation and a friendly closing. The direct organizational plan should be used under the following circumstances:

Prefer the direct organizational plan for communicating bad news to your superior.

- The bad news involves a small, insignificant matter and can be considered routine. If the reader is not likely to be emotionally involved and thus not seriously disappointed by the decision, use the direct approach.

- The reader prefers directness. Superiors typically prefer that *all* messages from subordinates be written in the direct style.

- The reader expects a "no" response. For example, mid-career job applicants know that job offers at their level are typically made by phone and job rejections by letter. Thus, upon receiving a letter from the prospective employer, the applicant expects a "no" response; under these circumstances, delaying the inevitable only causes ill will and makes the writer look less than forthright.

THE FAR SIDE® BY GARY LARSON

© 1984 FarWorks, Inc. All Rights Reserved/Dist. by Creators Syndicate

The Far Side® by Gary Larson © 1984 FarWorks, Inc. All Rights Reserved. Used with permission.

"You know what I'm sayin'? ... Me, for example. I couldn't work in some stuffy little office. ... The outdoors just calls to me."

"bombed" on stage.) But if there was ever an axiom to follow in this business, it would be this: Be honest to yourself, and—most important—respect your audience. So, in a nutshell (probably an unfortunate choice of words for me), I ask only that this respect be returned, and the way for anyone to do that is to please, please refrain from putting "The Far Side" out on the Internet. These cartoons are my "children" of sorts, and like a parent I'm concerned about where they go at night without telling me. And seeing them at someone's website is like getting the call at 2 a.m. that goes, "Uh, Dad, you're not going to like this much, but guess where I am."

I hope my explanation helps you to understand the importance this has for me personally and why I'm making this request.

Please send my "kids" home. I'll be eternally grateful.

Most respectfully,
Gary Larson

Did the letter achieve its objective? Log on to the Internet and search for "The Far Side." How many private sites still display one of Larson's cartoons? (By the way, Larson's letter is reprinted here with the permission of Gary Larson and FarWorks, Inc.)

- The writer wants to emphasize the negative news. Suppose that you have already refused a request once and the reader writes a second time; under these circumstances, a forceful "no" might be in order. Or consider the situation where negative information is to be included in a form letter—perhaps as an insert in a monthly statement. Because the reader might otherwise discard or only skim an "unimportant-looking" message, you should consider placing the bad news up front—where it will be noticed.

A message organized according to a direct plan is not necessarily any shorter than one organized according to an indirect plan. Both types of message may contain the same basic information but simply in a different order. For example, assume that the program chairman of the Downtown Marketing Club has written to ask you to be the luncheon speaker at its March 8 meeting, but because of a prior commitment, you must decline. If you have a close relationship with the reader, you might choose the direct approach, as follows:

Except for the fact that I'll be in Mexico on March 8, I would have enjoyed speaking to the Downtown Marketing Club. As you know, Hansdorf Industries is opening an outlet in Nogales, and I'll be there March 7–14 interviewing marketing representatives and setting up sales territories.

Presenting bad news directly

♦ Present a brief rationale along with the bad news.

♦ Follow with needed explanation.

♦ End with a friendly, off-the-topic closing.

9.4

■ See Slide 9.4.

Direct messages are not necessarily shorter than indirect messages.

If, however, you find yourself in need of a speaker during the summer months, please keep me in mind. My travel schedule thus far is quite light during June, July, and August.

As a long-time member of the Downtown Marketing Club, I've enjoyed and benefited from the luncheon speakers the club sponsors each month. Best wishes, Roger, for a successful year as program chairperson. (*114 words*)

Now assume the same situation, except that you do not know the reader. This time, you might choose the indirect approach, as follows:

> *Complex situations typically call for an indirect organizational pattern and require more explanation than simpler situations.*

As a long-time member of the Downtown Marketing Club, I've enjoyed and benefited from the luncheon speakers the club sponsors each month. Monica Foote's December talk on the pitfalls of international marketing was especially interesting and helpful.

As you may have read in the newspaper, Hansdorf Industries is opening an outlet in Nogales, Mexico, and I'll be there March 7–14 interviewing marketing representatives and setting up sales territories. Thus, you will need to select another speaker for your March 8 meeting.

If you find yourself in need of a speaker during the summer months, Mr. Caine, please keep me in mind. My travel schedule thus far is quite light during June, July, and August. (*113 words*)

Direct messages are often shorter than indirect messages only because the direct plan is often used for *simpler* situations, which require little explanation and background information.

Indirect Plan—Buffer the Bad News

Because the preceding conditions are *not* true for many bad-news situations, you will often want to use an indirect plan—especially when giving bad news to

- Subordinates
- Customers
- Readers who prefer the indirect approach
- Readers you don't know[3]

With the indirect approach, you present the reasons first, then the negative news. This approach emphasizes the *reasons* for the bad news, rather than the bad news itself.

Suppose, for example, a subordinate expects a "yes" answer upon receiving your e-mail message. Putting the negative news in the first sentence might be too harsh and emphatic, and your decision might sound unreasonable until the reader has heard the rationale. In such a situation, you should begin with a neutral and relevant statement—one that helps establish or strengthen the reader–writer relationship. Such a statement serves as a **buffer** between the reader and the bad news that will follow.

A S K Ober

Dear Dr. Ober:

In my class, the e-mail-letter format causes confusion as students begin to use this form also in memos. I'm assuming your standard memo continues in the traditional format. Because of this evolution, when students hand in assignments, they must specify whether the correspondence is meant to be a memo or e-mail. What are your thoughts on this?

—Andrea D.

Dear Andrea:

In the past, most e-mails were interoffice communications—thus the default memo headings that you see on most e-mail programs. E-mails today can be formatted as either memos or letters, depending on their receiver and company preference. The paper memo format remains unchanged. Because it must be filed manually (as opposed to being stored electronically), it must continue to show all of the identifying heading information. The assignment situation itself would make clear to the instructor whether the needed response is a memo (for internal correspondence within the same organization) or a letter (for external correspondence). Today, many traditionally formatted memos and letters are sent as e-mail attachments. This provides the more formal formatting of traditional correspondence with the speed of electronic transmission.

—Scot

E-mail your questions and comments to askober@ober.net.

These are the characteristics of an effective opening buffer for bad-news messages:

1. It is *neutral.* To serve as a true buffer, the opening must not convey the negative news immediately. On the other hand, guard against implying that the request will be *granted,* thus building up the reader for a big letdown.

   NOT NEUTRAL: Stores like Parker Brothers benefit from our policy of not providing in-store demonstrators for our line of microwave ovens.

   MISLEADING: Your tenth-anniversary sale would be a great opportunity for us to promote our products.

2. It is *relevant.* The danger with starting *too* far from the topic is that the reader might not recognize that the letter is in response to his or her request. In addition, an irrelevant opening seems to avoid the issue, thus sounding insincere or self-serving. To show relevance and to personalize the opening, you might include some reference to the reader's letter in your first sentence. A relevant opening provides a smooth transition to the reasons that follow.

   IRRELEVANT: Our new apartment-sized microwave oven means that young couples, retirees, and students can enjoy the convenience of microwave cooking.

3. It is *supportive.* The purpose of the opening is to help establish compatibility between reader and writer. If the opening is controversial or seems to lecture the reader, it will not achieve its purpose.

   UNSUPPORTIVE: You must realize how expensive it would be to supply an in-house demonstrator for anniversary sales such as yours.

4. It is *interesting.* Although buffer openings are not substitutes for the strong attention-getters that are used in persuasive messages, they should nevertheless be interesting enough to motivate the recipient to continue reading. Therefore, avoid giving obvious information.

   OBVIOUS: We have received your letter requesting an in-store demonstrator for your upcoming tenth-anniversary sale.

5. Finally, it is *short.* Readers get impatient if they have to wait too long to get to the major point of the message.

A buffer lessens the impact of bad news.

■ See Slide 9.5.

A buffer should be neutral, relevant, supportive, interesting, and short.

Relevant buffers provide a smooth transition to the discussion of reasons.

DILBERT

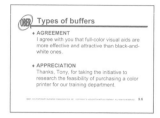

■ See Slides 9.6–9.9.

TOO LONG: As you may remember, for many years we provided in-store demonstrators for our line of microwave ovens. We were happy to do this because we felt that customers needed to see the spectacular results of our new browning element, which made microwaved food look as if it had just come from a regular oven. We discontinued this practice five years ago because . . .

Recall the earlier situation, introduced in Chapter 8, in which the owner of an appliance store wrote one of its suppliers, asking the supplier to provide an in-store demonstrator of the firm's products (even though it was against the company's policy to do so). In Chapter 8, we assumed the role of the appliance store owner and wrote a persuasive message. Now let's assume the role of the supplier, who, for good business reasons, must refuse the request. Because we're writing to a good customer, we decide to use an indirect plan. We might effectively start our message by using any of the following types of buffers:

Buffer Type	Example
Agreement	We both recognize the promotional possibilities that often accompany big anniversary sales such as yours.
Appreciation	Thanks for letting us know of your success in selling our microwaves. (*Avoid, however, thanking the reader for asking you to do something that you're going to refuse to do; such expressions of appreciation sound insincere.*)
Compliment	Congratulations on having served the community of Greenville for ten years.
Facts	Three-fourths of our distributors who held anniversary sales last year reported at least a 6 percent increase in annual sales of our home products.
General principle	We believe in furnishing our distributors a wide range of support in promoting our products.
Good news	Our upcoming 20 percent-off sale will be heavily advertised and will likely provide increased traffic for your February anniversary sale.
Understanding	I wish to assure you of our desire to help make your anniversary sale successful.

Ethical communicators use a buffer *not* in an attempt to manipulate or confuse the reader but in a sincere effort to help the reader accept the disappointing information in an objective manner.

Justifying Your Decision

Focus on the reasons for the refusal rather than on the refusal itself.

Presumably, you reached your negative decision by analyzing all the relevant information. Whether you began in a direct or an indirect manner, now explain your analysis to help convince the reader that your decision is reasonable. The major part of your message should thus focus on the reasons rather than on the bad news itself.

For routine bad-news messages (that is, those written in a direct approach), the reasons can probably be stated concisely and matter-of-factly. Indirectly written messages, however, require more careful planning—because the stakes are typically greater.

Provide a smooth transition from the opening buffer and present the reasons honestly and convincingly. If possible, explain how the reasons benefit the reader or, at least, benefit someone other than your organization. Thus:

- Refusing to exchange a worn garment might enable you to offer better-quality merchandise to your customers.

- Raising the price of your product might enable you to switch to nonpolluting energy for manufacturing it.

- Refusing to provide copies of company documents might protect the confidentiality of customer transactions.

Presenting reader benefits keeps your decision from sounding selfish. Sometimes, however, granting the request is simply not in the company's best interests. In such situations, don't "manufacture" reader benefits; instead, just provide whatever short explanation you can and let it go at that.

> Because this data would be of strategic importance to our competitors, we treat the information as confidential. Similar information about our entire industry (SIC Code 1473), however, is collected in the annual *U.S. Census of Manufacturing*. These census reports are available in most public and university libraries and online.

Show the reader that your decision was a *business* decision, not a personal one. Show that the request was taken seriously, and don't hide behind company policy. If the policy is a sound one, it was established for good reasons; therefore, explain the rationale for the policy.

NOT: Company policy prohibits our providing an in-store demonstrator for your tenth-anniversary sale.

BUT: A survey of our dealers three years ago indicated they felt the space taken up by in-store demonstrators and the resulting traffic problems were not worth the effort; they were also concerned about the legal liability of having someone cooking in their stores.

While executives are given wide leeway in promoting their companies and products, federal laws require that bad news regarding financial operations must be openly and fully disclosed. Scott Sullivan, the former chief financial officer at WorldCom, shown here following his booking on fraud charges, was once the highest paid chief financial officer in the United States.

Ten Reasons to Consult Your Lawyer

Because e-mail, memos, letters, and corporate communications may be used as evidence against you or your organization in a court of law, it is often wise to check with a lawyer to make sure that what you write doesn't violate state or federal law. You should consult legal counsel when a document that you have written:

1. Commits you to a legally binding contract.
2. Commits you to a warranty or guarantee of a product or service.
3. Makes an advertising claim.
4. Amends or modifies corporate policy.
5. Requests documents from an attorney.
6. Makes a statement to an insurance adjuster, the police, or a government agency.
7. Reports an accident involving a product, service, or employee.
8. Concerns the termination of an employee.
9. Concerns workers' compensation or insurance matters.
10. Concerns any product or process that will affect the environment.

The reasons justifying your decision should take up the major part of the message, but be concise or your readers may become impatient. Do not belabor a point and do not provide more background than is necessary. If you have several reasons for refusing a request, present the strongest ones first—where they will receive the most emphasis. If possible, avoid mentioning any weak reasons. If the reader feels he or she can effectively rebut even one of your arguments, you're simply raising false hopes and inviting needless correspondence. Finally, be aware of the ethical and legal aspects of your decisions and your justification of your decisions (see Spotlight 23, "Ten Reasons to Consult Your Lawyer," above).

Giving the Bad News

The reader should be able to infer the bad news before it is presented.

The bad news is communicated up front in directly written messages. Even in an indirectly written message, if you have done a convincing job of explaining the reasons, the bad news itself will come as no surprise; the decision will appear logical and reasonable—indeed the *only* logical and reasonable decision that could have been made under the circumstances.

To retain the reader's goodwill, state the bad news in positive or neutral language, stressing what you *are* able to do rather than what you are not able to do. Avoid, for example, such words and phrases as "cannot," "are not able to," "impossible," "unfortunately," "sorry," and "must refuse." To subordinate the bad news, put it in the middle of a paragraph, and include in the same sentence (or immediately afterward) additional discussion of reasons.

■ See Slide 9.10.

In response to these dealer concerns, we eliminated in-store demonstrations and now advertise exclusively in the print media. Doing so has enabled us to begin featuring a two-page spread in each major Sunday newspaper, including your local paper, the *Greenville Courier*.

When using the indirect plan, phrase the bad news in impersonal language, avoiding the use of *you* and *your*. The objective is to distance the reader from the bad news so that it will not be perceived as a personal rejection. So as not to point out the bad news that lies ahead, avoid using "but" and "however" to introduce it. The fact is, most readers won't remember what was written before the "but"—only what was written after it.

Resist any temptation to apologize for your decision. You may reasonably assume that if the reader were faced with the same options and had the same information available, he or she would act in a similar way. There is no reason to apologize for any reasonable business decision.

You do not need to apologize for making a rational business decision.

In some situations, the refusal can be implied, making a direct statement of refusal unnecessary. But don't be evasive. If you think a positive, subordinated refusal might be misunderstood, go ahead and state it directly. However, even under these circumstances, you should use impersonal language and include reader benefits.

Closing on a Pleasant Note

Any refusal, even when handled skillfully, has negative overtones. Therefore, you need to end your message on a more pleasant note. Avoid statements such as those listed here.

Problem to Avoid	Example of Problem
Apologizing	Again, I am sorry that we were unable to grant this request.
Anticipating problems	If you run into any other problems, please write me directly.
Inviting needless communication	If you have any further questions, please let me know.
Referring again to bad news	Although we are unable to supply an in-store demonstrator, we do wish you much success in your tenth-anniversary sale.
Repeating a cliché	If we can be of any further help, please don't hesitate to call on us.
Revealing doubt	I trust that you now understand why we made this decision.
Sounding selfish	Don't forget to feature Golden microwaves prominently in your anniversary display.

■ See Slides 9.11 and 9.12.

Make your closing original, friendly, and positive by using any of the following techniques. Avoid referring again to the bad news.

Do not refer to the bad news in the closing.

Technique	Example
Best wishes	Best wishes for success with your tenth-anniversary sale. We have certainly enjoyed our ten-year relationship with Parker Brothers and look forward to continuing to serve your needs in the future.

Counterproposal	To provide increased publicity for your tenth-anniversary sale, we would be happy to include a special 2-by-6-inch boxed notice of your sale in the *Greenville Courier* edition of our ad on Sunday, February 8. Just send us your camera-ready copy by January 26.
Other sources of help	A dealer in South Carolina switched from using in-store demonstrators to showing a video continuously during his microwave sale. He used the ten-minute film *Twenty-Minute Dinners with Pizzazz* (available for $45 from the Microwave Research Institute, P.O. Box 800, Chicago, IL 60625) and reported a favorable reaction from customers.
Resale or subtle sales promotion	You can be sure that the new Golden Mini-Micro we're introducing in January will draw many customers to your store during your anniversary sale.

> *Close the letter on a positive, friendly, helpful note.*

■ See Handout 9.1.

CO1. **Compose a message that rejects an idea.**

To sound sincere and helpful, make your ending original. If you provide a counterproposal or offer other sources of help, provide all information the reader needs to follow through. If you include sales promotion, make it subtle and reader-oriented.

In short, the last idea the reader hears from you should be positive, friendly, and helpful. Checklist 11 on page 317 summarizes guidelines for writing bad-news letters. The remainder of this chapter discusses strategies for writing bad-news replies and bad-news announcements.

■ Bad-News Replies

Despite the skill with which a persuasive message is written, circumstances of which the reader is unaware may require a negative response. Your organization's well-being (and your own) may depend on the skill with which you are able to refuse a request and still maintain the goodwill of the reader.

Rejecting an Idea

One of the more challenging bad-news messages to write is one that rejects someone's idea or proposal. Put yourself in the role of the person making the suggestion. He or she has probably spent a considerable amount of time in developing the idea, studying its feasibility, perhaps doing some research, and, of course, writing the original persuasive message.

Consider, for example, the persuasive memo presented in Model 7 on page 276, in which Jenson Peterson tries to persuade Elliott Lamborn to restrict the nearest parking lots to Ford vehicles. Peterson obviously thinks his idea has merit. He went to the trouble of having his staff count the number of non-Ford vehicles in the lots, getting a cost estimate for making the change, and contacting the union representative to get the union's position. Finally, he organized all of his information into an effectively written memo.

✓checklist 11

Bad-News Messages

Determine How to Start the Message

✓ **Direct Plan**—Use a direct organizational plan when the bad news is insignificant, the reader prefers directness (such as your superior) or expects a "no" response, or the writer wants to emphasize the bad news. Present the bad news (see "Give the Bad News" at right), along with a brief rationale, in the first paragraph.

✓ **Indirect Plan**—Use an indirect organizational plan when writing to subordinates, customers, readers who prefer the indirect plan, or readers you don't know. Start by buffering the bad news, following these guidelines:

- Remember the purpose: to establish a common ground with the reader.

- Select an opening statement that is neutral, relevant, supportive, interesting, and short.

- Consider establishing a point of agreement, expressing appreciation, giving a sincere compliment, presenting a fact or general principle, giving good news, or showing understanding.

- Provide a smooth transition from the buffer to the reasons that follow.

Justify Your Decision

✓ If possible, stress reasons that benefit someone other than yourself.

✓ State reasons in positive language.

✓ Avoid relying on "company policy"; instead, explain the reason behind the policy.

✓ State reasons concisely to avoid reader impatience. Do not overexplain.

✓ Present the strongest reasons first; avoid discussing weak reasons.

Give the Bad News

✓ If using the indirect plan, subordinate the bad news by putting it in the middle of a paragraph and including additional discussion of reasons.

✓ Present the bad news as a logical outcome of the reasons given.

✓ State the bad news in positive and impersonal language. Avoid terms such as *cannot* and *your*.

✓ Do not apologize.

✓ Make the refusal definite—by implication if appropriate; otherwise, by stating it directly.

Close on a Positive Note

✓ Make your closing original, friendly, off the topic of the bad news, and positive.

✓ Consider expressing best wishes, offering a counterproposal, suggesting other sources of help, or building in resale or subtle sales promotion.

✓ Avoid anticipating problems, apologizing, inviting needless communication, referring to the bad news, repeating a cliché, revealing doubt, or sounding selfish.

Having invested that much time and energy in the proposal, Peterson probably feels quite strongly that his proposal is valid, and he likely expects Lamborn to approve it. If—or in this case *when*—his proposal is rejected, Peterson will be surprised and disappointed.

Because Lamborn is Peterson's superior, he could send Peterson a directly written memo saying in effect, "I have considered your proposal and must reject it." But Peterson is obviously intelligent and enterprising, and Lamborn does not want to discourage future initiatives on his part. As with all such bad-news replies, then, Lamborn's twin objectives are to refuse the proposal and retain Peterson's goodwill.

To be successful, Lamborn has an educating job to do. He must give Peterson the reasons for the rejection, reasons of which Peterson is probably unaware. He must also show that he recognizes Peterson's proposal as carefully considered and that the rejection is based on business—not personal—considerations.

Given the amount of effort Peterson has put into this project, Lamborn's response will be most effective if written in the indirect pattern. This pattern will let Lamborn move his subordinate gradually into agreeing that the proposal is not in the best interests of the firm.

Lamborn's memo rejecting Peterson's proposal is shown in Model 11 on page 319. Although we label this memo a bad-news message, actually it is also a *persuasive* message. Like all bad-news messages, the memo seeks to persuade the reader that the writer's position is reasonable.

Refusing a Favor

CO2. Compose a message that refuses a favor.

Many favors are asked and granted almost automatically. Doing routine favors for others in the organization shows a cooperative spirit, and a spirit of reciprocity often prevails—we recognize that the person asking us for a favor today may be the person from whom we'll need a favor next week. Sometimes, however, for business or personal reasons, we are not able to accommodate the other person and must decline an invitation or a request for a favor.

The type of message written to refuse a favor depends on the particular circumstances. Occasionally, someone asks a "big" favor—perhaps one involving a major investment of time or resources. In that case, the person has probably written a thoughtful, reasoned message trying to persuade you to do as he or she asks. If you must refuse such a significant request, you should probably present your refusal indirectly, following the guidelines given earlier.

When refusing routine requests, give the refusal in the first paragraph.

Most requests for favors, however, are routine, and a routine request should receive a routine response—that is, a response written in the direct organizational plan. A colleague asking you to attend a meeting in her place, a superior asking you to serve on a committee, or a business associate inviting you to lunch is not going to be deeply disappointed if you decline. The writer probably has not spent a great deal of energy composing the request; the main thing he or she wants to know from you is "yes" or "no."

In such situations, give your refusal in the first paragraph, but avoid curtness and coldness. Courtesy demands that you buffer the bad news somewhat and that you at least give a quick, reasonable rationale for declining. Although the refusal itself might not lose the reader's goodwill, a poorly written refusal message might! The e-mail message in Model 12 on page 320 declines a request to serve on a corporate committee and is written using a direct plan.

Assume for a moment, however, that Peter Carmichael had decided, instead, that his best strategy would be to write the message (Model 12) in the indirect pattern, explaining his rationale before refusing. His opening buffer might then have been as follows:

> Like you, I believe our new Executive-in-Residence program will prove to be effective for both Utah State and the executives who participate.

Refusing a Claim

CO3. Compose a message that refuses a claim.

The indirect plan is almost always used when refusing an adjustment request because the reader (a dissatisfied customer) is emotionally involved in the situation. The customer is already upset by the failure of the product to live up to expectations. If you refuse the claim immediately, you risk losing the customer's goodwill. And, as

NEWTON
Electrical
Systems

1034 York Road
Baltimore, MD 21204
Phone: 301.555.1086
Fax: 301.555.3926
www.nes.com

+ — + — + — + — + — + — + — + — + — + — + — + — + — + — + — + —
Serving the automotive industry for more than 50 years

MEMO TO: Jenson J. Peterson, Marketing Supervisor

FROM: Elliott Lamborn, Vice President *EL*

DATE: April 15, 20—

SUBJECT: Employee Parking Lot Proposal

Your April 3 memo certainly enlightened me about the automobile habits of our employees. I had no idea that our workers drive such a variety of models.

The increasing popularity of foreign-made vehicles recently led management to conclude that we should consider taking advantage of this expanding market. President Wrede has appointed a task force to determine how we might also promote our electrical systems to Asian automakers, as well as to Ford.

Our successful push into the international automotive market will mean that many of the foreign-made vehicles our employees drive will, in fact, be supplied with Newton Electrical Systems components. Thus, our firm will benefit from the continuing presence of these cars in all our lots.

1   Your memo got me to thinking, Jenson, that we might be missing an opportunity to promote our products to headquarters visitors. Would you please develop some type of awareness campaign (such as a bumper sticker for employee cars that contain a Newton electrical system) that shows our employees support the products we sell. I would appreciate having a memo from you with your ideas by May 3
2   so that I might include this project in next year's marketing campaign.

amp

**BAD-NEWS REPLY—
REJECTING AN IDEA**

This memo responds to the persuasive request in Model 7 (see page 276).

Uses a neutrally worded subject line.

Starts with a supportive buffer; the second sentence provides a smooth transition to the reason.

Begins discussing the reason.

Presents the refusal in the last sentence of the paragraph, using positive and impersonal language.

Closes on a forward-looking, off-the-topic note.

Grammar and Mechanics Notes

1 *thinking, Jenson, that:* Set off nouns of direct address (*Jenson*) with commas.

2 *year's:* Use apostrophe plus *s* to form the possessive of a singular noun (*year*).

model12

**BAD-NEWS REPLY—
REFUSING A FAVOR**   1

**Gives a quick reason,
immediately followed by
the refusal.**

Provides additional details.

Closes on a helpful note.   2

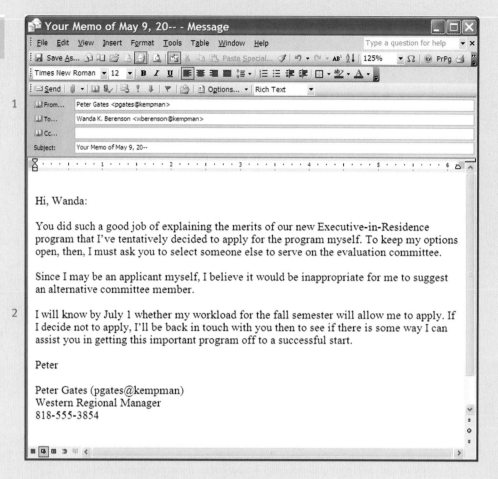

Hi, Wanda:

You did such a good job of explaining the merits of our new Executive-in-Residence program that I've tentatively decided to apply for the program myself. To keep my options open, then, I must ask you to select someone else to serve on the evaluation committee.

Since I may be an applicant myself, I believe it would be inappropriate for me to suggest an alternative committee member.

I will know by July 1 whether my workload for the fall semester will allow me to apply. If I decide not to apply, I'll be back in touch with you then to see if there is some way I can assist you in getting this important program off to a successful start.

Peter

Peter Gates (pgates@kempman)
Western Regional Manager
818-555-3854

Grammar and Mechanics Notes

1 Most e-mail programs will automatically insert the From: line in the header.

2 *July 1 whether:* Do not use a comma after an incomplete date.

noted previously, every dissatisfied customer tells nine or ten people about the bad experience and they, in turn, each tell four or five others. Clearly, you want to avoid the ripple effect of such situations.

The tone of your refusal must convey respect and consideration for the customer—even when the customer is at fault. To separate the reader from the refusal, begin with a buffer, using one of the techniques presented earlier (for example, showing understanding).

Use impersonal, neutral language to explain the basis for the refusal.

> Frequent travelers like you depend on luggage that "can take it"—luggage that will hold up for many years under normal use.

When explaining the reasons for denying the claim, do not accuse or lecture the reader. At the same time, however, don't appear to accept responsibility for the problem if the customer is at fault. In impersonal, neutral language, explain why the claim is being denied.

■ See Handout 9.2.

NOT: The reason the handles ripped off your Sebastian luggage is that you overloaded it. The tag on the luggage clearly states that you should use the luggage only for clothing, with a maximum of 40 pounds. However, our engineers concluded that you had put at least 65 pounds of items in the luggage.

BUT: On receiving your piece of Sebastian luggage, we sent it to our testing department. The engineers there found stretch marks on the leather and a frayed nylon stitching cord. They concluded that such wear could have been caused only by contents weighing substantially more than the 40-pound maximum weight that is stated on the luggage tag. Such use is beyond the "normal wear and tear" covered in our warranty.

Note that in the second example, the pronoun *you* is not used at all when discussing the bad news. By using third-person pronouns and the passive voice, the example avoids directly accusing the reader of misusing the product. The actual refusal, given in the last sentence, is conveyed in neutral language.

As with other bad-news messages, close on a friendly, forward-looking note. If you can offer a compromise, it will take the sting out of the rejection and show the customer that you are reasonable. It will also help the customer save face. Be careful, however, that your offer does not imply any assumption of responsibility on your part. The compromise can either come before or be a part of the closing.

An offer of a compromise, however small, helps retain the reader's goodwill.

> Although we replace luggage only when it is damaged in normal use, our repair shop tells me the damaged handle can easily be replaced. We would be happy to do so for $39.50, including return shipping. If you will simply initial this letter and return it to us in the enclosed, addressed envelope, we will return your repaired luggage within four weeks.

Somewhere in your letter you might also include a subtle pitch for resale. The customer has had a negative experience with your product. If you want your reader to continue to be a customer, you might restate some of the benefits that led him or her to buy the product in the first place. But use this technique carefully; a strong pitch may simply annoy an already unhappy customer.

Consider the persuasive request written by Oliver Arbin presented in Model 9 on page 281. Mr. Arbin, as you may remember, was upset that his family's flight to Indianapolis was canceled and that they were thus forced to make a six-hour drive instead. He wanted a refund of the $680 cost of his five nonrefundable tickets. It appears, on further investigation, that Mr. Arbin was not completely forthright.

figure 9.1
An Ineffective Bad-News Message

Uses a direct, negative subject line.

Begins by apologizing, giving the bad news first (where it is emphasized), and using personal language.

Uses an accusatory tone; hides behind company policy without explaining the reason for the policy.

Repeats the apology (thereby emphasizing the negative aspects), sounds insincere in its sales promotion, and ends with a cliché.

June 27, 20—

Mr. Oliver J. Arbin
518 Thompson Street
Saginaw, MI 48607

Dear Mr. Arbin

Subject: Denial of Your Claim of June 18, 20—

Although we were certainly sorry to learn of your troubles with Northern Airlines, I'm afraid that we won't be able to refund your money. Let me explain why.

Flight 126 was scheduled to depart at 8 p.m. and was canceled at 7:10 p.m. because of inclement weather. If you and your family had remained in the boarding area as requested, you would have been rebooked on Flight 3321, which arrived in Indianapolis just 75 minutes later than your scheduled flight. Company policy forbids our refunding money when a flight is canceled because of inclement weather.

Although I'm sorry we could not help you this time, Mr. Arbin, I hope you will call upon us in the future when your travel plans take you to one of the 200 cities Northern Airlines is proud to serve. Please let me know if you have any questions about this matter.

Sincerely

Madelyn Masarani

Madelyn Masarani
Service Representative

eta

How might the company respond to Mr. Arbin under these circumstances? Figure 9.1 above illustrates how *not* to write an effective bad-news message. Model 13 on the next page, a revised version of the ineffective example, illustrates the guidelines discussed earlier for writing an effective bad-news message.

■ Bad-News Announcements

CO4. Compose an announcement that conveys bad news.

The previous section discussed strategies for writing negative replies. Often, however, the bad news we have to present involves a new situation; that is, it is not in response to another message. And quite often, these messages go to a large audience,

NORTHERN
A I R L I N E S

June 27, 20—

Mr. Oliver J. Arbin
518 Thompson Street
Saginaw, MI 48607

1   Dear Mr. Arbin

Subject: Further Information About Flight 126

We make no money when our customers are forced to take long trips by car rather than by flying Northern Airlines; and when that happens, we want to find out why.

A review of the June 2 log of the aborted Flight 126 shows that it was scheduled to depart at 8 p.m. and was canceled at 7:10 p.m. because of inclement weather. Pas-
2   sengers were asked to remain in the boarding area; those who did were rebooked on Flight 3321, which departed at 9:15 p.m. Flight 3321 arrived in Indianapolis at 10:40 p.m., just 75 minutes later than the scheduled arrival of Flight 126. Given these circumstances, the ticket agent was correct in disallowing any refund on nonrefundable tickets.

Because you indicated that you're a frequent traveler on Northern, I've asked our scheduling department to add you to the mailing list to receive a complimentary subscription to our quarterly Saginaw flight schedule. A copy of the current schedule is enclosed. From now on, you'll be sure to know exactly when every Northern flight arrives at and departs from Tri-Cities Airport.

Sincerely

Madelyn Masarani

Madelyn Masarani
Service Representative

eta
3   Enclosure

P.O. BOX 6001, DENVER, CO 80240 • (303) 555-3990 • FAX (303) 555-3992

model 13

BAD-NEWS REPLY— REFUSING A CLAIM

This letter responds to the persuasive claim in Model 9 on page 280.

Opens on an agreeable and relevant note.

Begins the explanation; presents the refusal in impersonal language.

Closes on a helpful note; assumes that the reader will continue to fly on Northern Airlines.

Grammar and Mechanics Notes

1 Insert no punctuation after the salutation and complimentary closing when using open punctuation.

2 *boarding area;:* Use a semicolon to separate two closely related independent clauses not connected by a conjunction.

3 Use an enclosure notation to alert the recipient to look for some inserted material.

Bad-news announcements are not in response to any request.

as, for example, when you're announcing a major price increase or new rules and regulations. Such announcements may be either internal (addressed to employees) or external (addressed to customers, news media, stockholders, and the like).

As with other bad-news messages, you must decide whether to use the direct or the indirect plan of organization. Be guided by the effect the bad news will have on the recipients and on your relationship with them.

Bad News About Normal Operations

Assume that management has decided a price increase of 10 percent is justified on the Danforth cabin tent you manufacture. This price increase requires that you notify your order department, your wholesalers, and finally, a special retail customer.

To notify the order department of the price change (a routine matter), you would probably send a memo or e-mail message like this one, written in the direct pattern:

> Effective March 1, the regular price of our Danforth cabin tent (Item R-885) changes from $149.99 to $164.99, an increase of 10 percent. Any order postmarked before March 1 should be billed at the lower price, regardless of when the order is actually shipped.
>
> The new price will be shown in our spring catalog, and a notice is being sent immediately to all wholesalers. If you receive orders postmarked after March 1 but showing the old price, please notify the wholesaler before filling the order.

If the reader will not be disappointed, present the bad news directly.

The preceding message reflects the fact that the price increase will have minor negative consequences to the order department. Therefore, the news is given directly—in the first sentence—followed by the details. Because the person receiving this memorandum will not be personally disappointed in the news, you don't need to explain the price increase.

However, you also need to notify your wholesalers of this price increase. How will they react? They probably will not be personally disappointed because price increases are common in business and come as no surprise; thus a direct message is called for. But wholesalers *do* have a choice about where to buy tents for resale, so you need to justify your price increase.

A reason may be presented first—even in a message written in a direct pattern.

> Because of the prolonged strike in South African mines, we now must purchase the chrome used in our Danforth cabin tent elsewhere at a higher cost. Thus, effective March 1, the regular price of the Danforth tent (Item R-885) will change from $149.99 to $164.99.
>
> As a courtesy to our wholesalers, however, we are billing any orders postmarked prior to March 1 at the old price of $149.99. Use the enclosed form or call our toll-free number (800-555-9843) to place your order for what *American Camper* calls the "sock-it-to-me" tent.

Note how the bad news is cushioned by (1) presenting the reason first—a reason that is clearly beyond your control; (2) selling at the old price until March 1; and (3) including resale in the closing paragraph.

Finally, you need to write a third message about the price increase. For the past two years, you have had an exclusive marketing agreement with the Association for Backpackers and Campers. It promotes the Danforth cabin tent in each issue of *Field News*, its quarterly magazine, at no cost to you in exchange for your offering ABC members the wholesale price of $149.99 (instead of the retail price, which is about 35 percent higher).

ABC selected the Danforth tent because of its quality *and* because of this attractive price arrangement, and you want to make sure that your price increase does not endanger this relationship. Thus, you write an indirect-pattern letter, in which your major emphasis is on the reasons, not the results.

> The popularity of the Danforth cabin tent that you feature in each issue of *Field News* is based partly on our exclusive use of a chrome frame. Chrome is twice as strong as aluminum, yet weighs about the same.
>
> Because of the prolonged strike in South African mines, we were faced with the choice of either switching to aluminum or securing the needed chrome elsewhere at a higher cost. We elected to continue using chrome in our tent. This decision to maintain quality has resulted in a change in the wholesale price of the Danforth cabin tent (Item R-885) from $149.99 to $164.99.
>
> The Danforth tent promotion in the spring issue of *Field News* should be changed to reflect this new price. Since the spring issue usually arrives the last week of February, we will bill any orders postmarked before March 1 at the lower price of $149.99.
>
> We have enjoyed the opportunity to serve ABC members and extend best wishes to your organization for another successful year of providing such valuable service to American backpackers and campers.

Another situation that calls for indirect organization is one in which a change in organizational policy will adversely affect employees. It is just as important, of course, to retain the goodwill of employees as it is to retain that of customers. Acceptance of a new policy depends not only on the reasons for the policy but also on the skill with which the reasons are communicated. An example of such a situation is shown in Model 14 on page 326.

If the reader must be persuaded of the reasonableness of your decision, use the indirect approach.

When dealing with issues that are of such personal interest to the reader, don't hurry your discussion. Take as much space as necessary to show the reader that your decision was not made in haste, that you considered all options, and that the reader's interests were taken into account.

Explain thoroughly the basis for your decision.

Note, especially, the use of personal and impersonal language throughout the memo in Model 14. When discussing insurance programs that will be retained (third paragraph), *you* and *your* are used extensively. When discussing the program that will be dropped (fourth paragraph), impersonal language is used instead. The purpose is to closely associate the readers with the good news and to separate them from the bad news. Such deliberate use of language does not manipulate the reader; it simply uses good human relations to bring the reader to an understanding and appreciation of the writer's position.

Bad News About the Organization

If your organization is experiencing serious problems, your employees, customers, and stockholders should hear the news from you—not from newspaper accounts or through the grapevine. For extremely serious problems that receive widespread attention (for example, product recalls, unexpected operating deficits, or legal problems), the company's public relations department will probably issue a news release.

Often, some type of correspondence is also necessary. For example, owners of recalled products must be notified, customers must be notified if an impending strike will affect delivery dates, and employees must be notified if they will be affected by plant closings or layoffs. To show that these situations are receiving attention from top management, such messages should generally come from a high-level official.

Show that the situation is receiving top-management attention.

model14

GENERAL BAD-NEWS ANNOUNCEMENT

Uses a neutral subject line.

Begins with a compliment.

Provides a smooth transition to the explanation; uses figures for believability.

Uses the overall welfare of all employees as the reader benefit; presents the good news before the bad.

Implies that fairness demands a change; subordinates the bad news in the middle of a long paragraph.

Closes by discussing a different, but related, topic.

TO: All Blockbuster Employees

FROM: Mary Louis Lytle, Vice President *MLL*

DATE: July 8, 20—

1 **RE:**   Change in Insurance Coverage

2 Thanks to you, President Adams will announce a 13 percent increase in sales for the year that ended June 30. Six of the seven divisions met or exceeded their sales quotas for the year. What an example of the Blockbuster spirit!

Our pleasure at the 13 percent increase in sales is somewhat tempered by a corresponding increase in expenditures. In studying the reasons for this increase, we found that fringe benefits, especially insurance, were the largest factor. Medical insurance costs increased 23 percent last year and have risen 58 percent in the past three years.

To continue providing needed coverage for our employees and their families and still hold down costs, we've analyzed the use and cost of each benefit. Last year 89 percent of you used your health insurance. Clearly, this benefit is important to you and, therefore, to us. Similarly, although only 6 percent used your major medical insurance last year, protecting our employees from devastating health-care costs remains a top priority for us.

On the other hand, only 9 percent of you used dental coverage last year; yet dental insurance represented 19 percent of our total insurance costs. We believe the funds now being used for dental care for a small minority of our employees can better be used to pay the escalating costs of medical coverage for all of our employees. Thus, effective January 1, all company-paid insurance programs will include only health and major-medical coverage. All requests for reimbursement for dental bills submitted on or before December 31 will be paid at the normal rates.

3 The Benefits Office will hold an open forum on July 28 from 2 to 3 p.m. in the auditorium to solicit your views on all areas of employee benefits. Please come prepared with questions and comments. Your input will enable us to continue to provide our family of employees the kind of protection and options they deserve.

ama

Grammar and Mechanics Notes

1 You may use *RE:* instead of *SUBJECT:* in the memo heading.

2 *President Adams:* Capitalize a title that is used before a name.

3 *3 p.m.:* Use figures to express time; type the abbreviation *p.m.* in lowercase letters, with no space after the internal period.

If the situation about which you are writing has news value, assume that your communication may find its way to a reporter's desk. Thus, make sure not only that the overall tone of the letter is appropriate but also that individual sentences of the letter cannot be misinterpreted if they are lifted out of context.

Throughout your message, choose each word with care. In general, avoid using words with negative connotations and emphasize those with positive connotations. Effective communication techniques can help you control the emphasis, subordination, and tone of your *own* message; however, you cannot do so for a news item that quotes individual parts of your message. For example, note the following misinterpretation, in a published news item, of a sentence from a company president's letter.

Write in such a way as not to be misinterpreted.

President's actual statement:	Unlike several other firms in the area, we have always had a strict policy of not allowing any digging in residential areas. In fact, all our excavation sites are at least 2 miles from any paved road and are well marked by 10-foot signs. Because these sites are so isolated, our company does not require fences around these sites.
News item:	Although other drilling companies in the area erect 8-foot fences around their excavation sites, Owens-Ohio President Robert Leach admitted in a letter to stockholders yesterday that "our company does not require fences around these sites."

The last sentence of the president's statement would have been more effective had it been worded in positive, impersonal language.

Fences are unnecessary in such isolated sites and, in fact, can cause safety hazards of their own. For example, . . .

If the reader has already learned about the situation from other sources, your best strategy is to use a direct organizational pattern. In a spirit of helpfulness and forthrightness, confirm the bad news quickly and begin immediately to provide the necessary information to help the reader understand the situation. For example,

■ For an additional 3Ps model for a bad-news letter, see the Supplementary Teaching Materials section in the *Instructor's Resource Manual*.

As you entered the building this morning, you may have seen the evidence of a burglary last night. The purpose of this memo is to let you know exactly what happened and to outline steps we are taking to ensure the continued safety of our employees who work during evening hours.

If the reader is hearing the news for the first time, your best strategy is to use the indirect pattern, using a buffer opening and stressing the most positive aspects of the situation (in this case, the steps you're taking to prevent a recurrence of the problem).

Employees in our data-entry and maintenance departments who work at night perform a valuable service for Martin Company, and their safety and well-being are of prime concern to us. In that spirit, I would like to discuss with you several steps we are taking as a result of . . .

Model 15 on page 328 shows a letter written to alert customers to the possibility of a demonstration outside the site of a meeting announcing a new product. By showing a respectful attitude toward the demonstrators and by avoiding emotional language, the writer is able to convey the bad news with a minimum of fuss. And the fact that each customer received a personally typed letter from the president is in itself reassuring.

model 15

BAD-NEWS ANNOUNCEMENT— PERSONAL LETTER

A personal letter from the president draws the needed attention.

Uses sales promotion for the opening buffer.

Presents the company in a favorable light by using a reasoned and evenhanded approach.

Treats the news of the expected demonstrations (the bad news) objectively and unemotionally.

Closes with additional sales promotion and reader benefits.

PACIFIC LABORATORIES   *A LIFE-LABS COMPANY*

1   November 8, 20—

Ms. Michele Loftis
Planning Department
Crosslanes Pharmacies
1842 Le Pure Boulevard
El Toro, CA 92630

Dear Ms. Loftis:

The breakthrough in over-the-counter birth control that Pacific Laboratories will announce at 3 p.m. on December 5 at the Park Inn will present a very substantial marketing opportunity for Crosslanes Pharmacies. I'm pleased you can be with us for the announcement.

2   Like many scientific breakthroughs, our new product is generating quite a bit of media interest. Already, 12 newspapers and television stations have requested permission to cover this announcement. We welcome such coverage and believe that an open discussion will lead to more informed decisions by consumers.

3   In the same spirit, we have taken no steps to prevent any demonstrations outside the Park Inn on that day. It is likely that some pro-life and anti-abortion groups will march and distribute leaflets. So long as they do so peacefully, they are perfectly within their rights. We also are within our rights to hold a meeting without disruption, and there will be adequate security personnel on hand to ensure that everything runs smoothly. We do ask that you bring your original invitation (or this letter) to identify yourself.

We look forward to showing off the efforts of five years of research by our staff. The safety, convenience, and price of this product will make it a very popular item on your pharmacy shelves.

Sincerely,

Stephen Lynch

Stephen Lynch, President

924 Ninth Street, Santa Monica, CA 90403 • (415)555-2389

Grammar and Mechanics Notes

1 Begin the date and closing lines at the center point when using a modified block style of letter.

2 *coverage and:* Do not insert a comma before the conjunction (*and*) because what follows is not an independent clause.

3 *runs smoothly:* Use an adverb (*smoothly*) instead of an adjective (*smooth*) to modify a verb.

A BAD-NEWS MESSAGE

You are a facilities manager at General Mills. Your firm recently constructed a new administrative building on a 5-acre lot, and you've landscaped the unused 4 acres with lighted walkways, fountains, and ponds for employees to enjoy during their lunch hours and before and after work. Your lovely campus-like site is one of the few such locations within the city limits.

Joan Bradley, the mayor of your city, is running for reelection. She has written to you asking permission to hold a campaign fundraiser on your grounds on July 7 from 8 p.m. until midnight. This event will be for "heavy" contributors; as many as 150 people, each paying $500, are expected. Her reelection committee will take care of all catering, security, and cleanup.

You do not want to become involved in this event for numerous reasons. Write to the mayor (The Honorable Joan Bradley, Mayor of Clarkfield, Clarkfield, MN 56223) and decline her request.

1. Describe your primary audience.

   - Very important person (don't want to offend her)
   - Holds political views different from my own
   - Possibility of her losing the election (don't want to appear to be backing a loser)

2. Describe your secondary audience.

   - The 150 big contributors (What will be their reaction to my refusal?)
   - The other candidates (do not wish to offend anyone who might become the next mayor)

3. Brainstorm: List as many reasons as you can think of why you might refuse her request. Then, after you've come up with several, determine which one will be most effective. Underline that reason.

   - Other sites in the city offering a more suitable environment for the event
   - Would have to provide the same favor for every other candidate
   - Possible harm to lawn, plants, and animals
   - Company policy that prohibits outside use

4. Write your buffer opening—neutral, relevant, supportive, interesting, and short.

   Thank you for your kind comments about our lovely grounds. Our staff has been able to create an environment in which plants and animals not normally found in the Midwest are able to thrive.

5. Now skip to the actual refusal itself. Write the statement in which you refuse the request—making it positive, subordinated, and unselfish.

   To protect this delicate environment, we restrict the use of these grounds to company employees.

6. Write the closing for your letter—original, friendly, off the topic of the refusal, and positive. *Suggestions:* best wishes, counterproposal, other sources of help, or subtle resale.

   As an alternative, may I suggest the beautiful grounds at the Minnesota Educational Consortium on Lapeer Street. They were designed with a Minnesota motif by Larry Miller, the designer for our grounds.

General Mills
General Offices

Post Office Box 1113
Minneapolis, Minnesota 55440

May 20, 20—

The Honorable Joan Bradley
Mayor of Clarkfield
Clarkfield, MN 56223

Dear Mayor Bradley:

Thank you for your kind comments about our lovely grounds. Our staff has been able to create an environment here in which plants and animals not normally found in the Midwest are able to thrive.

For example, after much effort, we have finally been able to attract a family of Eastern Bluebirds to our site. At this very moment, the female is sitting on three eggs, and members of our staff unobtrusively check on her progress each day.

Similar efforts have resulted in the successful introduction of beautiful but sensitive flowers, shrubs, and marsh grasses. To protect this delicate environment, we restrict the use of these grounds to company employees, many of whom have contributed ideas, plants, and time in developing the grounds.

As an alternative, may I suggest the beautiful grounds at the Minnesota Educational Consortium on Lapeer Street. They were designed with a Minnesota motif by Larry Miller, who designed our grounds. Various public events have been held there without damage to the environment. Susan Siebold, their executive director (555-9832), is the person to contact about using MEC's facilities.

Sincerely,

J. W. Hudson

J. W. Hudson
Facilities Manager

tma

General Offices at Number One General Mills Boulevard

Being a part of the management team sometimes requires that you support decisions with which you personally disagree.

This letter also illustrates another common aspect of bad-news messages: occasionally, you may have to defend positions with which you personally disagree. Your disagreement may be strategic (it's not a smart move at this time) or philosophical (we shouldn't be selling and promoting this product). The issue, of course, goes much deeper than communicating. If you and your organization's philosophies consistently do not mesh, you might be happier finding employment in a more compatible environment. If you decide to stay, however, you should have no qualms about defending any legal and ethical position the organization decides to take.

 Visit the **BusCom Online Learning Center** (at http://college.hmco.com) for additional resources to help you with this course and with your future career.

■ Summary

■ A parallel BusCom Online Teaching Center is available for instructors using this text. Here you will find a monthly newsletter with additional teaching tips and hot-off-the-press current event items, lecture and supplemental discussion notes, additional application exercises and cases, PowerPoint slides, and a forum for idea exchange. Call your Houghton Mifflin representative for the free password to this important resource.

CO1. Compose a message that rejects an idea.

CO2. Compose a message that refuses a favor.

CO3. Compose a message that refuses a claim.

CO4. Compose an announcement that conveys bad news.

When writing a bad-news message, your goal is to convey the bad news and, at the same time, keep the reader's goodwill. A direct organizational plan is recommended when you are writing to superiors, when the bad news involves a small, insignificant matter, or when you want to emphasize the bad news. When using the direct plan, state the bad news in positive language in the first paragraph, perhaps preceded or followed by a short buffer or a reason for the decision. Then present the explanation or reasons, and close on a friendly and positive note.

When writing to subordinates, customers, or people you don't know, you should generally use an indirect plan. This approach begins with a buffer—a neutral and relevant statement that helps establish or strengthen the reader–writer relationship. Then follows the explanation of or reasons for the bad news. The reasons should be logical and, when possible, should identify a reader benefit. The bad news should be subordinated, using positive and impersonal language; apologies are not necessary. The closing should be friendly, positive, and off the topic.

When rejecting someone's idea, tact is especially important, inasmuch as the person presenting the idea is probably strongly convinced of its merits. Devote most of your message to presenting reasons for the rejection, reasons of which the reader is probably unaware. Show that the proposal was carefully considered and that the rejection is based on business, not personal, beliefs.

Most requests for favors are routine and should receive a routine response, that is, a response written in the direct organizational plan. Give your refusal in the first paragraph, but avoid curtness or coldness. Provide a quick, reasonable rationale for declining.

Use the indirect plan when refusing an adjustment request. The tone of your refusal must convey respect and consideration for the customer, even when the customer is at fault. When explaining the reasons for denying the claim, do not accuse or lecture the reader. Close on a friendly, forward-looking note.

Announcements of bad news may be either internal (addressed to employees) or external (addressed to those outside the organization). If the bad news will have little effect on the reader, use a direct organizational plan. If the reader will be personally affected by the announcement, use an indirect pattern, with a buffer opening and stress any positive aspects of the situation (that is, the steps you're taking to resolve the situation).

■ Key Term

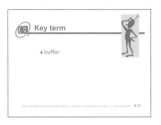

■ See Slide 9.13.

You should be able to define the following term in your own words and give an original example.

buffer (310)

■ Exercises

1   The 3Ps (Problem, Process, and Product) Model: Communication Applications at Intel   Taking the customers' perspective helps Howard High craft bad-news messages when Intel has to announce a problem. The company is careful to keep customers—and the media—informed about any problems as soon as they are discovered. This open disclosure policy allows High and his colleagues to minimize the possibility of a negative reaction to bad news.

■ Suggestions and sample solutions for exercises appear in the *Instructor's Resource Manual*.

Problem

Imagine that Intel is adding a variety of speed-enhancing features to the next generation of its Pentium Pro chip. To allow for extensive testing of these features, the new chip will not be available until March, four weeks later than originally announced. As an Intel communication specialist, you have been asked to convey this information in a letter to the production manager of Compaq, which buys Intel chips to install in its PCs. Although the delay may be disappointing, Compaq should know that the testing will bring out any flaws that need to be addressed before the new (and substantially improved) chips are shipped.

■ Sample solutions to the exercises are in the *Instructor's Resource Manual*.

Process

a. Describe your audience.
b. Should you use a direct or indirect organizational plan for this letter? Why?
c. Write your buffer opening, bearing in mind the need to retain Compaq's goodwill despite the delay.
d. What points should you make in discussing the reason for this delay?
e. Write the closing of your letter, striving for a positive, supportive tone.

Product

Using your knowledge of bad-news messages, draft this letter to John Cullinan, Production Manager, Compaq (P.O. Box 69200, Houston, TX 77269-2000).

■ See Handout 9.3.

2   The 3Ps (Problem, Process, and Product) Model: A Claim Refusal

Problem

You have just received a claim letter from John Stodel (306 Hyde Court, Kirkwood, MO 63122-4541). Mr. Stodel purchased a Clipper lawn mower (Model 306-B) from you two years ago. For the third time, he has written a claim letter requesting that you repair his $486 mower for free because its self-propelling mechanism stopped working after 15 months of use. Twice already, you've sent polite adjustment letters, denying the claim on the basis that the Model 306-B comes with a one-year warranty and the repair does not fall within the warranty period. You don't want to be rude, but you wish he would stop writing to you about a matter that you've already settled. Let him know.

Process

a. What is the purpose of your message?

b. Describe your audience.

c. Should you use a direct or indirect organizational plan? Why?

d. Write the first sentence of your letter. Be firm and businesslike—but polite and respectful. Remember that you want to retain the customer's goodwill.

e. How much space should you devote to discussing the reasons for your refusal to honor the claim? Why?

f. Write the last sentence of your letter. Again, strive for a firm, businesslike, polite, and respectful tone.

Product

Draft, revise, format, and proofread your letter. Then submit both your answers to the process questions and your revised letter to your instructor.

co1. Compose a message that rejects an idea.

3 Rejecting an Idea—Job Too Big   You are the owner of AMX Construction in Loveland, Colorado. You are putting together a proposal for a construction loan to build the Eagle's Nest apartments, a 100-unit apartment complex, in Fort Collins, Colorado. You will be the general contractor on the project, and you have accepted bids from subcontractors for the plumbing work on the apartments.

You reviewed the bids very carefully and narrowed the field of 15 to 2 bidders. The second lowest bid was from a plumbing firm in Denver. This firm specializes in plumbing for large apartment complexes. You have worked with them before, and their work is good.

The lowest bidder was Alpine Plumbing from Golden, Colorado. You have worked with Alpine before; and although their work was also good, the company took longer than expected to complete jobs. Alpine Plumbing is a small firm with only three plumbers. They usually work on small complexes of between 20 and 30 units and have never tackled a job this big.

You are concerned that Alpine wouldn't be able to meet the deadlines you have proposed. Therefore, you elected to go with the company from Denver rather than Alpine. You would be willing to work with Alpine Plumbing again on smaller jobs, but you believe that the Denver firm with its 10 plumbers is better suited to get this job done on schedule.

Write a letter to Mr. Alex Gephardt, General Manager, Alpine Plumbing, P.O. Box 245, Golden, CO 75221, giving him the bad news.

4 Refusing an Application—Bad Times for Raising Cattle   Cyndi Fallis is 28 years old and a real estate agent. She and her husband have purchased a small 50-acre farm just outside of Butte, Montana. She grew up in the area and wants to try her hand at raising cattle.

Yesterday, she applied to American West Bank for a loan to purchase 25 calves. She hopes to raise the calves and sell them for a profit. Cyndi has the land to accommodate the calves, and her flexible schedule selling real estate allows her time to feed and care for the calves. She also has a good credit history and good references. However, she has had no experience raising cattle.

The cattle industry is extremely hard to get into. Most of the ranchers in the area have huge operations with hundreds or thousands of cattle. With recent drought conditions in the area, ranchers have had to purchase most of their cattle feed from outside suppliers—at a very high price. In addition to the high price for feed, ranchers are currently getting very little for cattle when they do sell them. Several ranchers have quit the cattle business because of the hard times.

Now is not a good time for someone with limited experience to try to get into the cattle market. Write a letter to Cyndi, at 4810 West Star Route in Butte, MO 58944, denying her loan application for purchasing the calves. She might be a good loan candidate for some other investment.

5 **Refusing a Request—No Home-and-Home Schedule**   You are the Women's Athletic Director of Western State University. Paula Hernandez, an acquaintance whom you met 15 years ago in college, is now the assistant women's athletic director for Jacksonville State College in Jacksonville, Florida. She has written to you inquiring about the possibility of scheduling a home-and-home women's basketball series between Jacksonville State College and Western State University.

She has suggested that they would be willing to play on your home court next year, they would host you the following year. Last year Jacksonville State College made a jump from a two-year junior-college athletic program to a four-year NCAA program. Because of the jump to NCAA status, Jacksonville must serve a six-year probationary period before it is eligible for postseason play.

Therefore, scheduling Jacksonville during this probationary period would actually hurt your team's chances of qualifying for postseason play. You would be willing to play Jacksonville on a home-and-home basis after they have finished their probationary period, or you would play them on an exhibition basis at the beginning of next year on your home court.

Write a letter to Ms. Hernandez letting her know that you are unwilling to play them on a home-and-home basis at this time. Her address is 1400 West Waterford Avenue, Jacksonville, FL 32411.

6 **Refusing an Idea—Oversized Dressing Rooms**   You are Rebecca Lordstrom (see Exercise 8 of Chapter 8), and you certainly appreciate Robert Kilcline's memo recommending oversized dressing rooms for your new store in Fashion Square Mall. Robert has always been very customer-conscious, a trait you try to instill and nurture in all your employees.

After checking with the facility planner for the new store, you find that the Fashion Square Mall management has only a certain amount of space available for your store. Thus, any space taken up by the dressing rooms would have to be at the expense of the public store areas.

Write a memo to Robert, giving him this information. Perhaps he can suggest other ways to enhance customer service.

7 **Refusing Business—Hotel Reservation**   You are the manager of the Daytona 100, a 100-room hotel in Daytona, Florida, that caters to businesspeople. You've received a reservation from Alpha Kappa Psi fraternity at Ball State University to rent 24 double rooms during their spring break (April 6–13). They have offered to send a $1,000 deposit to guarantee the rooms if necessary.

As a former AKPsi, you know that these fraternity members are responsible students who would cause no problems. You also recognize that when these students graduate and assume positions in industry, they are the very type of people you hope will use your hotel. However, because of previous bad experiences, you now have a strict policy against accepting reservations from student groups. Write to the AKPsi treasurer (Scott Rovan, 40 Cypress Grove Court, No. 25, Muncie, IN 47304), conveying this information.

8 **Rejecting an Idea—Getting Around a Long Wait**   You're new to the management staff of Cedar Point, a large amusement park in Sandusky, Ohio. Cedar Point is renowned for its 14 roller coasters and dozens of other exciting rides. Each ride can accommodate many people at once, so the lines don't stand still for very long. Even so, on summer holidays and weekends, the wait for Cedar Point's most popular rides, such as the Millennium Force roller coaster, can be lengthy. In fact, when *Wall Street Journal* reporters sampled the midday waiting time at parks around the United States, they wound up standing for an hour in the line for the two-minute Millennium Force ride. At the other end of the spectrum, the reporters waited only 11 minutes or less to jump on rides at Coney Island in Brooklyn, New York, an old-fashioned park where the lines lengthen after dark.

Your boss, Cedar Point's top operational officer, has asked all employees to submit ideas for a system that would make the wait less onerous for customers. One employee suggests that parents with strollers be allowed to go to the front of the line, on the theory that this policy reduces the likelihood of noisy scenes with fussy youngsters. You believe that other customers would resent this system; you also don't believe that it would dramatically affect either the wait or customers' perceptions of it. With your boss's approval, you decide to reject this idea. What is your goal in writing this bad-news memo? What organizational pattern will you use? Write this memo, using your knowledge of bad-news replies (making up any details you need).

CO2. Compose a message that refuses a favor.

9 **No Magic**   Today you received in the mail a letter you have come to expect. The letter is from Olivia Frances, a close personal friend in Steubenville, Ohio. Olivia has been the chairperson of NHP, a nonprofit organization that helps raise money for a children's hospital near Steubenville.

Because of your national reputation as a magician and your friendship with Olivia, you have been invited for several years in a row to do a magic show at the organization's annual conference. The magic show has been a big money-maker for the hospital, and you have enjoyed volunteering your time to help such a worthy cause and to help a dear friend.

However, this year you have a prior family commitment and must deny your friend's request to do the magic show. Write a personal letter to Olivia letting her know the bad news. However, you know a friend who might volunteer to do a comedy show. Olivia's address is 965 West Cloverdale Avenue, Steubenville, OH 45810.

10 **Refusing a Favor—Summer Internship**   Assume the role of vice president of operations for Kolor Kosmetics, a small manufacturer in Biloxi, Mississippi. One of your colleagues from the local chamber of commerce, Dr. Andrea T. Mazzi, has written asking whether your firm can provide a summer internship in your department for her son Peter, a college sophomore who is interested in a manufacturing career. Kolor Kosmetics has no provisions for temporary summer employees and does not currently operate an internship program. Further, the factory shuts down for a two-week vacation every July.

Write Dr. Mazzi (at 3930 Lyman Turnpike, Biloxi, MS 39530) to let her know this information. Perhaps there are other ways that her son can gain firsthand experience in manufacturing during the summer.

11 Refusing a Favor—Field Trip   You are Donna Jo Luse and you have received the letter written by David Pearson (see Exercise 11 of Chapter 8). Lunch is, of course, your busiest time, and no one has the time then (or the patience) to provide a tour of the kitchens and help 23 youngsters make their salads. Perhaps, instead, they could come for a tour and snack midmorning or mid-afternoon. Write to Mr. Pearson (Jack 'n Jill Preschool, 113 Grenvale Road, Westminster, MD 21157), refusing his request.

12 Declining an Invitation—Dinner   You are the purchasing manager at your firm and have received an e-mail message from Barbara Sorrels, one of your firm's major suppliers. She will be in town on October 13 and would like to take you out to dinner that evening. However, you have an early morning flight on October 14 to Kansas City and will need to pack and make last-minute preparations on the evening of the 13th. Write to Ms. Sorrels (bsorrels@aol.com), declining her invitation.

13 Declining an Invitation—Public Speaking   You are Tanya Porrat, editor of *Autoimmune Diseases Monthly*. You just received an invitation from May Lyon to speak as the keynote speaker at the annual Multiple Sclerosis Congress (see Model 8 on page 279). In the past, you frequently accepted such invitations. However, your medical journal is in the process of being purchased by Triton Medical Research Group, and for the time being you have new rules to follow: you cannot speak in public until the sale is complete. Because you are unsure of the final date, you are refusing all speaking engagements until October. Tell this to Lyon in a letter.

14 Refusing a Claim—No Refund   Once again, assume you are the fulfillment representative at Paperbacks by Post (see Exercise 22 of Chapter 7). Roberto Valazquez has written to request that you take back a book he received three months ago. The problem is not the book itself, which he read and enjoyed, but the value for the money. He complains that the book is too short (162 pages) to justify the amount he paid ($10.95). Valazquez wants his money back, and he also wants the book club to refund the cost of shipping the book back.

This is the fourth time in five months that Valazquez has returned a book. Each time he had a different complaint—once he didn't like the cover illustration, another time he found the language offensive—and you agreed to send him his refunds. At this point, however, you believe that he is simply reading the books and then making up an excuse to avoid paying for them. You decide not to refund his money on this occasion (the number of pages and price of the book were both clearly noted in the announcement Valazquez received before the book was shipped). You also decide to cancel his membership. Write him a letter (at 717 North Walnut Street, Jacksonville, FL 32241) to let him know your decisions.

CO3. **Compose a message that refuses a claim.**

15 Refusing a Claim—Azaleas   You are a customer service representative for Jackson-Parsons Nurseries and have received the letter written by Vera Malcolm (see Exercise 14 of Chapter 8). Jackson-Parsons goes to great expense to use only the highest-quality patented stock and to pack each order in dampened sphagnum moss. However, there is no way that any nursery can control the care that plants receive on reaching their destination. Your obligation in this matter clearly ended when Ms. Malcolm did not notify you of the problem immediately. If she had, you would have cheerfully refunded her money. But evidently the azaleas are now thriving where they were planted, and you feel you have no further obligation. Tell this to Ms. Malcolm in a letter (Public Service Company of Arkansas, 189 Blackwood Lane, Little Rock, AR 72207).

16 Internet Exercise   Online auctions are increasingly popular, but not every transaction ends satisfactorily for both buyer and seller. That's why the auction site eBay posts written guidelines alerting consumers that they, not eBay, are responsible for safe trading. View these guidelines by following the "User Agreement" link at eBay (at http://www.ebay.com). Now assume the role of customer service representative at eBay. You have received an e-mail message from a buyer who misunderstood the description of an item she just purchased at auction—and she wants eBay to get her money back. Using the information in the User Agreement (and making up any reasonable details you need), draft an e-mail response breaking the bad news that the buyer is responsible for requesting additional information, understanding the terms of the auction, and communicating with the seller to resolve misunderstandings.

co4. Compose an announcement that conveys bad news.

17 Work-team Communication—A Slow Economy—No Bonus   You are the manager of a fitness equipment manufacturing plant called Muscles Galore located in Gary, Indiana. The plant has been in operation for seven years. Over the years your employees have been very productive, and sales have been high. Therefore, Muscles Galore has been able to give generous holiday bonuses (usually more than $1,000) to all of its employees for the last five years.

This year, however, because of a slow economy, you will not be able to offer the holiday bonus. Although the workers have been very productive, fitness equipment sales are down about 15 percent from last year. Your projections indicate that the economy is recovering, and sales should be up about 20 percent next year. If the projections are accurate, you should be able to offer the bonus again next year.

Write a memo to your employees letting them know the bad news. Add any additional details to make your message complete.

18 Bad-News Announcement—Mad Cow Disease—No Beef   You represent Triple M Meats in Chicago. As a meat packing plant, you supply meat to wholesalers throughout the Midwest. Blue Ribbon Meats of Grand Rapids, Michigan, has a standing order for 100 sides of beef to be delivered every week. Normally, filling this order is not a problem; however, because of new restrictions brought about because of the mad cow disease scare, you are going to have to make changes in your processing procedure. Starting March 1, 20—, your plant will be closed for two weeks to upgrade your facilities to allow for the new processing procedure. Blue Ribbon Meats has been a steady customer for over 20 years. You want to keep them as a customer, but you will not be able to fill its orders for beef from March 1 through March 14. You will still be able to fill orders for pork products. Write a letter to Mr. Larry Stokers, President of Blue Ribbon Meats, P.O. Box 435, Grand Rapids, MI 55091. Let him know the bad news, but try to keep his business. Add additional details to complete the letter.

19 **Bad-News Announcement—No Renewal**   Assume the role of Gene Harley, the leasing manager of Northern Plaza. You have decided not to renew the lease of T-shirts Plus, which operates a tiny T-shirt decorating outlet in the mall. Three times in the past 13 months, the store's employees have left their heat-transfer machinery switched on after closing. Each time, the smoke activated the mall's smoke alarms and brought the fire department to the mall during the late-night hours. Although no damage has occurred, your insurance agent warns that the mall's rates will rise if this situation continues.

The lease that T-shirts Plus signed five years ago specifies that either party can decide not to renew. All that is required is written notification to the other party at least 90 days in advance of the yearly anniversary of the contract date. By writing this week, you will be providing adequate notice. Convey this information to the store's manager, Henry D. Curtis (at Northern Plaza, Brook Parkway North, Cranbrook, BC, V1C 2Z3, Canada).

20 **Bad-News Announcement—Moving to Dallas—No Help at Thanksgiving**   You own Kitco Inc., a small financial consulting firm in Baton Rouge, Louisiana. For the last 12 years, some of your employees have voluntarily prepared and served a Thanksgiving meal at St. Benedict's homeless shelter in Baton Rouge. You paid for the turkeys, hams, and other trimming to feed the 100–150 people; your employees cooked the food at their homes and served the meal at a local church. This meal has been greatly appreciated by the St. Benedict staff and anticipated by the poor and homeless people in the area. However, you are closing your office in Baton Rouge and moving to Dallas in early October; therefore, no one from your company will be available in Baton Rouge to prepare and serve the meal. You have enjoyed your partnership with the homeless shelter, and you plan to continue the tradition in Dallas. Although you cannot prepare and serve the meal, you would be willing to donate $250 to the shelter to cover the cost of buying the food. Write a letter to Pastor Sullivan DeMarco, giving him the bad news. The address of the shelter is St. Benedict Parish, 1245 Edgewater Street, Baton Rouge, LA 34590.

21 **Bad-News Announcement—No Party**   Nobody likes a party more than Edgar Dunkirk, the president of Rockabilly Enterprises. In the early days, the company's holiday parties were legendary for their splendid food arrangements and outstanding entertainment (featuring the label's popular singing stars). Employees performed elaborate skits and competed for valuable prizes that included color television sets and videocassette recorders. These days, however, sales of the company's country and rockabilly recordings are down. In fact, Dunkirk recently had to lay off 150 of the company's 350 employees, the most severe austerity measure in the company's history.

Because so many employees had to be let go, including some who had helped Dunkirk found the company a decade ago, the president has decided that a lavish party would be inappropriate. He has therefore canceled the traditional holiday party. As Dunkirk's vice president of personnel, you must prepare a memo conveying this information to Rockabilly's employees.

22 **Bad-News Announcement—Fringe Benefits**   When your organization moved to its new building in Dallas three years ago, you negotiated a contract with the Universal Self-Parking garage a half-block away to provide free parking to all employees at Grade Level 11 or above. Your rationale was that these managerial employees often work long hours and that convenient, free parking was a justifiable fringe benefit.

Universal has just notified you that when your contract expires in three months, the monthly fee will increase by 15 percent. Given the state of the economy and your organization's declining profits, you feel that not only can you not afford the 15 percent increase but you must, reluctantly, discontinue the free parking altogether.

Therefore, beginning January 1, all employees must locate and pay for their own parking. Your organization continues to promote ride sharing; and the receptionist has copies of the city bus schedule—a bus stops a block from your building. Write a memo to these managerial employees giving them the information.

23 **Bad-News Announcement—Product Recall**   You have received two reports that users of your ten-stitch portable sewing machine, Sew-Now, have been injured when the needle broke off while sewing. One person was sewing lined denim and the other was sewing drapery fabric—neither of which should have been used on this small machine. Fortunately, neither injury was serious. Although your firm accepts no responsibility for these injuries, you decide to recall all Sew-Now machines to have a stronger needle installed.

Owners should take their machines to the store where they purchased them. These stores have been notified and already have a supply of the replacement needles. The needle can be replaced while the customer waits. Alternatively, users can ship their machines to you prepaid (Betsy Ross Sewing Machine Company, 168 West 17th Avenue, Columbus, OH 43210). Other than shipping, there is no cost to the user.

Prepare a form letter that will go out to the 1,750 Sew-Now purchasers. Customers can call your toll-free number (800-555-9821) if they have questions.

24 **Bad-News Announcement—From Free to Fee**   Kmart's e-commerce division, Bluelight.com, had a great idea for promoting its online shopping site: offer Internet access to Kmart shoppers. After attracting 7 million users, however, the company decided that providing entirely free, unlimited Internet access was too costly; first, the company tried a two-tiered plan, offering 12 hours of free access every month with an option to choose 100 hours of access for $8.95. Within a few months, the company—under pressure to improve efficiencies and become profitable—decided to do away with all free service. Under the new arrangement, customers who sign up for Internet access before September 1 will pay a discounted rate of $6.95 for their first three months, then pay the full $8.95 per month after that.

As director of customer service for Bluelight.com, it is your responsibility to notify all Internet access customers of this change. Will you use the direct or indirect organization plan? What kind of buffer will be most effective in this situation? How can you justify the company's change? How can you close your message on a positive note? Using your knowledge of bad-new messages, draft this e-mail announcement.

No Such Thing as a Free Flight

Diana has now received the memos she requested from Jean and Larry regarding the frequent-flyer program (see Continuing Case 8 in Chapter 8). She has thought about the issue quite a bit and discussed it with Marc, Tom, and Dave.

It seems to her that Larry has the more convincing argument: Company funds *were* used to purchase the tickets; therefore, the company logically owns the free tickets its employees earned. In addition, allowing traveling employees to keep their free tickets in effect amounts to an additional fringe benefit that equally hard-working nontraveling employees do not receive. So Diana decides to begin requiring US employees to use their frequent-flyer free tickets for business travel rather than personal travel.

Now she needs to write to Jean and Larry to communicate her decision. Larry, of course, will be pleased; Jean will be extremely disappointed—not only because she believes her position to be correct but because she will feel threatened by being turned down by her superior. Jean was promoted to her present position only several months ago and is still a little unsure of her abilities.

Diana also needs to issue a policy memo to all employees outlining the new program. The system will have to operate on trust; she does not intend to act as "Big Brother," policing the program and verifying mileage. Each employee will be required to join the frequent-flyer program for any airline he or she uses in connection with business travel. Employees can use different versions of their names if they also have a frequent-flyer number for their nonbusiness travel.

The expense report form will be revised to include a check-off question that asks if their frequent-flyer mileage for the flight was recorded. The clerk in OIS who makes all flight reservations will be instructed to ask each manager requesting tickets if he or she has accumulated enough miles on any airline to receive a free flight. Other details can be worked out.

Although many employees, especially those in marketing and R&D who travel extensively, will be upset, Diana is confident her decision is reasonable and in the best interests of Urban Systems.

■ A suggested solution to the Continuing Case can be found in the *Instructor's Resource Manual.*

Diana must now decide whether Larry or Jean presented the more compelling evidence regarding the use of frequent-flyer miles at Urban Systems.

Critical Thinking

1. Should Diana send Jean and Larry a joint memo or separate memos? Why?

Writing Projects

2. Write the needed memos: to Jean and Larry (either a joint memo or separate memos, depending on your response to Question 1) and to the staff.

3. Assume that Urban Systems employees do *not* travel extensively and that Diana's memo outlining the new restrictions will be considered a routine policy announcement. Write a second version of this memo to the staff using the direct pattern.

■ See Handout 9.4.

LABtest 9

Retype the following news item, correcting any mechanical errors (including misspellings) according to the rules introduced in LAB 5 on page 596.

A major educational campaign is under way to ~~prommote~~ *promote (SPELLING)* dimming, even though most designers are not using ~~flourescent~~ *fluorescent (SPELLING)* lamps with a dimming range as low as ~~eight~~ *8 (MEASUREMENT)* percent. ~~2~~ *Two (FIRST WORD IN SENTENCE)* recent developments, however, have broadened the range of possibilities for de-

5   signers—compact fluorescent lamps and electronic ballasts. The ~~national dimming institute~~ *National Dimming Institute (PROPER NAME)*, made up of leading electrical ~~mfrs~~ *manufacturers (SPELL OUT)*, seeks to increase awareness of the benefits of lighting controls. The group's ~~education~~ *Education (NOUN PLUS NUMBER)* 101 program has released a ~~C.D.R.O.M.~~ *CD-ROM (NO PERIODS)* that will be widely distributed.

10   Advanced Lighting Concepts started the group. In a recent Illuminating Engineering Society newsletter ~~artical~~ *article (SPELLING)* entitled "I am dim," ~~Dr~~ *Dr. (ABB—PERIOD)* Steve Purdy, ~~1~~ *one (BELOW 11)* of the group's founders and the company's ~~Director of Sales~~ *director of sales (TITLE AFTER NAME)*, noted, "~~we~~ *We (FIRST WORD OF QUOTATION)* intend for this new organization to mount a national educational outreach program."

15   Meetings have been ~~schedualed~~ *scheduled (SPELLING)* for different regions of the country, especially in the ~~northeast~~ *Northeast (REGION OF THE COUNTRY)*, to inform the design community about the many options available.

■ See Slides 9.14–9.17.

10

Planning the Report

communication
OBJECTIVES

After you have finished this chapter, you should be able to

1. **Describe the common types and purposes of business reports.**

2. **Analyze the audience for business reports.**

3. **Evaluate the quality of data already available.**

4. **Discuss the need for managing reports in the organization.**

As a link between the brand team—the people who develop and prepare the market for AstraZeneca's cardiovascular drugs—and the corporation's senior leadership, Anne Cobuzzi regularly plans and writes reports for different audiences. AstraZeneca is a $19 billion, London-based pharmaceutical company with more than 60,000 employees worldwide. In addition to cardiovascular drugs, the company offers medications to treat cancer, asthma, hypertension, high cholesterol, and other conditions.

Cobuzzi's first step in planning any report is to identify the audience and the purpose. "Once I know my audience, and I know whether this report will help them make a decision, provide them with information, or request their guidance, I have a direction," she says. Knowing the audience also helps her determine how much detail to include in the report. For top managers, Cobuzzi will summarize key points in the body of the report and then put all the supporting data in the appendix. Although she avoids reiterating information for readers who are knowledgeable about the topic, she also is aware that some readers may need the report's context and relevance explained. She often consults with colleagues when considering how much background to include because, she says, "having people who can give you that fresh perspective is very helpful."

an insider's
perspective

ANNE K. COBUZZI
Senior Brand Planning
Manager, Cardiovascular,
AstraZeneca
(Wilmington, Delaware)

In the exacting world of pharmaceuticals, facts and figures must be very precise. Cobuzzi gathers data from a variety of sources and takes particular care to ensure that her sources are recent, reliable, and meaningful to each audience. Depending on the report, she will plan and draft the body, then collaborate with other AstraZeneca experts who comment on the draft and write additional sections. In addition, she stresses the importance of examining every report for accuracy, logic, and proper organization. "If you can't challenge yourself," she suggests, "approach a colleague who is not involved in the report and say, 'Challenge me on this. Is this the right way to go? Have I convinced you?'"

Finally, Cobuzzi believes that business communicators sometimes concentrate too heavily on the end result of a report and miss some of the vital steps in between. Her advice: "Really plan the report by thinking it through, jotting down a number of ideas, deciding on a direction, and not getting bogged down by the ending. Once you've decided which direction to take, stay on that path, but don't be so rigid that you miss a good point."

"Plan the report by thinking it through, jotting down a number of ideas, deciding on a direction, and not getting bogged down by the ending."

■ Who Reads and Writes Reports?

Consider the following routine informational needs of management and other human resources in a large, complex, and perhaps multinational organization:

■ A sales manager at headquarters uses information provided by the field representatives to make sales projections.

■ A vice president asks subordinates to gather and analyze information needed to make an operational decision.

■ A human resources supervisor relies on the firm's legal staff to interpret government requirements for completing a compliance report.

■ A manager prepares a proposal for the company to bid on a government project.

■ An administrator informs all subordinates about a new company policy on hiring temporary personnel.

These common situations show why a wide variety of reports have become such a basic part of the typical management information system (MIS) of the contemporary organization. Because constraints are imposed by geography, time, and technical expertise, most managers often rely on others to provide the information, analysis, and recommendations they need for making decisions and solving problems. Reports travel upward, downward, and laterally within the organization, so reading and writing reports is a typical part of nearly every manager's duties.

Reports can range from a fill-in form to a one-page letter or memo to a multi-volume manuscript. For our purposes, we define a *business report* as an orderly and objective presentation of information that helps in decision making and problem solving. Note the different parts of our definition.

■ The report must be *orderly* so that the reader can locate the needed information quickly.

■ It must be *objective* because the reader will use the report to make decisions that affect the health and welfare of the organization.

■ It must present *information*—facts, data. Where subjective judgments are required, as in drawing conclusions and making recommendations, they must be presented ethically and be based squarely on the information presented in the report.

■ Finally, the report must aid in *decision making* and *problem solving*. There is a practical, "need-to-know" dimension in business reports that is sometimes missing in scientific and academic reports. Business reports must provide the specific information that management and other personnel need to make a decision or solve a problem. This goal should be uppermost in the writer's mind during all phases of the reporting process.

■ See Slide 10.1.

■ A chapter overview appears in the *Instructor's Resource Manual*.

A wide variety of reports helps managers solve problems.

■ See Slide 10.2.

■ See Slide 10.3.

■ Characteristics of Business Reports

To better understand your role as a reporter of business information, consider the following four characteristics of business reports:

■ Reports vary widely—in length, complexity, formality, and format.

■ The quality of the report process affects the quality of the product.

■ Accuracy is the most important trait of a report.

■ Reports are often a collaborative effort.

Reports Vary Widely

The typical business report is one to three pages long and written in narrative format.

There is no such document as a standard report—in length, complexity, formality, or format. The sales representative who spends five minutes completing a half-page call report showing which customers were contacted has completed a report. Likewise, the team of designers, engineers, and marketing personnel who spend six months preparing a six-volume proposal to submit to the U.S. Department of Defense has completed a report. The typical report lies somewhere in between. One analysis of 383 actual business reports found that 36 percent were one page, 37 percent were two to three pages, and 27 percent were four or more pages long.[1]

Most reports are written using a standard narrative (manuscript) format, but reports may also be in the form of letters, memos, e-mail, or preprinted forms. In addition to the body, a report may include such preliminary (prefatory) parts as a cover letter, title page, table of contents, and executive summary. Supplemental parts may include a list of references, appendixes, and an index.

Although reports may be either oral or written, most important reports are written; even most oral reports are written initially. In other words, many reports are first written and then presented orally. Having the report available in written format is important for several reasons: (1) the written report provides a permanent record, (2) it can be read and reread as needed, and (3) the reader can control the pace—rereading the complex parts, marking the important points, and skipping some sections.

The Quality of the Process Affects the Quality of the Product

A report may be well written and still contain faulty data.

Writing a report involves much more than "writing a report." As contradictory as this statement might seem, consider a fairly routine report assignment—determining whether to recommend the purchase of the Brand A, B, or C computer projection system for your organization's conference room. Before you can begin to write your recommendation, you must do your homework. At a minimum, you must (1) determine which technical features are most important to the users of the machines; (2) evaluate each brand in terms of these features; (3) compare the brands on such characteristics as cost, maintenance, reliability, and ease of use; and (4) draw a conclusion about which brand to recommend.

GRANTLAND®

If at any step you make a mistake, your report will be worse than useless; it will contain errors that the reader will in turn rely on to make a decision. Suppose you interviewed only 2 of the 50 managers who will be using the new system. The needs of these 2 managers may not be typical of the needs of the other 48. Or suppose you failed to consider the amount of downtime required by each brand. Regardless of its features, no machine can meet the needs of its users when it is inoperable.

As such situations show, your report itself (the end product of your efforts) can be well written and well designed, with appropriate charts and tables; yet if the process by which the information was gathered and analyzed was defective, erroneous, or incomplete, the report will be also. The final product can be only as good as the weakest link in the chain of events leading up to the report.

As indicated in Checklist 12 on page 348, the reporting process involves planning, data gathering and analysis, and writing. We cover the two major components of the planning stage—defining the purpose of the report and analyzing the audience—later in this chapter. The other steps are discussed in the following chapters.

■ See Handout 10.1.

Accuracy Is the Most Important Trait

No report weakness—including making major grammatical mistakes, misspelling the name of the report reader, or missing the deadline for submitting the report—is as serious as communicating inaccurate information. It's a basic tenet of management that bad information leads to bad decisions. And in such situations, the bearer of the "bad" news will surely suffer the consequences.

Your most important job is to ensure that the information you transmit is correct.

Suppose that while conducting the research for the computer projection system report, you inadvertently noted that the bulbs for Brand A had a 100-hour life when, in fact, they have a 300-hour life. If operating costs were a major criterion, your final recommendation might be incorrect because of this simple careless error. It doesn't even matter how the error occurred—whether you made it or the typist made it. You are responsible for the project, and the praise or criticism of the results of your efforts will fall on you.

To achieve accuracy, follow these guidelines:

1. *Report all relevant facts.* Errors of *omission* are just as serious as errors of *commission.* Don't mislead the reader by reporting just those facts that tend to support your position.

✓ checklist 12

The Reporting Process

Planning

✓ Define the purpose of the report.

- Determine why the issue is important; what use will be made of the report; and what the time, resource, and length constraints are.

- Decide whether the purpose is to inform, analyze, or recommend.

- Using neutral language, construct a one-sentence problem statement, perhaps in question form.

✓ Define the audience for the report.

- Is the report for an internal or an external reader?

- Did the reader authorize the report or is it voluntary?

- What is the level of knowledge and interest of the reader?

Data Gathering and Analysis

✓ Determine what data will be required.

- Factor the problem statement into its component parts, perhaps stating each subproblem as a question.

- Determine what data will be needed to answer each subproblem.

✓ Decide which methods to use to collect the needed data.

- Ensure that any secondary data used is current, accurate, complete, free from bias and misinterpretation, and relevant.

- If secondary data is not available, determine the most efficient means of collecting the needed data.

✓ Collect the data.

- Ensure that all informational needs have been identified.

- Allot sufficient time to gather the needed data.

- Ensure that the collection methods will produce valid and reliable data.

✓ Compile the data in a systematic and logical form, organizing the information according to the subproblems.

✓ Analyze each bit of data individually at first and then in conjunction with every other bit of data. Finally, look at all the data together to try to discern trends, contradictions, unexpected findings, areas for further investigation, and the like.

✓ Construct appropriate visual aids.

Writing

✓ Draft the report.

- Consider the needs of the reader and the nature of the problem.

- Determine the organization, length, formality, and format of the report.

- Make sure the report is clear, complete, objective, and credible.

✓ Revise the report for content, style, and correctness.

✓ Use generally accepted formatting conventions to format the report in an attractive, efficient, and effective style.

✓ Proofread to ensure that the report reflects the highest standards of scholarship, critical thinking, and care.

NOT: During the two-year period of 2003 and 2004, our return on investment averaged 13 percent.

BUT: Our return on investment was 34 percent in 2003 but 8 percent in 2004, for an average of 13 percent.

■ See Slide 10.4.

2. *Use emphasis and subordination appropriately.* Your goal is to help the reader see the relative importance of the points you discuss. If you honestly think a certain idea is of minor importance, subordinate it—regardless of whether it reinforces or weakens your ultimate conclusion. Don't emphasize a point simply because it reinforces your position, and don't subordinate a point simply because it weakens your position.

3. *Give enough evidence to support your conclusions.* Make sure that your sources are accurate, reliable, and objective and that there is enough evidence to support your position. Sometimes your evidence (the data you gather) may be so sparse or of such questionable quality that you are unable to draw a valid conclusion. If so, simply present the findings and don't draw a conclusion. To give the reader confidence in your statements, discuss your procedures thoroughly and cite all your sources.

Draw valid conclusions, if appropriate.

4. *Avoid letting personal biases and unfounded opinions influence your interpretation and presentation of the data.* Sometimes you will be asked to draw conclusions and to make recommendations, and such judgments inherently involve a certain amount of subjectivity. You must make a special effort to look at the data objectively and to base your conclusions solely on the data. Avoid letting your personal feelings influence the outcomes. Sometimes the use of a single word can unintentionally convey bias.

NOT: The accounting supervisor *claimed* the error was unintentional.

BUT: The accounting supervisor *stated* the error was unintentional.

Reports Are Often a Collaborative Effort

Short, informal reports are usually a one-person effort. Many recurring reports in an organization, however, are multiperson efforts. It is not likely, for example, that general management would ask a single person to study the feasibility of entering the generic-product market. Instead, a combination of talents would be needed—marketing, manufacturing, human resources, and the like.

Complex reports require the talents of many people.

Such joint efforts require well-defined organizational skills, time management, close coordination, and a genuine spirit of cooperation. Although more difficult to manage than individually written reports, team-written reports offer these advantages:

■ They draw on the diverse experiences and talents of many members.

■ They increase each manager's awareness of other viewpoints.

■ They typically result in higher-quality output than might be the case if a single person worked alone on a complex assignment.

■ They produce a final product in less time than would be possible otherwise.

■ They help develop important networking contacts.

■ They provide valuable experience in working with small groups.

■ Common Types of Reports

CO1. Describe the common types and purposes of business reports.

Management needs comprehensive, up-to-date, accurate, and understandable information to achieve the organization's goals. Much of this information is communicated in the form of reports. The most common types of business reports are periodic reports, proposals, policies and procedures, and situational reports. Each of these types is discussed and illustrated in the following sections.

Periodic Reports

Periodic reports are recurring routine reports submitted at regular intervals.

Three common types of periodic reports are routine management reports, compliance reports, and progress reports.

Routine Management Reports   Every organization requires its own set of recurring reports to provide the knowledge base from which decisions are made and problems are solved. Some of these routine management reports are statistical, consisting sometimes of just computer printouts; other management reports are primarily narrative. Routine management reports range from accounting, financial, and sales updates to various human resources and equipment reports.

Compliance Reports   Many state and federal government agencies require companies doing business with them to file reports showing that they are complying with regulations in such areas as affirmative action, contacts with foreign firms, labor relations, occupational safety, financial dealings, and environmental concerns. Com-

At Motorola's Communication (or Comm) Sector, employees and managers brainstorm to develop improvements for two-way radios. This scene is typical in business where a combination of talents joins to produce a collaborative report.

pleting these compliance reports is often mostly a matter of gathering the needed data and reporting the information honestly and completely. Typically, very little analysis of the data is required.

Progress Reports   Interim progress reports are often used to communicate the status of long-term projects. They are submitted periodically to management for internal projects, to the customer for external projects, and to the investor for an accounting of venture capital expenditures. Typically, these narrative reports (1) tell what has been accomplished since the last progress report, (2) document how well the project is adhering to the schedule and budget, (3) describe any problems encountered and how they were solved, and (4) outline future plans (see Model 16 on page 352).

Proposals

A **proposal** is a written report that seeks to persuade the reader to accept a suggested plan of action. Two common types of proposals in business are project proposals and research proposals.

Project Proposals   A manager may write a project proposal that, for example, seeks to persuade a potential customer to purchase goods or services from the writer's firm, persuade the federal government to locate a new research facility in the headquarters city of the writer's firm, or persuade a foundation to fund a project to be undertaken by the writer's firm.

Proposals may be solicited or unsolicited. Government agencies and many large commercial firms routinely solicit proposals from potential suppliers. For example, the government might publish an RFP (request for proposal) stating its intention to purchase 5,000 microcomputers, giving detailed specifications regarding the features it needs on these computers, and inviting prospective suppliers to bid on the project. Similarly, the computer manufacturer that submits the successful bid might itself publish an RFP to invite parts manufacturers to bid on supplying some component the manufacturer needs for these computers.

The unsolicited proposal differs from the solicited proposal in that the former typically requires more background information and more persuasion. Because the reader may not be familiar with the project, the writer must present more evidence to convince the reader of the merits of the proposal.

The proposal reader is typically outside the organization. The format for these external documents may be a letter report, a manuscript report, or even a form report, with the form supplied by the soliciting organization. If the soliciting organization does not supply a form, it will likely specify in detailed language the format required for the proposal. The reader's instructions should be followed explicitly. Despite the merits of a proposal, failure to follow such guidelines may be sufficient reason for the evaluator to reject it.

When writing a proposal, the writer must keep in mind that the proposal may become legally binding on the writer and the organization. In spelling out exactly what the writer's organization will provide, when, under what circumstances, and at what price, the proposal report writer creates the *offer* part of a contract which, if accepted, becomes binding on the organization.

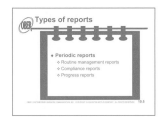

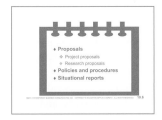

■ See Slides 10.5. and 10.6.

Both solicited and unsolicited proposals require persuasion.

■ See Slide 10.7.

model 16

PROGRESS REPORT

This progress report is sub-mitted in letter format.

Begins by giving the purpose and an overall summary.

Identifies the work com-pleted, in progress, and still to be done.

Uses enumerations to make the items stand out.

Uses first- and second-person pronouns (appropriate in a letter or memo report).

Identifies problems and needed decisions.

Closes on a goodwill note.

---

amazon.com

MEMO TO:	Mr. Ellis Shepherd, Manufacturing Department
FROM:	Mark Hansdorf, Project Manager
DATE:	May 9, 20—
SUBJECT:	Warehouse Status Report

This memo brings you up to date on the status of the construction of our new warehouse on Lafayette Street. As you will see, construction is on schedule and within budget, with no major problems foreseen.

Work Completed to Date: We have now completed the following jobs:

1. The foundation was poured on March 27.

2. The exterior of the building, including asphalt roofing and aluminum siding, was completed on April 23.

Work in Progress: The following work has been started but has not yet been completed:

1. The drywallers are installing the interior walls and partitions; they should be finished by the end of next week.

2. The plumbers have installed the necessary fixtures in the washrooms and are install-ing the Amana high-energy-efficient heating/cooling unit.

Work to Be Completed: From now until July 20, we will be completing these tasks:

1. The vinyl flooring will be installed by June 23.

2. The painters will paint the interior on July 1–3.

3. The city inspector and fire marshal will perform a final inspection on July 17.

Miscellaneous: The modular rack storage system was ordered on April 3 and should have been delivered two weeks ago. Our supplier assures me that the system will be de-livered by May 12. If so, we should have no problems installing it on schedule.

By June 25, you will need to make a final color selection for the interior walls. The plan calls for one color.

We appreciate the opportunity to build this facility for you and are sure you will enjoy using it. I will provide you another update in June.

hwc

P.O. BOX 81226, SEATTLE, WA 98108-1226
WWW.AMAZON.COM

Grammar and Mechanics Notes

1 *exterior . . . was:* Ignore intervening words when establishing subject/verb agreement.

2 *been started but:* Do not insert a comma between parts of a compound predicate.

3 *partitions; they:* Connect two closely related independent clauses with a semicolon—not a comma.

4 Use your word processing program's enumeration or bullet feature to format lists automatically.

Effective collaborative writing requires tact, patience, and a spirit of cooperation. Here, Jon Stewart and his Emmy-winning team of writers bat around ideas for an episode of *The Daily Show,* a highly successful fake news program filled with social satire that airs on the Comedy Central channel.

Proposals are persuasive documents, and all the techniques you learned about persuasion in correspondence apply equally here:

Proposals are persuasive reports written to an external audience.

- Give ample, credible evidence for all statements.

- Do not exaggerate.

- Provide examples, expert testimony, and specific facts and figures to support your statements.

- Use simple, straightforward, and direct language, preferring simple sentences and the active voice.

- Stress reader benefits. Remember that you are asking for something, usually a commitment of money; let the reader know what he or she will get in return.

Obviously, having a good idea is not enough. You must be able to present that idea clearly and convincingly so that it will be accepted. The benefits of clear and persuasive writing go far beyond the immediate goal of securing approval for your current project. A well-written proposal increases both your visibility and your credibility with the reader and with the organization on whose behalf you wrote the proposal.

Although proposals vary in length, organization, complexity, and format, the following sections are typical:

1. *Background:* Introduce the problem you're addressing and discuss why it merits the reader's consideration. Provide enough background information to show that a problem exists and that you have a viable solution.
2. *Objectives:* Provide specific information about what the outcomes of the project will be. Be detailed and honest in discussing what the reader will get in return for a commitment of resources.
3. *Procedures:* Discuss in detail exactly how you will achieve these objectives. Include a step-by-step discussion of what will be done, when, and exactly how much each component or phase will cost.
4. *Qualifications:* Show how you, your organization, and any others who would be involved in conducting this project are qualified to do so. If appropriate, include testimonials or other external evidence to support your claims.

Provide all the objective information the reader needs to make a decision.

5. *Request for approval:* Directly ask for approval of your proposal. Depending on the reader's needs, this request could come either at the beginning or at the end of the proposal.

6. *Supporting data:* Include as an appendix to your proposal any relevant but supplementary information that might bolster your arguments.

As with all persuasive writing, the use of clear and objective language, ample evidence, and logical organization will help you achieve your goals. An example of a proposal for a small project is shown in Model 17 (see pages 356–357).

■ See Slide 10.8.

Research Proposals   Because research is a cost to the organization in terms of personnel time and monetary expenses, superiors want to know what they will gain in return for expending these resources. Thus, a research proposal is a structured presentation of what you plan to do in research, why you plan to conduct the research, and how you plan to accomplish it. The proposal gives those concerned with your research effort an opportunity to evaluate your research approach. Every step of your proposal should be developed with extreme care. Once it has been accepted, any substantive changes you may wish to make must receive prior approval.

Research proposal formats vary depending on the desires and needs of those who will appraise your work. The format provided below is one effective format for simple report projects. It includes the following sections:

1. *Heading:* Provide a neutral, descriptive title for your project, being careful not to promise more than you can deliver. Include as a subtitle "A Research Proposal," your name, and the submission date.

2. *Introduction:* Establish a definite need for your study. Include here the background information about the problem, explaining enough to establish a situation and to orient the reader. For credibility, include any information from published sources that helps to establish a need for your project.

3. *Problem:* On the basis of what you said in the previous section, a problem needs answering. Introduce the problem statement and then, using neutral language, state in question form the specific problem to be investigated (avoid yes-or-no questions because your problem is probably more complex than that). Then introduce the subproblems, again in the form of questions, and list them in logical order. Taken together, the answers to your subproblems must provide a complete and accurate answer to your problem statement.

4. *Scope:* The scope of the problem describes the boundaries you have established for your research problem. The scope (also called "delimitations") indicates those parts of the topic that normally might be considered a part of such a study but that you do not wish to include in your study. Your report title and problem statement must reflect any major delimitations imposed on your study. If you are using any terms in your study that may be subject to different interpretations or that may be unfamiliar to the reader, define them here.

5. *Procedures:* Explain how you will conduct your investigation. Describe your sources of data and methods of collection. Regardless of how you organize this section, plan your procedures carefully and present them in such a way that the reader has confidence that they will enable you to provide an accurate and complete answer to your problem statement.

6. *Conclusion:* Don't leave the reader hanging by ending your report abruptly. Include an appropriate ending paragraph that provides a sense of closure for your research proposal.
7. *References:* Include here the published sources (including Internet citations) to which you actually referred in your proposal, using the citation style preferred by your reader or organization. For short or informal reports, footnotes may take the place of a separate References section.

Model 18 on pages 358–359 shows a typical research proposal.

Policies and Procedures

Policies are broad operating guidelines that govern the general direction and activities of an organization; **procedures** are the recommended methods or sequential steps to follow when performing a specific activity. Thus, an organization's attitude toward promoting from within the firm would constitute a policy, and the steps to be taken to apply for a promotion would constitute a procedure. Policy statements are typically written by top management; procedures are typically written by the managers and supervisors who are involved in the day-to-day operation of the organization.

Policy   Begin a policy statement by setting the stage; that is, justify the need for a policy. Your justification should be general enough that the policy covers a broad range of situations but not so general that it has no real "teeth." Ensure that the reader knows exactly who is covered by the policy, what is required, and any other needed information. Finally, show how the reader, the organization, or *someone* benefits from this policy.

> *Avoid making policies so general that they are of little practical help.*

Procedure   Write procedures in a businesslike but not formal manner, using the active voice. Imagine that you are explaining the procedure orally to someone. Go step by step through the process, explaining, when necessary, what should *not* be done as well as what should be done. Try to put yourself in the role of the reader. How much background information is needed; how much jargon can safely be used; what reading level is appropriate? Anticipate questions and problems. Show and tell; that is, use pictures and diagrams as appropriate.

> *Write procedures in a businesslike, step-by-step format.*

Don't assume that the reader knows anything about the process, but likewise don't assume that the reader is completely ignorant. Because it would be impossible to answer every conceivable question, concentrate on the high-risk components—those tasks that are difficult to perform or that have serious safety or financial implications if performed incorrectly.

Minimize the amount of conceptual information included, concentrating instead on the practical information. (Remember that a person can learn to drive a car safely without needing to learn how the engine actually propels the car forward.) Usually, numbered steps are appropriate, but use a narrative approach if it seems more effective.

After you have written a draft, have several employees who are typical of those who will use the document read and comment on it. If the document is a policy, ask them questions to see if they really understand the policy. If it is a procedure, have them follow the steps to see if they work. Revise as necessary.

> *Have typical users review and edit drafts of policies and procedures.*

An example of a procedure is given in Model 19 (see page 360). Could you follow this procedure and get the desired results?

model17

PROJECT PROPOSAL

This solicited proposal seeks to persuade an organization to sponsor a workshop.

Begins by identifying the purpose of the letter.

Provides specific examples to show that a need exists.

Suggests a reasonable solution.

Tells exactly what the proposal should accomplish.

WORDS etc

Business communication
and document processing

September 16, 20—

Ms. Carolyn Soule, Employee Manager
Everglades National Corporation
1407 Lincoln Road, Suite 15
Miami, FL 33139

Dear Ms. Soule:

1   Subject: Proposal for an In-house Workshop on Business Writing

I enjoyed discussing with you the business writing workshops you intend to sponsor for the engineering staff at Everglades National Corporation. As you requested, I am submitting this proposal to conduct a two-day workshop.

BACKGROUND

2   On September 4-5, I interviewed four engineers at your organization and analyzed samples of their writing. Your engineers are typical of many highly trained specialists who know exactly what they want to say but sometimes do not structure their communications in the most effective manner. Problems with audience analysis, organization, and overall writing style were especially apparent when they were communicating with nonspecialists either inside or outside the organization.

3   Thus, I propose that you sponsor a two-day writing workshop that I will develop entitled "The Process of Business Writing." The workshop could be held during any two days between November 26 and December 10.

OBJECTIVES

The workshop would help your engineers achieve these objectives:

1. Specify the purpose of a message and perform an audience analysis.

2. Determine what information to include and in what order to present it.

3. Set an appropriate overall tone by using confident language, using appropriate emphasis and subordination, and stressing the "you" attitude.

4. Revise a draft for content, style, correctness, and readability.

5. Format written communications in an efficient standard format.

10388 POWER DRIVE, CARMEL, IN 48033 • PHONE: 317.571.8766 • FAX: 317.575.8103 • EMAIL: WORDSetc@OBER.NET

Grammar and Mechanics Notes

1 Leave one blank line before and after a subject line.

2 *highly trained specialists:* Do not hyphenate a compound modifier when the first word (an adverb) ends in -*ly.*

3 *Business Writing.":* Place the period inside the closing quotation marks.

2

model 17

PROCEDURES

The enclosed outline shows the coverage of the course. The workshop would require a meeting room with participants seated at tables, an overhead projector, and a chalkboard or some other writing surface. The program would be divided into four half-day segments, each lasting three hours. The first two hours would be devoted to discussing the topics listed, followed by a 15-minute break. The final hour would consist of group and individual writing assignments, with appropriate guidance, discussion, and feedback provided.

Provides enough details to enable the reader to understand what is planned.

4   My fee for teaching the two-day workshop would be $2,000, plus expenses (including photocopying handouts, automobile mileage, and lunch on the workshop days). Your organization would be responsible for arranging and providing the morning and afternoon refreshments and lunch for the participants.

Discusses costs in an open and confident manner.

QUALIFICATIONS

I would be responsible for planning and conducting the workshop. As you can see from the enclosed data sheet, I've had 15 years of consulting experience in business communications and have spoken and written widely on the topic.

Highlights only the most relevant information from the enclosed data sheet.

SUMMARY

5   My experience in working with engineers has taught me that they recognize the value of effective business communications and are motivated to improve their writing skills. The course should help them become more effective communicators and more effective managers for Everglades National Corporation.

Shows how the reader will benefit from doing as asked.

I wish you much success in your efforts to upgrade your staff's writing skills. Please call me at 317-571-8766 to let me know your reactions to this proposal.

6   Sincerely yours,

Ann Skarzinski

Ann Skarzinski, Executive Trainer

mje
Enclosures

Closes on a friendly, confident note.

Grammar and Mechanics Notes

4 *$2,000:* Omit the decimal point and zeroes for even amounts of money. Use a comma in all numerals of four or more digits except years.

5 *engineers has:* Use the singular verb (*has*) because the subject is *experience,* not *engineers.*

6 *Sincerely yours,:* Capitalize only the first word of a complimentary closing.

model18

RESEARCH PROPOSAL

This research proposal is shown in manuscript format.

Uses a neutral, descriptive title.

Introduces the topic and establishes a need for the study.

Phrases the problem to be solved in question format.

Includes subproblems that, taken together, will answer the problem statement.

STAFF EMPLOYEES' EVALUATION OF THE BENEFIT PROGRAM AT MAYO MEMORIAL HOSPITAL

A Research Proposal by Lyn Santos
January 23, 20—

1   Employee benefits are a rapidly growing and an increasingly important form of employee compensation for both profit and nonprofit organizations. According to a recent U.S. Chamber of Commerce survey, benefits now constitute 37 percent of

2   all payroll costs, costing an average of $10,857 a year for each full-time employee.[1] As has been noted by two management consultants, "The success of employee benefit programs depends directly on whether employees need and understand the value of the benefits provided."[2] Thus, an organization's employee benefit program must be monitored and evaluated if it is to remain an effective recruitment and retention tool.

Mayo Memorial employs 2,500 staff personnel, who have not received a cost-of-living increase in two years. Thus, staff salaries may not have kept pace with industry, and the hospital's benefits program may become more important in attracting and retaining good workers. In addition, the contracts of three staff unions expire next year, and the benefit program is typically a major area of bargaining.

PROBLEM

To help ensure that the benefit program is operating as effectively as possible, the following problem will be addressed in this study: What are the opinions of staff employees at Mayo Memorial Hospital regarding their employee benefits? To answer this question, the following subproblems will be addressed:

1. How knowledgeable are the employees about the benefit program?
2. What are the employees' opinions of the benefits presently available to them?
3. What benefits would the employees like to have added to the program?

---

3   [1] Enar Ignatio, "Can Flexible Benefits Promote Your Company?" *Personnel Quarterly*, Vol. 20, September 2006, p. 812.

[2] Ramon Adams and Seymour Stevens, *Personnel Administration*, All-State, Cambridge, MA, 2002, p. 483.

Grammar and Mechanics Notes

1 Like most research proposals, this one is written in third-person language. Note the absence of "I" and "you" pronouns.

2 When using the business style citation method, use footnotes and include page numbers when citing statistics or a direct quotation. Omit page numbers if citing the entire work.

3 Format publications in italic; enclose parts of publications (such as article titles) in parentheses.

model18

2

SCOPE

Although staff employees at all state-supported hospitals receive the same benefits, no attempt will be made to generalize the findings beyond Mayo Memorial. In
addition, this study will attempt to determine employee preferences only. The
question of whether these preferences are economically feasible is not within the
scope of this study.

Identifies those parts of the problem the researcher has chosen *not* to investigate.

PROCEDURES

A random sample of 200 staff employees at Mayo Memorial Hospital will be surveyed to answer the three subproblems. In addition, personal interviews will be
held with a compensation specialist at Mayo and with the chair of the Staff Personnel Committee. Secondary data will be used to (a) provide background information for developing the questionnaire items and the interview questions, (b)
provide a basis for comparing the Mayo benefit program with that of other organizations, and (c) provide a basis for comparing the employees' opinions of the
Mayo benefit program with employee opinions of programs at other organizations.

Identifies the procedures needed to answer each subproblem.

CONCLUSION

This information will be analyzed, and appropriate tables and charts will be developed. Conclusions will be drawn and recommendations made as appropriate to
explain the staff employees' opinions about the benefit program at Mayo Memorial Hospital.

Provides a sense of closure.

model19

PROCEDURE

A step-by-step outline of who (Actor) does what (Action) when temporary help is hired.

Uses a descriptive title.

Begins with the act that starts the process and ends with the final result.

Contains only essential information.

Details clearly and concisely what steps are necessary and in what order.

Maintains parallel structure (complete sentences are not necessary).

PROCEDURE FOR HIRING A TEMPORARY EMPLOYEE

Actor	Action
Requester	1. Requests a temporary employee with specialized skills by filling out Form 722, "Request for a Temporary Employee."
	2. Secures manager's approval.
	3. Sends four copies of Form 722 to labor analyst in Human Resources.
Labor Analyst	4. Checks overtime figures of regular employees in the department.
	5. If satisfied that the specific people are necessary, checks budget.
	6. If funds are available, approves Form 722, sends three copies to buyer of special services in Human Resources, and files the fourth copy.
Buyer of Special Services	7. Notifies outside temporary help contractor by phone and follows up the same day with a confirming letter or e-mail.
	8. Negotiates a mutually agreeable effective date.
	9. Contacts Human Resources by phone, telling them of the number of people and the effective dates.
Human Resources	10. Notifies Security, Badges, and Gate Guards.
	11. Returns one copy of Form 722 to the requester.
	12. Provides a temporary ID.
Temporary Help Contractor	13. Furnishes assigned employee or employees with information on the job description, effective date, and the individual to whom to report.
Temporary Employee	14. Reports to receptionist one half-hour early on the effective date.

Grammar and Mechanics Note

The format used is optional. This procedure uses a playscript format that clearly specifies what role each person plays in the process.

Situational Reports

In any organization, unique problems and opportunities appear that require one-time-only reports. Many of these situations call for information to be gathered and analyzed and for recommendations to be made. These so-called *situational reports* are perhaps the most challenging for the report writer. Because they involve a unique event, the writer has no previous reports to use as a guide; he or she must decide what types of information and how much information are needed and how best to organize and present the findings.

A sample situational report is shown in Model 20 (see page 363). The guidelines presented in the upcoming report chapters are especially applicable to situational reports because of the many decisions that surround these one-of-a-kind projects.

■ See Slides 10.9. and 10.10.

■ Purposes of Reports

At the outset, you need to determine why you are writing the report. Business reports generally aim to inform, analyze, or recommend.

Informing

Informational reports relate objectively the facts and events surrounding a particular situation. No attempt is made to analyze and interpret the data, draw conclusions, or recommend a course of action. Most periodic reports, as well as policies and procedures, are examples of informational reports. In most cases, these types of reports are the easiest to complete. The report writer's major interest is in presenting all of the relevant information objectively, accurately, and clearly, while refraining from including unsolicited analysis and recommendations.

Informational reports present information without analyzing it.

Analyzing

One step in complexity above the informational report is the analytical report, which not only presents the information but also analyzes it. Data by itself may be meaningless; the information must be put into some context before readers can make use of it. As social forecaster John Naisbitt has remarked, "We are drowning in information, but starved for knowledge."[2]

Consider, for example, this informational statement: "Sales for the quarter ending June 30 were $780,000." Was this performance good or bad? We cannot possibly know unless the writer *analyzes* the information for us. Here are two possible interpretations of this statement:

Analytical reports interpret the information.

> Sales for the quarter ending June 30 were $780,000, up 7 percent from the previous quarter. This strong showing was achieved despite an industrywide slump and may be attributed to the new "Tell One—Sell One" campaign we introduced in January.

> Sales for the quarter ending June 30 were $780,000, a decline of 5.5 percent from the same quarter last year. All regions experienced a 3 percent to 5 percent increase except for the western region, which experienced an 18 percent decrease in sales. John Manilow, western regional manager, attributes his area's sharp drop in sales to the budgetary problems now being experienced by the state governments in California and Arizona.

The report writer must be careful that any conclusions drawn are reasonable, valid, and fully supported by the data presented. Although the writer must attempt to avoid inserting his or her own biases or preexisting opinions into the report, analysis and interpretation can never be completely objective. The report writer makes numerous decisions that call for subjective evaluations. Note the difference in effect of the following two statements, which contain the same information but in reversed order:

Original:

Although it is too early to determine the effectiveness of Mundrake's efforts, he believes the steps he is taking will bring Limerick's absentee rate down to the industry average of 3.6 percent by December.

Reversed:

Although Mundrake believes the steps he is taking will bring Limerick's absentee rate down to the industry average of 3.6 percent by December, it is too early to determine the effectiveness of his efforts.

Recommendation reports propose a course of action.

The original order leaves a confident impression of the probable success of the steps taken, whereas the reversed order leaves a much more skeptical impression. Only the report writer can determine which version leaves the more accurate impression.

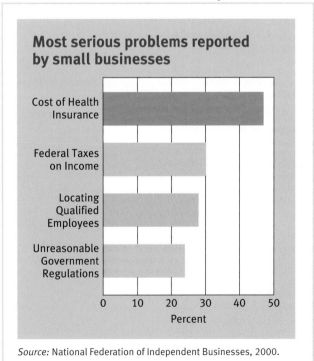

communication snapshot 10

Most serious problems reported by small businesses

Cost of Health Insurance

Federal Taxes on Income

Locating Qualified Employees

Unreasonable Government Regulations

0   10   20   30   40   50
Percent

Source: National Federation of Independent Businesses, 2000.

Recommending

Recommendation reports add the element of endorsing a specific course of action (see, for example, the situational report in Model 20). The writer presents the relevant information, interprets it, and then suggests a plan of attack. The important point is that you must let the *data* be the basis for any conclusions you draw and any recommendations you make. You want to analyze and present your data so that the truth, the whole truth, and nothing but the truth emerges. In other words, avoid the temptation of beginning with a preconceived idea and then marshaling and manipulating data to support it.

In a sense, your final recommendation is only the tip of the iceberg, but it is a very visible tip. The logic, clarity, and strength of your recommendation can have major implications for your career and for your organization's well-being.

Consider the most serious problems reported by small business, shown in Communication Snapshot 10. What types of reports might be written to help resolve these problems?

model20

THE FEASIBILITY OF AN MXD IN MEMPHIS

David M. Beall

1 Mixed-use development (MXD) integrates three or more land uses (e.g., office, retail, hotel, residential, and recreation) in a high-density configuration with uninterrupted circulation from one component to another. Interviews with seven local real estate developers and bankers and secondary sources provided information on the feasibility of constructing a mixed-use development in Memphis.

Low Land Prices and Low-Density Population Weaken Potential

2 Land prices are a key economic factor in real estate development. High prices force developers to develop land with intensive uses to justify land costs. The much more expensive cost of an MXD makes economic sense only when high land prices justify the investment. Land prices in Memphis, however, are relatively low compared to prices in other major U.S. cities. The Galleria in Houston and the Metrocenter in Phoenix are similar-sized developments that offer an excellent comparison of how land prices dictate development intensity. The Galleria site cost $85,000 per acre; six years later, the Metrocenter site cost only $10,000 per acre (Rogers, 1998, p. 148).

Successful MXDs tend to be located in high-density urban cores. The Memphis market, however, is a low-density environment. Approximately 67 percent of the Memphis housing stock is single-family homes, and relatively few commercial buildings reach over six stories high ("Inside Memphis," 2003).

3 **Financing Would Be Difficult**

The area bankers interviewed are reluctant to become involved with a new type of large-scale commercial development. Instead, they prefer to sponsor projects with which they have had experience. According to one banker, "A bank is only as successful as its last loan" (Weiss, 2004). The bankers believe the economic risks associated with developing an MXD outweigh the rewards. They cite such adverse factors as high development costs, complexity, and lack of expertise (Allen, 2003).

Davenport Should Delay MXD Project

Because of Memphis's relatively low land costs and low-density population and the difficulty of securing financing, Davenport Development Corp. should not pursue a mixed-use development in the Memphis area now. However, because the Southeast is growing so rapidly, we should reevaluate the Memphis market in three years.

SITUATIONAL REPORT

Begins by introducing the topic and discussing the procedures used. This report uses the indirect pattern, saving the recommendations until the end.

This situational report is shown in manuscript format.

Is organized according to the criteria used to solve the problem.

Uses the author-date format for citing references (see Reference Manual).

Closes by making a recommendation based on the findings presented.

Grammar and Mechanics Notes

1 *real estate developers:* Do not hyphenate a compound noun (*real estate*) that comes before another noun (*developers*).

2 *site:* location (*cite:* "to quote"; *sight:* "to view").

3 Be consistent in formatting report side headings; there is no one standard format (other than consistency). This report uses "talking" headings, which identify both the topic and the major conclusion of each section.

■ Audience Analysis

co2. **Analyze the audience for business reports.**

The audience for a report—the reader or readers—is typically homogeneous. Many times, of course, the audience is one person; but even when it is not, the audience usually consists of people with similar levels of expertise, background knowledge, and the like. Thus, you can, and should, develop your report to take into account the needs of your reader. In doing so, you will need to consider the following elements.

Internal Versus External Audiences

Internal reports are generally less formal and contain less background information than external reports.

Internal reports are written for readers within the organization and are usually less formal than external reports, for which the reader might be a customer, potential customer, or government agency. Internal reports also typically require less background information and can safely use more technical vocabulary than external reports, which are often more sensitive to public relations issues.

Internal reports are also directional and are aimed at the writer's superiors, peers, or subordinates. The strategy used must be appropriate for the audience's position. For example, reports often have a costs-and-profits tone when directed to superiors, a conversational tone when directed to peers, and an emphatic tone when directed to subordinates.

Authorized Versus Voluntary Reports

Voluntary reports require more background information and more persuasion than authorized reports.

Authorized reports are written at the specific request of some higher authority. Thus, the reader has an inherent interest in the report. Voluntary reports, on the other hand, are prepared on the writer's own initiative. Therefore, the reader needs more background information and frequently more persuasive evidence than do readers of authorized reports.

Authorized reports may be either periodic or situational. Periodic reports are submitted on a recurring, systematic basis. Very often they are form reports, with space provided for specific items of information. Readers of periodic reports need little introductory or background information because of the report's recurring nature. Readers of situational, one-time reports, on the other hand, need more explanatory material because of the uniqueness of the situation.

■ See Slide 10.11.

Gear the amount of information presented and the order in which it is presented to the needs of the reader.

Level of Knowledge and Interest

Is the reader already familiar with your topic? Will he or she understand the terms used, or will you need to define them? If you have a heterogeneous audience for your report, striking an appropriate balance in level of detail given will require careful planning.

Most reports are written in the direct pattern, with the major conclusions and recommendations given up front (but see, however, Spotlight 24, "Context in International Reports," on page 366). This situation is especially true when you know the reader is interested in your project or is likely to agree with your opinions and judgments. Reports that make a recommendation with which the reader may disagree are often written in the indirect pattern because you want the reader to study the reasons first. The reader will be more likely to accept or at least consider the recommendation if he or she has first had an opportunity to study its rationale.

■ What Data Is Already Available?

Before collecting any data, you must define the report purpose and analyze the intended audience. Then you must determine what data is needed to solve the problem. (*Note:* The word *data* is technically the plural form of *datum* and therefore technically requires a plural verb when referring to several individual items of data. In most cases in this text, however, the term is used in the sense of a collective noun and takes a singular verb. The Usage Panel for the *American Heritage Dictionary* endorses this position.) Sometimes the data you need will be in your mind or in documents you already have at hand, sometimes it will be in documents located elsewhere, and sometimes the data is not available at all but must be generated by you.

Start the data-collection phase by **factoring** your problem—that is, by breaking it down into its component parts so that you will know what data you need to collect. The easiest way to do this is to think about what questions you need to answer before you can solve the problem. The answers to these questions will ultimately provide the answer to the overall problem you're trying to solve, and the question topics may, in fact, ultimately serve as the major divisions of your report.

Research and report writing are a cost, just like other corporate expenses. Thus, you should use data-collection methods that will provide the needed data with the least expenditure of time and money but at the level of completeness, accuracy, and precision needed to solve your problem. There is a break-even point to data collection. You do not want to provide a $100 answer to a $5 question, but neither do you want to provide a $5 answer to a $100 question.

Common Types of Data

The two major types of data you will use are secondary and primary data. **Secondary data** is data collected by someone else for some other purpose; it may be published or unpublished. Published data includes any material that is widely disseminated, including the following:

- World Wide Web and other Internet resources

- Journal, magazine, and newspaper articles (*Note:* A *journal* is a scholarly periodical published by a professional association or a university, and a *magazine* is a commercial periodical published by a for-profit organization. Although the distinction is sometimes useful in evaluating secondary sources, the two terms are used interchangeably in this chapter to refer to any periodical publication.) These articles may be located in print format or may be retrieved from an electronic database.

CO3. **Evaluate the quality of data already available.**

Determine what questions must be answered to solve your report problem.

Dear Dr. Ober:

Hello. I am taking a business communication class in college using your book Contemporary Business Communication, and we have to write a business plan. The teacher says it is due in three weeks, but he did not explain how to do one. Do you have any suggestions? Please help because I need this class to graduate. Thank you so much.

—*Nancy G.*

Dear Nancy:

A quick search of Yahoo (at http://www.yahoo.com) or Google (at http://www.google.com) will turn up hundreds of useful sites to help guide you in thinking about, planning, and writing a business plan; and many of these sites contain complete sample plans, properly written and formatted. You'll find sites such as the following:

http://www.bplans.com/

http://www.businessplans.org/

http://www.sba.gov/starting_business/planning/basic.html

http://home3.americanexpress.com/smallbusiness/tool/biz_plan/index.asp

Cordial best wishes on your report project.

—Scot

E-mail your questions and comments to askober@ober.net.

Context in International Reports

Most business reports are written for a relatively homogeneous audience. However, in the international arena the reader and writer often have different cultural viewpoints. The greater the amount of knowledge, perceptions, and attitudes the reader and writer share (that is, the higher the *context* of the communication exchange), the less important it is for report writers to directly express *everything* they wish to communicate. Conversely, the less the reader and writer have in common, the more they need to convey every nuance of their meaning explicitly through words—that is, the less they can assume to be implicitly understood.

Contexting can be categorized as either high or low. When report writers have considerable knowledge and experience in common with their readers, their reports are generally *highly contexted*. In highly contexted reports, what the writer chooses *not* to put into words is still essential to understanding the actual message intended. But the writer assumes that what is not said is actually *already understood*.

When report writers rely relatively little on shared knowledge and experience, their report is *low contexted*. As a result, in low-context exchanges more information must be explicitly stated than in high-context ones. Thus,

low-context cultures tend to rely on *direct* communication; they often consider the indirect pattern a waste of time or a strain on the receiver's patience. High-context cultures, on the other hand, tend to rely on *indirect* communication to smooth over interpersonal differences and to keep from losing face in a conflict situation. They often consider directness rude and offensive.

To a large extent, contexting is a culturally learned behavior, with the degree of context varying from culture to culture. As shown below, Germans and German-speaking Swiss tend to be low-context cultures (all important information is explicitly stated), whereas the Japanese, Arabic, and Latin American people tend to be high-context cultures (much important information is implicitly assumed).

As Stella Ting-Toomey has noted, "In the HCC [high-context culture] system, what is not said is sometimes more important than what is said. In contrast, in the LCC [low-context culture] system, words represent truth and power."

Competent communicators ensure that the degree of explicitness, the amount of detail, and the assumptions built into their reports match the context expectations of their audience.[3]

Importance of Context in Different Cultures

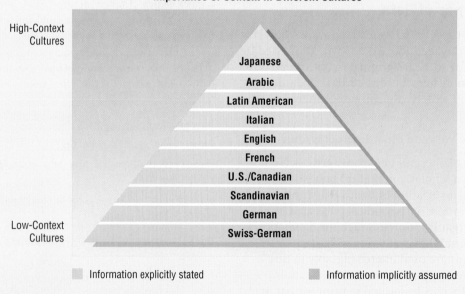

High-Context Cultures

Japanese
Arabic
Latin American
Italian
English
French
U.S./Canadian
Scandinavian
German
Swiss-German

Low-Context Cultures

Information explicitly stated   Information implicitly assumed

- Books

- Brochures and pamphlets

- Technical reports

Unpublished secondary data includes any material that is not widely disseminated, including the following:

- Company records (such as financial records, personnel data, and previous correspondence and reports)

- Legal documents (such as court records and minutes of regulatory hearings)

- Personal records (such as diaries, receipts, and checkbook registers)

- Medical records

Primary data is collected by the researcher to solve the specific problem at hand. Because you are collecting the data yourself, you have more control over its accuracy, completeness, objectivity, and relevance. The three main methods of primary data collection are surveys (questionnaires, interviews, and telephone inquiries), observation, and experimentation.

Although secondary and primary data are both important sources for business reports, we usually start our data collection by reviewing the data that is already available. Not all report situations require collecting new (primary) data, but it would be unusual to write a report that did not use some type of secondary data.

Studying what is already known about a topic and what remains to be learned makes the reporting process more efficient because the report writer can then concentrate scarce resources on generating new information rather than rediscovering existing information. Also, studying secondary data can provide sources for additional information, suggest methods of primary research, or give clues for questionnaire items—that is, provide guidance for primary research. For these reasons, our discussion of data collection first focuses on secondary sources.

Secondary data is neither better nor worse than primary data; it's simply *different*. The source of the data is not as important as its quality and its relevance for your particular purpose. The major advantages of using secondary data are economic: using secondary data is less costly and less time-consuming than collecting primary data. The disadvantages relate not only to the availability of sufficient secondary data but also to the quality of the data that is available. Never use any data before you have evaluated its appropriateness for the intended purpose.

Evaluating Secondary Data

By definition, secondary data was gathered for some purpose other than your particular report needs. Therefore, the categories used, the population sampled, and the analyses reported might not be appropriate for your use. In Chapter 3 we discussed guidelines for evaluating the quality of electronic data (see Checklist 3 on page 110). In addition, ask yourself the following questions about any secondary sources you're thinking about incorporating into your report.

What Was the Purpose of the Study?   If the study was undertaken to genuinely find the answer to a question or problem, you can have more confidence about the accuracy and objectivity of the results than if, for example, the study was undertaken

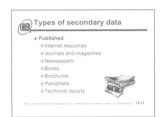

■ See Slides 10.12. and 10.13.

Nearly all reporting tasks use secondary data.

■ See Slide 10.14.

merely to prove a point. People seeking honest answers to honest questions are more likely to select their samples carefully, to ask clear and unbiased questions, and to analyze the data appropriately.

Be wary of secondary data if the researcher had a vested interest in the outcome of the study. For example, you would probably have more faith in a study extolling the merits of the Hubbard automobile that had been conducted by *Consumer Reports* than one conducted by Hubbard Motors, Inc.

> *Avoid using biased data in your report.*

How Was the Data Collected?
Were appropriate procedures used? Although you may not be an experienced researcher yourself, your reading of secondary data will likely alert you to certain standard research procedures that should be followed. For example, common sense should tell you that if you are interested in learning the reactions of all factory workers in your organization to a particular proposal, you would not gather data from just the newly hired workers. Likewise, if a questionnaire was sent to all the factory workers and only 10 percent responded, you would probably not be able to conclude that the opinions of these few respondents represented the views of all the workers.

How Was the Data Analyzed?
As we shall see in Chapter 11, different types of data lend themselves to different types of analyses. Sometimes the low number of responses to a particular question or ambiguity in the question itself prevents us from drawing any valid conclusions.

In some situations, even though the analysis was appropriate for the original study, it may not be appropriate for your particular purposes. For example, suppose you're interested in the reactions of teenagers and the only available secondary data used the category "younger than 21 years of age." You would not know whether the responses came mostly from those younger than 13 years old, those 13 to 19 years old (your target group), or those older than 19 years old.

> *Generally, the more consensus you find in secondary data, the more trustworthy the data.*

How Consistent Is the Data with That from Other Studies?
When you find the same general conclusions in several independent sources, you can have greater confidence in the data. On the other hand, if four studies of a particular topic reached

Knowledge-management software can help make sense of the abundance of information found in reports. David Gilmour founded Tacit Knowledge Systems, which makes software that automatically scans your documents to learn what you're interested in and then hooks you up with colleagues with similar interests. According to Gilmour, who pilots his own plane, "In most big companies, the left hand doesn't know what the right hand is doing."

one conclusion and a fifth study reached an opposite conclusion, you would need to scrutinize the fifth study carefully before accepting its findings.

Avoid accepting something as true simply because you read it in print or saw it on the Internet. Because the reader of your report will be making decisions based on the data you present, take care that the data in your report is accurate.

How Old Is the Data?   Data that was true at the time it was collected might or might not be true today. A job-satisfaction study completed at your organization last year may have yielded accurate data then. But if in the meantime your organization has merged with another company, moved its headquarters, or been torn by a strike, the job-satisfaction data may have no relevance today. On the other hand, some data may still be accurate years after its collection. For example, a thorough study of the origins of the labor movement in the United States may have almost permanent validity.

Your data must pass these five tests, whether it comes from company records or printed sources on the Internet. Data that fails even one of these tests should probably be discarded and not used in your report. At the very least, such data requires extra scrutiny and perhaps extra explanation in the report itself if you do choose to use it.

■ Managing Reports

Throughout this chapter we have made a strong case for the increasingly important role that business reports play in the successful management of the contemporary organization. However, too much of a good thing is a bad thing. Without proper management, reports—especially computer printouts—can backfire, becoming a nuisance and contributing to information overload.

With the increasing availability of data and the ease with which that data can be manipulated, copied, and distributed, managers sometimes tend to generate every type of report possible and then submit them all to higher-level management. Some managers seem to devote more energy to generating reports than to analyzing and making use of their contents.

Thus, someone in the organization—preferably someone in higher management—should be assigned the task of controlling reports. Periodically (typically, annually) this individual should make an inventory of all recurring reports and determine the continuing usefulness of each one. Some reports may be eliminated altogether, some modified, others merged, and, where justified, new reports authorized.

This review process will guarantee that business reports continue to serve management rather than the reverse. With or without such controls, all managers should ensure that the reports they write serve some actual purpose, stick to that purpose, and avoid including extraneous computer data just because it's easily available.

BY THE NUMBERS   *word*wise

- Forty is the only number that has its letters in alphabetical order.
- A *googol* is a 1 followed by 100 zeros.
- No number from one to nine hundred ninety-nine contains the letter a.
- The word *misunderstanding* contains at least 13 different words of 3 or more letters: *and, din, sun, tan, ding, erst, under, stand, sunder, standing, understand, understanding,* and *misunderstand.*

CO4. Discuss the need for managing reports in the organization.

■ In an effort to reduce information overload at AT&T, Victor A. Pelson, president of AT&T's General Markets Group, banned thick bound reports from offices and fancy slide shows from presentations. Because employees can digest only a limited amount of information, he wanted to be sure that they would be exposed only to information relevant to their jobs.

Ensure that all reports serve a specific purpose, that only needed information is included, and that all recipients actually need the report.

A PROJECT PROPOSAL

Problem

You and your colleagues who teach business communication at Valley State College are interested in setting up a business writer's hotline—a telephone and e-mail service that will provide answers to grammar, mechanics, and format questions from people who call in or write. You see it as a way of providing a much-needed service to local businesspeople, as well as a way of providing positive public relations for your institution.

Each faculty member is willing to donate time to answer the phones and e-mail, but you will need funds for telephone lines, answering machines, reference books, advertising, and the like. You decide to apply for a grant from the A. C. Reynolds Foundation to fund the project for one year. After that, if the hotline is successful, you will either reapply for funds or ask the Valley State College administration to fund the continuing costs. For requests of less than $3,000, the foundation requires a simple narrative report explaining and justifying the request.

Process

1. What is the background of the problem?

   Every writer has occasional questions about writing style but may not have a reference book or style manual available to answer the questions. We know there is a need for such a service because we frequently get calls from people on campus with these questions. Although several grammar hotlines operate nationally, none is available within a 200-mile radius of Portland.

2. What will be the outcome of the project?

   A telephone and e-mail service that will be available free of charge 24 hours a day to answer any question regarding business writing.

3. Describe the audience for this report and the implications for structuring your report.

   The A. C. Reynolds Foundation makes grants to nonprofit organizations in the Portland area, mostly for small projects of less than $10,000 each. Because of the foundation's small size and personal orientation, a direct and personal (rather than scholarly) writing style should be used. As there is no reason to expect that the foundation holds a negative attitude toward this project, the proposal will be written in a direct pattern—the request for funds will be made at the beginning of the report.

4. Describe how the hotline will work.

   a. Questions phoned in will be recorded on an answering machine. E-mail questions can, of course, be sent at any time.

   b. A separate phone line will be installed.

   c. The faculty will agree on which books should serve as the standards of reference.

   d. The faculty will attempt to answer any reasonable question about grammar, mechanics, format, and the like but will not review or edit anyone's writing and will not answer questions requiring extensive research.

5. What are the advantages of this project?

   a. Enhancing the college's reputation as an asset to the community.

   b. Providing a genuine service to business writers.

   c. Aiding business productivity by decreasing communication problems.

   d. Helping the business communication faculty members stay abreast of their fields.

6. What will the project cost?

   The faculty members will donate their time. Two copies of each of the reference books needed will cost $123.50. The telephone line will cost $61.30 monthly, and the long-distance charges for returning calls are estimated at $55 monthly. An answering machine costs $119.50. Monthly advertisements in the campus newspaper and in the local newspaper are estimated at $62.50.

7. What are the qualifications of those involved in this project?

   Each of the 12 faculty members has a doctoral degree and has taught business communication and related courses for an average of eight years.

Product

THE BUSINESS WRITER'S HOTLINE

A Proposal Submitted by Professor Steve Harland
Valley State College
March 15, 20—

All business writers have occasional questions about writing style. Indeed, the business communication faculty at Valley State College frequently receives calls asking questions about punctuation, subject-verb agreement, the correct format for business documents, and the like. Thus, the business communication faculty requests a grant of $2,388.60 to establish and operate a Business Writer's Hotline for one year to benefit students, faculty, and staff, as well as the Portland community in general.

OUTCOME OF THE PROJECT

The project will fund the operation of a Business Writer's Hotline in which faculty members answer telephone and e-mail inquires from business writers on the subject of grammar, mechanics, and format. The service will operate at no cost to users and will serve the following purposes:

1. Increase business productivity by lessening the chance that an error in writing will cause communication problems, delays, or even incorrect decisions.

2. Provide a service to business writers (including college students, faculty, staff, businesspeople, and the general community) who presently have no convenient way of getting their questions answered.

3. Enhance the college's reputation as an asset to the local community.

PROCEDURES

Questions may be phoned in or e-mailed at any time. Questions phoned in will be recorded on an answering machine. While the school is in session, questions will be answered by the end of the following business day.

A dedicated telephone line will be installed. Faculty consultants will attempt to answer any reasonable question regarding grammar, mechanics (including punctuation and spelling), document format, and the like. They will not review or edit

2

anyone's writing and will not be available to answer questions that require extensive research. Three books will serve as the standard references: *The Chicago Manual of Style, The Associated Press Stylebook and Libel Manual,* and the *American Heritage Dictionary.*

The hotline will begin operating the first day of the school year and will continue for one year. A small ad announcing the availability of the service will be placed monthly in the *Valley State Voice* and in the *Portland Herald.*

BUDGET

The following budget is projected for the first year of operation:

Purchase of two copies each of three reference books	$ 123.50
Purchase of one telephone-answering machine	119.50
Rental of one telephone line (12 mo. @ $61.30)	735.60
Long-distance charges (12 mo. estimated @ $55)	660.00
Newspaper advertisements (12 mo. @ 62.50)	750.00
Total	$ 2,388.60

PERSONNEL QUALIFICATIONS

Each of the 12 faculty members who will act as a voluntary consultant has a doctoral degree and an average of eight years of experience teaching business communication and related courses. Thus, they have had much experience in answering the types of questions likely to be encountered.

SUMMARY

The establishment of a Business Writer's Hotline will increase the communication skills of the local community. The recurring yearly cost of $2,145.60 is less than $10 per day and 40 cents per hour for the 45 weeks of 24-hour service. This cost is a small amount to pay for the benefits that will be provided.

Visit the **BusCom Online Learning Center** (at http://college.hmco.com) for additional resources to help you with this course and with your future career.

■ Summary

CO1. Describe the common types and purposes of business reports.

The most common types of reports are periodic reports (including routine management, compliance, and progress reports), proposals, policies and procedures, and situational reports. The purpose of each type of report may be either to inform, to analyze, or to recommend.

CO2. Analyze the audience for business reports.

Because the audience for a specific report is typically homogeneous, you should develop your report to take into account the reader's needs—in terms of level of knowledge and interest, internal versus external readers, and authorized versus voluntary reports.

CO3. Evaluate the quality of data already available.

Secondary data is collected by others for their own specific purposes. Therefore, the researcher who wants to use secondary data for his or her own study must first evaluate it in terms of why and how the data was collected, how it was analyzed, how consistent the data is with that found in other studies, and how old the data is.

CO4. Discuss the need for managing reports in the organization.

Reports can become a drain on the organization's resources if they are not controlled. Management should therefore periodically inventory and review all reports to ensure that only needed reports are being generated and distributed and that they contain the information needed to help solve problems and make decisions.

■ Consider treating this list as an end-of-chapter exercise for students to define and give an example of each term.

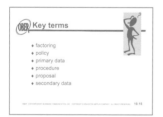

■ See Slide 10.15.

■ Suggestions and sample solutions for exercises appear in the *Instructor's Resource Manual.*

■ Key Terms

You should now be able to define the following terms in your own words and give an original example of each.

factoring (365)	procedure (355)
policy (355)	proposal (351)
primary data (367)	secondary data (365)

■ Exercises

1 **The 3Ps (Problem, Process, and Product) Model: Communication Applications at AstraZeneca.** As senior brand planning manager for AstraZeneca's cardiovascular drugs, Anne Cobuzzi writes reports to keep corporate executives informed, to support management decision making, and to obtain management guidance about a particular issue. Depending on the report's purpose, audience, and content, she will draft the body, ask colleagues for feedback, and, if needed, ask internal experts to draft additional sections.

Problem

Cobuzzi has asked you, the assistant brand planning manager, to draft a brief report for top AstraZeneca executives. She wants you to compare sales of your cardiovascular drugs for the first half of this year with sales during the same period last year. This data will help company executives monitor sales patterns and determine whether results are as expected. Your research shows that sales were much stronger in the first quarter of this year than in the first quarter of last year. You also find that this year's second-quarter sales were lower than last year's second-quarter sales. This year's pattern is atypical: for the past five years, sales of your drugs have been stronger in the second quarter than in the first quarter. You will need another two weeks to determine whether this year's sales were affected by changes in promotional activities, competition, or another cause. Cobuzzi wants you to draft your report now and mention that you will file a second report after researching all the details.

■ See Handout 10.2.

Process

a. What is the purpose of this report?
b. Describe your audience.
c. What points will you cover and in what order?
d. Which point(s) should you emphasize? Why?
e. Compose the specific headings for this report.
f. Draft an opening paragraph to introduce the report and bring the highlights to your readers' attention.

Product

Using your knowledge of reports, prepare a short report in memorandum format, inventing any reasonable data you need to complete this assignment.

2 The 3Ps (Problem, Process, and Product) Model: A Proposal—Starting a Student-Run Business

Problem

You are the president of the Hospitality Services Association, a campus organization made up of students planning careers in hotel and motel management, tourism, and the like. You've just received a copy of a memo from the provost at your university addressed to the presidents of all campus organizations. The university is seeking proposals from student organizations to run a part-time business, tentatively named University Hosts, which would provide local services and organize various events for campus visitors.

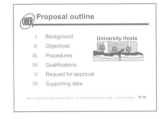

■ See Slide 10.16.

For example, when the admissions office lets University Hosts know that a prospective student and his or her family will be visiting the campus, UH would immediately contact the family and offer to provide any reasonable service to help campus visitors enjoy their stay and receive a favorable impression of the institution. The service would be aimed at potential students and their families, alumni, donors, prospective faculty and staff members, and visiting legislators.

You feel that HSA would be the most logical organization to run this enterprise for the university. Your executive council has authorized you to submit a proposal to the provost. Personnel time (to be supplied by student members of

HSA) would be billed at $15 per hour; a 10 percent surcharge would be added to the actual cost of all services provided (for example, tickets to campus or local events); automobile expenses would be billed at 22 cents per mile; and other charges would be billed at actual cost. Depending on the purpose of the campus visits, costs of the services would be billed either to the university or to the actual clients.

Process

a. What is the purpose of your report?
b. Describe your audience.
c. Is this a solicited or unsolicited proposal?
d. List the major advantages of this project and indicate how someone other than HSA will benefit from each advantage.
e. What costs are involved?
f. What qualifies HSA members to operate this business?
g. Will you request approval for this project at the beginning or end of your proposal? Why?
h. Compose an effective first sentence for your proposal.
i. What topics will you cover and in what order? Compose the specific headings for each topic.

Product

Prepare a three- to five-page typed proposal in memorandum format and submit it, along with your answers to the process questions, to your instructor. (You may invent any reasonable data needed.)

3 **Factoring Problems—Proposal Memo**   Write a proposal to your instructor seeking his or her approval of a topic and tentative content of an analytical report that could be prepared later in the semester. Submit the proposal as a one-page memo.

In the proposal identify what has happened in the past to create the problem, the purpose of the report, the scope of the report, how you would gather data (both primary data and secondary data) regarding the topic, and a plan of action for completing the report. Select appropriate headings to identify the problem statement, report purpose, report scope, data collection process, and report timeline.

co1. **Describe the common types and purposes of business reports.**

4 **Work-team Communication—Common Report Types**   Four types of business reports were identified in this chapter. Working in a group of three to five students, obtain a sample of three report types, perhaps from someone at the university or where you work. Analyze these reports for such factors as the following:

a. Purpose (to inform, analyze, or recommend)
b. Target audience
c. Length, format, and degree of formality
d. Clarity, completeness, and accuracy of the information
e. Authorship (individual or work-team)

Write a two-page memo report to your instructor summarizing your findings.

5 Progress Report—What Do You Already Know?   You are serving on a school hiring committee. The committee is planning to interview three candidates who are interested in teaching at your school. As part of the interview process, the candidates have been asked to teach a section of the business communication class. The topic to be taught is writing business reports.

One of the candidates has asked for a report on what the class has already covered during the semester so he knows what has been covered previously. As the only student on the committee who is currently taking the class, you have been asked to prepare a short progress report of what has been covered in the class during the semester. Write a two-page report summarizing the material covered in Chapters 1–9 of the book.

Submit the report to your instructor for evaluation.

6 Progress Report—Market Analysis   Your market research firm, National Collegiate Solutions, Inc. (NCSI), was recently hired by Archway Publications, a publisher of teen magazines. Edgar Martin, Archway's vice president of marketing, wants you to analyze the market for a proposed monthly magazine geared toward college students. As director of research for NCSI, you agreed to submit a progress report at the end of each month. It's April 30 (you started the project on April 5), so it's time to tell Martin what your firm has accomplished so far.

First, you developed an interview form to gather data on what college students like and dislike about the magazines currently available. After testing this interview form on 35 students to be sure the questions were clearly phrased, you made appropriate revisions and obtained Archway's approval of the final instrument. Then you began the lengthy process of conducting 50 face-to-face interviews on each of 12 campuses across the country. By April 29, you had scheduled and completed the 50 interviews on 3 campuses; you expect to schedule and complete the remainder of the interviews by June 1. All interviews are going according to schedule. You plan to submit a brief synopsis of your findings by June 6, and by June 20 you will submit a full report including conclusions and recommendations.

Using a letter format, write a progress report to Martin, whose company is located at 15097 Dana Avenue, Cincinnati, OH 45207.

7 Work-team Communication—Situational Report   You are one member of a four-student team that has volunteered to look into the advantages and disadvantages of extending the college library's hours the week before each long break and the final week of each term or semester. You have heard some students complain that the evening hours are too short; they would especially like to see the library open later during periods when most students are working on research papers, examinations, and projects. Of course, longer hours would have an effect on payroll, staff scheduling, and other aspects of the library's operation. Your team will examine the issues, report your findings, and suggest how the administration might proceed.

Team up with three other students to plan a situational report for your school's head of administrative services. Prepare a one- to two-page memo to your instructor indicating the purpose of your report, the audience, and the data that you will gather. Also list the issues you expect to examine. Will this situational report include recommendations? Why or why not?

8 **Procedure—Giving Directions**   As director of the student union at your institution, you frequently receive calls from for-profit and nonprofit organizations inquiring about reserving a room for special meetings. Sometimes these organizations want food service such as a meal or refreshments, sometimes they want a cash bar, and at other times they simply want an attractive meeting room. Of course, they're also interested in the cost, availability of parking, use of audiovisual equipment, deadlines, forms that need to be completed, and the like.

Prepare a procedure that can be distributed to inquirers that will answer their most frequent questions and that will take them through the reservation process from initial inquiry through paying the final bill (if there is one). Use the actual practices in effect at your institution. Decide on an effective format for the written procedure report.

9 **Policy—Using University Facilities**   Refer to Exercise 8. Assume that your institution is establishing a policy that only nonprofit organizations may reserve meeting rooms on campus and that reservations by any on-campus groups take precedence over those from off-campus groups. The reason for this policy is to avoid competing with local commercial establishments and to prevent overcrowding of campus facilities. Prepare a policy statement (University Policy No. 403) for the board of trustees to consider at its next meeting.

10 **Internet Activity**   In a group of three or four students, find and download a hard copy of a business report from the Internet. Try to get reports that are relatively short—fewer than 20 pages. Evaluate the report's effectiveness based on the principles covered in this chapter.

Answer the following question as you complete the evaluation: What type of report is it? What is the report's purpose? Who is the audience? Is the report formal or informal? Does it follow a direct or indirect plan? What are the report's strengths and weaknesses? How about content, spelling, grammar, punctuation, and other aspects of report writing? Does the report use primary and secondary data? Does the report appear to be written by one person or a group? What suggestions would you make to improve the quality of the report? Submit a memo to your instructor with your answers to the questions listed above and a copy of the report.

11 **Planning a Research Proposal**   If you were going to gather data to resolve each of the following problem situations, which factors would you consider to be the most important? Select at least three factors for each problem.

a. You are halfway through your college education and still undecided about what career path you should follow.
b. You are planning to get married in three months and need a place to live. You are wondering what considerations should be made in selecting the apartment.
c. You own a small convenience store. The store has been robbed twice in the last three months. You wonder what could be done to better protect against robberies.

CO2. **Analyze the audience for business reports.**

12 **Audience Analysis—Market Research**   Resume the role of director of research for National Collegiate Solutions, Inc. (see Exercise 6). Now that all the student

■ See Handout 10.3.

interviews have been completed and the data analyzed, you are planning the final report of your findings, conclusions, and recommendations. Analyze your audience for this report. Is the audience internal or external? Is this a solicited or unsolicited report? What is the level of interest of the reader? Should you use a formal or informal style? Will you use a memo, letter, or manuscript format for this report? What organizational plan is appropriate? Prepare a one- to two-page summary of your answers to these questions.

13 Evaluating Secondary Data—Looking Beyond the Numbers You're a summer intern in the Washington, D.C., office of Hillary Clinton, the junior U.S. senator from New York. You've been collecting data about high school and college graduation rates for a report recommending increased federal funding for loans and grants to high school graduates who go on to college. Unfortunately, you're not sure how strong a case you can make for this recommendation. During your research, you read an article in the *New York Times* citing research by Thomas G. Mortenson of Postsecondary Education Opportunity. This article indicated that New York has the second-highest college continuation rate in the nation (behind Massachusetts, which has the highest number of graduates continuing on to college). It also noted that New York has one of the country's lowest public high school graduation rates. In fact, only 61 percent of public school ninth-graders in New York stay long enough to graduate, compared with the U.S. average of 67.8 percent.

> **co3.** Evaluate the quality of data already available.

Step back and evaluate this secondary data. What questions should you ask about the study and the results? What conclusions can you draw, based on the statistics you read in this article? Does this research support your recommendation? Write a brief memo to the senator explaining your view of this research and describing how you think it should be discussed in your report.

14 Small Business—Reporting Needs Interview the owner/operator of a small business (with 10 to 50 employees) in your area. Determine the extent and types of reports written and received by employees in this firm. Write a memo report to your instructor summarizing your findings.

> **co4.** Discuss the need for managing reports in the organization.

15 Managing Reports—Large Business Interview the records manager at a large business in your area (personally or by phone). Determine what policies the organization follows to control reports, especially recurring reports, in terms of need, frequency, length, distribution, and the like. Write a memo to your instructor summarizing your findings.

16 Managing Reports—Procedures Managers are often uncertain about how to go about discontinuing a recurring report that doesn't seem to be needed anymore. When does a report become obsolete? For example, several departments or managers at several levels may be simply accustomed to seeing a given report, even if they no longer need it, but there may be one manager who actually needs and uses the information in the report. You decide to prepare a procedure that describes the steps to take before discontinuing a recurring report. Consider both the writer's and the readers' needs for information. What can you do before distributing your procedure statement to determine whether it is reasonable and appropriate?

continuing case 10

■ A suggested solution to the Continuing Case can be found in the *Instructor's Resource Manual*.

Urban Systems attempts to control photocopying costs by adopting appropriate policies and procedures.

■ See Handout 10.4.

The Copy Cat

Larry Haas has been surprised to learn when examining the quarterly departmental statements that photocopying costs have more than doubled from the previous quarter. In talking over the problem with others, he has learned that some workers photocopy nearly everything on their small departmental photocopier (there are five of these convenient, but relatively inefficient, copiers at headquarters) and other workers copy only small jobs on the departmental copiers and send larger jobs to the copy center, one of the departments managed by Eric Fox.

Jobs that are too big or too complicated for even the copy center to manage are sent to a local print shop. Some departments do the sending on their own; others rely on the copy center to do it. Regardless of where the copying is done, the individual department is charged for the job. From a company point of view, however, Larry is interested in ensuring that each job is completed in the most cost-effective way possible.

An additional problem that Larry has discovered is that the company's lax attitude about using the departmental photocopiers may have given the erroneous impression that employees have permission to photocopy personal documents. He has heard of numerous instances regarding the copying of personal insurance forms, recipes, sports stories, even kids' homework.

In speaking with the manager of the copy center, Larry learns that departmental copiers are designed for small jobs—no more than 30 copies of an original and no more than 20 originals per job. Any larger job should be sent to the copy center, which will decide whether to do the job in-house or send it outside. Generally, the in-house center handles one-color jobs on 8½-by-11-inch paper and up to 2,000 copies. Any job requiring more copies, more than one color, special binding, photographs, or the like is sent to the print shop.

Larry decides that a policy is needed on photocopying. Several specific procedures also need to be established to accomplish the legitimate photocopying efficiently.

Critical Thinking

1. Taking into account the absence of any formal organizational policy, what are the ethical implications of employees' copying personal insurance forms, recipes, sports stories, and the like on the office copier?

Writing Projects

2. Write a policy statement (General Guideline 72) on the topic of photocopying. You may assume any reasonable information needed.

3. Once a job is submitted to the copy center, a procedure must be in place for deciding whether it's an in-house or outside job. Write a procedure that covers the situation from when the job reaches the copy center until it is returned to the requester.

LABtest 10

Retype the following press release, correcting any word-usage problems according to the rules introduced in LAB 6 on page 603.

Unless you live in a glass house, you will need to throw

switches, because lighting up your life is ~~adviced~~ *advised* for safety and

vision. Depending on ~~it's~~ *its* function, lighting serves as general

illumination, task lighting, or accent lighting. ~~Irregardless,~~ *Regardless,* in a

5   ~~good~~-designed plan, all three types must interact. *well*

General illumination creates the ~~principle~~ *principal* seeing environment.

If you notice ~~any one~~ *anyone* groping around or tripping, if nobody

seems to want to be in a room, or if a ~~cite~~ *site* seems dull, then

~~you're~~ *your* general lighting probably needs improvement.

10 When it was installed, task lighting ~~should of~~ *should've* been glare-free

and directed to shine directly on the task area; ~~i.e.,~~ *e.g.,* reading

lamps should be aimed at the book, not at the reader. The reason

is ~~because~~ *that* task lighting prevents fatigue and eye strain.

In ~~passed~~ *past* years, a fixture hanging on a chain over the coffee

15 table was common. Today, these hanging lamps make a room look

gloomy and flat, so ~~its~~ *it's* important to be an informed consumer.

You can buy fluorescent lighting in colors that are close to

the ~~affect~~ *effect* of regular bulbs and that are easier on the eye than the

old fluorescent lights. ~~Try and~~ *Try to* avoid any kind of unshielded bare

20 light bulbs. When planning recessed lights, be ~~sure and~~ *sure to* give the

builder a sample fixture so he ~~may~~ *can* make the holes the correct size.

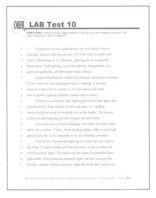

■ See Slides 10.17.–10.20.

■ See Handout 10.5.

Collecting and Analyzing Data

communication
OBJECTIVES

After you have finished this chapter, you should be able to

1. Develop an effective questionnaire and cover letter.

2. Conduct a data-gathering interview.

3. Construct clear, concise, and accurate tables.

4. Determine the most effective chart form and construct any needed charts.

5. Interpret the data for the report reader.

How can a nonprofit museum with a modest research budget and an ambitious mission collect and analyze data about half a million visitors yearly? If he could, Todd Mesek would like to survey everyone about the Rock and Roll Hall of Fame and Museum, which is dedicated to preserving the art form and showing its cultural significance in a fun way. The museum's exciting multimedia exhibits and educational programs celebrate the performers and personalities who have shaped rock and roll, such as recent inductees Prince and ZZ Top. As director of marketing and communications, Mesek is responsible for the museum's marketing, advertising, public relations, and website. He needs research to understand the public's view of the museum so management can determine how to allocate its resources most effectively.

an insider's perspective

TODD MESEK
Director of Marketing and Communications, Rock and Roll Hall of Fame and Museum (Cleveland, Ohio)

"Ideally, I would like to look at how the whole world sees us," Mesek says. "However, because of our resources, I have to focus on the people who come through our doors." Every year, he hires researchers to interview visitors and gather data about their demographics, satisfaction, and expectations. The museum also has experimented with interactive computer questionnaires, which visitors seem to enjoy. Another plus, says Mesek: "We suspect that people are more candid when they are facing a computer screen."

Other valuable sources of data are admission figures, museum shop sales, café sales, and customer complaints. Every complaint is logged, and if Mesek spots a consistent problem, he takes action. When preparing reports, he uses charts to help readers grasp the significance of the data. "I use bar graphs for age or basic demographic information," he explains. "When I want to show a trend or data movement over time, I use a line graph. Often, I use pie charts to show the origin of our visitors."

Where are the museum's visitors coming from? Staff members originally believed that approximately 40 percent of the visitors were local and that most out-of-town visitors were on day trips from nearby cities. Once the museum started asking visitors for their home zip codes and examined the annual survey results, a different picture emerged.

"I learned that more than 95 percent of our visitors were from out of town and about 10 percent were from outside the country," Mesek says. "The out-of-town audience is very different in terms of how they behave and how they approach the museum." Knowing this, the museum now invests more of its resources reaching out to potential visitors beyond Cleveland who want to see Eric Clapton's guitar and other artifacts of rock and roll.

"I use bar graphs for age or basic demographic information. When I want to show a trend or data movement over time, I use a line graph."

■ A chapter overview appears in the *Instructor's Resource Manual.*

CO1. Develop an effective questionnaire and cover letter.

Don't confuse the terms survey *and* questionnaire: *you* conduct *a survey by* administering *a questionnaire.*

■ See Slide 11.1.

The main disadvantage of surveys is a low response rate.

■ See Slides 11.2 and 11.3.

The question should not yield clues to the "correct" answer.

■ Collecting Data Through Questionnaires

Despite your best efforts, you will sometimes find that not enough high-quality secondary data is available to solve your problem. In such a situation, you will probably need to collect primary data.

A **survey** is a data-collection method that gathers information through questionnaires, telephone or e-mail inquiries, or interviews. The **questionnaire** (a written instrument containing questions designed to obtain information from the individual being surveyed) is the most frequently used method in business research. The researcher can economically get a representative sampling over a large geographical area. After all, it costs no more to mail a questionnaire across the country than across the street.

Also, the anonymity of a questionnaire increases the validity of some responses. Certain personal and economic data may be given more completely and honestly when the respondent remains unidentified. In addition, no interviewer is present to possibly bias the results. Finally, respondents can answer at a time convenient for them, which is not always the case with telephone or interview studies.

The big disadvantage of mail questionnaires is the low response rate, and those who do respond may not be representative (typical) of the population. Indeed, extensive research has shown that respondents tend to be better educated, have higher social status, are more intelligent, have higher need for social approval, and are more sociable than those who choose not to respond.[1] Thus, mail questionnaires should be used only under certain conditions:

■ *When the desired information can be provided easily and quickly.* Questionnaires should contain mostly yes-or-no questions, check-off alternatives, or one- to two-word fill-in responses. People tend not to complete questionnaires that call for lengthy or complex responses.

■ *When the target audience is homogeneous.* To ensure a high response rate, your study must interest the respondents and you must use language they understand. It is difficult to construct a questionnaire that would be clearly and uniformly understood by people with widely differing interests, education, and socioeconomic backgrounds.

■ *When sufficient time is available.* Three to four weeks is generally required from questionnaire mailing to final returns—including follow-ups of the nonrespondents. (E-mailing questionnaires, of course, requires less total time.) A telephone survey, on the other hand, can often be completed in one day.

Constructing the Questionnaire

Because the target audience's time is valuable, make sure that every question you ask is necessary—that it is essential to help you solve your problem and that you cannot acquire the information from other sources (such as through library or online research). Guidelines for constructing a questionnaire are provided in Checklist 13. Some of the more important points are illustrated in the following paragraphs.

Your language must be clear, precise, and understandable so that the questionnaire yields valid and reliable data. Moreover, each question must be neutral (unbiased). Consider the following question:

✓checklist 13

Content

✓ Do not ask for information that is easily available elsewhere.

✓ Have a purpose for each question. Make sure that all questions directly help you to solve your problem. Avoid asking for unimportant or merely "interesting" information.

✓ Use precise wording so that no question can possibly be misunderstood. Use clear, simple language, and define any term that may be unfamiliar to the respondent or that you are using in a special way.

✓ Use neutrally worded questions and deal with only one topic per question. Avoid loaded, leading, or multifaceted questions.

✓ Ensure that the response choices are both exhaustive and mutually exclusive (that is, that there is an appropriate response for every one and that there are no overlapping categories).

✓ Be especially careful about asking sensitive questions, such as information about age, salary, or morals. Consider using broad categories for such questions (instead of narrow, more specific categories).

✓ Pilot-test your questionnaire on a few people to ensure that all questions function as intended. Revise as needed.

Organization

✓ Arrange the questions in some logical order. Group together all questions that deal with a particular topic. If your questionnaire is long, divide it into sections.

✓ Arrange the alternatives for each question in some logical order—such as numerical, chronological, or alphabetical.

✓ Give the questionnaire a descriptive title, provide whatever directions are necessary, and include your name and return address somewhere on the questionnaire.

Format

✓ Use an easy-to-answer format. Check-off questions draw the most responses and are easiest to answer and tabulate. Use free-response items only when absolutely necessary.

✓ To increase the likelihood that your target audience will cooperate and take your study seriously, ensure that your questionnaire has a professional appearance:

■ Use a simple and attractive format, allowing for plenty of white (blank) space.

■ Ensure that the questionnaire is free from errors in grammar, spelling, and style.

■ Use a high-quality printer and make high-quality photocopies.

NOT: Do you think our company should open an on-site child-care center as a means of ensuring the welfare of our employees' small children?

  ___ yes
  ___ no

This wording of the question favors the "pro" side, thereby biasing the responses. A more neutral question is needed if valid responses are to result.

BUT: Which one of the following possible additional fringe benefits would you most prefer?

  ___ a dental insurance plan
  ___ an on-site child-care center
  ___ three personal-leave days annually
  ___ other (please specify: _____)

Questionnaire items *(cont'd)*

Unambiguous

Not: Do you think it takes a long time for the average start-up firm to secure financing?

But: How many months do you think it takes the average start-up company to secure financing?

11.4

■ See Slide 11.4.

■ See Slides 11.5 and 11.6.

Note several things about the revised question. First, it is more neutral than the original version; no "right" answer is apparent. Second, the alternatives are arranged in alphabetical order. To avoid possibly biasing the responses, always arrange the alternatives in some logical order—alphabetical, numerical, chronological, or the like.

Finally, note that an "other" category is provided; it always goes last and is accompanied by the request to "please specify." Suppose the one fringe benefit that the vast majority of employees really wanted most was for the company to increase its pension contributions. If the "other" category were missing, the researcher would never learn that important information. Ensure that your categories are *exhaustive* (that is, that they include all possible alternatives) by including an "other" category if necessary.

Also be certain that each question contains a single idea. Note the following question:

NOT: Our company should spend less money on advertising and more money on research and development.

      __ agree
      __ disagree

Suppose the respondent believes that the company should spend more (or less) money on advertising *and* on research and development? How is he or she supposed to answer? The solution is to put each of the two ideas in a separate question.

Finally, ensure that your categories are *mutually exclusive*—that is, that there are no overlapping categories.

Ask only one question in each item.

NOT: In your opinion, what is the major cause of high employee turnover?

      __ lack of air-conditioning
      __ noncompetitive financial package
      __ poor fringe benefits
      __ poor working conditions
      __ weak management

The problem with this item is that the "lack of air-conditioning" category overlaps with the "poor working conditions" category, and "noncompetitive financial package" overlaps with "poor fringe benefits." And all four of these probably overlap with "weak management." Such intermingling of categories will thoroughly confuse the respondent and yield unreliable survey results.

Recognize that respondents may be hesitant to answer sensitive questions (regarding age, salary, morals, and the like). Even worse, they may deliberately provide *inaccurate* responses. When it is necessary to gather such data, ensure that the respondent understands that the questionnaire is anonymous (by prominently discussing that fact in the cover letter). Respondents tend to be more cooperative in answering such questions when broad categories are used. Accurate estimates provided by broad categories are preferable to precise data that is incorrect.

■ See Handout 11.1.

Simply checking a broad range of figures might be less threatening than having to write in an exact figure.

NOT: What is your annual gross salary? $ _____

BUT: Please check the category that best describes your annual salary:

      __ Less than $25,000
      __ $25,000–$40,000
      __ $40,001–$70,000
      __ More than $70,000

Note that the use of the number "$40,001" in the third category is necessary to avoid overlap with the figure "$40,000" in the second category; remember that the categories must be mutually exclusive.

Even experienced researchers find it difficult to spot ambiguities or other problems in their own questionnaires. If time permits, administer the draft questionnaire to a small sample of potential respondents and then revise it as necessary. At a minimum, ask a colleague to edit your instrument with a critical eye. The sample questionnaire shown in Model 21 (on pages 388–389) illustrates a variety of question types, along with clear directions and efficient format.

Writing the Cover Letter

Unless you intend to distribute the questionnaires personally (in which case, you would be able to explain the purpose and procedures in person), include a cover letter like the one shown in Model 22 (on page 390) with your questionnaire. The cover letter should be written as a regular persuasive letter (see Chapter 8). Your job is to convince the reader that it's worth taking the time to complete the questionnaire.

■ Collecting Data Through Interviews

Personal interviews are generally considered to be the most valid method of survey research. In a personal interview, the interviewer can probe, ask for clarification, clear up any misunderstandings immediately, ensure that all questions are answered completely, and pursue unexpected avenues. Thus, data resulting from an interview is often of a higher quality than data resulting from a questionnaire.

Personal interviews are most appropriate when in-depth information is desired. The interview permits open-ended questions and gives the respondent free rein to answer as he or she desires. Respondents are likely to *say* more than they will write. Research into topics such as motives, deeply held feelings, and complex issues simply does not lend itself to the objective questions that are found in most questionnaires.

There are, however, several problems with interviews. First, interview research is expensive; it is time-consuming to schedule the interviews, conduct them, and analyze the subjective data that flows from them. Also, in-depth interviewing requires specially trained and experienced interviewers.

Second, the interviewer can consciously or unconsciously bias the results—by not recording the answers exactly, for instance, or showing a favorable or unfavorable reaction to a response, or hurrying through parts of the interview. Different interviewers may experience the same situation and "see" different things. Thus, analyzing interview data is often more difficult than analyzing questionnaire data. The subjective nature of the data given and of the data received affects the validity of the research.

Finally, a personal interview is not appropriate for eliciting information of a sensitive nature. Questions about age, salary, personal beliefs, and the like should generally not be used in face-to-face questioning where anonymity is not possible. (The alert interviewer can, however, sometimes get an estimate of these variables by carefully observing the interviewee and his or her environment.)

In most situations, the sample for a questionnaire study is selected so that each member is typical of the population. However, interviewees are often selected for just the opposite reason: they may have *unique* expertise or experiences to share, and the data they provide will serve as "expert testimony" and not be tabulated and generalized to the population.

CO2. **Conduct a data-gathering interview.**

Although expensive to conduct, personal interviews are most appropriate for gathering in-depth or complex data.

■ Advise students conducting interviews to give their subjects time to answer. Toby Fulwiler and Alan R. Hayakawa note in *The Blair Handbook* that while a brief silence might mean your question needs clarification, your interviewee might just be thinking over the question, considering a careful response.

model21

QUESTIONNAIRE

Uses a descriptive title.

Provides clear directions.

Note the variety of response formats used.

Uses check-off responses for Questions 1–3.

Uses fill-in-the-blank responses for Question 4.

Uses a qualification (branching) response for Question 6.

Lists alternatives in logical order (alphabetically, here).

Provides clear directions and an example for the complex response in Question 8.

---

1   # STUDENT USE OF COMPUTERS AT PCC

This survey is being conducted as part of a class research project. Please complete this questionnaire only if you (a) are a full-time junior or senior student at PCC, (b) attended PCC last semester, and (c) have declared a major.

A. DESCRIPTIVE INFORMATION

2   1. Grade level: 2. Gender: 3. Age:
          ___ junior   ___ female   ___ 20 or younger
          ___ senior   ___ male   ___ 21-24
                                                       ___ 25 or older

4. Are you pursuing a teaching or nonteaching major?
   ___ teaching *(Please write in the name of your major:* _____)
   ___ nonteaching *(Please write in the name of your major:* _____)

5. College where major is located:
   ___ Arts and Sciences
   ___ Business
   ___ Education
   ___ Other *(Please specify:* _____)

6. Did you use a computer in a PCC computer lab last semester?
   ___ yes   *(Please continue with Question 7.)*
   ___ no   *(Please disregard the following questions and return the questionnaire in the enclosed campus envelope to Matt Jones, 105 Woldt Hall.)*

B. EXTENT OF COMPUTER USE

7. Which on-campus computer labs were most convenient for completing your computer assignments? Please rank the labs from 1 (*most convenient*) to 4 (*least convenient*) by writing in the appropriate number in each blank. If you did not use a lab, leave that alternative blank.
   ___ business lab
   ___ dormitory lab
   ___ library lab
   ___ student center lab

3   8. Listed on the reverse side are different types of software. For each, first check the type of use you made of this software at any time during the previous semester. You may check both *Required* and *Personal* if appropriate. An example of personal use would be using a spreadsheet in a business assignment—if such use were not required. Then, if you used this software, check the total number of hours of use during the semester, including both in-class and out-of-class use.

Grammar and Mechanics Notes

1 Make the title and section heading stand out through the use of bold type and perhaps a larger font size.

2 If space is at a premium, you may group shorter questions on the same line (as in Questions 1–3).

3 Although not always possible (as illustrated here), try to avoid splitting a question between two pages.

model21

(CONTINUED)

8. *(continued)*

Software	Type of Use			Hrs. Used Per Semester		
	None	Required	Personal	<5	5-15	>15
Example: Games	__	__	✓	__	__	✓
Accounting/Financial	__	__	__	__	__	__
Database						
Educational/Tutorial	__	__	__	__	__	__
E-mail	__	__	__	__	__	__
Graphics/Presentation	__	__	__	__	__	__
Internet	__	__	__	__	__	__
Programming	__	__	__	__	__	__
Spreadsheet	__	__	__	__	__	__
Word Processing	__	__	__	__	__	__
Other *(Please specify:*						
_____)	__	__	__	__	__	__

4

C. OPINIONS

Please check whether you agree with, have no opinion about, or disagree with each of the following statements.

	Agree	No Opinion	Disagree
9. I am receiving adequate training in the use of computers and software.	__	__	__
10. I have to wait an unreasonable length of time to get onto a computer in the lab.	__	__	__
11. The computer labs at PCC are up to date.	__	__	__
12. Lab attendants are not very helpful.	__	__	__
13. Most instructors provide adequate instruction in the use of the software they require.	__	__	__

Uses attitude-scale responses for Questions 9–13, with both positive and negative statements.

D. IMPROVEMENTS NEEDED

5   14.   How could the university administration improve computer services at PCC?

_____

_____

_____

Thanks so much for your help. Please return the completed questionnaire in the enclosed campus envelope to Matt Jones, 105 Woldt Hall.

Places the open-ended question last.

Expresses appreciation and provides the name and address of the researcher.

Grammar and Mechanics Notes

4 Label different sections if the questionnaire is more than one or two pages long.

5 Provide sufficient space for the respondent to answer open-ended questions.

model22

QUESTIONNAIRE COVER LETTER

This cover letter would accompany the questionnaire shown in Model 21.

Begins with a short attention-getter.

Provides a smooth transition to the purpose of the letter.

Provides reasons for cooperating.

Makes the requested action easy to take.

PEACE COMMUNITY COLLEGE

P.O. BOX 0049   FAIRBANKS, ALASKA 99701

February 8, 20—

1   Dear Fellow Student:

"Oh no—not another computer project!"

Have you ever felt this way during the first day of class when the instructor makes course assignments? Or, instead, do you sometimes wonder, "Why is the instructor making us do this project manually when it would be so much easier to do on a
2   computer?"

Either way, here is your chance to provide the PCC administration with your views on student computer and software use at Peace Community College. This research project is a class project for BEOA 249 (Business Communication), and the results will be shared with Dr. Dan Rulong, vice president for academic computing.

3   If you are a full-time junior or senior student, attended PCC last semester, and have declared a major, please take five minutes to complete this questionnaire. Then simply return it by February 19 in the enclosed envelope. You'll be doing yourself and your fellow students a big favor.

Sincerely,

Matt Jones

Matt Jones, Project Leader
105 Woldt Hall

Enclosures

Training the mind.
body, and spirit

Grammar and Mechanics Notes

1 *Dear Fellow Student:* Use a generic salutation for form letters that are not individually prepared.

2 *on a computer?":* Position the question mark inside the closing quotation mark if the entire quoted matter is a question.

3 The word *questionnaire* contains two *n*'s and one *r*.

Types of Questions

In most ways, your interview questions should follow the guidelines given in Checklist 13 on page 385 for questionnaire items; they should be clear and unbiased and deal with only one topic per question. However, because of the increased complexity of many interview topics, you now have other choices to make.

Open-ended Versus Closed Questions   Open-ended questions allow the interviewee flexibility in responding, whereas closed questions limit the subject matter of the response:

Use both open-ended and closed questions.

Open: What is your opinion of the NAFTA treaty?

Closed: How much of your firm's business is attributable to Canadian or Mexican sales?

Open questions expose the interviewee's priorities and frame of reference and may uncover information that the interviewer may never have thought to ask about. Interviewees like open questions because they are easy to answer (there is no wrong answer), and they give recognition to the interviewee—by letting him or her talk through ideas while the interviewer listens intently. The drawbacks to open questions are that they are time-consuming and the responses may be rambling, difficult to record, and difficult to tabulate later.

Closed questions save time and are very useful when you know exactly what type of information you want, when you intend to tabulate the responses, and when the responses don't require elaborate explanation by the interviewee. The amount of interview information that can be obtained by closed questions, however, is fairly restricted. After all, if all your questions lend themselves to the closed format, a questionnaire would probably yield just as valid results for much less expense.

In actual practice, the interviewer usually uses both open and closed questions, often following up a closed question with an open one.

Closed: Do you agree or disagree with the proposal?

Open: Why?

Closed: Will it have any effect on your own firm?

Open: In what way?

Direct Versus Indirect Questions   Most questions may be asked directly. In threatening or sensitive situations, however, you may want to resort to indirect questions, which are less threatening because they let the interviewee camouflage his or her response.

■ See Slides 11.7–11.9.

Direct: How would you evaluate your boss's people skills?

Indirect: How do you think most people in this department would evaluate your boss's people skills?

Conducting the Interview

As an interviewer, you must wear two hats—that of an observer and that of a participant. You participate by asking questions, but you must also analyze the responses to ensure that the interviewee is indeed answering the question asked and

Listening in an interview involves much more than simply hearing what is being said.

Michael Dell, who at 38 years of age is the longest-serving CEO of a Fortune 500 company (he founded the company when he was 19 years old), is often interviewed by the business press. He admits to being shy. According to him, "My natural tendency is to be introverted, so when you see me in front of an audience, I'm really trying hard at it."

It is difficult to listen actively if you are busy taking notes.

to determine whether follow-up questions are needed. Fulfilling this dual role requires concentration, preparation, and flexibility.

To secure the greatest cooperation from interviewees, make them feel comfortable and important (they are!). The first few minutes of the interview are crucial for establishing rapport. Begin with a warm greeting; reintroduce yourself; and explain again the purpose of the interview, how the information will be used, and how much time will be required.

One of the barriers to effective listening during an interview is the need for note taking. Keep note taking to a minimum by using a small portable cassette recorder when possible. Always get permission first, assuring the interviewee that the purpose is to make certain that he or she is not misquoted and to let you give his or her responses your full attention. Keep the recorder out of sight (perhaps on the floor beside you) so that the interviewee is not constantly reminded that his or her remarks are being recorded. Test the recording level beforehand to ensure that the responses will be audible.

Always use an **interview guide**—a list of questions to ask, with suggested wording and possible follow-up questions. Mark off each question as it is asked and answered (don't assume that just because a question was asked, it was answered). Nothing is more embarrassing than repeating a question that has already been answered, and nothing is more frustrating than learning after the interview is over that you failed to ask an important question.

Provide smooth transitions when moving from topic to topic by using periodic summaries of what has been covered and previews of what will be covered next—for example,

> We've covered the start-up and initial funding for your firm. Next, I'd like to investigate any problems your firm experienced during its early years.

Follow up a point if the interviewee's response is inadequate in some way; for example, the interviewee may have consciously or unconsciously failed to answer all or part of a question, given inaccurate information, or given a response you did not understand completely. When the response needs amplification, you can probe by asking for more information, by asking for clarification, or simply by repeating the question.

Indicate when the interview is over—either by a direct statement or by such nonverbal gestures as putting your papers away or standing up. Experienced interviewers often end an interview by asking these two questions:

Is there some question you think I should have asked that I didn't ask? *(to uncover unexpected information)*

May I call you if I need to verify some information? *(to enable the checking of some fact or spelling or to ask a quick follow-up question)*

Leave the interviewee with a sense of accomplishment by quickly summarizing the important points you've gathered (to show that you've listened) or by restating how the information will be used. Finally, express appreciation once more for the time granted.

MARRIAGE NAMES   *word***wise**

If Dolly Parton married Salvador Dali, she'd be Dolly Dali.
If Bo Derek married Don Ho, she'd be Bo Ho.
If Ella Fitzgerald married Darth Vader, she'd be Ella Vader.
If Bea Arthur married Sting, she'd be Bea Sting.
If Tuesday Weld married Hal March III, she'd be Tuesday, March 3.
If Liv Ullman married Judge Lance Ito, then divorced him and married Jerry Mathers, she'd be Liv Ito Beaver.

Constructing Tables

At some point in the reporting process, you will have gathered enough data from your secondary and primary sources to enable you to solve your problem. (It is always possible, of course, that during data analysis and report writing you may find that you need additional information on a topic.)

CO3. Construct clear, concise, and accurate tables.

Tables are often the most economical way of presenting numerical data.

Your job at this point, then, is to convert your raw data, which might be represented by your notes, photocopies of journal articles, completed questionnaires, audiotapes of interviews, Internet and computer printouts, and the like, into *information*—meaningful facts, statistics, and conclusions—that will help the reader of your report make a decision. In addition to interpreting your findings in narrative form, you will also likely prepare some **visual aids**—tables, charts, photographs, or other graphic materials—to aid comprehension and add interest.

Data analysis is not a step that can be accomplished at one sitting. The more familiar you become with the data and the more you pore over it, the more different things you will see. Data analysis is usually the part of the report process that requires the most time as well as the most skill. The more insight you can provide the reader about the *meaning* of the data you've collected and presented, the more helpful your report will be.

Analysis and interpretation turn data into information.

A **table** is an orderly arrangement of data into columns and rows (see Model 23 on page 394). It represents the most basic form of statistical analysis and is useful for showing a large amount of numerical data in a small space. A table presents numerical data more efficiently and more interestingly than narrative text and provides more information than a graph, albeit with less visual impact. Because of its orderly arrangement of information into vertical columns and horizontal rows, a table also permits easy comparison of figures. However, trends are more obvious when presented in graphs.

Figure 11.1 shows a computer printout of an attitude-scale item (Question 9) on a questionnaire and the corresponding table constructed from this printout. Apex Company, a manufacturer of consumer products headquartered in Des Moines, Iowa, is considering building an addition to its factory there and wants to gauge local opinion before making a commitment.

Consider first the computer printout at the top of Figure 11.1 and the meaning of each column.

- *Value Label:* Shows the five alternatives given on the questionnaire.

- *Value:* Shows the code used to identify each of these five alternatives.

model 23

TABLE

Use tables to present a large amount of data clearly and concisely.

Table number and title

Subtitle (optional)

Column Headings

Body

Source (optional)

Footnote (optional)

the market leader for the past three years. As shown in Table 4, the Central Region led the company's sales force again in 2006.

1

2

3

4

Table 4. RECYCLED PAPER PRODUCTS				
Sales Through September 20				
Region	Year-to-Date Sales*		Percent Change	Goal Met?
	2006	2005		
Northeast	$ 20	17	15	No
Southeast	183	285	-56	No
Central	2,076	1,986	4	Yes
West	984	759	23	Yes
Totals	$3,263	3,047	7	No

Source: *Insurance Leaders DataQuest*, National Insurance Institute, New York, 2006, p. 663.

* Sales in thousands.

All regions but the Southeast experienced an increase in sales through September. According to Wanda Sánchez, regional manager, the main reason for the region's low performance during the past year was primarily the poor local economies in

Grammar and Mechanics Notes

1 Position the table below the first paragraph that makes reference to the table. Leave one to two blank lines before and after the table.

2 There is no one standard table format; the goal is readability and consistency.

3 Align all column headings horizontally at the bottom.

4 Align word columns at the left and number columns at the right.

Computer Printout

Q.9   "APEX COMPANY IS AN ASSET TO OUR COMMUNITY"

VALUE LABEL	VALUE	FREQ	PCT	VALID PCT	CUM PCT
Strongly agree	1	41	15.0	15.1	15.1
Agree	2	175	63.8	64.6	79.7
No opinion	3	34	12.4	12.6	92.3
Disagree	4	15	5.5	5.5	97.8
Strongly disagree	5	6	2.2	2.2	100.0
	•	3	1.1	MISSING	
TOTAL		274	100.0	100.0	100.0
VALID CASES	271	MISSING CASES 3			

figure11.1

From Computer Printout to Report Table

Corresponding Report Table

Table 4.   Response to Statement, "Apex Company is an asset to our community."

Response	No.	Pct.
Strongly agree	41	15
Agree	175	65
No opinion	34	13
Disagree	15	5
Strongly disagree	6	2
Total	**271**	**100**

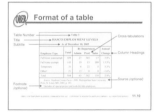

■ See Slide 11.10.

- *Freq:* Shows the number of respondents who checked each alternative.

- *Pct:* Shows the percentage of each response, based on the total number of respondents ($N = 274$), including those who left this particular item blank.

- *Valid Pct:* Shows the percentage of each response, based on the total number of respondents who actually answered this particular question ($N = 271$).

- *Cum Pct:* Shows the cumulative percentage—that is, the sum of this response plus those above it (for example, 79.7% of the respondents either agreed or strongly agreed with the statement).

The researcher must determine whether the "Pct" or "Valid Pct" column is more appropriate for the analysis. In most cases, the "Valid Pct" column, which ignores any blank responses, would be the one to choose. That is the case in Table 4, shown in the lower half of Figure 11.1.

Your reader must be able to understand each table on its own, without having to read the surrounding text. Thus, at a minimum, each table should contain a table number, a descriptive but concise title, column headings, and body (the items under each column heading). If you need footnotes to explain individual items within the table, put them immediately below the body of the table, not at the bottom of the page. Similarly, if the table is based on secondary data, type a source note below the body, giving the appropriate citation. Common abbreviations and symbols are acceptable in tables.

Cross-tabulation analysis enables you to look at two or more groups of data simultaneously.

Cross-Tabulation Analysis

In some cases, the simple question-by-question tabulation illustrated in Table 4 of Figure 11.1 would be sufficient analysis for the reader's purpose. However, in most cases, such simple tabulations would not yield all of the "secrets" the data holds. Most data can be further analyzed through **cross-tabulation,** a process by which two or more pieces of data are analyzed together. The table in Figure 11.2 shows not only the total responses (both the number and the percentages) but also the percentage responses for the subgroups according to marital status, sex, and age. A quick "eyeballing" of the table shows that there do not seem to be any major differences in the perceptions of married versus single respondents. However, there does seem to be a fairly sizable difference between male and female respondents: males have a much more positive view of the company than do females.

Sometimes tabular data needs to be condensed for easier and faster comprehension.

If the table in Figure 11.2 were one of only a few tables in your report, it would be just fine the way it is shown. However, suppose the statement "Apex Company is an asset to our community" is one of a dozen attitude items, each of which requires a similar table. It is probably too much to expect the reader to study a dozen similar tables; in such a situation, you should consider simplifying the table.

There are a number of ways to simplify a table. You should recognize right from the start, however, that whenever you simplify a table (that is, whenever you merge rows or columns or simply delete data), your table loses some of its detail. The goal is to gain more in comprehensibility than you lose in specificity. Your knowledge of the readers and their needs will help you determine how much detail to present.

With that in mind, consider the simplified version of this table shown in Figure 11.3. The two positive responses ("strongly agree" and "agree") have been combined into one "agree" row, as have the two negative responses. Combining not only simplifies the table but also prevents some possible interpretation problems. Given the original table in Figure 11.2, for example, would you consider the following statement to be accurate: "Less than half of the females agree that Apex Company is an asset to their community"? Technically, the statement is accurate, since the 46.3 percent who "agree" is *less* than half. However, the statement leaves an incorrect impression because more than half of the females (57 percent—those who "agree" *and* who "strongly agree") believe that Apex Company is an asset to their community. This conclusion is made clear in Figure 11.3.

Note also that the two center age groups ("21–35" and "36–50") have been combined into one age group ("21–50"). Because the company's products are geared mainly to this large age group, the company wanted to compare the responses of this important group with the responses of the less-important younger and older groups.

Two other changes help simplify the table. First, only percentages are provided, which eliminates the need for

figure 11.2   Cross-Tabulation Analysis

Table 4. Response to Statement, "Apex Company is an asset to our community."										
	Total		Marital Status		Sex		Age			
	Total	Pct.	Married	Single	Male	Female	Under 21	21–35	36–50	Over 50
Strongly agree	41	15.1%	14.0%	17.6%	15.7%	10.4%	21.7%	8.4%	12.0%	28.4%
Agree	175	64.6%	67.5%	58.8%	67.6%	46.3%	47.8%	65.1%	69.1%	61.0%
No opinion	34	12.6%	11.2%	15.4%	11.4%	20.9%	17.5%	13.0%	14.3%	9.2%
Disagree	15	5.5%	5.1%	5.5%	4.0%	13.4%	13.0%	8.4%	4.0%	0.7%
Strongly disagree	6	2.2%	2.2%	2.7%	1.3%	9.0%	0.0%	5.1%	0.6%	0.7%
Total	271	100.0%	100.0%	100.0%	100.0%	100.0%	100.0%	100.0%	100.0%	100.0%

the percentage sign after each number (interested readers can compute the raw numbers for themselves, since the sample size is shown in the table subtitle). Second, each percentage is rounded to its nearest whole—a practice recommended for most business reports when presenting percentages that total 100 percent.

More data is not always better than less data.

Follow these practices when rounding numbers:

- Any number with a decimal less than .50 gets rounded *down* to the next nearest whole number; any number with a decimal greater than .50 gets rounded *up*.

- Odd numbers with a decimal of exactly .50 get rounded *up;* even numbers with a decimal of exactly .50 get rounded *down.*

If the decimal is exactly 0.50, round to the nearest even number.

- If your table shows the total percentages and your rounding efforts result in totals that do not equal 100 percent (such as 99 percent or 101 percent), you have the option of either (1) showing the actual resulting totals or (2) readjusting one of the rounded numbers (the one that will cause the least distortion to the number) to "force" a 100 percent total. Thus, 86.4 percent, which would normally be rounded to 86 percent, might need to be rounded to 87 percent to force a 100 percent total. This practice is often used in business reports. You may also add a footnote to your table stating that your numbers are rounded.

This simplification of Table 4 has deleted two of the ten columns and two of the five rows—for a net decrease of 49 percent in the number of individual bits of data presented. When this reduction is multiplied by the number of similar tables in the report, the net effect is rather dramatic.

figure 11.3
Simplified Table

Table 4. Response to Statement "Apex Company is an asset to our community." (N = 271; all figures in percent)									
		Marital Status		Sex		Age			
	Total	Married	Single	Male	Female	Under 21	21–50	Over 50	
Agree	80	82	77	83	57	69	77	90	
No opinion	12	11	15	12	21	18	14	9	
Disagree	8	7	8	5	22	13	9	1	
Total	100	100	100	100	100	100	100	100	

figure 11.4

Arranging Data in Tables

Arrange the data in logical format—usually from high to low.

From This Survey Response:

6. In which of the following categories of clerical workers do you expect to hire additional workers within the next three years? (Check all that apply.)

211	bookkeepers and accounting clerks
31	computer operators
30	data-entry keyers
24	file clerks
247	general office clerks
78	receptionists and information clerks
323	secretaries/administrative assistants
7	statistical clerks
107	typists and word processors

To This Report Table:

TABLE 2.   COMPANIES PLANNING TO HIRE ADDITIONAL CLERICAL WORKERS, BY CATEGORY ($N = 326$)

Category	Pct.*
Secretaries/administrative assistants	99
General office clerks	76
Bookkeepers and accounting clerks	65
Typists and word processors	33
Receptionists and information clerks	24
Miscellaneous	28

*Answers total more than 100% because of multiple responses.

Arranging Data in Tables

As discussed earlier, the check-off alternatives in your questionnaire items should be arranged in some logical order, most often either numerical or alphabetical, to avoid possibly biasing the responses. Once you have the data in hand, however, it is often helpful to the reader if you rearrange the data from high to low.

In Figure 11.4, for example, the categories have been rearranged from their original *alphabetical* order in the questionnaire into *descending* order in the report table. Note also that the four smallest categories have been combined into a miscellaneous category, which always goes last, regardless of its size. Finally, note the position and format of the table footnote, which may be used to explain an entry in the table.

■ Preparing Charts

CO4. Determine the most effective chart form and construct any needed charts.

The appropriate use of well-designed charts and graphs (technically, *graphs* are shown on graph paper; however, the two terms are used interchangeably) can aid in reader comprehension, emphasize certain data, create interest, and save time and space because the reader can perceive immediately the essential meaning of large masses of statistical data.

Because of their visual impact, charts receive more emphasis than tables or narrative text. Therefore, you should save them for presenting information that is important and that can best be grasped visually—for example, when the overall picture is more important than the individual numbers. Also, recognize that the more charts your report contains, the less impact each individual chart will have. (Communication Snapshot 11 shows the number of charts included in annual reports for different countries.)

The cardinal rule for designing charts is to keep them simple. Trying to cram too much information into one chart will merely confuse the reader and lessen the impact of the graphic. Well-designed charts have only one interpretation, and that interpretation should be clear immediately; the reader shouldn't have to study the chart at length or refer to the surrounding text.

Regardless of their type, label all your charts as *figures,* and assign them consecutive numbers, separate from table numbers. Although tables are captioned at the top, charts may be captioned at the top or bottom. Charts used alone (for example, as an overhead transparency or slide) are typically captioned at the top. Charts preceded or followed by text or containing an explanatory paragraph are typically captioned at the bottom. As with tables, you may use commonly understood abbreviations.

Today, many microcomputer software programs are able to generate special charts automatically from data contained in spreadsheets or from data entered at the keyboard. The professional appearance and ready availability of such charts often make up for the loss of flexibility in designing graphics precisely to your wishes.

The main types of charts used in business reports and presentations are line charts, bar charts, and pie charts.

Keep charts simple. Immediate comprehension is the goal.

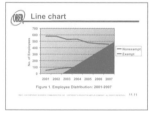

■ See Slide 11.11.

Line Charts

A **line chart** is a graph based on a grid of uniformly spaced horizontal and vertical lines. The vertical dimension represents values; the horizontal dimension represents time. Line charts are useful for showing changes in data over long periods of time and for emphasizing the movement of the data— the trends. (Model 24 on page 400 shows three kinds of line charts.) Both axes should be marked off at equal intervals and clearly labeled. The vertical axis should begin with zero, even when all the amounts are quite large. In some situations, it may be desirable to show a break in the intervals. Fluctuations of the line over time indicate variations in the trend; the distance of the line from the horizontal axis indicates quantity.

More than one variable may be plotted on the same chart (see Model 24A). For example, both sales and net profits can be plotted on one chart, using either different-colored lines or different types of lines (solid, dotted, and dashed, for example) to avoid confusion. Each line should be labeled clearly.

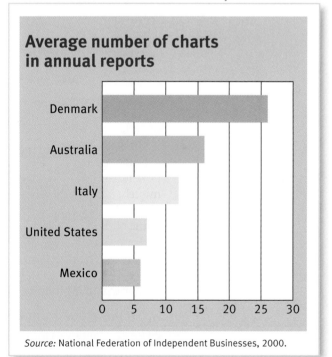

communication snapshot 11

Average number of charts in annual reports

Source: National Federation of Independent Businesses, 2000.

model24

LINE CHARTS

Source: "A Nation Online: How Americans Are Expanding Their Use of the Internet," National Telecommunications and Information Administration, n.d., retrieved from http://www.ntia.doc.gov/ntiamone/dn/ (December 21, 2004).

A. Simple Line Chart

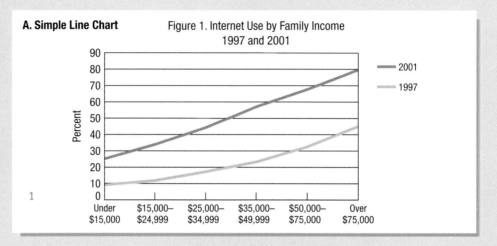

Figure 1. Internet Use by Family Income 1997 and 2001

1

B. Area Chart

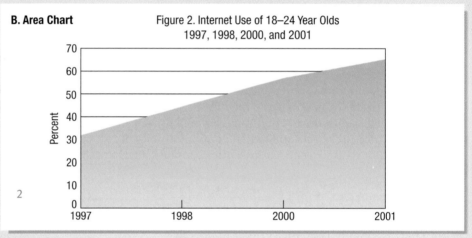

Figure 2. Internet Use of 18–24 Year Olds 1997, 1998, 2000, and 2001

2

C. Segmented Area Chart

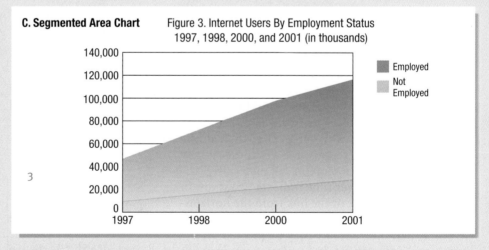

Figure 3. Internet Users By Employment Status 1997, 1998, 2000, and 2001 (in thousands)

3

Grammar and Mechanics Notes

1 Start the vertical axis at the zero point.

2 Use equal intervals for the time periods.

3 Clearly differentiate between two trend lines, and label each.

Visual aids extend far beyond PowerPoint slides. President Bush, Defense Secretary Donald Rumsfeld, and the U.S. military all use a universal-touch-screen remote panel, shown here, that allows the speaker not only to display slides but also to download satellite photos, online news articles, and even adjust camera angle and lighting.

A variation of the line chart is the area (or surface) chart, which uses shading to emphasize the overall picture of the trend (see Model 24B). A second variation is the segmented area chart, which contains several bands that depict the components of the total trend (see Model 24C). Because the individual components cannot be read accurately, the segmented area chart should be used only to give an overall picture.

Bar Charts

A **bar chart** is a graph with horizontal or vertical bars representing values. Bar charts are one of the most useful, simple, and popular graphic techniques. They are particularly appropriate for comparing the magnitude or size of items, either at a specified time or over a period of time (see Model 25 on page 402). The vertical bar chart (sometimes called a *column chart*) is typically used for portraying a time series when the emphasis is on the individual amounts rather than on the trends (see Model 25A).

The bars should all be the same width, with the length changing to reflect the value of each item. The spacing between the bars should generally be about half the width of the bars themselves.

Bars may be grouped to compare several variables over a period of time (see Model 25B) or may be stacked to show component parts of several variables (see Model 25C). As with tables, the bars should be arranged in some logical order. If space permits, include the actual value of each bar for quicker comprehension.

Bar charts compare the magnitude of items. Use vertical bars for comparing items over time.

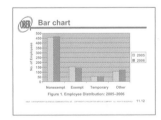

■ See Slide 11.12.

Pie Charts

A **pie chart** is a circle graph whose area is divided into component wedges (see Model 26 on page 403). It compares the relative parts that make up a whole. Some software charting programs permit you to "drag out" a particular wedge of the pie chart for special emphasis.

Although pie charts rank very high in popular appeal, graphics specialists hold them in somewhat lower esteem because of their lack of precision and because of the difficulty in differentiating more than a few categories and in comparing component values across several pie charts. However, pie charts are useful for showing how component

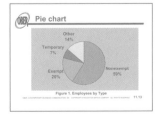

■ See Slide 11.13.

model25

BAR CHARTS

Source: "A Nation Online: How Americans Are Expanding Their Use of the Internet," National Telecommunications and Information Administration, n.d., retrieved from http://www.ntia.doc.gov/ntiamone/dn/ (December 21, 2004).

A. Vertical Bar Chart

1

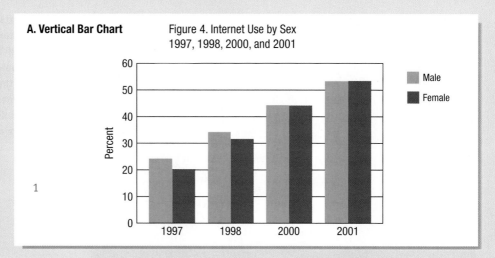

Figure 4. Internet Use by Sex 1997, 1998, 2000, and 2001

B. Horizontal Bar Chart

2

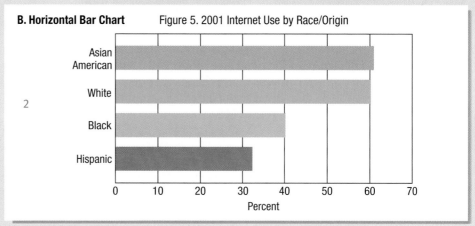

Figure 5. 2001 Internet Use by Race/Origin

C. Stacked Bar Chart

3

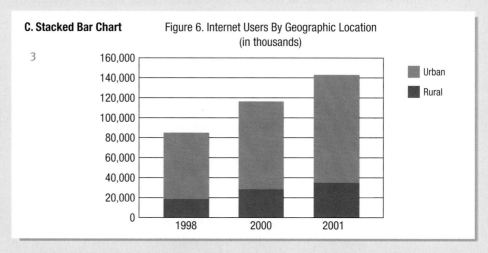

Figure 6. Internet Users By Geographic Location (in thousands)

Grammar and Mechanics Notes

1 Make all bars the same width; show value differences by varying the length or height.

2 Position the bars either vertically or horizontally.   3 Label all charts (regardless of type) as "figures"; place the figure number and title either above or below the chart.

A. Simple Pie Chart

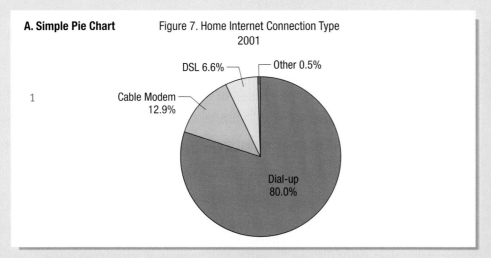

Figure 7. Home Internet Connection Type
2001

1

B. Three-Dimensional Pie Chart

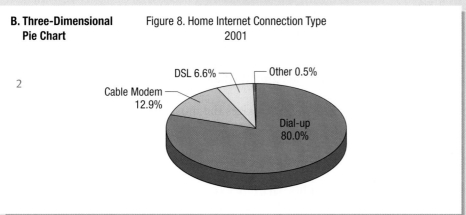

Figure 8. Home Internet Connection Type
2001

2

C. Three-Dimensional Exploded Pie Chart

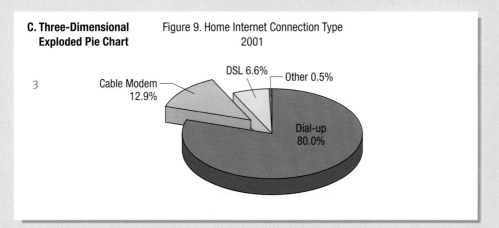

Figure 9. Home Internet Connection Type
2001

3

model26

PIE CHARTS

Source: "A Nation Online: How Americans Are Expanding Their Use of the Internet," National Telecommunications and Information Administration, n.d., retrieved from http://www.ntia.doc.gov/ntiamone/dn/ (December 21, 2004).

Grammar and Mechanics Notes

1 Begin slicing the pie at the 12 o'clock position and move clockwise in a logical order; the order here is by size.

2 Provide the percentage or other value shown by each wedge.

3 Generally use between three and five wedges.

As a rule, use between three and five components in a pie chart.

parts add up to make a total when the whole contains three to five component parts. A chart is generally not needed for presenting only two component parts; more than five or so can present visual difficulties in perceiving the relative value of each wedge.

It is customary to begin "slicing" the pie at the 12 o'clock position and move clockwise in some logical order (often in order of descending size). When used, a miscellaneous category goes last, regardless of its size. The labels should be placed either inside each wedge, directly opposite the wedge but outside the pie, or in a legend or key.

It is also customary to include the percentages or other values represented by each wedge and to distinguish each wedge by shading, cross-hatched lines, different colors, or some similar device.

Three-dimensional graphics, although attention grabbing, are difficult to interpret because they are often used to display only two-dimensional data (horizontal and vertical), with the third dimension (depth) having no significance. Similarly, three-dimensional pie charts, which are shown slanted away from the viewer rather than vertically, can be misleading because of perspective—the slices farthest away appear smaller than they actually are. Such graphics are effective for gaining attention and providing a general impression but are less effective for conveying the precise meanings needed in business communications. One recent laboratory experiment found that two-dimensional graphs communicated information more quickly and accurately than corresponding three-dimensional graphs.[2]

Checklist 14 on page 405 summarizes the most important points to consider when constructing tables and charts.

A Word of Caution

Do not overuse visual aids; they will detract from your message.

As the name *visual aids* implies, charts act as a *help*—not a substitute—for the narrative presentation and interpretation. Never use visual aids simply to make your report "look prettier."

Recent research indicates that the format of the data (tables versus graphs) has little effect on the quality of the decisions made when the task requires a thorough analysis of financial data; both formats are judged to be equally effective. Managers appear to have more confidence in their decisions when such decisions are based on data from tables alone as opposed to data from graphs alone, but managers have the most confidence when both formats are used.[3]

These research findings indicate that graphic devices should be used as an *adjunct* to textual and tabular presentations. Although most numerical data can be presented more efficiently in tables, the competent business communicator uses charts to call attention to particular findings. Rarely should the same data be presented in both tabular and graphic formats.

In *The Visual Display of Quantitative Information*, Edward Tufte warns against *chartjunk*—charts that call attention to themselves instead of to the information they contain.[4] With the ready availability and ease of use of computer graphics, the temptation might be to "overvisualize" your report. Avoid using too many, too large, too garish, or too complicated charts. If the impact is not immediate or if interpretations vary, the chart loses its effectiveness. As with all other aspects of the report project, the visual aids must contribute directly to telling your story more effectively. Avoid chartjunk; strive to *express*—not to *impress*.

■ See Handout 11.2.

✓checklist14

Visual Aids

Tables

✓ Use tables to present a large amount of numerical data in a small space and to permit easy comparisons of figures.

✓ Number tables consecutively and use concise but descriptive table titles and column headings.

✓ Ensure that the table is understandable by itself—without reference to the accompanying narrative.

✓ Arrange the rows of the table in some logical order (most often, in descending order).

✓ Combine smaller, less important categories into a miscellaneous category and put it last.

✓ Use cross-tabulation analysis to compare different subgroups.

✓ Use only as much detail as necessary; for example, rounding figures off to the nearest whole increases comprehension. Align decimals (if used) vertically on the decimal point.

✓ Use easily understood abbreviations and symbols as needed.

✓ Ensure that the units (dollars, percentages, or tons, for example) are identified clearly.

Charts

✓ Use charts only when they will help the reader interpret the data better—never just to make the report "look pretty."

✓ Label all charts as *figures*, and assign them consecutive numbers (separate from table numbers).

✓ Keep charts simple. Strive for a single, immediate, correct interpretation, and keep the reader's attention on the *data* in the chart rather than on the chart itself.

✓ Prefer two-dimensional charts; use three-dimensional charts only when generating interest is more important than precision.

✓ Use the most appropriate type of chart to achieve your objectives. Three of the most popular types of business charts are line, bar, and pie charts.

Line Charts: Use line charts to show changes in data over a period of time and to emphasize the movement of the data—the trends.

- Use the vertical axis to represent amount and the horizontal axis to represent time.

- Mark off both axes at equal intervals and clearly label them.

- Begin the vertical axis at zero; if necessary, use slash marks (//) to show a break in the interval.

- If you plot more than one variable on a chart, clearly distinguish between the lines and label each clearly.

Bar Charts: Use bar charts to compare the magnitude or relative size of items (rather than the trend), either at a specified time or over a period of time.

- Make all bars the same width; vary the length to reflect the value of each item.

- Arrange the bars in a logical order and clearly label each.

Pie Charts: Use pie charts to compare the relative parts that make up a whole.

- Begin slicing the pie at the 12 o'clock position, moving clockwise in a logical order.

- Label each wedge of the pie, indicate its value, and clearly differentiate the wedges.

■ Interpreting Data

CO5. Interpret the data for the report reader.

When analyzing the data, you must first determine whether the data does, in fact, solve your problem. It would make no sense to prepare elaborate tables and other visual aids if your data is irrelevant, incomplete, or inaccurate. To help yourself make this initial evaluation of your data, assume for the sake of simplicity that you have gathered only three bits of information—a paraphrase from a secondary source, a chart you developed, and a computer printout, labeled Findings A, B, and C, respectively (see Figure 11.5). Now, you are ready to analyze this data, using the following process:

1. Look at each piece of data in isolation (Step 1). If Finding A were the only piece of data you collected, what would it mean in terms of solving the problem? What conclusions, if any, could you draw from this one bit of data? Follow the same process for Findings B and C, examining each in isolation, without considering any other data.

2. Look at each piece of data in combination with the other bits (Step 2). For example, by itself Finding A might lead to one conclusion, but when viewed in conjunction with B and C, it might take on a different shade of meaning. In other words, does adding Findings B and C to your data pool *reinforce* your initial conclusion? If so, you can use stronger language in drawing your conclusion. Or does it *weaken* your initial conclusion? If so, you might wish to qualify your conclusion with less certain language or refrain from drawing any conclusion at all.

Determine the meaning of each finding by itself, in conjunction with each other finding, and in conjunction with all other findings.

3. Synthesize all the information you've collected (Step 3). When you consider all the facts and their relationships together, what do they mean? For example, if Findings A, B, and C all point in the same direction, you might be able to define a trend. More important, you must determine whether all the data taken together provide an accurate and complete answer to your problem statement. If so, you're then ready to begin the detailed analysis and presentation that will help the reader understand your findings. If not, you must backtrack and start the research process again.

figure 11.5 **The Three Steps in Interpreting Data**

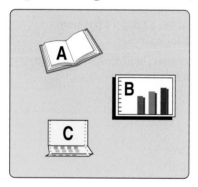

Step 1
Isolation

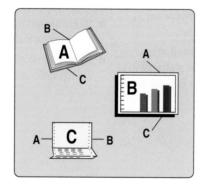

Step 2
Context

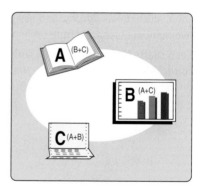

Step 3
Synthesis

Table 4. Response to Statement "Apex Company is an asset to our community."
(*N* = 271; all figures in %)

	Total	Marital Status		Sex		Age		
		Married	Single	Male	Female	Under 21	21–50	Over 50
Agree	80	82	77	83	57	69	77	90
No opinion	12	11	15	12	21	18	14	9
Disagree	8	7	8	5	22	13	9	1
Total	100	100	100	100	100	100	100	100

figure11.6

Simplified Table

Making Sense of the Data

As a report writer, you cannot simply present the raw data without interpreting it. The data in your tables and charts helps to solve a problem, and the report writer must make the connection between that data and the solution to the problem. In the report narrative, you need not discuss *all* the data in the tables and charts; that would be boring and insulting to the reader's intelligence. But you must determine what you think the important implications of your data are, and then you must identify and discuss them for the reader.

What types of important points do you look for? Almost always, the most important finding is the overall response to a question (rather than the responses of the cross-tabulation subgroups). And almost always the category within the question that receives the largest response is the most important point. So discuss this question and this category first. Let's take another look at Apex's Table 4 presented earlier in Figure 11.3 and above as Figure 11.6.

In Table 4, the major finding is this: four-fifths of the respondents believe that Apex Company is an asset to their community. Note that if you give the exact figure given in the table (here, 80 percent), you can use less precise language in the narrative— "four-fifths" in this case, or in other cases "one in four," "a slight majority," and the like. Doing so helps you avoid presenting facts and figures too quickly. Pace your analysis because the reader will not be able to comprehend data that is presented too quickly or in too concentrated a format.

Once you've discussed the overall finding, begin discussing the cross-tabulation data as necessary. Look for any of these features:

- Trends
- Unexpected findings
- Data that reinforces or contradicts other data
- Extreme values
- Data that raises questions

If these features are important, discuss them. In our example, there were no major differences in the responses by marital status, so you would probably not need to discuss them. However, you would need to discuss the big difference in responses between males and females. If possible, present data or draw any valid conclusions regarding the *reasons* for these differences.

Don't just present tables and figures. Interpret their important points.

■ According to philosopher Friedrich Nietzsche, "There are no facts, only interpretations."

At a minimum, discuss the overall response and any important cross-tab findings.

Everyone involved in the reporting situation has a responsibility to act in an ethical manner.

Finally, point out the trend that is evident with regard to age: the older the respondent, the more positive the response. If it's important enough, you might display this trend in a graph for more visual effect.

Sometimes you will want to include descriptive statistics (such as the mean, median, range, and standard deviation). At other times, the nature of your data will necessitate the use of inference (significance) testing—to determine whether the differences found in your sample data are also likely to exist in the general population. By now, you probably know more about the topic on which you're writing than the reader knows. Assist the reader, then, by pointing out the important implications, findings, and relationships of your data. Help your reader reach the same conclusions you have reached.

The Ethical Dimension

In gathering, analyzing, reporting, and disseminating data, everyone involved has both rights and obligations. For example, the researcher (1) has the right to expect that respondents will be truthful in their responses and (2) has an obligation not to deceive the respondent. Similarly, the organization that is paying for the research (1) has the right to expect that the researcher will provide valid and reliable information and (2) has an obligation not to misuse that data.

Emerging technology will no doubt provide even greater ethical dilemmas (see Spotlight 25, "When Is a Picture *Not* Worth a Thousand Words?"). If your research and corresponding report are to help solve problems and aid in decision making, all parties involved must use common sense, good judgment, goodwill, and an ethical mindset to make the project successful.

CROCK

spotlight25
ON LAW AND ETHICS

When Is a Picture *Not* Worth a Thousand Words?

"Seeing is believing" may no longer be the case. Granted, commercial photographers have long used the airbrush to touch up portraits, wedding scenes, and advertising layouts, but only recently has the technology to manipulate photos come to the desktop computer. Today, any computer user, with the appropriate software, can electronically alter photographs—even to the extent that they no longer reflect reality.

As an indication of the extent to which photographs can be manipulated, the cover of a *Texas Monthly* magazine showed former Texas governor Ann Richards in a computer-altered photograph. The head of Ms. Richards had been electronically superimposed on the body of a biker. And, as you can see below, for this Spotlight box the head of Marc Kaplan was put onto Dave's body. (The doctored photo is on the left; see also page 7.)

It does not take a wide stretch of the imagination to ponder the ethical dilemmas report writers may soon face. Suppose, as an adjunct to your report on the status of a building project, you use a digital camera to take a photo of the partially completed building. The digital camera stores the image directly on a compact disc rather than on film. You pop the CD into your personal computer and view the image on the screen. You notice that a worker is standing next to the building, providing a distraction. So you use your software to digitally remove the worker from the image. Then you notice that the sign on the building, which contained a typographical error, had not been fixed when you took the photo (it has since been corrected). Should you digitally correct it on the photo? How about changing the color of the building's exterior, which you plan to paint next week?

By allowing us to capture, store, and manipulate photographs, emerging computer technology is going to have an enormous impact on business communications.[5]

Doctored Photo

Actual Photo

The 3Ps
Problem, Process, Product

A QUESTIONNAIRE

You are Martha Halpern, assistant store manager for Just Pool Supplies, a small firm in San Antonio, Texas. You have been asked by Joe Cox, store owner, to determine the feasibility of expanding into the spa supply business. To help yourself determine whether there is a sufficient demand for spa (hot tub) supplies, you decide to develop and administer a short questionnaire to potential customers.

Process

1. What is the purpose of your questionnaire?

   To determine whether there are enough potential customers to make it profitable for us to expand into the spa supply business.

2. Who is your audience?

   The theoretical population for my study would be all spa owners in the San Antonio area. However, because our major business will still be pool supplies, I'll assume that most of my spa supply business would come from my present pool supply customers.

   Thus, the real population for my survey will be the approximately 1,500 existing customers that I have on my mailing list. I don't need to contact every customer, only a representative sample. I'll have my database program generate address labels for every fifth customer.

3. What information do you need from these customers?

   a. Whether they presently own a spa or intend to purchase one in the near future

   b. Where they typically purchase their spa supplies

   c. How much money they typically spend on spa supplies each year

   d. How satisfied they are with their suppliers

   e. What the likelihood is that they'd switch their spa supply business to us

   f. How many spa supply firms are located in the area

4. Is all this information necessary? Can any of it be secured elsewhere?

   I can probably determine the number of spa supply firms and their volume of business from secondary data or from the local chamber of commerce, so I won't need to address that question (3f) in my survey. All of the other information is needed and none of it can be obtained elsewhere.

5. Do any of these questions ask for sensitive information, or are any of them difficult to answer?

   No. The question asking about the amount of money spent on spa supplies depends a little on memory; because most people buy spa supplies only four or five times a year, however, respondents should be able to provide a fairly accurate estimate.

6. Is there any logical order to the questions in Item 3?

The question about spa ownership must come first, because respondents cannot answer the other questions unless they own a spa. In reviewing the other questions, I think the logical order appears to be a, c, b, d, and e.

7. Will the questionnaire require a cover letter?

Yes, because it will be mailed to the respondents, instead of being administered personally. I'll use my word processing program to generate a personalized form letter to each of the customers selected.

Product

Cover Letter

JUST POOL SUPPLIES

P.O. Box 2277 San Antonio, TX 78298
Phone: (512) 555-0083 Fax: (512) 555-2994

February 22, 20—

Mr. Frederic J. Diehl
Rio Rancho Estates
1876 Anderson Road
San Antonio, TX 79299

Dear Mr. Diehl:

We miss you during the winter!

Although you're a frequent shopper at Just Pool Supplies during the summer months when you're using your pool, we miss having the opportunity to serve you during the rest of the year. Therefore, we're considering adding a complete line of spa supplies to our inventory.

Would you please help us make this decision by answering the enclosed five questions and then returning this form to us in the enclosed stamped envelope.

Thanks for sharing your views with us. We look forward to seeing you during our traditional Pool Party Sale in March.

Sincerely,

Martha Halpern

Martha Halpern
Assistant Manager

swm
Enclosures

Questionnaire

SPA SUPPLIES

1. Do you presently own a spa?
   ___ yes
   ___ no (Please skip the remaining questions and return this form to us
         in the enclosed envelope.)

2. Considering the number of times you purchased spa supplies last year and
   the average amount of each purchase, how much do you estimate you spent
   on spa supplies last year (include all types of purchases—chemicals, accessories, decorative items, and the like).
   ___ less than $100
   ___ $100–$300
   ___ $301–$500
   ___ more than $500

3. Where did you purchase <u>most</u> of your spa supplies last year? (Please check
   only one.)
   ___ at a general-merchandise store (e.g., Kmart or Sears)
   ___ at a pool- or spa-supply store
   ___ from a mail-order firm
   ___ other (please specify: _____)

4. How satisfied were you with each of these factors at the store where you
   purchased most of your spa supplies?

Factor	Very Satisfied	Satisfied	Very Dissatisfied
Customer service	___	___	___
Hours of operation	___	___	___
Location of store	___	___	___
Prices	___	___	___
Quality of products	___	___	___
Quantity of products	___	___	___

5. If Just Pool Supplies were to sell spa supplies, how likely would you be to
   purchase most of your spa supplies there, assuming that the quality, selection, and pricing would be similar to those for its pool supplies?
   ___ very likely
   ___ somewhat likely
   ___ don't know
   ___ somewhat unlikely
   ___ very unlikely

*Thanks for your cooperation. Please return the completed questionnaire in the enclosed envelope
to Martha Halpern, Just Pool Supplies, P.O. Box 2277, San Antonio, TX 78298.*

Visit the **BusCom Online Learning Center** (at http://college.hmco.com) for additional resources to help you with this course and with your future career.

■ Summary

Primary data is collected by various survey methods, mainly questionnaires, telephone inquiries, and interviews. Mail questionnaires are an economical and convenient way to gather primary data when the desired information can be supplied easily and quickly. Care should be taken to ensure that all questions are necessary, clearly worded, complete, and unbiased. The questions and their alternatives should be organized in a logical order, the directions should be clear, and the overall format should be attractive and efficient. The cover letter should be a persuasive letter explaining why it is in the reader's interest to answer the survey.

CO1. Develop an effective questionnaire and cover letter.

Personal interviews are preferable to questionnaires when the information desired is complex or requires extensive explanation or elaboration. The interviewer must determine whether to use open-ended or closed questions and whether to use direct or indirect questions. The use of a cassette recorder will enable the interviewer to minimize note taking, thereby enabling him or her to listen more attentively.

CO2. Conduct a data-gathering interview.

Data is converted into information by careful analysis and is interpreted in the report in narrative form and by visual aids. Each table you construct from the data should be interpretable by itself, without reference to the text. Often you will want to analyze two or more fields of data together in the same table to help identify relationships. Include only as much data in a table as is helpful, keeping the table as simple as possible.

CO3. Construct clear, concise, and accurate tables.

Use well-designed line, bar, and pie charts to aid in reader comprehension, emphasize certain data, create interest, and save time and space. Avoid using too many, too large, too garish, or too complicated charts.

CO4. Determine the most effective chart form and construct any needed charts.

Arrange the data in logical order, most often in order of descending value. Do not analyze every figure from the table in your narrative. Instead, interpret the important points from the table, pointing out the major findings, trends, contradictions, and the like. Avoid misrepresenting your information. The competent reporter of business information is an ethical reporter of business information.

CO5. Interpret the data for the report reader.

■ Key Terms

You should be able to define the following terms in your own words and give an original example of each.

bar chart (401)

cross-tabulation (396)

interview guide (392)

line chart (399)

pie chart (401)

questionnaire (384)

survey (384)

table (393)

visual aids (393)

■ See Slide 11.14.

■ Consider treating this list as an end-of-chapter exercise for students to define and give an example of each term.

■ See Handout 11.3.

■ Suggestions and sample solutions for exercises appear in the *Instructor's Resource Manual.*

■ Exercises

1 **The 3Ps (Problem, Process, and Product) Model: Communication Applications at the Rock and Roll Hall of Fame and Museum**   Todd Mesek and his researchers are constantly collecting and interpreting information to support decisions about serving visitors to the Rock and Roll Hall of Fame and Museum. Mesek uses both personal interviews and interactive computer questionnaires to profile visitors, understand their needs, and gauge their satisfaction with the museum. Then Mesek presents the results in reports illustrated by informative charts to help management grasp the data's significance.

Problem

Imagine that Mesek asks you to develop a computer interactive questionnaire for gathering data about the museum's weekday visitors compared with weekend visitors. You will be researching the ratio of local visitors to out-of-town visitors; the age, gender, family status, and household income of visitors; and the most popular exhibits and programs. The results will help management identify any key differences between weekday and weekend visitors in preparation for planning appropriate marketing activities, exhibits, and programs.

Process

a. Brainstorm about possible questions. What specific information will each question uncover? What might the museum's management be able to do as a result of knowing the answer to each question?
b. Choose the most appropriate questions and arrange them in a logical order.
c. Edit the wording of each question for clarity. Is every question bias-free? Does each deal with only one element?
d. Consider how to format each question for the respondents' convenience in answering. Which questions should be open-ended and which should be closed?
e. Should you revise or eliminate some questions or change some formats to speed up the survey and encourage more respondents to participate?

Product

Using your knowledge of data collection and analysis, prepare, format, and proofread a suitable questionnaire. Submit your questionnaire and the answers to these process questions to your instructor.

CO1. Develop an effective questionnaire and cover letter.

2 **The 3Ps (Problem, Process, and Product) Model: A Questionnaire**

Problem

The dean of your school of business has asked you, as director of the Bureau of Business Research at your college, to survey typical businesses in your state that have hired your business graduates within the past five years. The purpose of the survey is to determine whether your business graduates have competent communication skills.

Process

a. Brainstorm for 10 minutes. List every possible question you might ask these businesses; don't worry at this point about the wording of the questions or their sequence.

b. Review your questions. Are all of them necessary? Can any of the information be secured elsewhere?

c. Edit your questions to ensure that they are clear and unbiased.

d. Arrange the questions in some logical order.

e. Where possible, format each question with check-off responses, arranging the responses in some logical order.

f. Do any of the questions ask for sensitive information, or are any of them difficult to answer? If so, how will you handle these questions?

g. What information other than the questions themselves should you include on the questionnaire?

h. Should you add a questionnaire cover letter?

Product

Draft, revise, format, and proofread your questionnaire. Submit both your questionnaire and your answers to the process questions to your instructor.

3 **Seafood Restaurant Survey**   As the marketing vice president of Piedmont Seafood Restaurants, you are considering opening a new restaurant in Ft. Collins, Colorado. You currently have 15 restaurants in surrounding states, and last year you opened a Piedmont in Denver. The Denver restaurant has been very successful, so you want to expand to other suitable areas.

To determine the suitability of a seafood restaurant in Ft. Collins, you are preparing a short survey to be completed by people living in the Ft. Collins area. Your restaurant features a full seafood menu with fresh seafood flown in daily. You are a full-service restaurant with a family-style atmosphere. Your prices range from $5.99 for a children's combo plate to $17.99 for your top-priced meal. Average price for a lunch or dinner would be $12.50.

Working with a partner, prepare a short questionnaire to be completed by the residents of Ft. Collins. You should have a title for your questionnaire and a brief introduction. Then ask six to ten appropriate questions that are clearly worded and unbiased. Put the questions in a logical sequence and make sure the options they are given are mutually exclusive and exhaustive. Submit the questionnaire to your instructor for evaluation.

4 **Seafood Restaurant Cover Letter**   Prepare a cover letter to introduce the questionnaire prepared for Exercise 3. The letter should encourage readers to complete the questionnaire and return it quickly in the stamped, addressed envelope. It should also lay some groundwork for establishing potential customers if the restaurant becomes a reality. If the demand is sufficient, a Piedmont Seafood Restaurant could be coming soon.

5 **Exhaustive and Mutually Exclusive**   You are planning to open an ice cream parlor. You want to have a wide variety of flavors for your patrons to select from, so you are going to ask potential customers to identify their favorite flavors of ice cream. (A) Write a question that presents an exhaustive list of ice cream flavors.

You also want to know how much people are willing to pay for a single scoop of ice cream and a double scoop of ice cream. (B) Prepare questions that list the various price ranges people would be willing to pay for a single scoop of ice cream and a double scoop of ice cream. Make sure the questions are exhaustive and mutually exclusive.

Finally, you want to know what other ice cream novelty items your store should offer. (C) Write a question that gathers this information. The question should be exhaustive, and it should follow a logical sequence.

Make sure the options for each question are listed in an appropriate order.

6 **Work-team Communication—Questionnaire**   Assume that you have been asked to write a report on the feasibility of opening a frozen yogurt store in your town. As the student body at your institution would provide a major source of potential customers for your yogurt store, you decide to survey the students to gather relevant data. Working in a group of four or five, develop a two-page questionnaire and a cover letter that you will mail to a sample of these students.

Ensure that the content and appearance of the questionnaire follow the guidelines given in Checklist 13 (page 385). Pilot-test your questionnaire and cover letter on a small sample of students; then revise it as necessary and submit it to your instructor.

7 **Online Surveys**   By creating your questionnaire so that it can be read and completed online, you'll save time and mailing expenses. Navigate to a free online survey site (such as http://freeonlinesurveys.com), and reformat the questionnaire you developed in Exercise 6 for administering online. Your instructor may ask you to actually administer this questionnaire online by e-mailing it to selected students.

co2. Conduct a data-gathering interview.

8 **Primary Data—Interview**   Refer to Exercise 6. You decide to get some firsthand information from the owner-manager of a premium ice cream or frozen yogurt store in your area (such as Dairy Queen, Baskin-Robbins, TCBY, or I Can't Believe It's Yogurt).

Think of the type of information he or she might be able to provide that would help you solve your research problem. Then prepare an interview guide, listing questions in a logical order and noting possible follow-up questions.

Schedule an interview with the owner-manager and conduct the interview, recording it on tape. Write up your findings in a one- or two-page memo report to your instructor. Retain your tape of the interview until after this assignment has been returned to you.

9 **Internet Exercise**   How does a well-known research firm handle interviews and questions? Gallup has been polling people about all kinds of issues since 1935. To learn more about its methodology, visit the FAQ (frequently asked questions) page of Gallup's website (at http://www.gallup.com//help/FAQs/poll1.asp). Scroll down to read about the interview, the questions, and interpreting the results. Compare Gallup's methodology with the guidelines in this chapter. Why does Gallup test the wording of some questions? Why does Gallup say that "public opinion on a given topic cannot be understood by using only a single poll question asked a single time"? Do you agree or disagree? Write one paragraph explaining and justifying your reaction.

10 **Constructing Tables**   Next year Broadway Productions will move its headquarters from Manhattan to Stamford, Connecticut, in the building where Tri-City Bank occupies the first floor. The bank hopes to secure many Broadway Productions employees as customers and has conducted a survey to determine their banking habits. The handwritten figures on the questionnaire in Figure 11.7 show the number of respondents who checked each alternative.

co3. **Construct clear, concise, and accurate tables.**

figure11.7

Survey Results

BROADWAY PRODUCTIONS SURVEY

1. Do you currently have an account at Tri-City Bank?
    _58_ yes
    _170_ no

2. At which of the following institutions do you currently have an account?
    (Please check all that apply.)
    _201_ commercial bank
    _52_ employee credit union
    _75_ savings and loan association
    _6_ other (please specify: _____)
    _18_ none

3. In terms of convenience, which one of the following bank locations do you consider most important in selecting your main bank?
    _70_ near home
    _102_ near office
    _12_ near shopping
    _31_ on way to and from work
    _13_ other (please specify: _____)

4. How important do you consider each of the following banking services?

	Very Important	Somewhat Important	Not Important
Bank credit card	88	132	8
Check-guarantee card	74	32	122
Convenient ATM machines	143	56	29
Drive-in service	148	47	33
Free checking	219	9	0
Overdraft privileges	20	187	21
Personal banker	40	32	156
Telephone transfer	6	20	202
Trust department	13	45	170

5. If you have changed banks within the past three years, what was the major reason for the change?
    _33_ relocation of residence
    _4_ relocation of bank
    _18_ dissatisfaction with bank service
    _7_ other (please specify: _____)

Thank you so much for your cooperation. Please return this questionnaire in the enclosed envelope to Customer Service Department, Tri-City Bank, P.O. Box 1086, Stamford, CT 06902.

a. Is a table needed to present the information in Question 1?

b. Would any cross-tabulation analyses help readers understand the data in this questionnaire? Explain.

c. Construct a table that presents the important information from Question 4 of the questionnaire in a logical, helpful, and efficient manner. Give the table an appropriate title and arrange it in final report format.

co4. **Determine the most effective chart form and construct any needed charts.**

11 **What Color Is Your M&M?**   According to Mars, Inc., each bag of M&Ms should contain the percentage of colors shown in Figure 11.8. Purchase five small bags of M&Ms and separate the M&Ms in each bag by color. Compare your percentage of occurrence of colors to that shown as the M&M standard. Create a chart showing the comparison.

12 **Visual Aids in Business Articles**   Find three or more visual aids in business articles from newspapers or magazines. Make a copy of each visual and the written information associated with it. Evaluate the visual aids based on the principles presented in this chapter. What are the strengths and weaknesses of each visual? What changes, if any, should be made to the visuals to make them more understandable and helpful? Submit a copy of each article and your evaluation of the visual aid's effectiveness to your instructor for evaluation.

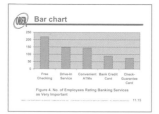

■ See Slide 11.15.

13 **Constructing Charts**   Refer to Exercise 10. You decide to use a chart rather than a table to convey the data in Question 4 of the questionnaire.

a. Can you use a line chart to present the data? Why or why not? If a line chart is appropriate, construct it and label the vertical and horizontal axes.

b. Can you use a bar chart to present the data? Why or why not? If a bar chart is appropriate, construct it, arranging the bars in a logical order and clearly labeling each bar as well as the vertical axis.

c. Can you use a pie chart to present the data? Why or why not? If a pie chart is appropriate, construct it, label each wedge, and clearly differentiate the wedges.

14 **Which Visual Is Best?**   For the following situations select the most appropriate visual aid for presenting the data, and explain why it is the best option.

figure11.8
M&M Color Breakdown

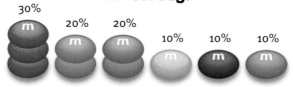

What Colors Come in Your Bag?

30%   20%   20%   10%   10%   10%

"M&M's"® Milk Chocolate Candies Color Chart
Source: http://global.mms.com/us/about/products/milkchocolate.jsp.

a. To show the daily sales for your small computer business.

b. To show the proportion of your budget spent on each of the four fixed costs for your company during the year.

c. To show the results of six survey questions asking people's opinion regarding the economy.

d. To show the comparisons of the first quarter's net sales for departments A, B, and C.

e. To show the locations of your international offices.

f. To show total sales by region and the percent of increase or decrease from the previous year

g. To show the average annual rainfall in selected cities in the nation.

15 **Constructing Charts**   Refer to Exercise 10. You want to construct a visual aid to emphasize the proportion of respondents who have changed banks within the past three years. Calculate this percentage using the survey results shown in Figure 11.7. Decide which type of chart would most effectively convey this information. Then construct the chart, using appropriate values and helpful labels.

16 **Making Sense of Data**   As a marriage counselor, you have gathered the following statistics.

- The average age at which women marry for the first time has increased by 1.5 years in the last decade.

- The average age at which men marry for the first time has increased by 2.5 years in the last decade.

- The number of people getting married for the first time has dropped by 13 percent in the last decade.

- The number of divorces has increased by 22 percent in the last decade.

- The average number of years couples remain married has decreased by 2.8 years in the last decade.

- The number of people who were divorced more than once has increased 26 percent in the last decade.

- The number of women between the ages of 20 and 50 entering the workforce has increased by 12 percent in the last decade.

- The number of men between the ages of 20 and 50 entering the workforce has decreased by 8 percent.

- The amount of debt for married couples has increased by more than 31 percent (an all-time high) during the last decade.

This is a lot of data, but what does it all mean? In groups of five or six people, discuss possible answers to the following questions: What trends can be identified in the data? What could the trends mean? How do the pieces of data relate to each other? Could one factor be causing another? If so, which ones? Before drawing any conclusions, what additional information would be helpful? What kind of visual aid would be best for showing these changes in the last decade?

CO5. **Interpret the data for the report reader.**

17 **Interpreting Data**   Give a one- or two-sentence interpretation of the data for each of the five questions shown in Figure 11.7 (page 417). Assume you need to present the important information from this questionnaire in one paragraph of no more than 50 or 60 words. Compose this summary paragraph.

18 **Misrepresenting Data—Interpreting a Table**   The following sentences interpret the table in Figure 11.6 on page 407. Analyze each sentence to determine whether it represents the data in the table accurately.

a. Males and females alike believe Apex is an asset to the community.
b. More than one-fifth of the females (22 percent) did not respond.
c. Age and the generation gap bring about different beliefs.
d. Married males over age 50 had the most positive opinions.
e. Females disagree more than males—probably because most of the workers at Apex are male.
f. Female respondents tend to disagree with the statement.
g. Apex should be proud of the fact that four-fifths of the residents believe the company is an asset to the community.
h. Thirteen percent of the younger residents have doubts about whether Apex is an asset to the community.
i. More single than married residents didn't care or had no opinion about the topic.
j. Overall, the residents believe that 8 percent of the company is not an asset to the community.

19 **Misrepresenting Data—Use of Statistics**   Politicians, businesspeople, and others love to quote statistics to support their viewpoints. Locate three news stories in which someone quotes statistics to support a particular case. Then find an unbiased source that either confirms or refutes those statistics. Write a memo to your instructor discussing your findings. Include a photocopy of both the original news articles and your supporting statistics.

The Keyboard Strikes Back

The manufacturing facility in Charlotte employs three data-entry operators who work full-time keyboarding production, personnel, and inventory data into a terminal. This data is then sent over telephone lines to the Urban Systems minicomputer, where it becomes part of the corporate database for financial, production, and personnel management.

As required by the labor agreement, in addition to a one-hour lunch period, these three operators receive two 15-minute breaks daily; they may take them at any convenient time, once in the morning and once in the afternoon. Otherwise, they generally work at their keyboards all day.

Last year, Arlene Berkowitz, one of the operators, was absent from work for two weeks for a condition diagnosed as carpal tunnel syndrome, a neuromuscular disorder of the tendons and tissue in the wrists caused by repeated hand motions. Her symptoms included a dull ache in the wrist and excruciating pain in the shoulder and neck. Her doctor treated her with anti-inflammatory medicine and a cortisone injection, and she has had no further problems. However, just last week a second data-entry operator experienced similar symptoms; her doctor diagnosed her ailment as

■ A suggested solution to the Continuing Case can be found in the *Instructor's Resource Manual.*

Increasing automation requires contemporary companies like Urban Systems to address such ergonomic issues as carpal tunnel syndrome. Here, Arlene Berkowitz, a data-entry operator, wears wrist splints to ease the pain of this disability.

"repeated-motion illness" or RSI (repetitive stress injury) and referred to it informally as the "VDT (video display terminal) disease."

Because the company anticipates further automation in the future, with more data-entry operators to be hired, Jean Tate asked her assistant, Pat Robbins, to gather additional information on this condition. In fact, Jean wants Pat to survey all workers at US who use a computer to determine the type and degree of their use and to identify any related health problems. Once the extent of the problem is known, she wants Pat to make any appropriate recommendations regarding the work environment—posture, furniture, work habits, rest breaks, and the like—that will alleviate this problem.

Critical Thinking

1. Assume the role of Pat Robbins. Define the problem of the report and then identify the component subparts (that is, *factor* the problem).

2. What are the ethical implications of this case?

Writing Projects

3. Search the appropriate sources and identify five relevant journal articles and five Internet resources on this topic. Photocopy or download each article and save the articles for a future assignment. Evaluate each article using the criteria given in this chapter; write a one-paragraph summary of your *evaluation* of each article. Make notes of these articles.

4. Develop an employee questionnaire that elicits the information requested by Jean, plus whatever additional information you believe would be helpful, based on your reading of the journal articles and Internet sources you located. In lieu of a cover letter, include a short introductory paragraph at the top of the questionnaire explaining the purpose of the study and giving any needed directions.

LABtest 11

Retype the following news item, correcting any grammar and mechanics errors according to the rules introduced in LABs 2–6 beginning on page 576.

    Not too many years ago, computers were something of an of-

novelty. Most (RUN-ON)

fice ~~novelty, most~~ office workers then performed one major visual

task:^(EXP)

~~task~~ the reading of black characters printed on white paper laid

flat or nearly flat on a desk.

their (WORD)

5   Office workers now spend ~~there~~ days looking into a monitor

whose (WORD)

~~who's~~ screen is almost perpendicular to the desk. Some screens
^

still display low-contrast green characters on a dark background.

easier, faster, (SER)

The higher the contrast, the ~~easier faster~~ and more accurately a

his or her ^ (AGR)

worker can perform ~~their~~ visual tasks.
^

building's (SING. POSS.)

10   While the electric illumination produced by a ~~buildings~~

tasks, (INTRO) ^it (AGR)

system may be ideal for performing paper ~~tasks they~~ could create

conditions inappropriate for computer-based tasks. Managers must

has (AGR)   qualities, (IND)

recognize that office lighting ~~have~~ many ~~qualities~~ but the dif-
^   ^

ferences aren't apparent in a cursory survey of the work area.

discomfort, which (FRAG)

15   Glare creates visual ~~discomfort.Which~~ is often subtle, due

eyes' (PLUR POSS.) ^   accept (WORD) relatively poor (ADJ)

to your ~~eyes~~ amazing ability to ~~except relatively-poor~~ viewing
^   ^

cause (AGR)

conditions. Tiny ocular muscles react to lighting and ~~causes~~ the

Long-term (COMP)

eyes to adapt, minimizing viewing problems. ~~Long term~~ viewing

problems, however, (TRAN)

~~problems however~~ cause these muscles to become strained. These
^

hospitable (NO COMMA)

20   conditions can make the workplace far less ~~hospitable,~~ and can

effect (WORD)   ^morale (SPELL)

have a damaging ~~affect~~ on productivity and ~~moral~~. In addition, a

1 percent (NO.-FIGURE) $1 million (NO.-FIGURE)

productivity loss of ~~one percent~~ in a payroll of ~~$1,000,000.00~~
^   ^

^$10,000 (NO.-FIGURE)

costs the company ~~$10000~~ annually.
^

■ Handout 11.4.

■ See Slides 11.16–11.19.

12

Writing the Report

When Steve Messinetti writes a report, he wants to do more than simply inform, analyze, or recommend—he also wants to touch his readers in a very personal way. Messinetti is the director of campus chapters and youth programs at the Americus, Georgia, headquarters of Habitat for Humanity International, a nonprofit, ecumenical organization dedicated to eliminating poverty housing throughout the world. Through the efforts of 1,916 local affiliates and millions of volunteers, Habitat has built more than 80,000 homes in 64 countries. Messinetti and his staff coordinate special events and training for more than 600 high school and college chapters as well as programs for younger groups.

an insider's perspective

STEVE MESSINETTI
Director, Campus Chapters and Youth Programs Habitat for Humanity International

Messinetti writes a variety of reports, including periodical management reports, progress reports, proposals for new programs, and one-time reports about special events. Whether writing for internal or external audiences, he brings his reports to life by including photos and quotes that capture the feelings of program participants. "We're not writing reports just to give the information," he explains. "Our readers are less interested in the statistics and more interested in what the facts really mean. So our reports are more personal because we show the emotions brought out by our programs and show how lives were affected."

Reports written for senior Habitat leaders and other internal audiences also provide an opportunity to strengthen the connections between Messinetti's department and other departments. "We are constantly looking for ways to spread the vision of student involvement to other departments," he says. "A report can get other departments think-ing about how their day-to-day work affects student involvement in Habitat. This is an internal sales pitch."

One of Messinetti's longer reports summarizes the results of Habitat's Spring Break Collegiate Challenge, an annual event in which college students volunteer to work on Habitat homes. This 15-page report opens with a transmittal document bound directly into the report. "We use the letter to introduce the report, summarize the program, rec-ognize the participants, and catch the reader's attention by mentioning a few high-lights," Messinetti says. Next comes the table of contents, comprising the report's generic headings, which helps readers quickly locate sections of par-ticular interest. Throughout the report, graphs and charts inter-spersed with the narrative offer a visual snapshot of the program's success.

His department's reports rarely include an appendix or ref-erence list, but when Messinetti quotes from other documents, he is careful to provide a com-plete citation on the same page. In addition to stating the date, author, and other relevant details, he explains why the information is being included in the report. He also describes the group responsible for the information: "The documen-tation gives proper credit to the source and confirms the validity of the information, so readers don't wonder where it came from."

Before distributing any widely circulated report, Messinetti sends a draft to Habi-tat's editorial manager, who ensures that it meets Habitat's style guidelines and has no grammatical errors. Messinetti also asks a few readers to comment on the draft. Be-cause these readers are representative of the audience, they "usually offer some good suggestions on what to include," he observes. "We pay close attention to this feedback so we don't miss the mark."

"We're not writing reports just to give the information. Our readers are less interested in the statistics and more interested in what the facts really mean."

co1. Determine an appropriate report structure and organization.

Most reports are formatted as manuscripts, memos, or letters.

■ Planning

As we have seen throughout our study of business communication, the writing process consists of planning, drafting, revising, formatting, and proofreading. You follow this same process when writing a report.

Although much of the planning in the report process is, of necessity, done even before collecting the data, the written presentation of the results requires its own stage of planning. You need to make decisions about the structure of the report, the organization of the content, and the framework of the headings before and as you write.

Determining the Report Structure

The physical structure of the report and such general traits as complexity, degree of formality, and length depend on the audience for the report and the nature of the problem that the report addresses. The three most common formats for a report are manuscript, memorandum, and letter format.

Manuscript reports (see, for example, Model 18 on page 358), the most formal of the three, are formatted in narrative (paragraph) style, with headings and subheadings separating the different sections. If the problem that the report addresses is complex and has serious consequences, the report will likely follow a manuscript format and a formal writing style. A formal writing style typically avoids the use of first- and second-person pronouns, such as *I* and *you*. In addition, the more formal the report, the more supplementary parts are included (such as a table of contents, executive summary, and appendix) and, therefore, the longer the report.

Memorandum and letter reports (see, for example, Model 16 on page 352) contain the standard correspondence parts (for example, lines identifying the names of the sender and receiver). They use a more informal writing style and may or may not contain headings and subheadings.

So that your written presentation will have an overall sense of proportion and unity, decide beforehand on the complexity, formality, length, and format of the report. The "right" decision depends on the needs and desires of the reader.

Organizing the Report

A sculptor creating a statue of someone doesn't necessarily start at the head and work down to the feet in lock-step fashion. Instead, he or she may first create part of the torso, then part of the head, then another part of the torso, and so on. Likewise, a movie director may film segments of the movie out of narrative order. But in the end, both creations are put together in such a way as to show unity, order, logic, and beauty.

Similarly, you may have organized the collection and analysis of data in a way that suited the investigation of various subtopics of the problem. But now that it is time to put the results of your work together into a coherent written presentation, you may need a *new* organization, one that integrates the whole and takes into account what you have learned through your research.

Planning your written presentation to show unity, order, logic, and yes, even beauty, involves selecting an organizational basis for the findings (the data you've collected and analyzed) and developing an outline. You must decide in what order

to present each piece of the puzzle and when to "spill the beans," that is, when to present your overall **conclusions** (the answers to the research questions raised in the introduction) and any recommendations you may wish to make.

As shown in Figure 12.1, the four most common bases for organizing your findings are *time, location, importance,* and *criteria.* There are, of course, other patterns for organizing data; for example, you can move from the known to the unknown or from the simple to the complex. The purpose of the report (information, analysis, or recommendation), the nature of the problem, and your knowledge of the reader will help you select the organizational framework that will be most useful.

Most reports are organized by time, location, importance, or criteria.

Topic	Basis	Format	Heading
A. Eastern Electronics: A Case Study 1. Start-up of Firm: 1999 2. Rapid Expansion: 1999–2005 3. Industrywide Slowdown: 2003 4. Retrenchment: 2004–2005 5. Return to Profitability: 2006	Time	Noun phrases	Generic
B. Renovation Needs 1. Expanding the Mailroom 2. Modernizing the Reception Area 3. Installing a Humidity System in Warehouse C 4. Repaving the North Parking Lot	Location	Participial phrases	Generic
C. Progress on Automation Project 1. Conversion on Budget 2. Time Schedule Slipped One Month 3. Branch Offices Added to Project 4. Software Programs Upgraded	Importance	Partial statements	Talking
D. Evaluation of Applicants for Communications Director 1. Sefcick Has Higher Professional Training. 2. Jenson Has More Relevant Work Experience. 3. Jenson's Written Work Samples Are More Effective.	Criteria	Statements	Talking
E. Establishing a Policy on AIDS in the Workplace 1. What Are the Firm's Legal and Social Obligations? 2. What Policies Have Other Firms Established? 3. What Policies Are Needed to Deal with the Needs of AIDS-Infected Employees? 4. What Policies Are Needed to Deal with the Concerns of Noninfected Employees? 5. How Should These Policies Be Implemented?	Criteria	Questions	Generic

figure**12.1**

Organizing the Data

Organize your report by time only when it is important for the reader to know the sequence of events.

Time   The use of chronology, or time sequence, is appropriate for agendas, minutes of meetings, programs, many status reports, and similar projects. Discussing events in the order in which they occurred or in the order in which they will or should occur is an efficient way to organize many informational reports—those whose purpose is simply to inform.

Despite its usefulness and simplicity, time sequence should not be overused. Because events *occur* one after another, chronology is often the most efficient way to *record* data, but it may not be the most efficient way to *present* that data to your readers. Assume, for example, that you are writing a progress report on a recruiting trip you made to four college campuses. Each day you interviewed candidates for the three positions you have open. The first passage, given in time sequence, requires too much work of the reader. The second version saves the reader time.

NOT: On Monday morning, I interviewed one candidate for the budget-analyst position and two candidates for the junior-accountant position. Then, in the afternoon, I interviewed two candidates for the asset-manager position and another for the budget-analyst position. Finally, on Tuesday, I interviewed another candidate for budget analyst and two for junior accountant

BUT: On Monday and Tuesday, I interviewed three candidates for the budget-analyst position, four for the junior-accountant position, and two for the asset-manager position.

A blow-by-blow description is not necessarily the most efficient means of communicating information to the reader. Sometimes it forces the reader to do too much work. Organize your information in time sequence only when it is important for the reader to know the sequence in which events occurred.

Larry Page (left) and Sergey Brin founded the search firm Google in 1999. Today it earns roughly $1 billion a year and accounts for 48 percent of all Internet queries. Yet, according to them, their first business plan wasn't much more than a series of notes scribbled on a whiteboard.

Location   Like the use of time sequence, the use of location as the basis for organizing a report is often appropriate for simple informational reports. Discussing topics according to their geographical or physical location (for example, describing an office layout) may be the most efficient way to present the data. Again, however, be sure that such an organizational plan helps the reader process the information most efficiently and that it is not merely the easiest way for you to report the data. Decisions should be based on reader needs rather than on writer convenience.

Importance   For the busy reader, the most efficient organizational plan may be to have the most important topic discussed first, followed in order by topics of decreasing importance. The reader then gets the major idea up front and can skim the less-important information as desired or needed. This organizational plan is routinely used by newspapers, where the most important points are discussed in the lead paragraph.

For some types of reports, especially recommendation reports, the opposite plan might be used effectively. If you've analyzed four alternatives and will recommend the implementation of Alternative 4, you might first present each of the other alternatives in turn (starting with the least-viable solution) and show why they're *not* feasible. Then, you save your "trump card" until last, thus making the alternative you're recommending the freshest in the reader's mind because it is the last one read. If you use this option, make sure that you effectively "slay all the dragons" except your own so the reader will agree that your recommendation is the most logical one.

> **MAKE UP YOUR MIND!**   *word***wise**
>
> An *antagonym* is a single word that has meanings that contradict each other. Examples:
>
> Bound: Moving ("I was bound for Chicago") or unable to move ("I was bound to a post").
>
> Buckle: To hold together ("Buckle your belt") or to fall apart ("to buckle under pressure").
>
> Cut: Get in ("Cut in line") or to get out ("cut a class").
>
> Replace: Take away ("replace the worn carpet") or put back ("replace the papers in the file").
>
> Trim: To add things to ("trim a Christmas tree") or take pieces off ("trim your hair").

Criteria   For most analytical and recommendation reports, where the purpose is to analyze the data, draw conclusions, and possibly recommend a solution, the most logical arrangement is to organize the data by criteria. One of the important steps in the reporting process is to develop hypotheses regarding causes of or solutions for the problem you're exploring. This process requires factoring, or breaking down, your problem into its component subproblems. These factors, or criteria, then, become the basis for organizing the report.

The most logical organization for most analytical and recommendation reports is by criteria.

In Example D in Figure 12.1 on page 427, for instance, the three factors presented—professional training, work experience, and written work samples—are the bases on which you will evaluate each candidate. Thus, they should also form the bases for presenting the data. By focusing attention on the criteria, you help lead the reader to the same conclusion you reached. For this reason, organizing data by criteria is an especially effective organizational plan when the reader might be initially resistant to your recommendations.

If you're evaluating three sites for a new facility, for example, avoid the temptation to use the *locations* of these sites as the report headings. Such an organizational plan focuses attention on the sites themselves instead of on the criteria by which you evaluated them and on which you based your recommendations. Instead, use the criteria as the headings. Similarly, avoid using "Advantages" and "Disadvantages" as headings. Keep your reader in step with you by helping the reader focus on the same topics—the criteria—that you focused on during the research and analysis phases of your project.

In actual practice, you might use a combination of these organizational plans. For instance, you might organize your first-level headings by criteria but your second-level headings in simple-to-complex order. Or you might organize your first-level headings by criteria but present these criteria in their order of importance. Competent communicators select an organizational plan with a view toward helping the reader comprehend and appreciate the information and viewpoints being presented in the most efficient manner possible.

Presenting Conclusions and Recommendations   Once you've decided how to organize the findings of your study, you must decide where to present the conclusions and any recommendations that have resulted from these findings. The differences among findings, conclusions, and recommendations can be illustrated by the following examples:

In general, prefer the direct plan (conclusions and recommendations first) for most business reports.

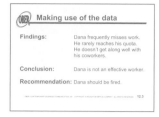

Making use of the data

Findings:	Dana frequently misses work. He rarely reaches his quota. He doesn't get along well with his coworkers.
Conclusion:	Dana is not an effective worker.
Recommendation:	Dana should be fired.

■ See Slide 12.3.

The conclusions answer the research questions raised in the introduction.

Finding:	The computer monitor sometimes goes blank during operation.
Conclusion:	The computer is broken.
Recommendation:	We should repair the computer before May 3, when payroll processing begins.
Finding:	Our Statesville branch has lost money four out of the past five years.
Conclusion:	Our Statesville branch is not profitable.
Recommendation:	We should close our Statesville branch.

Academic reports and many business reports have traditionally presented the conclusions and recommendations of a study at the end of the report, the rationale being that conclusions cannot logically be drawn until the data has been presented and analyzed; similarly, recommendations cannot be made until conclusions have been drawn.

Although hard-and-fast rules cannot be given for when to use the direct and indirect organizational plans in reports, some guidance can be given. Generally, it is better to use the direct organizational plan (in which the conclusions and recommendations are presented at the beginning of the report) when

- The reader prefers the direct plan for reports (as is typically the case when preparing a business report for your superior).

- The reader will be receptive to your conclusions and recommendations.

- The reader can evaluate the information in the report more efficiently if the conclusions and recommendations are given up front.

Similarly, the indirect plan (in which the evidence is presented first, followed by conclusions and recommendations) is more appropriate when

- The reader prefers the indirect plan for reports.

- The reader will be initially uninterested in or resistant to the conclusions and recommendations.

- The topic is so complex that detailed explanations and discussions are needed for the conclusions and recommendations to be understood and accepted.

The decision isn't necessarily an either/or situation. Instead of putting all the conclusions and recommendations either first or last, you may choose to split them up, discussing each in the appropriate subsection of your report. Similarly, even though you write a report using an indirect plan, you may add an executive summary or letter of transmittal that communicates the conclusions and recommendations to the reader before the report itself has been read.

Outlining the Report

Although we've not used the term *outlining* thus far, whenever we've talked about organizing, we've actually been talking about outlining as well. For example, early in the report process you factored your problem statement into its logical component subproblems. Thus, your problem statement and subproblems served as your first working outline.

Many business writers find it useful at this point in the report process to construct a more formal outline. A formal outline provides an orderly visual representation of the report, showing clearly which points are to be covered, in what order they are to be covered, and what the relationship of each is to the rest of the report. The purpose of the outline is to guide you, the writer, in structuring your report logically and efficiently. Consider it a working draft, subject to being revised as you compose the report.

Use the working title of your report as the title of your outline. Then use uppercase roman numerals for the major headings, uppercase letters for first-level subheadings, arabic numerals for second-level subheadings, and lowercase letters for third-level subheadings. Only rarely will you need to use all four levels of headings. Model 27 on page 432 shows an outline for a formal report.

As part of the process of developing a formal outline, you should compose the actual wording for your headings and decide how many headings you will need. Headings play an important role in helping to focus the reader's attention and in helping your report achieve unity and coherence, so plan them carefully, and revise them as needed as you work toward a final version of your report.

Talking Versus Generic Headings   **Talking headings** identify not only the topic of the section but also the major conclusion. For instance, Example C in Figure 12.1 on page 427 uses talking headings to indicate not only that the first section of the report is about the budget for the conversion but also that the conversion is proceeding on budget.

Talking headings, which are typically used in newspapers and magazines, are often also useful for business reports, where they can serve as a preview or executive summary of the entire report. They are especially useful when directness is desired—the reader can simply skim the headings in the report (or in the table of contents) and get an overview of the topics covered and each topic's conclusions.

Generic headings, on the other hand, identify only the topic of the section, without giving the conclusion. Most formal reports and any report written in an indirect pattern would use generic headings, similar to the headings used for Examples A and B in Figure 12.1 and used throughout Model 27 on page 432.

Parallelism   As illustrated in Figure 12.1, you have wide leeway in selecting the formats of headings you wish to use in your report. Noun phrases are probably the most common form of heading, but you may also choose participial phrases, partial statements (in which a verb is missing—the kind often used in newspaper headlines), statements, or questions. Perhaps there are other forms you might choose as well.

Regardless of the form of heading you select, be consistent within each level of heading. If the first major heading (a first-level heading) is a noun phrase, all first-level headings should be noun phrases. If the first major heading is a talking heading, the others should be too. As you move from level to level, you may switch to another form of heading if it would be more appropriate. Again, however, the headings within the same level must be parallel.

Length and Number of Headings   Four to eight words is about the right length for most headings. Headings that are too long lose some of their effectiveness; the shorter the heading, the more emphasis it receives. Yet headings that are too short are ineffective because they do not convey enough meaning.

The outline provides a concise visual picture of the structure of your report.

Use descriptive and parallel headings for unity and coherence.

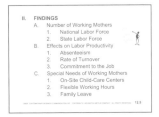

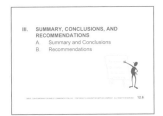

■ See Slides 12.4–12.6.

model27

REPORT OUTLINE

Uses the working title of the report as the outline title

Organizes the findings by criteria.

Contains at least two items in each level of subdivision.

Uses generic, not talking, headings.

Uses parallel structure (noun phrases are used for each heading and subheading).

STAFF EMPLOYEES' EVALUATION
OF THE BENEFIT PROGRAM
AT MAYO MEMORIAL HOSPITAL
Loretta J. Santorini

1 **I. INTRODUCTION**
  A. Purpose and Scope
  B. Procedures

II. FINDINGS
2 A. Knowledge of Benefits
    1. Familiarity with Benefits
    2. Present Methods of Communication
       a. Formal Channels
       b. Informal Channels
    3. Preferred Methods of Communication
  B. Opinions of Present Benefits
    1. Importance of Benefits
    2. Satisfaction with Benefits
  C. Desirability of Additional Benefits

III. SUMMARY, CONCLUSIONS, AND RECOMMENDATIONS
  A. Summary of the Problems and Procedures
  B. Summary of the Findings
  C. Conclusions and Recommendations

APPENDIX
3 A. Cover Letter
  B. Questionnaire

Grammar and Mechanics Notes

1 Align the roman numerals vertically on the periods.

2 Type each entry in upper- and lowercase letters.

3 Identify each appendix item by letter.

Similarly, choose an appropriate number of headings. Having too many headings weakens the unity of a report—they chop the report up too much, making it look more like an outline than a reasoned analysis. Having too few headings, however, confronts the reader with page after page of solid copy, without the chance to stop periodically and refocus attention on the topic.

In general, consider having at least one heading or visual aid to break up each single-spaced page or each two consecutive, double-spaced pages. Make your report inviting to read.

Use headings to break up a long report and refocus the reader's attention.

Balance   Maintain a sense of balance within and among sections. It would be unusual to give one section of a report eight subsections (eight second-level headings) and give the following section none. Similarly, it would be unusual to have one section ten pages long and another section only half a page long. Also, ensure that the most important ideas appear in the highest levels of headings. If you're discussing four criteria for a topic, for example, all four should be in the same level of heading—presumably in first-level headings.

When you divide a section into subsections, it must have at least two subsections. You cannot logically have just one second-level heading within a section because when you divide something, it divides into more than one "piece."

■ Drafting

Although it is the last step of a long and sometimes complex process, the written presentation of your research is the only evidence your reader has of the effort you have invested in the project. The success or failure of all your work depends on this physical evidence. Prepare the written report carefully to bring out the full significance of your data and to help the reader reach a decision and solve a problem.

Everything that you learned in Chapter 6 about the writing process applies directly to report writing—choosing a productive work environment; scheduling a reasonable block of time to devote to the drafting phase; letting ideas flow quickly during the drafting stage, without worrying about style, correctness, or format; and revising for content, style, correctness, and readability. However, report writing requires several additional considerations as well.

CO2. **Draft the report body and supplementary pages.**

The final product—the written report—is the only evidence the reader has of your efforts.

Drafting the Body

The report body consists of the introduction; the findings; and the summary, conclusions, and recommendations. As stated earlier, the conclusions may go first or last in the report. Each part may be a separate chapter in long reports or a major section in shorter reports.

Introduction   The introduction sets the stage for understanding the findings that follow. In this section, present such information as the following:

- Background of the problem

- Need for the study

- Authorization for the report

The introduction presents the information the reader needs to make sense of the findings.

- Hypotheses or problem statement and subproblems
- Purpose and scope (including definition of terms, if needed)
- Procedures used to gather and analyze the data

The actual topics and amount of detail presented in the introductory section will depend on the complexity of the report and the needs of the reader. For example, if the procedures are extensive, you may want to place them in a separate section, with their own first-level heading. Model 28 on page 435 is an example of an introductory section for a formal report.

Don't just present your findings; analyze and interpret them for the reader.

Findings   The findings of the study represent the major contribution of the report and make up the largest section of the report. Discuss and interpret any relevant primary and secondary data you gathered. Organize this section using one of the plans discussed earlier (for example, by time, location, importance, or, more frequently, criteria). Using objective language, present the information clearly, concisely, and accurately.

Many reports will display numerical information in tables and figures (such as bar, line, or pie charts). The information in such displays should be self-explanatory; that is, readers should understand it without having to refer to the text. Nevertheless, all tables and figures must be mentioned and explained in the text so that the text, too, is self-explanatory. All text references should be by number (for example, "as shown in Table 4")—never by a phrase such as "as shown below," because the table or figure might actually appear at the top of the following page.

Summarize the important information from the display (see Model 29 on page 436). Give enough interpretation to help the reader comprehend the table or figure, but don't repeat all the information it contains. Discussing display information in the narrative *emphasizes* that information, so discuss only what merits such emphasis.

The table or figure should be placed immediately *below* the first paragraph of text in which the reference to the display occurs. (Of course, if the display contains supplementary information, you may place it in an appendix rather than in the body of the report itself.) Avoid splitting a table or figure between two pages. If not enough space is available on the page for the display, continue with the narrative to the bottom of the page and then place the display at the very top of the following page.

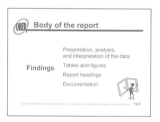

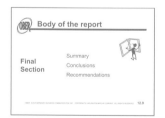

For all primary and secondary data, point out important items, implications, trends, contradictions, unexpected findings, similarities and differences, and the like. Use emphasis, subordination, preview, summary, and transition to make the report read clearly and smoothly. Avoid presenting facts and figures so fast that the reader is overwhelmed with data. Keep the reader's needs and desires uppermost in mind as you organize, present, and discuss the information.

■ See Slides 12.7–12.9.

Findings lead to conclusions; conclusions lead to recommendations.

Summary, Conclusions, and Recommendations   A one- or two-page report may need only a one-sentence or one-paragraph summary. Longer or more complex reports, however, should include a more extensive summary. Briefly review the problem and the procedures used to solve the problem, and provide an overview of the major findings. Repeating the main points or arguments immediately before presenting the conclusions and recommendations reinforces the reasonableness of those conclusions and recommendations. To avoid monotony when summarizing, use wording that is different from the original presentation.

If your report only analyzes the information presented and does not make recommendations, you might label the final section of the report "Summary" or "Summary and Conclusions," as appropriate. If your report includes both conclusions and

1   **INTRODUCTION**

Employee benefits are a rapidly growing and an increasingly important form of employee compensation for both profit and nonprofit organizations. According to a recent U.S. Chamber of Commerce survey, benefits now constitute 37 percent of all payroll costs, averaging $10,857 yearly for each employee (Ignatio, 2006, p. 812). Thus, on the basis of cost alone, an organization's benefit program must be carefully monitored and evaluated.

To ensure that the benefit program for Mayo Memorial Hospital's 2,500 staff personnel is operating as effectively as possible, David Riggins, director of personnel, authorized this report on February 15, 20—.

PURPOSE AND SCOPE

Specifically, the following problem was addressed in this study: What are the opinions of staff employees at Mayo Memorial Hospital regarding their employee benefits? To answer this question, the following subproblems were addressed:

2   1. How knowledgeable are the employees about the benefit program?
2. What are the employees' opinions of the value of the benefits already available?
3. What benefits, if any, would the employees like to have added to the program?

This study attempted to determine employee preferences only. Whether or not employee preferences are economically feasible is not within the scope of this study. As used in this study, employee benefits (also called fringe benefits) means an employment benefit given in addition to one's wages or salary.

PROCEDURES

A list of the 2,489 staff employees eligible for benefits was generated from the
3   January 15 payroll run. Using a 10 percent systematic sample, 250 employees were selected for the survey. On March 3, each of these employees was sent the cover letter and questionnaire shown in Appendixes A and B via campus mail. A total of 206 employees completed usable questionnaires, for a response rate of 82 percent.

In addition to the questionnaire data, personal interviews were held with three benefits managers. The primary data provided by the survey and personal interviews was then analyzed and compared with findings from secondary sources to determine the staff employees' opinions of the benefits program at Mayo.

REPORT INTRODUCTION

Provides a citation for statistics, direct quotations, or paraphrases.

Identifies who authorized the report.

Provides the problem statement in the form of a question to be answered.

Identifies the subproblems that must be answered to solve the problem.

Identifies the *delimitations* of the study and defines terms, as needed.

Provides concise, but complete, discussion of the procedures used to answer the problem statement.

Ends with an appropriate sense of closure for this section.

Grammar and Mechanics Notes

1 Center the first-level headings in bold and all caps. Type second-level headings in bold at the left margin.

2 In a single-spaced report, single-space numbered and bulleted lists if every item comprises a single line. Otherwise, single-space lines within an item but double-space between items.

3 Be consistent in using either the word *percent* or the percent sign (%). Regardless, use figures for the actual percentage.

model29

REPORT FINDINGS

Refers to tables and charts by number.

Discusses only the most important data from the table.

Subordinates the reference to tables and charts by placing it in a dependent clause ("As shown in Figure 1").

Recent studies (Egan, 2003; Ignatio, 2006) have shown that employees' satisfaction with benefits is directly correlated with their knowledge of such benefits. Thus, the Mayo staff employees were asked to rate their level of familiarity with each benefit. As shown in Table 2, most staff employees believe that most benefits have been adequately communicated to them.

1

TABLE 2. LEVEL OF FAMILIARITY WITH BENEFIT PROGRAM

Benefit	Level of Familiarity (%)				
	Familiar	Unfamiliar	Undecided	No Response	Total
Sick leave	94	4	1	1	100
Vacation	94	4	1	1	100
Paid holidays	92	4	3	1	100
Hospital/Medical insurance	90	7	2	0	100
Life insurance	84	10	5	1	100
Retirement	84	11	4	1	100
Long-term disability insurance	55	33	12	1	100
Auto insurance	36	57	6	15	100

At least four-fifths of the employees are familiar with all major benefits except for long-term disability insurance, which is familiar to only a slight majority. The low level of knowledge about auto insurance (36 percent familiarity) may be explained by the fact that this benefit started just six weeks before the survey was taken.

In general, benefit familiarity is not related to length of employment at Mayo. Most employees are familiar with most benefits regardless of their length of employment. However, as shown in Figure 1, the only benefit for which this is not true is life insurance. The longer a person has been employed at Mayo, the more likely he or she is to know about this benefit.

2

FIGURE 1. KNOWLEDGE OF LIFE INSURANCE BENEFIT

3

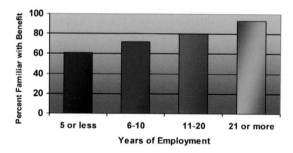

Grammar and Mechanics Notes

1 Position tables and charts immediately below the paragraph that introduces them.

2 Label charts as "figures" and number them independently of table numbers.

3 If a display does not fit completely at the bottom of the page, continue with the text to the bottom of the page and then place the display at the top of the following page.

recommendations, ensure that the conclusions stem directly from your findings and that the recommendations stem directly from the conclusions. Provide ample evidence to support all your conclusions and recommendations. An example of a closing section of a report is shown in Model 30 on page 438.

As shown, you should end your report with an overall concluding statement that provides a definite sense of project completion. Don't leave your reader wondering if additional pages will follow.

Drafting the Supplementary Sections

The length, formality, and complexity of the report, as well as the needs of the reader, affect the number of report parts that precede and follow the body of the report. Use any of the following components that will help you achieve your report objectives. Each of these parts is illustrated in the Reference Manual at the end of the text.

Title Page   A title page is typically used for reports typed in manuscript (as opposed to letter or memorandum) format. It shows such information as the title of the report, the names (and perhaps titles and departments) of the reader and writer, and the date the report was transmitted to the reader. Other information may be included at the writer's discretion. The information on the title page should be arranged attractively on the page.

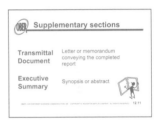

■ See Slides 12.10 and 12.11.

Transmittal Document   Formal reports and all reports that are not hand-delivered to the reader should be accompanied by a **transmittal document.** As its name implies, a transmittal document conveys the report to the reader. If the reader is outside the organization, you would use a transmittal letter; if the reader is within the organization, you would typically use a transmittal memo. Whether the report is written in formal or informal style, use a conversational, personal style of writing for the transmittal document.

Because the completion of the report assignment is good news (whether the information it contains is good or bad news), use the direct organizational plan. Begin by actually transmitting the report. Briefly discuss any needed background information, and perhaps give an overview of the conclusions and recommendations of the report (unless you want the reader to read the evidence supporting these conclusions and recommendations first). Include any other information that will help the reader understand, appreciate, and make use of the information presented in the report. End with such goodwill features as an expression of appreciation for being given the report assignment, an offer of willingness to discuss the report further, or perhaps an offer of assistance in the future. Model 31 on page 439 shows a sample transmittal memo.

The letter or memo may simply be transmitted along with the report, or it may be a part of the report. In the latter case, it is placed immediately after the title page but before the executive summary or table of contents.

Write the transmittal memo or letter in a direct pattern.

Executive Summary   An **executive summary,** also called an *abstract* or *synopsis,* is a condensed version of the body of the report (including introduction, findings, and any conclusions or recommendations). Although some readers may simply scan the report itself, most will read the executive summary carefully. Like the transmittal document, the executive summary is an optional part of the report. It is especially appropriate when the conclusions and recommendations will be welcomed by the reader, when the report is long, or when you know your reader appreciates having such information up front.

The report summary may be read more carefully than the report itself.

model30

REPORT SUMMARY, CONCLUSIONS, AND RECOMMENDATIONS

Quickly summarizes the need for the study.

Summarizes the problem and procedures used to solve the problem.

Summarizes the findings.

Presents the recommendations based on the findings and conclusions.

Provides an appropriate concluding statement.

1   **SUMMARY, CONCLUSIONS, AND RECOMMENDATIONS**

Nationwide, employee benefits now account for more than a third of all payroll costs. Thus, on the basis of cost alone, an organization's benefit program must be carefully monitored and evaluated.

The problem in this study was to determine the opinions of the nearly 2,500 staff employees at Mayo Memorial Hospital regarding the employee benefit program. Specifically, the investigation included determining the employees' present level of knowledge about the program, their opinions of the benefits presently offered, and their preferences for additional benefits. A survey of 206 staff employees and interviews with three managers familiar with the Mayo employee benefit program provided the primary data for this study.

2   The findings show that staff employees at Mayo Memorial Hospital are extremely knowledgeable about all benefits except long-term disability and automobile insurance; however, a majority would prefer to have an individualized benefit statement instead of the brochures now used to explain the benefit program. They consider paid time off the most important benefit and automobile insurance the least important. A majority are satisfied with all benefits, although retirement benefits generated substantial dissatisfaction. The only additional benefit desired by a majority of the employees is compensation for unused sick leave.

The following recommendations are based on these conclusions:

1. Determine the feasibility of generating an annual individualized benefit statement for each staff employee.

3

2. Reevaluate the attractiveness of the automobile insurance benefit in one year to determine staff employees' knowledge about, use of, and desire for this benefit. Consider the feasibility of substituting compensation for unused sick leave for the automobile insurance benefit.

3. Conduct a follow-up study of the retirement benefits at Mayo to determine how competitive they are with those offered by comparable public and private institutions.

These recommendations, as well as the findings of this study, should help the hospital administration ensure that its benefit program is accomplishing its stated objectives of attracting and retaining high-quality employees and meeting their needs once employed.

Grammar and Mechanics Notes

1 If necessary, break a long heading at a logical point and single-space the lines of the heading. Try to make the second line shorter than the first.

2 Note the use of the present tense when summarizing the findings.

3 Leave a blank line between multiline numbered items.

model31

TRANSMITTAL MEMO

MEMO TO: David Riggins, Director of Human Resources

FROM: Loretta J. Santorini, Assistant Director of Human Resources *LJS*

DATE: March 30, 20—

SUBJECT: Staff Employees' Evaluation of the Benefit Program at Mayo Memorial Hospital

Here is the report on our staff benefit program that you requested on February 15.

The report shows that the staff is familiar with and values most of the benefits we offer. At the end of the report, I've made several recommendations regarding issuing individualized benefit statements annually and determining

1   the usefulness of the automobile insurance benefit, the feasibility of offering compensation for unused sick leave, and the competitiveness of our retirement program.

2   I enjoyed working on this assignment, Dave, and learned quite a bit from my analysis that will help me during the upcoming labor negotiations. Please let me know if you have any questions about the report.

mek
3 Attachment

Uses a memo format because the reader is from within the organization.

Uses the same date on the memo as is used on the title page of the report.

Uses a direct organizational style for the transmittal document—regardless of whether the report is organized directly or indirectly.

Grammar and Mechanics Notes

1 *the usefulness . . . , the feasibility . . . , the competitiveness . . .* : Ensure that items in a series are stated in parallel format.

2 *assignment, Dave,:* set off nouns of address with commas.

3 Use the term *Attachment* for memos rather than *Enclosure.*

■ See Slides 12.12 and 12.13.

An appendix might include supplementary reference material not important enough to go in the body of the report.

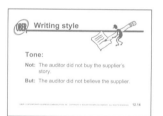

■ See Slide 12.14.

CO**3.** **Use an effective writing style.**

■ See Slide 12.15.

Because the purpose of the executive summary is to save the reader time, the summary should be short—generally no more than 10 percent of the length of the report. The summary should contain the same emphasis as the report itself and should be independent of the report; that is, you should not refer to the report itself in the summary. Assume that the person reading the summary will not have a chance to read the whole report, so include as much useful information as possible.

Use the same writing style for the summary as you used in the report. Position the summary immediately before the table of contents.

Table of Contents   Long reports with many headings and subheadings usually benefit from a table of contents. The wording used in the headings in the table of contents must be identical to the wording used in the headings in the body of the report. Typically, only two or three levels of headings are included in the table of contents—even if more levels are used in the body of the report. The page numbers identify the page on which the section heading appears, even though the section itself may comprise many pages. Obviously, the table of contents cannot be written until after the report itself has been typed.

Appendix   The appendix is an optional report part that contains supplementary information or documents. For example, in an appendix you might include a copy of the questionnaire and cover letter used to collect data, supplementary tables, forms, or computer printouts that might be helpful to the reader but that are not important enough to include in the body of the report. Label each appendix separately, by letter—for example, "Appendix A: Questionnaire" and "Appendix B: Cover Letter." In the body of the report, refer by letter to any items placed in an appendix.

References   The reference list contains the complete record of any secondary sources cited in the report. Different disciplines use different formats for citing these references; whichever you choose, be consistent and include enough information so that the reader can easily locate any source if he or she wants to do so.

A good indication of a report writer's scholarship is the accuracy of the reference list—in terms of both content and format—so proofread this part of your report carefully. The reference list is the very last section of the report.

Developing an Effective Writing Style

You can enhance the effectiveness of your written reports by paying attention to your writing style.

Tone   Regardless of the structure of your report, the writing style used is typically more objective and less conversational than, for example, the style of an informal memorandum. Avoid colloquial expressions, attempts at humor, subjectivity, bias, and exaggeration.

NOT: The company *hit the jackpot* with its new MRP program.

BUT: The new MRP program saved the company $125,000 the first year.

NOT: He *claimed* that half of his projects involved name-brand advertising.

BUT: He stated that half of his projects involved name-brand advertising.

Pronouns   For most business reports, the use of first- and second-person pronouns is not only acceptable but also quite helpful for achieving an effective writing style. Formal language, however, focuses attention on the information being conveyed instead of on the writer; therefore, reports written in the formal style should use third-person pronouns and avoid using *I, we,* and *you.*

You can avoid the awkward substitute "the writer" by recasting the sentence. Most often, it is evident that the writer is the person doing the action communicated.

Informal: I recommend that the project be canceled.

Awkward: The writer recommends that the project be canceled.

Formal: The project should be canceled.

Using the passive voice is a common device for avoiding the use of *I* in formal reports, but doing so weakens the impact. Instead, recast the sentence to avoid undue use of the passive voice.

Informal: I interviewed Jan Smith.

Passive: Jan Smith was interviewed.

Formal: In a personal interview, Jan Smith stated . . .

You will probably also want to avoid using *he* as a generic pronoun when referring to an unidentified person. Chapter 5 discusses many ways to avoid such discriminatory language.

Verb Tense   Use the verb tense (past, present, or future) that is appropriate at the time the reader *reads* the report—not necessarily at the time that you *wrote* the report. Use past tense to describe procedures and to describe the findings of other studies already completed, but use present tense for conclusions from those studies.

When possible, use the stronger present tense to present the data from your study. The rationale for doing so is that we assume our findings continue to be true; thus, the use of the present tense is justified. (If we cannot assume the continuing truth of any findings, we should probably not use them in the study.)

NOT: These findings *will be discussed* later in this report.

BUT: These findings *are discussed* later in the report. (*But:* These findings *were discussed* earlier in this report.)

NOT: Three-fourths of the managers *believed* quality circles *were* effective at the plant.

BUT: Three-fourths of the managers *believe* that quality circles *are* effective at the plant.

Procedure: Nearly 500 people *responded* to this survey.

Finding: Only 11 percent of the managers *received* any specific training on the new procedure. (*The event happened in the past.*)

Conclusion: Most managers *do not receive* any specific training on the new procedures.

Emphasis and Subordination   Only rarely does all of the data consistently point to one conclusion. More likely, you will have a mixed bag of data from which you

First- and second-person pronouns can be used appropriately in most business reports.

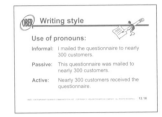

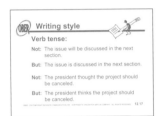

■ See Slides 12.16 and 12.17.

Verb tenses should reflect the reader's (not the writer's) time frame.

will have to evaluate the relative merits of each point. For your report to achieve its objective, the reader must evaluate the importance of each point in the same way that you did. At the very least, your reader must be *aware* of the importance you attached to each point. Therefore, you should employ the emphasis and subordination techniques learned in Chapter 5 when discussing your findings.

By (a) making sure that the amount of space devoted to a topic reflects the importance of that topic, (b) carefully positioning your major ideas, and (c) using language that directly tells what is more and less important, you can help ensure that you and your reader have the same perspective when your reader analyzes the data.

Use emphasis and subordination ethically—not to pressure the reader.

Use emphasis and subordination to let the reader know what you consider most and least important—but *not* to unduly sway the reader. If the data honestly leads to a strong, definite conclusion, then by all means make your conclusion strong and definite. But if the data permits only a tentative conclusion, then say so.

Coherence   One of the difficulties of writing any long document—especially when the document is drafted in sections and then put together—is making the finished product read smoothly and coherently, like a unified presentation rather than a cut-and-paste job. The problem is even greater for team-written reports (see "Team Writing" on page 46 of Chapter 2).

Use previews, summaries, and transitions to achieve coherence and unity.

One effective way to achieve coherence in a report is to use previews, summaries, and transitions regularly. At the beginning of each major section, preview what is discussed in that section. At the conclusion of each section, summarize what was presented and provide a smooth transition to the next topic. For long sections, the preview, summary, and transition might each be a separate paragraph; for short sections, a sentence might suffice.

Note how preview, summary, and transition are used in the following example of a report section opening and closing.

Training of System Users

The training program can be evaluated in terms of the opinions of the users and in terms of the cost of training in relation to the cost of the system itself. . . . (*After this topic preview, several paragraphs follow that discuss the opinions of the users and the cost of the training program.*)

Even though a slight majority of users now feel competent in using the system, the training provided falls far short of the 20 percent of total system cost recommended by experts. This low level of training may have affected the precision of the data generated by the MRP system. (*The first sentence contains the summary of this section; the second, the transition to the next.*)

Don't depend on your heading structure for coherence. Your report should read smoothly and coherently without the headings. Avoid repeating the exact words of the heading in the subsequent narrative, and avoid using the heading as part of the narrative.

NOT: **THE TWO DEPARTMENTS SHOULD BE MERGED.** The reason is that there is a duplication of services.

NOT: **THE TWO DEPARTMENTS SHOULD BE MERGED.** The two departments should be merged. The reason is that there is a duplication of services.

BUT: **THE TWO DEPARTMENTS SHOULD BE MERGED.** Merging the two departments would eliminate the duplication of services.

Always introduce a topic before dividing it into subtopics. Thus, you should never have one heading following another without some intervening text. (The exception to this guideline is that the heading "Introduction" may be used immediately after the report title or subtitle.) Preview for the reader how the topic will be divided before you actually make the division.

Paraphrasing Versus Direct Quotation

When including the ideas of another person in your report, avoid the temptation to become lazy and simply repeat everything in the author's exact words. It is unlikely that the problem you're trying to solve and the problem discussed by the author mesh exactly. More than likely, you'll need to take bits and pieces of information from numerous sources and integrate them into a context appropriate for your specific purposes.

A **paraphrase** is a summary or restatement of a passage in your own words. A **direct quotation,** on the other hand, contains the exact words of another. Use direct quotations (always enclosed in quotation marks) only for definitions or for text that is so precise, clear, or otherwise noteworthy that it cannot be improved on. Most of your references to secondary data should be in the form of paraphrases. Paraphrasing involves more than just rearranging the words or leaving out a word or two. It requires, instead, that you understand the writer's idea and then restate it in your own language.

CO4. Provide appropriate documentation when using someone else's work.

Use direct quotations sparingly.

Documenting Your Sources

Documentation is the identification of sources by giving credit to another person, either in the text or in the reference list, for using his or her words or ideas. You may, of course, use the words and ideas of others, provided such use is properly documented; in fact, for many business reports such secondary information may be the *only* data you use. You must, however, provide appropriate documentation whenever you quote, paraphrase, or summarize someone else's work (see Spotlight 26, "Who Said So?" on page 444).

Plagiarism is the use of another person's words or ideas without giving proper credit. Writings are considered the writer's legal property; someone else who wrongfully uses such property is guilty of theft. Plagiarism, therefore, carries stiff penalties. In the classroom, the penalty ranges from failure in a course to expulsion from school. On the job, the penalty for plagiarism ranges from loss of credibility to loss of employment.

■ Various plagiarism-detection technologies and websites boast that they can identify term papers copied from other sources. See, for example, http://www. plagiarism.org and http://www.canexus.com/eve (featuring the essay verification engine).

Provide a reference citation for material that came from others, unless that material is common knowledge or can be verified easily.

What Needs to Be Documented   Except as noted here, all material in your report that comes from secondary sources must be documented; that is, enough information about the original source must be given to enable the reader to locate the source if he or she so desires. If the secondary source is published (for example, a journal article), the documentation should appear as a reference citation. If the source is unpublished, sufficient documentation can generally be given in the narrative, making a formal citation unnecessary, as in these examples:

According to Board Policy 91-18b, all position vacancies above the level of C-3 must be posted internally at least two weeks prior to being advertised.

Who Said So?

Jay Leno, in his book *Leading with My Chin,* tells a humorous story about himself on the old Dinah Shore television show. The only problem is that the incident didn't happen to Leno but to a fellow comedian. When questioned later about the incident, Leno said he liked the story so much that he paid the comedian $1,000 for the right to publish it as his own.

Plagiarism is a potential problem for anyone who communicates. Consider, for example, these other recent incidents:

- The *Wall Street Journal* reported that almost half of one of the best-selling business books in history, *The One-Minute Manager,* was lifted nearly verbatim by the authors without attribution from another writer's *Wall Street Journal* article.

- The head of the Harvard University psychiatric hospital resigned when it was found he had committed plagiarism in four papers he had published.

- A nationally known minister was accused of plagiarizing numerous sections from someone else's book to include in his own popular book.

- A best-selling romance novelist admitted that she copied some of her passionate love scenes from her major rival author and blamed a psychological disorder for the transgression.

- The director of a university law school resigned immediately after admitting he used "substantial unattributed quotations" in a law-review article.

- In *Pacific Rim Trade,* a book published by the American Management Association, the writers stated that Lakewood Industries in Minnesota sells the most chopsticks in Japan. *Forbes* magazine investigated and found that the company doesn't sell the most chopsticks in Japan, never did, and never will— because it went bankrupt trying to perfect a technique for manufacturing chopsticks.

Cite and Check Your Sources

To avoid problems of dishonesty, always cite your secondary sources of information. You can, of course, go too far and provide excessive documentation. Such a practice not only is distracting but also leaves the impression that the writer is not an original thinker. As an example of excessive documentation, a study of criminal procedure published in the *Georgetown Law Journal* was accompanied by 3,917 footnotes!

In addition to citing your sources, you should also verify any information you include in a report, regardless of who said it. For example, despite widespread belief to the contrary,

- Voltaire never said, "I disapprove of what you say, but I will defend to the death your right to say it."

- Leo Durocher never said, "Nice guys finish last."

- W. C. Fields never said, "Anybody who hates children and dogs can't be all bad."

- James Cagney never used the line "You dirty rat" in any of his movies. Nor did Humphrey Bogart ever say the line "Play it again, Sam."

- Sherlock Holmes never uttered "Elementary, my dear Watson" in any of Arthur Conan Doyle's novels.

Give Credit Where Credit Is Due

As a competent communicator, you must give appropriate credit to your sources and ensure the accuracy of your data. Make certain that you have answered completely and fairly the question "Who said so?" Your organization's reputation and welfare—not to mention your own—demand no less.[1]

The contractor's letter of May 23, 2003, stated, "We agree to modify Blueprint 3884 by widening the southeast entrance from 10 feet to 12 feet 6 inches for a total additional charge of $273.50."

Occasionally, enough information can be given in the narrative so that a formal citation is unnecessary even for published sources. This format is most appropriate when only one or two sources are used in a report.

Widmark made this very argument in a guest editorial entitled "Here We Go Again" in the May 4, 2002, *Wall Street Journal* (p. A12).

After a study has been cited once, it may be mentioned again in continuous discussion on the same page or even on the next pages without further citation if no ambiguity results. If several pages intervene or if ambiguity might result, the citation should be given again.

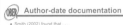

■ See Slide 12.18.

What Does Not Need to Be Documented   The use of two types of material by others does not need to be documented: (1) facts that are common knowledge to the readers of your report and (2) facts that can be verified easily.

Dell Computer is a large manufacturer of microcomputers.

The stock market closed at 10,506 on November 8.

But such statements as "Sales of the original Dell computer were disappointing" and "Only 4,000 Dell computers were sold last year" would need to be documented. If in doubt about whether you need to document, provide the citation.

Forms of Documentation   The three major forms for documenting the ideas, information, and quotations of other people in a report are endnotes, footnotes, and author-date references (see the Reference Manual at the back of this text for examples and formatting conventions). Let the nature of the report and the needs of the reader dictate the documentation method used. Regardless of the method you select, ensure that the citations are accurate, complete, and consistently formatted and that your bibliography format is consistent with your documentation format.

1. *Endnotes:* The endnote format uses superscript (raised) numbers to identify secondary sources in the text and then provides the actual citations in a numbered list entitled "Notes" at the end of the report. The endnotes are numbered consecutively throughout the report. Some readers prefer the endnote format because it avoids the clutter of footnotes and because it's easy to use.

    In the past, using endnotes for a long or complex report was somewhat risky because of the possibility of introducing errors when revising text. Every time text with a reference was inserted, deleted, or moved, all following endnote references in the text and in the list at the back

A S K Ober

Dear Dr. Ober:

I would like to know whether the business style for citation and documentation that you have included in your book Contemporary Business Communication *is commonly used in the world of business nowadays more than the APA or MLA styles. We have been using your book at the American University of Beirut for the last four years and have in the past asked students to use the APA or MLA style.*

—Sawsan M.

Dear Sawsan:

The business style illustrated in *Contemporary Business Communication* is, in fact, the most common style for citation and documentation in business—at least in U.S. business. It is based on the *Gregg Reference Manual*, 9th edition, published by Glencoe/McGraw-Hill. Another advantage of this style is that it is much simpler than APA or MLA for students to format.

—Scot

E-mail your questions and comments to askober@ober.net.

■ The author-date format discussed in this chapter is also known as the APA method and is fully documented in the *Publication Manual of the American Psychological Association*. Students who are not sure of the format for a citation should consult this manual.

The author-date format is preferred by many users of business reports.

of the report had to be renumbered. Today, however, word processors have an endnote feature that automatically numbers and keeps track of endnote references. Still, some readers prefer one of the other formats because endnotes provide no clues in the text regarding the source.

2. *Footnotes:* For years, footnotes were the traditional method of citing sources, especially in academic reports. A bibliographic footnote provides the complete reference at the bottom of the page on which the citation occurs in the text. Thus, a reader interested in exploring the source does not have to turn to the back of the report. Today's word processors can format footnotes almost painlessly—automatically numbering and positioning each note correctly. Some readers, however, find the presence of footnotes on the text page distracting.

3. *Author-Date Format:* Some business report readers prefer the author-date format of documentation, regarding the method as a reasonable compromise between endnotes (which provide *no* reference information on the text page) and footnotes (which provide *all* the reference information on the text page). In the author-date format, the writer inserts at an appropriate point in the text the last name of the author and the year of publication in parentheses. Complete bibliographic information is then included in the Notes or References section at the end of the report.

Distortion by Omission

Do not use quotations out of context.

It would be unethical to leave an inaccurate impression, even when what you do report is true. Sins of *omission* are as serious as sins of *commission*. Distortion by omission can occur when using quotations out of context, when omitting certain relevant background information, or when including only the most extreme or most interesting data.

It would be inappropriate, for example, to quote extensively from a survey that was conducted 15 years ago without first establishing for the reader that the findings are still valid. Likewise, it would be inappropriate to quote a finding from one study and not discuss the fact that four similar studies reached opposite conclusions.

Be especially careful to quote and paraphrase accurately from interview sources. Provide enough information to ensure that the passage reflects the interviewee's *intention*. Here are examples of possible distortions:

■ In addition to revising for content, style, and correctness, remind students to review their drafts for unintentional plagiarism. They should be sure they have cited their sources not only for direct quotations but also for summaries and paraphrases.

Original Quotation:	"I think the Lancelot is an excellent car for anyone who does not need to worry about fuel economy."
Distortion:	Johnson stated that the Lancelot "is an excellent car."
Worse Distortion:	Johnson stated that the Lancelot "is an excellent car for anyone."

■ Revising

CO5. Revise, format, and proofread the report.

Once you have produced a first draft of your report, put it away for a few days. Doing so will enable you to view the draft with a fresh perspective and perhaps find a more effective means of communicating your ideas to the reader. Don't try to correct all problems in one review. Instead, look at this process as having three steps—revising first for content, then for style, and finally for correctness.

Revise first for content. Make sure you've included sufficient information to support each point, that you've included no extraneous information (regardless of how interesting it might be or how hard you worked to gather the information), that all information is accurate, and that the information is presented in an efficient and logical sequence. Keep the purpose of the report and the reader's needs and desires in mind as you review for content.

Once you're satisfied with the content of the report, revise for style (refer to Checklist 5 on page 183). Ensure that your writing is clear and that you have used short, simple, vigorous, and concise words. Check to see whether you have used a variety of sentence types and have relied on active and passive voice appropriately. Do your paragraphs have unity and coherence, and are they of reasonable length? Have you maintained an overall tone of confidence, courtesy, sincerity, and objectivity? Finally, review your draft to ensure that you have used nondiscriminatory language and appropriate emphasis and subordination.

After you're confident about the content and style of your draft, revise once more for correctness. This revision step, known as *editing*, identifies and resolves any problems with grammar, spelling, punctuation, and word usage—the topics covered in the LABs in the Reference Manual at the back of this text. (See Communication Snapshot 12 on page 448 for information about which writing distractions executives consider most serious.) Do not risk losing credibility with the reader by careless English usage. If possible, have a colleague review your draft to catch any errors you may have overlooked.

Kevin Cohee, chairman of OneUnited Bank, the largest black-owned bank in the country, stands in front of his new $370 million headquarters. According to Cohee, one secret to the successful acquisitions his bank has made has been a thorough and impartial analysis of the operating data of the companies he has purchased.

Adopt a consistent, logical format, keeping the needs of the reader in mind.

■ Formatting

The physical format of your report (margins, spacing, and the like) depends to a certain extent on the length and complexity of the report and the format preferred by either the organization or the reader.

Consistency and readability are the hallmarks of an effective format. For example, be sure that all of your first-level headings are formatted consistently; if they are not, the reader may not be able to tell which headings are superior or subordinate to other headings. Regardless of the format used, make sure the reader can instantly tell which

Shanks

"Richard, let's have a talk about margins and report lengths."

communication snapshot 12

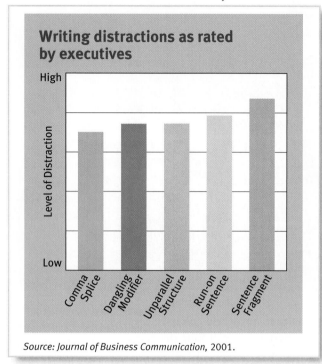

Writing distractions as rated by executives

Source: Journal of Business Communication, 2001.

Do not risk destroying your credibility by failing to proofread carefully.

■ See Handout 12.1.

are major headings and which are minor headings. You can differentiate among headings by using different fonts, font sizes, styles (such as bold or italic), and horizontal alignment.

If the organization or reader has a preferred format style, use it. Otherwise, follow the report formatting guidelines provided in the Reference Manual at the back of this text. Finally, consider designing your report to include the document-design principles discussed in Chapter 5.

■ Proofreading

First impressions are important. Even before reading the first line of your report, the reader will have formed an initial impression of the report—and of *you.* Make this impression a positive one by ensuring that the report carries with it a professional appearance.

After making all your revisions and formatting the various pages, give each page one final proofreading. Check closely for typographical errors. Check for appearance. Have you arranged the pages in correct order and stapled them neatly? If you're submitting a photocopy, are all the copies legible and of even darkness? Is each page free of wrinkles and smudges?

Ensure that in moving passages about, you did not inadvertently delete a line or two or repeat a passage. Run the spelling checker a final time after making all changes. (Remember, however, that a spelling checker will not locate an incorrect word that is spelled correctly.) If you have a grammar software program, evaluate your writing electronically. The grammar checker will check for use of passive voice, sentence length, misuse of words, unmatched punctuation (for example, an opening parenthesis not followed by a closing parenthesis), and readability. Use every aid at your disposal to ensure that your report reflects the highest standards of scholarship, critical thinking, and care.

In short, let your pride of authorship show through in every facet of your report. Appearances and details count. Review your entire document to ensure that you can answer "yes" to every question contained in Checklist 15.

✔checklist 15

Reviewing Your Report Draft

Introduction

✔ Is the report title accurate, descriptive, and honest?

✔ Is the research problem or the purpose of the study stated clearly and accurately?

✔ Is the scope of the study identified?

✔ Are all technical terms, or any terms used in a special way, defined?

✔ Are the procedures discussed in sufficient detail?

✔ Are any questionable decisions justified?

Findings

✔ Is the data analyzed completely, accurately, and appropriately?

✔ Is the analysis free of bias and misrepresentation?

✔ Is the data *interpreted* (its importance and implications discussed) rather than just presented?

✔ Are all calculations correct?

✔ Is all relevant data included and all irrelevant data excluded?

✔ Are visual aids correct, needed, clear, appropriately sized and positioned, and correctly labeled?

Supplementary Pages

✔ Is the executive summary short, descriptive, and in proportion to the report itself?

✔ Is the table of contents accurate, with correct page numbers and wording that is identical to that used in the report headings?

✔ Is any appended material properly labeled and referred to in the body of the report?

✔ Is the reference list accurate, complete, and appropriately formatted?

Writing Style and Format

✔ Does the overall report take into account the needs and desires of the reader?

✔ Is the material appropriately organized?

✔ Are the headings descriptive, parallel, and appropriate in number?

✔ Are emphasis and subordination used effectively?

✔ Does each major section contain a preview, summary, and transition?

✔ Has proper verb tense been used throughout?

✔ Has an appropriate level of formality been used?

✔ Are all references to secondary sources properly documented?

✔ Is each needed report part included and in an appropriate format?

✔ Is the length of the report appropriate?

✔ Are the paragraphs of an appropriate length?

✔ Have the principles of document design been followed to enhance the report's effectiveness?

✔ Is the report free from spelling, grammar, and punctuation errors?

✔ Does the overall report provide a positive first impression and reflect care, neatness, and scholarship?

Summary, Conclusions, and Recommendations

✔ Is the wording used in the summary different from that used earlier to present the data initially?

✔ Are the conclusions drawn supported by ample, credible evidence?

✔ Do the conclusions answer the questions or issues raised in the introduction?

✔ Are the recommendations reasonable in light of the conclusions?

✔ Does the report end with a sense of completion and convey an impression that the project is important?

The 3Ps
Problem, Process, Product

A SECTION OF A REPORT

You are a manager at a software-development house that publishes communication software for the HAL and Pear microcomputers. Together, these two computers account for about 90 percent of the business market. In 2005, you were asked to survey users of communication software—a repeat of a similar study you undertook in 2001.

You conducted the survey using the same questionnaire and same procedures from the 2001 study. Now you've gathered the data, along with the comparable data collected in 2001, and have organized it roughly into draft tables, one of which is shown in Figure 12.2. You're now ready to put this table into final report format and analyze its contents.

FIGURE 12.2   Draft Table

Q. From what source did you obtain your last software program?												
	2001						2006					
	Total		HAL		Pear		Total		HAL		Pear	
Source	N	%	N	%	N	%	N	%	N	%	N	%
Online	28	21.2	24	26.1	4	10.0	60	41.1	25	30.9	35	53.9
Mail-order company	3	2.3	2	2.2	1	2.5	4	2.7	2	2.5	2	3.1
Retail outlet	70	53.0	46	50.0	24	60.0	63	43.2	44	54.3	19	29.2
Software publisher	9	6.8	4	4.3	5	12.5	10	6.8	4	4.9	6	9.2
Unauthorized copy	21	15.9	15	16.3	6	15.0	6	4.1	3	3.7	3	4.6
Other	1	.8	1	1.1	0	0.0	3	2.1	3	3.7	0	0.0
Total	132	100.0	92	100.0	40	100.0	146	100.0	81	100.0	65	100.0

1. **Table Format**

   a. Examine the format of your draft table—the arrangement of columns and rows. Should you change anything for the final table?

      First, the year columns (2001 and 2006) should be transposed. The new data is more important than the old data, so putting it first will emphasize it.

      Second, the rows need to be rearranged. They're now in alphabetical order but should be rearranged in descending order according to the first amount column—the 2006 total column. Doing this will put the most important data first in the table.

   b. Assuming that you will have many tables in your final report, is there some way to condense the information in this table without undue loss of precision or detail?

      Although the number of respondents is important, the readers of my report will be much more interested in the percentages. Therefore, I'll give only the total number of respondents for each column and put that figure immediately under each column heading.

      Also, I see immediately that very few people obtained their software from mail-order companies either in 2001 or 2006, so I'll combine that category with the "Other" category.

      These changes are shown in Figure 12.3.

FIGURE 12.3   Draft Report Table

Source	2006			2001		
	Total (N = 146)	HAL (N = 81)	Pear (N = 65)	Total (N = 132)	HAL (N = 92)	Pear (N = 40)
Retail outlet	43	54	29	53	50	60
Online	41	31	54	21	26	10
Software publisher	7	5	9	7	4	13
Unauthorized copy	4	3	5	16	17	15
Other	5	7	3	3	3	2
Total	100	100	100	100	100	100

2. **Table Interpretation**

   a. Study the table in Figure 12.3. If you had space to make only one statement about this table, what would it be?

      Retail outlets and online companies are equally important sources for obtaining software, together accounting for more than four-fifths of all sources.

b. What other 2006 data should you discuss in your narrative?

HAL and Pear users obtain their software in different ways: the majority of HAL users obtain theirs from retail outlets, whereas the majority of Pear users obtain theirs from online firms.

c. What should you point out in comparing 2006 data with 2001 data?

The market share for retail outlets decreased by almost 20 percent from 2001 to 2006, whereas the market share for online companies almost doubled, increasing by 95 percent.

Also, the use of unauthorized copies appears to be decreasing (although the actual figures are probably somewhat higher than these self-reported figures).

3. **Report Writing**

a. Develop an effective talking heading and an effective generic heading for this section of the report. Which one will you use?

Talking Heading: **ONLINE ORDERS CATCHING UP WITH RETAIL SALES**

Generic Heading: **SOURCES OF SOFTWARE PURCHASES**

Because I do not know personally the readers of the report and their preferences, I'll make the conservative choice and use a generic heading.

b. Compose an effective topic (preview) sentence for this section.

Respondents were asked to indicate the source of the last software program they purchased.

c. Where will you position the table for this section?

At the end of the first paragraph that refers to the table.

d. What verb tense will you use in this section?

Past tense for the procedures; present tense for the findings.

e. Assume that the next report section discusses the cost of software. Compose an effective summary/transition sentence for this section of the report.

Perhaps the increasing reliance on online purchases is one reason that the cost of communication software has decreased since 2001.

SOURCES OF SOFTWARE PURCHASES

Respondents were asked to indicate the source of the last software program they purchased. As shown in Table 8, retail outlets and online companies are now equally important sources for obtaining software, together accounting for more than four-fifths of all sources. HAL and Pear users obtain their software in different ways: the majority of HAL users obtain theirs from retail outlets, whereas the majority of Pear users obtain theirs online.

TABLE 8. SOURCE OF LAST SOFTWARE PROGRAM
(In Percentages)

Source	2006			2001		
	Total (N = 146)	HAL (N = 81)	Pear (N = 65)	Total (N = 132)	HAL (N = 92)	Pear (N = 40)
Retail outlet	43	54	29	53	50	60
Online	41	31	54	21	26	10
Software publisher	7	5	9	7	4	13
Unauthorized copy	4	3	5	16	17	15
Other	5	7	3	3	3	2
Total	100	100	100	100	100	100

Retail outlets have decreased in popularity (down 10 percent) since 2001, whereas online sources have dramatically increased in popularity (up 20 percent). Also, the use of unauthorized copies appears to be decreasing (although the actual figure is probably somewhat higher than these self-reported figures).

Perhaps the increasing reliance on online purchases is one reason that the cost of communication software has declined since 2001.

COST OF SOFTWARE

Visit the **BusCom Online Learning Center** (at http://college.hmco.com) for additional resources to help you with this course and with your future career.

■ Summary

CO1. Determine an appropriate report structure and organization.

The most common report formats are manuscript (for formal reports) and letter or memorandum (for informal reports). The most common plans for organizing the findings of a study are by time, location, importance, and criteria. Conclusions should be presented at the beginning of the report unless the reader prefers the indirect plan, the reader will not be receptive toward the conclusions, or the topic is complex. Report headings should be composed carefully—in terms of their type, parallelism, length, and number.

CO2. Draft the report body and supplementary pages.

The body of the report consists of the introduction, findings (the major part of the report), and, as needed, the summary, conclusions, and recommendations. Long, formal reports might also require such supplementary components as a title page, transmittal document, executive summary, table of contents, appendix, and reference list.

CO3. Use an effective writing style.

Use an objective writing style, appropriate pronouns, and verb tenses that reflect the reader's time frame (rather than the writer's). Use emphasis and subordination techniques to help alert the reader to what you consider important; and use preview, summary, and transitional devices to help maintain coherence.

CO4. Provide appropriate documentation when using someone else's work.

Use direct quotations sparingly; most references to secondary data should be paraphrases. Provide appropriate documentation whenever you quote, paraphrase, or summarize someone else's work by using endnotes, footnotes, or the author-date method of citation. Do not omit important, relevant information from the report.

CO5. Revise, format, and proofread the report.

Delay revising the report until a few days after completing the first draft. Revise in three distinct steps: first for content, then for style, and finally for correctness. The report's format should enhance the report's appearance and readability and should be based on the organization's and reader's preferences. Unless directed otherwise, follow generally accepted formatting guidelines for margins, report headings, and pagination. Use a simple, consistent design and make generous use of white space. After all revisions and formatting have been completed, give each page one final proofreading. Make sure the final report reflects the highest standards of scholarship, critical thinking, and pride of authorship.

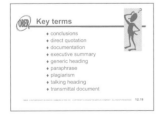

■ See Slide 12.19.

■ Consider treating this list as an end-of-chapter exercise for students to define and give an example of each term.

■ Key Terms

You should be able to define the following terms in your own words and give an original example of each.

conclusions (427)

direct quotation (443)

documentation (443)

executive summary (437)

generic heading (431)

paraphrase (443)

plagiarism (443)

talking heading (431)

transmittal document (437)

■ Exercises

1 The 3Ps (Problem, Process, and Product) Model: Communication Applications at Habitat for Humanity International   When Steve Messinetti writes a report about a Habitat for Humanity campus event, he goes beyond the bare facts and figures. He touches his readers in a very personal way by including photos and quotes that show how people's feelings and lives were affected. Before Messinetti begins to draft any report, he starts by analyzing his audience, selecting an appropriate report structure, and organizing his points in a logical order. No report leaves his office without being proofread to catch the tiniest error.

Problem

As a member of Messinetti's staff, you coordinate special events for all of Habitat's campus chapters in California. Last weekend, 20 students from two San Francisco–area colleges worked on a bake sale that raised $500 for a local Habitat house under construction. This was such a success that you think other campus chapters might want to stage their own bake sales. You also want to show appreciation for the volunteers who ran the bake sale. As you sit down at your computer to write a wrap-up report for Habitat management and the students who head all the California campus chapters, you look again at the nine bake sale photos you received from one of the students.

Process

a. What is the purpose of your report?
b. Describe your audience.
c. What data will you include in your report?
d. Will you use talking or generic headings? Why?
e. Will you use a transmittal letter or memo? Why?

Product

Using your knowledge of reports, research and prepare this two-page report in memorandum format.

■ See Handout 12.2.

2 The 3Ps (Problem, Process, and Product) Model: A Report Section

Problem

Review Exercise 10c of Chapter 11 (page 418). You have constructed your report table and analyzed the data. Now you are ready to write this section of the report.

All exercises require the application of all five chapter objectives shown at the beginning of this chapter.

Process

a. Compose an effective talking heading and an effective generic heading for this section of the report. Which one will you use?
b. Compose an effective topic sentence for this section.
c. Compose the sentence that contains your recommendation.
d. Assume that the next section of the report discusses reasons for changing banks. Compose an effective summary/transition sentence for this section of the report.

Product

Prepare this section of your report (one to three paragraphs). Include the table in the appropriate position. Submit both your report section and your responses to the process activities to your instructor.

3 **Organizing the Report—Outlining**   Using the method of outlining discussed in the chapter, develop an outline of Chapter 12 using the headings and sub-headings.

4 **Report Section—Secondary Statistical Data Furnished**   You are the vice president of marketing for Excelsior, a small manufacturer located in Asheboro, North Carolina. Although your firm manufactures consumer products such as toothpaste, plastic food wrap, and floor wax, you have the capability of manufacturing numerous different types of small, inexpensive products. The CEO of your firm has asked you to prepare an extensive report on the feasibility of Excelsior's entering the international market.

One strategy that you're considering is the possibility of becoming a supplier for a large multinational company. As part of your research, you have located data on the world's 100 largest public companies (see Figure 12.4). You are interested, first, in the nonbanking firms in this group that have the largest sales, and, second, in the percentage change in sales from the previous year. (You are not interested in market value and profit data because they are too much affected by extraneous market conditions that are irrelevant to your purposes, and you are not interested in banks, mortgage companies, and holding companies because they would not be potential purchasers of your products.)

■ Consider having students surf the Internet to use the most up-to-date information.

Compose the section of your report that presents and discusses this data. Include a table of the 25 largest firms (in terms of sales) that meet your criteria. Discuss the data in terms of the largest companies, their countries of origin, changes in sales from the previous year, and similar factors. Format the section in appropriate report format (beginning with page 5 of your report), provide an effective heading for this section, a topic sentence, summary, and transition to the next section, which discusses the largest companies in terms of the major products they sell.

5 **Supplementary Sections—Going International**   Resume the role of vice president of marketing for Excelsior (see Exercise 4). Your report to Victor Trillingham, Excelsior's CEO, needs several supplementary sections.

a. Assuming that the report will be submitted tomorrow, prepare a title page.
b. Using the data you analyzed in Exercise 4, draw conclusions and make recommendations. Then write a transmittal memo to accompany this report. Include brief statements of your conclusions and recommendations.
c. Decide whether you need an appendix; if so, note what it should contain.

6 **Short Memorandum Report—New Analysis**   Excelsior's CEO has read your report (see Exercise 5). He would like the data on the 25 companies you identified as potential purchasers analyzed from a different perspective: he wants you to group the companies according to the country in which they are based. Put the data into a table and, from your findings, draw conclusions about the geographic concentration of prospects. Write a brief memorandum report to the CEO; include your table and your conclusion.

figure12.4 The World's 100 Largest Public Companies

Ranked by market value as of August 29, 2003, as determined by The Wall Street Journal Market Data Group (in millions of U.S. dollars at Dec. 31, 2002, exchange rates; percentage changes based on home currencies)

RANK 2003	RANK 2002	COMPANY (COUNTRY)	MARKET VALUE	FISCAL 2002 SALES*	PERCENT CHANGE FROM 2001	FISCAL 2002 PROFIT†	PERCENT CHANGE FROM 2001
1	1	General Electric (U.S.)	$294,206	$130,732	4%	$15,133	7%
2	2	Microsoft (U.S.)	283,576	32,187	13	9,993	28
3	3	Wal-Mart Stores (U.S.)	259,501	244,524	12	8,039	21
4	4	Exxon Mobil (U.S.)	251,813	204,506	-4	11,011	-27
5	5	Pfizer (U.S.)	236,203	32,373	12	9,459	21
6	8	Citigroup (U.S.)	222,849	92,556	-7	15,276	8
7	21	Intel (U.S.)	187,003	26,764	1	3,117	141
8	9	American International Group (U.S.)	155,382	67,482	9	5,519	3
9	10	Royal Dutch/Shell (Netherlands/U.K.)	154,194	235,598	33	9,419	-13
10	7	BP (U.K.)	151,431	178,721	3	6,845	4
11	6	Johnson & Johnson (U.S.)	147,194	36,298	12	6,597	16
12	16	International Business Machines (U.S.)	141,713	81,186	-2	3,579	-54
13	19	HSBC Holdings (U.K.)	137,526	44,365	-18	6,239	25
14	28	Cisco Systems (U.S.)	134,409	18,878	0	3,578	89
15	25	NTT DoCoMo (Japan)	128,766	40,479	3	1,789	N.A.
16	23	Vodafone Group (U.K.)	124,425	48,949	33	-15,823	N.A.
17	18	Bank of America (U.S.)	118,613	46,724	-12	9,249	36
18	12	GlaxoSmithKline (U.K.)	114,811	34,183	4	6,309	28
19	13	Procter & Gamble (U.S.)	112,858	43,377	8	5,186	19
20	15	Merck (U.S.)	112,834	51,790	9	7,150	-2
21	11	Coca-Cola (U.S.)	107,201	19,564	12	3,050	-23
22	20	Total (France)	105,437	107,554	-3	6,232	-22
23	14	Novartis (Switzerland)	99,873	23,453	2	5,292	4
24	22	Toyota Motor (Japan)	99,429	130,479	9	6,321	35
25	17	Berkshire Hathaway (U.S.)	98,255	41,970	12	4,286	439
26	29	Verizon Communications (U.S.)	96,368	67,625	1	4,079	949
27	24	Nestlé (Switzerland)	87,872	64,515	5	5,473	13
28	46	Amgen (U.S.)	84,232	5,523	10	-1,392	N.A.
29	27	Wells Fargo (U.S.)	83,990	28,790	1	5,430	59
30	40	Dell Computer (U.S.)	83,803	35,404	14	2,122	70
31	26	Altria Group (U.S.)	83,464	80,408	-1	11,102	30
32	37	Nokia (Finland)	78,458	31,484	-4	3,546	54
33	30	ChevronTexaco (U.S.)	77,831	98,691	-5	1,132	-71
34	34	PepsiCo (U.S.)	76,525	25,112	7	3,313	24
35	38	Eli Lilly (U.S.)	74,738	11,078	-4	2,708	-4
36	32	SBC Communications (U.S.)	74,671	43,138	-6	5,653	-19
37	39	Home Depot (U.S.)	73,891	58,247	9	3,664	20
38	33	Viacom (U.S.)	72,953	24,606	6	2,207	N.A.
39	53	Roche Holding (Switzerland)	72,562	21,509	2	-2,913	N.A.
40	44	Royal Bank of Scotland (U.K.)	71,808	35,678	0	3,176	6
41	31	United Parcel Service (U.S.)	70,628	31,272	3	3,254	34
42	50	AOL Time Warner (U.S.)	70,219	40,961	10	-44,461	N.A.
43	45	Nippon Telegraph & Telephone (Japan)	70,048	91,942	-1	1,964	N.A.
44	73	J.P. Morgan Chase (U.S.)	69,461	25,283	-3	1,612	-1
45	48	UBS (Switzerland)	67,766	48,914	-21	2,558	-29
46	61	Oracle (U.S.)	67,005	9,475	-2	2,307	4
47	47	AstraZeneca (U.K.)	65,896	17,841	10	2,836	-2
48	42	Comcast (U.S.)	65,380	12,460	27	-274	N.A.
49	42	Fannie Mae (U.S.)	63,483	52,901	4	4,520	-21
50	36	Abbott Laboratories (U.S.)	62,907	17,685	9	2,794	80
51	79	Hewlett-Packard (U.S.)	$60,785	$56,588	25%	$ -923	N.A.
52	43	ENI (Italy)	60,478	50,265	-2	4,818	-41%
53	49	Medtronic (U.S.)	60,284	7,665	20	1,600	63
54	84	Deutsche Telekom (Germany)	59,935	56,314	11	-25,789	N.A.
55	77	Telefonica (Spain)	59,540	29,801	-9	-5,850	N.A.
56	65	American Express (U.S.)	58,790	23,807	5	2,671	104
57	62	Wyeth (U.S.)	56,782	14,584	4	4,447	95
58	57	Wachovia (U.S.)	56,699	23,591	5	3,560	121
59	75	Samsung Electronics (South Korea)	55,843	50,216	28	5,946	131
60	60	3M (U.S.)	55,565	16,382	2	1,974	38
61	41	Unilever (Netherlands/U.K.)	55,458	50,630	-6	2,233	16
62	—	France Telecom (France)	55,357	48,910	8	-16,109	N.A.
63	99	Siemens (Germany)	55,153	88,124	-3	2,724	24
64	76	Morgan Stanley (U.S.)	52,967	32,242	-26	2,988	-16
65	35	Kraft Foods (U.S.)	51,450	29,723	2	3,394	80
66	56	China Mobile (Hong Kong)	50,571	14,630	28	3,726	17
67	—	Merrill Lynch (U.S.)	49,851	28,253	-27	2,475	363
68	55	Bristol-Myers Squibb (U.S.)	49,143	18,119	1	2,066	-57
69	87	Nissan Motor (Japan)	48,412	57,477	10	4,168	33
70	71	Barclays (U.K.)	47,677	28,515	-8	3,594	-10
71	52	L'Oreal (France)	47,001	14,987	4	1,475	18
72	85	BellSouth (U.S.)	46,540	22,440	-7	2,708	5
73	59	Bank One (U.S.)	45,791	22,171	-10	3,295	25
74	81	U.S. Bancorp (U.S.)	45,755	15,422	-6	3,326	95
75	—	Orange (France)	44,682	17,920	13	664	N.A.
76	—	BNP Paribas (France)	44,651	47,668	-17	3,456	-18
77	78	DuPont (U.S.)	44,440	24,006	-3	-1,103	N.A.
78	58	Anheuser-Busch (U.S.)	43,002	13,566	5	1,934	13
79	90	Lowe's (U.S.)	42,695	26,491	20	1,471	44
80	—	BHP Billiton (Australia/U.K.)	42,465	17,506	15	1,920	3
81	83	HBOS (U.K.)	41,987	32,700	5	3,088	31
82	—	Canon (Japan)	41,841	24,748	1	1,605	16
83	97	Walt Disney (U.S.)	41,839	25,329	1	1,236	930
84	88	Telstra (Australia)	41,825	12,141	4	1,926	-6
85	92	Goldman Sachs (U.S.)	41,554	22,854	-27	2,114	-8
86	—	Texas Instruments (U.S.)	41,243	8,383	2	-344	N.A.
87	67	Sanofi-Synthelabo (France)	41,183	7,812	15	1,845	11
88	—	Tyco International (Bermuda)	41,061	35,590	5	-9,180	N.A.
89	—	News Corporation (Australia)	40,865	16,801	3	1,015	N.A.
90	—	Grupo Santander Central Hispano (Spain)	40,693	30,225	-18	2,357	-10
91	—	Genentech (U.S.)	40,506	2,719	23	64	-58
92	69	Honda Motor (Japan)	39,590	67,097	8	3,591	18
93	—	Taiwan Semiconductor (Taiwan)	39,552	4,684	29	624	49
94	94	ING Group (Netherlands)	38,997	94,582	0	4,698	-2
95	64	Aventis (France)	38,845	21,630	-10	2,198	39
96	86	DaimlerChrysler (Germany)	38,588	156,898	-2	5,115	N.A.
97	—	SAP (Germany)	37,812	7,775	1	527	-13
98	—	Telecom Italia Mobile (Italy)	37,790	11,398	6	1,222	23
99	96	ConocoPhillips (U.S.)	37,743	57,224	-14	-295	N.A.
100	—	United Technologies (U.S.)	37,548	27,980	2	2,234	15

N.A.=Not applicable

*March 31, 2002, results are used for Japanese companies

†Figures reflect the July 2002 acquisition of Immunex

NOTE: Rank calculated for Royal Dutch/Shell Group by combining market value of the Netherlands' Royal Dutch Petroleum and Britain's Shell Transport & Trading. Rank calculated for Unilever by combining market value of Netherlands' Unilever NV. and Britain's Unilever PLC. Rank calculated for BHP Billiton by combining market value of Australia's BHP Billiton Ltd. and Britain's BHP Billiton PLC.

Source: The Wall Street Journal Reports, World Business, August 29, 2003.

7 Secondary Data—International Competition

Excelsior CEO Victor Trillingham (see Exercises 4, 5, and 6) is concerned about the international activities of Nestlé, which competes with Excelsior in the United States and would be a formidable rival in international markets. Conduct secondary research on the Internet to uncover the answers to Trillingham's questions.

a. In how many countries does Nestlé sell its products? List the countries.
b. What percentage of Nestlé's overall sales are made outside the United States?
c. What companies (if any) has Nestlé acquired during the past 12 months?
d. What major new consumer products has Nestlé introduced in the United States during the past 12 months?

Using talking headings, outline an informational report in manuscript format to present your findings. Prepare visual aids to convey the answers to Questions 7a and b. Include a reference list of secondary sources used in your research. Then draft a transmittal memorandum to Trillingham (assume that the report will be submitted next Monday).

8 Report Section—Document Design   Reformat the report section shown on page 453 to incorporate the elements of document design discussed in Chapter 5. You may edit the report as needed, as long as you do not change the basic information.

9 Short Formal Report—Primary and Secondary Statistical Data Furnished
North Star is a producer of consumer products with annual sales of $847.2 million. It has 4.5 percent of the consumer market for its six consumer products (soap, deodorant, ammonia, chili, canned ham, and frozen vegetables).

On July 8 of this year, Paul Gettisfield, sales manager, asked you, a product manager, to study the feasibility of North Star's entering the generic-products market. Generic products are products that do not have brand names but instead carry a plain generic label, such as "Paper Towels." Generic products are typically not advertised; they involve less packaging, less processing, and cheaper ingredients than brand names; and they compete both with private brands (those distributed solely by individual store chains such as A&P and Kroger) and with national brands (those available for sale at all grocery stores and advertised nationally). At the present time, North Star produces only national brands.

Paul specifically asked you *not* to explore whether North Star had the necessary plant capacity. He wanted you only to provide up-to-date information on the generic market in general and to explore likely consumer acceptance of generic brands for the products that North Star produces. He is quite interested in learning the results of your research.

In August you conducted a mail survey of 1,500 consumers in the three states (California, Texas, and Arizona) that constitute your largest market. Responses were received from 832 consumers to the following questions; responses are provided for all 832 consumers and for the 237 largest consumers (those who indicated that they did 51 percent to 100 percent of their household shopping):

Have you purchased a food generic product (such as canned fruit or vegetables) in the last month?

All consumers: 36 percent yes, 64 percent no
Largest consumers: 29 percent yes, 71 percent no

Was this the first time you had purchased a food generic product?

All consumers: 18 percent yes, 82 percent no
Largest consumers: 20 percent yes, 80 percent no

Have you purchased a nonfood generic product (such as paper towels or soap) in the last month?

All consumers: 60 percent yes, 40 percent no
Largest consumers: 59 percent yes, 41 percent no

Was this the first time you had purchased a nonfood generic product?

All consumers: 5 percent yes, 95 percent no
Largest consumers: 7 percent yes, 93 percent no

If you could save at least 30 percent by purchasing a generic brand rather than a national brand, would you purchase a generic brand of any of the following products?

Bar of soap: 43 percent yes, 57 percent no, 0 percent don't use this product
Deodorant: 31 percent yes, 67 percent no, 2 percent don't use this product
Ammonia: 80 percent yes, 10 percent no, 10 percent don't use this product
Chili: 34 percent yes, 52 percent no, 14 percent don't use this product
Canned ham: 19 percent yes, 44 percent no, 37 percent don't use this product
Frozen vegetables: 54 percent yes, 30 percent no, 16 percent don't use this product

You also asked the local North Star sales representatives to audit 20 randomly selected chain supermarkets in each of these three states in August. Personal observation showed that 39 of the stores stocked generic brands, 37 of these 39 stocked 100 or more generic items, and 15 had separate generic-product sections. All but 3 of the 60 stores stocked all six products that North Star produces.

In gathering your data, you also made the following notes from three secondary sources:

1. *Hammond's Market Reports,* Gary, IN, 2006, pp. 1027–1030: This annual index lists various information for more than 2,000 consumer products. The percentages of market share for the six products North Star produces are as follows:

	2000	2003	2006
Generic brands	1.5%	2.6%	7.3%
Private labels	31.6%	30.7%	27.8%
National brands	66.9%	66.7%	64.9%

2. H. R. Nolan, "No-Name Brands: An Update," *Supermarket Management,* April 2005, pp. 31–37.
   a. Generic brands are typically priced 30 percent to 50 percent below national brands. (p. 31)
   b. Consumers require a 36 percent saving on a bar of soap and 40 percent savings on deodorant to motivate them to switch to a generic. (p. 32)
   c. Consumer awareness of generics has tripled since 1978. (p. 33)

    d. "The easiest way to become a no-name store is to ignore no-name brands." (direct quotation from p. 33)

    e. Many leading brand manufacturers feel compelled to produce the lower-profit generic brands because either the market has grown too big to ignore or the inroads generic brands have made on their own brands have left them with idle capacity. (p. 35)

3. Edward J. Rauch and Pamela G. McCleary, "National Brands to Play a Bit Part in the Future," *Grocery Business,* Fall 2004, pp. 118–120.

    a. Eight out of ten food-chain officers believe their costs will rise more than their prices this year. (p. 118)

    b. Generics are now available in 84 percent of the stores nationwide and account for about 4 percent of the store space. (p. 118)

    c. "Supermarket executives foresee a drop in shelf space allocated to brand products and an increase in the space allocated to generics and private labels. Many experts predict that supermarkets will ultimately carry no more than the top two brands in a category plus a private label and a generic label." (direct quotation from p. 119)

    d. Today, 37 percent of the grocery stores have switched from paper bags to the less expensive plastic bags for packaging customer purchases, even though the plastic bags are nonbiodegradable. (p. 119)

    e. Starting from nearly zero in 1977, generics have acquired 7 percent of the $275 billion grocery market. Many observers predict they will go up to 25 percent within the next five years. (p. 120)

Analyze the data, prepare whatever visual aids would be helpful, and then write a formal report for Gettisfield. Include any supplementary report pages you think would be helpful.

10 Short Memorandum Report—Findings, Conclusions, and Recommendations
Welfare Services is concerned about the increasing number of single-parent households in the United States. It has conducted a study to look into this matter. It has gathered, among other findings, the following facts:

a. The divorce rate in the United States has doubled in the last 20 years.

b. The average age for women getting married has increased from 20 to 23 in the last 20 years, and the average age for men getting married has increased from 22 to 24 in the last 20 years.

c. The number of people getting married has only increased by 5 percent in the last 20 years.

d. The number of married women working full time has increased by 60 percent in the last 20 years.

e. The consumer debt of married couples in the United States has increased by 150 percent in the last 20 years.

Working in groups of two or three, draw conclusions about these findings and, based on additional research, make recommendations as to what should or should not be done to deal with the Welfare Services' concern.

Share your conclusions and recommendations with the rest of the class. Are the other groups' conclusions and recommendations similar or different? What additional information, if any, would have been helpful? What are the differences between conclusions and recommendations?

11 **Work-team Communication—Long Formal Report Requiring Additional Research**   Assume that your group of four has been asked by Jim Miller, executive vice president of Jefferson Industries, to write an exploratory report on the feasibility of Jefferson's opening a frozen yogurt store in Akron, Ohio. If the preliminary data your group gathers warrants further exploration of this project, a professional venture-consultant group will be hired to conduct an in-depth "dollars-and-cents" study. Your job, then, is to recommend whether such an expensive follow-up study is warranted. Assume that Jefferson has the financial resources to support such a venture if it looks promising.

You can immediately think of several areas you'll want to explore: the general market outlook for frozen yogurt stores, the demographic makeup of Akron (home of the University of Akron), the local economic climate, franchise opportunities in the industry, and the like. Undoubtedly, other topics (or criteria) will surface as you brainstorm the problem.

Working as a group, carry through the entire research process for this project—planning the study, collecting the data, organizing and analyzing the data, and writing the report. (*Note:* If you gathered any data by completing Exercises 6, 7, and 8 in Chapter 11, integrate that data into your study as needed.)

Write the body of the report using formal language, organize the study by criteria, and place the conclusions and recommendations at the end. Include a title page, transmittal memo (addressed to James H. Miller), executive summary, table of contents, and reference list (use the author-date method of citation).

Regardless of how your group decides to divide up the work, everyone should review and comment on the draft of the final report. If different members write different parts, edit as needed to ensure that the report reads smoothly and coherently.

12 **Documenting Using Endnotes**   Assume you are writing a report and have used the following secondary sources.

An article written by John J. Richer on pages 45–48 of the April 2, 20—, edition of *Sports Weekly* entitled "The Big Profit Breakdown."

A quotation by Scott Taylor in an article entitled "Winter Olympics—Boom or Bust" on page A2, column 1, of the April 17, 20—, edition of the *Salt Lake Herald.*

Statistics from page 233 in a book entitled *How to Win at the Service Game* written by James Michaels in 20—and published by Ammiden Publishing in New York.

A quote from an interview conducted with T. Winkle Towes, a professor of economics at the University of Utah conducted on March 31, 20—.

Using these sources of information and the examples shown in Section B (see pages 620–624), prepare the bibliography for your report.

13 **Secondary Data—The Female Manager**   Using the appropriate business indexes (print or computer), identify three women who are presidents or CEOs of companies listed on the New York Stock Exchange. Provide information on their backgrounds. Did they make it to the top by rising through the ranks, by starting the firm, by taking over from another family member, or by following some other path?

Analyze the effectiveness of these three individuals. How profitable are the firms they head in relation to others in the industry? Are their firms more or less profitable now than when they assumed the top job? Finally, try to uncover

For Exercises 13–16, follow the desires of your instructor (the audience) in terms of length, format, degree of formality, number of report parts, and the like.

data regarding their management styles—how they see their role, how they relate to their employees, what problems they've experienced, and the like.

From your study of these three individuals, are there any valid conclusions you can draw? Write a report objectively presenting and analyzing the information you've gathered.

14 Secondary Data—Keyboarding Skills   You are the director of training for an aerospace firm located in Seattle. Your superior, Charles R. Underwood, personnel manager, is concerned that so many of the firm's 2,000 white-collar employees use their computers for hours each day but still do not know how to touch-keyboard. He believes the hunt-and-peck method is inefficient and increases the possibility of making errors when inputting data, thus lowering its reliability.

He has asked you to recommend a software program that teaches the user how to type. He is specifically interested in a program that is IBM-compatible, is geared to adults, is educationally sound, and can be learned on an individual basis without an instructor present.

Identify and evaluate three to five keyboarding software programs that meet these criteria, and write a report recommending the best one to Underwood. Justify your choice.

15 Primary Data—Career Choices   Explore a career position in which you are interested. Determine the job outlook, present level of employment, salary trends, typical duties, working conditions, educational or experience requirements, and the like. If possible, interview someone holding this position to gain firsthand impressions. Then write up your findings in a report to your instructor. Include at least five secondary sources and at least one table or visual aid in your report.

16 Primary Data—Intercultural Dimensions   To what extent does network and cable television accurately portray members of cultural, ethnic, and racial minorities? To what extent are they portrayed at all during prime time (8 p.m. to 11 p.m.)? In what types of roles are they shown, and what is their relationship with nonminority characters? As assistant to the director of public relations of the National Minority Alliance, you are interested in such questions.

Locate and review at least three journal articles on this topic. Then develop a definition of the term *minority.* Randomly select and view at least ten prime-time television shows, and develop a form for recording the needed data on minority representation in these shows. As part of your research, compare the proportion of minority members in this country with their representation on prime-time television. Integrate your primary and secondary data into a report. Use objective language, being careful to present ample data to support any conclusions or recommendations you may make.

17 Primary Data—Student Living Arrangements   Darlene Anderson, a real estate developer and president of Anderson and Associates, is exploring the feasibility of building a large student-apartment complex on a lot her firm owns two blocks from campus. Even though the city planning commission believes there is already enough student housing, Anderson thinks she can succeed if she addresses specific problems of present housing. She has asked you, her executive assistant, to survey students to determine their views of off-campus living.

Specifically, she wants you to develop a ranked listing of the most important attributes of student housing. How important to students are such criteria as price, location (access to campus, shopping, public transportation, and the like), space and layout, furnishings (furnished versus unfurnished), social activities, parking, pets policy, and the like?

In addition, the architect has drawn a plan that features the following options: private hotel-like rooms (sleeping and sitting area and private bath but no kitchen); private one-room efficiency apartments; one-bedroom two-person apartments; and four-bedroom four-person apartments. Which of these arrangements would students most likely rent, given their present economic situation? Would another alternative be more appealing to them?

Develop a questionnaire and administer it to a sample of students. Then analyze the data and write a report for Anderson.

18 **Writing the Report—Going Back in Time**   Procter & Gamble has long been known for its product development prowess. You were recently hired by the company's public affairs department to manage the development of a new and unusual product: a book about the history of P&G's product development efforts. The company plans to use this book for training purposes. You believe that making the book available to a wider audience would enhance P&G's reputation without giving away any of its secrets. You also know that you will need professional help to research the book—based on information in your archives and on interviews with current and former employees—and to write it.

Doing a bit of research, you learn that you can choose among four companies specializing in corporate histories: Winthrop Group in Cambridge, Massachusetts; History Associates in Rockville, Maryland; History Factory in Chantilly, Virginia; and Business History Group in Columbia, Maryland. Before your boss will approve this expensive project, you need to prepare a brief report showing the services offered by each company, some clients served by each, and your recommendations for which company seems the best fit given P&G's requirements. How will you conduct more research? What do you need to know to make a recommendation? What is the purpose of your report? Describe your audience. What data will you include in the report? Using your knowledge of report writing, draft an introduction to this report.

19 **Proofreading—Selling Business on Business Software**   Assume that the following passage is part of an informational report that you have prepared. Proofread it carefully for spelling errors, misused words, and grammar errors. Rewrite the passage showing the correction you made.

Our lawyers have reviewed the wording of the contacts you sent us. They're advise is to except provisions 1 thru 8 and 11 thorough 15. The remainder of the provisions (9 and 10) require farther negotiation.

The number of people we want to include in these talks has not yet been determined. We do expect, however, to have fewer people involved now then in our proceeding meetings.

Marcia Nash, our chief legal council, will be your principal contact during these negotiations. Please telephone her at 555-7376 to sit a mutualy beneficial time for us too meet early next month. We are eager to settle this matter soon.

continuing
case 12

■ A suggested solution to the Continuing Case can be found in the *Instructor's Resource Manual.*

URBAN SYSTEMS

Reporting—A Pain in the Wrist

Review the Continuing Case account at the end of Chapter 11, in which Jean Tate asked Pat Robbins to write a report on carpal tunnel syndrome, a neuromuscular wrist ailment caused by repeated hand motions as in typing.

Now, administer the questionnaire you developed in Chapter 11 to a sample of at least 30 clerical workers at your institution, where you work, or at some other office. For the purposes of this assignment, assume that the responses you receive were actually those from Urban Systems clerical workers. Then analyze the questionnaire data carefully. Construct whatever tables and charts would be helpful to the reader.

Critical Thinking

1. Considering the findings from your questionnaire and the secondary sources you checked, what does all this information mean in terms of your problem statement?

2. For each subproblem you specified (see Chapter 11), what conclusion can you draw? In view of each of these individual conclusions, what overall conclusion is merited? In view of your individual and overall conclusions, what recommendations are appropriate?

Writing Project

3. Prepare a recommendation report in manuscript format for Tate. Use formal language for the body of the report, organize the study by criteria, and place the conclusions and recommendations at the end. Include a title page, transmittal memo, executive summary, table of contents, abstract, appendix (copy of the questionnaire), and reference list (use the author-date method of citation).

[OBER LAB Test 12 form]

■ See Handout 12.3.

Pat analyzes the results of secondary research, primary data, and Internet searching to draft her recommendation report on carpal tunnel syndrome.

LABtest 12

Retype the following news item, correcting any grammar and mechanics errors according to the rules introduced in LABs 2–6 beginning on page 576.

Even on the brightest of ~~evenings~~ *evenings, (INTRO)* navigating your garden

can be a challenge at ~~best. At~~ *best or, ^ at(FRAG)* worst, the cause of a nasty spill.

Today, ~~alot~~ *a lot (WORD)* of people are discovering the ~~benifits~~ *benefits (SPELL)* of ~~low voltage~~ *low-voltage (COMP)*

lighting as an ~~economical effective~~ *economical, effective, (SER)* and energy-efficient source

5 of exterior lighting.

    Many ~~Lighting Systems~~ *lighting systems (COMMON NOUNS)* are sold in kits for do-it-yourself

~~installation, many~~ *installation. ^ Many (RUN-ON)* folks who ~~would'nt~~ *wouldn't (SPELL)* otherwise fool with an

electrical outlet ~~is~~ *are (AGR)* now installing a lighting system.

    Essentially, there ~~is~~ *are (AGR)* only ~~3~~ *three (NO.–FIGURE)* basic types of ~~fixtures~~ *fixtures: (EXP)* spot

10 lighting, path lighting, and general lighting. Spot lighting

~~consist~~ *consists (AGR)* of a floodlight that is used to direct light to a spe-

cific location so as to illuminate a tree, decorative shrub, or

architectural element of the ~~homes~~ *home's (SING POSS.)* exterior. Path lighting and

accent lighting ~~is~~ *are (AGR)* the most popular styles used by ~~homeowners'~~ *homeowners (PLURAL)*

15 today.

    One aspect of design that deserves creative ideas ~~are~~ *is (AGR)* the

maximum distance that the wire will travel. The ~~further~~ *farther (WORD)* the wire

travels, the more the voltage ~~drops. Which,~~ *drops, which, (FRAG)* in turn, creates a

drop in illumination. To avoid this ~~condition~~ *condition, (INTRO)* experts ~~advice~~ *advise (WORD)* us-

20 ing several wires of varying lengths.

    Some transformers are ~~equiped~~ *equipped (SPELL)* with a photoelectric cell

that automatically ~~turn~~ *turns (AGR)* the lights on and off. Another ~~poplar~~ *popular (SPELL)* ac-

cessory is a dimmer to control the ~~lights'~~ *light's (SING POSS.)* intensity.

■ See Slides 12.20–12.24.

13

Planning the Business Presentation

After you have finished this chapter, you should be able to

1. Describe the important role that business presentations play in the organization.

2. Plan a presentation by determining its purpose, analyzing the audience, and deciding the timing and method of delivery.

3. Write a presentation by collecting the data and organizing it in a logical format.

4. Plan a team presentation.

5. Plan a video presentation.

6. Plan other types of business presentations.

an insider's
perspective

SARA GONZÁLEZ
President & CEO,
Georgia Hispanic Chamber of
Commerce (Atlanta, Georgia)

When Sara González makes a presentation, she starts with the past and ends with the future. González is president and CEO of the Georgia Hispanic Chamber of Commerce. This Atlanta-based nonprofit organization promotes and supports the economic development of Georgia's Hispanic business community. Also, because Chamber officials are both bicultural and bilingual, they provide a vital link between local Hispanic businesses and corporations throughout the United States and Latin America.

González receives invitations to address all kinds of audiences, from graduate students to international women's groups, about the Chamber's background, achievements, and goals. "My presentation usually starts with a brief history of who we are, when we started, and how I came to be in this position," she says. "Then I talk about all the things we have accomplished over the years." Next, she quotes official statistics that demonstrate the dramatic growth of the Hispanic population and Hispanic-owned companies within Georgia. In closing, she reinforces the Chamber's unique role within the business world and its goal of putting more Hispanic entrepreneurs on the road to business success.

Although González avoids using slides, overhead transparencies, or electronic slides, she brings business cards, Chamber brochures, and newsletters as handouts. "I prefer to make my presentations interactive rather than following a formal script, and I make a point of following up on audience questions. I love questions. I always invite people to ask me questions. Usually I know the answer because I know my topic so well. If by chance I don't have an answer, I say that I don't know but I'll find out." After taking the questioner's business card or noting the name and phone number, she heads back to the office, researches the answer, and calls the questioner right away.

Good presentations have the power to change lives, as González knows from her experience at the Chamber. Several years ago, she organized a "How to Open Your Own Business" panel presentation featuring an attorney, an accountant, a banker, and a business owner. Despite extensive advance publicity, the presentation drew an audience of one—but the lone attendee went on to open an auto mechanic shop. "It was very rewarding, better than if 50 people had attended and done nothing," González remembers. Now the Chamber sponsors such presentations every month, and a number of attendees have founded businesses. González invites these entrepreneurs to join her panels as a way of inspiring as well as informing audiences. "I want to include someone with a success story," she explains. "What better example?"

"I prefer to make my presentations interactive rather than following a formal script, and I make a point of following up on audience questions."

■ A chapter overview appears in the *Instructor's Resource Manual*.

CO1. Describe the important role that business presentations play in the organization.

Almost everyone in business is required to give a presentation occasionally.

Planning the business presentation

● Describe the role of business presentations.
● Plan and write a presentation.
● Plan a team presentation.
● Plan a video presentation.
● Plan other types of presentations.

■ See Slide 13.1.

■ The Role of Business Presentations

Anyone who plans a career in sales, training, or education expects to make many oral presentations to customers, employees, or students each week. What you may not realize, though, is that just about *everyone* in business will probably give at least one major presentation and many smaller ones each year, to customers, superiors, subordinates, or colleagues—not to mention presentations at PTA meetings, home-owners' association meetings, civic clubs, and the like.

The costs of ineffective presentations are immense. With many managers earning six-figure salaries, a presentation that discusses ideas incompletely and inefficiently wastes time and money. Sales are lost, vital information is not communicated, training programs fail, policies are not implemented, and profits fall.

Technology is undoubtedly changing the physical characteristics of oral presentations in business—for example, by making possible presenting via videotape, interactive television, or the Internet rather than in person. Competent communicators recognize, however, that the compelling effects of verbal and nonverbal communication strategies that are possible in oral presentations will continue to make them a critical communication competency in the contemporary business organization.

Written Versus Oral Presentations

Written reports and oral presentations both play important roles in helping an organization achieve its objectives. An oral presentation may be made either in conjunction with or in place of a written report. Effective communicators must recognize the advantages and disadvantages of presenting business information orally.[1]

Oral presentations provide immediate feedback, allow speaker control, and require little work of the audience.

Advantages of Oral Presentations   Probably the most important advantage of live oral presentations is the *immediate feedback* that is possible from the audience. Questions can be answered and decisions can be made on the spot. In addition, the speaker can pick up cues from audience members regarding how well they understand and agree with his or her points and can then adjust content and delivery accordingly.

A second advantage concerns *speaker control*. A written report may never even be read, let alone studied carefully. But speakers have a captive audience. They can control the pace of the presentation; question the audience to ensure attention and understanding; and use nonverbal cues such as pauses, gestures, and changes in voice speed and volume to add emphasis. In addition, visual aids used in an oral presentation are often more effective than those used in a written report.

A third advantage of the oral presentation has to do with the listener: presentations are simply *less work for the audience*. Listening is less strenuous and often more enjoyable than reading. The written report presents mostly verbal clues, whereas the oral presentation is filled with a variety of verbal and nonverbal clues to make comprehension easier and more interesting.

Advantages

● Immediate feedback
● Impact
● Control
● Less work for audience

Disadvantages

● Impermanence
● Expense
● Limited audience size
● Speaker-controlled pace

Disadvantages of Oral Presentations   Considering the advantages of immediate feedback, speaker control, and reduced audience effort, why isn't *all* business

■ See Slides 13.2 and 13.3.

information communicated orally? The major reason is that oral presentations are temporary. They "disappear," and within hours of delivery much of the information presented has been forgotten. Also, listeners have only one opportunity to understand what they're hearing. In contrast, the written report provides a permanent record that can be reread and referred to in the future. Video presentations, of course, avoid this problem; they are discussed later in this chapter.

Oral presentations may also be very expensive. It is much more cost-effective to have 1,000 managers scattered around the country read a written report than to have them hear the same information in a mass meeting. In addition to the expense, the sheer logistics of assembling such a large group can be overpowering. Furthermore, the visual aids used in oral presentations are often more expensive than those used in written reports (which is perhaps one reason that they're also usually more effective).

Oral presentations do not provide a permanent record and often are very expensive.

It's not surprising, then, that many presentations include both an oral and a written component. As a business communicator, you'll need to weigh a number of factors when you decide whether to communicate orally or in writing: the complexity of the material, the size of the audience, your need for immediate feedback, and the cost of the presentation, among others.

The Process of Making a Business Presentation

As you will remember, we followed a specific process when learning to communicate business information in written form; the process consisted of planning, drafting, revising, formatting, and finally proofreading the written document. We follow a similar logical process for making an oral presentation.

1. *Planning:* Determining the purpose of the presentation, analyzing the audience, and deciding the timing and method of delivery.
2. *Organizing:* Collecting the data and arranging it in a logical order.
3. *Developing visual aids:* Selecting the appropriate type, number, and content of visual aids.
4. *Practicing:* Rehearsing by simulating the actual presentation conditions as closely as possible.
5. *Delivering:* Dressing appropriately, maintaining friendly eye contact, speaking in an effective manner, and answering questions confidently.

The presentation process requires planning, organizing, developing visual aids, practicing, and delivering the presentation.

Planning and organizing the presentation are covered in this chapter. Developing visual aids and practicing and delivering the presentation are covered in Chapter 14.

■ Planning the Presentation

When assigned the task of making a business presentation, your first impulse might be to sit down at your desk or computer and begin writing. Resist the temptation. As in written communications, several important steps precede the actual writing. These steps involve determining the purpose of the presentation, analyzing the audience, planning the timing of the presentation, and selecting a delivery method.

co2. Plan a presentation by determining its purpose, analyzing the audience, and deciding the timing and method of delivery.

In addition to helping you decide what to include in your presentation, these planning tasks will give you important information about the degree of formality appropriate for the situation. The more formal the presentation, the more time you'll devote to the project. In general, complex topics or proposals with "high stakes" demand more formal presentations—with well-planned visuals, a carefully thought-out organizational plan, and extensive research. Likewise, the larger the audience and the greater the audience's opposition to your ideas, the more formal the presentation should be. A presentation you will deliver more than once is likely to be more formal than a one-time speech, as is a presentation on a complex topic. Finally, if the audience is made up of nationals from other countries, you will need to take their needs and expectations into consideration and will probably prepare a more formal presentation (see Spotlight 27, "Presenting Abroad").

Purpose

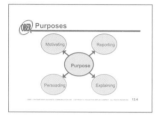

■ See Slide 13.4.

Most presentations seek either to report, explain, persuade, or motivate.

Keeping your purpose uppermost in mind helps you decide what information to include and what to omit, in what order to present this information, and which points to emphasize and subordinate. (See Communication Snapshot 13 for a look at the most popular topics of professional speakers.)

Most business presentations have one of these four purposes:

■ *Reporting:* Updating the audience on some project or event.

■ *Explaining:* Detailing how to carry out a procedure or how to operate a new piece of equipment.

■ *Persuading:* Convincing the listeners to purchase something or to accept an idea you're presenting.

■ *Motivating:* Inspiring the listeners to take some action.

Assume, for example, that you have been asked to make a short oral presentation on the topic of absenteeism at the Fremont Manufacturing Plant. If you're speaking to the management committee, your purpose would be to *report* the results of your research. Using a logical organization, you would discuss the effects of the problem on productivity, its causes, and possible solutions.

If you're speaking to the union personnel, however, your purpose might be to *motivate* the employees to reduce their absenteeism. You might then briefly discuss the extent of the problem, devote your major efforts to showing how the employees ultimately benefit from lower absenteeism, and finally introduce a monthly recognition program.

After your presentation is over, your purpose provides a criterion—the *only* important criterion—by which to judge the success of your presentation.

communication snapshot 13

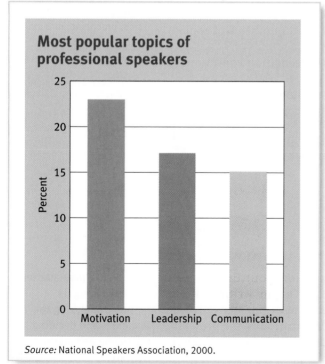

Most popular topics of professional speakers

Source: National Speakers Association, 2000.

spotlight27
ACROSS CULTURES

Presenting Abroad

Increasingly, managers are being required to make presentations abroad to nationals from other countries. Many of the principles discussed in this chapter hold true; however, those discussed in Chapter 2 regarding international communications also apply. Because each culture is different, we cannot make broad generalizations. The following discussion, then, simply points out some factors you will want to be aware of as you try to make your presentation appropriate for the specific country.

Planning the Presentation

Planning the presentation should really begin with deciding *who* should make the presentation. In Asian cultures, age is highly respected and the credibility of a younger presenter, regardless of his or her expertise or communication skills, may be questioned by an older audience. Similarly, female presenters may experience difficulty in some Middle Eastern countries.

The culture also affects the content and organization of your presentation, and you should adopt a strategy that will help you accomplish your goal. The most successful communicators adopt strategies that reflect both their culture and that of their host country.

Well-planned visual aids and printed handouts are especially desirable in helping an audience for whom English is a second language to follow your presentation. The use of examples and frequent preview and summary is also helpful. Know the customs and attitudes of your audience. For example, beginning a presentation with a joke, discussing incidents from one's private life, or holding a question-and-answer period might or might not be considered appropriate. However, projecting a cordial nature is appropriate everywhere.

Giving the Presentation

In many cultures, a formal presentation will be expected, with the presenter speaking from a full script and using elaborate visual aids. Some audiences may misinterpret an extemporaneous speech given from notes as implying the speaker didn't respect the audience enough to prepare his or her remarks fully.

Writing out your remarks in full beforehand will also help you plan your choice of words carefully. Restrict your vocabulary to the most common English words and your word meanings to the most common ones. Avoid using jargon, slang, and clichés.

Speak lowly and clearly, using uncomplicated language, and keep gestures to a minimum. Do not be surprised if some members of the audience do not look at you directly as you speak. Eye contact is not as important in some cultures as it is to many Americans. If possible, try to include some phrase from the local language in your remarks. When using overhead and slide projectors, the American custom is normally to stand next to the projector, whereas the European custom is to present while seated, with the projector alongside on a low table.

An overall attitude of sensitivity, empathy, respect, and flexibility will help you achieve success in giving presentations—both here and abroad.[2]

In other words, did the management committee understand the results of your research? Were the union members motivated to reduce their absenteeism? No matter how well or how poorly you spoke and no matter how impressive or ineffective your visual aids, the important question is whether you accomplished your purpose.

Audience Analysis

In addition to identifying such demographic factors as the size, age, and organizational status of your audience, you will also need to determine their level of knowledge

■ There is an ancient Greek saying, "When Demostracles speaks, the people say, 'My, what a wonderful speaker he is,' but when Pericles speaks, the people say, 'Let us march!' "

Analyze the audience in terms of demographics, level of knowledge, and psychological needs.

about your topic and their psychological needs (values, attitudes, and beliefs). These factors provide clues to everything from the overall content, tone, and types of examples you should use to the types of questions to expect and even the way you should dress.

The principles by which you analyze your audience are the same as those we discussed in the chapters on writing letters, memos, and reports. Consider the effect of your message on your audience and your credibility with them. The key is to put yourself in your audience's place so that you can anticipate their questions and reactions. The "you" attitude applies to oral as well as to written communication.

Large audiences require a more formal presentation.

The larger your audience, the more formal your presentation will be. When you speak to a large group, you should speak more loudly and more slowly and use more emphatic gestures and larger visuals. Usually, you should allow questions only at the end of your talk. If you're speaking to a small group, you can be more flexible about questions, and your tone and gestures will be more like those used in normal conversation. Furthermore, when presenting to small groups, your options in terms of visual aids increase.

If your audience is unfamiliar with your topic, you will need to use clear, easy-to-understand language, with extensive visual aids and many examples. If the audience is more knowledgeable, you can proceed at a faster pace. Suppose, however, that you have an audience composed of both novices and experts. One option, of course, would be to separate the two groups and to give two presentations—each geared to the level of that particular audience.

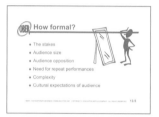

■ See Slide 13.5.

If the gulf in understanding is not quite that wide, you should determine who the key decision maker is in the group—frequently, but not always, the highest-ranking member present—and then provide a level of detail necessary to secure that person's understanding. Take time especially to understand this decision maker's needs, objectives, and interests as they relate to your objective.

The audience's psychological needs will also affect your presentation. If, for example, you think your listeners will be hostile—either to you personally or to your message—then you'll have to oversell yourself or your idea. Instead of giving one or two examples, you'll need to give several. In addition to establishing your own credibility, you may need to quote other experts to bolster your case.

In the presentation on absenteeism discussed earlier, the first audience was the management committee. The members of this committee have very high organizational status and probably expect a somewhat formal presentation. Although they may not be familiar with the specific problem, they are very familiar with the organization overall and are probably quite interested in the bottom-line implications of the problem.

Regarding the second presentation, however, the union members are probably a more heterogeneous group than the management committee. Thus, you must make sure that the language and examples used are appropriate for a broad range of knowledge, interests, and attitudes. In addition, you'll probably want to use a more informal, conversational style for the presentation. Sample slides that might be used for each of these two presentations are shown in Figure 13.1.

Once you've identified your audience, it is often helpful to meet with key people before your presentation, especially with the key decision makers. These meetings can help you predispose the audience in your favor or, at the very least, help you discover sources of opposition. Knowing ahead of time about their concerns

figure 13.1   The Audience and Purpose Determine the Content

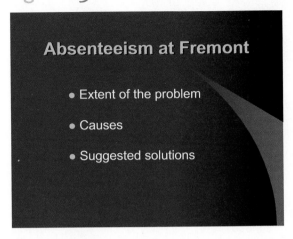

Absenteeism at Fremont

- Extent of the problem
- Causes
- Suggested solutions

OR

Absenteeism at Fremont

- How we stack up
- Full attendance = Full employment
- And the winner is ...

Audience: Management Committee
Purpose: Reporting

Audience: Union Members
Purpose: Motivating

will let you build relevant information into your presentation to address those concerns.

Timing of the Presentation

Often the timing of a presentation is beyond your control. If you've been asked to update the management committee about the absenteeism problem and the committee typically meets at 2 p.m. on the first Tuesday of each month, that is the precise time you must be available. Sometimes, however, you will have some flexibility. For example, if you want to present a proposal for a pet project to several managers whose cooperation is crucial for your success, you will be in charge of scheduling the meeting.

Consider two factors when scheduling presentations. First, allow yourself enough time to prepare—including gathering data, writing and revising, producing visual aids, and practicing the presentation. Second, consider the needs of your audience. Avoid times when they need to be away or are so occupied with other matters that they will not be able to concentrate on your presentation. In general, early or midmorning presentations are preferable to late afternoon sessions. Try to avoid giving a presentation immediately before lunch, when the audience may be hungry or eager to make lunch appointments, or, worse, immediately after lunch, when the audience may be late or not very alert.

Time the presentation to allow adequate preparation and to avoid rushed periods.

Delivery Method

At some point during your planning, you must decide on the method of delivery— that is, will you memorize your speech, read it, or speak from notes? Your choice will be determined by the answers to such questions as, How long is your talk? How complex is the content? How formal is the presentation? And, with what method (or combination of methods) are you most comfortable?

During his 2004 presidential campaign, Senator John Kerry of Massachusetts gave hundreds of speeches. Yet, he spent hours fiddling with drafts of each new speech. "Polishing and polishing and polishing until he's satisfied," is how one aide described the process.

Memorizing   Unless a presentation is short and significant, memorizing an entire speech is risky, not to mention time-consuming. You always run the risk (a very real one if you're nervous) of forgetting your lines and perhaps ruining your entire presentation. In addition, memorized presentations often sound mechanical and do not let you adapt the material to the needs of the audience. However, memorizing the first or last section of your presentation, a telling quotation, or a humorous story may be extremely effective for presenting a key part of your talk.

Reading   Reading speeches is quite common in academic and scientific settings, where a professor or researcher might be asked to read a paper at a professional conference. Writing out a speech and reading from the prepared text is helpful if you're dealing with a highly complex or technical topic, if the subject is controversial (making a statement to the press, for example), or if you have a lot of information to present in a short time. Such delivery is *not* recommended for most business settings because the presenter's eyes are typically too much on the paper and not enough on the audience and because spontaneity and flexibility are lost. After all, if the speech is going to be read word for word, why not just duplicate and distribute it to the audience for them to read at their leisure?

Of the three common methods of presentation (memorizing, reading, and speaking from notes), the last is the most common for business presentations.

Speaking from Notes   By far the most common (and generally the most effective) method for delivering business presentations is speaking from prepared notes, such as an outline. The notes contain key phrases rather than complete sentences, and you compose the exact wording as you speak. Although you may occasionally stumble in choosing a word, the spontaneous, conversational quality and the close audience rapport that result are generally superior to those of other presentation methods. The notes help ensure that you will cover all the material and cover it in a logical order; yet this method provides enough flexibility that you can adapt your remarks in reaction to verbal and nonverbal cues from the audience.

The specific content and format of the notes is not important; choose whatever works best for you. Some people use a formal outline on full sheets of paper; others prefer notes jotted on index cards. Some use complete sentences; others, short phrases. If desirable, include notes to yourself, such as when to pause, which phrases to emphasize, and when to change a slide or transparency.

Whether you use full sheets or index cards, be sure to number each page (in case the pages are dropped). For ease in moving from sheet to sheet or card to card, write on just one side and do not staple. Typed copy is better than handwritten copy and large type is better than small type. Type your notes in standard upper- and lowercase letters rather than in all capitals, which are more difficult to read because all the letters are the same size.

Use larger type and upper- and lowercase letters for outline notes.

Examples of excerpts from a written report, a complete script for an oral presentation, and outline notes for an oral presentation are shown in Figure 13.2 (see page 476). Note several things about the content and format of the excerpts:

- Both the complete script and the outline notes are typed in larger type for ease of reading, and both contain prompts showing when to display each visual aid (slide).

- The complete script is written in a more informal, conversational style than the written report and uses a shorter line length and extra spacing between paragraphs (to help the speaker find his or her place easily).

- The outline notes contain mostly phrases, with each subtopic indented to show its relationship to the main idea.

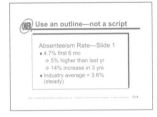

■ See Slide 13.6.

Of course, you can tailor any combination of these methods to suit your needs. Some people, especially those who give speeches only occasionally, do best by writing out the entire speech and then practicing it until they can recite whole paragraphs or thoughts with ease. Doing so enables them to maintain eye contact with the audience. Some insert delivery cues, indicating when to pause, smile, make a gesture, display a visual aid, slow down, and the like.

Some speakers start off by writing out the entire speech and then practice extensively from the prepared script. Only after they are thoroughly familiar with their verbatim script do they condense it into an outline and then speak from the outline. Most experienced speakers work directly from notes right from the beginning. Whatever method you use, the key to a successful delivery is practice, practice, practice.

■ Organizing the Presentation

For most presentations, the best way to begin is simply to brainstorm: write down every point you can think of that might be included in your presentation. Don't worry about the order or format—just get it all down. During the next several days, carry a pen and some paper with you so that you can jot down random thoughts as they occur—during a meeting, at lunch, going to and from work, or in the evening at home.

CO3. Write a presentation by collecting the data and organizing it in a logical format.

figure 13.2
Complete Script Versus Outline Notes

Original Written Report Page

Note the formal language.

> The staff employees were asked to rate their level of familiarity with each benefit. As shown in Table 1, most staff employees believe that most benefits have been adequately communicated to them.
>
> At least three-fourths of the employees are familiar with all major benefits except for long-term disability insurance, which is familiar to only a slight majority. The low level of knowledge about automobile insurance can be explained by the fact that this benefit had been in effect for only six weeks at the time of the survey.
>
> In general, benefit familiarity is not related to length of employment at Mayo. Most employees are familiar with most benefits, regardless of their length of employment. However, as shown in Figure 1, the one benefit for which this is not true is life insurance. The longer a person has been employed at Mayo, the more likely he or she is to know about this benefit.

Excerpt of a Complete Script of an Oral Presentation

Note the conversational language, larger type size, and shorter line length.

> We asked our employees how familiar they are with our benefits (SLIDE 1). As you can see, most employees know about most of our benefits.
>
> At least three-fourths of them are familiar with all but two of our benefits, and these two are long-term disability and automobile insurance. Only a slight majority know about our long-term disability insurance, and slightly more than a third know about our automobile insurance. As you may remember, we began offering automobile insurance just six weeks before conducting this survey.
>
> In general, there's no correlation between how long employees have worked and how familiar they are with our benefits. Most employees are familiar with our benefits, no matter how long they've worked here. The one exception is life insurance (SLIDE 2). The longer a person has worked for us, the more

Outline Notes for an Oral Presentation

Note the incomplete sentences and abbreviations.

FAMILIARITY WITH BENEFITS—SLIDE 1
• Most know about most benefits
• −3/4 know about all but 2 benefits:
—Long-term disability = slight majority
—Auto insur. = +1/3 (begun 6 wks before survey)
• No correlation between employment length & familiarity
—Not true for life insur.—SLIDE 2
—Life insur.: Longer employ. = more familiarity

Later, separate your notes into three categories: opening, body, and ending. As you begin to analyze and organize your material, you may find that you need additional information. You may need to retrieve records from files, consult with a colleague, visit your corporate or local library to fill in the gaps, or perhaps go online to retrieve data from the World Wide Web.

See Slide 13.7.

The Opening

The purpose of the opening is to capture the interest of your audience, and the first 90 seconds of your presentation are crucial. The audience will be observing every detail about you—your dress, posture, facial features, and voice qualities, as well as what you're actually saying—for clues about you and your topic, and they will be making preliminary judgments accordingly.

Your opening should introduce the topic, identify the purpose, and preview the presentation.

Begin immediately to establish rapport and build a relationship with your audience—not just for the duration of your presentation but for the long term. If you're making a proposal, you need not only the audience's attention during your presentation but also their cooperation later to implement your proposal. Because the opening is so crucial, many professionals write out the entire opening and practice it until they are extremely familiar with it.

The kind of opening that will be effective depends on your topic, how well you know the audience, and how well they know you. If, for example, you're giving a status report on a project about which you've reported before, you can immediately announce your main points (for example, that the project is on schedule and proceeding as planned) and go immediately to the body of your remarks. If, however, you're presenting a new proposal to your superiors, you'll first have to introduce the topic and provide background information.

See Slide 13.8.

If most of the listeners don't know you, you'll have to gain their attention with a creative opening. The following types of attention-getting openings have proven successful for business presentations; the examples given are for the presentation to union employees on the topic of absenteeism:

Spreading her money knowledge, Jacquette Timmons, president and CEO of Sterling Investment Management Inc., conducts a "Meet Your Money" workshop. She spices her presentations with hard data. According to her, "The numbers reveal the facts, the facts tell a story, and the story gives clues about what to do next."

Effective openings include a quotation, question, hypothetical situation, story, startling fact, or visual aid.

- *Quote a well-known person:* "Comedian Woody Allen once noted that 90 percent of the job is just showing up."

- *Ask a question:* "If we were able to cut our absenteeism rate by half during the coming six months, exactly how much do you think that would mean for each of us in our end-of-year bonus checks?"

- *Present a hypothetical situation:* "Assume that as you were leaving home this morning to put in a full day at work, your son came up to you and said he was too tired to go to school because he had stayed up so late last night watching *Wrestle Mania*. What would be your reaction?"

- *Relate an appropriate anecdote, story, joke, or personal experience:* "George, a friend of mine who had recently changed jobs, happened to meet his former boss and asked her whom she had hired to fill his vacancy. 'George,' his former boss said, 'when you left, you didn't *leave* any vacancy!' Perhaps the reason George didn't leave any vacancy was that . . ."

- *Give a startling fact:* "During the next 24 hours, American industry will lose $136 million because of absenteeism."

- *Use a dramatic prop or visual aid:* (holding up a paper clip) "What do you think is the *true* cost of this paper clip to our company?"

Don't apologize or make excuses (for example, "I wish I had had more time to prepare my remarks today" or "I'm not really much of a speaker"). The audience may agree with you! At any rate, you'll turn them off immediately and weaken your credibility.

Your opening should lead into the body of your presentation by previewing your remarks: "Today, I'll cover four main points. First, . . ." Let the audience know the scope of your remarks. For example, if you're discussing the pros and cons of a plant closing from a strictly dollars-and-cents standpoint, advise the audience immediately that your analysis does not include political or human relations considerations. If you don't first define the scope of your remarks, you may invite needless questions and second-guessing during your presentation.

For most business presentations, let the audience know up front what you expect of them. Are you simply presenting information for them to absorb, or will the audience be expected to react to your remarks? Are you asking for their endorsement, their resources, their help, or what? Let the audience know what their role will be so that they can then place your remarks in perspective.

The Body

The body of your presentation conveys the real content. Here you'll develop the points you introduced in the opening, giving background information, specific evidence, examples, implications, consequences, and other needed information.

Organize the body logically, according to your topic and audience needs.

Choose a Logical Sequence   Just as you do when writing a letter or report, choose an organizational plan that suits your purpose and your audience's needs. The most commonly used organizational plans are these:

- *Criteria:* Introduce each criterion in turn and show how well each alternative meets that criterion (typically used for presenting proposals).

- *Direct sequence:* Give the major conclusions first, followed by the supporting details (typically used for presenting routine information).

- *Indirect sequence:* Present the reasons first, followed by the major conclusion (typically used for persuasive presentations).

- *Chronology:* Present the points in the order in which they occurred (typically used in status reports or when reporting on some event).

- *Cause/effect/solution:* Present the sources and consequences of some problem and then pose a solution.

- *Order of importance:* Arrange the points in order of importance and then pose each point as a question and answer it (an effective way of ensuring that the audience can follow your arguments).

- *Elimination of alternatives:* List all alternatives and then gradually eliminate each one until only one option remains—the one you're recommending.

Whatever organizational plan you choose, make sure that your audience knows at the outset where you're going and is able to follow your organization. In a written document, signposts such as headings tell the reader how the parts fit together. In an oral presentation, you must compensate for the lack of such aids by using frequent and clear transitions that tell your listeners where you are. Pace your presentation of data so that you do not lose your audience.

Establish Your Credibility   Convince the listener that you've done a thorough job of collecting and analyzing the data and that your points are reasonable. Support your arguments with credible evidence—statistics, actual experiences, examples, and support from experts. Use objective language; let the data—not exaggeration or emotion—persuade the audience. Be guided by the same principles you use when writing a persuasive letter or report.

Avoid saturating your presentation with so many facts and figures that your audience won't be able to absorb them. Regardless of their relevance, statistics will not strengthen your presentation if the audience is unable to digest all the data. A more effective tactic is to prepare handouts of detailed statistical data to distribute for review at a later time.

Deal with Negative Information   It would be unusual if *all* the data you've collected and analyzed support your proposal. (If that were the case, persuasion would not be needed.) What should you do, then, about negative information, which, if presented, might weaken your argument? You cannot simply ignore negative information. To do so would surely open up a host of questions and subsequent doubts that would seriously weaken your position.

Think about your own analysis of the data. Despite the negative information, you still concluded that your solution has merit. Your tactic, then, is to present all the important information—pro and con—and to show through your analysis and discussion that your recommendations are still valid, in spite of the

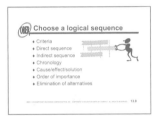

■ See Slide 13.9.

Do not ignore negative information.

DILBERT

disadvantages and drawbacks. Use the techniques you learned in Chapter 5 about emphasis and subordination to let your listeners know which points you considered major and which you considered minor.

Although you should discuss the important negative points, you may safely omit discussing minor ones. You must, however, be prepared to discuss these minor negative points if any questions about them arise at the conclusion of your presentation.

The Ending

Finish on a strong, upbeat note, leaving your audience with a clear and simple message.

The ending of your presentation is your last opportunity to achieve your objective. Don't waste it. A presentation without a strong ending is like a joke without a punch line.

Your closing should summarize the main points of your presentation, especially if it has been a long one. Even if the members of your audience have had an easy time following the structure of your talk, they won't necessarily remember all your important points. Let the audience know the significance of what you've said. Draw conclusions, make recommendations, or outline the next steps to take. Leave the audience with a clear and simple message.

To add punch to your ending, you may want to use one of the same techniques discussed for opening a presentation. You might tell a story, make a personal appeal, or issue a challenge. However, resist the temptation to end with a quotation. It won't sound dramatic enough. Besides, you want your listeners to remember *your* words and thoughts—not someone else's. Also avoid fading out with a weak "That's about all I have to say" or "I see that our time is running out."

After you've developed some experience in giving presentations, you will be able to judge fairly accurately how long to spend on each point so as to finish on time. Until then, practice your presentation with a stopwatch. If necessary, insert reminders at critical points in your notes indicating where you should be at what point in time. Avoid having to drop important sections or rush through the conclusion of your presentation because you misjudged your timing.

Because your audience will remember best what they hear last, think of your ending as one of the most important parts of your presentation. Finish on a strong, upbeat note. Also remember that no one ever lost any friends by finishing a minute or two ahead of schedule. As Toastmasters International puts it, "Get up, speak up, shut up, and sit down."

The Use of Humor in Business Presentations

Memory research indicates that when ideas are presented with humor, the audience not only is able to recall more details of the presentation but also is able to retain the information longer.[3]

Most of us are not capable of being a David Letterman, even if we wanted to be. If you know you do not tell humorous stories well, the moment you're in front of an audience is not the time to try to rectify that situation. Both you and your audience will suffer. If, however, you feel that you can use humor effectively, doing so might add just the appropriate touch to your presentation.

Use humor if it is appropriate and you are adept at telling humorous stories.

Jokes, puns, satire, and especially amusing real-life incidents are just a few examples of humor, all of which serve to form a bond between speaker and audience. Humor can be used anywhere in a presentation—in the opening to get attention, in the body to add interest, or in the closing to drive home a point. Humor should be avoided, of course, if the topic is very serious or has negative consequences for the audience.

If you tell an amusing story, it must always be appropriate to the situation and in good taste. Never tell an off-color or sexist joke; never use offensive language; never single out an ethnic, racial, or religious group; and never use a dialect or foreign accent in telling a story. Such tactics are always in bad taste. The best stories are directed at yourself; they show that you are human and can laugh at yourself.

Personalize an amusing story to make it relate more directly to your topic.

Before telling a humorous story, make sure you understand it and think it's funny. Then personalize it for your own style of speaking and for the particular situation. Avoid beginning jokes by saying, "I heard a funny story the other day about . . ." A major element of humor is surprise, so don't warn the audience a joke is coming. If you do, they're mentally preparing for a funny punch line, and you may disappoint them. If, on the other hand, you're already halfway into the story before the audience even realizes it's a joke, your chances of success are greater.

Resist the temptation to laugh at your own stories. A slight smile is more effective. Wait for the (hoped-for) laughter to subside; then continue your presentation by relating the punch line to the topic at hand.

Regardless of your expertise as a joke teller, do not use humor too frequently. Humor is a means to an end—not an end in itself. When all is said and done, you don't want your audience to remember that you were funny. You want them to remember that what you had to say was important and made sense.

■ Work-Team Presentations

Work-team presentations are common strategies for communicating about complex projects. For example, when presenting the organization's marketing plan to management or when updating the five-year plan, it is unlikely that any one person will have the expertise or time to prepare the entire presentation. Instead, a cooperative effort will be most effective.

CO4. **Plan a team presentation.**

Work-team presentations, whether written or oral, require extensive planning, close coordination, and a measure of maturity and goodwill. If you are responsible for coordinating such efforts, allow enough time and assign responsibilities on the basis of individual talents and time constraints.

Your major criterion for making assignments is the division of duties that will result in the most effective presentation. Tap into each member's strengths. Some members may be better at collecting and analyzing the information to be presented, others may be better at developing the visual aids, and others may be

■ See Slide 13.10.

better at delivering the presentation. Does any work-team member have a knack for telling good stories or connecting with strangers? Maybe he or she should begin the presentation. Or pick a "diplomat" to moderate the question-and-answer session.

Make individual assignments for a team presentation based on individual strengths and preferences.

Everyone need not share equally in each aspect of the project. As coordinator, you should ensure that all efforts are recognized publicly and equally during the actual presentation, regardless of how much "podium time" is assigned to each person.

The Role of the Team Leader

Every team needs a leader—someone who will assume overall responsibility for the project. The team leader should be organized, knowledgeable about the topic, and well liked and respected by the rest of the team.

The effective team leader will lead the group in developing a cohesive strategy for the entire presentation and preparing a tentative schedule. Delay dividing up individual responsibilities until all team members are aware of and support the basic framework for the presentation. Assigning roles too early in the process is, in fact, one of the most common problems encountered with team presentations.

The team leader will want to give each member a written assignment of his or her responsibilities for content, visual aids, audience handouts, deadlines, rehearsals, and the like. In setting deadlines, work backward from the presentation date—not forward from the starting date.

Achieving Coherence

Make your team presentation look as though it were prepared and given by a single person.

Just as people have different writing styles, so also they have different speaking styles. You must ensure that your overall presentation has coherence and unity—that is, that it sounds as if it were prepared and given by one individual. Thus, the group members should decide beforehand the most appropriate tone, format, organization, style for visual aids, manner of dress, method of handling questions, and similar factors that will help the presentation flow smoothly from topic to topic and from speaker to speaker.

Use a presentation template (either one that comes with your software package or one developed by your team) to maintain a consistent "look-and-feel" across everyone's slides. These templates define backgrounds and colors, slide heading formats, and font styles and sizes. Someone must also monitor for semantic consistency—both in the visual aids and in the verbal portion. Do you refer to people by first and last names, last names only, or a personal title and last name? Do you refer to your visual aids as charts, slides, overheads, graphics, or something else? If an unfamiliar term is used, ensure that the first person using the term (and only the first person) defines it.

Practicing the Team Presentation

A full-scale rehearsal—in the room where the presentation will be made and using all visual aids—is crucial for work-team presentations. If possible, videotape this rehearsal for later analysis by the entire group. Schedule your final practice session early enough that you will have time to make any changes needed—and then to run through the presentation once more, if necessary.

Critiquing the performance of a colleague requires tact, empathy, and goodwill; accepting such feedback requires grace and maturity. For the entire presentation to succeed, each individual element must succeed. If it does, each contributor shares in the success and any rewards that may result.

If dividing up the team parts prematurely is the most common problem of team presentations, then surely the failure to plan and coordinate introductions and transitions is the second most frequently encountered dilemma. Will the first speaker introduce all team members at the beginning, or will speakers introduce themselves as they get up to speak?

If a question comes up during the presentation that you know a team member will answer during a subsequent segment, avoid stealing the team member's thunder. Instead, respond that "Alice will be covering that very point in a few minutes." If a question is asked of the group itself, the team leader should determine who will answer it. Refrain from adding to another member's response unless what you have to contribute is truly an important point not covered in the original answer.

Finally, consider yourself on stage during the entire team presentation—no matter who is presenting. If you're on the sidelines, stand straight, pay attention to the presenter (even though you may have heard the content a dozen times), and try to read the audience for nonverbal signs of confusion, boredom, disagreement, and the like.

■ Video Presentations

Increasingly, organizations are videotaping presentations, which can then be shown on a television monitor using a videocassette recorder (VCR), CD-ROM, computer projection, or even the Internet. For example, as part of an orientation program for new employees, the president of the organization may videotape a welcome speech and a personnel specialist may tape a presentation of employee benefits. A marketing manager may also videotape a new product announcement to be sent to important customers and the news media around the country. In fact, any presentation that must be given many times is a candidate for videotaping.

Most of the same principles mentioned earlier apply equally well to video presentations. In addition, peculiar effects may result when the presenter faces the camera, because gazing into the eye of the camera for a long time is such an unnatural situation. The only solution is to practice. Fortunately, handheld videocameras and VCRs are now so common that you can practice easily in the comfort of your own home or office.

The best colors to wear when participating in a video presentation are shades of blue; a light blue shirt or blouse with a blue jacket or blazer is ideal. Avoid contrasting colors and stripes. Makeup is recommended for both men and women to reduce sweat and even out skin tone. When recording, sit or stand straight and look into the camera as long as possible while talking. Always focus your eyes on one of two places—either directly at the camera or at your notes; never gaze off to the side or over the camera. Because television exaggerates movements, stand or sit as still as possible and keep gestures to a minimum. Also, stay within an established area

co5. **Plan a video presentation.**

■ See Slide 13.11.

of movement (determined beforehand with the person who will be doing the videotaping).

If possible, use actual color printouts of your visuals instead of an overhead or computer projection; the camera will pick up the image much better. Use at least one-inch lettering, printed on a light blue or pastel background rather than white. Try to group your visuals so that the camera is not zooming in and out too much, as it can be distracting to the audience.

The increasing use of video presentations also means that you may be called upon to operate the videocamera. As a camera operator:

- Control the noise level in the room; even an air conditioner can add distracting background noise. Also, make sure that the room has good overall lighting, although it does not have to be "spotlights."

- Check your camera batteries beforehand and perhaps have a spare on hand.

- Use a tripod for stability. If you do not have access to a tripod, use your body as a brace for the camera, tucking it in against your body to steady it.

- Zoom in on the visual when the speaker mentions it.

- Minimize camera movement, but don't be afraid to move the camera. Use smooth, slow movement rather than fast, jerky movement.

- Try to "frame" or block the person in the camera (waist up, for example); don't get a shot that is too wide, covering too much area. A good rule of thumb is to provide a one-inch border around the subject. If the presenter plans to move around, establish the area for movement with him or her before filming. Then let the person move within this frame while keeping the camera still, instead of always following the person with the camera.

- Think in terms of what will be viewed by the audience rather than what will be filmed by the camera operator (that is, think in terms of showing, not shooting). Rarely will you use all of the footage shot; consider it the raw material from which to select and organize an effective presentation.

Contemporary businesspeople need to become not only "computer literate," but also "video literate." If you're unfamiliar with videotaping procedures, visit a local video studio and observe a shoot to see how the process is handled and how directors and camera crews work with the presenter.

■ See Slide 13.12.

co6. **Plan other types of business presentations.**

■ Other Business Presentations

In the standard types of business presentations discussed so far, you, the presenter, are the star of the show: you present information that is necessary to conduct the business of the organization, and you prepare your presentation carefully. Occasionally, however, you may be asked to participate in other types of presentations—ones in which you act as a supporting player. Such situations include giving impromptu remarks, making introductions, and making or receiving special recognitions.

Impromptu Remarks

During the course of a meeting or in conjunction with another person's presentation, you may unexpectedly be asked to come to the podium to "say a few words about" or "bring us up to date on" some topic. In truth, most such situations are not a complete surprise; you can often predict when you may be called on and should prepare accordingly. (Remember the words of Mark Twain: "It takes three weeks to prepare a good impromptu speech.")

Do not be put off by the fact that you may sometimes prepare remarks that will never be given because you were not asked to speak. Reviewing a situation and defining your ideas about it are always helpful, both as a management strategy and as preparation for future speaking opportunities.

If you truly have no warning, stay calm. You would not have been called on unless you had something positive to contribute. Remember that the audience knows you are giving impromptu remarks, so they won't expect you to demonstrate the same polish as a person who is giving a prepared presentation. You have no need to apologize. Keep to the topic, limiting your remarks to those areas in which you have some real expertise or insight, and speak for no more than a few minutes.

A S K Ober

Dear Dr. Ober:

I am a student at Illinois State University and don't know how to type. Can you tell me this: Is the Dvorak keyboard or the Qwerty keyboard better to learn? Are there any statistics to support or refute why individuals should change to the Dvorak keyboard from the Qwerty?

—Bryan F.

Dear Bryan:

I'm not aware of any recent actual research in this area. My suspicion is that this is an issue whose time has come and gone. Voice-recognition technology may be the next hot issue in data entry. Two good sources of previous research analysis are (a) Lee Gomes, "Economists Decide to Challenge Facts of the QWERTY Story," *Wall Street Journal*, February 25, 1998, p. B1, and (b) Stan Libowitz and Stephen Margolis, "Typing Errors: QWERTY Typewriter Keyboard Reform," *Reason*, Vol. 28, 1996, pp. 28–35.

—Scot

E-mail your questions and comments to askober@ober.net.

Introductions

If you're the host of a presentation given by someone else, your actions can set the stage for a successful performance, which reflects well on both the speaker and the host. Make sure that you request background information about the speaker ahead of time, including correct pronunciations for all proper names. Also, communicate to the speaker the audience needs and interests, the nature of the expected presentation, its preferred length, the type of physical accommodations, and the like.

When introducing someone, remember that the speaker is the main event—not you. All of your remarks should be directed at welcoming the speaker and establishing his or her qualifications to speak on the topic being addressed. Avoid inserting your own opinions about the topic or speaking for too long, thereby cutting into the speaker's time.

Briefly introduce the speaker, keeping the emphasis on the speaker and his or her qualifications.

Select from the speaker's data sheet those accomplishments that are particularly relevant to the current topic, add any personal asides such as hobbies or family information to show the speaker as a human being, and conclude with a statement such as "We're honored to have with us Ms. Jane Doe, who will now speak on the topic of . . . Ms. Doe." Lead the applause as the speaker rises; then step back from the podium and welcome the speaker with a handshake.

After the presentation, return to the podium and extend your appreciation to the person once again with another handshake and some brief remarks about the importance and relevance of the speaker's comments. Also, lead the question-and-answer session if one is planned, and be prepared to ask the first question in case no one in the audience wants to go first. At the conclusion, extend a sincere "thank you" to the speaker.

If you are responsible for seating and introducing a head table, you and the speaker should be seated on opposite sides of the podium, with the speaker sitting at the immediate left as you face the audience and you, as master of ceremonies, sitting at the immediate right side of the podium. When making the introductions, indicate whether each person should stand when introduced or remain seated, and ask the audience to hold any applause until everyone has been introduced. Then introduce each person, making a few appropriate remarks about each. Proceed from your extreme right to the podium and then from your extreme left to the podium.

Give similar types and amounts of information about each person and ensure that all names are pronounced correctly. Be consistent in identifying each person—all first names or all personal titles and last names. When you get to the speaker, introduce him or her in a similar manner, indicating that a more complete introduction will follow. Lead the applause when all members of the head table have been introduced.

Introduce the head table, beginning from the speaker's extreme right to the podium and then from the extreme left to the podium.

Special Recognitions

When presenting an award or recognizing someone for special achievement, first provide some background about the award—its history and criteria for selection. Then discuss the awardee's accomplishments, emphasizing those most relevant to the award. Under such happy circumstances, extensive praise is appropriate. Lead the applause as the awardee rises.

When accepting an honor, show genuine appreciation and graciously thank those responsible for the award. You may briefly thank people who helped you in your accomplishments, but do not bore the audience by thanking a long list of individuals who may be unknown to the audience.

The **3Ps**
Problem, Process, Product

A BUSINESS PRESENTATION

Problem

You are Matt Kromer, an information specialist at Lewis & Smith, a large import/export firm in San Francisco. Your company publishes three major external documents—a quarterly customer newsletter, a semiannual catalog, and an annual report. All three are currently prepared by an outside printing company. However, the decision was recently made to switch to some form of in-house publishing for these publications.

Your superior asked you to research the question of whether your firm should use word processing or desktop publishing software to create these documents. Considering the importance of these external documents, you have been asked to make a formal 20-minute presentation of your findings and recommendations to the firm's administrative committee.

Process

1. What is the purpose of your presentation?

   To present the findings from my research, to recommend a type of software program, and to persuade the audience that my recommendations are sound.

2. Describe your audience.

   The administrative committee consists of the five managers (including my superior) who report to the vice president for administration. I have met them all, but with the exception of my own superior, I do not know any of them well.

   Their role will be to make the final decision regarding which type of software program to use. Once that decision has been made, the actual users will decide which brand to purchase. Four of the five managers are casual users of word processing software. They've all likely heard of desktop publishing but have never used it.

3. What type of presentation will be most appropriate?

   This will be a normal business presentation to a small audience, so I'll speak from notes and use slides. Because I have only 20 minutes to present, I'll hold off answering questions until the end—to make sure I have enough time to cover the needed information.

4. What kind of data have you collected for your presentation?

> I studied each publication's formatting requirements, analyzed the features of the most popular word processing (Microsoft Word) and desktop publishing (Adobe PageMaker) programs, and spoke with a colleague from a firm that recently began publishing its documents in-house.
>
> On the basis of the criteria of cost, ease of use, and features, I'll recommend the use of word processing software to publish our three documents.

5. How will you organize the data?

> First, I'll present the background information. Then, I could organize my research data by presenting the advantages and disadvantages of each type of program. However, I think it would be more effective to organize my findings by criteria instead; that is, I will show how each program rates in terms of cost, ease of use, and features.

6. Outline an effective opening section for your presentation.

> a. Introduction: "Freedom of the Press" (Computer software now gives us the freedom to publish our own documents at lower cost and with greater flexibility.)
>
> b. Purpose: to recommend whether to use WP or DTP software
>
> c. Organization: by criteria (cost, ease of use, and features)
>
> d. Audience role: to make the final decision

7. How will you handle negative information?

> Although I'm recommending word processing software, the desktop publishing program has more features. However, I'll show that (a) we don't necessarily need those features and (b) those features make the program more difficult to learn.

Note: This 3Ps activity continues in Chapter 14.

SELECTING DESKTOP PUBLISHING SOFTWARE
Presented to the Administrative Committee
Matt Kromer, 10/3/—

I. OPENING

A. I'd like to talk to you today about <u>freedom of the press</u>—specifically about our recent decision to switch to in-house publishing. And though our publications won't be completely "free," desktop publishing <u>will</u> provide us with more flexibility—at a greatly reduced price.

B. <u>Purpose</u>: To recommend whether to use word processing or desktop publishing software to publish our company newsletter, catalog, and annual report.

SLIDE 1—FREEDOM OF THE PRESS

C. <u>Preview</u>:

   1. Background information

   2. Criteria for decision:
      a. Cost
      b. Ease of use
      c. Features

   3. My recommendation

D. <u>Your Job</u>: Make final decision.
   Will <u>not</u> have to decide which brand of software.

E. Will take questions at the end.
   Will distribute handout.

II. BODY

SLIDE 2—PUBLICATIONS

A. <u>Background</u>:

Provides identifying information in the opening—in case of loss or for future reference.

Uses an attention-getting opening that is written verbatim for a stress-free start.

Uses the opening to give the purpose, preview the topics, and identify the audience's role.

Alerts the audience to prevent interrupting questions and unnecessary note taking.

Marks the slide references for easy identification.

Grammar and Mechanics Notes

Type the outline in large upper- and lowercase letters, either on individual note cards or on full sheets of paper. Leave plenty of white space between sections so that you can easily find your place.

Makes a note to hold up copies of documents.

1. 3 major external documents; all have strategic marketing value:

   a. <u>Newsletter</u> *(Show copy)*: <u>The Forum</u>
      — 2,000 copies quarterly
      — 8 pp. 1-color (black) on ivory stock, with brown masthead
      — Photos and line art

   b. <u>Catalog</u> *(Show copy)*:
      — 4,000 copies semiannually
      — 36-44 pp.
      — 1-color (black) interior with 4-color cover

   c. <u>Annual Report</u> *(Show copy)*:
      — 1,500 copies annually
      — 24-28 pp.
      — 1-color (blue) interior on gray stock with 4-color cover

2. All 3 presently published by Medallion Printing Company

Discusses research procedures to help establish credibility.

3. <u>Research</u>:

   a. Analyzed each pub. to determine formatting reqs.

   b. Analyzed features of <u>Microsoft Word,</u> the WP program we now support, and <u>Adobe PageMaker,</u> the most popular DTP program.

   c. Spoke with Paula Henning from Crown Busch.
      Her co. began producing documents in-house using DTP last year.

Organizes the main part of the speech body by the criteria used for making the decision.

B. <u>Criteria</u>:

SLIDE 3—COST COMPARISON

1. <u>Cost</u>:

   a. Either program will require:
      (1) One flatbed scanner and software: $375
      (2) One digital camera: $475

   b. Microsoft Word: $175—But we already own.

   c. Adobe PageMaker: $495—Have to buy.

Grammar and Mechanics Notes

You do not have to write your presentation notes in parallel format; no one will see them but you. You may need complete sentences to jog your memory for some parts but only partial sentences, individual words, or abbreviations for other parts.

    d. <u>Conclusion</u>: PageMaker costs $495 more than Microsoft Word.

  2. <u>Ease of Use</u>:

    a. <u>Microsoft Word</u>:
      (1) Operators already know how to use.
      (2) ½-day seminar to teach advanced features—$500

    b. <u>Adobe PageMaker</u>:
      (1) Difficult to learn because of adv. features
      (2) Danger of forgetting—used infrequently
      (3) 2-day seminar needed—$2,000

    c. Conclusion: Word cost $1,500 less than PageMaker.

Presents both positive and negative information and discusses the importance and implications of each feature.

SLIDE 4—FEATURE COMPARISON

  3. <u>Features</u>:

a. Font flexibility	Both have.
b. Column feature	Both have.
c. Import/manipulate graphics	PM has more options.
d. Color separations	PM has; Word doesn't. Don't need now; maybe in future.
e. Predesigned templates	Both have; PM better.
f. Ease of revisions	Important criterion Both have; easier in Word.

Underline important points for easy referral. Use columns when needed for easy reference.

III. CLOSING

SLIDE 5—RECOMMENDATION

A. <u>Recommendation:</u> Microsoft Word

  1. Cheaper (by $1,500)

  2. Easier to use/less training needed

  3. Has all the features we presently need

Puts the final recommendation and the rationale on a slide—for emphasis.

Closes by giving the recommendation and telling what happens next. Ends on a confident, forward-looking note.

Follows presentation with a question-and-answer session.

Leaves room for taking notes during question-and-answer session.

<u>**SLIDE 6—SCHEDULE**</u>

B. <u>Schedule</u>:

Today	Make software decision
November	Purchase and install hardware and software
December	Conduct user training
January	Begin producing 3 docs. in-house

C. <u>Conclusion</u>:

Our entry into DTP is an exciting project because it gives us greater control over our publications at less cost. In addition, DTP will open up opportunities for even more publishing projects in the future to help us better fulfill our corporate mission.

<u>**HANDOUT—SELECTING DESKTOP PUBLISHING SOFTWARE**</u>

IV. QUESTIONS

NOTES *(to be taken during presentation)*

Grammar and Mechanics Notes

Double-space the conclusion because it will be given verbatim. *Note:* You would no doubt have to insert some last-minute handwritten changes in your final outline prior to actually giving the presentation.

Visit the **BusCom Online Learning Center** (at http://college.hmco.com) for additional resources to help you with this course and with your future career.

Summary

Oral business presentations are a vital part of the contemporary organization because they provide immediate feedback, give the presenter full control of the situation, and require less audience effort than do written presentations. However, oral presentations are also impermanent and expensive, and the speaker-controlled pace means that some people in the audience may not be able to keep up with the flow of information. Managers need to develop their presentation skills so as to take advantage of these strengths and to minimize these weaknesses.

Planning the presentation requires determining the purpose, analyzing the audience, and planning the timing and method of presentation appropriate for the situation. Organizing the presentation requires developing an effective opening, developing each point logically in the middle, and closing on a strong, confident note.

Use your opening remarks to capture the interest of your audience and build rapport. In the body, choose a logical sequence and deal effectively with any negative information. At the end, summarize your main points and outline the next steps to be taken. At any point in your presentation, you may use humor if it is appropriate to the situation.

When making a work-team presentation, allow enough time to prepare, assign responsibilities on the basis of individual talents, and rehearse sufficiently to ensure that the overall presentation has coherence and unity.

When giving a video presentation, wear appropriate clothing, look directly into the camera, avoid exaggerated movements, and stay within an established area of movement.

Other common types of business presentations include impromptu remarks, introductions, and special recognitions. Plan for and practice these so that you can make coherent, effective remarks as appropriate.

co1. Describe the important role that business presentations play in the organization.

co2. Plan a presentation by determining its purpose, analyzing the audience, and deciding the timing and method of delivery.

co3. Write a presentation by collecting the data and organizing it in a logical format.

co4. Plan a team presentation.

co5. Plan a video presentation.

co6. Plan other types of business presentations.

Exercises

1 **The 3Ps (Problem, Process, and Product) Model: Communication Applications at Georgia Hispanic Chamber of Commerce**   When Sara González plans a presentation to a local audience, she determines the purpose, analyzes what the audience needs to know, and thinks about the questions listeners are likely to ask. Before finalizing her presentation, she gathers the most recent statistics to support her main points.

Problem

Your job as the assistant director of the Georgia Hispanic Chamber of Commerce is to promote the organization to industry groups and entrepreneurial

■ Suggested and sample solutions for exercises appear in the *Instructor's Resource Manual.*

organizations. The Georgia chapter of a national association for women business owners has invited you to speak about the Chamber's mission and accomplishments. You believe that many of the audience members would be good mentors for new business owners in the state's Hispanic community. This is your first appearance in front of the group, and you have only ten minutes in which to speak.

Process

a. What is the purpose of your presentation?
b. Describe your audience.
c. What level of knowledge is your audience likely to have about your topic?
d. How will you capture your audience's attention in the first minute of your presentation? Draft your opening section.
e. What points will you cover in the body of your speech, and in what order? How will you link these points to audience benefits?
f. Write a closing section that summarizes your points and reinforces the purpose of your presentation.

Product

Using your knowledge of oral presentations, prepare a complete outline for this speech.

■ See Handout 13.1.

② The 3Ps (Problem, Process, and Product) Model: A Proposal Presentation

Problem

Review Exercise 2 of Chapter 10 (pages 375–376), in which the Hospitality Services Association at your university proposes to start University Hosts, a business that would provide hospitality services for campus visitors. Assume that you have been given ten minutes to present your proposal orally to the President's Council at your institution.

Process

a. What is the purpose of your presentation?
b. Describe your audience.
c. What type of delivery would be most appropriate—reading, memorizing, or speaking from notes?
d. Because of the importance of both the topic and the audience, you decide to write in full your opening remarks. Write a 1- to 1½-minute opening section for your presentation. Include an attention-getter.
e. Outline the topics you will discuss and the order in which you will discuss them. Be sure to include reader benefits.
f. Write a 1- to 1½ -minute closing section for your presentation.
g. Prepare rough drafts of the slides you will use for your presentation.

■ See Slide 13.13.

Product

Prepare a complete presentation outline, including where the slides will be used.

CO1. Describe the important role that business presentations play in the organization.

③ Understanding the Role of Business Presentations   Interview two business-people in your community who hold positions in your area of interest to learn more about their experiences in making oral presentations. Write a

memorandum to your instructor summarizing what you've learned. You may want to ask such questions as the following:

a. How important has the ability to make effective oral presentations been to your career?
b. What kinds of oral presentations do you make in and out of the office and how often?
c. How do you typically prepare for oral presentations?

4 **The Opening**   Chapter 13 lists six types of effective openings for an oral presentation—quotation, question, hypothetical situation, story, startling fact, or visual aid. Select two of these methods and develop effective openings for the same oral presentation. Plan your presentation by first describing your purpose for the presentation; second, perform an audience analysis by identifying the demographics, the knowledge level, and the psychological needs of a potential audience; third, prepare two effective openings for your presentation and explain why you selected these types.

CO2. **Plan a presentation by determining its purpose, analyzing the audience, and deciding the timing and method of delivery.**

5 **Planning a Presentation**   You decided at the last minute to apply to the graduate school at your institution to work toward a master's degree in public administration. Even though you have a 3.4 GPA (on a 4.0 scale), you were denied admission because you had not taken the GMAT, which is a prerequisite for admission. You have, however, been given ten minutes to appear before the Graduate Council to try to convince them to grant you a temporary waiver of this requirement and permit you to enroll in graduate classes next term, during which time you will take the GMAT. The Graduate Council consists of the director of the public administration program and two senior faculty members, one of whom is your business communication professor.

a. What is the purpose of your presentation?
b. What do you know or what can you surmise about your audience that might help you prepare a more effective presentation?
c. What considerations affect the timing of your presentation?
d. What method of delivery should you use?

6 **Presenting Research Data**   Review the analytical or recommendation report you prepared in Chapter 12. Assume that you have been given 15 minutes to present the important information from your written report to a committee of your superiors who will not have an opportunity to read the written report. Write your presentation notes, using either full sheets of paper or note cards.

CO3. **Write a presentation by collecting the data and organizing it in a logical format.**

7 **Presentation Notes**   Prepare a three-minute oral presentation on the business topic of your choice. First, write out the complete presentation. Next, select several excerpts of the complete script to be used as notes for your presentation. Then, prepare an outline of notes for your presentation. Submit all three versions of the presentation to your instructor for evaluation.

8 **Self-Presentation**   A big part of any company's success is the ability to sell its goods or services. As a new sales associate in Pinkston Inc., you have been asked to work with other new sales associates to improve your selling skills. You are to prepare a three-minute oral presentation in which you attempt to sell yourself as a product to a group of buyers. The buyers will be members of your class. You will be placed in groups of five or six people, and each person will have three minutes to sell himself or herself to the other group members.

The other group members will evaluate the seller using an evaluation sheet that will rate him or her in eight areas: (1) effectiveness of opening, (2) ability to hold buyers' interest, (3) appropriateness of eye contact, (4) logical sequence of presentation, (5) quality of voice, (6) clear identification of talents and skills, (7) motivational level of buyers, and (8) overall impression of the presentation. You will be evaluated in each area as being Poor, Fair, Good, or Excellent.

To prepare for your sales presentation, you might follow the following steps:

a. List at least three skills and/or talents you have (e.g., playing the guitar, playing tennis, and reciting the alphabet backward in less than 10 seconds).
b. Turn your skills and talents into buyer benefits.
c. Prepare an outline that identifies talents and skills you will be selling, and why these benefits would appeal to your buyers.

9 Presenting to an International Audience   The West Coast manager of Honda has approached your school of business about the possibility of sending 30 of its Japanese managers to your institution to pursue a three-month intensive course in written and oral business communication. The purpose of the course is to make the Japanese managers better able to interact with their American counterparts.

You, as the assistant provost at your institution, have been asked to give a six- to eight-minute presentation to the four Japanese executives who will decide whether to fund this program at your institution. The purpose of your presentation is to convince them to select your school.

Because of the care with which you will want to select your wording for this international audience and because of the high stakes involved, you decide to prepare a full script of your presentation (approximately 1,000 words).

10 Business Presentation Role Play   Prepare a data sheet and a two-minute speech (using note cards) on the business topic of your choice. Then form into groups of six or seven to make up the head table. A few minutes before starting, randomly select roles to be played: host, head table guests (with professional titles), and a guest speaker. The rest of the class will serve as the audience.

The person selected to be the host should quickly obtain and review the data sheet of the speaker and the professional titles and names of the people at the head table. Then the host should seat the members of the head table in their chairs. The host should then introduce the people at the head table—including the speaker. The speaker should then give his or her two-minute speech. After the speech is finished, the host should present the speaker with a token of appreciation.

Next, a member of the audience should be selected for an award such as employee of the year, and he or she should be invited to the podium by the host to receive the award and to make a short impromptu acceptance speech. Roles can be changed to allow others to be host, guest at the head table, speaker, or employee of the year. Have everyone submit his or her notes for the two-minute speech whether or not he or she actually spoke.

11 International Presentation   Working in teams of three or four people, prepare and make a presentation to the class. Each member of the group should take approximately the same amount of time in the presentation. The presentation should be at least 9 minutes, but no more than 12 minutes, long.

CO4. Plan a team presentation.

The audience consists of wealthy individuals from a foreign country who are being persuaded to invest in a new product to be sold in their country. The product being sold and the country should be selected by the students.

The students should plan the presentation and determine the timing and method of delivery (the purpose and audience have already been determined). The students should give evidence of data collected regarding the presentation. Visual aids should be used in the presentation—if possible in the language of the audience members. Evidence of rehearsing should be included—videotaped if possible. The final presentation to the class should also be videotaped for critiquing the presentation.

Groups should submit their notes for the presentation to the instructor after making the presentation. In addition to the notes, the group should detail why particular things were done regarding cultural differences.

12 Work-team Presentation   Divide into teams of four or five students. Your instructor will assign you to either the pro or the con side of one of the following topics:

- Drug testing should be mandatory for all employees.

- All forms of smoking should be banned completely from the workplace—including outside the building.

- Employers should provide flextime (flexible working hours) for all office employees.

- Employers should provide on-site child-care facilities for the preschool children of their employees.

- Employees who deal extensively with the public should be required to wear a company uniform.

- Employers should have the right to hire the most qualified employees without regard to affirmative action guidelines.

Assume that your employee group has been asked to present its views to a management committee that will make the final decision regarding your topic. The presentations will be given as follows:

a. Each side (beginning with the pro side) will have eight minutes to present its views.
b. Each side will then have three minutes to confer.
c. Each side (beginning with the con side) will deliver a two-minute rebuttal—to refute the arguments and answer the issues raised by the other side.
d. Each side (beginning with the pro side) will give a one-minute summary.
e. The management committee (the rest of the class) will then vote by secret ballot regarding which side (pro or con) presented its case more effectively.

Gather whatever data you think will be helpful to your case, organize it, divide up the speaking roles as you deem best, and prepare speaker notes. (*Hint:* It might be helpful to gather information on both the pro and the con sides of the issue in preparation for the rebuttal session, which will be given impromptu.)

co5. Plan a video presentation.

⑬ Video Presentation   Assume the role of Danielle K. Kizer, who, as a graduate student at Central Michigan University, conducted a research project entitled "A Comparison of the Physical Fitness Levels of Mount Pleasant Academy Students with National Norms." Shown below is a part of her research report (reprinted with the permission of the researcher). She has been asked to make a 15-minute presentation of the results of her research to an all-faculty meeting of the school. Because she has other commitments that day, Danielle has decided to videotape her presentation.

Chapter 3
Summary, Conclusions, and Recommendations

Recent studies reveal a nation of physically unfit children. One research study revealed that one-third of the youth were not physically active enough for aerobic benefit.[4] As past fitness studies have shown schoolchildren to be unfit, the purpose of this study was to determine how Mount Pleasant Academy (MPA) students (encompassing grades three through six) compared to national norms in physical fitness. To make this comparison, MPA students were administered the American Alliance for Health, Physical Education, Recreation, and Dance (AAHPERD) Health-Related Physical Fitness Test. This test consisted of four subtests, each of which was treated as a subproblem of this study.

Throughout the findings that follow, higher scores relate to better physical fitness and lower scores relate to lower fitness.

The cardiorespiratory maximum functional capacity and endurance of the students was measured by the Distance-Run Test. Students were instructed to run one mile in the fastest possible time. Walking was permitted, but the objective was to cover the distance in the shortest time possible.

Boys' scores tended to exceed the girls' scores, indicating better fitness for the boys. The weakest age group was the 11-year-old students; all of the students in this age group scored in the lower two quartiles. Seventy percent of the boys and 87 percent of the girls scored at or below the 50th percentile. Overall, the scores displayed by MPA students were below average.

The second test administered was the Skinfold Fat Test. This test measured the level of fat in a student's body. Two skinfold fat sites (triceps and subscapular) were used because they are easily measured and are highly correlated with total body fat.

The majority of the students scored below the 50th percentile for healthfulness. In fact, three-fourths of the students evidenced higher-than-average levels of body fat. The leanest group of students comprised the 11-year-old boys and girls. As a whole, boys had higher levels of body fat than girls.

The Modified Sit-Up Test, the third test used in this study, evaluated a student's abdominal muscular strength and endurance. Students completed their sit-ups lying on their backs with knees flexed, feet on the floor, and heels 12"–18" above the buttocks.

The 8- and 9-year-old students scored the highest—specifically, the 8-year-old boys and the 9-year-old girls. When students' scores were compared by sex, 55 percent of the boys and 45 percent of the girls scored above the 50th percentile. However, when the students were compared to national norms as a group, half of the students scored at or below the 50th percentile. The students appeared most physically fit when this test was used, but half of the class still scored at or below national averages.

The final test, the Sit-and-Reach Test, was used to measure flexibility of the lower back and posterior thighs. The students sat with knees fully extended and reached directly forward, palms down, as far as they could along the measuring scale.

The girls' scores on this test were higher than the boys' scores. The younger age groups also showed greater levels of flexibility than the other students. Eighty percent of the 8-year-old girls and 86 percent of the 9-year-old girls scored in the top two quartiles. Overall, 68 percent of the girls scored above the 50th percentile compared to 27 percent of the boys. Mount Pleasant Academy students' Sit-and-Reach Test scores for the girls were above average, but the boys' scores were markedly low.

To answer the problem posed at the beginning of this study, the four subproblems were analyzed jointly. As a group, all of the students at MPA scored well below the 50th percentile on both the Distance-Run Test and the Skinfold Test. Stronger scores were shown on the Modified Sit-Ups Test, but half of the class still scored below average. The boys' Sit-and-Reach Test scores were well below average, but 68 percent of the girls scored above the 50th percentile.

On the whole, the physical-fitness level of the students at Mount Pleasant Academy is below the average set by the American Alliance for Physical Education, Health, Recreation, and Dance.

Students who scored below average on any test should be encouraged to strive for higher performance—through counseling, individualized exercise routines, and all-school activities.

In summary, Mount Pleasant Academy students demonstrated below-average levels of physical fitness. Improvements in physical fitness should become a priority to help reduce the risk of injury or disease and to improve overall health and physical fitness.

a. Describe precisely what you plan to wear for this videotaped presentation.
b. Describe your audience for this presentation, especially in terms of their level of knowledge about and their interest in your topic.
c. Describe the kinds of visual aids you will prepare (such as printed posters, transparencies, or computer projection) and why.
d. Prepare your speech notes for this 15-minute presentation. Ensure that your opening and closing sections are detailed.

Note: You will actually deliver this videotaped presentation after completing Chapter 14, as well as videotape a partner's presentation. In the meantime, learn as much as you can about how to operate a videocamera effectively.

14 **Impromptu Presentation**   Your instructor will randomly call on members of the class to come to the front of the room and give a one-minute impromptu presentation on a topic that he or she selects from the following list. As you give your presentation, be aware of the time limits and your body language. Recognize that the audience doesn't expect a polished spur-of-the-moment

CO6. Plan other types of business presentations.

presentation, but do your best, recognizing that surprises like this one occasionally happen in business.

a. How I feel about giving impromptu presentations
b. My career plans after college
c. My most embarrassing experience on a date
d. My opinion of Microsoft
e. The college course I enjoyed most
f. The cost of college
g. What bugs me about e-mail
h. What I like (or dislike) about the current U.S. president
i. What I've learned from the Internet
j. Where I grew up
k. Why I do (or do not) live on campus
l. Why I enjoy (or dislike) team projects

15 **Presenting and Accepting an Honor**   Your instructor will divide you into two-member teams for this exercise. By a flip of the coin, determine which one of you has just been named Business Student of the Month for this month and will be recognized at the business faculty meeting next week. Prepare a one-minute acceptance of this award. The other student should assume the role of president of the business faculty and prepare to present the Business Student of the Month award. Prepare a one- or two-minute introduction.

16 **Special Recognition—Honoring Crossword Accomplishments**   You're the assistant executive director of the American Crossword Puzzle Tournament, an annual three-day event in which 400 contestants compete to be the fastest to accurately solve seven crossword puzzles. Will Shortz, the crossword editor of *The New York Times,* founded this event and remains its executive director. Over the years, the tournament—the oldest and largest of its type in the United States—has grown into something of a media event. National Public Radio features live play-by-play coverage, and the results are widely reported in crossword publications.

Imagine that the board of directors has asked you to present Shortz, your boss, with an artistically framed, hand-lettered copy of the crossword puzzle he created for the first tournament. You are to make this presentation at the special 25th anniversary banquet that closes the next tournament. Browsing through the tournament Web site at http://www.crosswordtournament.com, you find a lot of data about Shortz and his involvement with the tournament, as well as his background and accomplishments. Use this information to prepare a two-minute presentation honoring Shortz as you hand over the framed puzzle.

The Typists Who Lost Their Touch

Review the Continuing Case presented at the ends of Chapters 11 and 12. As you recall, in response to increasing sick-leave among data-entry personnel, Jean Tate asked Pat Robbins to write a report on carpal tunnel syndrome, a neuromuscular wrist injury caused by repeated hand motions such as those used in typing.

■ A suggested solution to the Continuing Case can be found in the *Instructor's Resource Manual.*

Pat's staff helps her plan how to organize her presentation to the executive committee at Urban Systems.

Assume the role of Pat Robbins. You have now been asked to present the results of your research in a 20-minute session to the executive committee, composed of Dave Kaplan and the three vice presidents. This occasion is your first opportunity to speak to this high-ranking group, and the speech is on a topic about which you developed strong feelings over the past few months as you researched the topic in depth.

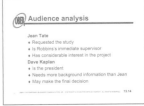

■ See Slide 13.14.

Critical Thinking

1. Analyze your audience. Specifically, what do you know (or what can you learn) about each of the executive committee members that will affect your presentation?
2. How will your strong feelings about this topic affect your presentation—either positively or negatively?

Speaking/Writing Projects

If you did not conduct any primary research for this project, base your presentation on secondary data.

3. Write your presentation notes, using either full sheets of paper or note cards.

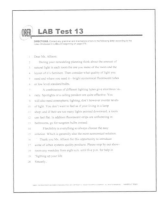

■ See Handout 13.2.

LABtest 13

Retype the following letter, correcting any grammar and mechanics errors according to the rules introduced in LABs 2–6 beginning on page 576.

■ See Slides 13.15–13.17.

Dear Ms. Allison:

During your remodeling ~~planning~~ *planning, (INTRO)* think about the amount of natural light in each ~~room~~ *room, (SER)* the use you make of the ~~room~~ *room, (SER)* and the

layout of ~~it's~~ *its (WORD)* furniture. Then consider what quality of light you

5   need and where you need it—~~bright~~ *bright, (ADJ)* economical fluorescent tubes or ~~low level~~ *low-level (ADJ)* standard bulbs.

A combination of different lighting types ~~give~~ *gives (AGR)* enormous

variety. Spotlights or a ceiling pendant ~~are~~ *is (AGR)* quite ~~affective~~ *effective (SPELL)*. You

will also need atmospheric ~~lighting, don't however~~ *lighting. (RUN-ON) Don't, however, (TRAN)* overdo levels

10   of light. You don't want to feel as if ~~your~~ *you're (WORD)* living in a lamp

shop; and if ~~their~~ *there (WORD)* are too many lights pointed downward, a room

can feel flat. In ~~addition~~ *addition, (INTRO or TRAN)* fluorescent strips are unflattering in ~~bathrooms,~~ *bathrooms; (NO^CONJ)* go for tungsten bulbs instead.

Flexibility is ~~everything~~ *everything, (IND)* so always choose the easy

15   ~~solution. Which~~ *solution, which (FRAG)* is generally also the most economical solution.

Thank ~~you Ms. Allison~~ *you, Ms. Allison, (DIR AD)* for this opportunity to introduce

some of ~~urban systems~~ *Urban Systems' (PLURAL POSS.)* quality products. Please stop by our

showroom any weekday from ~~eight~~ *8 (NO.-FIG)* a.m. until ~~five~~ *5 (NO.-FIG)* p.m. for help in

"lighting up your ~~life.~~ *life." (PUNC)*

~~Sincerly,~~ *Sincerely, (SPELL)*

14

Illustrating and Delivering the Business Presentation

communication
OBJECTIVES

After you have finished this chapter, you should be able to

1. Develop effective visual aids for a presentation.

2. Develop effective audience handouts.

3. Practice a presentation to develop an effective speaking style.

4. Deliver a presentation in a clear, confident, and efficient manner.

5. Critique your performance as a presenter.

an insider's perspective

PATRICIA DIAZ DENNIS
Senior Vice President,
SBC Communications

atricia Diaz Dennis never forgets that the speaker is the most important visual aid in any presentation. As senior vice president for regulatory and public affairs in Texas-based SBC Communications, Dennis and her staff help to shape the firm's policy positions on regulatory, legislative, and governmental issues at the federal and state levels. They also maintain an ongoing dialogue about telecommunications issues with government officials, lawyers, consumer advocates, special-interest groups, and other audiences. Not surprisingly, public speaking is an integral part of Dennis's job. One week, she may be dissecting Internet access issues for an audience of lobbyists; the next, she may be speaking to members of the U.S. Hispanic Chamber of Commerce about contemporary management challenges.

Dennis minimizes her use of visual aids to avoid distracting the audience. "I like to keep the focus on the speaker," she says. This approach helps listeners concentrate on each point as she presents it, instead of reading ahead to see what is coming next. When covering technical topics, Dennis sometimes distributes an outline of her talk so that audience members can jot down notes as she speaks. Or, depending on the audience, she may display a single slide during her presentation to reinforce a handful of key points. On occasion, she also uses summary handouts—but only after she's finished her presentation: "After people have heard you, they can refer to the take-away to better recall what you said and how it affected them."

Dennis practices before every presentation by reading her speech aloud more than once. "Some points may be beautifully written, but when you say them aloud, they don't sound as good," she explains. She is careful to use short, declarative sentences and to vary her word choices for interest. However, Dennis stays away from jargon, knowing it can confuse the audience. "If a decision maker has to stop and think about what you mean, you're never going to drive home your point," she says. "I try to speak in metaphors and use word pictures so people can easily visualize what I'm telling them." Rather than using an industry acronym such as DSL, for example, Dennis helps her audiences visualize a digital subscriber line by describing it as "a bigger pipe connecting your computer to your Internet service provider so you can get more information a lot faster."

The SBC executive frequently practices in front of family members who don't know her subject, to be sure she is getting her message across. "If my mother understands what I'm talking about, then I know my presentation has succeeded," she says. During her actual presentation, Dennis saves at least a few minutes for audience questions. When she doesn't know the answer to a particular question, she's not afraid to say "I don't know" and offer to find out later. "I never pretend I know something I don't," she notes. "That's the road to ruination, because it undercuts your credibility. If somebody in the audience really knows the answer, your credibility is shot. And when you're making a presentation, your credibility is a large part of what you're really selling."

"Some points may be beautifully written, but when you say them aloud, they don't sound as good."

■ Visual Aids for Business Presentations

■ A chapter overview appears in the *Instructor's Resource Manual*.

Today's audiences are accustomed to multimedia events that bombard the senses. They often assume that any formal presentation must be accompanied by some visual element, whether it is a flipchart, overhead transparency, slide, film, videotape, or actual model.

Visual aids are relatively simple to create and help the audience understand the presentation, especially if it includes complex or statistical material. A University of Pennsylvania study found that presenters who used visual aids successfully persuaded 67 percent of their audience, whereas those who did not use such aids persuaded only 50 percent of their audience. In addition, meetings in which visual aids were used were 28 percent shorter than those that lacked such aids. Similarly, a University of Minnesota study found that the use of graphics increased a presenter's persuasiveness by 43 percent. Presenters who used visual aids were also perceived as being more professional, better prepared, and more interesting than those who didn't use visual aids.[1] (For an indication of how much your sense of sight contributes to your knowledge, see Communication Snapshot 14.)

CO1. Develop effective visual aids for a presentation.

Use visual aids to enhance audience interest and comprehension and to help tell your story.

Transparencies and Slides

Figure 14.1 on page 506 compares features of the most common types of visual aids. Inexpensive, easy to produce, and simple to update, transparencies for overhead projection can be used without darkening the room and while you face the audience. Thus, your audience can see to take notes, and you can maintain eye contact with them. Thanks to presentation software, overhead transparencies easily take advantage of color, designed fonts, charts, artwork, and preplanned layouts (called *templates*). Although the installed base of overhead projectors numbers more than 2 million, the availability and low cost of computer projectors, combined with growing sales of notebook computers, has brought a significant drop in the use of transparencies in recent years.[2]

Although 35-mm slides are best projected in a somewhat darkened room, their high quality adds a distinctly professional touch to a presentation, and they can be effectively used with very large audiences. Unfortunately, slides lack the flexibility of other media; it is difficult to review an earlier slide or skip forward several slides during a presentation. Slides are moderately expensive to produce and require somewhat more preparation time than transparencies. As with overhead transparencies, the use of 35-mm slides has dramatically decreased due to the increasing popularity of electronic presentations.

■ See Slide 14.1.

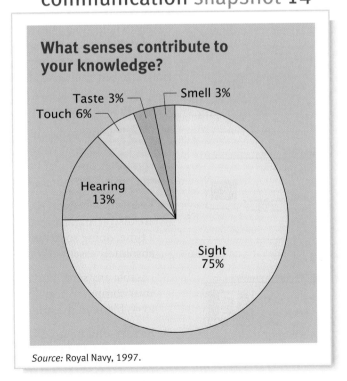

communication snapshot 14

What senses contribute to your knowledge?

Taste 3%
Touch 6%
Smell 3%
Hearing 13%
Sight 75%

Source: Royal Navy, 1997.

figure14.1

Criteria for Selecting Visual Aids

Criteria	Electronic presentations	Transparencies	35-mm slides	Films	Videotape	Flipcharts	Handouts
Quality	Good	Good	Excellent	Excellent	Excellent	Poor	Good
Cost	Moderate	Low	Moderate	High	High	Low	Low
Ease of use	Difficult	Easy	Moderate	Moderate	Easy	Easy	Easy
Ease of preparation	Easy	Easy	Moderate	Difficult	Difficult	Easy	Easy
Ease of updating	Easy	Easy	Moderate	Difficult	Difficult	N/A	Easy
Degrees of formality	Formal	Either	Formal	Either	Either	Informal	Either
Adaptability to audience size	Moderate	Excellent	Excellent	Excellent	Moderate	Poor	Moderate
Dependence on equipment	High	Moderate	Moderate	Moderate	Moderate	Low	None

Electronic presentations are fast becoming the method of choice for business presenters.

■ See Slides 14.2–14.4.

Electronic Presentations

Today, electronic presentations are the newest medium for visual aids. They consist of slides or video shown directly from a computer and projected onto a screen via a projector. Because the slide images come directly from the computer file, actual transparencies and slides do not have to be made. Electronic presentations enable you to easily add multimedia effects to your presentation—if doing so helps you tell your story more effectively. You could, for example, show a short video, move text across the screen, or play background sound effects. Electronic slide presentations offer greater flexibility than traditional slide presentations do, but their use also requires high-powered projectors to obtain the best results.

When giving an electronic presentation, follow these guidelines:

■ Check colors for accuracy. If precise color matching is important (for example, with the color of your corporate logo), ensure that the color projected on the computer on which you designed the presentation matches the color shown on the projection system on which you will display it.

■ Keep special effects simple. Elaborate or random transition effects, for example, are distracting. Nevertheless, consider using builds to reveal one bullet point at a time; doing so helps focus the audience's attention. Avoid sound effects unless absolutely essential for understanding.

■ Disable any screen savers and energy-saving automatic shutdown features of your computer. You don't want your screen to begin displaying a screen saver or to go blank in the middle of your presentation.

■ Be seen and heard. Stand on the left side from the audience's point of view—in the light and away from the computer—using a remote mouse if necessary. Make sure that you're still easily visible when the projection screen is dark.

Preparing Visual Aids

Avoid using too many visual aids. Novice presenters sometimes use them as a crutch. Such overuse keeps the emphasis on the visual aid rather than on the presenter. Use visual aids only when they will help the audience grasp an important point, and remove them when they're no longer needed. One or two relevant, helpful visual aids are better than an entire armload of irrelevant ones—no matter how attractive they are.

One of the most common mistakes presenters make in developing visual aids is to simply photocopy tables or illustrations from reports, printouts, or journals and project them on a screen. Print graphics usually contain far too much information to serve effectively as presentation graphics. Using print graphics in a presentation will often do more to hinder your presentation than to help it.

As a general rule, each slide or transparency should contain no more than 40 characters per line, no more than six or seven lines per visual, and no more than three columns of data (think of your slide as a highway billboard rather than a memo). Use upper- and lowercase letters (rather than all capitals) in a large, simple typeface and plenty of white (empty) space. Use bulleted lists to show a group of related items that have no specific order and numbered lists to show related items in a specific order.

Establish a color scheme and stay with it for all your visual aids; that is, use the same background color for each slide or transparency. For handouts and overheads, use dark type on a light background; for slides, use light type on a dark background.

If you do not keep your visual aids clear and simple, your audience can easily become overwhelmed, with their attention drawn to the technology rather than to the content. As always, seek to *express*—not to *impress*. With visual aids, less is more. In his book *PowerPoint Is Evil,* Yale professor Edward R. Tufte makes the point that "the PowerPoint style routinely disrupts, dominates, and trivializes

Visual aids should be used only when needed and should be simple, readable, and of high quality.

Today a wide variety of visual aids are available to enhance the speaker's presentation—from video and graphic display to leave-behind audience handouts.

content." And according to Joan Detz, speaker, trainer, and author of *How to Write and Give a Speech*:[3]

> A successful presentation has little to do with technical wizardry. The single biggest mistake I see is overusing technology. Most of the time, visuals are used as a security blanket for people who haven't thought through a presentation. It's easier to have an audience look at a slide or other visual rather than at you.

The only real way to ensure that your visual aids are readable is to test them beforehand from the back seat of the room in which you will be presenting. If that is not possible, follow the guidelines presented in Figure 14.2.

The quality of your visual aids sends a nonverbal message about your competence and your respect for your audience. Just as you don't want your audience's attention distracted by the razzle-dazzle of your slides, neither do you want their attention distracted by poor quality. If the visual aid isn't readable or attractive, don't use it.

■ See Slide 14.5.

Practice using your visual aids smoothly and effectively.

Using Visual Aids

Even the best visual aid will not be effective if it is not used properly during the presentation or if the equipment doesn't work. Using equipment smoothly does not come naturally; it takes practice and a keen awareness of audience needs, especially when using a slide or overhead projector. Ensure that the image is readable from every seat and that neither you nor the projector blocks anyone's view (see Figure 14.3).

Confirm that your equipment is in top working order and that you know how to operate it and how to secure a spare bulb or spare machine quickly if one becomes necessary. Adjust the projector and focus the image so that it is clearly readable from the farthest seat. However, do not make the image larger than necessary; the presenter should be the center of attention. The image should be a square or rectangle. Avoid the common keystoning effect (where the top of the image is wider than the bottom) by tilting the top of the screen forward slightly toward the projector.

When using slide projectors, have a blank opaque slide or a generic title slide as the last slide so that the audi-

figure14.2

What Size Screen Do You Need?

What size screen do you need?

The width of the blue screen should be half the distance to the first row of seats (yellow dots.)

The distance from the blue screen to the last row of seats (red dots) should be six times the width of the screen or greater.

The height of the screen should be at least 1/8 the distance from the back row.

THE SCREEN SHOULD BE **AT LEAST 1/8 THIS DISTANCE TALL**

screen

THIS **WIDTH**...

...SHOULD BE **HALF THIS DISTANCE**...

...AND **1/6 THIS DISTANCE OR MORE.**

audience

ence is not suddenly hit with a bright flash of light when you finish your presentation. And with all types of projectors, avoid walking in front of the projected image.

Try to avoid problems. Lock your slides in place in the tray; number your slides and transparencies so that they can be restored quickly if dropped; have your film already threaded into the projector; clean the overhead projector glass before using it; tape to the lectern the device used to advance the slides to avoid having it tumble off; and have an extra bulb handy (and know how to insert it). Finally, be prepared to give your presentation without visual aids if that should become necessary.

With practice, you can learn to stand to the side of the screen, facing the audience with your feet pointed toward them. Then, when you need to refer to an item on the screen, point with either a finger, pointer, or pen. (Many people find the use of laser pointers distracting.) Turn your body from the waist, keeping your feet pointed toward the audience. Doing so enables you to maintain better eye contact with the audience as well as better control of the presentation.

When showing slides, be sure to avoid walking in front of the projector. Also, avoid including too much information on each slide. Here, Attorney Philip Beck violates these guidelines as he testifies at a court hearing on the contested presidential election results in Florida.

Be prepared to give your presentation without visual aids if necessary.

figure14.3

Positioning the Projector Correctly

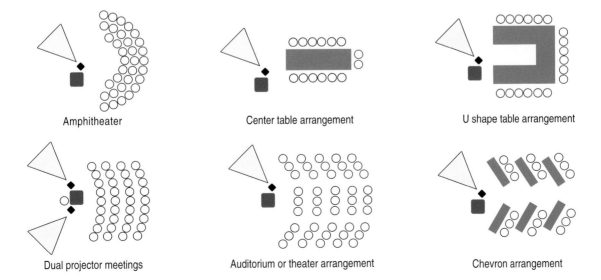

Amphitheater

Center table arrangement

U shape table arrangement

Dual projector meetings

Auditorium or theater arrangement

Chevron arrangement

■ Audience Handouts

CO2. Develop effective audience handouts.

Audience handouts supplement your oral information, provide space for note taking, and represent a permanent record of your presentation.

Audience handouts—printed copies of notes, tables, or illustrations—are often important in helping the audience follow a presentation. They are a standard part of most business presentations, because they provide a review and new information for the audience long after your presentation is over. In addition, they represent a permanent record of the major points of the presentation and reduce or eliminate the need for note taking. Handouts are especially helpful when you are dealing with complex information such as detailed statistical tables, which would be ineffective if projected as a slide or transparency.

What to Include

Handouts may, of course, contain miniature versions of the slides containing the most important points of your presentation. As a rule, however, you should avoid including them all. It's also much better if you can annotate each slide you do include. Include additional information that would not fit on the projected slide—for examples, details, background data, summaries, more complete charts, or sources of extra information. Keep the content simple, concise, and to the point. Avoid padding with irrelevant information.

Organize your handout topics in the sequence in which you present them. Use a generous number of headings and number pages so that you can easily refer your audience to the section you're presenting. Also, provide plenty of white space—both as a design element for readability and as space for note taking. If a high-quality color printer or copier is available, use color within reason—for the cover page, headings, charts, and the like—but not for body type, which should be black on a white background.

Provide good photocopies, avoiding off-center, smudged, gray, or faint copies. Retype a document that is unattractive or difficult to read or that contains nonessential information. Use a legible font—at least 12 points in size—to facilitate reading in a somewhat darkened room during an audiovisual presentation.

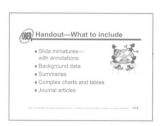

■ See Slide 14.6.

■ See Slide 14.7.

The content and purpose of your handout determine when it should be distributed.

When to Distribute

You must decide the most effective time to distribute your handout—either before, during, or after your presentation. Some handouts contain complex data or extensive information that should be read before your presentation as a framework for understanding your remarks (for example, a complex proposal). In that case, send the handout to the audience members prior to their arrival for the presentation. In a cover letter, tell them the purpose of the handout and ask them to read it before attending your presentation. Obviously, you must then ensure that you do not merely repeat the information in the handout during your presentation.

You should distribute your handout immediately before the presentation if you will be referring to material in it as you speak. Ensure that the audience members

spotlight28
ON TECHNOLOGY

Converting Presentation Slides into an Audience Handout

Darlene Zhang is the strategic manager for a company that is on a "buying spree." She has been asked to identify several small companies as possible acquisition targets and then to perform a preliminary SWOT analysis on each company. SWOT analysis is a standard strategic management tool that analyzes a company's internal s̲trengths and w̲eaknesses and its external o̲pportunities and t̲hreats.

After performing a preliminary SWOT analysis on one acquisition candidate, Oakleaf Industries, Darlene has prepared a presentation that she will give to the management committee of her company. The purpose of her presentation is to persuade the management committee to continue pursuing Oakleaf as an acquisition candidate.

As part of her planning, Darlene has developed a slide program. In following the advice to always "say more than you show," she has kept the information on the slides to a minimum and created only 11 slides for her one-hour presentation. Knowing that PowerPoint is the standard presentation software used at her company, she wanted to ensure that her visual aids did not look exactly like everyone else's. Consequently, instead of using one of PowerPoint's standard templates to design her slide program, Darlene modified the Blends template by inserting Oakleaf's logo into the master slide and by changing the title color to match the logo color. The result is a unique look for her audiovisuals.

Darlene is now ready to develop her presentation handout. She could, of course, simply use PowerPoint's handout feature and quickly print out miniatures of all of her slides to be distributed as a two-page handout. Given the critical nature of the decision to be made and the importance of her audience, however, she decides to analyze each slide to determine whether it would be an effective component for the handout. Shown below is her decision-making process:

1. Darlene begins with Slide 1, the title slide. Obviously, the handout needs some identifying title information. If she were preparing an extensive handout (of, perhaps, five or more pages), Darlene would create a separate title page to show this information. A separate title page for her two-page handout (actually, one page duplicated on both sides) would be overkill, however, so she decides to keep the title slide in her handout. Similarly, she realizes that the "snapshot" information

about the company contained on Slide 2 would make an effective addition to her handout. Darlene does decide to add a short annotation to each slide in her handout.

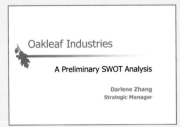

2. Slides 3 to 7 outline the results of her SWOT analysis—the heart of her presentation. She wants the audience to have this information for future reference because she will be presenting the results of her SWOT analyses of other companies in the coming weeks. Darlene decides that she can present this information in a more condensed and useful format in her handout by combining the four factors into a single table for her handout.

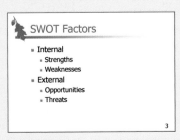

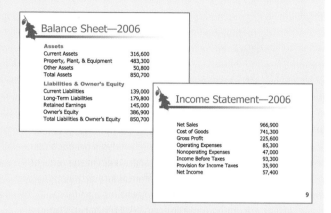

Slides 10 and 11 summarize her research and present her recommendation—obviously important information. Because graphics are more appealing than textual information, she decides to include these two slides in her handout—accompanied by short annotations.

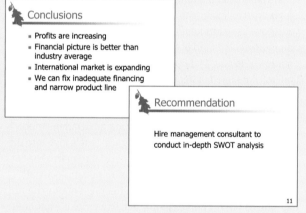

3. Slides 8 and 9 summarize the most recent financial data for Oakleaf. This information, of course, will be critical in the management committee's decision-making process, but Darlene realizes that she cannot include the complete balance sheet and income statement on a slide. Instead, she decides to include only the most important figures on the slides; to further simplify, she rounds each figure off to the nearest hundred. She then includes the complete statements in an appendix to her handout. Because she will refer to these figures during her presentation, Darlene plans to distribute the handout at the beginning of her session—thereby ensuring that the audience can follow along with her reasoning.

She considered whether it would be even better to distribute the handout a few days before her presentation to give the audience members time to study the statements in advance. Because she has only a two-page handout and plans to walk the audience through the financial statements, she decides instead to distribute it at the beginning of her session. After all, Darlene can count on at least some committee members forgetting to bring their marked-up copies to the session.

Having made these decisions, Darlene has created much more work for herself. Instead of simply printing out her slides six to a page in PowerPoint, she must now cut and paste the four slides she decides to use into a Word document, develop a table containing the complete SWOT analysis, and type out the two financial statements. She briefly considered simply photocopying the six pages of financial statements included in the company's latest annual report but decided that these pages provided too much detail; besides, the tables were printed in a small font and in a color that would not photocopy well.

Shown on page 513 is the actual handout (one page duplicated on both sides) that Darlene used in her successful presentation to the management committee.

Oakleaf Industries

A Preliminary SWOT Analysis

Darlene Zhang
Strategic Manager

Presentation made before the Management
Committee on May 3, 20--

About Oakleaf Industries

Business	Drill-bit manufacturer
Location	Ashland, OR
President/Owner	Howard Oakes
Employees	17
Revenue	$967,000
Income	$57,000

Oakes has indicated an interest in selling his
profitable firm.

SWOT Analysis

	Internal	External
Advantages	**Strengths** ❑ Acknowledged market leader ❑ Good public relations ❑ Stable and trained work force ❑ Innovative advertising	**Opportunities** ❑ Increased market demand ❑ Favorable demographic changes ❑ Emerging technologies
Disadvantages	**Weaknesses** ❑ Inadequate financing ❑ Narrow product line	**Threats** ❑ Increased domestic competition ❑ Vulnerability to recession and business cycles ❑ Public trade policies

Pro Forma	Industry
8.2%	14.7%
9.8%	
3.6%	8.1%
14.0%	28.5%
1.5%	4.8%
37.0%	56.1%
56.4%	
4.0%	
1.91%	
100.0%	100.0%
3.0%	2.9%
5.4%	12.8%
7.9%	
16.3%	30.4%
1.5%	0.1%
19.4%	
0.2%	
37.5%	
45.5%	
17.0%	
100.0%	100.0%

Conclusions

- Profits are increasing
- Financial picture is better than industry average
- International market is expanding
- We can fix inadequate financing and narrow product line

The preliminary analysis is positive.

Recommendation

Hire management consultant to
conduct in-depth SWOT analysis

SmithBarnes can prepare a detailed analysis for
us in 90 days.

				Pro Forma	Industry
Net Sales	966,946	696,481	465,213	100.0%	100.0%
Cost of Goods	741,323	546,493	360,064	76.7%	
Gross Profit	225,623	149,988	105,149	23.3%	41.0%
Sales Gen. & Admin. Exp.	85,260	57,045	42,547	8.8%	
Income Before Dep. & Amort.	140,363	92,943	62,602	14.5%	
Depreciation & Amortization	52,141	35,950	22,486	5.4%	
Nonoperating Income	12,393	20,247	6,792	1.3%	
Interest Expense	7,266	8,739	3,765	0.8%	
Income Before Taxes	93,349	68,501	43,143	9.6%	
Provision for Income Taxes	35,937	26,373	17,041	3.7%	
Net Income	57,412	42,128	26,102	5.9%	3.6%

■ See Slides 14.8–14.9.

have time to browse the material before the session starts so that you will have their complete attention when you begin speaking. Many audience members prefer to have the handout available during the presentation as a handy means of taking notes. In this scenario, your message will be reinforced three times—once when you present it, once when the audience views your handout, and again when they take notes.

Finally, if your handout merely summarizes your message, you may decide to distribute it immediately after your presentation—to ensure that you have the audience's complete attention during your remarks. Do, however, tell the audience that you intend to do so to prevent them from taking unnecessary notes.

Handouts provide a tangible, permanent record of the temporal presentation. In addition, they give a nonverbal message about you and your organization. Ensure that you leave behind a positive impression. Spotlight 28, "Converting Presentation Slides into an Audience Handout," on pages 511–513, takes you through the process of developing an effective handout for a specific presentation.

■ Practicing the Presentation

co3. **Practice a presentation to develop an effective speaking style.**

Use appropriate language, voice qualities, gestures, and posture.

The language of oral presentations must be simple. Because the listener has only one chance to comprehend the information presented, shorter sentences and simpler vocabulary should be used for oral presentations than for written presentations. Presenters have trouble articulating long, involved sentences with complex vocabulary, and listeners have trouble understanding them. A long sentence that reads easily on paper may leave the speaker breathless when he or she says it aloud. Avoid such traps. Use short, simple sentences and a conversational style. Use contractions freely, and avoid using words that you may have trouble pronouncing. (Compare, for example, the different styles used in the excerpts from the written report and the oral presentation script shown in Figure 13.2 on page 476.)

Use frequent preview, summary, transition, and repetition to help your audience follow your presentation. The old advice to preachers is just as pertinent for business presenters: "Tell them what you're going to tell them, tell them, and then tell them what you told them."

Whether you plan to speak from a complete script or from notes or an outline, begin practicing by simulating the conditions of the meeting room as closely as possible. Always practice standing, with your notes at the same level and angle as at a podium, and use any visual aids that will be a part of your presentation.

■ See Slides 14.10 and 14.11.

Videotaping your rehearsal can help you review and modify your voice qualities, gestures, and speech content. If videotaping is not possible, two good substitutes are a large mirror and a tape recorder. The mirror can help you judge the appropriateness of your posture, facial expressions, and gestures. Remember that 55 percent of your credibility with an audience comes from your body language, 38 percent comes from your voice qualities, and only 7 percent comes from the actual words you use.[4] Play back the tape several times, paying attention to your voice qualities (especially speed and pitch), pauses, grouping of words and phrases, and pronunciation.

For important presentations, plan on a minimum of three run-throughs. The first run-through should focus on continuity (does everything you say make

sense when you say it aloud?) and approximate timing. For each run-through, record how much time it takes on each section of your outline. If necessary, cut out a key point so that you have time for a solid, well-rehearsed, and nonrushed summary and conclusion. Schedule your practice sessions far enough ahead of time to allow you to make any needed changes. Start small and add on later. Your first run-through should probably be private, or perhaps with one close colleague in attendance to give feedback. Then, when you're satisfied, move up to the next step.

Become familiar enough with your message that a few notes or a graphic will keep you on track. Practice the most important parts (introduction, summary of key points, conclusion) the most number of times.

Speak in a conversational tone, but at a slightly slower rate than normally used in conversation. For interest and to fit the situation, vary both your volume and your rate of speaking, slowing down when presenting important or complex information and speeding up when summarizing. Use periodic pauses to emphasize important points. Use correct diction, avoid slurring or dropping off the endings of words, and practice pronouncing difficult names.

Speak in a conversational tone—but slightly slower.

Occasional hand and arm gestures are important for adding interest and emphasis, but only if they are appropriate and appear natural. If you never "talk with your hands" in normal conversation, it is unlikely you will do so naturally while presenting. Generally, one-handed gestures are more effective and less distracting than two-handed ones.

Use appropriate gestures if you are comfortable doing so.

Avoid annoying and distracting mannerisms and gestures, such as jingling coins or keys in your pocket; coughing or clearing your throat excessively; wildly waving your hands; gripping the lectern tightly; nervously swaying or pacing; playing with jewelry, pens, or paper clips; or peppering your remarks with "and uh" or "you know."

Establish an anchor. Position your body on the left side of the room (the left side from the audience's point of view) when speaking in English, which reads from left to right. With this setup, the audience looks toward the left to view the speaker, glances slightly to the right to begin reading the visual aid, and then moves back left to the speaker again. For most of your presentation, you should stand at a 45-degree angle to the audience.

Practice smiling occasionally, standing tall and naturally, with the body balanced on both feet. Rest your hands on the podium, by your side, or in any natural, quiet position. Your voice and demeanor should reflect professionalism, enthusiasm, and self-confidence.

■ Delivering the Presentation

CO4. Deliver a presentation in a clear, confident, and efficient manner.

Dress comfortably—just slightly dressier than your audience.

Your clothing is a part of the message you communicate to your audience, so dress appropriately—in comfortable and businesslike attire. Different clothes give us different energy levels, and if you can feel it, so can your audience. Follow these guidelines:[5]

- Dress just slightly better than the audience; the audience will be complimented by your efforts.

- Make sure your shoes are the same color or darker than the hemline of your pants or skirt.

- Always wear long sleeves when presenting. They project authority and a higher level of professionalism and respect. Short sleeves create a more casual appearance.

- Ensure that the tip of a man's tie hits the middle of his belt buckle.

- Be aware that the higher the stage, the shorter a woman's skirt will appear. The best skirt length is mid-knee for women of short or medium height and a few inches below mid-knee for taller women.

If you're speaking after a meal, eat lightly, avoiding heavy sauces, desserts, and alcoholic beverages. As you're being introduced, take several deep breaths to clear your mind, walk confidently to the front of the room, take enough time to arrange yourself and your notes, look slowly around you, establish eye contact with several members of the audience, and then, in a loud, clear voice, begin your presentation.

In most environments, a microphone is not needed if you're speaking to a group smaller than 150 people—10 to 12 rows of people. Your voice should carry that far. Not using a microphone gives you more freedom to move about and avoids problems with audio feedback and volume adjustments. If you will need to use a microphone, test it beforehand to see how it operates and to determine the appropriate setting and height; the microphone normally should be 4 to 6 inches from your mouth.

You should know your presentation well enough that you can maintain eye contact easily with your audience, taking care to include members in all corners of the room. Lock in on one person and maintain eye contact for at least three seconds—or until you have completed a thought.

If you lose your place in your notes or script, relax and take as much time as you need to regroup. If your mind actually does go blank, try to keep talking—even if you repeat what you've just said. The audience will probably think you intentionally repeated the information for emphasis, and the

A S K Ober

Dear Dr. Ober:

I am a student at Robert Morris College in Springfield, Illinois, and am currently enrolled in a business English course using your textbook. Is there an online version that I can access so that I don't have to retype sentences and risk typos? Our instructor requires hard copy, so I would appreciate very much the ability to cut and paste from an online site.

—Kay C.

Dear Kay:

I wish I could help make your job easier, but there is no online version of the text. The same economic principle works here as with music. If you can download it for free, why purchase it? And if you don't purchase it, publishers (and authors) have no financial incentive to write and make the text available to the public.

—Scot

E-mail your questions and comments to askober@ober.net.

extra time may jog your memory. If this doesn't work, simply skip ahead to another part of your presentation that you do remember; then come back later to the part you omitted.

Stage Fright

According to author Mark Twain, "There are two types of speakers—those who are nervous and those who are liars." For some people, making a presentation is accompanied by such symptoms as these:

- Gasping for air

- Feeling faint or nauseated ("butterflies in the stomach")

- Having shaking hands or legs and sweaty palms

- Feeling the heart beat rapidly and loudly

- Speaking too rapidly and in a high-pitched voice

If you've ever experienced any of these symptoms, take comfort in the fact that you're not alone. Fear of giving a speech is the Number 1 fear of most Americans. In a national poll of 3,000 people, 42 percent said the one thing they're most afraid of in life—even more than having cancer or a heart attack—is giving a speech.[6] Fortunately, behavior-modification experts have found that of the full range of anxiety disorders, people can most predictably overcome their fear of public speaking.[7]

Recognize that you have been asked to make a presentation because someone obviously thinks you have something important to say. You should feel complimented. Unless you are an exceptionally good or exceptionally bad speaker, the audience will more likely remember *what* you say rather than how you say it. Most of us fall somewhere between these two extremes as presenters.

The best way to minimize any lingering anxiety is to overprepare. For the anxious presenter, there is no such thing as overpractice. The more familiar you are with the content of your speech and the more trial runs you've made, the better you'll be able to concentrate on your delivery once you're actually in front of the group. You may want to memorize the first several sentences of your presentation just so you can approach those critical first moments (when anxiety is highest) with more confidence.

Practice mental imagery. Several times before your big presentation, sit in a comfortable position, close your eyes, and visualize yourself giving your speech. Picture yourself speaking confidently, loudly, and clearly in an assured voice. If you can imagine yourself giving a successful speech, you will be able to do so.

Before your presentation, take a short walk to relax your body. While waiting for your presentation to begin, let your arms drop loosely by your sides and shake your wrists gently, all the while breathing deeply several times. As you begin to speak, look for friendly faces in the crowd, and concentrate on them initially.

Some nervousness, of course, is good. It gets the adrenaline flowing and gives your speech an edge. If you do find that you're exceedingly nervous as you begin your speech, don't say something like, "I'm so nervous this morning, my hands are shaking." Probably your audience hadn't noticed; but as soon as you bring it to their attention, their eyes will immediately move to your shaking hands, thus creating a needless distraction and weakening your credibility.

■ Stand-up comic Jerry Seinfeld interprets this statistic this way: "This means that at a funeral, the average person would rather be lying in the casket than delivering the eulogy."

To avoid anxiety, practice, develop a positive attitude, and concentrate on friendly faces.

■ See Slide 14.12.

The homepage for Toast-masters International is found at http://www. toastmasters.org.

Finally, the professional who is anxious about speaking in public should consider taking a public speaking course or joining Toastmasters International, the world's oldest and largest nonprofit educational organization. The purpose of Toastmasters is to improve the speaking skills of its members. Members meet weekly or monthly and deliver prepared speeches, evaluate one another's oral presentations, give impromptu talks, develop their listening skills, conduct meetings, and learn parliamentary procedure.

Answering Questions

One advantage of oral presentations over written reports is the opportunity to engage in two-way communication. The question-and-answer session is a vital part of your presentation; plan for it accordingly.

Normally, you should announce at the beginning of your presentation that you will be happy to answer any questions when you're through. Holding questions until the end helps you avoid being interrupted and losing your train of thought or possibly running out of time and not being able to complete your prepared remarks. Also, there is always the possibility that the listener's question will be answered later in the course of your presentation.

The exception to a questions-at-the-end policy is when your topic is so complex that a listener's question must be answered immediately if he or she is to follow the rest of the presentation. Another exception is informal (and generally small) meetings, where questions and comments naturally occur throughout the presentation.

Plan your answers to possible questions ahead of time.

As you prepare your presentation, anticipate what questions you might expect from the audience. Make a list of them and think through possible answers. If necessary, make notes to refer to while answering. If your list of questions is very long, you should probably consider revising your presentation to incorporate some of the answers into your prepared remarks.

Always listen carefully to the question; repeat it, if necessary, for the benefit of the entire audience; and look at the entire audience as you answer—not just at the questioner. Treat each questioner with unfailing courtesy. If the question is antagonistic, be firm but fair and polite.

■ Writer and cartoonist James Thurber once said, "It is better to know some of the questions than all of the answers."

If you don't know the answer to a question, freely say so and promise to have the answer within a specific period. Then write down the question (and the name of the questioner) to remind yourself to find the answer later. Do not risk embarrassing another member of the audience by referring the question to him or her.

If your call for questions results in absolute silence, you may conclude either that you did a superb job of explaining your topic or that no one wishes to be the first to ask a question. If you suspect the latter, to break the ice, you might start the questions yourself, by saying something like, "One question I'm frequently asked that might interest you is. . . ." Or you may ask the program chair ahead of time to be prepared to ask the first question if no one in the audience begins.

■ See Handout 14.1.

CO5. **Critique your performance as a presenter.**

■ Post-Presentation Activities

After the presentation is over and you're back in your office, evaluate your performance using the guidelines presented in Checklist 16 so that you can benefit from the experience. What seemed to work well and what not so well? Analyze each aspect of your performance—from initial research through delivery. Regardless of how well the presentation went, vow to improve your performance next time.

✓checklist 16

The Oral Presentation Process

Planning

✓ Determine whether an oral presentation will be more effective than a written report.

✓ Determine your purpose: What response do you want from your audience?

✓ Analyze your audience in terms of demographic factors, level of knowledge, and psychological needs.

✓ If possible, schedule the presentation to permit adequate preparation and to avoid inconvenience for the audience.

✓ Select an appropriate delivery method.

Organizing

✓ Brainstorm. Write down every point you think you might cover in the presentation.

✓ Separate your notes into the opening, body, and ending. Gather additional data if needed.

✓ Write an effective opening that introduces the topic, discusses the points you'll cover, and tells the audience what you hope will happen as a result of your presentation.

✓ In the body, develop the points fully, giving background data, evidence, and examples.

- Organize the points logically.
- To maintain credibility, discuss any major negative points and be prepared to discuss any minor ones.
- Pace the presentation of data to avoid presenting facts and figures too quickly.

✓ Finish on a strong, upbeat note by summarizing your main points, adding a personal appeal, drawing conclusions and making recommendations, discussing what needs to be done next, or using some other logical closing.

✓ Use humor only when appropriate and only if you are effective at telling amusing stories.

✓ Ensure that your visual aids are needed, simple, easily readable, and of the highest quality.

✓ Ensure that your audience handout contains useful and new information and is attractive and readable.

Practicing

✓ Rehearse your presentation extensively, simulating the actual speaking conditions as much as possible and using your visual aids.

✓ Use simple language and short sentences, with frequent preview, summary, transition, and repetition.

✓ Stand tall and naturally, and speak in a loud, clear, enthusiastic, and friendly voice. Vary the rate and volume of your voice.

✓ Use correct diction and appropriate gestures.

Delivering

✓ Dress appropriately—in comfortable, businesslike, conservative clothing.

✓ If needed, use a microphone effectively.

✓ Maintain eye contact with the audience, including all corners of the room in your gaze.

✓ To avoid anxiety, practice extensively, develop a positive attitude, and concentrate on the friendly faces in the audience.

✓ Plan your answers to possible questions ahead of time. Listen to each question carefully and address your answer to the entire audience.

A BUSINESS PRESENTATION (continued from page 487)

Problem

Recall from the 3Ps activity in Chapter 13 (pages 487–492) that Matt Kromer is preparing to present the findings of his research, to recommend a type of software for publishing in-house documents, and to persuade the audience that his recommendations are sound. The process continues below.

Process

8. What types of visual aids will you use?

   Slides (in the form of an electronic presentation)

   a. Two slides at the beginning—to preview the topic and to illustrate our three publications

   b. Two in the middle—to compare the costs and features of the two programs

   c. Two at the end—to give my recommendations and to show what needs to be done next

9. Will you develop an audience handout?

   I could, of course, easily develop a one-page handout showing miniature copies of the six slides—as a summary of my important points and for future reference. Because the purpose of my presentation is to get a decision made today and I have no supplementary information to present, however, a handout isn't necessary.

10. How will you practice your presentation?

    I'll do a dry run in the conference room where I'll be speaking, standing where I'll actually be giving the presentation and using my computer and projector. I'll also set up a cassette recorder at the far end of the conference table to tape my practice presentation to ensure that I can be heard, to check for clarity and voice qualities, and to time my presentation. In addition, I'll practice answering any questions I think the managers might ask.

11. Afterward, how will you determine whether your presentation was a success?

    If the administrative committee votes to accept my recommendation and schedule, I will have achieved my purpose and the presentation will have been successful.

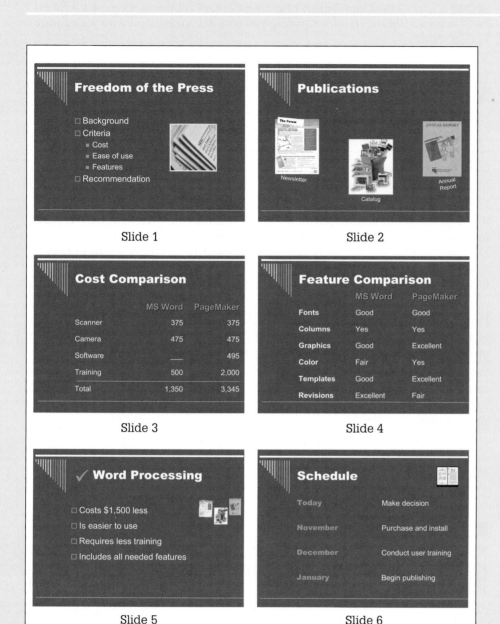

Product

Actual documents can be scanned into the computer, sized to fit, and positioned as desired.

Tables and charts are created easily using presentation software.

During the presentation, each bulleted point and each schedule line is projected one at a time—for emphasis.

Grammar and Mechanics Notes

This presentation uses a standard template in Microsoft PowerPoint. All font faces, sizes, and locations are preselected for you. Do not try to crowd too much information on each slide.

Visit the **BusCom Online Learning Center** (at http://college.hmco.com) for additional resources to help you with this course and with your future career.

■ Summary

CO1. Develop effective visual aids for a presentation.

Visual aids are a component of most business presentations. Although overhead transparencies and 35-mm slides were traditionally the format of choice, today presenters are making electronic presentations, with the slides or video being shown directly from the computer connected to a projector. Regardless of the format used, your visual aids should be relevant, simple, easily readable, and of high quality.

CO2. Develop effective audience handouts.

Audience handouts can supplement the oral information presented, provide space for audience note taking, and represent a permanent record of your presentation. Distribute the handout prior to the presentation if the audience needs to read the information beforehand, during the presentation if you will be referring to the handout during your remarks, or afterward if the handout simply contains a recap of what you presented.

CO3. Practice a presentation to develop an effective speaking style.

Practice your presentation as much as necessary. Speak in a conversational tone, but at a slightly slower rate than normal. Use appropriate arm and hand gestures, but avoid annoying and distracting mannerisms and gestures.

CO4. Deliver a presentation in a clear, confident, and efficient manner.

When actually delivering your presentation, dress appropriately, speak in a clear and confident manner, and maintain eye contact with the audience. If needed, follow the recommended techniques for dealing with stage fright. Plan answers to possible questions and determine beforehand when you will take questions.

CO5. Critique your performance as a presenter.

Finally, evaluate your performance afterward to ensure that your presentation skills improve with each opportunity to speak. Try to determine what worked well and what worked not so well.

■ Exercises

■ Suggested and sample solutions for exercises appear in the *Instructor's Resource Manual*.

① **The 3Ps (Problem, Process, and Product) Model: Communication Applications at SBC Communications** Although Patricia Diaz Dennis doesn't use many visual aids during presentations on behalf of SBC Communications, she knows that audiences benefit from seeing key points reinforced on a slide or in a handout. She also keeps jargon out of her speeches, relying on simple but vivid word pictures to help her audience grasp complex issues and technical concepts.

Before she makes a presentation to any group, Dennis practices in front of family members and times herself to be sure she isn't speaking for too long or, just as bad, finishing her speech much too early.

Problem

Dennis has been invited to address local entrepreneurs and city officials at a widely publicized small business seminar in San Antonio, Texas, where SBC Communications is headquartered. She sees this as a good opportunity to build goodwill and provide information that will help attendees make better choices about new Internet access technology. As Dennis's assistant, you are in charge of researching this presentation and developing the visual aids. You learn that the seminar organizers expect an audience of 100 and have allotted 20 minutes for this presentation, which will take place in the ballroom of a nearby hotel. Now you have to get to work on the visual aids for this speech.

Process

a. What is the purpose of your presentation?
b. Describe your audience.
c. What type of visual aids are most appropriate, given the presentation length, the audience, the information to be conveyed, and the speaker's preferences?
d. If you decide to prepare handouts for Dennis, when do you recommend that she distribute them?

Product

Using your knowledge of presentations, prepare rough drafts of the visual aids you will provide for Dennis's speech, making up any details you need to complete this assignment.

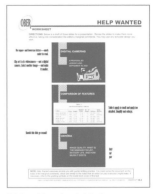

■ See Handout 14.2.

2 Visual Aids   You are the owner of a midsized company. You have 25 agents who travel throughout the country making presentations to small groups of people (10 to 20) regarding retirement programs. Many of your agents have been weak in their presentations. You are concerned that they need to improve their oral presentations because their presentations seem to be a little stale.

Your agents have been making their own visual aids—most of them have used only flipcharts and transparencies. Needless to say, the visuals are not very professionally done; they probably hurt more than they help. You are going to hold a one-day seminar with your agents to work on their oral presentation skills.

One of the things you plan to cover in the seminar is the use of visual aids in oral presentations. Using the information shown in Figure 14.1 on page 506, develop one or more visual aids to illustrate to your agents the criteria for selecting visual aids. You will be presenting in a typical classroom that is able to accommodate all 25 agents.

CO1. Develop effective visual aids for a presentation.

3 Visualizing a Proposal   Review Exercise 2 of Chapter 10 (pages 375–376) and Exercise 2 of Chapter 13 (page 494). Using a presentation software program, prepare a handout (four slides per page) of the slides you will develop for this presentation.

4 Planning the Visual Element   You are the trainer for an in-house survey course in effective advertising techniques that is being offered to franchise owners of your Mexican fast-food chain. As part of the course, you are scheduled to present a 30-minute session on writing effective sales letters. You decide to use the sales letter section of Chapter 8 in this text (beginning on page 264) as the basis for your presentation. Prepare four to six slides that you might use for your presentation to the 25 participants in the course. Submit full-sized color copies of the transparencies to your instructor.

5 Presentation Handout   Prepare a handout to be distributed at the one-day seminar for your company's agents (see Exercise 2). The handout should present helpful tips for making good oral presentations.

CO2. Develop effective audience handouts.

6 **Planning the Audience Handout**   Refer to Exercise 4, in which you prepared slides for your presentation on writing effective sales letters. Using the techniques discussed in this chapter, prepare a handout that not only highlights the important points of your presentation but also provides useful supplementary information.

7 **Evaluating Visuals**   Attend a business meeting, a city council meeting, a student council meeting, a business conference, an executive lecture presentation, or some other event where oral presentations will be taking place. Evaluate the visual aids that were used in the presentation. What kind, if any, visuals were used? Did the presenter have handouts? When were the handouts distributed? How effective were the visuals? What changes could have improved the visuals? Was the presenter trying to impress or express? Write a one-page memo to your instructor addressing these and other aspects regarding the delivery of the presentation.

8 **Stage Fright**   Working in groups of three or four, develop at least three slides for an electronic presentation on how to overcome stage fright. The presentation would be to 10 people in a small boardroom. Use the Internet and other outside sources as well as information from the textbook for your slides. Remember to use an appropriate background color and to keep the special effects simple. Submit the slides to your instructor for evaluation.

CO3 Practice your presentation to develop an effective speaking style.

CO4. Deliver a presentation in a clear, confident, and efficient manner.

9 **Presenting Research Data**   Review the analytical or recommendation report that you prepared in Chapter 12 and the presentation notes that you prepared for this 15-minute oral presentation in Exercise 6 in Chapter 13 (page 495).

a. Develop four to six slides to use during your presentation.
b. Practice your presentation several times—at least once in the classroom where you will actually give it.
c. Give your presentation to the class.

Your instructor may ask the audience to evaluate each presentation in terms of the effectiveness of its content, use of visual aids, and delivery.

10 **Answering Questions**   Prepare a three-minute presentation, using an outline, on any section of any chapter in this text. Before making the presentation make a list of the questions you anticipate being asked and possible answers to those questions. Then form into groups of four or five students, with group members taking turns delivering their presentation to the group.

After each presentation the group members should ask the presenter questions about his or her topic. Did the presenter anticipate the questions the group asked? If so, did he or she have effective answers? If not, how did he or she handle the questions that were asked?

Submit a memo to your instructor. The memo should include your outline, a list of the questions you anticipated, your answers to those questions, the actual questions asked if different from the ones anticipated, and your answers to those questions. Also give your instructor a short post-presentation evaluation of how you think you did and what changes you would make to improve your presentation.

11 Video Presentation   For this exercise, your instructor will assign a partner to you and let you know how you may temporarily secure a videocamera (perhaps from your college audiovisual center). Review the video presentation assignment on physical fitness for which you prepared presentation notes in Exercise 13 in Chapter 13 (pages 498–499), and then complete the following assignments.

a. Develop your audiovisual program, taking into account that you will be presenting on video.
b. Practice your presentation several times, at least once in the location where you will actually have it videotaped.
c. Have a partner videotape a full-scale dress rehearsal (save this videotape to submit to your instructor).
d. Make any needed adjustments to your presentation, rehearse again off-camera, then have your partner videotape your final performance.
e. Repeat this process with your partner being the presenter and you acting as camera operator.
f. Submit a videotape containing both your rehearsal and your final performance, along with your self-evaluation and your partner's evaluation.

12 Answering Questions—Raising Head Count   Ken Shwartz wants you, the new director of human resources, to recruit more production workers for his hat embroidery company, Ahead Headgear. Based in New Bedford, Massachusetts, Ahead creates caps and visors for golf courses, resorts, and tournaments. Founder and CEO Shwartz has turned Ahead into one of the fastest-growing small businesses in the United States. In just a few years, the company has gone from a start-up operation to a firm that rings up more than $18 million in annual sales. However, filling open production jobs can be a struggle. "We have a very high-tech company, but younger workers don't seem to want our production jobs," he tells you. "They equate us with the old, dirty sewing factories."

You decide to make a presentation about Ahead at the next Southern Massachusetts Job Fair, which typically attracts 1,000 high school graduates. You are allotted five minutes to speak to the audience and another five minutes for a question-and-answer period. What kinds of questions do you anticipate? List at least six questions you expect to be asked. Using the Internet or other sources, research Ahead Headgear to find the answers to these questions. If some information is unavailable, determine who at Ahead could answer the question for you.

■ See Handout 14.3.

13 Providing Feedback   Using the presentation feedback form provided by your instructor:

a. Provide a self-evaluation of your performance in a classroom presentation.
b. Evaluate the performance of other classroom presenters.
c. Evaluate the performance of another speaker assigned by your instructor.

CO5. **Critique your performance as a presenter.**

continuing case 10

■ A suggested solution to the Continuing Case can be found in the *Instructor's Resource Manual*.

URBAN SYSTEMS

Picture the Pain

Review the Continuing Case presented at the end of Chapter 13, where you planned an oral presentation on carpal tunnel syndrome.

Critical Thinking

1. Considering the audience and topic, which type of audiovisual aid would be most effective—transparencies, 35-mm slides, or electronic projection directly from your computer?

2. Would a photograph of a sufferer of this ailment (or even a short videotaped interview) be effective for this audience? Why or why not? After much preparation and several rehearsals, Pat gives her presentation.

Speaking/Writing Projects

Prepare as many of the following projects as are assigned by your instructor. (*Note:* If you did not conduct any primary research for this project, base your presentation on secondary data.)

3. Develop five to eight visual aids to use during your presentation.

4. Arrange to have a full-scale practice session of your presentation videotaped. Evaluate your taped practice session in light of the guidelines presented in this chapter. Prepare a memo to your instructor critiquing your performance. Submit both your memo and the videotape.

5. Divide into groups of five students, with each student in turn giving his or her presentation to the other four. Each presenter should conduct a question-and-answer session immediately after each presentation. Be prepared to ask a question of the presenter and to answer any questions directed to you when you present. Prepare a memo to your instructor critiquing the performance of each presenter.

After much preparation and several rehearsals, Pat gives her presentation.

LABtest 14

Retype the following news release, correcting any grammar and mechanics errors according to the rules introduced in LABs 2-6 beginning on page 576.

Lighting is often seen as one of those practical

necessities (SP)
~~necessitys~~, something that's put in place simply to illuminate
                    do and (NO COMMA)
what we ~~do, and~~ protect us against unwelcome intruders.
Psychologically, however, (TRAN)   *us and (FRAG)*
~~Psychologically however~~ we need light to comfort ~~us. And~~ to send
                              welcome, vitality, (SER)
5   out signals of ~~welcome vitality~~ and warmth. From the decorating
              view, (INTRO) there's (WORD)
point of ~~view theres~~ no doubt lighting can make or break an

interior.
                are (AGR)
There ~~is~~, in fact, no limits to how imaginative you can be.
                                      effects (WORD)
Lighting design can create special ~~affects~~ according to the
                              its (WORD)
10   architecture of your home, ~~it's~~ interior styling, and even
              personal (WORD)
your ~~personnel~~ moods.
              increasingly influential (NO HYPHEN)   *is (AGR)*
One ~~increasingly-influential~~ trend in lighting circles ~~are~~
                                      invisible (SP)
for fittings that are almost ~~invizible~~. Another is the sleek
                        low-voltage (ADJ)
contemporary lines of ~~low voltage~~ halogen spotlights. The reason
      that (WORD)   *stainless-steel (ADJ)*
15   is ~~because~~ white walls, modular furniture, and ~~stainless steel~~

industrial kitchens are now so popular. There's also a craze for
do-it-yourself (ADJ) fittings that (FRAG)
~~do it yourself fittings. That~~ come in kit form ready for you to

assemble at home.
      "There's (QUOT)   *before," (QUOT)*
~~There's~~ more freedom in lighting than ever ~~before~~ says David
              president (POSITION TITLE)   *Ultra Light (PROPER NOUN)*
20   Kaplan, ~~President~~ of Urban Systems (the developer of ~~ultra light~~,
              paper-thin (ADJ)
a new ~~paper thin~~-light source). "The look is light-hearted and

sometimes even slightly mad."

■ See Handout 14.4.

■ See Slides 14.13–14.16.

15

Employment Communication

After you have finished this chapter, you should be able to

1. **Determine the appropriate length, format, and content for your résumé.**

2. **Compose solicited and unsolicited job-application letters.**

3. **Conduct yourself appropriately during an employment interview.**

4. **Complete the communication tasks needed after the employment interview.**

an insider's
perspective

JEFF TAYLOR
Founder and Chief Monster,
Monster.com (Maynard,
Massachusetts)

Jeff Taylor may be Chief Monster, but he still takes time to interview applicants for certain jobs. Taylor launched The Monster Board in 1994 as the Web's first online recruiting site, and he remains responsible for its strategy, product, and marketing. Today the company, renamed Monster, has more than 1,400 employees in 19 countries and a database of more than 30 million résumés. The site (at http://www.monster.com) features hundreds of thousands of job postings plus expert advice on career management.

When Taylor and his staff want to fill a position, they begin—where else?—with résumés in their own database. "We hire 70 percent of our candidates from the Monster database," he says. Depending on the position, they search by skills, work experience, and other qualifications. Then the interview process begins.

Taylor likes to start interviews with an open-ended question: "Tell me about yourself—not necessarily what's on your résumé, but who you are." The point is to "see how people react when they are not scripted," he explains. During the interview, Taylor mentions specifics from the résumé to "establish that I'm taking an interest and offer clues that will help the candidate ad lib around particular subjects." For example, when interviewing a graduate of the University of Massachusetts, he might say, "Tell me about your UMass experience." This offers an opportunity for the candidate to stand out by talking about grades, extracurricular activities, or other aspects of the college experience.

Candidates for Monster jobs are expected to come prepared with questions of their own. "I like to see that the candidate has done a little research about the position, about our company, or about me," Taylor says. "One of the worst things you can do at the end of a rigorous interview is to have no questions to ask. If you're interested in the company, you should find out enough about it to ask creative questions during the interview."

Finally, Taylor stresses the importance of following up after the interview. "Some sort of correspondence is appropriate, whether it's handwritten or typed, mailed or e-mailed," he says. He prefers that candidates jog his memory by mentioning the date of the interview or a particular topic they discussed: "On a busy day, I might interview several people, so I appreciate it when a candidate mentions something from our conversation to take my mind back to that interview." He offers this advice to job-seekers: "Don't procrastinate. When you see a job you want, don't just talk about sending your résumé. Do it—now."

"One of the worst things you can do at the end of a rigorous interview is to have no questions to ask."

■ A chapter overview appears in the *Instructor's Resource Manual.*

CO1. Determine the appropriate length, format, and content for your résumé.

Communication skills play an important role in the job campaign.

The purpose of a résumé is to get you a job interview— not to get you a job.

■ For more on résumés, see the supplemental lecture/discussion notes in the *Instructor's Resource Manual.*

■ Preparing Your Résumé

A **résumé** is a brief record of one's personal history and qualifications that is typically prepared by an applicant for a job. The emphasis in the résumé should be on the future rather than on the past: you must show how your education and work experience have prepared you for future jobs—specifically, the job for which you are applying.

Right from the start, be realistic about the purpose of your résumé. Few people are actually hired on the basis of their résumés alone. (However, many people are *rejected* because of their poorly written or poorly presented résumés.) Instead, applicants are generally hired on the basis of their performance during one or more job interviews.

Thus, the purpose of the résumé is to get you an interview, and the purpose of the interview is to get you a job. Remember, however, that the résumé and accompanying application letter (cover letter) are crucial in advancing you beyond the mass of initial applicants and into the much smaller group of potential candidates invited to an interview. (See Communication Snapshot 15 for information on how workers typically find their jobs.)

Résumé Length

Decisions about résumé length become much easier when you consider what happens on the receiving end: recruiters typically spend no more than 35 seconds looking at each résumé during their initial screening to pare down the perhaps hundreds of applications for a position into a manageable number to study in more detail.[1] How much information can the recruiter be expected to read in less than a minute? It won't matter how well qualified you are if no one ever reviews those qualifications.

How much is too much? Surveys of employment and human resources executives consistently show that most managers prefer a one-page résumé for the entry-level positions typically sought by recent college graduates, with a two-page résumé being reserved for unusual circumstances or for higher-level positions.[2] True or not, take note of the old career-services adage, "The thicker the résumé, the thicker the applicant."

(It should be noted, however, that a recent survey of personnel recruiters from Big Five accounting firms found that recruiters ranked candidates with two-page résumés more favorably than candidates with one-page résumés. The researchers recommended that graduating seniors with accounting majors *and outstanding credentials* consider writing two-page résumés when applying for entry-level Big Five accounting positions.[3])

communication snapshot 15

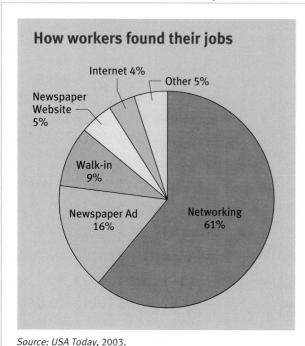

How workers found their jobs

Internet 4%
Other 5%
Newspaper Website 5%
Walk-in 9%
Newspaper Ad 16%
Networking 61%

Source: USA Today, 2003.

In addition to the all-important job interview, some positions also require auditions. That's how Tara Strong, shown here with her two-year-old son Sammy, got her job as a voiceover artist for TV cartoon characters. According to Strong, "You don't just get in a room and read—you have to bring these cartoon characters to life." Enthusiasm is an asset for any type of job application.

According to one survey of 200 executives from major U.S. firms, the most serious mistake job candidates make is including too much information in their résumés. Their ranking (in percentages of the whole) of the most serious résumé errors is as follows:[4]

■ See Slide 15.1.

Most recruiters prefer a one-page résumé for entry-level positions.

Too long	32 percent
Typographical or grammatical errors	25 percent
No description of job functions	18 percent
Unprofessional appearance	15 percent
Achievements omitted	10 percent
	100 percent

Accounting graduates with outstanding credentials should consider creating a two-page résumé.

A one-page résumé is *not* the same as a two-page résumé crammed onto one page by means of small type and narrow margins. Your résumé must be attractive and easy to read. Shorten your résumé by making judicious decisions about what to include and then by using concise language to communicate what is important.

Do not, on the other hand, make your résumé *too* short. A résumé that does not fill one page may tell the prospective employer that you have little to offer. It has been estimated that one page is ideal for 85 percent of all résumés, and that is the length you should target.[5]

Résumé Format

Although the content of your résumé is obviously more important than the format, remember that first impressions are lasting. As pointed out earlier, those first impressions are formed during the half-minute that is typically devoted to the initial

Use a clear, simple design, with plenty of white space.

screening of each résumé. Therefore, even before you begin writing your résumé, think about the format, because some format decisions will affect the amount of space available to discuss your qualifications and background.

Choose a simple, easy-to-read typeface, and avoid the temptation to use a lot of "special effects" just because they're available on your computer. One or two typefaces in one or two different sizes should be enough. Use a simple format, with lots of white space, short paragraphs, and a logical organization. Through the use of type size and style, indentation, bullets, and the like, make clear which parts are subordinate to main features. One of your word processor's built-in résumé templates is a good place to start.

Format your résumé on standard-sized paper (8½ by 11 inches) so that it can be filed easily. Avoid brightly colored papers: they'll get attention but perhaps the wrong kind. Dark colors do not photocopy well, and you want photocopies of your résumé (whether made by you or by the potential employer) to look professional.

ASK Ober

Choose white or an off-white (cream or ivory) paper of good quality—at least 20-pound bond.

Unless you're applying for a creative position (such as a copywriter of advertising material) and know your intended audience well, avoid being too artistic and original in formatting your résumé. If you are applying for the typical business position, the overall appearance of your résumé should present a professional, conservative appearance—one that adds to your credibility. Don't scare off your readers before they have a chance to meet you.

Finally, your résumé and application letter must be 100 percent free from error—in content, spelling, grammar, and format. Ninety-nine percent accuracy is simply not good enough when seeking a job. One survey of large-company executives showed that fully 80 percent of them had decided against interviewing a job seeker simply because of poor grammar, spelling, or punctuation in his or her résumé.[6] Don't write, as one job applicant did, "Education: Advanced Curses in Accounting," or as another did, "I have an obsession for detail; I make sure that I cross my i's and dot my t's." Show right from the start that you're the type of person who takes pride in your work.

Résumé Content

Fortunately, perhaps, there is no such thing as a standard résumé; each is as individual as the person it represents. There are, however, standard parts of the résumé—those parts recruiters expect and need to see to make valid judgments. For example, one survey of 152 *Fortune* 500 company personnel indicated that 90 percent or more wanted the following information on a résumé:[7]

- Name, address, and telephone number

- Job objective

- College major, degree, name of college, and date of graduation

- Jobs held, employing company or companies (but not complete mailing address or the names of your supervisors), dates of employment, and job duties

- Special aptitudes and skills

Similarly, items *not* wanted on the résumé (items rated unimportant by more than 90 percent of those surveyed) related primarily to possible bases for discrimination: religion, ethnicity, age, gender, photograph, and marital status. Additionally, most of the employers questioned thought high school activities should not be included on the résumés of college graduates.

The standard and optional parts of the résumé are discussed here in the order in which they typically appear on the résumé of a recent (or soon-to-be) college graduate.

Include the information employers want; exclude the information they do not want.

Identifying Information   It doesn't do any good to impress a recruiter if he or she cannot locate you easily to schedule an interview; therefore, your name and complete address (including phone number and e-mail address) are crucial.

Your name should be the very first item on the résumé, arranged attractively at the top. Use whatever form you typically use for signing your name (for example, with or without initials). Give your complete name, avoiding nicknames, and do not use a personal title such as *Mr.* or *Ms.*

It is not necessary to include the heading "Résumé" at the top (any more than it is necessary to use the heading "Letter" at the top of a business letter). The purpose of the document will be evident to the recruiter. Besides, you want your name to be the main heading—where it will stand out in the recruiter's mind.

If you will soon be changing your address (as from a college address to a home address), include both, along with the relevant dates for each. If you are away from your telephone most of the day and no one is at home to answer it and take a message, you would be wise to secure voice mail or an answering machine (and make sure your recorded message is businesslike). The important point is to be available for contact.

Display your name, address, and phone number in a prominent position.

■ See Slides 15.2 and 15.3.

Job Objective   The job objective is a short summary of your area of expertise and career interest. Most recruiters want the objective stated so that they will know where you might fit into their organization. Don't force the employer to guess about your career goals.

Furthermore, don't waste the objective's prominent spot at the top of your résumé by giving a weak, over-general goal like these:

NOT: "A position that offers both a challenge and an opportunity for growth"

"Challenging position in a progressive organization"

"A responsible position that lets me use my education and experience and that provides opportunities for increased responsibilities"

The problem with such goals is not that they're unworthy objectives; they are *very* worthwhile. That is why everyone—perhaps including the recruiter—wants such positions. The problem is that such vague, high-flown goals don't help the

Include a job objective if you have specific requirements.

■ See Slides 15.4–15.6.

recruiter find a suitable position for *you*. They waste valuable space on your résumé.

For your objective to help you, it must be personalized—both for you and for the position you're seeking. Also, it must be specific enough to be useful to the prospective employer but not so specific as to exclude you from many types of similar positions. The following job objectives meet these criteria:

BUT: "A paid, one-semester internship in marketing or advertising in the Atlanta area"

"Position in personal sales in a medium-sized manufacturing firm"

"Opportunity to apply my accounting education and Spanish-language skills outside the United States"

"A public relations position requiring well-developed communication, administrative, and computer skills"

Note that after reading these objectives, you feel you know a little about each candidate, a feeling you did not get from reading the earlier general objectives. If your goals are so broad that you have difficulty specifying a job objective, consider either eliminating this section of your résumé or developing several résumés, each with a different job objective and emphasis.

You should be aware that an increasing number of large corporations have begun scanning the résumés they receive into their computer systems and then searching this computerized database by keyword. Be certain, therefore, that the title of the actual position you desire and other relevant terms are included somewhere in your résumé. (Later in this chapter, we discuss electronic résumés.)

Education Unless your work experience has been extensive, fairly high level, and directly related to your job objective, your education is probably a stronger job qualification than your work experience and should therefore come first on the résumé.

List the title of your degree, the name of your college and its location if needed, your major and (if applicable) minor, and your expected date of graduation (month and year).

List your grade-point average if it will set you apart from the competition (generally, at least a 3.0 on a 4.0 scale). If you've made the dean's list or have financed any substantial portion of your college expenses through part-time work, savings, or scholarships, mention that. Unless your course of study provided distinctive experiences that uniquely qualify you for the job, avoid including a lengthy list of college courses.

Work Experience Today, almost half of all full-time college students are employed, most of them working between 15 and 29 hours per week.[8] And most other students have had at least some work experience—for example, summer jobs. Thus, most students will have some work experience to bring to their future jobs.

Work experience—*any* work experience—is a definite plus. It shows the employer that you've had experience in satisfying a superior, following directions, accomplishing objectives through team effort, and being rewarded for your labors. If your work experience has been directly related to your job objectives, consider putting it ahead of the education section, where it will receive more emphasis.

■ See Slides 15.7–15.9.

In relating your work experience, use either a chronological or a functional organizational pattern.

■ *Chronological:* In a chronological arrangement, you organize your experience by date, describing your most recent job first and working backward. This format is most appropriate when you have had a strong continuing work history and much of your work has been related to your job objective (see Model 32, page 536). About 95 percent of all résumés are chronological, beginning with the most recent information and working backward.[9]

■ *Functional:* In a functional arrangement, you organize your experience by type of function performed (such as *supervision* or *budgeting*) or by type of skill developed (such as *human relations* or *communication skills*). Then, under each, are specific examples (evidence), as illustrated in Model 33 on page 537. Functional résumés are most appropriate when you're changing industries, moving into an entirely different line of work, or reentering the work force after a long period of unemployment, because they emphasize your skills rather than your employment history and let you show how these skills have broad applicability to other jobs.

In actual practice, the two patterns are not mutually exclusive; you can use a combination. And regardless of which arrangement you ultimately select, remember that more than 90 percent of the employers in the survey cited earlier want to see on a résumé the jobs held, employing company or companies, dates of employment, and job duties.

Remember that the purpose of describing your work history is to show the prospective employer what you've learned *that will benefit the organization.* No matter what your previous work, you've developed certain traits or had certain experiences that can be transferred to the new position. On the basis of your research into the duties of the job you are seeking, highlight those transferable skills.

If you can honestly do so, show in your résumé that you have developed as many of the following characteristics as possible:

■ Ability to work well with others

■ Communication skills

■ Competence and good judgment

■ Innovation

■ High-level computer proficiency

■ Reliability and trustworthiness

■ Enthusiasm

■ Honest and moral character

■ Increasing responsibility

VANITY PLATES   *word*wise

According to the website
http://www.chaos.umd.edu/misc/origplates.html,
these are actual license plates held by professionals:

10R SAX	"Tenor sax"—Professional musician
2 3PAIR	"Tooth repair"—Dentist
2N2R4	"2 and 2 are 4"—Schoolteacher
4CASTR	"Forecaster"—Meteorologist
CALQL8	"Calculate"—Auditor
DR IIII	"Doctor Four-Eyes"—Optometrist
I CD8EM	"I sedate 'em"—Anesthesiologist

Regardless of which type of organizational pattern you use, provide complete information about your work history.

Show how your work experience qualifies you for the type of job for which you are applying.

model 32

RÉSUMÉ IN CHRONOLOGICAL FORMAT

Provides specific enough objective to be useful.

Places work experience before education because applicant considers it to be her stronger qualification.

Uses action words like *assisted* and *conducted*; uses incomplete sentences to emphasize the action words and to conserve space.

Provides additional data to enhance her credentials.

Omits actual names and addresses of references.

---

225 West 70 Street
New York, NY 10023
Phone: 212-555-3821
Email: agomez@nyu.edu

1
2   # Aurelia Gomez

Objective		Entry-level staff accounting position with a public accounting firm

3 **Experience** | Summer 2005 | ***Accounting Intern***: Coopers & Lybrand, New York City
- Assisted in preparing corporate income tax returns
- Attended meetings with clients
- Conducted research in corporate tax library and wrote research reports

4 | Nov. 2001-Aug. 2003 | ***Payroll Specialist:*** City of New York
- Worked in civil service position in Department of Administration
- Used payroll software on both DEC 1034 minicomputer and on personal computers
- Audited all overtime billing
- Developed two new forms for requesting independent-contractor status that are now used city-wide
- Represented 28-person work unit on the department's management-labor committee
- Left job to pursue college degree full-time

Education | Jan. 1999-Present | Pursuing a 5-year bachelor of business administration degree (major in accounting) from New York University
- Will graduate June 2006
- Attended part-time from 1999 until 2003 while holding down a full-time job
- Have financed 100% of all college expenses through savings, work, and student loans
- Plan to sit for the CPA exam in May 2007

Personal Data
- Helped start the Minority Business Student Association at NYU and served as program director for two years
- Have traveled extensively throughout the Caribbean
- Am a member of the Accounting Society
- Am willing to relocate

References | Available upon request

Grammar and Mechanics Notes

1 The name is formatted in larger type for emphasis.

2 Horizontal and vertical rules separate the heading information from the body of the résumé.

3 The major section headings are parallel in format and in wording.

4 The side headings for the dates are formatted in a column for ease of reading. Note that abbreviations may be used.

RAYMOND J. ARNOLD

1   **OBJECTIVE**

Labor relations position in a large multinational firm that requires well-developed labor relations, management, and communication skills

SKILLS

LABOR RELATIONS
- Majored in labor relations; minored in psychology
2
- Belong to Local 463 of International Office Workers Union
- Was crew chief for the second-shift work team at Wainwright Bank

MANAGEMENT
- Learned time-management skills by working 30 hours per week while attending school full-time
- Was promoted twice in three years at Wainwright Bank
- Practiced discretion while dealing with the financial affairs of others; treated all transactions confidentially

COMMUNICATION
3
- Developed a webpage for Alpha Kappa Psi business fraternity
- Ran for senior class vice president, making frequent campaign speeches and impromptu remarks
- Took elective classes in report writing and business research
- Am competent in Microsoft Office 2003 and Internet research

4   **EDUCATION**

B.S. Degree from Boston University to be awarded June 2006
Major: Labor Relations; Minor: Psychology

EXPERIENCE

Bank teller, Wainwright Bank, Boston, Massachusetts: 2003-Present
Salesperson, JC Penney, Norfolk, Nebraska: Summer 2001

REFERENCES

Available from the Career Information Center
Boston University, Boston, MA 02215; phone: 617-555-2000

15 TURNER HALL, BOSTON UNIVERSITY, BOSTON, MA 02215 • PHONE: 617-555-9833 • E-MAIL: RJARN@BU.EDU

RÉSUMÉ IN FUNCTIONAL FORMAT

Introduces three skill areas in objective and expands on each with bulleted examples.

Relates each listed item directly to the desired job.

Provides specific evidence to support each skill.

Weaves work experiences, education, and extracurricular activities into the skill statements.

Avoids repeating the duties given earlier.

Grammar and Mechanics Notes

1 Putting the headings along the side and indenting the copy opens up the résumé, providing more white space. (This document is based on the "Elegant" résumé template in Microsoft Word.)

2 Bullets are used to highlight the individual skills; asterisks would have worked just as well.

3 All items are in parallel format.

4 More space is left *between* the different sections than *within* sections (to clearly separate each section).

Complete sentences are not necessary. Instead, start your descriptions with action verbs, using present tense for current duties and past tense for previous job duties or accomplishments. Concrete words such as the following make your work experience come alive:

Use concrete, achievement-oriented words to describe your experience.

accomplished	constructed	increased	produced
achieved	contracted	instituted	purchased
administered	controlled	interviewed	recommended
analyzed	coordinated	introduced	reported
applied	created	investigated	researched
approved	delegated	led	revised
arranged	designed	maintained	scheduled
assisted	determined	managed	screened
authorized	developed	marketed	secured
balanced	diagnosed	modified	simplified
budgeted	directed	motivated	sold
built	edited	negotiated	studied
changed	established	operated	supervised
collected	evaluated	ordered	taught
communicated	forecast	organized	trained
completed	generated	oversaw	transformed
conceived	guided	planned	updated
concluded	handled	prepared	wrote
conducted	hired	presented	
consolidated	implemented	presided	

Avoid weak verbs such as *attempted, endeavored, hoped,* and *tried,* and avoid sexist language such as *manpower* and *chairman.* When possible, ensure credibility by listing specific accomplishments, giving numbers or dollar amounts. Highlight especially those accomplishments that have direct relevance to the desired job. Here are some examples:

Stress specific accomplishments directly related to the desired job.

NOT: I was responsible for a large sales territory.

BUT: Managed a six-county sales territory; increased sales 13 percent during first full year.

NOT: I worked as a clerk in the cashier's office.

BUT: Balanced the cash register every day; was the only part-time employee entrusted to make nightly cash deposits.

NOT: Worked as a bouncer at a local bar.

BUT: Maintained order at Nick's Side-Door Saloon; learned firsthand the importance of compromise and negotiation in solving problems.

NOT: Worked as a volunteer for Art Reach.

BUT: Personally sold more than $1,000 worth of tickets to annual benefit dance; introduced an "Each one, reach one" membership drive that increased membership every year during my three-year term as membership chairperson.

As illustrated in the last example, if you have little or no actual work experience, show how your involvement with professional, social, or civic organizations has helped you develop skills that are transferable to the workplace. Volunteer work, for example, can help develop valuable skills in time management, working with groups, handling money, speaking, accepting responsibility, and the like. In addition, most schools offer internships in which a student receives course credit and close supervision while holding down a temporary job.

Work experience need not be restricted to paid positions.

It has been said that the closest any of us comes to perfection is when we develop our résumé, which has also been called "a balance sheet without any liabilities." Employers recognize your right to put your best foot forward in your résumé—that is, to highlight your strengths and minimize your weaknesses. However, you must never lie about anything and must never take credit for anything you did not do. A simple telephone call can verify any statement on your résumé. Don't risk destroying your credibility before being hired, and don't risk the possibility of being dismissed later for having misrepresented your qualifications.

Be ethical in all aspects of your résumé.

Other Relevant Information If you have special skills that might give you an edge over the competition (such as knowledge of a foreign language or webpage-creation competence), list them on your résumé. Although employers assume that college graduates today have competence in word processing, you should specify any other particular software skills you possess.

Include any honors or recognitions that have relevance to the job you're seeking. Memberships in business-related organizations demonstrate your commitment to your profession, and you should list them if space permits. Likewise, involvement in volunteer, civic, and other extracurricular activities gives evidence of a well-rounded individual and reflects your values and commitment.

Avoid including any data that can become grounds for a discrimination suit—such as information about age, gender, race, religion, handicaps, marital status, and the like. Do not include a photograph with your application papers. Some employers like to have the applicant's Social Security number included as an aid in verifying college or military information. If you have military experience, include it. If your name stereotypes you as a possible noncitizen and citizenship is important for the job you want, you may want to explicitly state your citizenship.

Other optional information includes hobbies and special interests, travel experiences, willingness to travel, and health status. (However, because it is unlikely that anyone has ever written "Health—Poor" on a résumé, a health statement may be meaningless.) Such information may be included if it has direct relevance to your desired job and if you have room for it, but it may be safely omitted if you need space for more important information.

As space permits, include other information that uniquely qualifies you for the type of position for which you're applying.

References A **reference** is a person who has agreed to provide information to a prospective employer regarding a job applicant's fitness for a job. As a general rule,

■ See Handout 15.1.

the names and addresses of references need not be included on the résumé itself. Instead, give a general statement that references are available. This policy ensures that you will be contacted before your references are called. The exception to this practice is if your references are likely to be known by the person reading the résumé; in this case, list their names.

Your references should be professional references rather than character references. The best ones are employers, especially your present employer. University professors with whom you have had a close and successful relationship are also valuable references. When asking for references, be prepared to sign a waiver stating that you forgo your right to see the recommendation or that you won't claim that a reference prevented you from getting a job. Many firms are becoming reluctant to authorize their managers to provide reference letters because of the possibility of being sued.

Study the two résumés shown in Models 32 and 33. Note the different formats that can be used to present the data. As stated earlier, there is no standard résumé format. Use these résumés or others to which you have access (available from your college career-center office or from job-hunting books) to glean ideas for formatting your own.

Note also the different organizational patterns used to convey work experience. The résumé in Model 32 is arranged in a chronological pattern (with the most recent work experience listed first), whereas the one in Model 33 is arranged in a functional pattern that stresses the skills learned rather than the jobs held. Note how job descriptions and skills are all geared to support the applicant's qualifications for the desired job. Note also the concise, concrete language used and the overall tone of quiet confidence.

Electronic Résumés

An **electronic résumé** is a résumé that is stored in a computer database designed to help manage and initially screen job applicants. These résumés come from a variety of sources; applicants may simply mail or fax a paper copy of their standard résumé, which is then scanned into a database; they may fill out (type in) an online résumé form and submit it; they may send the résumé as an e-mail message; or they may post their résumé on the Internet, using a bulletin board system, a newsgroup, or a personal home page on the World Wide Web.

Electronic résumés provide many benefits—both to the recruiter and to the job seeker:

Submitting an electronic résumé makes you available to more people and for more positions.

- The job seeker's résumé is potentially available to a large number of employers.

- The job seeker may be considered for positions of which he or she wasn't even aware.

- The initial screening is done by a bias-free computer.

- Employers are relieved of the drudgery of having to manually screen and acknowledge résumés.

- A focused search can be conducted quickly.

- Information is always available until the individual résumé is purged from the system (often in six months).

When jobs need to be filled, the computer is fed a list of keywords and phrases. It then looks through the database and prints out a list of candidates with the most keyword matches. A person picks it up from there, manually studying each se-lected résumé to determine whom to invite for an interview. (So far, electronic tools alter only the screening, not the selection, process. People are still hired by people.)

Building appropriate keywords into your résumé is essential to successfully us-ing automated résumé systems. Keywords are the descriptive terms that employers search for when trying to fill a position. They are the words and phrases employers believe best summarize the characteristics that they are seeking in candidates for particular jobs, such as college degree, foreign language skills, job titles, specific job skills, software packages, or the names of competitors for whom applicants may have worked. Examples of key terms include *human resources manager, Hughes Air-craft, Windows XP, teamwork,* or *ISO 9000.*

Electronic résumés must be picked up by a computer search before they are even seen by human eyes. OCR software creates an ASCII (text) file of your résumé, and artificial intelligence software then "reads" the text and extracts important informa-tion about you. Thus, your first hurdle is *to be selected by the computer.*

One type of electronic résumé that *is* designed to look attractive is the online HTML (or XML) résumé, which can be viewed on your home page on the Web. Many providers, such as Yahoo! Geocities, will host your home page for free or little cost. (To locate other websites with free Web space hosting, log on to http://freewebspace.net.)

HTML résumés offer these advantages:

- Potential employers can access your résumé at any time. Assume, for example, you're talking to a potential employer who expresses an interest in your qualifi-cations. You can simply refer him or her to your Web address for instant reviewing.

- You can include hypertext links to work samples you've completed. For exam-ple, instead of merely saying that you wrote extensive reports in your job or that you have top-level communication skills, you can prove it by providing links to actual documents you have created.

- You can highlight your creativity because the online language provides enough formatting options to enable you to produce a very attractive page (your HTML résumé also provides evidence of your technical expertise).

Note the attractive appearance and numerous links in the online résumé shown in Model 34. Pay particular attention to the marginal notations and mechanics notes at the bottom.

Because you can never be sure how your résumé will be treated, you should pre-pare two résumés—one for the computer to read and one for people to read. When mailing a résumé, you may wish to include both versions, making note of that fact in your cover letter. Differences between the two versions concern both content and format.

Content Guidelines for Electronic Résumés   Using your standard résumé as a starting point, make these modifications to ensure that your résumé is "computer-friendly" and to maximize the chance that your résumé will be picked by the computer for further review by humans:

Using appropriate key words is essential in an electronic résumé.

HTML résumés send a subtle message about your online skills.

model34

ONLINE RÉSUMÉ

Provides appropriate identification information in an attractive heading.

Allows the reader to view, download, and print the résumé in different formats.

Provides links to make it easy to navigate the page.

Links to a copy of her transcript for viewing courses taken and grades.

Contains underlined links throughout the page that bring up copies of the actual documents for viewing.

Anna Swan

103 Dayton Street, West Alexandria, OH 45381

937-839-4362

aswan@yahoo.com

1

[MS Word Version]   [Scannable Plain-Text Version]   [PDF Version]

▶ Education
▶ Experience
▶ Certifications
▶ Computer Skills
▶ References
▶ Contact me

OBJECTIVE

To apply my community health, organizational, and communication skills to help people improve their health and lifestyles

EDUCATION

Bachelor of Science Degree, Ohio University, Athens, OH, Jun 06
- Major: Community Health
- GPA: 3.8 in major on 4.0 scale [Transcript]

2

EXPERIENCE

Volunteer Instructor, American Red Cross, Eaton, OH, Jul 06-Present

- Taught First Aid and CPR
- Exposed to individual learning styles

Assistant Pool Manager, Village of West Alexandria, OH, May 05-Aug 05

- Assisted the manager with everyday duties of running a community swimming pool
- Applied first-aid skills as needed

Intern, Health Center, Indiana University East, Richmond, IN, Sep 04-Dec 04

3

- Developed and presented PowerPoint health programs
- Produced resource folders to be used as supplemental materials in existing programs

---

Grammar and Mechanics Notes

1 Use color—but in moderation; ensure that your webpage projects a professional image.

2 Avoid the tendency to include a photograph of yourself on your webpage.

3 Do not underline any part of your webpage. Save underlining to indicate links.

Anna Swan • 937-839-4362 • aswan@yahoo.com

4

● Assisted in conducting corporate health appraisals

Nursing Assistant, Hudson Center, Ohio University, Athens, OH, Jan 03-Aug 04
   ● Assisted physicians and nurses in performing medical exams and charting
   ● Wrote Procedures Handbook for the staff

CERTIFICATIONS
   ● First Aid and CPR Instructor
   ● Professional Rescuer Instructor

COMPUTER SKILLS

   ● Microsoft Word, PowerPoint, and Excel (Ver. 2003)

   ● Microsoft Publisher

   ● Print Shop

   ● All aspects of Internet research

5

REFERENCES

Available on request

CONTACT ME

Please contact me by e-mail at aswan@yahoo.com or by phone at 937-839-4362.

Created on April 3, 2006
Last updated on April 21, 2006

Return to Top • Education • Experience

Certifications • Computer Skills • References

model34

(CONTINUED)

Provides links to a sample of her report-writing skills.

Provides links to actual copies of the certification documents.

Shows the currency of the information.

Repeats the navigation links.

Grammar and Mechanics Notes

4 Use Google or some other search engine to search the Web for "resumes + HTML." You'll find a wide variety of actual HTML résumés to review. When you see one you like, download it and adjust it to fit your own needs.

5 Leave plenty of white space and make your section headings stand out.

Prefer nouns for describing your work experience.

1. Think "nouns" instead of "verbs" (users rarely search for verbs). Use concrete words rather than vague descriptions. Include industry-specific descriptive nouns that characterize your skills accurately and that people in your field use and commonly look for. (Browse other online résumés, newspaper ads, and industry publications to see what terms are currently being used.)

2. Put keywords in proper context, weaving them throughout your résumé. (This strategy is considered a more polished and sophisticated approach than listing them in a block at the beginning of the résumé.)

3. Use a variety of different words to describe your skills, and don't overuse important words. In most searches, each word counts once, no matter how many times it is used.

4. Because your résumé is going to look very bland in plain ASCII text, stripped of all formatting, consider adding a sentence such as this one to the end of your posted résumé: "An attractive and fully formatted hard-copy version of this résumé is available upon request."

Format Guidelines for Electronic Résumés   The following guidelines will ensure that your résumé is in a format that can be scanned accurately and transmitted accurately as an e-mail message.

1. Save your traditionally formatted résumé as a text-only file; most word processors allow you to save a file in ASCII format, which has a file name with a .txt extension.

2. Reopen the text file and make any needed changes to your résumé (see the remaining guidelines). Make sure you always save the document as a text file—not as a word processing document.

3. To ensure accurate reading by computer software, make the format as plain as possible. Do not change typefaces, justification, margins, tabs, font sizes, and the like; do not insert underlines, bold, or italic; and do not use horizontal or vertical rules, graphics, boxes, tables, or columns. None of these will show up in a scan of a text file.

4. Use a line length of no more than 70 characters per line. Because you can't change margins in a text file, press Enter at the ends of lines if necessary.

5. Do not divide (hyphenate) words at the end of a line.

6. Change bullets to * or + signs at the beginning of the line; then insert spaces at the beginning of runover lines to make all lines of a bulleted paragraph begin at the same point.

7. Press the space bar (instead of the tab) to show any needed indentions.

8. Type your name on the first line by itself, use a standard address format below your name, and type your phone number and e-mail address, each on its own line.

9. Make the résumé as long as necessary (most database résumés average 2–3 pages).

10. After making all needed changes, as a test, mail your text file in the body of an e-mail message to yourself to see how it looks after being mailed. This step will help you identify any more formatting problems before you send it out to possible employers.

11. Use white 8½-by-11-inch paper, printed on one side only. Do not use textured paper and do not fold or staple.

■ See Handout 15.2.

12. If responding via e-mail, use the job title or noted reference number as the subject of your message. Always send the résumé in the body of the e-mail message. Don't assume that you can attach a word-processed document to an e-mail message; it may or may not be readable.

13. Whenever you update your résumé, remember to update both versions.

These guidelines are illustrated in Model 35—an electronic version of the standard résumé shown in Model 32. The savvy job seeker would probably send both versions to a prospective employer. When formatted in plain ASCII text, an electronic résumé can be sent as an e-mail message with the assurance that it will arrive in readable format.

Because your résumé is about you, it is perhaps the most personal business document you'll ever write. Use everything you know about successful communication techniques to ensure that you tell your story in the most effective manner possible. After you're satisfied with the content and arrangement of your résumé, proofread your document carefully and have several others proofread it also. Then have it printed on high-quality white or off-white 8½-by-11-inch paper, and turn your attention to your cover letters.

The guidelines for developing a résumé are summarized in Checklist 17 on page 547.

■ See Handout 15.3.

■ Writing Job-Application Letters

A résumé itself is all that is generally needed to secure an interview with an on-campus recruiter. However, you will likely not want to limit your job search to those employers that interview on campus. Campus recruiters typically represent large organizations or regional employers. Thus, if you want to work in a smaller organization or in a distant location, you will need to contact those organizations by writing application letters.

An **application letter** communicates to the prospective employer your interest in and qualifications for a position within the organization. The letter is also called a *cover letter,* because it introduces (or "covers") the major points in your résumé, which you should include with the application letter. A **solicited application letter** is written in response to an advertised vacancy, whereas an **unsolicited application letter** (also called a *prospecting letter*) is written to an organization that has not advertised a vacancy.

Most job applicants use the same résumé when applying for numerous positions and then use their application letter to personalize their qualification for the specific job for which they are applying.

Because the application letter is the first thing the employer will read about you, it is of crucial importance. Make sure the letter is formatted appropriately, looks attractive, and is free from typographical, spelling, and grammatical errors. Don't forget to sign the letter and enclose a copy of your résumé (or perhaps both versions—formatted and plain-text).

Your cover letter is a sales letter—you're selling your qualifications to the prospective employer. You should use the same persuasive techniques you learned earlier: provide specific evidence, stress reader benefits, avoid exaggeration, and show confidence in the quality of your product.

CO2. Compose solicited and unsolicited job-application letters.

Use the application letter, which is often your first contact with the potential employer, to personalize your qualifications for one specific job.

model35

ELECTRONIC RÉSUMÉ

Runs longer than one page (acceptable with electronic résumés).

Includes notice of availability of a fully formatted version.

Begins with name at the top, followed immediately by addresses (both an e-mail address and a home address).

Emphasizes, where possible, nouns as keywords.

```
PERSONAL DATA
     * Helped start the Minority Business Student
       Association at New York University and served as
       program director for two years
     * Have traveled extensively throughout South America
     * Am a member of the Accounting Society
     * Am willing to relocate

REFERENCES
     Available upon request

NOTE
     An attractive and fully formatted hard-copy version of
     this resume is available upon request.
```

```
AURELIA GOMEZ

225 West 70 Street
New York, NY 10023
Phone: 212-555-3821
E-mail: agomez@nyu.edu

OBJECTIVE
     Entry-level staff accounting position with a public
     accounting firm


EXPERIENCE
     Summer 2005
     Accounting Intern: Coopers & Lybrand, NYC
     * Assisted in preparing corporate tax returns
     * Attended meetings with clients
     * Conducted research in corporate tax library and
       wrote research reports

     Nov. 2001-Aug. 2003
     Payroll Specialist: City of New York
     * Full-time civil service position in the Department
       of Administration
     * Proficiency in payroll and other accounting software
       on DEC 1034 minicomputer and on personal computers
     * Representative for a 28-person work unit on the
       department's management-labor committee
     * Reason for leaving job: To pursue college degree
       full-time


EDUCATION
     Jan. 1999-Present
     Pursuing a 5-year bachelor of business administration
     degree (major in accounting) from NYU
     * Will graduate June 2001
     * Attended part-time from 1999 until 2003 while
       holding down a full-time job
     * Have financed 100% of all college expenses through
       savings, work, and student loans
     * Plan to sit for the CPA exam in May 2007
```

Grammar and Mechanics Notes

Only ASCII characters are used; all text is one size with no special formatting; no rules, graphics, columns, tables, and the like are used. Vertical line spaces (Enter key) and horizontal spacing (space bar) show relationship of parts. Lists are formatted with asterisks instead of bullets.

✔checklist 17

Résumés

Length and Format

✔ Use a one-page résumé (neither longer nor shorter) when applying for most entry-level positions.

✔ Use a simple format, with lots of white space and short blocks of text. By means of type size, indenting, bullets, boldface, and the like, show which parts are subordinate to other parts.

✔ Print your résumé on standard-sized (8½ by 11 inches), good-quality, white or off-white (cream or ivory) paper.

✔ Make sure the finished document looks professional, attractive, and conservative and that it is 100 percent error-free.

Content

✔ Type your complete name without a personal title at the top of the document (omit the word *résumé*), followed by an address, a daytime phone number, and an e-mail address.

✔ Include a one-sentence job objective that is specific enough to be useful to the employer but not so specific as to preclude consideration for similar jobs.

✔ Decide whether your education or work experience is your stronger qualification, and list it first. For education, list the title of your degree, the name of your college and its location, your major and minor, and your expected date of graduation (month and year). List your grade-point average if it is impressive and any academic honors. Avoid listing college courses that are part of the normal preparation for your desired position.

✔ For work experience, determine whether to use a chronological (most recent job first) or a functional (list of competencies and skills developed) organizational pattern. For either, stress those duties or skills that are transferable to the new position. Use short phrases and action verbs, and provide specific evidence of the results you achieved.

✔ Include any additional information (such as special skills, professional affiliations, and willingness to travel or relocate) that will help to distinguish you from the competition. Avoid including such personal information as age, gender, ethnicity, religion, disabilities, or marital status.

✔ Provide a statement that references are available on request.

✔ Throughout, highlight your strengths and minimize any weaknesses, but always tell the truth.

Electronic Résumés

✔ In general, describe your qualifications and experiences in terms of nouns rather than verbs. Weave these keywords throughout your résumé—do not list them in a block at the beginning of the résumé.

✔ Save the electronic résumé in plain ASCII text.

✔ Use a line length of no more than 70 characters—manually press the Enter key if necessary.

✔ Include a note at the end of your text résumé that a fully formatted version is available upon request.

✔ Print your résumé on plain 8½-by-11-inch smooth white paper (print on one side only) and mail it unfolded and unstapled.

✔ For HTML résumés, choose an open, attractive design and create links to your actual work samples.

An application letter should be no longer than one page. Let's examine each part of a typical letter. Model 36 (on page 549) shows a solicited application letter, written to accompany the résumé presented in Model 32. (An unsolicited application letter appears in the 3Ps model on page 563.)

Address and Salutation

Your letter should be addressed to an individual rather than to an organization or department. Remember, the more hands your letter must go through before it reaches the right person, the more chance for something to go wrong. Ideally, your letter should be addressed to the person who will actually interview you and who will likely be your supervisor if you get the job.

If you do not know enough about the prospective employer to know the name of the appropriate person (the decision maker), you have probably not gathered enough data. If necessary, call the organization to make sure you have the right name—including the correct spelling—and position title. In your salutation, use a courtesy title (such as *Mr.* or *Ms.*) along with the person's last name.

Some job-vacancy ads are blind ads; they do not identify the hiring company by name and provide only a box number address, often in care of the newspaper or magazine that contains the ad. In such a situation, you (and all others responding to that ad) have no choice but to address your letter to the newspaper and to use a generic salutation, such as "Dear Human Resources Manager." Insert a subject line to identify immediately the purpose of this important message.

Opening

The opening paragraph of a solicited application letter is fairly straightforward. Because the organization has advertised an opening, it is eager to receive quality applications, so use a direct organization: state (or imply) the reason for your letter, identify the particular position for which you're applying, and indicate how you learned about the opening.

Gear your opening to the job and to the specific organization. For positions that are widely perceived to be somewhat conservative (such as in finance, accounting, and banking), use a restrained opening. For more creative work (like sales, advertising, and public relations), you might start out on a more imaginative note. Here are two examples:

Conservative:

Mr. Adam Storkel, manager of your Fleet Street branch, has suggested that I submit my qualifications for the position of assistant loan officer that was advertised in last week's *Indianapolis Business*.

Creative:

If quality is Job 1 at Ford, then Job 2 must surely be communicating that message effectively to the public. My degree in journalism and work experience at the Kintzell Agency will enable me to help you achieve that objective. The enclosed

■ See Slides 15.10 and 15.11.

Use the direct organizational plan for writing a solicited application letter.

■ See Handout 15.4.

■ For more on application letters, see the supplemental lecture/discussion notes in the *Instructor's Resource Manual*.

model36

JOB-APPLICATION LETTER

This model is an example of a solicited application letter; it accompanies the résumé in Model 32 on page 536.

March 13, 20—

Mr. David Norman, Partner
Ross, Russell & Weston
452 Fifth Avenue
New York, NY 10018

1   Dear Mr. Norman:

Subject: EDP Specialist Position (Reference No. 103-G)

2   My varied work experience in accounting and payroll services, coupled with my accounting degree, has prepared me for the position of EDP specialist that you advertised in the March 9 *New York Times.*

3   In addition to taking required courses in accounting and management information systems as part of my accounting major at New York University, I also took an elective course in EDP auditing and control. The training I received in this course in applications, software, systems, and service-center records would enable me to immediately become a productive member of your EDP consulting staff.

My college training has been supplemented by an internship in a large accounting firm. In addition, my two and one-half years of experience as a payroll specialist for the city of New York have given me firsthand knowledge of the operation and needs of nonprofit agencies. This experience should help me to contribute to your large consulting practice with governmental agencies.

4   After you have reviewed my enclosed résumé, I would appreciate having the opportunity to discuss with you why I believe I have the right qualifications and personality to serve you and your clients. I can be reached by phone after 3 p.m. daily.

Sincerely,

Aurelia Gomez

Aurelia Gomez
225 West 70 Street
New York, NY 10023
Phone: 212-555-3821
E-mail: agomez@nyu.edu

5

Enclosure

Begins by identifying the job position and the source of advertising.

Emphasizes a qualification that might distinguish her from other applicants.

Relates her work experience to the specific needs of the employer.

Provides a telephone number (may be done either in the body of the letter or in the last line of the address block).

Grammar and Mechanics Notes

1 This letter is formatted in modified-block style with standard punctuation (colon after the salutation and comma after the complimentary closing).

2 *New York Times:* Italicize the names of newspapers.

3 *accounting and management information systems:* Do not capitalize the names of college courses unless they include a proper noun.

4 *résumé:* This word may also properly be written without the accent marks: *resume.*

5 Putting the writer's name and address together at the bottom of the letter makes it convenient for the reader to respond.

résumé further describes my qualifications for the position of advertising copywriter posted in the June issue of *Automotive Age*.

For unsolicited application letters, you must first get the reader's attention. You can gain that attention most easily by talking about the company rather than about yourself. One effective strategy is to show that you know something about the organization—its recent projects, awards, changes in personnel, and the like—and then show how you can contribute to the corporate effort.

> Now that Russell Industries has expanded operations to Central America, can you use a marketing graduate who speaks fluent Spanish and who knows the culture of the region?

Make the opening short, original, interesting, and reader-oriented.

Your opening should be short, interesting, and reader-oriented. Avoid tired openings such as "This is to apply for . . ." or "Please consider this letter my application for . . ." Maintain an air of formality. Don't address the reader by a first name and don't try to be cute. Avoid such attention-grabbing (but unsuccessful) stunts as sending a worn, once-white running shoe with the note "Now that I have one foot in the door, I hope you'll let me get the other one in" or writing the application letter beginning at the bottom of the page and working upward (to indicate a willingness to start at the bottom and work one's way up). Such gimmicks send a nonverbal message to the reader that the applicant may be trying to deflect attention from a weak resumé.

Body

Don't repeat all the information from the résumé.

In a paragraph or two, highlight your strongest qualifications and show how they can benefit the employer. Show—don't tell; that is, provide specific, credible evidence to support your statements, using wording different from that used in the résumé. Tell an anecdote about yourself ("For example, recently I . . ."). Your discussion should reflect modest confidence rather than a hard-sell approach. Avoid starting too many sentences with *I*.

NOT: I am an effective supervisor.

BUT: Supervising a staff of five counter clerks taught me . . . .

NOT: I am an accurate person.

BUT: In my two years of experience as a student secretary, none of the letters, memorandums, and reports I typed were ever returned with a typographical error marked.

NOT: I took a course in business communication.

BUT: The communication strategies I learned in my business communication course will enable me to help solve customer problems as a customer-service representative at Allegheny Industries.

Refer the reader to the enclosed résumé. Subordinate the reference to the résumé, and emphasize instead what the résumé contains.

NOT: I am enclosing a copy of my résumé for your review.

BUT: As detailed in the enclosed résumé, my extensive work experience in records management has prepared me to help you "take charge of this paperwork jungle," as headlined in your classified ad.

Closing

You are not likely to get what you do not ask for, so close by asking for a personal interview. Indicate flexibility regarding scheduling and location. Provide your phone number and e-mail address, either in the last paragraph or immediately below your name and address in the closing lines.

Politely ask for an interview.

> After you have reviewed my qualifications, I would appreciate your letting me know when we can meet to discuss further my employment with Connecticut Power and Light. I will be in the Hartford area from December 16 through January 4 and could come to your office at any time that is convenient for you.

or

> I will call your office next week to see if we can arrange a meeting at your convenience to discuss my qualifications for working as a financial analyst with your organization.

Use a standard complimentary closing (such as "Sincerely"), leave enough space to sign the letter, and then type your name, address, phone number, and e-mail address. Even though you may be sending out many application letters at the same time, take care with each individual letter. You never know which one will be the one that actually gets you an interview. Sign your name neatly in blue or black ink, fold each letter and accompanying résumé neatly, and mail.

The guidelines for writing an application letter are summarized in Checklist 18.

■ Preparing for a Job Interview

Ninety-five percent of all employers require one or more employment interviews before extending a job offer, resulting in as many as 150 million employment interviews being conducted annually.[10] The employer's purpose in these interviews is to verify information on the résumé, explore any issues raised by the résumé, and get some indication of the probable chemistry between the applicant and the organization. (It is estimated that 90 percent of all job failures result from personality clashes or conflicts—not incompetence.[11]) The job applicant will use the interview to glean important information about the organization and to decide whether the culture of the organization meshes with his or her personality (see Spotlight 29, "The Ethical Dimensions of the Job Campaign," on page 553, for some ethical considerations when applying for a job).

CO3. Conduct yourself appropriately during an employment interview.

✓checklist18

Job-Application Letters

✓ Use your job-application letter to show how the qualifications listed in your résumé have prepared you for the specific job for which you're applying.

✓ If possible, address your letter to the individual in the organization who will interview you if you're successful.

✓ When applying for an advertised opening, begin by stating (or implying) the reason for the letter, identify the position for which you're applying, and tell how you learned about the opening.

✓ When writing an unsolicited application letter, first gain the reader's attention by showing that you are familiar with the company and can make a unique contribution to its efforts.

✓ In one or two paragraphs, highlight your strongest qualifications and relate them directly to the needs of the specific position for which you're applying. Refer the reader to the enclosed résumé.

✓ Treat your letter as a persuasive sales letter: provide specific evidence, stress reader benefits, avoid exaggeration, and show confidence in the quality of your product.

✓ Close by tactfully asking for an interview.

✓ Maintain an air of formality throughout the letter. Avoid cuteness.

✓ Make sure the finished document presents a professional, attractive, and conservative appearance and that it is 100 percent error-free.

■ See Handout 15.5.

Learn as much as you can about the organization— your possible future employer.

Consider the employment interview as a sales presentation. Just as any good sales representative would never attempt to walk into a potential customer's office without having a thorough knowledge of the product, neither should you. You are both the product and the product promoter, so do your homework—both on yourself and on the potential customer.

Researching the Organization

As a result of having developed your résumé and written your application letters, you have probably done enough general homework on yourself. You are likely to have a reasonably accurate picture of who you are and what you want out of your career. Now is the time to zero in on the organization.

It is no exaggeration to say that you should learn everything you possibly can about the organization. Research the specific organization in depth, using the research techniques you developed in Chapter 11. Search the current business periodical indexes and go online to learn what has been happening recently with the company. Many libraries maintain copies of the annual reports from large companies. Study these or other sources for current product information, profitability, plans for the future, and the like. Learn about the company's products and services, its history, the names of its officers, what the business press has to say about the organization, its recent stock activity, financial health, corporate structure, and the like.

The Ethical Dimensions of the Job Campaign

Most recruiters have heard the story about the job applicant who, when told that he was overqualified for a position, pleaded in vain, "But I lied about my credentials." When constructing your résumé and application letter, when completing an application form, and when answering questions during an interview, you will constantly have to make judgments about what to divulge and what to omit. Everyone would agree that outright lying is unethical (and clearly illegal as well). But when is hedging or omitting negative information about yourself simply being smart, and when is it unethical?

The Ethics of Constructing a Résumé

Recruiters believe that the problem they call "résumé inflation" has increased in recent years, and plenty of research backs them up. One survey of executives found that 26 percent of them reported hiring employees during the previous year who had misrepresented their qualifications, education, or salary history. By far, the most frequent transgression is misrepresenting one's qualifications.

Acting ethically does not, of course, require that you emphasize every little problem that has occurred in your past. Indeed, one study showed that the majority of *Fortune* 500 human resources directors agree with the statement "Interviewees should stress their strengths and not mention their weaknesses unless the interviewer asks for information in an area of weakness."

Recognize, however, that some employers have a standard policy of terminating all employees who are found to have falsely represented their qualifications on their résumés. Generally, the employer must show evidence that the employee intentionally misrepresented his or her qualifications so as to fraudulently secure a job. Claiming to have a college degree when, in fact, one does not would likely be grounds for termination, whereas an unintentional mistake in the dates of previous employment would probably not be.

The Ethics of Accepting a Position

For some applicants, another ethical dilemma occurs when they receive a second, perhaps more attractive, job offer after having already accepted a prior offer. Most professionals believe that such a situation should not present a dilemma. A job acceptance is a promise that the applicant is expected to keep. The hiring organization has made many decisions based on the applicant's acceptance, not the least of which was to notify all other candidates that the job had been filled. Reneging on the commitment to the employer not only puts the applicant in a bad light (and don't underestimate the power of the network in spreading such information) but also puts the applicant's school in a bad light.

If you're unsure about whether to accept a job offer, ask for a time extension. Once you've made your decision, however, stick to it and have no regrets. If you decide to accept the job, immediately notify all other employers that you are withdrawing from further consideration. If you decide to decline the job, move on to your next interviews without looking back. Learn to live with your decisions.[12]

Relate what you discover about the individual company to what you've learned about competing companies and about the industry in general. By trying to fit what you've learned into the broader perspective of the industry, you will be able to discuss matters more intelligently during your interview instead of just having a bunch of jumbled facts at your disposal.

If you're interviewing at a governmental agency, determine its role, recent funding levels, recent activities, spending legislation affecting the agency, and the extent to which being on the "right" side (that is, the official side) of a political question

DILBERT

matters. If you're interviewing for a teaching position at an educational institution, determine the range of course offerings, types of students, conditions of the facilities and equipment, professionalism of the staff, and funding levels. In short, every tidbit of information you can learn about your prospective employer will help you make the most appropriate career decision.

You will use this information as a resource to help you understand and discuss topics with some familiarity during the interview. No one is impressed by the interviewee who, out of the blue, spouts, "I see your stock went up 5½ points last week." However, in response to the interviewer's comment about the company's recent announcement of a new product line, it would be quite appropriate to respond, "That must have been the reason your stock jumped so high last week."

In short, bring up such information only if it flows naturally into the conversation. Even if you're never able to discuss some of the information you've gathered, the knowledge itself will still provide perspective in helping you to make a reasonable decision if a job offer is extended.

Avoid "showing off" your knowledge of the organization.

Practicing Interview Questions

Practice your response to typical interview questions.

Following is a sample of typical questions that are often asked during an employment interview. Questions such as these provide the interviewer with important clues about the applicant's qualifications, personality, poise, and communication skills. The interviewer is interested not only in the content of your responses but also in *how* you react to the questions themselves and *how* you communicate your thoughts and ideas.

Before going for your interview, practice dictating a response to each of these questions into a cassette recorder. Then assume the role of the interviewer and play back your responses. How acceptable and appropriate was each response?

- Tell me about yourself.

- How would you describe yourself?

- Tell me something about yourself that I won't find on your résumé.

- What do you take real pride in?

- Why would you like to work for our organization?

- Why should we hire you?

- What are your long-range career objectives?

- What types of work do you enjoy doing most? Least?

- What accomplishment has given you the greatest satisfaction?

- What would you like to change in your past?

- What courses did you like best and least in college?

- Specifically, how does your education or experience relate to this job?

These questions are fairly straightforward and not especially difficult to answer if you have practiced them. Not infrequently, however, interviewers may pose more difficult questions—ones that seemingly have no "right" answer. Sometimes they even try to create a stressful situation by asking pointed questions, interrupting, or feigning disbelief in an attempt to gauge your behavior under stress.

The strategy to use in such a circumstance is to keep the desired job firmly in mind and to formulate each answer—no matter what the question—so as to highlight your ability to perform the desired job competently. You don't have to accept each question as asked. You can ask the interviewer to be more specific or to rephrase the question. Doing so not only will provide guidance for answering the question but will give you a few additional moments to prepare your response.

Preparing Your Own Questions

During the course of the interview, many of the questions you may have about the organization or the job will probably be answered. However, an interview is a two-way conversation, so it is legitimate for you to pose relevant questions at appropriate moments, and you should prepare those questions beforehand.

Questions such as the following will provide useful information on which to base a decision if a job is offered:

- How would you describe a typical day on the job?

- How is an employee evaluated and promoted?

- What types of training are available?

- What are your expectations of new employees?

- What are the organization's plans for the future?

- To whom would I report? Would anyone report to me?

- What are the advancement opportunities for this position?

Each of these questions not only secures needed information to help you make a decision but also sends a positive nonverbal message to the interviewer that you are interested in this position as a long-term commitment. Do not, however, ask so many questions that the roles of the interviewer and the interviewee become blurred, and avoid putting the interviewer on the spot.

Finally, avoid asking about salary and fringe benefits during the initial interview. There will be plenty of time for such questions later, after you've convinced the organization that you're the person it wants. In terms of planning, however,

■ See Slides 15.12 and 15.13.

Answer each question honestly, but in a way that highlights your qualifications.

■ Employers tend to hire applicants who spend about half the interview speaking and half listening, revealed a Massachusetts Institute of Technology study. Another study suggested that applicants who make the best impression speak no longer than two minutes at a time during the interview. (Richard Bolles, *What Color Is Your Parachute?* Ten Speed Press, Berkeley, CA, 2001.)

Ensure that any relevant questions you may have are answered during the interview.

Avoid appearing to be overly concerned about salary.

you should know ahead of time the market value of the position for which you're applying. Check the classified ads, reports collected by your college career service, and library and Internet sources to learn what a reasonable salary figure for your position would be.

Dressing for Success

Prefer a well-tailored, clean, conservative outfit for the interview.

The importance of making a good first impression during the interview can hardly be overstated. One study has shown that 75 percent of the interviewees who made a good impression during the first five minutes of the interview received a job offer, whereas only 10 percent of the interviewees who made a bad impression during the first five minutes received a job offer.[13]

The most effective strategy for making a good impression is to pay careful attention to your dress, grooming, and posture. Dress in a manner that flatters your appearance while conforming to the office norm. The employment interview is not the place for a fashion statement. You want the interviewer to remember what you had to say and not what you wore. Although different positions, different companies, different industries, and different parts of the country and world have different norms, in general prefer well-tailored, clean, conservative clothing for the interview.

For most business interviews, men should dress in a blue or gray suit and a white or pale blue shirt with a subtle tie, dark socks, and black shoes. Women should dress in a blue or gray tailored suit with a light-colored blouse and medium-height heels. Avoid excessive or distracting jewelry, heavy perfumes or after-shave lotions, and elaborate hairstyles. Impeccable grooming is a must, including clothing clean and free of wrinkles, shoes shined, teeth brushed, and hair neatly styled and combed. Blend in; you will have plenty of opportunity to express your individual style once you've been hired.

■ Conducting Yourself During the Interview

■ Try this simple tip to help you project a good first impression: Notice the color of a person's eyes as you shake hands. Why it works: You'll gain strong eye contact in a way that shows you care. (Roger Dawson, *Secrets of Power Persuasion*, Prentice-Hall.)

Observe the organizational environment very carefully and treat everyone you meet, including the receptionist and the interviewer's assistant or secretary, with scrupulous courtesy. Maintain an air of formality. When shown into the interview room, greet the interviewer by name, with a firm handshake, direct eye contact, and a smile.

At the beginning, address the interviewer as "Mr." or "Ms.," switching to a first-name basis only if specifically requested to do so. If you're not asked to be seated immediately, wait until the interviewer is seated and then take your seat. Sit with your feet planted firmly on the floor, lean forward a bit in your seat, and maintain comfortable eye contact with the interviewer. Avoid taking notes, except perhaps for a specific name, date, or telephone number.

Assume a confident, courteous, and conservative attitude during the interview.

Recognize that certain parts of the office are off-limits—especially the interviewer's desk and any area behind the desk. Do not rest your hands, purse, or notes on the desk and never wander around the office. Show interest in everything the interviewer is saying; don't concentrate so hard on formulating your response that you miss the last part of any question. Answer each question in a positive, confident, forthright manner. Recognize that more than yes-or-no answers are expected.

Control nervousness during the interview the same way you control it when making an oral presentation; that is, practice until you're confident you can face whatever the interviewer throws your way. The career centers at many colleges conduct mock interviews to prepare prospective interviewees. If yours does not, ask a professor or even another student to interview you. Practice answering lists of common questions.

Throughout the interview, your attitude should be one of confidence and courtesy. Assume a role that is appropriate for you. Don't go in with the attitude that "You're lucky to have me here." The interviewer might not agree. Likewise, you needn't fawn or grovel. You're *applying*—not begging—for a job. If the match works, both you and the employer will benefit. Finally, don't try to take charge of the interview. Follow the interviewer's lead, letting him or her determine which questions to ask, when to move to a new area of discussion, and when to end the interview.

Answer each question put to you as honestly as you can (see Spotlight 30, "The Legal Dimensions of the Job Campaign"). Keep your mind on the desired job and how you can show that you are qualified for that job. Don't try to oversell yourself, or you may end up in a job for which you're unprepared. However, if the interviewer doesn't address an area in which you believe you have strong qualifications, be ready to volunteer such information at the appropriate time, working it into your answer to one of the interviewer's questions.

If asked about your salary expectations, try to avoid giving a salary figure, indicating that you would expect to be paid in line with other employees at your level of expertise and experience. If pressed, however, be prepared to reveal your salary expectations, preferably using a broad range.

When discussing salary, talk in terms of what you think the position and responsibilities are worth rather than what you think *you* are worth. If salary is not discussed, be patient. Few people have ever been offered a job in industry without first being told what they would be paid.

You might participate in a group interview, in which several people interview you at once. If possible, find out about this practice ahead of time so that you can learn the name, position, and rank of each interviewer. Address your responses to everyone, not just to the person who asked the question or to the most senior person present.

It is also likely that you will be interviewed more than once—having either multiple interviews the same day or, if you survive the initial interview, a more intense set of interviews to be scheduled for some later date. Be on the alert for clues you can pick up from your early interviews that might be of use to you in later interviews and be sure to provide consistent responses to the same questions asked by different interviewers. The different interviewers will typically get together later to discuss their reactions to you and your responses.

When the interview ends, if you've not been told, you have a right to ask the interviewer when you might expect to hear from him or her. You will likely be evaluated on these four criteria:

- *Education and experience:* Your accomplishments as they relate to the job requirements, evidence of growth, breadth and depth of your experiences, leadership qualities, and evidence of your willingness to assume responsibility.

Overpreparation is the best way to control nervousness.

■ An activity test may be administered as part of an interview. Dave Wiegand, president of Advance Network Design, tests his sales candidates during an interview by setting up a simulated sales call. The candidate must go into a separate room, call Wiegand's office, and try to make an appointment. Wiegand makes the candidate ask for an appointment three times. Activity tests help employers identify weak candidates.

Job-interview bloopers

- A job applicant challenged the interviewer to arm wrestle.
- A job candidate said he had never finished high school because he was kidnapped and kept in a closet in Mexico.
- A balding candidate excused himself and then returned wearing a full hairpiece.
- A clumsy candidate fell and broke an arm during the interview.

- A candidate said he didn't have time for lunch and then started to eat a hamburger and fries in the interviewer's office.
- An applicant interrupted the questioning to phone her therapist for advice.
- A candidate dozed during the interview.
- A candidate muttered, "Would it be a problem if I'm angry most of the time?"
- An applicant wore headphones to the interview and, when asked to remove them, explained that she could listen to the interviewer and the music at the same time.

■ See Slides 15.14 and 15.15.

You will likely be evaluated on education and experience, mental qualities, manner and personal traits, and appearance.

spotlight 30
ON LAW AND ETHICS

The Legal Dimensions of the Job Campaign

I applied for a job and was told I will be hired if I take a lie-detector test. Must I take this test?
In most states, yes, if you want the job. A few states, however, prohibit employers from requiring a lie-detector test as a condition of employment.

The computer firm where I want to work requires all job applicants to take a psychological test as part of the application process. Is this legal?
Yes. Aptitude, personality, and psychological tests are legal as long as the results are accurate, are related to success on the job, and do not tend to eliminate anyone on the basis of gender, age, race, religion, or national origin.

I work full-time and have been offered a dream job by another employer—if I can start the new job immediately. Do I have to give my current employer a certain number of days' notice?
No. You are not legally required to do so unless the contract you signed specifies how far in advance you must notify the company.

I'm an older student who will be applying for positions along with much younger ones. Can the interviewer ask my age?
No, not unless the employer can show that most people beyond a certain age cannot perform the job competently or safely. If you're worried about the possible impact of your age, you might wish to volunteer certain information to allay the interviewer's concerns—mentioning some vigorous physical activity you regularly engage in, for example.

What types of information may not be asked for on an application form or during a job interview?

- Race or national origin (including origin of a surname or place of birth; however, you may be asked to prove that you have legal authorization to work in the United States)
- Family information (including marital status, plans for marriage or children, number of children or their ages, child-care arrangements, spouse's occupation, roommate arrangements, and home ownership)
- Disabilities (unless they relate directly to the job)
- Arrests (you may, however, be asked about convictions for serious offenses)

How should I respond to an illegal question during a job interview?
The best response, assuming you want to continue to be considered for the position, may be to deflect the question by focusing on how you can contribute to the job. For example, if you were asked about your plans to have children in the immediate future, you might respond, "I assure you that I'm fully committed to my career and to making a real contribution to the organization for which I work." Or you may respond by saying you don't believe such questions are relevant to your ability to do the job, or by asking the interviewer to explain the relevance of the question. You could also, of course, file a complaint with the Equal Employment Opportunity Commission.

- *Mental qualities:* Intelligence, alertness, judgment, logic, perception, creativity, organization, and depth.

- *Manner and personal traits:* Social poise, sense of humor, mannerisms, warmth, confidence, courtesy, aggressiveness, listening ability, manner of oral expression, emotional balance, enthusiasm, initiative, energy, ambition, maturity, stability, and interests.

- *Appearance:* Grooming, dress, posture, cleanliness, and apparent health.

■ See Handout 15.6.

■ Communicating After the Interview

Immediately after the interview, conduct a self-appraisal of your performance. Try to recall each question that was asked and evaluate your response. If you're not satisfied with one of your responses, take the time to formulate a more effective answer. Chances are that you will be asked a similar question in the future.

Also reevaluate your résumé. Were any questions asked during the interview that indicated some confusion about your qualifications? Does some section need to be revised or some information added or deleted?

Determine too whether you can improve your application letter on the basis of your interview experience. Were the qualifications you discussed in your letter the ones that seemed to impress the interviewers the most? Were these qualifications discussed in terms of how they would benefit the organization? Did you provide specific evidence to support your claims?

You should also take the time to send the interviewer (or interviewers) a short thank-you note or e-mail message as a gesture of courtesy and to reaffirm your interest in the job. The interviewer, who probably devoted quite a bit of time to you before, during, and after the interview session, deserves to have his or her efforts on your behalf acknowledged.

Recognize, however, that your thank-you note may or may not have any effect on the hiring decision. Most decisions to offer the candidate a job or to invite him or her back for another round of interviewing are made the day of the interview, often during the interview itself. Thus, your thank-you note may arrive after the decision, good or bad, has been made.

The real purpose of a thank-you note is to express genuine appreciation for some courtesy extended to you; you do not write to earn points. Also, avoid trying to resell yourself. You've already made your case through your résumé, cover letter, and interview. Your note might sound similar to the following:

> Thank you for the opportunity to interview for the position of EDP specialist yesterday. I very much enjoyed meeting you and Arlene Worthington and learning more about the position and about Ross, Russell & Weston.
>
> I especially appreciated the opportunity to observe the long-range planning meeting yesterday afternoon and to learn of your firm's plans for increasing your consulting practice with nonprofit agencies. My experience working in city government leads me to believe that nonprofit agencies can benefit greatly from your expertise.
>
> Again, thank you for taking the time to visit with me yesterday. I look forward to hearing from you.

Your thank-you note should be short and may be either typed or handwritten. Consider it a routine message that should be written in a direct organizational pattern. Begin by expressing appreciation for the interview; then achieve credibility by mentioning some specific incident or insight gained from the interview. Close on a hopeful, forward-looking note.

CO4. Complete the communication tasks needed after the employment interview.

OBER. **Interview Follow-up Letter**

Dear Mr. Reagan

Interviewing with you and Mr. Larson yesterday for the position of administrative assistant was certainly an enjoyable and informative experience. Thanks for giving me the opportunity to learn more about the Hudson Institute.

After sitting in more detail the kinds of projects on which your staff is working, I feel even more confident that my desktop publishing and presentation software skills would enable me to contribute immediately to your effort. They are the kind of projects I've frequently worked on and enjoyed in my previous job.

Thanks also for that wonderful lunch at Della Court. I look forward to a return visit.

Sincerely,

■ See Handout 15.7.

Send a short thank-you note immediately after the interview.

✔checklist 19

Employment Interviews

Preparing for an Employment Interview

✔ Before going on an employment interview, learn everything you can about the organization.

✔ Practice answering common interview questions and prepare questions of your own to ask.

✔ Select appropriate clothing to wear.

✔ Control your nervousness by being well prepared, well equipped, and on time.

Conducting Yourself During the Interview

✔ Throughout the interview, be aware of the nonverbal signals you are communicating through your body language.

✔ Answer each question completely and accurately, always trying to relate your qualifications to the specific needs of the desired job.

✔ Whether you are interviewed by one person or a group of people, you will likely be evaluated on your education and experience, mental qualities, manner and personal traits, and general appearance.

Communicating After the Interview

✔ Immediately following the interview, critique your performance, your résumé, and your application letter.

✔ Send a thank-you note or e-mail message to the interviewer.

If you have not heard from the interviewer by the deadline date he or she gave you for making a decision, telephone or e-mail the interviewer for a status report. If no decision has been made, your inquiry will keep your name and your interest in the position in the interviewer's mind. If someone else has been selected, you need to know so that you can continue your job search. The steps of the interview process are summarized in Checklist 19.

The 3Ps
Problem, Process, Product

AN APPLICATION LETTER

Problem

You are Ray Arnold, a senior labor relations major at Boston University. You have analyzed your interests, strengths and weaknesses, and preferred lifestyle and have decided you would like to work in some area of labor relations for a large multinational firm in southern California. Because you attend a school in the East, you decide not to limit your job search to on-campus interviewing.

In your research you learned that Precision Systems, Inc. (PSI) has recently been awarded a $23 million contract by the U.S. Department of State to develop a high-level computerized message system to provide fast and secure communications among U.S. government installations throughout Europe. PSI, which is headquartered in Los Angeles, will build a new automated factory in Ciudad Juárez, Mexico, to assemble the electronic components for the new system.

You decide to write to PSI to see whether it might have an opening for someone with your qualifications. You will, of course, include a copy of your résumé with your letter. (See Model 36 for the résumé.) Send your letter to Ms. Phyllis Morrison, Assistant Director of Human Resources, Precision Systems, Inc., P.O. Box 18734, Los Angeles, CA 90018.

Process

1. Will this letter be a solicited or unsolicited (prospecting) letter?

   Unsolicited—I don't know whether PSI has an opening.

2. Write an opening paragraph for your letter that gets attention and that relates your skills to PSI's needs. Make sure the purpose of your letter is made clear in your opening paragraph.

   PSI's recently accepted proposal to the State Department estimated that you would be adding up to 3,000 new staff for the Ciudad Juárez project. With this dramatic increase in personnel, do you have an opening in your human resources department for a college graduate with a major in labor relations and a minor in psychology?

3. Compare your education with PSI's likely requirements. What will help you stand out from the competition?

   ■ It's somewhat unusual for a labor relations major to have a psychology minor.

   ■ My course work in my major and minor were pretty standard, so there's no need to list individual courses.

4. Compare your work experiences with PSI's likely requirements. What qualifications from your résumé should you highlight in your letter?

   ■ The interpersonal and human relations skills developed as a teller will be an important asset in labor management.

   ■ Written and oral communications skills developed through work and extracurricular activities will enable me to communicate effectively with a widely dispersed work force.

5. What other qualifications should you mention?

   My degree in labor relations, combined with my union membership, will help me look at each issue from the perspective of both management and labor.

6. Write the sentence in which you request the interview.

   I would welcome the opportunity to come to Los Angeles to discuss with you the role I might play in helping PSI manage its human resources in an efficient and humane manner.

Product

1   15 Turner Hall
Boston University
Boston, MA 02215
February 7, 20—

This prospecting letter accompanies the résumé in Model 33 on page 537.

Ms. Phyllis Morrison
Assistant Human Resources Director
Precision Systems, Inc.
P.O. Box 18734
Los Angeles, CA 90018

2   Dear Ms. Morrison

PSI's recent proposal to the State Department estimated that you would be adding up to 3,000 new positions for the Ciudad Juárez project. With this increase in personnel, will you have an opening in your human resources department for a recent college graduate with a major in labor relations and a minor in psychology?

Begins with an attention-getting opening that relates the writer's skills to the needs of the company.

3

My combination of course work in business and liberal arts will enable me to approach each issue from both a management and a behavioral point of view. Further, my degree in labor relations along with my experience as a union member will help me consider each issue from the perspective of both management and labor.

Shows how the writer's unique qualifications will benefit the company.

During my term as webmaster for a student association, the Scholastic Internet Association recognized our site for its "original, balanced, and refreshingly candid writing style and format." On the job, dealing successfully with customers' overdrawn accounts, bank computer errors, and delayed-deposit recording has taught me the value of active listening and has provided me experience in explaining and justifying the company's position. As detailed on the enclosed résumé, these communication and human relations skills will help me to interact and communicate effectively with PSI employees at all levels and at widely dispersed locations.

Provides specific evidence to support his claims: *shows* rather than *tells*.

4

I would welcome the opportunity to come to Los Angeles at your convenience to discuss with you the role I might play in helping PSI manage its human resources in an efficient and humane manner. I will call your office on February 21, or you may call me at any time after 2 p.m. daily at 617-555-9833.

Gives the reader the option of phoning the applicant or having him phone her.

Sincerely

Raymond J. Arnold

Raymond J. Arnold

Enclosure

Grammar and Mechanics Notes

1 In a personal business letter, the writer's return address may be typed above the date (as shown here) or below the sender's name in the closing.

2 This letter is formatted in block style, with all lines beginning at the left margin, and in open punctuation style, with no punctuation after the salutation and complimentary closing.

3 *major in labor relations:* Do not capitalize the names of college majors and minors.

4 *writing style and format."*: A period goes inside the closing quotation marks.

Visit the **BusCom Online Learning Center** (at http://college.hmco.com) for additional resources to help you with this course and with your future career.

■ Summary

One of the most important communication tasks you will ever face is securing a rewarding and worthwhile job. The job-seeking campaign thus requires considerable time, effort, and thought.

CO1. **Determine the appropriate length, format, and content for your résumé.**

The purpose of your résumé is to get you a job interview. Strive for a one-page document, typed in a simple, readable format on a computer and output on a laser printer. Include your name, address, phone number, job objective, information about your education and work experience, and special aptitudes and skills. Include other information only if it will help distinguish you favorably from the other applicants. Use either a chronological or functional organization for your work experience, and stress those skills and experiences that can be transferred to the job you want. Consider formatting an electronic version of your résumé for e-mailing or computer scanning. This version should be in plain text, with no special formatting, printed on standard white paper (one side only) and mailed unfolded and unstapled.

CO2. **Compose solicited and unsolicited job-application letters.**

You will typically use the same résumé when applying for numerous positions and then compose an application letter that discusses how your education and work experience qualify you specifically for the job at hand. If possible, address your letter to the person who will interview you for the job. When writing a solicited application letter, begin by stating the reason for your letter, identify the position for which you're applying, and tell how you learned about the position. When writing an unsolicited letter, first gain the reader's attention. Then use the body of your letter to highlight one or two of your strongest qualifications, relating them to the needs of the position for which you're applying. Close by politely asking for an interview.

CO3. **Conduct yourself appropriately during an employment interview.**

If your application efforts are successful, you will be invited to come for an interview. To succeed at the interview phase of the job campaign, prepare for the interview and conduct yourself appropriately during the interview. Be prepared to ask some questions of your own.

CO4. **Complete the communication tasks needed after the employment interview.**

After the interview is over, evaluate your performance and resolve to do better the next time. Also evaluate your résumé and cover letter and revise them if necessary. Finally, take the time to write a thank-you note to express appreciation to the courtesies extended to you.

■ See Slide 15.16.

■ Consider treating this list as an end-of-chapter exercise for students to define and give an example of each term.

■ Key Terms

You should be able to define the following terms in your own words and give an original example of each.

application letter (545)	résumé (530)
electronic résumé (540)	solicited application letter (545)
reference (539)	unsolicited application letter (545)

■ Exercises

1 **The 3Ps (Problem, Process, and Product) Model: Communication Applications at Monster.com**   When Jeff Taylor and his colleagues need to fill an open position, they use keywords to search through Monster's huge résumé database for candidates with the appropriate education and experience. During interviews, Taylor asks open-ended questions so candidates can talk about strengths and interests beyond the basic facts on their résumés. He also expects candidates to ask creative questions about the company, the position, or his role as founder and Chief Monster.

Problem

Imagine that you are getting ready to apply to Monster for a full-time job in human resources, marketing, information technology, or another functional area. In preparation, you need to find out more about Monster and its industry. This research will help you understand the company's direction and its employment needs, both immediate and long-term, so you can tailor your résumé accordingly and ask relevant questions during an interview.

Process

a. What kinds of job opportunities with Monster are you interested in researching?
b. Visit Monster's website (at http://www.monster.com) and search for company information. What industry is Monster in, and what is its strategy? Who are its customers? Where are its offices?
c. How do your skills and personal interests match up with what you have learned about Monster?
d. Look at the types of open positions that Monster wants to fill. Are your education and work experience appropriate for the positions that interest you? What other qualifications do you need to apply for the most promising positions?

Product

Using your knowledge of employment communication, write a brief analysis of Monster and one open position that you find interesting. Mention details that will help you customize your résumé for this job and prepare for a personal interview with Jeff Taylor.

2 **The 3Ps (Problem, Process, and Product) Model: Developing A Résumé—Getting to Know You**

Problem

Assume that you are beginning your last term of college before graduating. Using factual data from your own education, work experience, and so on (include any data that you expect to be true at the time of your graduation), prepare a résumé in an effective format.

Process

a. How will you word your name at the top of your résumé—for example, with or without any initials? (Remember *not* to include a personal title before your name.)

> ■ Suggestions and sample solutions for exercises appear in the *Instructor's Resource Manual.*

> **CO1.** Determine the appropriate length, format, and content for your résumé.

b. What is your mailing address? If you will be changing addresses during the job search, include both addresses, along with the effective dates of each.

c. What is your daytime phone number? When can you typically be reached at this number? What is your e-mail address?

d. For what type of position are you searching? Prepare an effective one-sentence job objective—one that is neither too general nor too specific.

e. What is the title of your degree? the name of your college? the location of the college? your major and minor? your expected date of graduation (month and year)?

f. What is your grade-point average overall and in your major? Is either one high enough to be considered a personal selling point?

g. Have you received any academic honors throughout your collegiate years, such as scholarships or being named to the dean's list? If so, list them.

h. Did you take any elective courses (courses that most applicants for this position probably did *not* take) that might be especially helpful in this position? If so, list them.

i. List in reverse chronological order (most recent job first) the following information for each job you've held during your college years: job title, organizational name, location (city and state), inclusive dates of employment, and full- or part-time status. Describe your specific duties in each position, stressing those duties that helped prepare you for your job objective. Use short phrases, beginning each duty or responsibility with one of the action verbs on page 538 and showing, where possible, specific evidence of the results you achieved.

j. Will your education or your work experience be more likely to impress the recruiter?

k. What additional information might you include, such as special skills, professional affiliations, offices held, or willingness to relocate or travel?

l. Are your reference letters on file at your school's placement office? If so, provide the office name, address, and phone number. (If not, include a statement such as "References available on request" at the bottom of your résumé.)

Product

Using the preceding information, draft, revise, format, and then proofread your résumé. Then prepare an electronic version of this résumé for computer scanning. Submit both of your résumés and your responses to the process questions to your instructor.

3 **Job Objectives**   Working in groups of three or four, come up with 20 to 25 jobs that group members might consider. From the list of jobs, select four and write an appropriate job objective for that job. Compare your job objectives with those of the other group members. Do your objectives clearly identify your career goals? Are the objectives personalized? Evaluate the job objectives of the other group members. How do they compare to yours? Prepare a one-page memo for your instructor listing the four jobs you selected, your objective for each job, and how you think your objectives compared to those of others in the group. Briefly describe how your objectives identify your career goals. End the memo with a summary statement of what you learned from this exercise.

■ See Handout 15.8.

4 **Internet Exercise**   Electronic résumés are an increasingly important part of the job search. Point your browser to Rebecca Smith's eRésumés and Resources website and look at her erésumé gallery (at http://www.eresumes.com), which features a number of creative examples of electronic résumés. Review one of the creative résumés, and then return to the erésumé gallery to view an electronic résumé selected from the listing of individuals' résumés. How do these résumés differ? Which do you think would be more attractive to an employer? Why? What ideas can you glean from these examples that would be appropriate and effective for your own résumé?

5 **Reference List** You have been scheduled for a job interview for an entry-level position with Stay Fit Gym. As part of the interview process, you have been asked to bring a list of references. Prepare a reference sheet with the names, professional titles, addresses, e-mail addresses, and phone numbers for at least four people who could recommend you for employment. This should be an actual list of references (real people) that could be left after your interview. Assume your instructor is the interviewer. Submit the reference sheet to him or her for evaluation.

6 **Application Letter Project** This project consists of writing both a solicited and an unsolicited application letter. Prepare each letter in an appropriate format and on appropriate paper. Include a copy of your résumé with each letter. Submit each letter to your instructor folded and inserted into a correctly addressed envelope (don't forget to sign your letter).

CO2. Compose solicited and unsolicited job-application letters.

a. Identify a large prospective employer—one that has not advertised for an opening in your field. Using one of the résumés you developed earlier, write an unsolicited application letter.

b. For various reasons, you might not secure a position directly related to your college major. In such a situation, it is especially important to be able to show how your qualifications (no matter what they are) match the needs of the employer. Using your own background, apply for the following position, which was advertised in last Sunday's *New York Times:* MANAGER-TRAINEE POSITION. Philip Morris is looking for recent college graduates to enter its management-trainee program in preparation for an exciting career in one of the diversified companies that make up Philip Morris. Excellent beginning salary and benefits, good working conditions, and a company that cares about you. (Reply to Box 385-G in care of this newspaper.)

7 **Job-Application Letters—Looking for a Spring Internship** You're looking for an internship where you can work part-time from February to May during your final college semester. One of your friends at Duquesne University has mentioned that Carnegie Learning hires interns throughout the year. Through research, you find out that Carnegie Learning makes math software for use by elementary school, middle school, and high school students. Interns get involved in product development and many other projects. Although you're not a math or education major, your friend says that the company is most interested in interns who are willing to test new programs and handle other tasks that regular employees simply don't have enough time to tackle.

You decide to apply for an internship at Carnegie Learning. Browse the company's website at http://www.carnegielearning.com, reading about its products and its employment needs. Then draft a job-application letter in which you highlight your qualifications and ask to be considered for an internship in the spring. As far as possible, base this letter on your actual educational background and work qualifications, but stress your interest in Carnegie Learning's industry and products.

CO3. Conduct yourself appropriately during an employment interview.

8 **Interview Evaluation**   You are employed by EverGreen Inc., a plant nursery, in Plano, Texas. You and two other people in the human resource department have been asked to prepare an interview evaluation form to be used for hiring new employees. Based on what you have learned regarding interviewing skills, develop a form that could be used to rate applicants' interviewing skills.

9 **Researching the Employer**   Refer to Exercise 5. Assume that Philip Morris has invited you to interview for the manager-trainee position. Research this company prior to your interview. Prepare a two-page, double-spaced report on your findings. You will concentrate, of course, on that information most likely to help you during the interview. As you're conducting your research, some questions are likely to occur to you that you'll want to get answered during the interview. Prepare a list of these questions and attach it as an appendix to your report.

10 **Work-team Communication—Mock Interviews**   This project uses information collected as part of Exercise 10. Divide into groups of six students. Draw straws to determine which three members will be interviewers and which three will be job applicants. Both groups now have homework to do. The interviewers must get together to plan their interview strategy (10 to 12 minutes for each candidate); and the applicants, working individually, must prepare for this interview.

The interviews will be conducted in front of the entire class, with each participant dressed appropriately. On the designated day, the three interviewers as a group will interview each of the three job applicants in turn (while the other two are out of the room). Given the short length of each interview, the applicant should refrain from asking any questions of his or her own, except to clarify the meaning of an interviewer's question.

After each round of interviews, the class as a whole will vote for the most effective interviewer and interviewee.

CO4. Complete the communication tasks needed after the employment interview.

11 **Thank-You Letters—Pedaling Toward Employment**   As your friends interview for jobs with investment banking firms and corporate giants, you decide on a different career path: retailing. You recently bought a Trek mountain bike at Zane's Cycles, a high-volume bicycle retailer located near New Haven, Connecticut. You were impressed by the store's huge selection, knowledgeable salespeople, and customer service culture. Customers can have their bikes adjusted or repaired for free, and the prices they pay are guaranteed to be the lowest available. Zane's also operates a highly successful business selling bikes to businesses that give the cycles away as rewards for sales performance and other achievements. This operation suggests that there are other opportunities beyond the retail side of the business. Another reason Zane's seems so appealing is that the founder, Chris Zane, lets his staff run the day-to-day operation—which means that managers have the responsibility and authority to do their jobs as they see fit.

You sent an unsolicited job-application letter and résumé to the store's human resources director, asking about a management trainee position. After going through an initial interview with two human resource experts, you're called back for a second interview. This time, you meet directly with Chris Zane to hear his vision for the store and his expectations for new managers. As soon as you get home, you turn on your computer to write a brief but professional thank-you note. What should you say in this letter? Should you send a printed letter or an e-mail message? Should you communicate with the human resources director at this time, even though you didn't see him during your second interview? Using your knowledge of employment communication, draft this thank-you note (making up appropriate details if needed).

continuing
case**15**

"Help Wanted"

When Diana Coleman accepted the position of vice president of administration at Urban Systems, she knew that she would have to work closely with Marc Kaplan, vice president of marketing. Diana had originally believed that the differences in their personalities, attitudes, and political biases would be outweighed by their commitment to Urban Systems. The subtle tensions between Diana and Marc have begun to escalate lately, however, and Diana is tired of working in that atmosphere.

Diana is savvy enough to recognize that she is highly marketable and that many organizations would be eager to create a position for her even if they had no advertised openings. She is interested in finding a position in information management at a large organization located in a metropolitan area. She is free to relocate anywhere in the country. She would like to become associated with a progressive organization, preferably one whose top-level officers are active in social and political causes. An organization with other women in prominent executive positions who could serve as her mentors would be especially attractive.

Note: Although you already know quite a bit about Diana, you may assume any additional, reasonable information you need to complete this project.

■ A suggested solution to the Continuing Case can be found in the *Instructor's Resource Manual.*

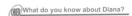

What do you know about Diana?
• She is single, willing to relocate, likes a large-city atmosphere, and prefers to work in a large organization.
• She has highly marketable skills and a master's degree in MIS from Stanford.
• She is self-confident and very interested in the welfare of her subordinates.
• She is a feminist and is politically active.

■ See Slide 15.17.

Critical Thinking

1. Is Diana making the right decision in leaving? Why or why not?

2. Review what you know about Diana—both from the background information contained in the Appendix to Chapter 1 and from the case studies in previous chapters. Develop a list of short phrases that describe her. What implication might each of these characteristics have for choosing a suitable new work environment?

Writing Project

3. Locate three organizations that would be top prospects for Diana to explore for a career move. Identify the organizations for Diana in terms of the criteria just discussed. Present a balanced view of the organizations, incorporating both positive and negative information. Finally, provide the name, address, and phone number of an appropriate person for Diana to contact. Organize your information in a logical manner, and present it as a letter report to Diana.

Diana contemplates working for a large, progressive organization with an activist social agenda.

LABtest 15

■ See Handout 15.9.

■ See Slides 15.18–15.21.

Retype the following news release, correcting any grammar and mechanics errors according to the rules introduced in LABs 2–6 beginning on page 576. Be especially alert for misused punctuation and misspellings.

Of all the elements that ~~effect~~ *affect (WORD)* the ambiance of a ~~room;~~ *room, (INTRO)* none ~~are~~ *is (AGR-PRO)* more important ~~then~~ *than (WORD)* lighting. Beyond ~~it's mood enhancing qualities good-lighting~~ *it's mood-enhancing (ADJ)* *qualities, (INTRO) good lighting (NO HYPHEN)* is essential for ~~safety reading~~ *safety, reading, (SER)* and spotlighting points of ~~interest,~~ *interest (NO COMMA)* and for such basics as cleaning.

5　　Many people associate ~~chandeleirs~~ *chandeliers (SP)* with elegant hotels or ~~old,~~ *old (NO COMMA)* movie palaces. But many ~~dinning~~ *dining (SP)* rooms need a fixture over the ~~table,~~ *table; (NO CONJ)* it may be brass and ~~glass,~~ *glass (NO COMMA)* or metal.

In contrast to chandeliers, ~~pendant's~~ *pendants (SP)* are hanging ~~lights.~~ *lights* ~~that~~ *that (FRAG)* represent one of ~~todays'~~ *today's (SING)* hottest lighting styles. Because

10　　~~their~~ *they're (WORD) they (AGR-^GEN)* small, ~~it~~ can be placed over ~~object's~~ *objects (WORD)* without overpowering ~~it.~~ *them. (AGR-G^EN)* In small spaces such as ~~entries,~~ *entries (NO COMMA)* or ~~above-kitchen~~ *above kitchen (NO HYPHEN)* islands or counters, glass shades add punch. ~~Its~~ *Their (AGR-GEN)* shapes are ~~intresting.~~ *interesting (SP)*.

If classical designs are ~~you're~~ *your (WORD)* favorite, there are many ~~time-less~~ *timeless (SP)* designs. Classic designs can be used like contemporary

15　　fixtures. They add elegance as they ~~preform~~ *perform (SP)* task lighting. In ~~an other~~ *another (SP)* part of the ~~room, maybe~~ *room (NO COMMA) may be* a carved fixture with ~~6~~ *six (NO.-WORD)* candle lights covered with silk shades with a ~~scalloped,~~ *scalloped (NO COMMA)* trim. ~~Shades incidently,~~ *Shades, (TRAN) incidentally,* also play a key role in the story. With their ~~high's and low's,~~ *highs and lows (NO APOSTROPHE)* pendant ~~lights,~~ *lights (NO COMMA)* and shades are ~~given~~ *giving* us

20　　~~alot~~ *a lot ^(WORD)* to look up ~~too.~~ *to (WORD)*.

Reference Manual

■ LAB 1: Parts of Speech

We use words, of course, to communicate. Of the hundreds of thousands of words in an unabridged dictionary, each can be classified as one of just eight parts of speech: noun, pronoun, verb, adjective, adverb, preposition, conjunction, or interjection. These eight parts of speech are illustrated in the sentence below:

| Interjection | Pronoun | Adverb | Verb | Preposition | | Adjective | Noun | | Conjunction | Noun |

Oh, I eagerly waited for new computers and printers.

Many words can act as different parts of speech, depending on how they are used in a sentence. (A *sentence* is a group of words that contains a subject and predicate and that expresses a complete thought.)

Consider, for example, the different parts of speech played by the word *following:*

We agree to do the *following. (noun)*

I was only *following* orders. *(verb)*

We met the *following* day. *(adjective)*

Following his remarks, he sat down. *(preposition)*

All words do not serve more than one function, but many do. Following is a brief introduction to the eight parts of speech.

1.1 Nouns A *noun* is a word that *names* something—for example, a person, place, thing, or idea:

Person:	employee, Mr. Watkins
Place:	office, Chicago
Thing:	animal, computer
Idea:	concentration, impatience, week, typing

The words in italics in the following sentences are all nouns.

Roger promoted his *idea* to the *vice president* on *Wednesday.*

Word processing is just one of the *skills* you'll need as a *temp.*

How much does one *quart* of *water* weigh on our bathroom *scales?*

The animal *doctor* treated my *animal* well in *Houston.*

If you were asked to give an example of a noun, you would probably think of a *concrete noun*—that is, a *physical* object that you can see, hear, feel, taste, or smell. An *abstract noun,* on the other hand, names a quality or concept and not something physical.

Concrete Noun	*Abstract Noun*
book	success
stapler	patience

computer	skills
dictionary	loyalty

A *common noun*, as its name suggests, is the name of a *general* person, place, thing, or idea. If you want to give the name of a *specific* person, place, thing, or idea, you would use a *proper noun.* Proper nouns are always capitalized.

Common Noun	*Proper Noun*
man	Lon Adams
city	Los Angeles
car	Corvette
religion	Judaism

A *singular noun* names one person, place, thing, or idea. A *plural noun* names more than one.

Singular Noun	*Plural Noun*
Smith	Smiths
watch	watches
computer	computers
victory	victories

1.2 Pronouns   A *pronoun* is a word used in place of a noun. Consider the following sentence:

> *Anna* went to *Anna's* kitchen and made *Anna's* favorite dessert because *Anna* was going to a party with *Anna's* friends.

The noun *Anna* is used five times in this awkward sentence. A smoother, less monotonous version of the sentence substitutes pronouns for all but the first *Anna:*

> Anna went to *her* kitchen and made *her* favorite dessert because *she* was going to a party with *her* friends.

The words in italics in the following sentences are pronouns. The nouns to which they refer are underlined:

> <u>Mary</u> thought *she* might get the promotion.
>
> *None* of the <u>speakers</u> were interesting.
>
> <u>Juan</u> forgot to bring *his* slides.

1.3 Verbs   A *verb* is a word (or group of words) that expresses either action or a state of being. The first kind of verb is called an *action verb;* the second kind is known as a *linking verb.* Without a verb, you have no sentence because the verb makes a statement about the subject.

Most verbs express action of some sort—either physical or mental—as indicated by the words in italics in the following sentences:

> Courtland *planted* his garden while Carol *pulled* weeds.
>
> I *solved* my problems as I *baked* bread.
>
> Jeremy *decided* he should *call* a meeting.

A small (but important) group of verbs do not express action. Instead, they simply link the subject with words that describe it. The most common linking verbs are forms of the verb *to be*, such as *is, am, are, was, were,* and *will.* Other forms of linking verbs involve the senses, such as *feels, looks, smells, sounds,* and *tastes.* The following words in italics are verbs (note that verbs can comprise one or more words):

Rosemary *was* angry because Dennis *looked* impatient.

If Lauren *is having* a party, I *should have been* invited.

Jason *had* already *seen* the report.

1.4 Adjectives   You can make sentences consisting of only nouns or pronouns and verbs (such as "Dogs bark."), but most of the time you'll need to add other parts of speech to make the meaning of the sentence clearer or more complete. An *adjective* is a word that modifies a noun or pronoun. Adjectives answer questions about the nouns or pronouns they describe, such as *how many?, what kind?,* and *which one? (Articles* are a special group of adjectives that include the words *a, an,* and *the.)*

As shown by the words in italics in the following sentences, adjectives may come before or after the nouns or pronouns they modify:

Seventeen applicants took the *typing* test.

The interview was *short,* but *comprehensive.*

She took the *last* plane and landed at a *small Mexican* airport.

1.5 Adverbs   An *adverb* is a word that modifies a verb (usually), an adjective, or another adverb. Adverbs often answer the questions *when?, where?, how?,* or *to what extent?* The words in italics in the following sentences are adverbs:

Please perform the procedure *now. (When?)*

Put the papers *here. (Where?)*

Alice performed *brilliantly. (How?)*

I am *almost* finished. *(To what extent?)*

The *exceedingly* expensive car was *very carefully* protected.

In the last sentence, the adverb *exceedingly* modifies the adjective *expensive* (how expensive?) and the adverb *very* modifies the adverb *carefully* (how carefully?).

Many (but, by no means, all) adverbs end in –*ly,* such as *loudly, quickly, really,* and *carefully.* However, not all words that end in –*ly* are adverbs; for example, *friendly, stately,* and *ugly* are all adjectives.

1.6 Prepositions   A *preposition* is a word (such as *to, for, from, of,* and *with*) that shows the relationship between a noun or pronoun and some other word in the sentence. The noun or pronoun following the preposition is called the *object* of the preposition, and the entire group of words is called a *prepositional phrase.* In the following sentences, the preposition is shown in italics; the entire prepositional phrase is underlined:

The ceremony occurred *on* the covered bridge.

The ceremony occurred *under* the covered bridge.

Marsha talked *with* Mr. Hines.

Marsha talked *about* Mr. Hines.

1.7 Conjunctions   A *conjunction* is a word (such as *and, or,* or *but*) that joins words or groups of words. For example, in the sentence "Ari and Alice are brokers," the conjunction *and* connects the two nouns *Ari* and *Alice.* In the following sentences, the conjunction is shown in italics; the words it joins are underlined:

Francesca *or* Teresa will attend the conference. (*joins two nouns*)

Howard spoke quietly *and* deliberately. (*joins two adverbs*)

Harriet tripped *but* caught her balance. (*joins two verbs*)

1.8 Interjections   An *interjection* is a word that expresses strong emotions. Interjections are used more often in oral communication than in written communication. If an interjection stands alone, it is followed by an exclamation point. If it is a part of the sentence, it is followed by a comma. You should not be surprised to learn that some words can serve as interjections in some sentences and as other parts of speech in other sentences. In the following sentences, the interjection is shown in italics:

Good! I'm glad to learn that the new employee does good work.

Oh! I didn't mean to startle you.

My, I wouldn't do that.

Gosh, that was an exhausting exercise. *Whew!*

APPLICATION

Note: For all LAB application exercises, first photocopy the exercise and then complete the exercise on the photocopied pages.

DIRECTIONS Label each part of speech in Sentences 1–8 with the abbreviation shown below.

adjective	*adj.*
adverb	*adv.*
conjunction	*conj.*
interjection	*interj.*
noun	*n.*
preposition	*prep.*
pronoun	*pron.*
verb	*v.*

interj   v   pron   pron
1. Oh, don't tell me I missed my flight.
     v/adv   pron   v   n

interj   adj   v
2. My, your new chair is comfortable.
   pron   n   adj

adv   v   n   v   interj
3. When I received your package, I was relieved. Whew!
   pron   pron   pron   v

interj   v   v   n   adj   n   adj
4. Gosh! I could not believe the depth of the raging water in the river.
   pron   adv   adj   prep   adj   prep   n

adv   n   pron   v   adj   adj   adv
5. When the quail and her chicks came into the yard, the hen carefully
   adj   conj   n   prep   n   n

adj   prep
checked the area for predators.
 v   n   n

interj   adj   pron   pron   adj   v   v
6. Alas! By the time he received her report, the decision had been made.
   prep   n   v   n   n   v

pron   v   v   n   adj   n
7. I was disappointed we missed your input to the decision-making process,
  v   pron   pron   prep   adj

pron pron v   n   n
but I hope you can meet the deadline next time.
conj v   v   adj   adj

n   adj   adj   v   prep   conj
8. Valerie Renoir, the major conference speaker, was delayed at O'Hare and
   n   adj   n   v   n

adv   prep   n   n
did not arrive at the hall until 2 p.m.
 v   v   adj   prep

■ LAB 2: Punctuation—Commas

Punctuation serves as a roadmap to help guide the reader through the twists and turns of your message—pointing out what is important (italics or underscores), subordinate (commas), copied from another source (quotation marks), explained further (colon), considered as a unit (hyphens), and the like. Sometimes correct punctuation is absolutely essential for comprehension. Consider, for example, the different meanings of the following sentences, depending on the punctuation:

What's the latest, Dope?
What's the latest dope?

The social secretary called the guests names as they arrived.
The social secretary called the guests' names as they arrived.

Our new model comes in red, green and brown, and white.
Our new model comes in red, green, and brown and white.

The play ended, happily.
The play ended happily.

A clever dog knows it's master.
A clever dog knows its master.

We must still play Michigan, which tied Ohio State, and Minnesota.
We must still play Michigan, which tied Ohio State and Minnesota.

"Medics Help Dog Bite Victim"
"Medics Help Dog-Bite Victim"

The comma rules presented in LAB 2 and the other punctuation rules presented in LAB 3 do not cover every possible situation; comprehensive style manuals, for example, routinely present more than 100 rules just for using the comma rather than just the 12 rules presented here. These rules cover the most frequent uses of punctuation in business writing. Learn them—because you will be using them frequently.

Commas are used to connect ideas and to set off elements within a sentence. When typing, leave one space after a comma. Many writers use commas inappropriately. No matter how long the sentence, make sure you have a legitimate reason before inserting a comma.

COMMAS USED *BETWEEN* EXPRESSIONS

Three types of expressions (an expression is words or groups of words) typically require commas between them: independent clauses, consecutive adjectives, and items in a series.

2.1 Independent Clauses   Use a comma between two independent clauses   *, ind*
joined by a coordinate conjunction (unless both clauses are short and closely related).

> Mr. Karas discussed last month's performance, and Ms. Daniels presented the sales projections.
> The meeting was running late, but Mr. Mears was in no hurry to adjourn.
> *But:* The firm hadn't paid and John was angry.

The major coordinate conjunctions are *and, but, or,* and *nor.* An independent clause is a subject-predicate combination that can stand alone as a complete sentence.

Do not confuse two independent clauses joined by a coordinate conjunction and a comma with a compound predicate, whose verbs are not separated by a comma. *Hint:* Cover up the conjunction with your pencil. If what's on both sides of your pencil could stand alone as complete sentences, a comma is needed.

> *No comma:*   Mrs. Ames had read the report_but had not discussed it with her colleagues. *("Had not discussed it with her colleagues" is not an independent clause; it lacks a subject.)*

Comma: Mrs. Ames had read the report, but she had not discussed it with her colleagues.

, adj   **2.2 Adjacent Adjectives**   Use a comma between two adjacent adjectives that modify the same noun.

> He was an aggressive, unpleasant manager.
>
> *But:* He was an aggressive_and unpleasant manager. *(The two adjectives are not adjacent; they are separated by the conjunction "and.")*

Do not use a comma if the first adjective modifies the combined idea of the second adjective plus the noun. *Hint:* Mentally insert the word "and" between the two consecutive adjectives. If it does not make sense, do not use a comma.

> Please order a new bulletin board for the executive_conference room.
>
> Do not use a comma between the last adjective and the noun.
>
> Wednesday, was a long, hot, humid_day.

, ser   **2.3 Items in a Series**   Use a comma between each item in a series of three or more. Do not use a comma after the last item in the series.

> The committee may meet on Wednesday, Thursday, or Friday_of next week.
>
> Carl wrote the questionnaire, Anna distributed the forms, and Tim tabulated the results_for our survey on employee satisfaction.

Some style manuals indicate that the last comma before the conjunction is optional. However, to avoid ambiguity in business writing, you should insert this comma.

> *Not:* We were served salads, macaroni and cheese and crackers.
>
> *But:* We were served salads, macaroni and cheese, and crackers.
>
> *Or:* We were served salads, macaroni, and cheese and crackers.

COMMAS USED *AFTER* EXPRESSIONS

Two types of expressions typically require commas after them: introductory expressions and complimentary closings in letters.

, intro   **2.4 Introductory Expressions**   Use a comma after an introductory expression. An *introductory expression* is a word, phrase, or clause that comes before the subject and verb of the independent clause. When the same expression occurs at the end of the sentence, no comma is used.

> No, the status report is not ready. *(introductory word)*
>
> Of course, you are not required to sign the petition. *(introductory phrase)*
>
> When the status report is ready, I shall call you. *(introductory clause)*
>
> *But:* I shall call you when the status report is ready.

Do not use a comma between the subject and verb—no matter how long or complex the subject is.

To finish that boring and time-consuming task in time for the monthly sales meeting_was a major challenge.

The effort to bring all of our products into compliance with ISO standards and to be eligible for sales in Common Market countries_required a full year of detailed planning.

2.5 Complimentary Closing   Use a comma after the complimentary closing of a business letter formatted in the standard punctuation style.   *, clos*

Sincerely,	Cordially yours,
Yours truly,	With warm regards,

With standard punctuation, a colon follows the salutation (such as "Dear Ms. Jones:" and a comma follows the complimentary closing. With open punctuation, no punctuation follows either the salutation or complimentary closing.

COMMAS USED *BEFORE* AND *AFTER* EXPRESSIONS

Numerous types of expressions typically require commas before *and* after them. Of course, if the expression comes at the beginning of a sentence, use a comma only after the expression; if it comes at the end of a sentence, use a comma only before it.

2.6 Nonrestrictive Expressions   Use commas before and after a nonrestric-   *, nonr*
tive expression. A *restrictive expression* is one that limits (restricts) the meaning of the noun or pronoun that it follows and is, therefore, essential to complete the basic meaning of the sentence. A *nonrestrictive expression,* on the other hand, may be omitted without changing the basic meaning of the sentence.

Restrictive:	Anyone *with some experience* should apply for the position. *("with some experience" restricts which "anyone" should apply.)*
Nonrestrictive:	Anne Cosgrave, *a clerk with extensive experience,* should apply for the position. (Because Anne Cosgrave can be only one person, the phrase "a clerk with extensive experience" does not serve to further restrict the noun and is, therefore, not essential to the meaning of the sentence.)
Restrictive:	Only the papers *left on the conference table* are missing. (identifies which papers are missing)
Nonrestrictive:	Lever Brothers, *one of our best customers,* is expanding in Europe. ("One of our best customers" could be omitted without changing the basic meaning of the sentence.)
Restrictive:	Ellis, *using a great deal of tact,* disagreed with her.
Nonrestrictive:	The manager *using a great deal of tact* was Ellis.

An *appositive* is a noun or noun phrase that identifies another noun or pronoun that comes immediately before it. If the appositive is nonrestrictive, insert commas before and after the appositive.

Restrictive:	The word *plagiarism* strikes fear into the heart of many. ("Plagiarism" is an appositive that identifies which word.)
Nonrestrictive:	Mr. Bayrami, *president of the corporation*, is planning to resign. ("President of the corporation" is an appositive that provides additional, but nonessential, information about Mr. Bayrami.)

, inter   **2.7 Interrupting Expressions**   Use commas before and after an interrupting expression. An *interrupting expression* breaks the normal flow of a sentence. Common examples are *in addition, as a result, therefore, in summary, on the other hand, however, unfortunately,* and *as a matter of fact*—when these expressions come in the middle of the sentence.

> You may, of course, cancel your subscription at any time.
>
> One suggestion, for example, was to undertake a leveraged buyout.
>
> I believe it was John, not Nancy, who raised the question.
>
> It is still not too late to make the change, is it?
>
> Anna's present salary, you must admit, is not in line with those of other network managers.
>
> *But:* You must admit_Anna's present salary is not in line with those of other network managers.

If the expression does not interrupt the normal flow of the sentence, do not use a comma.

> There is no doubt that you are qualified for the position.
>
> *But:* There is, no doubt, a good explanation for his actions.

, date   **2.8 Dates**   Use commas before and after the year when it follows the month and day. Do not use a comma after a partial date or when the date is formatted in day-month-year order. If the name of the day precedes the date, also use a comma *after* the name of the day.

> The note is due on May 31, 2007, at 5 p.m.
>
> *But:* The note is due on May 31 at 5 p.m.
>
> *But:* The note is due in May 2007.
>
> *But:* The note is due on 31 May 2007 at 5 p.m.
>
> Let's plan to meet on Wednesday, December 15, 2007, for our year-end review.

, place   **2.9 Places**   Use commas before and after a state or country that follows a city and between elements of an address in narrative writing.

> The sales conference will be held in Phoenix, Arizona, in May.
>
> Our business agent is located in Brussels, Belgium, in the P.O.M. Building.
>
> You may contact her at 500 Beaufort Drive, LaCrosse, VA 23950. *(Note that there is no comma between the state abbreviation and the ZIP code.)*

2.10 Direct Address   Use commas before and after a name used in direct address. A name is used in *direct address* when the writer speaks directly to (that is, directly addresses) another person.   *, dir ad*

Thank you, Ms. Cross, for bringing the matter to our attention.

Ladies and gentlemen, we appreciate your attending our session today.

2.11 Direct Quotation   Use commas before and after a direct quotation in a sentence.   *, quote*

The president said, "You have nothing to fear," and then changed the subject.

"I assure you," the human resources director said, "that no positions will be terminated."

If the quotation is a question, use a question mark instead of a comma.

"How many have applied?" she asked.

APPLICATION

DIRECTIONS Insert any needed commas in the following sentences. Above each comma, indicate the reason for the comma. If the sentence needs no commas, leave it blank.

intro

Example: As a matter of fact, you may tell her yourself.

ind

1. A comma comes between two adjacent adjectives that modify the same noun, but do not use a comma if the first adjective modifies the combined idea of the second adjective and the noun.

2. Stephen generated questions and I supplied responses.

intro

3. At the request of your accountant, we are summarizing all charitable deductions in a new format.

intro

4. By asking the right questions, we gained all the pertinent information we needed.

dir ad

5. Everyone, please use the door in the rear of the hall.

6. His bid for the congressional seat was successful this time.

7. I disagree with Beverly but do feel some change in policy is needed.

inter

8. I feel, as a matter of fact, that the proposed legislation will fall short of the required votes.

9. Ethan will prepare the presentation graphics and let you know when they are ready.

10. Determining purpose, *ser* analyzing the audience, and making content and organization decisions are critical planning steps.

11. It is appropriate, *inter* I believe, to make a preliminary announcement about the new position.

12. A goodwill message is prompt, *ser* direct, sincere, specific, and brief.

13. Look, *intro* this decision affects me as much as it does you.

14. The teacher, *nonr* using one of her favorite techniques, prompted the student into action.

15. Subordinate bad news by using the direct plan, *ser* by avoiding negative terms, and by presenting the news after the reasons are given.

16. My favorite destination is Atlanta, *place* Georgia.

17. The team presented a well-planned, *adj* logical scenario to explain the company's status.

18. Evan plans to conclude his investigation and explain the results by Friday but would not promise a written report until Tuesday.

19. We appreciate your business.

Sincerely, *clos*

Jason P. Smith

20. Those instructors, *nonr* who were from southern schools, were anxious to see the results of the study completed in Brimingham.

21. A group of teachers from Michigan attended the conference this year.

22. Our next training session will be located in Madison, *place* Wisconsin, sometime in the spring.

23. The next meeting of our professional organization will be held in the winter, *inter*

not in the spring.

24. The brochure states, *quote* "Satisfaction guaranteed, *ind* or your money back."

25. The department meeting, *inter* you will note, will be held every other Monday.

26. This assignment is due on April 20, *nonr* which is one week before the end of the

semester.

27. I need the cabinets installed by the week before my family arrives.

28. To qualify for promotion will require recommendations and long hours of

preparation.

29. To qualify for promotion, *intro* you will need recommendations from previous

managers.

30. To earn an award for outstanding sales is an achievable goal for Mary.

31. To earn an award for outstanding sales, *intro* Mary must set intermittent goals

that are attainable.

32. Dave was promoted in his job by working hard.

33. Harriet's sister was born on June 6, *date* 1957, in Munster, *place* Indiana.

34. Ted could paint the house himself, *ind* or he could hire a professional to do

the job.

35. I am telling you, *dir ad* Esther, that your report has been misplaced.

■ LAB 3: Punctuation—Other Marks

HYPHENS

Hyphens are used to form some compound adjectives, to link some prefixes to root words (such as *quasi-public*), and to divide words at the ends of lines. When typing, do not leave a space before or after a regular hyphen. Likewise, do not use a hyphen with a space before and after to substitute for a dash. Make a dash by typing two hyphens with no space before, between, or after. Most word processing programs automatically reformat two hyphens into a printed dash.

3.1 Compound Adjective   Hyphenate a compound adjective that comes *before* a noun (unless the adjective is a proper noun or unless the first word is an adverb ending in -*ly*).

> We hired a first-class management team.
>
> *But:* Our new management team is first_class.
>
> The long-term outlook for our investments is excellent.
>
> *But:* We intend to hold our investments for the long_term.
>
> *But:* The General_Motors warranty received high ratings.
>
> *But:* Alice presented a poorly_conceived proposal.

Note: Don't confuse compound adjectives (which are generally temporary combinations) with compound nouns (which are generally well-established concepts). Compound nouns (such as *Social Security, life insurance, word processing,* and *high school*) are not hyphenated when used as adjectives that come before a noun; thus, use *income_tax form, real_estate agent, public_relations firm,* and *data_processing center.*

3.2 Numbers   Hyphenate fractions and compound numbers 21 through 99 when they are spelled out.

> Nearly three-fourths of our new applicants were unqualified.
>
> Seventy-two orders were processed incorrectly last week.

SEMICOLONS

Semicolons are used to show where elements in a sentence are separated. The separation is stronger than a comma but not as strong as a period. When typing, leave one space after a semicolon and begin the following word with a lowercase letter.

; comma   **3.3 Independent Clauses with Commas**   If a misreading might otherwise occur, use a semicolon (instead of a comma) to separate independent clauses that contain internal commas. Make sure that the semicolon is inserted *between* the independent clauses—not *within* one of the clauses.

> *Confusing:* I ordered juice, toast, and bacon, and eggs, toast, and sausage were sent instead.
>
> *Clear:* I ordered juice, toast, and bacon; and eggs, toast, and sausage were sent instead.
>
> *But:* Although high-quality paper was used, the photocopy machine still jammed, and neither of us knew how to repair it. *(no misreading likely to occur)*

; no conj   **3.4 Independent Clauses Without a Conjunction**   Use a semicolon between independent clauses that are not connected by a coordinate conjunction (such as *and, but, or,* or *nor*). You have already learned to use a comma before coordinate

conjunctions when they connect independent clauses. This rule applies to independent clauses *not* connected by a conjunction.

> The president was eager to proceed with the plans; the board still had some reservations.
>
> *But:* The president was eager to proceed with the plans, but the board still had some reservations. *(Use a comma instead of a semicolon if the clauses are joined by a coordinate conjunction.)*

> Bannon Corporation exceeded its sales goal this quarter; furthermore, it rang up its highest net profit ever.
>
> *But:* Bannon Corporation exceeded its sales goal this quarter, and, furthermore, it rang up its highest net profit ever. *(Use a comma instead of a semicolon if the clauses are joined by a coordinate conjunction.)*

3.5 Series with Internal Commas   Use a semicolon after each item in a series   *; ser*
if any of the items already contain a comma. Normally, we separate items in a series with commas. However, if any of those items already contain a comma, we need a stronger mark (semicolon) between the items.

> The human resources department will be interviewing in Dallas, Texas; Stillwater, Oklahoma; and Little Rock, Arkansas, for the new position.
>
> Among the guests were Henry Halston, our attorney; Lisa Hart-Wilder; and Edith Grimes, our new controller.

COLONS

A colon is used after an independent clause that introduces explanatory material and after the salutation of a business letter that uses the standard punctuation style. When typing, leave one space after a colon; do not begin the following word with a capital letter unless it begins a quoted sentence.

3.6 Explanatory Material   Use a colon to introduce explanatory material that   *: exp*
is preceded by an independent clause.

> His directions were as follows: turn right and proceed to the third house on the left.
>
> I now have openings on the following dates: January 18, 19, and 20.
>
> Just remember this: you may need a reference from her in the future.
>
> The fall trade show offers the following advantages: inexpensive show space, abundant traffic, and free press publicity.

Expressions commonly used to introduce explanatory material are *the following, as follows, this,* and *these.* Make sure the clause preceding the explanatory material can stand alone as a complete sentence. Do not place a colon after a verb or a preposition that introduces a listing.

> *Not:* My responsibilities were: opening the mail, sorting it, and delivering it to each department.

But: My responsibilities were opening the mail, sorting it, and delivering it to each department.

: salut **3.7 Salutations** Use a colon after the salutation of a business letter that uses the standard punctuation style.

Dear Ms. Havelchek: Ladies and Gentlemen: Dear Lee:

Never use a comma after the salutation in a business letter. (A comma is appropriate only in a personal letter.) With standard punctuation, a colon follows the salutation and a comma follows the complimentary closing. With *open* punctuation, no punctuation follows the salutation or complimentary closing.

APOSTROPHES

Apostrophes are used to show that letters have been omitted (as in contractions) and to show possession. When typing, do not space before or after an apostrophe (unless a space after is needed before another word).

Remember this helpful hint: Whenever a noun ending in *s* is followed by another noun, the first noun is probably a possessive, requiring an apostrophe. However, if the first noun *describes* rather than establishes ownership, no apostrophe is used.

Bernie's department *(shows ownership; therefore, an apostrophe)*

the sales department *(describes; therefore, no apostrophe)*

' sing **3.8 Singular Nouns** To form the possessive of a singular noun, add an apostrophe plus *s.*

my accountant's fee	a child's toy
the company's stock	Ellen's choice
Alzheimer's disease	Mr. and Mrs. Dye's home
a year's time	the boss's contract
Ms. Morris's office	Liz's promotion
Gil Hodges's record	Carl Bissett Jr.'s birthday

' plur + s **3.9 Plural Nouns Ending in S** To form the possessive of a plural noun that ends in *s* (that is, most plural nouns), add an apostrophe only.

our accountants' fees	both companies' stock
the Dyes' home	two years' time

' plur − s **3.10 Plural Nouns Not Ending in S** To form the possessive of a plural noun that does not end in *s*, add an apostrophe plus *s* (just as you would for singular nouns).

the children's hour	the men's room
The alumni's contribution	

Hint: To avoid confusion in forming the possessive of plural nouns, first form the plural; then apply the appropriate rule.

Singular	*Plural*	*Plural Possessive*
employee	employees	employees' bonuses
hero	heroes	heroes' welcome
Mr. and Mrs. Lake	the Lakes	the Lakes' home
lady	ladies	ladies' clothing

3.11 Pronouns   To form the possessive of an indefinite pronoun, add an apostrophe plus *s*. Do not use an apostrophe to form the possessive of personal pronouns.   *' pro*

It is *someone's* responsibility
But: The responsibility is *theirs.*

I will review *everybody's* figures.
But: The bank will review *its* figures.

Note: Examples of indefinite possessive pronouns are *anybody's, everyone's, no one's, nobody's, one's,* and *somebody's.* Examples of personal possessive pronouns are *hers, his, its, ours, theirs,* and *yours.* Do not confuse the possessive pronouns *its, theirs,* and *whose* with the contractions *it's, there's,* and *who's.*

It's time to put litter in *its* place.
There's no reason to take *theirs.*
Who's determining *whose* jobs will be eliminated?

3.12 Gerunds   Use the possessive form for a noun or pronoun that comes before a gerund. (A gerund is the *–ing* form of a verb used as a noun.)   *' ger*

Garth questioned *Karen's* leaving so soon.
Stockholders' raising so many questions delayed the adjournment.
Mr. Matsumoto knew Karl and objected to *his* going to the meeting.

PERIODS

Periods are used at the ends of declarative sentences and polite requests and in abbreviations. When typing, leave one space after a period (or any other punctuation mark).

3.13 Polite Requests   Use a period after a polite request. Consider a statement a polite request if you expect the reader to respond by *acting* rather than by giving a yes-or-no answer.   *. req*

Would you please sign the form on page 2.
May I please have the report by Friday.
But: Would you be willing to take on this assignment? *(This sentence is a real question, requiring a question mark. You expect the reader to respond by saying "yes" or "no.")*

QUOTATION MARKS

Quotation marks are used around direct quotations, titles of some publications and conferences, and special terms. Type the closing quotation mark after a period or comma but before a colon or semicolon. Type the closing quotation mark after a question mark or exclamation point if the quoted material itself is a question or an exclamation; otherwise, type it before the question mark or exclamation. Capitalize the first word of a quotation that begins a sentence.

"quote   **3.14 Direct Quotation**   Use quotation marks around a direct quotation—that is, around the exact words of a person.

> "When we return on Thursday," Luis said, "we need to meet with you."
>
> *But:* Luis said that when we return on Thursday, we need to meet with you. *(no quotation marks needed in an indirect quotation)*
>
> Did Helen say, "He will represent us"?
>
> Helen asked, "Will he represent us?"

"term   **3.15 Term**   Use quotation marks around a term to clarify its meaning or to show that it is being used in a special way.

> Net income after taxes is known as "the bottom line"; that's what's important around here.
>
> The job title changed from "chairman" to "chief executive officer."
>
> The president misused the word "effect" in last night's press conference.

"title   **3.16 Title**   Use quotation marks around the title of a newspaper or magazine article, chapter in a book, report, conference, and similar items.

> Read the article entitled "Wall Street Recovery."
>
> Chapter 4, "Market Segmentation," of *Industrial Marketing* is of special interest.
>
> The theme of this year's sales conference is "Quality Sells."
>
> The report "Common Carriers" shows the extent of the transportation problems.

> *Note:* The titles of *complete* published works are shown in italics (see below). The titles of *parts* of published works and most other titles are enclosed in quotation marks.

ITALICS (OR UNDERLINING)

Before the advent of word processing software, underlining was used to emphasize words or indicate certain titles. Today, the use of italics is preferred for these functions.

Title   **3.17 Titles**   Italicize the title of a book, magazine, newspaper, and other *complete* published works.

> Roger's newest book, *All That Glitters,* was reviewed in *The New York Times* and in the *Washington Post.*

The cover story in last week's *Time* magazine was "Is the Economic Expansion
Over?"

ELLIPSES

An ellipsis is an omission. Three periods, with one space before and after each, are
used to show that something has been left out of a quotation. Four periods (the
sentence period plus the three ellipsis periods) indicate the omission of the last part
of a quoted sentence, the first part of the next sentence, or a whole sentence or paragraph. Here is an example:

Complete Quotation:

The average age of our homebuyers has risen from 29.6 years in 1998 to 31.5
years today. This increase is partly due to the rising cost of new home mortgages.
Adjustable-rate mortgages now account for 20% of all our new mortgages.

Shortened Quotation:

The average age of our homebuyers has risen . . . to 31.5 years today. . . .
Adjustable-rate mortgages now account for 20% of all our new mortgages.

Note: The typing sequence for the first ellipsis is *space period space period space period space.* The sequence for the second ellipsis is *period space period space period
space period space.*

3.18 Omission   Use ellipsis periods to indicate that one or more words have
been omitted from quoted material.

According to *Business Week,* "A continuing protest could shut down . . . Pemex,
which brought in 34% of Mexico's dollar income last year."

APPLICATION

DIRECTIONS   Insert any needed punctuation (including commas) in the following
sentences. Underline any expression that should be italicized. Above each mark of
punctuation, indicate the reason for the punctuation. If the sentence needs no
punctuation, leave it blank.

Example: We received our money's worth.
sing

1. Bernice tried to use the new software, but she had trouble with the
computer.
ind

2. James Johnson's raising the expectations for promotion was hotly debated.
ger

3. The short-term goal of the department was improvement in software
utilization.
adj

4. It was a poorly designed office.

5. Approximately one-half of the orders came from Spokane, Washington.
adj   *place*

6. Bertram preferred soda*ser*, hamburgers, and fries*ser*, but*conj* iced tea, hot dogs, and onion rings were served instead.

7. The classes started on time;*no conj* the school was entirely on schedule.

8. Did you met Sally Henley, our manager*nonr*; Paul Krause*ser*; and Gina South*ser*, our attorney*nonr*?

9. Remember this:*exp* the best recommendation is a job well done.

10. Dear Mr. Weatherby:*salut*

11. Did you get the total from the sales department?

12. Jason's*sing* boss will distribute the new guidelines for his department.

13. Within two years'*plur + s* time,*intro* the neighborhood will double in size.

14. Locking the door to the department was someone's*pro* responsibility.

15. Madelyn's*sing* guiding the discussion was a departure from the regular procedure.

16. Would you please sort these responses for me.*req*

17. The teacher said,*quote* "The samples you submitted were excellent."*quote*

18. Would you believe he misspelled the word "their"*term* in his report?

19. The article entitled "Technology for Fitness"*title* should be required reading.

20. *Time*Title* magazine features a person of the year each December.

21. I want her to know she is a highly respected employee.

22. It's*pro* a good thing the meeting was rescheduled.

23. If the tickets sell,*intro* we will tell Mrs. Zimfer;*no conj* she will take it from there.

24. The hotel's*sing* guests thought the conference rooms'*plur + s* temperatures were too cold.

25. They were watching the demonstration;*no conj* nevertheless,*intro* they didn't understand the last section.

26. Can we keep this off the record?

27. You will receive the materials tomorrow,*conj* but stop by today to see Alberto,*nonr* our corporate trainer,*nonr* for a quick preview.

28. I can do this for you either on December 5, 2005, or January 13, 2006.
     date   *date*

29. This is a once-in-a-lifetime opportunity for our employees' families.
          adj   *plur + s*

30. Mr. Henry will see you after the meeting; Mr. Perez will not be available.
                                  no conj

■ LAB 4: Grammar

Suppose the vice president of your organization asked you, a systems analyst, to try to locate a troublesome problem in a computer spreadsheet. After some sharp detective work, you finally resolved the problem and wrote a memo to the vice president saying, "John and myself discovered that one of the formulas were incorrect, so I asked he to revise it."

Instantly, you've turned what should have been a "good-news" opportunity for you into, at best, a "mixed-news" situation. The vice president will be pleased that you've uncovered the bug in the program but will probably focus entirely too much attention on your poor grammar skills.

Grammar refers to the rules for combining words into sentences. The most frequent grammar problems faced by business writers are discussed below. Learn these common rules well so that your use of grammar will not present a communication barrier in the message you're trying to convey.

COMPLETE SENTENCES

4.1 Fragment   Avoid sentence fragments.

NOT: He had always wanted to be a marketing representative. Because he liked to interact with people.

BUT: He had always wanted to be a marketing representative because he liked to interact with people.

Note: A fragment is a part of a sentence that is incorrectly punctuated as a complete sentence. Each sentence must contain a complete thought.

DRABBLE

4.2 Run-on Sentences   Avoid run-on sentences.

NOT: Karen Raines is a hard worker she even frequently works through lunch.

NOT: Karen Raines is a hard worker, she even frequently works through lunch.

BUT: Karen Raines is a hard worker; she even frequently works through lunch.

OR: Karen Raines is a hard worker. She even frequently works through lunch.

Note: A run-on sentence is two independent clauses run together without any punctuation between them or with only a comma between them (the latter error is called a *comma splice*).

MODIFIERS (ADJECTIVES AND ADVERBS)

An adjective modifies a noun or pronoun; an adverb modifies a verb, an adjective, or another adverb.

4.3 Modifiers   Use a comparative adjective or adverb (*-er, more,* or *less*) to refer to two persons, places, or things and a superlative adjective or adverb (*-est, most,* or *least*) to refer to more than two.

The Datascan is the fast**er** of the two machines.
The XR-75 is the slow**est** of all the machines.

Rose Marie is the **less** qualified of the two applicants.
Rose Marie is the **least** qualified of the three applicants.

Note: Do not use double comparisons, such as "more faster."

AGREEMENT (SUBJECT/VERB/PRONOUN)

Agreement refers to correspondence in number between related subjects, verbs, and pronouns. All must be singular if they refer to one, plural if they refer to more than one.

4.4 Agreement   Use a singular verb or pronoun with a singular subject and a plural verb or pronoun with a plural subject.

The four **workers have** a photocopy of **their** assignments.
Roger's **wife was** quite late for **her** appointment.
Mr. Tibbetts and Mrs. Downs plan to forgo **their** bonuses.
Included in this envelope **are a contract and an affidavit.**

Note: This is the general rule; variations are discussed below. In the first sentence, the plural subject (*workers*) requires a plural verb (*have*) and a plural pronoun (*their*). In the second sentence, the singular subject (*wife*) requires a singular verb (*was*) and a singular pronoun (*her*). In the third sentence, the plural subject (*Mr. Tibbetts and Ms. Downs*) requires a plural verb (*plan*) and a plural pronoun (*their*). In the last sentence, the subject is *a contract and an affidavit*—not *envelope*.

4.5 Company Names   Treat company names as singular.

NOT: Bickley and Bates **has** paid for **its** last order. **They** are ready to reorder.

BUT: Bickley and Bates **has** paid for **its** last order. **It** is now ready to reorder.

4.6 Expletives   In sentences that begin with an expletive, the true subject follows the verb. Use *is* or *are*, as appropriate.

There **is** no **reason** for his behavior.

There **are** many **reasons** for his behavior.

Note: An expletive is an expression such as *there is, there are, here is,* and *here are* that comes at the beginning of a clause or sentence. Because the topic of a sentence that begins with an expletive is not immediately apparent, such sentences should be used sparingly in business writing.

4.7 Intervening Words   Disregard any words that come between the subject and verb when establishing agreement. See, however, Rule 4.8 regarding special treatment of certain pronouns.

Only **one** of the mechanics **guarantees his** work. (not *their work*)

The **appearance** of the workers, not their competence, **was** being questioned.

The **secretary,** as well as the clerks, **was** late filing **her** form. (not *their forms*)

Note: First determine the subject; then make the verb agree. Other intervening words that do not affect the number of the verb are *together with, rather than, accompanied by, in addition to,* and *except.*

4.8 Pronouns   Some pronouns (*anybody, each, either, everybody, everyone, much, neither, no one, nobody,* and *one*) are always singular. Other pronouns (*all, any, more, most, none,* and *some*) may be singular or plural, depending on the noun to which they refer.

Each of the laborers **has** a different view of **his or her** job.

Neither of the models **is** doing **her** job well.

Everybody is required to take **his or her** turn at the booth. (not *their turn*)

All the **pie has** been eaten.   **None** of the **work is** finished.

All the **cookies have** been eaten.   **None** of the **workers are** finished.

4.9 Subject Nearer to Verb   If two subjects are joined by correlative conjunctions (*or, either/or, nor, neither/nor,* or *not only/but also*), the verb and any pronoun should agree with the subject that is nearer to the verb.

Either Robert or **Harold is** at **his** desk.

Neither the receptionist nor the **operators were** able to finish **their** tasks.

Not only the actress but also the **dancer has** to practice **her** routine.

The tellers or the **clerks have** to balance **their** cash drawers before leaving.

Note: The first noun in this type of construction may be disregarded when determining whether the verb should be singular or plural. Pay special attention to using the correct pronoun; do not use the plural pronoun *their* unless the subject and verb are plural. Note that subjects joined by *and* or *both/and* are always plural: *Both* **the actress and the dancer have** to practice **their** routines.

4.10 Subjunctive Mood   Verbs in the subjunctive mood require the plural form, even when the subject is singular.

> I wish the situation **were** reversed.
>
> If I **were** you, I would not mention the matter.

Note: Verbs in the subjunctive mood refer to conditions that are impossible or improbable.

CASE

Case refers to the form of a pronoun and indicates its use in a sentence. There are three cases: nominative, objective, and possessive. (Possessive-case pronouns are covered under "Apostrophes" in the section on punctuation in LAB 3.) Reflexive pronouns, which end in *-self* or *-selves*, refer to nouns or other pronouns.

4.11 Nominative Case   Use nominative pronouns (*I, he, she, we, they, who, whoever*) as subjects of a sentence or clause and with the verb *to be*.

> The customer representative and **he** are furnishing the figures. (**he** *is furnishing*)
>
> Mrs. Quigley asked if Oscar and **I** were ready to begin. (**I** *was ready to begin*)
>
> **We** old-timers can provide some background. (**we** *can provide*)
>
> It was **she** who agreed to the proposal. (**she** *agreed*)
>
> **Who** is chairing the meeting? (**he** *is chairing*)
>
> Mr. Lentzner wanted to know **who** was responsible. (**she** *was responsible*)
>
> Anna is the type of person **who** can be depended upon. (**she** *can be depended upon*)

Note: If you have trouble determining which pronoun to use, ignore the plural subject or substitute another pronoun. See the reworded clauses in parentheses above.

4.12 Objective Case   Use objective pronouns (*me, him, her, us, them, whom, whomever*) as objects in a sentence, clause, or phrase.

> Thomas sent a fax to Mr. Baird and **me.** (*sent a fax to* **me**)
>
> This policy applies to Eric and **her.** (*applies to* **her**)
>
> Joe asked **us** old-timers to provide some background. (*Joe asked* **us** *to provide*)
>
> The work was assigned to **her** and **me.** (*the work was assigned to* **me**)
>
> To **whom** shall we mail the specifications? (*mail them to* **him**)
>
> Anna is the type of person **whom** we can depend upon. (*we can depend upon* **her**)

Note: For *who/whom* constructions, if *he* or *she* can be substituted, *who* is the correct choice; if *him* or *her* can be substituted, *whom* is the correct choice. Remember: *who-he, whom-him.* The difference is apparent in the final examples shown here and under "Nominative Case," Rule 4.11: **who** *can be depended upon* versus **whom** *we can depend upon.*

4.13 Reflexive Pronouns   Use reflexive pronouns (*myself, yourself, himself, herself, itself, ourselves, yourselves,* or *themselves*) to refer to or emphasize a noun or pronoun *that has already been named.* Do not use reflexive pronouns to *substitute for* nominative or objective pronouns.

I **myself** have some doubts about the proposal.

You should see the exhibit **yourself.**

NOT: Virginia and **myself** will take care of the details.

BUT: Virginia and **I** will take care of the details.

NOT: Mary Louise administered the test to Thomas and **myself.**

BUT: Mary Louise administered the test to Thomas and **me.**

APPLICATION

DIRECTIONS   Select the correct words or words in parentheses.

1. (Who/Whom) is your favorite new chef? Laura Buraston, who along with Frederico Fox, (are/is) new chefs in Tucson. Some of my friends (has/have) eaten at their restaurants. Laura, they say, is the (better/best) of the two.

   1. Who, are, have, better

2. Merchant Associates is presenting (its/it's/their/there) seminar in Kansas City. The associates will work with seven or eight participants in developing (their/there) portfolios. Not only Dr. Merchant, but also his associates (is/are) willing to mentor faculty members. Dr. Merchant asked all participants to acknowledge the invitation with written responses to (he/him).

   2. its, their, are, him

3. If I (was/were) you, I would be (more/most) helpful with organizing the conference. You can work directly with Sandra and (me/myself). After all, Sandra knows that it was (I/me) (who/whom) made key contacts. This opportunity is open to the type of person (who/whom) we can depend on.

   3. were, more, me, I, who, whom

4. The report on sales volume (is/are) finally on my desk. (Us/We) managers may be somewhat apprehensive about these reports, but sales results tend to predict (who/whom) can be depended upon.

   4. is, We, who

5. Not only the lawyer but also the manager (was/were) able to attend the conference on ethics. Everybody in the firm (is/are) trying to participate as a way to improve (their/his or her) performance. Each of the employees (is/are) eager to attend the next session.

   5. were, is, his or her, is

6. were, who, was, us

6. There (was/were) several students in the class (who/whom) challenged whether each of the assignments (was/were) comparable in complexity. The professor asked (us/we) group leaders to evaluate the student's concerns.

7. was, was, is

7. Neither the professors nor the dean (was/were) able to meet Dr. Phyllis Hart, the conference speaker, at the airport. In fact, neither of the professors (was/were) able to pick him up at the hotel either. However, Dean Dye, as well as two other professors, (is/are) escorting him to the banquet.

8. quickest, slower, have

8. Martin's and Jay's groups are the (more quicker/most quicker/quicker/quickest) in the class. Jay's group is the (more slow/most slow/slower/slowest) of these two groups. In any case, all of the jobs (has/have) been submitted for both groups.

9. Whom, were, most, who

9. (Who/Whom) will you ask to participate in the evaluation process? If I (was/were) you I'd consider Hillary. While Jane is the (more/most) competent software expert we have available, Hillary is the type of team player (who/whom) can provide the leadership we need.

10. were, me, their, I, is, who

10. I wish it (was/were) possible for Jim and (I/me/myself) to see both Marty and Alex in (his/their) last performance this season. Jim and (I/me/myself) have always had a gathering in our home after they finished. Watching their reactions to the reviewers' comments as they were given (is/are) exciting, but as we are leaving too, it remains to be seen (who/whom) will assume that function next year.

DIRECTIONS   Revise the following paragraph to eliminate any fragments and run-on sentences.

plans, members
destination. With

year. Up

advance. These

FunTimes by Travel Log is a prepaid vacation program designed with families in mind. Club owners have permanent usage rights in a continually growing system of outstanding resorts. Unlike the traditional time-share plans. Members may select any of the club resorts as a destination with optional access to other resorts through exchange programs, the owners may select additional vacation sites, both in the United States and internationally. The membership fee entitles an owner to a fixed number of points each year, up to three years worth can be accumulated so a selected vacation can be upgraded or lengthened. Future points can be "borrowed" for use on a current vacation. Reservations may be made up to 13 months in advance these features make this plan an economical and flexible way to create family vacation memories.

■ LAB 5: Mechanics

Writing mechanics refer to those elements in communication that are evident only in written form: abbreviations, capitalization, number expression, spelling, and word division. (Punctuation, also a form of writing mechanics, was covered in LABs 2 and 3.) While creating a first draft, you need not be too concerned about the mechanics of your writing. However, you should be especially alert during the editing and proofreading stages to follow these common rules.

ABBREVIATIONS

Use abbreviations sparingly in narrative writing; many abbreviations are appropriate only in technical writing, statistical material, and tables. Consult a dictionary for the correct form for abbreviations, and follow the rule "When in doubt, write it out." When typing, do not space within abbreviations except to separate each initial of a person's name. Leave one space after an abbreviation unless another mark of punctuation follows immediately.

5.1 Not Abbreviated In narrative writing, do not abbreviate common nouns (such as *acct., assoc., bldg., co., dept., misc.,* and *pkg.*) or the names of cities, states (except in addresses), months, and days of the week.

5.2 With Periods Use periods to indicate many abbreviations.

No.	8 a.m.	4 ft.
Dr. M. L. Peterson	P.O. Box 45	e.g.

5.3 Without Periods Write some abbreviations in all capitals, with no periods—including all two-letter state abbreviations used in addresses with ZIP codes.

CPA	IRS	CT
TWA	UNESCO	OK

Note: Use two-letter state abbreviations in bibliographic citations.

CAPITALIZATION

The function of capitalization is to emphasize words or to show their importance. For example, the first word of a sentence is capitalized to emphasize that a new sentence has begun.

5.4 Compass Point Capitalize a compass point that designates a definite region or that is part of an official name. (Do not capitalize compass points used as directions.)

Margot lives in the **S**outh.

Our display window faces **w**est.

Is **E**ast Orange in **W**est Virginia?

5.5 Letter Part Capitalize the first word and any proper nouns in the salutation and complimentary closing of a business letter.

Dear **M**r. **S**mith:	**S**incerely **y**ours,
Dear **M**r. and **M**rs. **A**mes:	**Y**ours **t**ruly,

5.6 Noun Plus Number

Capitalize a noun followed by a number or letter (except for page and size numbers).

Table 3	page 79
Flight 1062	size 8D

5.7 Position Title

Capitalize an official position title that comes before a personal name, unless the personal name is an appositive set off by commas. Do not capitalize a position title used alone.

Vice President Alfredo Tenegco	Shirley Wilhite, dean,
our president, Joanne Rathburn,	The chief executive officer retired.

5.8 Proper Noun

Capitalize proper nouns and adjectives derived from proper nouns. Do not capitalize articles, conjunctions, and prepositions of four or fewer letters (for example, *a, an, the, and, of,* and *with*). The names of the seasons and the names of generic school courses are not proper nouns and are not capitalized.

Xerox copier	Amherst College (*but:* the college)
New York City (*but:* the city)	the Mexican border
the Fourth of July	Friday, March 3,
Chrysler Building	Bank of America
First-Class Storage Company	Margaret Adams-White
business communication	the winter holidays

5.9 Quotation

Capitalize the first word of a quoted sentence. (Do not capitalize the first word of an indirect quotation.)

According to Hall, "The goal of quality control is specified uniform quality."

Hall thinks we should work toward "specified uniform quality."

Hall said that uniform quality is the goal.

5.10 Title

In a published title, capitalize the first and last words, the first word after a colon or dash, and all other words except articles, conjunctions, and prepositions of three or fewer letters.

"A Word to the Wise"

Pricing Strategies: The Link With Reality

NUMBERS

Authorities do not agree on a single style for expressing numbers—whether to spell out a number in words or to write it in figures. The following guidelines apply to typical business writing. (The alternative is to use a *formal* style, in which all numbers that can be expressed in one or two words are spelled out.) When typing numbers in figures, separate thousands, millions, and billions with commas; and leave a space between a whole-number figure and its fraction unless the fraction is a character on the keyboard.

5.11 General   Spell out numbers for zero through ten and use figures for 11 and higher.

the first three pages	ten complaints
18 photocopies	5,376 stockholders

Note: Follow this rule only when none of the following special rules apply.

5.12 Figures   Use figures for

- dates. (Use the endings *-st, -d, -rd,* or *-th* only when the day precedes the month.)
- all numbers if two or more *related* numbers both above and below ten are used in the same sentence.
- measurements—such as time, money, distance, weight, and percentage. Be consistent in using either the word *percent* or the symbol %.
- mixed numbers.

May 9 (or the 9th of May)	10 miles
4 men and 18 women	*But:* The **18** women had **four** cars.
$6	5 p.m. (or 5 o'clock)
5 percent (or 5%)	6½
	But: 6 3/18

5.13 Words   Spell out

- a number used as the first word of a sentence.
- the smaller number when two numbers come together.
- fractions.
- the words *million* and *billion* in even numbers.

Thirty-two people attended.	nearly two-thirds of them
three 37-cent stamps	150 two-page brochures
37 million	$4.8 billion

Note: When fractions and the numbers 21 through 99 are spelled out, they should be hyphenated.

SPELLING

Correct spelling is essential to effective communication. A misspelled word can distract the reader, cause misunderstanding, and send a negative message about the writer's competence. Because of the many variations in the spelling of English words, no spelling guidelines are foolproof; there are exceptions to every spelling rule. The five rules that follow, however, may be safely applied in most business writing situations. Learning them will save you the time of looking up many words in a dictionary.

5.14 Doubling a Final Consonant   If the last syllable of a root word is stressed, double the final consonant when adding a suffix.

Last Syllable Stressed		*Last Syllable Not Stressed*	
prefer	preferring	happen	happening
control	controlling	total	totaling
occur	occurrence	differ	differed

5.15 One-Syllable Words   If a one-syllable word ends in a consonant preceded by a single vowel, double the final consonant before a suffix starting with a vowel.

Suffix Starting with Vowel		*Suffix Starting with Consonant*	
ship	shipper	ship	shipment
drop	dropped	glad	gladness
bag	baggage	bad	badly

5.16 Final *E*   If a final *e* is preceded by a consonant, drop the *e* before a suffix starting with a vowel.

Suffix Starting with Vowel		*Suffix Starting with Consonant*	
come	coming	hope	hopeful
use	usable	manage	management
sincere	sincerity	sincere	sincerely

Note: Words ending in *ce* or *ge* usually retain the *e* before a suffix starting with a vowel: *noticeable, advantageous.*

5.17 Final *Y*   If a final *y* is preceded by a consonant, change *y* to *i* before any suffix except one starting with *i.*

Most Suffixes		*Suffix Starting with* i	
company	companies	try	trying
ordinary	ordinarily	forty	fortyish
hurry	hurried		

5.18 *EI* and *IE* Words   Remember the rhyme:

Use *i* before *e*	believe	yield
Except after *c*	receive	deceit
Or when sounded like *a*	freight	their
As in *neighbor* and *weigh.*		

WORD AND PARAGRAPH DIVISION

When possible, avoid dividing words at the end of a line, because word divisions tend to slow down or even confuse a reader (for example, *rear- range* for *rearrange* or *read- just* for *readjust*). However, when necessary to avoid grossly uneven right margins, use the following rules. Most word processing software programs have a hyphenation feature that automatically divides words to make a more even right margin; you can change these word divisions manually if necessary. When you are typing, do not space before a hyphen.

5.19 Compound Word   Divide a compound word either after the hyphen or where the two words join to make a solid compound.

self- service   free- way   battle- field

5.20 Division Point   Leave at least two letters on the upper line and carry at least three letters to the next line.

ex- treme   typ- ing

5.21 Not Divided   Do not divide a one-syllable word, contraction, or abbreviation.

straight   shouldn't
UNESCO   approx.

5.22 Syllables   Divide words only between syllables.

per- sonnel   knowl- edge

Note: When in doubt about where a syllable ends, consult a dictionary.

5.23 Web Addresses   If necessary, break an online address (either an e-mail address or a webpage address) *before* (but never after) a dot (.), single slash (/), double slash (//), hyphen (-), underscore (_), *at* symbol (@), or any other mark of punctuation. Do not insert a hyphen within an online address to signify an end-of-line break.

For further information, check out this online source: http://college.hmco.com /business/ober/Sources/.

5.24 Paragraphs   If it is necessary to divide a paragraph between two pages, leave at least two lines of the paragraph at the bottom of the first page and carry forward at least two lines to the top of the next page. Do not divide a three-line paragraph.

APPLICATION

DIRECTIONS   Rewrite the following paragraphs so that all words and numbers are expressed correctly. Do not change the wording in any sentences.

1. 100 of our elementary students will receive passes to Holly's Heartland Amusement Park today. Mrs. freda t. albertson, principal, indicated students from every grade were randomly selected to receive the free passes. The students represent about a 1/5 of the school's population.

1. One hundred, Freda T. Albertson, fifth

2. September 1, three-quarters, school psychologist, 96

2. As of Sept. 1ˢᵗ, nearly ¾ of our parents have attended at least one learning style orientation seminar. The School Psychologist, John Sibilsky, summarized the response of the participants and reported a favorable evaluation by ninety-six parents.

3. 12 two-hour, three-week, East St. Louis

3. The Athletes for Freedom participants sponsored 12 2-hour presentations in a 3-week period. The last stop was east St. Louis, before the long ride home.

4. page 2, President Victoria Payton, 1½

4. As reported on Page 2 of today's newspaper, the price of a barrel of oil has continued to climb. According to president Victoria payton, the price is 1 ½ times higher than last year.

5. *Time*, Justin Lake, one of the most, 295

5. This month's issue of Time magazine reports an interview with justin lake who said, "Service to our country is measured by many things, but a gift of time is one of the more significant." Our employees gave a total of two-hundred-ninety-five hours.

DIRECTIONS Correct the one misspelling in each line.

Answers			
1. occurrence	1. preferring	controlling	occurence
2. dropped	2. shipper	droped	baggage
3. totaling	3. totalling	badly	shipment
4. differed	4. differred	happening	gladness
5. sincerely	5. sincerity	sincerly	noticeable
6. ordinarily	6. trying	fortyish	ordinarly
7. yield	7. deceit	yeild	believe
8. advantageous	8. advantagous	hopeful	companies
9. argument	9. changeable	boundary	arguement
10. category	10. catagory	apparent	criticize
11. accommodate	11. recommend	accomodate	weird
12. plausible	12. plausable	indispensable	allotted
13. separately	13. camouflage	innocence	seperately
14. nickel	14. nickle	miniature	embarrassing
15. inadvertent	15. liaison	exhilarated	inadvertant

DIRECTIONS Write the following words, inserting a hyphen or blank space at the first correct division point. If a word cannot be divided, write it without a hyphen.

Examples: mis-spelled
              thought

1. free-way, chair-person, level

1. freeway   chairperson   level

2. ex-press, ex-ploi-ta-tion, right

2. express   exploitation   right

3. MADD   soared   solitary

4. wouldn't   mayor-elect   reliance

5. agree   recourse   Ohio

6. www.homemadesimple.com/newsletter/index.shtml

7. Saddlebrooke_tripticket@yahoo.com

3. MADD, soared,
sol-i-tary

4. wouldn't, mayor-elect,
re-li-ance

5. agree, re-course, Ohio

6. www .homemadesimple
.com /newsletter /index
.shtml

7. Saddlebrooke _tripticket
@yahoo.com

■ LAB 6: Word Usage

The following words and phrases are often used incorrectly in everyday speech and in business writing. Learn to use them correctly to help achieve your communication goals.

In some cases in the following list, one word is often confused with another similar word; in other cases, the structure of our language requires that certain words be used only in certain ways. Because of space, only brief and incomplete definitions are given here. Consult a dictionary for more complete or additional meanings.

6.1 Accept/Except   *Accept* means "to agree to"; *except* means "with the exclusion of."

I will **accept** all the recommendations **except** the last one.

6.2 Advice/Advise   *Advice* is a noun meaning "counsel"; *advise* is a verb meaning "to recommend."

If I ask for her **advice,** she may **advise** me to quit.

6.3 Affect/Effect   *Affect* is most often used as a verb meaning "to influence" or "to change"; *effect* is most often used as a noun meaning "result" or "impression."

The legislation may **affect** sales but should have no **effect** on gross margin.

6.4 All Right/Alright   Use *all right.* (*Alright* is considered substandard.)

The arrangement is **all right** (not *alright*) with me.

6.5 A Lot/Alot   Use *a lot.* (*Alot* is considered substandard.)

We used **a lot** (not *alot*) of overtime on the project.

6.6 Among/Between   Use *among* when referring to three or more; use *between* when referring to two.

Among the three candidates was one manager who divided his time **between** London and New York.

6.7 Amount/Number   Use *amount* to refer to money or to things that cannot be counted; use *number* to refer to things that can be counted.

> The **amount** of consumer interest was measured by the **number** of coupons returned.

6.8 Anxious/Eager   Use *anxious* only if great concern or worry is involved.

> Jon was **eager** to get the new car although he was **anxious** about making such high payments.

6.9 Any One/Anyone   Spell as two words when followed by *of;* spell as one word when the accent is on *any.*

> **Anyone** is allowed to attend **any one** of the sessions.

> **Between**   See *Among/Between.*

6.10 Can/May   *Can* indicates ability; *may* indicates permission.

> I **can** finish the project on time if I **may** hire an additional secretary.

6.11 Cite/Sight/Site   *Cite* means "to quote" or "to mention"; *sight* is either a verb meaning "to look at" or a noun meaning "something seen"; *site* is most often a noun meaning "location."

> The **sight** of the high-rise building on the **site** of the old battlefield reminded Monica to **cite** several other examples to the commission members.

6.12 Complement/Compliment   *Complement* means "to complete" or "something that completes"; *compliment* means "to praise" or "words of praise."

> I must **compliment** you on the new model, which will **complement** our line.

6.13 Could of/Could've   Use *could've* (or *could have*). (*Could of* is incorrect.)

> We **could've** (not *could of*) prevented that loss had we been more alert.

6.14 Different from/Different than   Use *different from.* (*Different than* is considered substandard.)

> Your computer is **different from** (not *different than*) mine.

6.15 Each Other/One Another   Use *each other* when referring to two; use *one another* when referring to three or more.

> The two workers helped **each other,** but their three visitors would not even look at **one another.**

Eager   See *Anxious/Eager.*

Effect   See *Affect/Effect.*

6.16 e.g./i.e.   The abbreviation *e.g.* means "for example"; *i.e.* means "that is." Use *i.e.* to introduce a restatement or explanation of a preceding expression. Both abbreviations, like the expressions for which they stand, are followed by commas. (Many writers prefer the full English terms to the abbreviations because they are clearer.)

> The proposal has merit; **e.g.,** it is economical, forward-looking, and timely.
>
> *Or:* The proposal has merit; for example, it is economical, forward-looking, and timely.
>
> Unfortunately, it is also a hot potato; **i.e.,** it will generate unfavorable publicity.
>
> *Or:* Unfortunately, it is also a hot potato; that is, it will generate unfavorable publicity.

6.17 Eminent/Imminent   *Eminent* means "well-known"; *imminent* means "about to happen."

> The arrival of the **eminent** scientist from Russia is **imminent.**

6.18 Enthused/Enthusiastic   Use *enthusiastic.* (*Enthused* is considered substandard.)

> I have become quite **enthusiastic** (not *enthused*) about the possibilities.

Except   See *Accept/Except.*

6.19 Farther/Further   *Farther* refers to distance; *further* refers to extent or degree.

> We drove 10 miles **farther** while we discussed the matter **further.**

6.20 Fewer/Less   Use *fewer* to refer to things that can be counted; use *less* to refer to money or to things that cannot be counted.

> Alvin worked **fewer** hours at the exhibit and therefore generated **less** interest.

Further   See *Farther/Further.*

6.21 Good/Well   *Good* is an adjective; *well* is an adverb or (with reference to health) an adjective.

> Joe does a **good** job and performs **well** on tests, even when he does not feel **well.**

i.e.   See *e.g./i.e.*

Imminent   See *Eminent/Imminent.*

6.22 Imply/Infer   *Imply* means "to hint" or "to suggest"; *infer* means "to draw a conclusion." Speakers and writers *imply;* readers and listeners *infer.*

> The president **implied** that changes will be forthcoming; I **inferred** from his tone of voice that these changes will not be pleasant.

6.23 Irregardless/Regardless   Use *regardless.* (*Irregardless* is considered substandard.)

> He wants to proceed, **regardless** (not *irregardless*) of the costs.

6.24 Its/It's   *Its* is a possessive pronoun; *it's* is a contraction for "it is."

> **It's** time to let the department increase **its** budget.

6.25 Lay/Lie   *Lay* (principal forms: *lay, laid, laid, laying*) means "to put" and requires an object to complete its meaning; *lie* (principal forms: *lie, lay, lain, lying*) means "to rest."

> Please **lay** the supplies on the shelf.   I **lie** on the couch after lunch each day.
> I **laid** the folders in the drawer.   The report **lay** on his desk yesterday.
> She had **laid** the notes on her desk.   The job has **lain** untouched for a week.

> **Less**   See *Fewer/Less.*

> **Lie**   See *Lay/Lie.*

6.26 Loose/Lose   *Loose* means "not fastened"; *lose* means "to be unable to find."

> Do not **lose** the **loose** change in your pocket.

> **May**   See *Can/May.*

> **Number**   See *Amount/Number.*

> **One Another**   See *Each Other/One Another.*

6.27 Passed/Past   *Passed* is a verb (the past tense or past participle of *pass,* meaning "to move on or by"); *past* is an adjective, adverb, or preposition meaning "earlier."

> The committee **passed** the no-confidence motion at a **past** meeting.

6.28 Percent/Percentage   With figures, use *percent;* without figures, use *percentage.*

> We took a commission of 6 **percent** (or 6%), which was a lower **percentage** than last year.

6.29 Personal/Personnel   *Personal* means "private" or "belonging to one individual"; *personnel* means "employees."

I used my **personal** time to draft a memo to all **personnel.**

6.30 Principal/Principle   *Principal* means "primary" (adjective) or "sum of money" (noun); *principle* means "rule" or "law."

The guiding **principle** is fair play, and the **principal** means of achieving it is a code of ethics.

6.31 Real/Really   *Real* is an adjective; *really* is an adverb. Do not use *real* to modify another adjective.

She was **really** (not *real*) proud that her necklace contained **real** pearls.

6.32 Reason Is Because/Reason Is That   Use *reason is that.* (*Reason is because* is considered substandard.)

The **reason** for such low attendance **is that** (not *is because*) the weather was stormy.

> **Regardless**   See *Irregardless/Regardless.*

6.33 Same   Do not use *same* to refer to a previously mentioned item. Use *it* or some other wording instead.

We have received your order and will ship **it** (not *same*) in three days.

6.34 Set/Sit   *Set* (principal forms: *set, set, set, setting*) means "to place"; *sit* (principal forms: *sit, sat, sat, sitting*) means "to be seated."

Please **set** your papers on the table.	Please **sit** in the chair.
She **set** the computer on the desk.	She **sat** in the first-class section.
I have **set** the computer there before.	I had not **sat** there before.

6.35 Should of/Should've   Use *should've* (or *should have*). (*Should of* is incorrect.)

We **should've** (not *should of*) been more careful.

> **Sight**   See *Cite/Sight/Site.*

> **Sit**   See *Set/Sit.*

> **Site**   See *Cite/Sight/Site.*

6.36 Stationary/Stationery   *Stationary* means "remaining in one place"; *stationery* is writing paper.

I used my personal **stationery** to write them to ask whether the minicomputer should remain **stationary.**

6.37 Sure/Surely   *Sure* is an adjective; *surely* is an adverb. Do not use *sure* to modify another adjective.

I'm **surely** (not *sure*) glad that she is running and feel **sure** that she will be nominated.

6.38 Sure and/Sure to   Use *sure to*. (*Sure and* is considered substandard.)

Be **sure to** (not *sure and*) attend the meeting.

6.39 Their/There/They're   *Their* means "belonging to them"; *there* means "in that place"; and *they're* is a contraction for "they are."

They're too busy with **their** reports to be **there** for the hearing.

6.40 Theirs/There's   *Theirs* is a possessive pronoun; *there's* is a contraction for "there is."

We finished our meal but **there's** no time for them to finish **theirs.**

They're   See *Their/There/They're.*

6.41 Try and/Try to   Use *try to*. (*Try and* is considered substandard.)

Please **try to** (not *try and*) attend the meeting.

Well   See *Good/Well.*

6.42 Whose/Who's   *Whose* is a possessive pronoun; *who's* is a contraction for "who is."

Who's going to let us know **whose** turn it is to make coffee?

6.43 Your/You're   *Your* means "belonging to you"; *you're* is a contraction for "you are."

You're going to present **your** report first.

APPLICATION

DIRECTIONS   Select the correct words in parentheses.

1. accept, advice, effect, a lot

1. I will (accept/except) your (advice/advise), but the (affect/effect) of doing

so may bring (alot/a lot) of change.

2. The seminar was (all right/alright), but (among/between) Jamie and me, most participants were (anxious/eager) to complete the training.

   2. all right, between, eager

3. The (amount/number) of political activity generated (fewer/less) interest than anticipated.

   3. amount, less

4. (Any one/Anyone) of the students (may/can) apply that (principal/principle) if (theirs/there's) time.

   4. Anyone, can, principle, there's

5. The first (sight/cite/site) for the new office (could of/could've) (complimented/complemented) the surrounding community, mainly because it is (different from/different than) the typical building.

   5. site, could've, complemented, different from

6. The program will succeed; (e.g./i.e.), it is positive, forward-looking, and cost effective.

   6. e.g.

7. The group members supported (each other/one another) and were enthused/enthusiastic) about their presentation.

   7. one another, enthusiastic

8. The CEO (implied/inferred) that arrangements with an (eminent/imminent) scientist have been finalized, and (irregardless/regardless of the number who are invited, we will be included.

   8. implied, eminent, regardless

9. How much (farther/further) can we pursue this if (its/it's) not (passed/past) on through regular channels?

   9. further, it's, passed

10. Please (lay/lie) your (loose/lose) change on the dresser and I'll be (real/really) pleased.

    10. lay, loose, really

11. You (should of/should've) taken advantage of the opportunity to refinance your home under the lower (percent/percentage) rates.

    11. should've, percentage

12. The new investment program is open to all (personal/personnel) and will (sure/surely) build security for (their/there) future.

    12. personnel, surely, their

13. The reason for the increase in deli foods in grocery stores is (that/because) more people are buying food prepared outside the home.

    13. that

14. stationery, try to

15. sure to, set

16. it, your

17. Whose, surely

18. advise, except, imminent

19. between,
    one another

20. anxious

21. cites, good

22. infer, compliment

23. principal, their,
    who is

24. stationary,
    complemented

25. fewer, amount

14. I use my personal (stationery/stationary) and please (try to/try and) use yours.

15. Tell Henry to be (sure and/sure to) lock up before he leaves and (sit/set) the late afternoon mail on my desk.

16. We have the document and will forward (it/same) to the actuary so that (you're/your) department is included in the transaction.

17. (Who's/Whose) turn is it to clean the refrigerator because it (sure/surely) needs it?

18. I'll follow the guidelines you (advise/advice), (except/accept) the one involving the (eminent/imminent) staff change in sales.

19. There was wide disparity (between/among) the five candidates, but they supported (each other/one another).

20. Dr. Zhoa was excited about the new job but (eager/anxious) about the research required.

21. Be sure the (cites/sights/sites) are done correctly because we want to do a (good/well) job.

22. What did you (imply/infer) from her (compliment/complement)?

23. The (principle/principal) reason for (their/there/they're) success is the lawyer, (whose/who is) a specialist in international law.

24. A (stationery/stationary) pump for the well was (complemented/complimented) by a mobile emergency back up.

25. They wanted us to work (less/fewer) hours so the (number/amount) of savings could be increased.

◼ Formatting Correspondence and Memos

The most common features of business letters, memos, and e-mail are discussed in the following sections and illustrated in Figures 1 and 2.

LETTER AND PUNCTUATION STYLES

The *block style* is the simplest letter style to type because all lines begin at the left margin. In the *modified block style,* the date and closing lines begin at the center point. Offsetting these parts from the left margin enables the reader to locate them quickly.

The *standard punctuation style*—the most common format—uses a colon (never a comma) after the salutation and a comma after the complimentary closing. The *open punctuation style,* on the other hand, uses no punctuation after these two lines.

STATIONERY AND MARGINS

Most letters are typed on standard-sized stationery, $8\frac{1}{2}$ by 11 inches. The first page of a business letter is typed on letterhead stationery, which shows company information printed at the top. Subsequent pages of a business letter and all pages of a personal business letter (a letter written to transact one's personal business) are typed on good-quality plain paper.

Side, top, and bottom margins should be 1 to $1\frac{1}{4}$ inches (most word processing programs have default margins of $1\frac{1}{4}$ inches, which works just fine). Vertically center one-page letters and memos. Set a tab at the center point if you're formatting a modified block style letter.

REQUIRED LETTER PARTS

The required letter parts are as follows:

Date Line   Type the current month (spelled out), day, and year on the first line. Begin either at the center point for modified block style or at the left margin for all other styles.

figure1

CORRESPONDENCE FORMATS

Block style letter

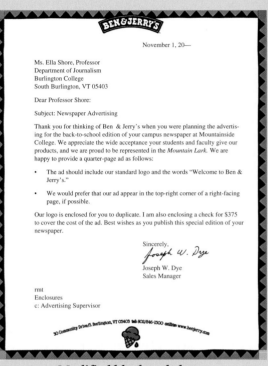

Modified block style letter

Interoffice memorandum

E-mail message

Inside Address   The inside address gives the name and location of the person to whom you're writing. Include a personal title (such as *Mr.*, *Mrs.*, *Miss*, or *Ms.*). If you use the addressee's job title, type it either on the same line as the name (separated from the name by a comma) or on the following line by itself. In the address, use the two-letter U.S. Postal Service abbreviation, typed in all capitals with no period, and leave one space between the state and the ZIP code. Type the inside address at the left margin four lines below the date; that is, press Enter four times. For international letters, type the name of the country in all-capital letters on the last line by itself.

Salutation   Use the same name in both the inside address and the salutation. If the letter is addressed to a job position rather than to a person, use a generic but nonsexist greeting, such as "Dear Human Resources Manager." If you typically address the reader in person by first name, use the first name in the salutation (for example, "Dear Lois:"); otherwise, use a personal title and the surname only (for example, "Dear Ms. Lane:"). Leave one blank line before and after the salutation.

Body   Single-space the lines of each paragraph and leave one blank line between paragraphs.

Page 2 Heading   Use your word processor's page-numbering command to insert the page number in the top right margin. Suppress the page number on page 1. You should carry forward to a second page at least two lines of the body of the message.

Complimentary Closing   Begin the complimentary closing at the same horizontal point as the date line, capitalize the first word only, and leave one blank line before and three blank lines after, to allow room for the signature. If a colon follows the salutation, use a comma after the complimentary closing; otherwise, no punctuation follows.

Signature   Some women insert the personal title they prefer (*Ms.*, *Miss*, or *Mrs.*) in parentheses before their signature. Men never include a personal title.

Writer's Identification   The writer's identification (name or job title or both) begins on the fourth line immediately below the complimentary closing. Do not use a personal title. The job title may go either on the same line as the typed name, separated from the name by a comma, or on the following line by itself.

Reference Initials   When used, reference initials (the initials of the typist) are typed at the left margin in lowercase letters without periods, with one blank line before. Do not include reference initials if you type your own letter.

Envelopes   Business envelopes have a printed return address. You may type your name above this address, if you wish. Use plain envelopes for personal business letters; you should type the return address (your home address) at the upper left corner. Envelopes may be typed either in standard upper- and lowercase style or in all-capital letters without any punctuation. On large (No. 10) envelopes, begin typing the mailing address 2 inches from the top edge and 4 inches from the left edge. On small (No. 6¾) envelopes, begin typing the mailing address 2 inches from the top edge and 2½ inches from the left edge. Fold letters as shown in Figure 2.

B

figure 2

**ENVELOPES AND
FOLDING LETTERS**

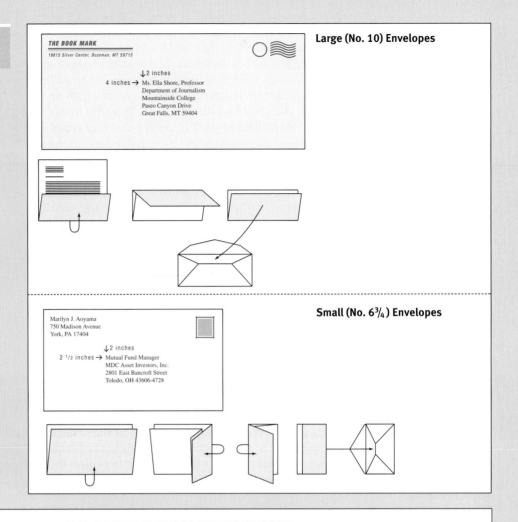

Large (No. 10) Envelopes

THE BOOK MARK
18615 Silver Center, Bozeman, MT 59715

↓2 inches
4 inches → Ms. Ella Shore, Professor
Department of Journalism
Mountainside College
Paseo Canyon Drive
Great Falls, MT 59404

Small (No. 6³/₄) Envelopes

Marilyn J. Aoyama
750 Madison Avenue
York, PA 17404

↓2 inches
2 ¹/₂ inches → Mutual Fund Manager
MDC Asset Investors, Inc.
2801 East Bancroft Street
Toledo, OH 43606-4728

U.S. POSTAL SERVICE ABBREVIATIONS
FOR STATES, TERRITORIES, AND CANADIAN PROVINCES

States and Territories

Alabama............AL	Kansas...............KS	North Dakota...........ND	Wyoming ....WY
Alaska..............AK	Kentucky ....KY	Ohio...................OH	
Arizona.............AZ	Louisiana..............LA	Oklahoma ....OK	
Arkansas ....AR	Maine ....ME	Oregon................OR	
California ....CA	Maryland..............MD	Pennsylvania...........PA	*Canadian Provinces*
Colorado............CO	Massachusetts ....MA	Puerto Rico ....PR	Alberta.............AB
Connecticut ....CT	Michigan ....MI	Rhode Island..........RI	British Columbia .....BC
Delaware ....DE	Minnesota............MN	South Carolina ....SC	Labrador ....LB
District of Columbia...DC	Mississippi ....MS	South Dakota ....SD	Manitoba...........MB
Florida ....FL	Missouri ....MO	Tennessee.............TN	New Brunswick ......NB
Georgia............GA	Montana ....MT	Texas ....TX	Newfoundland.......NF
Guam ....GU	Nebraska.............NE	Utah..................UT	Northwest Territories..NT
Hawaii ....HI	Nevada ....NV	Vermont..............VT	Nova Scotia ....NS
Idaho ....ID	New Hampshire ....NH	Virgin Islands VI	Ontario.............ON
Illinois IL	New Jersey............NJ	Virginia ....VA	Prince Edward Island..PE
Indiana.............IN	New Mexico...........NM	Washington............WA	Quebec ....PQ
Iowa ....IA	New York ....NY	West Virginia ....WV	Saskatchewan.......SK
	North Carolina..........NC	Wisconsin ....WI	Yukon Territory.......YT

OPTIONAL LETTER PARTS

Optional letter parts are as follows:

Subject Line   You should include a subject line in most letters (identified by the words *Subject, Re,* or *In Re* followed by a colon) to identify the topic of the letter. Type it below the salutation, with one blank line before and one after.

Numbered or Bulleted Lists in the Body   Use your word processor's number/bullet feature to insert a numbered list (if the sequence of the items is important) or a bulleted list (when the sequence is not important). If every item takes up only a single line, single-space the items; otherwise, single-space the lines within each item and double-space between items. Either way, leave one blank line before and after the list.

Enclosure Notation   Use an enclosure notation if any additional items are to be included in the envelope. Type "Enclosure" on the line immediately below the reference initials, and as an option, add the description of what is enclosed. (*Note:* For memos, the appropriate term is "Attachment" instead of "Enclosure" if the items are to be physically attached to the memo instead of being enclosed in an envelope.)

Delivery Notation   Type a delivery notation (such as *By Certified Mail, By Fax, By Federal Express*) a single space below the enclosure notation.

Copy Notation   If someone other than the addressee is to receive a copy of the letter, type a copy notation ("c:") immediately below the enclosure notation or reference initials, whichever comes last. Then follow the copy notation with the names of the people who will receive copies.

Postscript   If you add a postscript to a letter, type it as the last item, preceded by one blank line. The heading "PS:" is optional. Postscripts are used most often in sales letters.

■ Formatting Reports and Documenting Sources

If the reader or organization has a preferred format style, use it. Otherwise, follow these generally accepted guidelines for formatting business reports. Make use of your computer's automatic or formatting features to enhance the appearance and readability of your report and to increase the efficiency of the process. A sample report in business style is shown in Figure 3; MLA and APA styles are shown in Figure 4.

MARGINS

Memo and letter reports use regular correspondence margins as discussed earlier in this manual. For reports typed in manuscript (formal report) format, use a 2-inch top margin for the first page of each special part (for example, the table of contents, the executive summary, the first page of the body of the report, and the first page of the reference list). Leave a 1-inch top margin for all other pages and at least a 1-inch bottom margin on all pages. Use 1- to $1\frac{1}{4}$ -inch side margins on all pages.

SPACING

Memo and letter reports are typed single-spaced. Manuscript reports may be either single- or double-spaced. Double spacing is preferred if the reader will likely make many comments on the pages. Note that double spacing leaves one blank line between each line of type; do not confuse double spacing with $1\frac{1}{2}$ spacing, which leaves only *half* a blank line between lines of type.

Regardless of the spacing used for the body of the report, single spacing is typically used for the table of contents, the executive summary, long quotations, tables, and the reference list. Use a $\frac{1}{2}$-inch paragraph indention for double-spaced paragraphs. Do not indent single-spaced paragraphs; instead, double-space between them. Unless directed otherwise, use a 12-point serif font (such as Times New Roman 12).

REPORT HEADINGS

The number of levels of headings used will vary from report to report. Memo reports may have only first-level subheadings, with no part titles or other headings. Long reports may have as many as four levels of headings. One standard format for the various levels is given here. Recognize, however, that the format presented here is only one of several that might be used. Again, consistency and readability should be your major goals. Regardless of the format used, make sure that the reader can instantly tell which are major headings and which are subordinate headings.

Part Title   Using a slightly larger font size than used for the body of the report, center a part title (for example, "Contents" or "References") in all capitals and in bold on a new page, leaving a 2-inch top margin. Double-space titles of two or more lines, using an inverted pyramid style (the first line longer). Triple-space after the part title.

First-Level Subheading   Using the same font size as that used in the body of the report, center and bold the first-level subheading in all capitals. Double-space before and after the heading.

Second-Level Subheading   Begin the second-level subheading at the left margin. Use bold type and all capitals as in first-level headings. Double-space before and after the heading.

Third-Level Subheading   Double-space before the third-level subheading, indent, and bold. Capitalize the first letter of the first and last words and all other words except articles, prepositions with four or fewer letters, and conjunctions. Leave a period and one space after the subheading; begin typing the text on the same line.

PAGINATION

Number the preliminary pages, such as the table of contents, with lowercase roman numerals centered on the bottom margin. The title page is counted as page i, but no page number is shown. Page numbers appear on all other preliminary pages, centered at the bottom margin. For example, the executive summary might be page ii and the table of contents might be page iii.

Number all pages beginning with the first page of the body of the report with arabic numerals. The first page of the body is counted as page 1, but no page number is typed (in word processing terminology, the page number is *suppressed*). Beginning with page 2 of the body and continuing through the reference pages, number all pages consecutively at the top right of the page.

SAMPLE REPORT IN BUSINESS STYLE

EVALUATION OF THE STAFF BENEFIT PROGRAM

AT MAYO MEMORIAL HOSPITAL

Lyn Santos

I. INTRODUCTION
    A. Purpose and Scope of the Study
    B. Procedures

II. FINDINGS
    A. Knowledge of Benefits
        1. Familiarity with Benefits
        2. Present Methods of Communication
            a. Formal Channels
            b. Informal Channels
        3. Preferred Methods of Communication
    B. Opinions of Present Benefits
        1. Importance of Benefits
        2. Satisfaction with Benefits
    C. Desirability of Additional Benefits

III. SUMMARY, CONCLUSIONS, AND RECOMMENDATIONS
    A. Summary of the Problem and Procedures
    B. Summary of the Findings
    C. Conclusions and Recommendations

APPENDIX
    A. Cover Letter
    B. Questionnaire

Outline

EVALUATION OF THE STAFF BENEFIT PROGRAM

AT MAYO MEMORIAL HOSPITAL

Prepared for

David Riggins
Director of Human Resources
Mayo Memorial Hospital

Prepared by

Lyn Santos
Assistant Director of Human Resources
Mayo Memorial Hospital

December 8, 20—

Title page

MEMO TO: David Riggins, Director of Human Resources

FROM: Lyn Santos, Assistant Director of Human Resources

DATE: December 8, 20—

SUBJECT: Evaluation of the Staff Benefit Program at Mayo Memorial Hospital

Here is the report evaluating our staff benefit program that you requested on October 15.

The report shows that overall the staff is familiar with and values most of the benefits we offer. At the end of the report, I've made several recommendations regarding the possibility of issuing individualized benefit statements annually and determining the usefulness of the automobile insurance benefit, the feasibility of offering compensation for unused sick leave, and the competitiveness of our retirement program.

I enjoyed working on this assignment, Dave, and learned quite a bit from my analysis of the situation that will help me during the upcoming labor negotiations. Please let me know if I can provide further information.

emc
Attachment

Transmittal document

CONTENTS

Table of contents

figure3

SAMPLE REPORT IN BUSINESS STYLE *(continued)*

**EVALUATION OF THE STAFF BENEFIT PROGRAM
AT MAYO MEMORIAL HOSPITAL**

Lyn Santos

INTRODUCTION

Employee benefits are a rapidly growing and increasingly important form of employee compensation for both for profit and nonprofit organizations. According to a recent U.S. Chamber of Commerce survey, benefits now constitute 37 percent of all payroll cost, averaging $11,857 per year for each full-time employee.[1] Thus, on the basis of cost alone, an organization's employee benefit program must be carefully monitored and evaluated.

Mayo Memorial Hospital employs nearly 2,500 staff personnel, and these employees have not received a cost-of-living increase in two years. As a result, staff salaries may not have kept pace with private industry, and the hospital's employee benefit program may become more important in attracting and retaining good workers. In addition, the contracts of three of the four staff unions expire next year, and the benefit program is typically a major area of bargaining.

PURPOSE AND SCOPE OF THE STUDY

To help ensure that the staff benefit program at Mayo operates as effectively as possible, the director of personnel authorized this report on October 15, 20—. Specifically, this problem was addressed in this study: What are the opinions of staff employees at Mayo Memorial Hospital regarding their employee benefits? To answer this question, the following subproblems were addressed:

1. How knowledgeable are the employees about the benefit program?

2. What are the employees' opinions of the value of the benefits that are presently available to them?

[1]Sarah Berelson et al., *Managing Your Benefit Program*, 13th ed., Novak-Siebold, Chicago, 2002, p. 183.

First page

3

FINDINGS

For a benefit program to achieve its goals, employees must be aware of the benefits provided. Thus, the first section that follows discusses the employees' familiarity with their benefits as well as the effectiveness of the hospital's present method of communicating benefits and those methods that employees would prefer. An effective benefit package must also include benefits that are relevant to employee needs. Thus, the employees' opinions of the importance of and their satisfaction with each benefit offered are discussed next. The section concludes with a discussion of those benefits employees would like to see added to the benefit program at Mayo.

KNOWLEDGE OF BENEFITS

One study[3] has shown that employees' satisfaction with benefits is directly correlated with their knowledge of such benefits. Thus, an indication of the staff employees' level of familiarity with their benefits and suggestions for improving communication were solicited.

Familiarity with Benefits. Numerous methods are presently being used to communicate the fringe benefits to employees. According to Lewis Rigby, director of the State Personnel Board, every new state employee views a 30-minute video entitled "In Addition to Your Salary" as part of the new-employee orientation. Also, the major benefits are explained during one-on-one counseling during the first day of the orientation session.

The staff employees were asked to rate their level of familiarity with each benefit. As shown in Table 1, most staff employees believe that most benefits have been adequately communicated to them. At least three-fourths of the employees are familiar with all major benefits except for long-term disability insurance, which is familiar to only a slight majority, and auto insurance, which is familiar to only one-third of the respondents. This low level of knowledge is

[3]Donna Jean Egan and Annette Kantelzoglou (eds.), *Human Resources*, Varsity Books, New Haven, CT, 2005.

New-section page

4

TABLE 1. LEVEL OF FAMILIARITY WITH THE BENEFIT PROGRAM

Employee Benefit	Level of Familiarity			
	Familiar	Unfamiliar	Undecided	Total
Sick leave	94%	4%	2%	100%
Vacation/paid holidays	93%	4%	3%	100%
Hospital/medical insurance	90%	7%	3%	100%
Life insurance	84%	10%	6%	100%
Long-term disability insurance	53%	33%	14%	100%
Retirement	76%	14%	10%	100%
Auto insurance*	34%	58%	8%	100%

*This benefit started six weeks before the survey was taken.

In general, benefit familiarity is not related to length of employment. Most employees are familiar with most benefits regardless of their length of employment. As shown in Figure 1, however, the longer a person has been employed at Mayo, the more likely he or she is to know about the life insurance benefit.

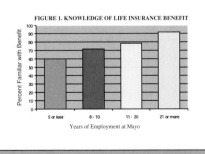

FIGURE 1. KNOWLEDGE OF LIFE INSURANCE BENEFIT

Page with audiovisual aids

18

BIBLIOGRAPHY

Abbey Petroleum Industries, *2005 Annual Report,* API, Inc., San Francisco, 2006.

Adams, Josiah B., *Compensation Systems,* Brunswick Press, Boston, 2005.

Berelson, Sarah, et al., *Managing Your Benefit Program,* 13th ed., Novak-Siebold, Chicago, 2006.

Directory of Business and Financial Services, Corporate Libraries Assoc., New York, 2005.

Egan, Donna Jean, and Annette Kantelzoglou (eds.); *Human Resources,* Varsity Books, New Haven, CT, 2005.

Ignatio, Enar, "Can Flexible Benefits Promote Your Company?" *Personnel Quarterly,* Vol. 20, September 2004, pp. 804–816.

"Let Employees Determine Their Own Benefits," *Manhattan Times,* January 12, 2006, p. C17, col. 2.

"Market Research," *Encyclopedia of Business,* 2d ed., 2006.

National Institute of Mental Health, *Who Pays the Piper? Ten Years of Passing the Buck,* DHHS Publication No. ADM 82-1195, U.S. Government Printing Office, Washington, 2005.

Preminger, Larry (Executive Producer), *The WKVX-TV Evening News,* Valhalla Broadcasting Co., Los Angeles, August 5, 2004.

Quincy, Dinah J., "Maxwell Announces New Health Benefit," *Maxwell Corp.* November 13, 2004, <http://www.maxcorp.com/NEWS/2004/f93500.html>, accessed on January 14, 2005.

Young, Laurel <lyoung2@express.com>, "Training Doesn't Always Last," June 3, 2004, <http://groups.l/groups.yahoo.com/group/personnel/message/51>, accessed on April 20, 2003.

Bibliography

SAMPLE REPORT IN APA AND MLA STYLES

Staff Benefit Program 2

Evaluation of the Staff Benefit Program

at Mayo Memorial Hospital

Lyn Santos

Introduction

Employee benefits are a rapidly growing and increasingly important form of employee compensation for both profit and nonprofit organizations. According to a recent U.S. Chamber of Commerce survey, benefits now constitute 37 percent of all payroll cost, costing an average of $11,857 per year for each full-time employee (Adhams & Stevens, 2004, p. 183). Thus, on the basis of cost alone, an organization's employee benefit program must be carefully monitored and evaluated.

Mayo Memorial Hospital employs nearly 2,500 staff personnel, and they have not received a cost-of-living increase in two years. As a result, staff salaries may not have kept pace with private industry, and the hospital's employee benefit program may become more important in attracting and retaining good workers. In addition, the contracts of three of the four staff unions expire next year, and the benefit program is typically a major area of bargaining (Ivarson, 2005, p. 28).

Purpose and Scope of the Study

As has been noted by J. B. Adams (2005), a management consultant, "The success of employee benefit programs depends directly on whether employees need, understand, and appreciate the value of the benefits provided" (p. 220). Thus, to ensure that the benefit program is operating as effectively as possible, David Riggins, director of personnel, authorized this report on October 15, 20—. Specifically, the following problem was addressed in this study: What are the opinions of staff employees at Mayo Memorial Hospital regarding their employee

Report page in APA style

Staff Benefit Program 18

References

Abbey Petroleum Industries. (2006). *2005 annual report.* San Francisco: Author.

Adams, J. B. (2005). *Compensation systems.* Boston: Brunswick Press.

Adhams, R., & Stevens, S. (2000). *Personnel management.* Cambridge, MA: All-State.

Directory of business and financial services. (2005). New York: Corporate Libraries Association.

Ivarson, A., Jr. (2005, September 29). Creating your benefit plan: A primer. *Business Month, 75,* 19–31.

Let employees determine their own benefits. (2006, January 12). *Manhattan Times,* p. C17.

Market research. (2006). In *The encyclopedia of business* (2nd ed., Vol. 2, pp. 436–441). Cleveland, OH: Collins.

National Institute of Mental Health. (2005). *Who pays the piper? Ten years of passing the buck* (DHHS Publication No. ADM 82-1195). Washington, DC: U.S. Government Printing Office.

Preminger, L. (Executive Producer). (2006, August 5). *The WKVX-TV evening news* [Television broadcast]. Los Angeles: Valhalla Broadcasting Co.

Quincy, D. J. (2004, November 13). Maxwell announces new health benefit. New York: Maxwell. Retrieved January 14, 2005, from http://www.maxcorp.com /NEWS/2004/f93500.html

Salary survey of service industries. (n.d.). Retrieved July 8, 2006, from BizInfo database, http://www.bizinfo.com/census.gov/ind.lib/tab-0315.html

Young, L. (2004, June 3). Training doesn't always last. Message posted to http://groups.yahoo.com/group/personne1/message/51

References in APA style

Santos 2

Lyn Santos

Professor Riggins

Management 348

8 December 20—

Evaluation of the Staff Benefit Program

at Mayo Memorial Hospital

Employee benefits are a rapidly growing and increasingly important form of employee compensation for both profit and nonprofit organizations. According to a recent U.S. Chamber of Commerce survey, benefits now constitute 37 percent of all payroll cost, costing an average of $11,857 per year for each full-time employee (Adhams and Stevens 183). Thus, on the basis of cost alone, an organization's employee benefit program must be carefully monitored and evaluated.

Mayo Memorial Hospital employs nearly 2,500 staff personnel, and they have not received a cost-of-living increase in two years. As a result, staff salaries may not have kept pace with private industry, meaning the university's employee benefit program may become more important in attracting and retaining good workers. In addition, the contracts of three of the four staff unions expire next year, and the benefit program is typically a major area of bargaining (Ivarson 28).

As has been noted by Adams, a management consultant, "The success of employee benefit programs depends directly on whether the employees need, understand, and appreciate the value of the benefits provided" (220). Thus, to ensure that the benefit program is operating as effectively as possible, David Riggins, director of personnel, authorized this report on 15 October 20—. Specifically, the following problem was addressed in this study: What are the

Report page in MLA style

Santos 18

Works Cited

Abbey Petroleum Industries. *2005 Annual Report.* San Francisco: Abbey Petroleum Industries, 2006.

Adams, Josiah B. *Compensation Systems.* Boston: Brunswick, 2005.

Adhams, Ramon, and Seymour Stevens. *Personnel Management.* Cambridge: All-State, 2004.

Corporate Libraries Association. *Directory of Business and Financial Services.* New York: Corporate Libraries Association, 2005.

Ivarson, Andrew, Jr. "Creating Your Benefit Plan: A Primer." *Business Month* 29 Sept. 2005: 19–31.

"Let Employees Determine Their Own Benefits." *Manhattan Times* 12 Jan. 2006: C17.

"Market Research." *Encyclopedia of Business.* 2nd ed. Cleveland: Collins, 2006.

National Institute of Mental Health. *Who Pays the Piper? Ten Years of Passing the Buck.* DHHS Publication No. ADM 82-1195. Washington: GPO, 2006.

O'Brian, Douglas. Personal interview. 13 May 2006.

Preminger, Larry (Executive Producer). *The WKVX-TV Evening News.* Los Angeles: Valhalla Broadcasting Co. 5 Aug. 2006.

Quincy, Dinah J. "Maxwell Announces New Health Benefit." *Maxwell Corp. Home Page.* 13 Nov. 2004. 14 Jan. 2005 <http://www.maxcorp.com/news/2004 /f93500.html>.

Waerov, Denis V. E-mail to the author. 18 Aug. 2005.

Works cited page in MLA style

■ Citation Styles

Shown below is a representative list of different types of citations formatted in the three most common citation styles—business style (also appropriate for most academic reports), APA style, and MLA style. Although the list is quite extensive, you may occasionally encounter a type of citation not illustrated here. In that case, simply find a similar type of citation and adapt it to your specific source.

Within Document	
	Business Style[1]
One author—not named in text	In fact, fringe benefits are growing in importance as a part of an overall salary package.[1]
One author—named in text	Adams argues that health insurance is the most important benefit of all.[2]
Multiple authors—not named in text	The personalized benefit statement shown in Figure 3 contains all necessary legal information.[3]
Multiple authors—named in text	According to Berelson, Lazarsfield, and Connell,[4] the personalized benefit statement shown in Figure 3 contains all necessary legal information.
Multiple sources	Numerous research studies[5] have shown that white-collar employees prefer an increase in benefits to an increase in salary.
Author not identified	Another variation that is growing in popularity is the cafeteria-style program.[6]
Direct quotation	According to Ivarson, "There is no such creature as a 'fringe benefit' anymore."[7]
	[1]William A. Sabin, *The Gregg Reference Manual*, 9th ed., Westerville, Ohio, Glencoe/McGraw-Hill, 2001.

End of Report	
	Bibliography
Annual report	Abbey Petroleum Industries, *2005 Annual Report*, API, Inc., San Francisco, 2006.
Book—one author	Adams, Josiah B., *Compensation Systems*, Brunswick Press, Boston, 2005.
Book—two authors	Adhams, Ramon, and Seymour Stevens, *Personnel Management*, All-State, Cambridge, MA, 2004.
Book—three or more authors	Berelson, Sarah, et al., *Managing Your Benefit Program*, 13th ed., Novak-Siebold, Chicago, 2006.
Book—organization as author	*Directory of Business and Financial Services*, Corporate Libraries Assoc., New York, 2005.

References

Business Style: William A. Sabin, *The Gregg Reference Manual,* 10th ed., McGraw-Hill/Irwin, New York, 2005.

APA Style: *Publication Manual of the American Psychological Association,* 5th ed., Washington, D.C., American Psychological Association, 2001.

MLA Style: Joseph Gibaldi, *MLA Handbook for Writers of Research Papers,* 6th ed. New York, Modern Language Association of America, 2003; "MLA Style," *MLA Home Page,* September 9, 2003, http://www.mla.org (June 14, 2004).

APA Style	**MLA Style**
In fact, fringe benefits are growing in importance as a part of an overall salary package (Ignatio, 2006).	In fact, fringe benefits are growing in importance as a part of an overall salary package (Ignatio 813).
Adams (2005) argues that health insurance is the most important benefit of all.	Adams argues that health insurance is the most important benefit of all (386–87).
The personalized benefit statement shown in Figure 3 contains all necessary legal information (Berelson, Lazarsfield, & Connell, 2006).	The personalized benefit statement shown in Figure 3 contains all necessary legal information (Berelson, Lazarsfield, and Connell 563).
According to Berelson, Lazarsfield, and Connell (2006, p. 563), the personalized benefit statement shown in Figure 3 contains all necessary legal information.	According to Berelson, Lazarsfield, and Connell, the personalized benefit statement shown in Figure 3 contains all necessary legal information (563).
Numerous research studies have shown that white-collar employees prefer an increase in benefits to an increase in salary (Adhams & Stevens, 2004; Ivarson, 2005; White, 2005).	Numerous research studies have shown that white-collar employees prefer an increase in benefits to an increase in salary (Adhams and Stevens 76; Ivarson 29; White).
Another variation that is growing in popularity is the cafeteria-style program ("Let Employees," 2006).	Another variation that is growing in popularity is the cafeteria-style program ("Let Employees").
According to Ivarson (2005), "There is no such creature as a 'fringe benefit' anymore" (p. 27).	According to Ivarson, "There is no such creature as a 'fringe benefit' anymore" (27).

APA Style—References	**MLA Style—Works Cited**
Abbey Petroleum Industries. (2006). *2005 annual report.* San Francisco: Author.	Abbey Petroleum Industries. *2005 Annual Report, Abbey Petroleum Industries, 2006.* San Francisco: API, Inc., 2006.
Adams, J. B. (2005). *Compensation systems.* Boston: Brunswick Press.	Adams, Josiah B. *Compensation Systems.* Boston: Brunswick; Press, 2005.
Adhams, R., & Stevens, S. (2004). *Personnel management.* Cambridge, MA: All-State.	Adhams, Ramon, and Seymour Stevens. *Personnel Management.* Cambridge: All-State, 2004.
Berelson, S., Lazarsfield, P. F., & Connell, W., Jr. (2006). *Managing your benefit program* (13th ed.). Chicago: Novak-Siebold.	Berelson, Sarah, Paul Lazarsfield, and Will Connell, Jr. *Managing Your Benefit Program.* 13th ed. Chicago: Novak-Siebold, 2006.
Directory of business and financial services. (2005). New York: Corporate Libraries Association.	Corporate Libraries Association. *Directory of Business and Financial Services.* New York: Corporate Libraries Association, 2005.

End of Report (*continued*)

	Business Style—Bibliography
Journal article—paged continuously throughout the year	Ignatio, Enar, "Can Flexible Benefits Promote Your Company?" *Personnel Quarterly,* Vol. 20, September 2006, pp. 804–816.
Magazine article—paged starting anew with each issue	Ivarson, Andrew, Jr., "Creating Your Benefit Plan: A Primer," *Business Month,* September 29, 2005, pp. 19–31.
Newspaper article—unsigned	"Let Employees Determine Their Own Benefits," *Manhattan Times,* January 12, 2006, p. C17, col. 2.
Reference work article	"Market Research," *Encyclopedia of Business,* 2d ed., 2006.
Government document	National Institute of Mental Health, *Who Pays the Piper? Ten Years of Passing the Buck,* DHHS Publication No. ADM 82-1195, U.S. Government Printing Office, Washington, 2005.
Interview	O'Brian, Douglas, Interview by author, May 13, 2006.
Paper presented at a meeting	Patts, Regina. *Tuition Reimbursement,* paper presented at the meeting of the National Mayors' Conference, Trenton, NJ, August 5, 2006.
Television/radio broadcast	Preminger, Larry (Executive Producer), *The WKVX-TV Evening News,* Valhalla Broadcasting Co., Los Angeles, August 5, 2006.
CD-ROM article	Petelin, Rosana, "Wage Administration," *Martindale Interactive Business Encyclopedia* (CD-ROM), Martindale, Inc., Pompton Lakes, NJ, 2005.
World Wide Web page	Quincy, Dinah J., "Maxwell Announces New Health Benefit," *Maxwell Corp.,* November 13, 2004, ≤http://www.maxcorp.com/NEWS/2004/f93500 .html≥< accessed on January 14, 2005.
Online database article	"Salary Survey of Service Industries," *BizInfo,* n.d., ≤http://www.bizinfo.com/census.gov/ind.lib /tab-0315.html≥< accessed on July 8, 2004.
E-mail	Waerov, Denis V., "Reaction to Management's Offer," e-mail message, August 19, 2005.
Electronic discussion message (including Listservs and newsgroups)	Young, Laurel <lyoung2@express.com>, "Training Doesn't Always Last," June 3, 2004, ≤http:l//groups.yahoo.com/group/personnel /message/51≥< accessed on April 20, 2005.

APA Style—References

Ignatio, E. (2006). Can flexible benefits promote your company?" *Personnel Quarterly, 20,* 804–816.

Ivarson, A., Jr. (2005, September 29). Creating your benefit plan: A primer. *Business Month, 75,* 19–31.

Let employees determine their own benefits. (2006, January 12). *Manhattan Times,* p. C17.

Market research. (2006). In *The encyclopedia of business* (2nd ed., Vol. 2, pp. 436–441). Cleveland, OH: Collins.

National Institute of Mental Health. (2005). *Who pays the piper? Ten years of passing the buck* (DHHS Publication No. ADM 82-1195). Washington, DC: U.S. Government Printing Office.

[Not cited in reference list. Cited in text as "D. O'Brian (personal interview, May 13, 2006) suggest that...]

Patts, R. (2005, August). *Tuition reimbursement.* Paper presented at the meeting of the National Mayors' Conference, Trenton, NJ.

Preminger, L. (Executive Producer). (2006, August 5). *The WKVX-TV Evening News* [Television broadcast]. Los Angeles: Valhalla Broadcasting Co.

Petelin, R. (2005). *Wage administration.* Pompton Lakes, NJ: Martindale, Inc. Retrieved from Martindale database (Martindale Interactive Business Encyclopedia, CD-ROM).

Quincy, D. J. (2004, November 13). Maxwell announces new health benefit. New York: Maxwell. Retrieved January 14, 2005 from http://www.maxcorp.com/NEWS/2004/f93500.html

Salary survey of service industries. (n.d.). Retrieved July 8, 2004, from BizInfo database, http://www.bizinfo.com/census.gov/ind.lib /tab-0315.html

[Not cited in reference list. Cited in text as "D. V. Waerov (personal communication, August 18, 2003) proposes that . . ."]

Young, L. (2004, June 3). Training doesn't always last. Message posted to http://groups.yahoo.com/group /personnel/message/51

MLA Style—Works Cited

Ignatio, Enar. "Can Flexible Benefits Promote Your Company?" *Personnel Quarterly* 20 (2006): 804–16.

Ivarson, Andrew, Jr. "Creating Your Benefit Plan: A Primer." *Business Month* 29 Sept. 2005: 19–31.

"Let Employees Determine Their Own Benefits." *Manhattan Times* 12 Jan. 2006: C17.

"Market Research." *Encyclopedia of Business,* 2nd ed., Cleveland: Collins, 2006.

National Institute of Mental Health. *Who Pays the Piper? Ten Years of Passing the Buck.* DHHS Publication No. ADM 82-1195. Washington: GPO, 2005.

O'Brian, Douglas. Personal interview, 13 May 2006.

Patts, Regina. *Tuition Reimbursement.* Paper presented at the meeting of the National Mayors' Conference. Trenton, NJ, 5 Aug. 2005.

Preminger, Larry (Executive Producer). *The WKVX-TV Evening News.* Los Angeles: Valhalla Broadcasting Co., 5 Aug. 2006.

Petelin, Rosana. "Wage Administration," *Martindale Interactive Business Encyclopedia.* CD-ROM. Pompton Lakes, NJ: Martindale, Inc., 2005.

Quincy, Dinah J. "Maxwell Announces New Health Benefit." *Maxwell Corp. Home Page.* 13 Nov. 2004. 14 Jan. 2005 <http://www.maxcorp.com /NEWS/2004/f93500.html>.

"Salary Survey of Service Industries." *BizInfo.* n.d. 8 July 2004 <http://www.bizinfo.com/census.gov/ind.lib /tab-0315.html>.

Waerov, Denis, V. "Reaction to Management's Offer," E-mail to the author. 19 Aug 2005.

Young, Laurel. <lyoung2@express.com> "Training Doesn't Always Last." Online posting. 3 June 2004. 20 Apr. 2005 <http://groups.yahoo.com/group /personnel/message/51>.

BUSINESS STYLE POINTERS

❑ The major differences between footnote and bibliographic entries are that (a) footnotes use the normal order for author names (e.g., "Raymond Stevens and Seymour Adams"), whereas bibliographies invert the order of the first author (e.g., "Stevens, Raymond, and Seymour Adams"); and (b) page numbers are included in bibliographic entries only when the material being cited is part of a larger work (for example, a journal or newspaper article).

❑ Type the authors' names exactly as they appear in print. For publications by two authors, arrange only the first name in last-name/first-name order. With three or more authors, type only the first name followed by *et al.* (not in italics). Arrange publications by the same author in alphabetical order, according to the publication title.

❑ Include page numbers only when the material being cited is part of a larger work. Do not italicize edition numbers. Be consistent in formatting the ordinal in raised position (13th) or in normal position (13th).

❑ Include the two-letter state name (using the USPS abbreviation) only if confusion might result. Use a shortened form of the publisher's name; e.g., *McGraw-Hill* rather than *McGraw-Hill Book Company,* and use common abbreviations (such as *Assoc.* or *Co.*).

❑ For online citations:

■ For e-mail, insert the type of e-mail (e.g., "office communication" or "personal e-mail").

■ If the date of an online posting cannot be determined, insert the abbreviation *n.d.* (no date)—not in italics.

■ Enclose in parentheses as the last section of the citation the date you accessed the site, followed by a period.

■ Follow the capitalization, punctuation, and spacing exactly as given in the original online address.

■ You may break an online citation *before* (but never after) a dot (.), single slash (/), double slash (//), hyphen (-), underscore (_), at symbol (@), or any other mark of punctuation. Do *not* insert a hyphen within an online address to signify an end-of-line break.

Abstract word   A word that identifies an idea or feeling as opposed to a concrete object.

Active voice   The sentence form in which the subject performs the action expressed by the verb.

Adjustment letter   A letter written to inform a customer of the action taken in response to the customer's claim letter.

Agenda   An ordered list of topics to be considered at a meeting, along with the name of the person responsible for each topic.

Application letter   A letter from a job applicant to a prospective employer explaining the applicant's interest in and qualifications for a position within the organization; also called a *cover letter*.

Audience   The person or persons with whom you're communicating.

Audience analysis   Identification of the needs, interests, and personality of the receiver of a communication.

Bar chart   A graph with horizontal or vertical bars representing values.

Brainstorming   Jotting down ideas, facts, possible leads, and anything else that might be helpful in constructing a message.

Buffer   A neutral and supportive opening statement designed to lessen the impact of negative news.

Business etiquette   The practice of polite and appropriate behavior in a business setting.

Buzz word   An important-sounding term used mainly to impress people.

Central selling theme   The major reader benefit that is introduced early and emphasized throughout a sales letter.

Claim letter   A letter from the buyer to the seller, seeking some type of action to correct a problem with the seller's product or service.

Cliché   An expression that has become monotonous through overuse.

Communication   The process of sending and receiving messages.

Complex sentence   A sentence that has one independent clause and at least one dependent clause.

Compound-complex sentence   A sentence that has two or more independent clauses and one or more dependent clauses.

Compound sentence   A sentence that has two or more independent clauses.

Conclusions   The answers to the research questions raised in the introduction to a report.

Concrete word   A word that identifies something the senses can perceive.

Connotation   The subjective or emotional feeling associated with a word.

Cross-tabulation   A process by which two or more items of data are analyzed together.

Dangling expression   Any part of a sentence that does not logically connect to the rest of the sentence.

Defamation   Any false and malicious statement that is communicated to others and that injures a person's good name or reputation.

Denotation   The literal, dictionary meaning of a word.

Derived benefit   The benefit a potential customer would receive from using a product or service.

Direct organizational plan   A plan in which the major purpose of the message is communicated first, followed by any needed explanation.

Direct quotation   The exact words of another.

Documentation   Giving credit to another person for his or her words or ideas that you have used.

Drafting   Composing a preliminary version of a message.

Editing   The stage of revision which ensures that writing conforms to standard English.

Electronic database   A computer-searchable collection of information on a general subject area, such as business, education, or psychology.

Electronic résumé   A résumé that is stored in a computer database designed to help manage and initially screen job applicants.

E-mail   A message transmitted electronically over a computer network most often connected by cable, telephone lines, or satellites.

Ethics   Rules of conduct.

Ethnocentrism   The belief that one's own cultural group is superior.

Euphemism   An inoffensive expression used in place of an expression that may offend or suggest something unpleasant.

Executive summary   A condensed version of the report body; also called an *abstract* or *synopsis*.

Expletive   An expression such as *there is* or *it has been* that begins a clause and for which the pronoun has no antecedent.

Factoring   Breaking a problem down into its component parts so that data-collection needs are known.

Feedback   The receiver's reaction or response to a message.

Filter   The mental process of perceiving stimuli based on one's knowledge, experience, and viewpoints.

Form letter   A letter with standardized wording that is sent to different people.

Formal communication network   The transmission of prescribed information through downward, upward, horizontal, and cross-channel routes.

Fraud   A deliberate misrepresentation of the truth that is made to induce someone to give up something of value.

Free writing   Writing continuously for 5 to 10 minutes without stopping as a means of generating a large quantity of material that will be revised later.

Generic heading   A report heading that identifies only the topic of a section without giving the conclusion.

Goodwill message   A message that is sent strictly out of a sense of kindness and friendliness.

Groupthink   A barrier to communication that results from an overemphasis on group cohesiveness, which stifles opposing ideas and the free flow of information.

Groupware   A form of software that automates information sharing between two or more remote users and enables them to communicate electronically and coordinate their efforts.

Indirect organizational plan   A plan in which the reasons or rationale are presented first, followed by the major idea.

Informal communication network   The transmission of information through nonofficial channels within the organization; also called the *grapevine*.

Internet   A worldwide collection of interconnected computers housed in university labs, business offices, government centers, and the like—all filled with massive amounts of information that is accessible to anyone with an Internet account.

Interview guide   A list of questions to ask, with suggested wording and possible follow-up questions.

Invasion of privacy   Any unreasonable intrusion into the private life of another person or denial of a person's right to be left alone.

Jargon   The technical terminology used within specialized groups.

Letter   A written message mailed to someone outside the organization.

Libel   Defamation in a permanent form such as in writing or on videotape.

Line chart   A graph based on a grid, with the vertical axis representing values and the horizontal axis representing time.

Mailing list   An Internet discussion group in which messages are sent directly to members via e-mail; also called a *listserv*.

Mechanics   Those elements in communication that show up only in written form, including spelling, punctuation, abbreviations, capitalization, number expression, and word division.

Medium   The form of a message—for example, a memo or telephone call.

Memorandum   A written message sent to someone within the organization.

Message   The information (either verbal or nonverbal) that is communicated.

Mind mapping   Generating ideas for message content by first writing the purpose of the message in the center of a page and circling it and then writing possible points to include, linking each one to either the purpose or to another point; also called *clustering*.

Minutes   An official record of the proceedings of a meeting that summarizes what was discussed and what decisions were made.

Misrepresentation   A false statement made innocently with no intent to deceive the other party.

Newsgroup   An Internet discussion group in which messages (called *articles*) are posted at the newsgroup site, rather than being sent directly to the members as e-mail.

Noise   Environmental or competing elements that distract one's attention during communication.

Nondiscriminatory language   Language that treats everyone equally, making no unwarranted assumptions about any group of people.

Nonverbal message   A nonwritten and nonspoken signal consisting of facial expressions, gestures, voice qualities, and the like.

Organization   The sequence in which topics are presented in a message.

Parallelism   Using similar grammatical structure to express similar ideas.

Paraphrase   A summary or restatement of a passage in one's own words.

Parliamentary procedure   Written rules of order that permit the efficient transaction of business in meetings.

Passive voice   The sentence form in which the subject receives the action expressed by the verb.

Persuasion   The process of motivating someone to take a specific action or to support a particular idea.

Pie chart   A circle graph whose area is divided into component wedges.

Plagiarism   Using another person's words or ideas without giving proper credit.

Platitude   A trite, obvious statement.

Policy   A broad operating guideline that governs the general direction or activities of an organization.

Primary audience   The receiver of a message whose cooperation is most crucial if the message is to achieve its objective.

Primary data   Data collected by the researcher to solve the specific problem at hand.

Procedure   The recommended methods or sequential steps to be followed when performing a specific activity.

Proposal   A written report that seeks to persuade a reader outside the organization to do as the writer wants.

Questionnaire   A written instrument containing questions designed to obtain information from the individual being surveyed.

Readability   The ease with which a passage can be understood, based on its style of writing.

Receiver benefits   The advantages a reader would derive from granting the writer's request or from accepting the writer's decision.

Redundancy   The unnecessary repetition of an idea that has already been expressed or intimated.

Reference   A person who has agreed to provide information to a prospective employer regarding a job applicant's fitness for a job.

Report   An orderly and objective presentation of information that assists in decision making and problem solving.

Resale   Information that reestablishes a customer's confidence in the product purchased or in the company that sold the product.

Résumé   A brief record of one's personal history and qualifications that is typically prepared by a job applicant.

Revising   The process of modifying the content and style of a draft to increase its effectiveness.

Rhetorical question   A question asked strictly to get the reader thinking about the topic; a literal answer is not expected.

Secondary audience   Any receiver of a message other than the primary audience who will be affected by the message.

Secondary data   Data collected by someone else for some other purpose; it may be published or unpublished.

Simple sentence   A sentence that has one independent clause.

Slander   Defamation in a temporary form such as in oral communication.

Slang   An expression, often short-lived, that is identified with a specific group of people.

Solicited sales letter   A reply to a request for product information from a potential customer.

Solicited application letter   An application letter written in response to an advertised job vacancy.

Stimulus   An event that creates within an individual the need to communicate.

Style   The manner in which an idea is expressed (rather than the *substance* of the idea).

Survey   A data-collection method that gathers information through questionnaires, telephone inquiries, or interviews.

Table   An orderly arrangement of data into columns and rows.

Talking heading   A report heading that identifies not only the topic of the report section but also the major conclusion.

Team   A group of individuals who depend on one another to accomplish a common objective.

Teleconference   A meeting of three or more people, at least some of whom are in different locations, who communicate via telephone.

Tone   The writer's attitude toward the reader and the subject of the message.

Transmittal document   A letter or memorandum that conveys the finished report to the reader.

Unsolicited application letter   An application letter written to an organization that has not advertised a vacancy; also called a *prospecting letter*.

Unsolicited sales letter   A letter promoting a firm's products mailed to a potential customer who has not expressed any prior interest in the product; also called a *prospecting letter*.

Verbal message   A message comprising spoken or written words.

Videoconference   An interactive meeting between two or more people using video linkups at two or more sites.

Visual aids   Tables, charts, photographs, and other graphic materials used in communication to aid comprehension and add interest.

Website   The location of one or more pages of related information that is posted on the World Wide Web and is accessed via the Internet (the main page of a website is called its "home page").

World Wide Web   The newest and fastest-growing segment of the Internet; comprises documents (called *pages*) containing text, graphics, sounds, and video, as well as electronic links (called *hypertext*) that let the user move quickly from one document to another.

Writer's block   The inability to focus one's attention on the writing process and to draft a message.

"You" attitude   A viewpoint that emphasizes what the reader wants to know and how the reader will be affected by the message.

references

Chapter 1

1. Faridah Awang, Marcia A. Anderson, and Clora Mae Baker, "Entry-Level Information Services and Support Personnel: Needed Workplace and Technology Skills," *Delta Pi Epsilon Journal*, Vol. 45, Winter 2003, p. 55; Leland V. Gustafson, Jack E. Johnson, and David H. Hovey, "Preparing Business Students—Can We Market Them Successfully?" *Business Education Forum*, Vol. 47, April 1993, pp. 23–26; "It's All Just Bossiness," *Indianapolis Star*, April 4, 1992, p. C3; "Mediocre Memos," *Detroit Free Press*, May 26, 1990, p. 9A; "Speak the Language," *Indianapolis Star*, January 30, 1991, p. A9; "Workplace Literacy," *USA Today*, September 21, 1992, p. B1; Edith Paal, "MBA Programs Talk Up Communications Skills," *Indianapolis Star*, November 23, 1996, p. B5; "The Job Market for the Class of 2001," in *Planning Job Choices: 2001*, 4th ed., National Association for Colleges and Employers, Bethlehem, PA, 2000.
2. Mark H. McCormack, "Words You Use Tell a Lot About You," *Arizona Republic*, April 13, 2000, p. D4.
3. Watson Wyatt Worldwide, *Linking Communications with Strategy to Achieve Business Goals*, Bethesda, MD, 1999, p. 6.
4. Kathleen Driscoll, "Your Voice Can Make or Break You," *Democrat and Chronicle*, August 26, 1993, p. 10B.
5. Robert L. Montgomery, *Listening Made Easy: How to Improve Listening on the Job, at Home, and in the Community*, American Management Association, New York, 1981, p. 6.
6. David Shenk, *Data Smog: Surviving the Information Glut*, HarperCollins, San Francisco, 1997.
7. David Shenk, *Data Smog: Surviving the Information Glut*, HarperCollins, San Francisco, 1997; David Stipp, "Intellectual Hedonism: Richard Saul Wurman, the King of Access," *Fortune*, June 23, 1997, p. 106; Richard Saul Wurman, *Information Architects*, Graphics Press Corp., New York, 1996; Richard Saul Wurman, *Information Anxiety*, Doubleday, Garden City, NY, 1989; Peter Lyman and Hal R. Varian, "How Much Information?", *University of California–Berkeley Home Page*, October 18, 2000, retrieved from http://www.sims.berkeley.edu /research/projects/how-much-info (April 2, 2001).
8. John Gerstner, "Executives Evaluate the Importance of Grapevine Communication," *Communication World*, March 1994, p. 17; James P. Miller, "Work Week," *Wall Street Journal*, February 1, 2000, p. A1.
9. Donald B. Simmons, "The Nature of the Organizational Grapevine," *Supervisory Management*, Vol. 30, November 1985, p. 40; Alan Zaremba, "Working with the Organizational Grapevine," *Personnel Journal*, Vol. 67, July 1988, p. 40; Carol Hymowitz, "Spread the Word: Gossip Is Good," *Wall Street Journal*, October 4, 1988, p. B1.
10. Stephen Karel, "Learning Culture the Hard Way," *Consumer Markets Abroad*, Vol. 7, May 1988, pp. 1, 15.
11. Donald Harris, "A Matter of Privacy: Managing Personal Data in Company Computers," *Personnel*, Vol. 65, June 1988, p. 52.
12. The Hanson Group, a corporate-ethics consultancy in Los Altos, California.
13. This case was adapted from Brenda R. Sims, "Linking Ethics and Language in the Technical Communication Classroom," *Technical Communication Quarterly*, Vol. 2, No. 3, Summer 1993, p. 285.

Chapter 2

1. Andrea Kay, "Craft Communication to Tasks," *Indianapolis Star*, June 18, 2003, p. C3.
2. John R. Pierce, "Communication," *Scientific American*, Vol. 227, September 1972, p. 36.
3. "Conflict Resolution: Don't Get Mad, Get Promoted," *Training*, June 2002, p. 20.
4. Irving R. Janis, *Victims of Groupthink*, Houghton Mifflin, Boston, 1972.
5. These guidelines are based on principles contained in Peter R. Scholtes, *The Team Handbook: How to Use Teams to Improve Quality*, Joiner Associates, Madison, WI, 1988, pp. 6.23–6.28.
6. Peter F. Drucker, quoted by Bill Boyers in *A World of Ideas*, Doubleday, Garden City, NY, 1990.
7. Albert Mehrabian, "Communicating Without Words," *Psychology Today*, September 1968, pp. 53–55.
8. Judee K. Burgoon and Thomas Saine, *The Unspoken Dialogue: An Introduction to Nonverbal Communication*, Houghton Mifflin, Boston, 1978, p. 123.
9. Buck Wolf, "The Pinocchio Effect," *ABCNews.com Home Page*, December 17, 2000, http://abcnews.go.com/sections/us /WolfFiles/wolffiles68.html (September 11, 2003).
10. See, for example, Mark L. Knapp, *Essentials of Nonverbal Communication*, Holt, Rinehart & Winston, New York, 1980, pp. 21–26; "Study: Good Looks Bring Bigger Bucks in Business World," *USA Today*, August 8, 1989, p. 2B.
11. David B. Givens, "Tones of Voice," *The Nonverbal Dictionary of Gestures, Signs, and Body Language Cues*, http://members.aol .com/nonverbal2/diction1.htm (April 12, 2001).
12. Curt Suplee, "Get Outta My Face," *The Washington Post*, June 9, 1999, p. H-1.
13. Edward T. Hall, *The Hidden Dimension*, Doubleday, Garden City, NY, 1966, pp. 107–122.
14. "CulturallyCorrectPapers.com," *ibiztips.com Home Page*, March 12, 2001, retrieved from http://www.ibiztips.com /business12MAR01.htm (September 12, 2003).
15. *The Universal Almanac: 1992*, Andrews and McMeel, Kansas City, MO, p. 316.
16. *2000 Statistical Abstract of the United States*, U.S. Government Printing Office, Washington, DC, 2000, Table 11.
17. Genaro C. Armas, "Hispanics, Black Populations Almost Equal," *Indianapolis Star*, March 13, 2001, p. A4.
18. Stephen Lieb, "Adults as Learners," *Principles of Adult Learning*, retrieved from http://www.hcc.hawaii.edu (July 13, 2001); "Overcoming Adult-Sized Obstacles," *Channel 3000*, retrieved from http://www.channel3000.com (July 13, 2001); Susan Imel,

"Guidelines for Working with Adult Learners," *ERIC Digest*, No. 154, 1994, pp. 1–3; Nevzer Stacey, "Overview of the Conference," *How Adults Learn*, September 1999, retrieved from http://www.ed.gov/pubs/HowAdultsLearn/overview.html.

19. Genaro C. Armas, "Hispanics, Black Populations Almost Equal," *Indianapolis Star*, March 13, 2001, p. A4.

20. Sondra Thiederman, "The Diverse Workplace: Strategies for Getting 'Culture Smart,'" *The Secretary*, March 1996, p. 8.

21. *2000 Statistical Abstract of the United States*, U.S. Government Printing Office, Washington, DC, 2000, Table 16.

22. Copyright © 1999 by Bruce A. Jacobs. Reprinted from *Race Manners*, published by Arcade Publishing, New York.

23. Jennifer Coates, *Women, Men, and Language*, Longman, New York, 1986; Deborah Tannen, *You Just Don't Understand*, Ballantine, New York, 1990; John Gray, *Men Are from Mars, Women Are from Venus*, HarperCollins, New York, 1992; Patti Hathaway, *Giving and Receiving Feedback*, rev. ed., Crisp Publications, Menlo Park, CA, 1998; Susan Herring, "Making the Net 'Work,'" retrieved from http://www.cs.nott.ac.uk/,azq97c/gender.htm (May 12, 1999); Deborah Tannen, *Talking from 9 to 5*, William Morrow, New York, 1994.

24. Alice Sargeant, *The Androgynous Manager*, American Management Association, New York, 1983, p. 37.

25. Ralph G. Nichols, "Listening Is a Ten-Part Skill," *Nation's Business*, September 1987, p. 40; "Listen Up!" *American Salesman*, July 1987, p. 29.

26. *Clear Communication*, Vol. 1, No. 2, Fall 1993, p. 2.

27. Federal Communications Commission, *Trends in Telephone Service*, U.S. Government Printing Office, Washington, DC, 2003; "International Long Distance Calling," *Consumer and Governmental Affairs Bureau Home Page*, retrieved from http://www.fcc.gov/cgb/consumerfacts/hello.html (September 13, 2003); Maggie Jackson, "Turn Off That Cellphone. It's Meeting Time," *New York Times*, March 2, 2003, p. BU-12.

28. John T. Molloy, "Dress for Success," *Detroit Free Press*, December 19, 1989, p. 3C.

29. "Telephone On-Hold Statistics," *National Telephone Message Corporation*, retrieved from http://www.ihearditonhold.com/statistics.html (September 13, 2003).

30. "Phone Calls Waste a Month Each Year," *Office Systems*, September 1989, p. 14.

31. Stephanie Armour, "Meetings Inspire High-Tech Survival Skills," *USA Today*, January 22, 1999, p. B1; Michael Doyle and David Straus, *How to Make Meetings Work*, Wyden Books, New York, 1976, p. 4; Marcy E. Mullins, "Are Meetings Worthwhile?" *USA Today*, August 28, 1989, p. B1; "Profile of the Typical Meeting," *Presentation Products Magazine*, February 1990, p. 8; E. F. Wells, "Rules for a Better Meeting," *Mainliner*, May 1978, p. 56; E. J. McGarry, "Presentations Can Be Economical and Effective," *Office Dealer 92*, March/April 1992, p. 18.

32. "Managing Meetings: A Critical Role," *The Office*, November 1989, p. 20.

33. "Managing Meetings," p. 20.

34. Henry Martyn Robert, Sarah Corbin Robert, and William J. Evans, *The Scott, Foresman Robert's Rules of Order, Newly Revised*, HarperCollins, New York, 1991.

35. Robert, p. xiii.

36. T. Brown, "The Dress-Down Debate," *Industry Week*, June 20, 1994, p. 43.

37. *Casual Clothing in the Workplace*, Levi Strauss & Co., San Francisco, 1995.

38. "Business Etiquette," *Keying In*, National Business Association, Reston, VA, January 1996, p. 6; Dean Foster, "Business Across Borders: International Etiquette for the Effective Global Secretary," *The Secretary*, October 1992, pp. 20–24; "Gift Giving Japanese-Style," *Business Tokyo*, November 1990, pp. 9–12; Yumiko Ono, "There's an Old Saying: Never Look for a Gift, of Course, in the Mouth," *Wall Street Journal*, December 13, 1989, p. 81.

39. Jeff Fee, "Practicing Cubicle Courtesy," *Indianapolis Star*, August 11, 2002, p. F1.

Chapter 3

1. Mary Kaufman, "There's No Denying the Fax," *Informationweek*, February 20, 1995, p. 32; "Paperless Office? Fortune 500 Computer-Created Documents End Up on Paper," *Edge*, September 21, 1998, retrieved from http://www.findarticles.com/cf_0/m0WUB/1998_Sept_21/53030074/p1/article.jhtml. (April 14, 2000); David Shenk, *Data Smog: Surviving the Information Glut*, HarperCollins, San Francisco, 1997; Traci Watson, "Paperless Office Still a Pipe Dream," *USA Today*, March 8, 1999, p. 128.

2. Byron J. Finch, *The Management Guide to Internet Resources*, McGraw-Hill, New York, 1997, pp. 6–7.

3. "What Makes a Successful Online Student?," *Illinois Online Network*, April 27, 2001, retrieved from http://www.ion.illinois.edu/IONresources/onlineLearning/StudentProfile.asp; Susan Imel "Distance Learning: Myths and Realities" *ERIC*, 1998, http://ericacve.org Barry Willis, "Guide #8: Strategies for Learning at a Distance," *Distance Education at a Glance*, College of Engineering, University of Idaho, December 11, 2000, retrieved from http://www.uidaho.edu/evo/dist8.html>; "Is Distance Ed Right for You?," *Channel 3000*, retrieved from http://www.channel3000.com> (July 13, 2001).

4. Donald T. Hawkins, "What Is Credible Information?," *Online*, September 1999, retrieved from http://www.onelineinc.com/OL1999/technomonitor9.html (April 14, 2001).

5. "Caslon Analytics Profile: E-mail, SMS, IM & Chat," *Caslon Analytics Home Page*, retrieved from http://www.caslon.com.aue-mailprofile5.htm (September 20, 2003).

6. This material was compiled from a set of five checklists created by Jan Alexander and Marsha Tate, "Teaching Critical Evaluation Skills for World Wide Web Resources," April 9, 1999. Retrieved from http://www.widener.edu/?pageId=86. (Select link "Evaluating Web Resources.") Copyright Widener University 2003.

7. Charles McGoon, "Speed Versus Accuracy in Cyberspace," *Communication World*, January/February 1996, p. 23.

8. David Shenk, *Data Smog: Surviving the Information Glut*, HarperCollins, San Francisco, 1997, p. 97.

9. Quoted in David Stipp, "Intellectual Hedonism," *Fortune*, June 23, 1997, p. 106.

Chapter 4

1. Marilyn vos Savant, "Ask Marilyn," *Parade Magazine*, November 3, 1996, p. 8.

2. Scot Ober, "The Difficulty Level of Typewritten Copy in Industry," *Delta Pi Epsilon Journal*, Vol. 25, January 1983, p. 5.

3. Ge-Lin Zhu, Chief Editor, *Practical Commercial English Handbook*, Commercial Publishing Company, Beijing, China.

4. Richard A. Lanham, *Revising Business Prose,* Scribner's, New York, 1981, p. 2.
5. Dave Ellis, *Becoming a Master Student,* Houghton Mifflin, Boston, 2000, p. 128; Carol C. Kanar, *The Confident Student,* Houghton Mifflin, Boston, 2001, p. 12.
6. Eve Nagler, "A Macaroni Company with Homespun Appeal," *New York Times,* December 12, 1993, sec. 13, p. 22.

Chapter 5

1. "The Core Rules of Netiquette," retrieved from http://www .albion.com /netiquette/corerules.html (February 6, 1997); "Intranet Intellectual Property Guide," retrieved from http://www.abitec.com/home/IPguide.htm (February 6, 1997); "The Ten Commandments for Computer Ethics," retrieved from http://www.fau.edu/netiquette/net/ten.html (February 6, 1997); "Social Climes/The Buzz: A Netiquette No-No Spams Back On-Line," *Los Angeles Times,* June 18, 1995, p. E5.
2. Michael E. Miller, "A Story of the Type That Turns Heads in Computer Circles," *Wall Street Journal,* September 15, 1992, pp. A1, A8; Michael E. Miller, "Sidelong Remarks That May Interest Propellerheads," *Wall Street Journal,* September 15, 1992, p. A8; Daniel Will-Harris, "Electronic Punctuation and Hieroglyphics," *PC Publishing and Presentations,* August–September 1991, p. 40; Barbara Yost, "BTW, What Did He Say?," *Arizona Republic,* June 4, 2000, p. J1.

Chapter 6

1. Marshall Cook, "Seven Steps to Better Manuscripts," *Writer's Digest,* September 1987, p. 30.
2. Julie Schmit, "Continental's $4 Million Typo," *USA Today,* May 25, 1993, p. B1.

Chapter 7

1. "Unhappy News Travels Fast," *USA Today,* May 21, 1996, p. 10B.

Chapter 8

1. Herschell Gordon Lewis, *Direct Mail Copy That Sells!* Prentice-Hall, Englewood Cliffs, NJ, 1984, p. iii.
2. Ed Cerny, "Listening for Effect," *American Salesman,* May 1986, p. 28.
3. Linda Lynton, "The Fine Art of Writing a Sales Letter," *Sales & Marketing Management,* August 1988, p. 55.

Chapter 9

1. B. P. Elzer, "They're Closing the Site," July 1, 1997, retrieved from http://members.aol.com/BPElzer/letter.html (November 18, 1999).
2. "Delivering Bad News by Email Is More Accurate, Less Painful, Study Suggests," *Informs Online,* June 23, 2001.
3. For a discussion of the empirical rationale for using an indirect versus a direct approach, see Marsha Bayless, "Business and Education: Perceptions of Written Communication," *NABTE Review,* 1991, pp. 32–35; D. Brent, "Indirect Structure and Reader Response," *Journal of Business Communication,* Spring 1985, pp. 5–7; Mohan Limaye, "Buffers in Bad News Messages

and Recipient Perceptions," *Management Communication Quarterly,* August 1988, pp. 90–101; Kitty O. Locker, "The Rhetoric of Negative Messages," *English for Specific Purposes,* July 1984, pp. 1–2; Douglas Salerno, "An Interpersonal Approach to Writing Negative Messages," *Journal of Advanced Composition,* 1985–1986, pp. 139–149.

Chapter 10

1. Scot Ober, "The Physical Format of Memorandums and Business Reports," *Business Education World,* November–December 1981, pp. 9–10, 24.
2. John Naisbitt, *Megatrends: Ten New Directions Shaping Our Lives,* Warner Books, New York, 1984, p. 17.
3. Martin J. Gannon, *Understanding Global Cultures,* Sage, Beverly Hills, CA, 1994, pp. 3–16; Martin Rosch and Kay Segler, "Communicating with the Japansese," *Management International Review,* Winter 1987, pp. 56–57; Stella Ting-Tommey, "Toward a Theory of Conflict and Culture," *Communication, Culture, and Organizational Processes,* Sage, Beverley Hills, CA, 1985, pp. 71–86; David A. Victor, *International Business Communication,* HarperCollins, New York, 1992, pp. 137–168.

Chapter 11

1. Robert Rosenthal and Ralph L. Rosnow, *The Volunteer Subject,* John Wiley, New York, 1975, pp. 195–196.
2. Theophilus B. A. Aldo, "The Effects of Dimensionality in Computer Graphics," *Journal of Business Communication,* Vol. 31, December 1994, pp. 253–265.
3. See, for example, "Tabling the Move to Computer Graphics," *Wall Street Journal,* January 30, 1991, p. B1; Jeremiah J. Sullivan, "Financial Presentation Format and Managerial Decision Making: Tables Versus Graphs," *Management Communication Quarterly,* Vol. 2, November 1988, pp. 194–216.
4. Edward Tufte, *The Visual Display of Quantitative Information,* Graphics Press, Cheshire, CT, 1983.
5. Sean Callahan, "Eye Tech," *Forbes ASAP,* Spring 1993, pp. 57–67; Jane Hundertmark, "When Enhancement Is Deception," *Publish,* October 1991, pp. 51–55; Jim Meade, "Graphics That Tell the Truth," *Personal Computing,* January 1989, pp. 79–84; Daryl Moen, "Misinformation Graphics," *Aldus Magazine,* January/February 1990, pp. 62–63.

Chapter 12

1. Kenneth H. Bacon, "U.S. Issues Rules Aimed at Policing Fraud in Research," *Wall Street Journal,* August 8, 1989, p. B3; Paul M. Barrett, "To Read This Story in Full, Don't Forget to See the Footnotes," *Wall Street Journal,* May 10, 1988, p. 1; Paul Boller and John George, *They Never Said It,* Oxford University Press, Oxford UK, 1989; Christopher Cook, "Judge Reportedly Plagiarized in Article," *Detroit Free Press,* March 19, 1989, p. 3A; John Entine, "Uh-oh: The Feckless Defense of Fabulists," *Chicago Tribune,* July 27, 2001, p. 19; John Harris, "Chop-Stuck," *Forbes,* August 21, 1989, p. 14; Ralph Keyes, "The Greatest Quotes Never Said," *Reader's Digest,* June 1993, pp. 97–100; Rob Stein, "Plagiarism Charges End in Departure at Harvard," *Detroit Free Press,* November 29, 1988, p. 8A;

Nanci Hellmich, "Stolen Passion: Author Plagiarized Her Rival," *USA Today*, July 30, 1997, p. 1D; Jay Leno (with Bill Zehme), *Leading with My Chin*, Mass Market Paperbacks, New York, 1997.

Chapter 13

1. Adapted from Leonard F. Meuse, Jr., *Mastering the Business and Technical Presentation*, CBI Publishing, Boston, 1980, pp. 2–7.
2. Philip R. Harris and Robert T. Moran, *Managing Cultural Differences*, 5th ed., Gulf Publishing, Houston, TX, 2000; Dona Z. Meilach, "Visually Speaking," *Presentation Products Magazine*, undated supplement, pp. A–L; Merna Skinner, "Presenting to International Audiences Effectively," *Public Relations Tactics*, January 2001, p. 12.
3. Kerry L. Johnson, "You Were Saying," *Managers Magazine*, February 1989, p. 19.

Chapter 14

1. Wharton Applied Center, "A Study of the Effects of the Use of Overhead Transparencies on Business Meetings, Final Report," Philadelphia: University of Pennsylvania, September 14, 1981; Tad Simons, "Study Shows Just How Much Visuals Increase Persuasiveness," *Presentations Magazine*, March 1998, p. 20.
2. Scott Heimes, "Is the LCD Panel Headed for the Technology Scrap Heap?" *Presentations Magazine Home Page*, March 19, 1998, retrieved from http://www.presentations.com/techno/rpod_w11_spot.html (November 28, 1999).
3. Betty A. Marton, "How to Construct a Winning Presentation," *Harvard Management Communication Letter*, April 2000, p. 5.
4. Albert Mehrabian, "Communicating Without Words," *Psychology Today*, September 1968, pp. 53–55.
5. Dawn E. Waldrop, "What You Wear Is Almost as Important as What You Say," *Presentations*, July 2000, p. 74.
6. David Wallechinsky, Irving Wallace, and Amy Wallace, *The Book of Lists*, William Morrow, New York, 1977, pp. 469–470.
7. Jolie Solomon, "Executives Who Dread Public Speaking Learn to Keep Their Cool in the Spotlight," *Wall Street Journal*, May 4, 1990, p. B1.

Chapter 15

1. Sandra L. Latimer, "First Impressions," *Mt. Pleasant (MI) Morning Sun*, May 8, 1989, p. 6.
2. See, for example, Jules Harcourt and A. C. "Buddy" Krizan, "A Comparison of Résumé Content Preferences of *Fortune* 500 Personnel Administrators and Business Communication Instructors," *Journal of Business Communication*, Spring 1989, pp. 177–190; Rod Little, "Keep Your Résumé Short," *USA Today*, July 28, 1989, p. B1; Darlene C. Pibal, "Criteria for Effective Résumés as Perceived by Personnel Directors," *Personnel Administrator*, May 1985, pp. 119–123.
3. Elizabeth Blackburn-Brockman and Kelly Belanger, "One Page or Two? A National Study of CPA Recruiters' Preferences for Résumé Length," *Journal of Business Communication*, January 2001, pp. 29–57.
4. "Most Serious Résumé Gaffes," *Communication Briefings*, March 1991, p. 6.
5. "To Be or Not to Be," *The Secretary*, April 1991, p. 6.
6. Albert P. Karr, "Labor Letter," *Wall Street Journal*, September 1, 1992, p. A1.
7. Harcourt and Krizan, pp. 177–190.
8. "Flashcard," *Education Life* (supplement to *New York Times*), November 5, 1989, p. 21.
9. Therese Droste, "Executive Résumés: The Ultimate Calling Card," *Hospitals*, March 5, 1989, p. 72.
10. Lynn Ulrich and Don Trumbo, "The Selection Interview Since 1949," *Psychological Bulletin*, Vol. 43, 1956, p. 100.
11. Shelley Liles, "Wrong Hire Might Prove Costly," *USA Today*, June 6, 1989, p. 6B.
12. Mary Bakeman et al., *Job-Seeking Skills Reference Manual*, 3d ed., Minnesota Rehabilitation Center, Minneapolis, MN, 1971, p. 57.
13. "Creative Résumés," *Dun's Business Month*, June 1985, p. 20; Nelda Spinks and Barron Wells, "Employment Interviews: Trends in the *Fortune* 500 Companies—1980–1988," *ABC Bulletin*, December 1988, p. 17; "Will Ethical Conflicts Undo Your Career?" *Mt. Pleasant (MI) Morning Sun*, May 12, 1988, p. 9.

credits

Grateful acknowledgment is made to the following companies and individuals for allowing their interviews and photographs to be included in this book:

Chapter 1: Nissan North America, Inc./Debra Sanchez Fair. *Chapter 2:* The Nucon Group/Gilbert C. Morrell Jr.. *Chapter 3:* Texas Instruments/Scott Roller. *Chapter 4:* World Wrestling Entertainment/Gary Davis. *Chapter 5:* Barnes & Noble/Bobbie Kroman. *Chapter 6:* PriceWaterhouseCoopers/Noel McCarthy. *Chapter 7:* Annie's Homegrown/Ann Withey. *Chapter 8:* Wurzburg, Inc./Patrick Vijiarungam. *Chapter 9:* Intel Corporation/Howard High. *Chapter 10:* AstraZeneca/Ann K. Cobuzzi. *Chapter 11:* Rock and Roll Hall of Fame/Todd Mesek. *Chapter 12:* Habitat for Humanity/Steve Messinetti. *Chapter 13:* Georgia Hispanic Chamber of Commerce/Sara González. *Chapter 14:* SBC Communications/Patricia Diaz Dennis. *Chapter 15:* Monster.com/Jeff Taylor.

Grateful acknowledgment is made to the following companies for allowing their letterheads to be included in this book. These letters are for text example only; they were not written by employees of the companies.

Chapter 6: Courtesy of Baker College of Owosso. *Chapter 7:* Courtesy of Sir Speedy, Inc.; Courtesy of Ralston Purina Company; Courtesy of Dillard's, Inc. *Chapter 8:* Courtesy of National Multiple Sclerosis Society; Courtesy of The Home Depot, ©2004 Homer TLC, Inc. All Rights Reserved. *Chapter 9:* BLOCKBUSTER name, design, and related marks are trademarks of Blockbuster Inc. ©2004 Blockbuster Inc. All rights reserved.; Courtesy of General Mills. *Chapter 10:* Courtesy of Amazon.com, Inc. Amazon, Amazon.com and the Amazon.com logo are registered trademarks of Amazon.com or its affiliates. *Reference Manual (page 612):* Used with permission of Ben & Jerry's Homemade Holdings, Inc. 2004.

TEXT CREDITS

Screen shots reprinted with permission from Microsoft Corporation.

AltaVista screen shots reproduced with permission of Yahoo! Inc. © 2004 by Yahoo! Inc. YAHOO! and the YAHOO! logo are trademarks of Yahoo! Inc.

Clip art reprinted from "Screen Beans" collections, published by A Bit Better Corporation (phone: 650-948-4766, Web: www .bitbetter.com).

Chapter 2: *Page 45, Figure 2.2:* From Peter S. Scholtes, *The Team Handbook,* 1998, pp. 6–27. Copyright © 1988 by Joiner Associates, Inc., Madison, WI; 1-800-669-8326. Reprinted with permission.

Chapter 3: *Page 103, Figure 3.1:* Listserv E-mail Posting screen shot reprinted with permission of AT&T.

Chapter 12: *Page 457, Figure 12.4:* Copyright 1998 by DOW JONES & CO INC. Reproduced with permission of DOW JONES & CO INC in the format Textbook via Copyright Clearance Center.

Chapter 13: *Page 470, Snapshot 13:* Most Popular Topics of Professional Speakers reprinted by permission of National Speakers Association, Tempe, AZ.

Chapter 14: *Page 508, Figure 14.2:* What size screen do you need? from *Presentations by Eric Gill,* June, 2001, page 8. Copyright © 2001 by V N U BUS publications USA. Reproduced with permission of V N U BUS Publications USA in the format Textbook via Copyright Clearance Center.

PHOTO CREDITS

Chapter 1: *Page 4:* © Chris Chapman. *Page 17:* © Robert Houser. *Page 20:* NON SEQUITUR © 1999 Wiley Miller. Distributed by UNIVERSAL PRESS SYNDICATE. Reprinted with permission. All rights reserved. *Page 25:* © Safia Fatimi. *Page 36:* © Bill Varie.

Chapter 2: *Page 45:* © Jonathan Chick. *Page 47:* © Marc Asnin/Redux. *Page 50:* © Andy Freeberg. *Page 56:* © John Abbott. *Page 58:* © Ray/Cartoon Features Syndicate. *Page 80:* © CJ Gunther/ZUMA Press. *Page 84:* Los Angeles Times Photo by Ricardo Dearatanha (TMS Reprints).

Chapter 3: *Page 98:* © Karen Moscowitz. *Page 104:* © Marc Asnin/Redux. *Page 111:* © J. Kohl. *Page 116:* Brian Davis Photography.

Chapter 4: *Page 136:* DILBERT reprinted by permission of United Feature Syndicate, Inc. *Page 138:* © Robyn Twomey. *Page 143:* © Robert Houser.

Chapter 5: *Page 171:* © Misha Gravenor Photography. *Page 174:* By permission of John L. Hart FLP, and Creators Syndicate, Inc. *Page 176:* AP/Wide World Photos.

Chapter 6: *Page 197:* © Michael Lewis. *Page 201:* Rose Palmisano/Reprinted by permission of the Orange County Register, copyright 2004. *Page 206:* © The New Yorker Collection 1987. J.B. Handelsman from cartoonbank.com. All Rights Reserved. *Page 207:* © Misha Gravenor Photography. *Page 224:* © LWA–Dann Tardif/CORBIS.

Chapter 7: *Page 232:* CATHY © 1982 Cathy Guisewite. Reprinted with permission of UNIVERSAL PRESS SYNDICATE. All rights reserved. *Page 236:* © David Strick/Redux–CA. *Page 241:* © Lisa Nipp. *Page 262:* © Neil Farren/Getty Images.

Chapter 8: *Page 267 (top):* By permission of Leigh Rubin and Creators Syndicate, Inc. *Page 267 (bottom):* © David Levenson. *Page 270:* © Kimberly Butler Photography. *Page 301:* © Dan Bosler/Getty Images.

Chapter 9: *Page 307:* AP/Wide World Photos. *Page 309:* The Far Side® by Gary Larson © 1984 FarWorks, Inc. All Rights Reserved. Used with permission. *Page 311:* DILBERT reprinted by permission of United Feature Syndicate, Inc. *Page 313:* AP/Wide World Photos.

Chapter 10: *Page 347:* Copyright Grantland Enterprises. www.grantland.net. *Page 350:* Courtesy of Motorola. *Page 353:* Charles Ommanney/Contact Press Images. *Page 368:* © Vance Jacobs. *Page 380:* Custom Medical Stock Photography.

Chapter 11: *Page 392:* Noah Berger/Bloomberg News/Landov. *Page 401:* © David Hume Kennerly/Getty Images. *Page 408:* Reprinted with special permission of King Features Syndicate.

Chapter 12: *Page 428:* © Brad Hines. *Page 444:* Reprinted with special permission of King Features Syndicate. *Page 447 (top):* © Steve Dunwell. *Page 447 (bottom):* © John Shanks. *Page 464:* Elie Bernager/Getty Images.

Chapter 13: *Page 474:* Kerry-Edwards 2004, Inc. from Sharon Farmer. *Page 477:* © Debra DeBoise. *Page 480:* DILBERT reprinted by permission of United Feature Syndicate, Inc. *Page 501:* Fisher/Thatcher/Getty Images.

Chapter 14: *Page 507:* Matthew Borkoski/IndexStock Photography. *Page 509:* © Reuters/CORBIS. *Page 515:* Copyright Grantland Enterprises; www.grantland.net. *Page 526:* Phil Boorman/Getty Images.

Chapter 15: *Page 531:* © Thomas Michael Alleman. *Page 554:* DILBERT reprinted by permission of United Feature Syndicate, Inc.

Reference Manual: *Page 591:* DRABBLE reprinted by permission of United Feature Syndicate, Inc.

index

sales letters and, 285
unauthorized-use issues and, 308–309
of work-team communication, 48
in written communication, 173
Ethnicity. *See* Cultural diversity
Ethnocentrism, 52
Ethos, 201, 202
Etiquette. *See* Business etiquette
Euphemism, 20–21
except/accept, 603
Executive summaries, 437, 440
Explanations
    colons with, 585–586
    in requests, 230–232
Expletives, 593
    explanation of, 142
Expressions
    dangling, 135
    inappropriate use of, 19–20
    interrupting, 580
    introductory, 578–579
    nonrestrictive, 579–580
    restrictive, 579
    transitional, 165
    wordy, 141
Eye contact/eye movement
    cultural diversity and, 53
    as nonverbal communication, 49
    during oral presentations, 516

Factoring, 365
Facts, in oral presentations, 478
Fair, Debra Sanchez, 2–3
farther/further, 605
Favors
    refusal of, 318, 320
    requests for, 274–275
Fax machines, etiquette related to, 85
Feedback
    explanation of, 9
    importance of, 44
    methods for giving, 44
    for oral presentations, 468
    on team writing, 48
fewer/less, 605
Filters, 7–8
Flaming, 170
Fonts, size of, 179
Footnotes, 446, 624
Ford Motor Company, 104
Foreign languages
    interaction with speakers of, 53
    miscommunications from translations
        of, 54
Formal communication network
    cross-channel communication and, 16
    downward communication and, 14
    explanation of, 13
    horizontal communication and, 14–16
    upward communication and, 14

Format
    for correspondence and memos,
        611–615
    for e-mail, 208, 612
    for justification, 181–182
    for lists, 181–182
    for memorandums, 611–615
    for paragraphs, 181
    proofreading for errors in, 210–211
    for report citations, 620–624
    for reports, 447–448, 615–619
    for résumés, 531–532, 536, 537, 544–545
    standards for, 208–209
Form letters, 233–234
Fragments, sentence, 591
Fraud, 23
Free writing, 206
Functional format, for résumés, 535, 537
further/farther, 605

Gender
    communication issues related to, 62–63
    sexist language and, 174–176
General Motors, 104
Generic headings, 431
Georgia Hispanic Chamber of Commerce,
    466–467
Gerunds, 587
Gestures
    cultural diversity and, 56
    as nonverbal communication, 49
    during oral presentations, 515
Gift giving, business etiquette for, 82, 83
González, Sara, 466–467
good/well, 605
Goodwill messages
    congratulatory, 247–248
    example of, 249
    explanation of, 245
    guidelines for, 245, 247
    sympathy, 248
    thank-you, 248
Grammar
    agreement, 592–594
    case, 594–595
    modifiers, 592
    sentences, 591–592
Grammar checkers, 210–211
Grapevine. *See* Informal communication
    network
Graphics. *See also* Charts; Tables; Visual aids
    charts as, 398–401, 403–405
    in documents, 182
    tables as, 393–398, 404, 405
Graphs. *See* Charts
Greetings, 77, 80
Grooming. *See* Personal
    appearance/grooming
Group communication. *See* Work-team
    communication

Groupthink, 43
Groupware, 111–112
Grove, Andrew, 306
Guindon, Richard, 308

Habitat for Humanity International,
    424–425
Handouts. *See* Audience handouts
Hawkins, Donald T., 105
Headings
    generic, 431
    length and number of, 431, 433
    in letters, 613
    in reports, 616
    talking, 431
High, Howard, 304–305
Horizontal communication, 14–16
Humor, in oral presentations, 478,
    480–481
Hypertext links, 102
Hyphens, 583–584
Hypothetical situations, in oral
    presentations, 478

i.e./e.g., 605
imminent/eminent, 605
Impatience, writer's block resulting from,
    205
imply/infer, 606
Importance, organizing data by, 428–429
Impromptu remarks, 485
Independent clauses
    commas between, 577–578
    run-on sentences with, 592
    semicolons with, 584–585
    without conjunctions, 584–585
Indirect organizational plans, 228
Individualism, cultural diversity and, 55
Individuals with disabilities,
    communication with, 63–64
infer/imply, 606
Informal communication network, 16
Informational reports, 361
Information anxiety, method to
    overcome, 15
-ing, 587
Intel Corporation, 304–305
Interjections, 575
Internal reports, 364
International Organization for
    Standardization, 54
International reports, 366
Internet
    access to, 100, 102
    browsing and searching on, 102–109
    distance learning and, 101
    e-mail and, 111, 112
    evaluation of information on, 105, 110,
        118–121

grading symbols

abb Do not abbreviate this word. *(page 597)*

acc Verify the accuracy of this statement or figure. *(pages 133–134, 347–349)*

act Prefer active voice. *(pages 132, 147–148, 172–173, 183)*

agr Make sure subjects, verbs, and pronouns agree; use plural verbs and pronouns with plural subjects and singular verbs and pronouns with singular subjects. *(pages 352, 357, 592–594)*

apol Do not apologize in this instance. *(pages 241–244)*

app Make sure that the appearance of your document does not detract from its effectiveness. *(pages 182, 208–209)*

aud Make sure the content and tone of your message are appropriate for your specific audience. *(pages 196–203, 363, 471–473)*

conc Be more concise; use fewer words to express this idea. *(pages 140–141)*

conf Use a more confident style of writing; avoid doubtful expressions. *(pages 168–170)*

cons Be consistent; do not contradict yourself.

dang Avoid dangling expressions; place modifiers close to the words they modify. *(page 135)*

disc Avoid discriminatory language. *(pages 173–177)*

emp Emphasize this point. *(pages 173–177)*

end Make the ending of your message more effective—more interesting, more positive, or more original. *(pages 232, 234, 240, 244–245, 286, 315–316, 480, 551)*

evid Give more evidence to support this point. *(pages 271–272, 283–286)*

expl Use expletive beginnings (such as *there are* or *it is*) sparingly. *(page 142)*

for Use correct format. *(pages 611–624)*

frag Avoid sentence fragments. Each sentence must contain a complete thought. *(page 591)*

head Use report headings effectively—descriptive, concise, parallel, and not too many or too few. *(pages 430–433, 616)*

info Use all the relevant information in the problem; make only reasonable assumptions.

int Interpret this point. Don't simply state facts or repeat data from tables and figures; give more information so that the reader understands the importance and implications. *(pages 406–408)*

list Consider putting these ideas in a numbered (sequence important) or bulleted (sequence not so important) list. *(pages 180, 611–624)*

mean Reword to make your meaning clearer or to be more precise. *(pages 133–135)*

mod Use modifiers (adjectives and adverbs) correctly. *(page 592)*

num Express numbers correctly (either in words or in figures). *(pages 598–599)*

obv Avoid obvious statements. *(page 171)*

org-dir Use a direct organizational pattern here—main idea before the supporting data. *(pages 228, 269–271, 307–310)*

org-ind Use an indirect organizational pattern here—supporting data before the main idea. *(pages 228–229, 269–271, 310–312)*

orig Use more original wording; avoid clichés and avoid copying the wording from the problem or text examples. *(pages 138–140)*

par Use parallel structure; express similar ideas in similar grammatical form. *(pages 166–167, 431–433)*

para Do not make paragraphs so long that they appear uninviting to read. *(pages 167–168)*

plur Do not confuse plurals and possessives. *(pages 586–587)*

pos Use positive language to express this idea. *(pages 142–144)*

pro Use pronouns and antecedents correctly. *(page 592)*

punc Use appropriate punctuation to help your reader understand your message. *(pages 576–592)*

quot Use direct quotations sparingly; paraphrasing is usually more effective. *(page 443)*